A-Level
Physics
Exam Board: AQA

Physics is a big subject — it covers *everything*. Minuscule subatomic particles? Check. Mind-bendingly enormous astronomical phenomena? Check. The broader socio-historical significance of heroic archetypes in classical Greek mythology? Oh.

But even without that last one, there are still plenty of challenging topics to tackle in the AQA A-Level Physics exams. Which is why you'll need this amazing CGP book...

It's packed with crystal-clear study notes, realistic exam questions and much more — there's even a free Online Edition you can read on your computer or tablet!

A-Level revision? It has to be CGP!

Published by CGP

Editors:
Emily Garrett, Sharon Keeley-Holden, Andy Park, Ethan Starmer-Jones, Hannah Taylor and Charlotte Whiteley.

Contributors:
Tony Alldridge, Jane Cartwright, Peter Cecil, Peter Clarke, Mark Edwards, Duncan Kamya, Barbara Mascetti, John Myers, Zoe Nye, Oliver Rigg, Frances Rooney, Moira Steven, Andy Williams and Tony Winzor.

With thanks to Matthew Benyohai, Mark Edwards and Duncan Lindsay for the proofreading.
With thanks to Jan Greenway for the copyright research.

ISBN: 978 1 78908 032 2

Contents

If you're revising for the **AS exams**, you'll need to revise Sections 1-6, and the Practical and Investigative Skills section at the back. If you're revising for the **A-level exams**, you'll need to revise the whole book — but only the option you've studied from Section 13. Option 13: "Electronics" isn't covered in this book.

Specification Map..i

Section 1 — Particles (AS)

Atomic Structure... 2
Stable and Unstable Nuclei 4
Particles and Antiparticles............................ 6
Forces and Exchange Particles....................... 8
Classification of Particles 10
Quarks 13

Section 2 — Electromagnetic Radiation and Quantum Phenomena (AS)

The Photoelectric Effect 16
Energy Levels and Photon Emission 18
Wave-Particle Duality 20
Extra Exam Practice for Sections 1 and 2 22

Section 3 — Waves (AS)

Progressive Waves 24
Longitudinal and Transverse Waves..................26
Superposition and Coherence.........................28
Stationary Waves 30
Diffraction...32
Two-Source Interference................................34
Diffraction Gratings 36
Refractive Index..38
Extra Exam Practice for Section 3 40

Section 4 — Mechanics (AS)

Scalars and Vectors.......................................42
Forces...44
Moments 46
Mass, Weight and Centre of Mass 48
Displacement-Time Graphs 50
Velocity-Time and Acceleration-Time Graphs ...52
Motion With Uniform Acceleration..................54
Acceleration Due to Gravity 56
Projectile Motion...58
Newton's Laws of Motion 60
Drag, Lift and Terminal Speed........................62
Momentum and Impulse.................................64
Work and Power..66
Conservation of Energy and Efficiency 68

Section 5 — Materials (AS)

Properties of Materials....................................70
Stress and Strain 72
The Young Modulus 74
Stress-Strain and Force-Extension Graphs..........76
Extra Exam Practice for Sections 4 and 5 78

Section 6 — Electricity (AS)

Current, Potential Difference and Resistance.....82
I/V Characteristics..84
Resistivity and Superconductivity.....................86
Electrical Energy and Power............................88
E.m.f. and Internal Resistance 90
Conservation of Energy and Charge 92
The Potential Divider......................................94
Extra Exam Practice for Section 6 96

Section 7 — Further Mechanics

Circular Motion 98

Simple Harmonic Motion 100

Simple Harmonic Oscillators....................... 102

Free and Forced Vibrations 104

Extra Exam Practice for Section 7 106

Section 8 — Thermal Physics

Thermal Energy Transfer............................... 108

Gas Laws..110

Ideal Gas Equation 112

The Pressure of an Ideal Gas.........................114

Kinetic Energy and the
Development of Theories.............................116

Extra Exam Practice for Section 8 118

Section 9 — Gravitational and Electric Fields

Gravitational Fields......................................120

Gravitational Potential 122

Orbits and Gravity......................................124

Electric Fields 126

Electric Potential and Work Done.................128

Comparing Electric and
Gravitational Fields.....................................130

Section 10 — Capacitors

Capacitors 132

Charging and Discharging 134

More Charging and Discharging.................. 136

Extra Exam Practice for Sections 9 and 10..... 138

Section 11 — Magnetic Fields

Magnetic Fields 140

Charged Particles in a Magnetic Field 142

Electromagnetic Induction 144

Induction Laws and Alternators.................... 146

Alternating Currents.................................... 148

Transformers... 150

Extra Exam Practice for Section 11 152

Section 12 — Nuclear Physics

Rutherford Scattering
and Atomic Structure.................................... 154

Nuclear Radius and Density 156

Radioactive Emissions 158

Investigations of Radioactive Emissions......... 160

Exponential Law of Decay 162

Nuclear Decay 164

Nuclear Fission and Fusion.......................... 166

Binding Energy 168

Extra Exam Practice for Section 12 170

Section 13: Option A — Astrophysics

Optical Telescopes......................................172

Non-Optical Telescopes...............................175

Distances and Magnitude 178

Stars as Black Bodies 180

Spectral Classes and the H-R Diagram...........182

Stellar Evolution 184

The Doppler Effect and Red Shift 188

Quasars and Exoplanets...............................190

The Big Bang Model of the Universe..............192

Section 13: Option B — Medical Physics

Physics of the Eye 194

Defects of Vision 196

Physics of the Ear...........................198

Intensity and Loudness 200

Electrocardiography (ECG)................202

Ultrasound Imaging.........................204

Endoscopy......................................206

X-Ray Production 208

X-Ray Imaging Techniques................210

Magnetic Resonance (MR) Imaging..............212

Medical Uses of Radiation.................214

Section 13: Option C — Engineering Physics

Inertia and Kinetic Energy................216

Rotational Motion............................218

Torque, Work and Power 220

Flywheels 222

Angular Momentum 224

The First Law of Thermodynamics.................226

p-V Diagrams 229

Four-Stroke Engines 232

Using Indicator Diagrams 234

Engine Efficiency 236

Reversed Heat Engines 238

Section 13: Option D — Turning Points in Physics

Specific Charge of the Electron 240

Millikan's Oil-Drop Experiment 242

Light — Particles vs Waves...............244

The Photoelectric Effect and the Photon Model 247

Wave-Particle Duality 250

The Speed of Light and Relativity.................252

Special Relativity 254

Extra Exam Practice for Section 13 256

Practical and Investigative Skills

Experiment Design 258

Uncertainty and Errors.....................260

Presenting and Evaluating Data 262

Do Well In Your Exams

Exam Structure and Technique.....................264

Working with Exponentials and Logarithms .. 266

Synoptic Practice 268

Answers..276

Index..310

Specification Map

This specification map tells you where each bit of the AQA specification is covered in the book.

3.1 — Measurements and their errors

3.1.1 — Use of SI units and their prefixes
covered throughout the book

3.1.2 — Limitation of physical measurements
p.259-261, p.263

3.1.3 — Estimation of physical quantities
covered throughout the book

3.2 — Particles and radiation

3.2.1 — Particles

3.2.1.1	p.2, p.3
3.2.1.2	p.4, p.5
3.2.1.3	p.6, p.7
3.2.1.4	p.8, p.9
3.2.1.5	p.8, p.10-15
3.2.1.6	p.13, p.14

3.2.1.7	p.14

3.2.2 — Electromagnetic radiation and quantum phenomena

3.2.2.1	p.16, p.17
3.2.2.2	p.18
3.2.2.3	p.18, p.19
3.2.2.4	p.20, p.21

3.3 — Waves

3.3.1 — Progressive and stationary waves

3.3.1.1	p.24, p.25
3.3.1.2	p.25-27
3.3.1.3	p.30, p.31

3.3.2 — Refraction, diffraction and interference

3.3.2.1	p.29, p.32, p.34, p.35
3.3.2.2	p.32, p.33, p.36, p.37
3.3.2.3	p.38, p.39

3.4 — Mechanics and materials

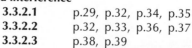

3.4.1 — Force, energy and momentum

3.4.1.1	p.42-45
3.4.1.2	p.46-49
3.4.1.3	p.50-57
3.4.1.4	p.58, p.59, p.62, p.63
3.4.1.5	p.60, p.61

3.4.1.6	p.64, p.65
3.4.1.7	p.66-68
3.4.1.8	p.68, p.69

3.4.2 — Materials

3.4.2.1	p.68, p.70-73, p.76, p.77
3.4.2.2	p.74, p.75

3.5 — Electricity

3.5.1 — Current electricity

3.5.1.1	p.82
3.5.1.2	p.82-85
3.5.1.3	p.85-87

3.5.1.4	p.88-90, p.92, p.93
3.5.1.5	p.94, p.95
3.5.1.6	p.90, p.91

3.6 — Further mechanics and thermal physics

3.6.1 — Periodic motion

3.6.1.1	p.98, p.99
3.6.1.2	p.100, p.101
3.6.1.3	p.100, p.102, p.103, p.105
3.6.1.4	p.104, p.105

3.6.2 — Thermal physics

3.6.2.1	p.108, p.109
3.6.2.2	p.110-113
3.6.2.3	p.110, p.114-117

3.7 — Fields and their consequences

3.7.1 — Fields
p.120, p.130, p.131

3.7.2 — Gravitational fields

3.7.2.1	p.120
3.7.2.2	p.120, p.121
3.7.2.3	p.122, p.123, p.129
3.7.2.4	p.122, p.124, p.125

3.7.3 — Electric fields

3.7.3.1	p.126, p.131
3.7.3.2	p.126-128
3.7.3.3	p.128, p.129

3.7.4 — Capacitance

3.7.4.1	p.132
3.7.4.2	p.132
3.7.4.3	p.133, p.134
3.7.4.4	p.134-137

3.7.5 — Magnetic fields

3.7.5.1	p.140, p.141
3.7.5.2	p.142, p.143
3.7.5.3	p.144, p.145
3.7.5.4	p.146, p.147
3.7.5.5	p.148, p.149
3.7.5.6	p.150, p.151

Specification Map

3.8 — Nuclear Physics

3.8.1 — Radioactivity
3.8.1.1	p.154
3.8.1.2	p.158-161
3.8.1.3	p.162, p.163, p.266
3.8.1.4	p.164, p.165
3.8.1.5	p.155-157
3.8.1.6	p.166-169
3.8.1.7	p.166
3.8.1.8	p.166, p.167

3.9 — Astrophysics

3.9.1 — Telescopes
3.9.1.1	p.172
3.9.1.2	p.173
3.9.1.3	p.175-177
3.9.1.4	p.173, p.174, p.177

3.9.2 — Classification of stars
3.9.2.1	p.178
3.9.2.2	p.178, p.179
3.9.2.3	p.180, p.181
3.9.2.4	p.182
3.9.2.5	p.183-185
3.9.2.6	p.186, p.187, p.190, p.192

3.9.3 — Cosmology
3.9.3.1	p.188-190
3.9.3.2	p.192, p.193
3.9.3.3	p.190
3.9.3.4	p.190, p.191

3.10 — Medical Physics

3.10.1 — Physics of the eye
3.10.1.1	p.194, p.195
3.10.1.2	p.194, p.196, p.197

3.10.2 — Physics of the ear
3.10.2.1	p.198, p.199
3.10.2.2	p.200, p.201
3.10.2.3	p.201

3.10.3 — Biological measurement
3.10.3.1	p.202, p.203

3.10.4 — Non-ionising imaging
3.10.4.1	p.204, p.205
3.10.4.2	p.206, p.207
3.10.4.3	p.212

3.10.5 — X-ray imaging
3.10.5.1	p.208, p.209
3.10.5.2	p.210, p.211
3.10.5.3	p.210
3.10.5.4	p.210

3.10.6 — Radionuclide imaging and therapy
3.10.6.1	p.214, p.215
3.10.6.2	p.214
3.10.6.3	p.214
3.10.6.4	p.215
3.10.6.5	p.215
3.10.6.6	p.213

3.11 — Engineering Physics

3.11.1 — Rotational dynamics
3.11.1.1	p.216
3.11.1.2	p.217, p.222, p.223
3.11.1.3	p.218, p.219
3.11.1.4	p.220
3.11.1.5	p.224, p.225
3.11.1.6	p.220, p.221

3.11.2 — Thermodynamics and engines
3.11.2.1	p.226
3.11.2.2	p.226-228
3.11.2.3	p.229-231
3.11.2.4	p.232-236
3.11.2.5	p.236, p.237
3.11.2.6	p.238, p.239

3.12 — Turning points in physics

3.12.1 — The discovery of the electron
3.12.1.1	p.240
3.12.1.2	p.240
3.12.1.3	p.240, p.241
3.12.1.4	p.242, p.243

3.12.2 — Wave-particle duality
3.12.2.1	p.244
3.12.2.2	p.245
3.12.2.3	p.245, p.246
3.12.2.4	p.247-249
3.12.2.5	p.250
3.12.2.6	p.251

3.12.3 — Special relativity
3.12.3.1	p.252
3.12.3.2	p.253
3.12.3.3	p.254
3.12.3.4	p.254
3.12.3.5	p.255

Option 13: "Electronics" isn't covered in this book.

Atomic Structure

"So what did you do today, Johnny?" "Particle physics, Mum." "How nice dear — done with times tables then?"
*Yeah, well, it's not exactly the **easiest** topic in the world, but it's a darn sight more interesting than biology.*

Atoms are made up of Protons, Neutrons and Electrons

Inside **every atom**, there's a **nucleus** containing **protons** and **neutrons**.
Protons and **neutrons** are both known as **nucleons**. **Orbiting** this core are the **electrons**.
This is the **nuclear model** of the atom.

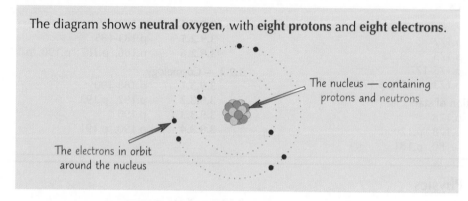

The diagram shows **neutral oxygen**, with **eight protons** and **eight electrons**.

The nucleus — containing
protons and neutrons

The electrons in orbit
around the nucleus

Tom dreamt of
becoming a nuclear
model when he grew up.

The particles in an atom have different **properties**. Their charges and masses are so **tiny**
that it's often easier to talk about their **relative charge** and **relative mass**.

*You need to learn
the values in the
orange columns —
you won't be given
them in the exam.*

Particle	Charge (coulombs, C)	Mass (kg)	Relative Charge	Relative Mass
Proton	$+1.60 \times 10^{-19}$	1.67×10^{-27}	$+1$	1
Neutron	0	1.67×10^{-27}	0	1
Electron	-1.60×10^{-19}	9.11×10^{-31}	-1	0.0005

The Proton Number is the Number of Protons in the Nucleus

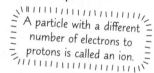 *No... really.*

The **proton number** is sometimes called the **atomic number**, and has the **symbol Z**
(I'm sure it makes sense to someone). **Z** is just the **number of protons** in the nucleus.

It's the **proton number** that **defines** the **element** — **no two elements** will have the **same** number of protons.

In a **neutral atom**, the number of **electrons equals** the number of **protons**.
The element's **reactions** and **chemical behaviour** depend on the number of **electrons**.
So the **proton number** tells you a lot about its **chemical properties**.

*A particle with a different
number of electrons to
protons is called an ion.*

The Nucleon Number is the Total Number of Protons and Neutrons

The **nucleon number** is also called the **mass number**, and has the **symbol A** (*shrug*).
It tells you how many **protons** and **neutrons** are in the nucleus. Since each **proton
or neutron** has a relative **mass** of (approximately) **1** and the electrons weigh virtually
nothing, the **number** of **nucleons** is the same as the **atom's relative mass**.

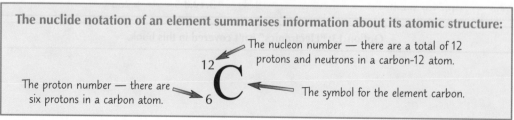

The nuclide notation of an element summarises information about its atomic structure:

The nucleon number — there are a total of 12
protons and neutrons in a carbon-12 atom.

$$^{12}_{6}C$$

The proton number — there are
six protons in a carbon atom.

The symbol for the element carbon.

Atomic Structure

Isotopes have the Same Proton Number, but Different Nucleon Numbers

Atoms with the **same number of protons** but **different numbers of neutrons** are called **isotopes**.

Example: Hydrogen has three natural isotopes — hydrogen, deuterium and tritium.
Hydrogen has 1 proton and 0 neutrons.
Deuterium has 1 proton and 1 neutron.
Tritium has 1 proton and 2 neutrons.

Changing the number of **neutrons doesn't affect** the atom's **chemical** properties.

The **number of neutrons** affects the **stability** of the nucleus though.

Unstable nuclei may be **radioactive** and **decay** over time into different nuclei that are more stable (see p.5).

Radioactive Isotopes Can be Used to Find Out How Old Stuff Is

1) All living things contain the same percentage of radioactive **carbon-14** taken in from the atmosphere.

2) After they die, the amount of carbon-14 inside them **decreases** over time as it **decays** to stable elements.

3) Scientists can calculate the **approximate age** of archaeological finds made from dead **organic matter** (e.g. wood, bone) by using the **isotopic data** (amount of each isotope present) to find the percentage of **radioactive carbon-14** that's **left in** the object.

The Specific Charge of a Particle is Equal to its Charge Over its Mass

The **specific charge** of a particle is the ratio of its charge to its mass, given in coulombs per kilogram ($C\,kg^{-1}$). To calculate specific charge, you just divide the charge in C by the mass in kg.

$$\text{Specific charge} = \frac{\text{charge}}{\text{mass}}$$

You could be asked to find the specific charge of any particle, from a **fundamental particle** like an electron, to the nucleus of an atom or an ion.

A fundamental particle is one that you can't break up into anything smaller.

Example: Calculate the specific charge of a proton.

A proton has a **charge** of $+1.60 \times 10^{-19}$ C and a **mass** of 1.67×10^{-27} kg (see p.2).
So specific charge = $(+1.60 \times 10^{-19}) \div (1.67 \times 10^{-27}) = 9.580... \times 10^7 = \mathbf{9.58 \times 10^7\ C\,kg^{-1}}$ **(to 3 s.f.)**

In calculations, always give your answer to the smallest number of significant figures used in the question.

Warm-Up Questions

Q1 List the particles that make up the atom and give their relative charges and relative masses.

Q2 Define the proton number and nucleon number.

Q3 Explain how the amount of carbon-14 in dead organic matter can tell scientists how old it is.

Q4 How could you calculate the specific charge of a particle?

Exam Questions

Q1 Describe the nuclear model of the atom.	[2 marks]
Q2 Write down the numbers of protons, neutrons and electrons in a neutral atom of oxygen, $^{16}_{8}O$.	[2 marks]
Q3 a) State what is meant by an 'isotope'.	[1 mark]
b) State the similarities and differences between the properties of two isotopes of the same element.	[2 marks]
Q4 An alpha particle is the nucleus of a $^{4}_{2}He$ atom. Calculate the specific charge of an alpha particle.	[4 marks]

"Proton no. = no. of protons" — hardly nuclear physics is it... oh wait...

Physics is the science of all things great and small — on these pages you saw the small (like, really really small). That's why it's useful to know about things like relative charge and relative mass — 'one point six seven times ten to the power of negative twenty-seven' is a bit more of a mouthful than 'one'. It all makes perfect sense.

Stable and Unstable Nuclei

Keeping the nucleus stable requires a lot of effort — a bit like Physics then...

The **Strong Nuclear Force** Binds Nucleons Together

There are several different **forces** acting on the nucleons in a nucleus. The two you already know about are **electrostatic** forces from the protons' electric charges, and **gravitational** forces due to the masses of the particles.

If you do the calculations (don't worry, *you* don't have to) you find the repulsion from the **electrostatic force** is much, much **bigger** than the **gravitational** attraction. If these were the only forces acting in the nucleus, the nucleons would **fly apart**. So there must be **another attractive force** that **holds the nucleus together** — called the **strong nuclear force**. (The gravitational force is so small, you can just ignore it.)

The **strong nuclear force** is quite **complicated**:

1) To **hold the nucleus together**, it must be an **attractive force** that's **stronger** than the electrostatic force.

2) Experiments have shown that the strong nuclear force has a **very short range**. It can only hold nucleons together when they're separated by up to **a few femtometres** (1 fm = 1×10^{-15} m) — the size of a nucleus.

3) The **strength** of the strong nuclear force **quickly falls** beyond this distance (see the graph below).

4) Experiments also show that the strong nuclear force **works equally between all nucleons**. This means that the size of the force is the same whether it's proton-proton, neutron-neutron or proton-neutron.

5) At **very small separations**, the strong nuclear force must be **repulsive** or it would **crush** the nucleus to a **point**.

The **Size** of the Strong Nuclear Force **Varies** with **Nucleon Separation**

The **strong nuclear force** can be plotted on a **graph** to show how it changes with the **distance of separation** between **nucleons**. If the **electrostatic force** is also plotted, you can see the **relationship** between these **two forces**.

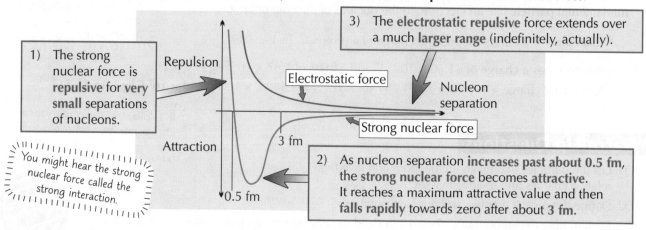

3) The **electrostatic repulsive** force extends over a much **larger range** (indefinitely, actually).

1) The strong nuclear force is **repulsive** for **very small** separations of nucleons.

You might hear the strong nuclear force called the strong interaction.

2) As nucleon separation **increases past about 0.5 fm**, the **strong nuclear force** becomes **attractive**. It reaches a maximum attractive value and then **falls rapidly** towards zero after about 3 fm.

α **Emission** Happens in **Very Big Nuclei**

1) **Alpha emission** only happens in **very big** nuclei, like **uranium** and **radium**.

2) The **nuclei** of these atoms are just **too massive** for the strong nuclear force to keep them stable.

3) When an alpha particle is **emitted**:

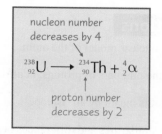

nucleon number decreases by 4

$$^{238}_{92}U \longrightarrow ^{234}_{90}Th + ^{4}_{2}\alpha$$

proton number decreases by 2

The **proton number decreases** by two, and the **nucleon number decreases** by four.

Alpha particles have a very **short range** — only a few cm in air. This can be seen by observing the tracks left by alpha particles in a **cloud chamber**. You could also use a **Geiger counter** (a device that measures the amount of ionising radiation). Bring it up close to the alpha source, then **move it away** slowly and observe how the **count rate drops**.

The thin line is a cosmic ray particle

Stable and Unstable Nuclei

β⁻ **Emission** Happens in **Neutron-Rich** Nuclei

1) **Beta-minus** (usually just called beta) decay is the emission of an **electron** from the **nucleus** along with an **antineutrino**.

2) Beta decay happens in isotopes that are unstable due to being **'neutron rich'** (i.e. they have too many more **neutrons** than **protons** in their nucleus).

3) When a nucleus ejects a beta particle, one of the **neutrons** in the nucleus is **changed** into a **proton**.

> The **proton number increases** by **one**, and the **nucleon number** stays **the same**.

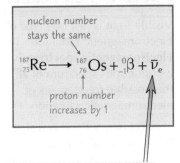

nucleon number stays the same

$$^{187}_{75}\text{Re} \longrightarrow \,^{187}_{76}\text{Os} + \,^{0}_{-1}\beta + \bar{\nu}_e$$

proton number increases by 1

Beta particles have a much greater range than alpha particles.

> In beta decay, you get a tiny neutral particle called an antineutrino released. This antineutrino carries away some energy and momentum.

Neutrinos Were First **Hypothesised** Due to Observations of **Beta Decay**

1) Scientists originally thought that the **only** particle emitted from the nucleus during beta decay was an **electron**.

2) However, observations showed that the **energy** of the particles **after** the **beta decay** was **less** than it was **before**, which didn't fit with the principle of **conservation of energy** (p. 68).

3) In 1930 Wolfgang Pauli suggested **another particle** was being emitted too, and it carried away the **missing energy**. This particle had to be **neutral** (or charge wouldn't be **conserved** in beta decay) and had to have **zero** or **almost zero** mass (as it had never been **detected**).

4) Other discoveries led to Pauli's theory becoming accepted and the particle was named the **neutrino**. (We now know this particle was an antineutrino — p. 6).

5) The neutrino was eventually observed 25 years later, providing evidence for Pauli's hypothesis.

Warm-Up Questions

Q1 What causes an electrostatic force inside the nucleus?

Q2 What evidence suggests the existence of a strong nuclear force?

Q3 Is the strong interaction attractive or repulsive at a nucleon separation of 2 fm?

Q4 Describe the changes that happen in the nucleus during alpha and beta-minus decay.

Q5 What observations led to the hypothesis of the existence of the neutrino?

PRACTICE QUESTIONS

Exam Questions

Q1 The strong nuclear force binds the nucleus together.

a) Explain why the force must be repulsive at very short distances.　　[1 mark]

b) Explain why a nucleus containing two protons in unstable, but one containing two protons and two neutrons is stable.　　[2 marks]

Q2 Radium-226 and potassium-40 are both unstable isotopes.

a) Radium-226 undergoes alpha decay to radon. Complete the balanced nuclear equation for this reaction:

$$^{226}_{88}\text{Ra} \longrightarrow \quad \text{Rn} +$$

[3 marks]

b) Potassium-40 (Z = 19, A = 40) undergoes beta decay to calcium. Write a balanced nuclear equation for this reaction.　　[4 marks]

The strong interaction's like nuclear glue...

Energy, momentum, charge and nucleon number (and several other things that you'll find out about in this section) are conserved in every nuclear reaction. That's why the antineutrino in beta decay has to be there.

Particles and Antiparticles

"I cannae do it Cap'n — their electron-antineutrino ray gun's interfering with my antineutron positron reading..."

Photons are Packets of Electromagnetic Radiation

Visible light is just one type of electromagnetic radiation. The **electromagnetic spectrum** is a continuous spectrum of **all** the possible frequencies of electromagnetic radiation.

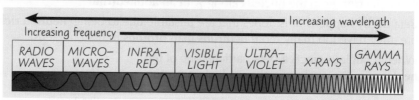

Increasing frequency → ← Increasing wavelength

| RADIO WAVES | MICRO-WAVES | INFRA-RED | VISIBLE LIGHT | ULTRA-VIOLET | X-RAYS | GAMMA RAYS |

The **frequency** f and **wavelength** λ are linked by $f = \frac{c}{\lambda}$, where $c = 3.00 \times 10^8$ ms^{-1} is the **speed of light** in a vacuum (sometimes called the speed of light **in vacuo**).

Electromagnetic radiation exists as **photons** of energy (page 16). The **energy** of a photon depends on the frequency of the radiation:

$$E = hf = \frac{hc}{\lambda}$$

h is the Planck constant, equal to 6.63×10^{-34} Js.

Every Particle has an Antiparticle

1) Each particle has a **matching antiparticle** with the **same mass** and **rest energy** (more later), but with **opposite charge** (amongst other things).

2) For instance, an **antiproton** is a **negatively-charged** particle with the same mass as the **proton**, and the **antineutrino** is the antiparticle of the **neutrino** — it doesn't do much either.

Particle/Antiparticle	Symbol	Relative Charge	Mass (kg)	Rest Energy (MeV)
proton	p	+1	$1.67(3) \times 10^{-27}$	938(.3)
antiproton	$\bar{p}$	−1		
neutron	n	0	$1.67(5) \times 10^{-27}$	939(.6)
antineutron	$\bar{n}$	0		
electron	e$^-$	−1	9.11×10^{-31}	0.51(1)
positron	e$^+$	+1		
neutrino	ν_e	0	0	0
antineutrino	$\bar{\nu}_e$	0		

These are actually an electron-neutrino and an electron-antineutrino (p. 12).

Luckily, in the exam you'll be given all the **masses** in kg and **rest energies** in MeV of each of these particles and their antiparticles. You just need to remember that the **mass** and **rest energy** are the **same** for a particle and its antiparticle. Neutrinos and antineutrinos are incredibly tiny — you can assume they have zero mass and zero rest energy.

1 MeV = 1×10^6 eV. There's more on eV (electron volts) on p. 18.

You can Create Matter and Antimatter from Energy

You've probably heard about the **equivalence** of energy and mass. It all comes out of Einstein's Special Theory of Relativity. **Energy** can turn into **mass** and **mass** can turn into **energy** if you know how. The **rest energy** of a particle is just the 'energy equivalent' of the particle's **mass**, measured in MeV. You can work it all out using the formula $E = mc^2$, but you won't be expected to do the calculations for AS.

When **energy** is converted into **mass** you get **equal amounts** of **matter** and **antimatter**.

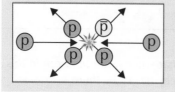

Fire **two protons** at each other at high speed and you'll end up with a lot of **energy** at the point of impact. This energy might be converted into **more particles**.

If an extra **proton** is formed then there will always be an **antiproton** to go with it. It's called **pair production**.

Particles and Antiparticles

Each **Particle-Antiparticle Pair** is Produced from a **Single Photon**

Energy that gets **converted** into **matter** and **antimatter** is in the form of a **photon** (p.16). Pair production only happens if **one photon** has enough energy to produce that much mass — only **gamma ray** photons have enough energy. It also tends to happen near a **nucleus**, which helps conserve momentum.
You usually get **electron-positron** pairs produced (rather than any other pair) — because they have a relatively **low mass**.

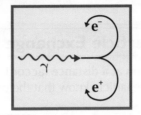

The particle tracks are curved because there's usually a magnetic field present in particle physics experiments. They curve in opposite directions because of the opposite charges on the electron and positron.

The **minimum energy** for a photon to undergo **pair production** is the **total rest energy** of the particles produced.
The particle and antiparticle each have a rest energy of E_0, so:

$$E_{min} = hf_{min} = 2E_0$$

The **Opposite** of **Pair-Production** is **Annihilation**

When a **particle** meets its **antiparticle** the result is **annihilation**. All the **mass** of the particle and antiparticle gets converted back to **energy**. Antiparticles can usually only exist for a fraction of a second before this happens, so you don't get them in ordinary matter.
An annihilation is between a particle-antiparticle pair, which both have a rest energy E_0. **Both** photons need to have a **minimum energy**, E_{min}, which when added together equals at least $2E_0$ for **energy** to be **conserved** in this interaction. So $2E_{min} = 2E_0$ and:

$$E_{min} = hf_{min} = E_0$$

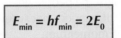

BANG

OR

The electron and positron annihilate and their mass is converted into the energy of a pair of gamma ray photons to conserve momentum.

Example: Calculate the maximum wavelength of one of the photons produced when an electron and positron annihilate each other.

For annihilation, minimum photon energy $E_{min} = hf_{min} = E_0$. Remember $f = \dfrac{c}{\lambda}$, so $\dfrac{hc}{\lambda_{max}} = E_0$.

So $\lambda_{max} = \dfrac{hc}{E_0} = \dfrac{(6.63 \times 10^{-34}) \times (3.00 \times 10^8)}{(0.511 \times 10^6) \times (1.60 \times 10^{-19})} = 2.432... \times 10^{-12} = \mathbf{2.43 \times 10^{-12}}$ **m (to 3 s.f.)**

The Planck constant is in J, so you need to convert E_0 from MeV to J.

Warm-Up Questions

Q1 Describe the properties of an electron-antineutrino.

Q2 Give one similarity and one difference between a proton and an antiproton.

Q3 What is pair production?

Q4 What happens when a proton collides with an antiproton?

PRACTICE QUESTIONS

Exam Questions

Q1 Write down an equation for the reaction between a positron and an electron and state the name for this type of reaction. [2 marks]

Q2 Explain what causes extra particles to be created when two particles collide. [2 marks]

Q3 Give a reason why the reaction: $p + p \rightarrow p + p + n$ is not possible. [1 mark]

Q4 A photon produces an electron-positron pair, each with 9.84×10^{-14} J of energy. Calculate the frequency of the photon. [2 marks]

This really is Physics at its ~~hardest~~ grooviest...

Inertial dampers are off-line Captain.........oops, no — it's just these false ears making me feel dizzy. Anyway — you'd need to carry an awful lot of antimatter to provide enough energy to run a spaceship. Plus, it's not the easiest to store...

Forces and Exchange Particles

*Having learnt about all those lovely particles and antiparticles, you now have the esteemed privilege of learning about yet another weirdy thing called a **gauge boson**. To the casual observer this might not seem **entirely fair**. And I have to say, I'd be with them.*

Forces are Caused by Particle Exchange

You can't have **instantaneous action at a distance** (according to Einstein, anyway). So, when two particles **interact**, something must **happen** to let one particle know that the other one's there. That's the idea behind **exchange particles**.

1) **Repulsion** — Each time the **ball** is **thrown or caught** the people get **pushed apart**. It happens because the ball carries **momentum**.

   Particle exchange also explains **attraction**, but you need a bit more imagination.

←——REPULSION——→

2) **Attraction** — Each time the **boomerang** is **thrown or caught** the people **get pushed together**. (In real life, you'd probably fall in first.)

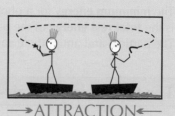

——→ATTRACTION←——

These exchange particles are called **gauge bosons**.

The **repulsion** between two **protons** is caused by the **exchange** of **virtual photons**, which are the gauge bosons of the **electromagnetic** force. Gauge bosons are **virtual** particles — they only exist for a **very short time**.

There are Four Fundamental Forces

All forces in nature are caused by four **fundamental** forces — the strong nuclear force, the weak nuclear force, the electromagnetic force and gravity. Each one has its **own gauge boson** and these are the ones you have to learn:

Type of Interaction	Gauge Boson	Particles Affected
electromagnetic	virtual photon (symbol, γ)	charged particles only
weak	W^+, W^-	all types
strong	pions (π^+, π^-, π^0)	hadrons only

Particle physicists never **bother** about **gravity** because it's so incredibly **feeble** compared with the other types of interaction. Gravity only really **matters** when you've got **big masses** like **stars and planets**.

In the **strong nuclear force**, pions are described as being exchanged between **nucleons**. You might also see it described as **gluons** being exchanged between **quarks** (p. 13).

The Larger the Mass of the Gauge Boson, the Shorter the Range of the Force

1) The **W bosons** have a **mass** of about **100 times that of a proton**, which gives the weak force a **very short range**. Creating a **virtual W particle** uses **so much energy** that it can only exist for a **very short time** and it **can't travel far**.

2) On the other hand, the **photon** has **zero mass**, which gives you a force with **infinite range**.

You can use Diagrams to Show What's Going In and What's Coming Out

Particle interactions can be hard to get your head around. A **neat way** of **solving problems** is by **drawing simple diagrams** of particle interactions rather than doing **calculations**.

1) **Gauge bosons** are represented by **wiggly lines** (technical term).

2) Other **particles** are represented by **straight lines**.

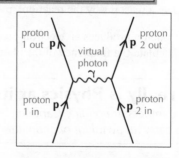

Forces and Exchange Particles

*You can draw simple diagrams of **loads** of interactions, but you **only** need to learn these ones for your exams.*

You Need to Be Able to **Draw Diagrams** of these **Interactions**

Electromagnetic Repulsion

This is the easiest of the lot. When two particles with **equal charges** get close to each other, they **repel**.

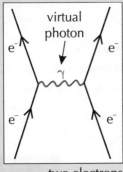

two electrons repelling each other

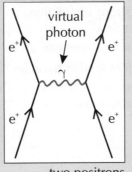

two positrons repelling each other

RULES FOR DRAWING PARTICLE INTERACTION DIAGRAMS:

1) **Incoming** particles start at the bottom of the diagram and move upwards.
2) The **baryons** (p.10) and **leptons** (p.12) can't cross from one side to the other.
3) Make sure the charges on both sides balance. The **W** bosons carry **charge** from one side of the diagram to the other.
4) A **W⁻** particle going to the **left** has the same effect as a **W⁺** particle going to the **right**.

Electron Capture and Electron-proton Collisions

Electrons and protons are of course attracted by the **electromagnetic interaction** between them, but if a proton **captures** an electron, the **weak interaction** can make this interaction happen.

$$p + e^- \rightarrow n + \nu_e$$

electron capture

You also need to know about **electron-proton collisions**, where an electron **collides** with a proton. The equation is just the same as electron capture but in the diagram a **W⁻ boson** goes from the **electron** to the **proton** instead of a W⁺ travelling the other way.

Beta-plus and Beta-minus Decay

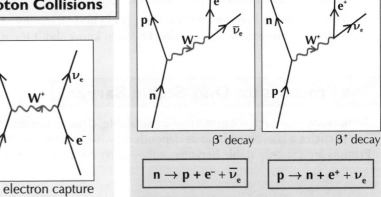

β⁻ decay   β⁺ decay

$$n \rightarrow p + e^- + \bar{\nu}_e$$ $$p \rightarrow n + e^+ + \nu_e$$

You get an **antineutrino** in β⁻ decay and a **neutrino** in β⁺ decay so that **lepton number** (p.12) is conserved.

You'll see on p.14 that when a proton changes to a neutron or vice versa, it has to be the weak interaction.

Warm-Up Questions

Q1 List the four fundamental forces in nature.
Q2 Explain what a virtual particle is.
Q3 Draw a simple diagram to show the particles involved in a beta-minus decay interaction.
Q4 Which gauge bosons are exchanged in weak interactions?

Exam Questions

Q1 Describe how the force of electromagnetic repulsion between two protons is explained by particle exchange. [2 marks]

Q2 Draw a diagram to show the particle interaction when an electron and a proton collide. Label all the particles involved and state clearly which type of interaction is involved. [3 marks]

I need a drink...
Urrrgghhhh... eyes... glazed... brain... melting... ears... bleeding... help me... help me...

help me...

Classification of Particles

There are loads of different types of particle apart from the ones you get in normal matter (protons, neutrons, etc.).
They only appear in cosmic rays and in particle accelerators, and they often decay very quickly so they're
difficult to get a handle on. Nonetheless, you need to learn about a load of them and their properties.
Stick with it — you'll get there.

Hadrons are Particles that Feel the Strong Nuclear Force (e.g. Protons and Neutrons)

1) The **nucleus** of an atom is made up of **protons** and **neutrons** (déjà vu).

2) Since the **protons** are **positively charged** they need a strong force to hold them together. This is called the **strong nuclear force** or the **strong interaction** (who said physicists lack imagination...). See page 4 for details.

(Leptons are an example of particles that can't. See page 12.)

3) **Not all particles** can **feel** the **strong nuclear force** — the ones that **can** are called **hadrons**.

4) Hadrons aren't **fundamental** particles. They're made up of **smaller particles** called quarks (see pages 13–15).

5) There are **two** types of **hadrons** — **baryons** (and anti-baryons) and **mesons**. They're classified according to the number of **quarks** that make them up, but don't worry about that for now.

Protons and Neutrons are Baryons

1) It's helpful to think of **protons** and **neutrons** as **two versions** of the **same particle** — the **nucleon**. They just have **different electric charges**.

2) **Protons** and **neutrons** are both **baryons**.

3) There are **other baryons** that you don't get in normal matter — like **sigmas** (Σ) — they're **short-lived** and you **don't** need to **know about them** (woohoo!).

Baryon and Meson felt the strong interaction.

The Proton is the Only Stable Baryon

All **baryons** — except the proton — are **unstable**. This means that they **decay** to become other **particles**.
The **particles** a baryon ends up as depends on what it started as, but it **always** includes a **proton**.
Protons are the only **stable** baryons — they don't decay (as far as we know).

> **All** baryons except protons decay to a **proton**.

Some theories predict that protons should decay with a very long half-life, but there's no evidence for it at the moment.

Antiprotons and Antineutrons are Antibaryons

The **antiparticles** of protons and neutrons — **antiprotons** and **antineutrons** — are **antibaryons**.
But, if you remember from page 7, **antiparticles** are **annihilated** when they meet the corresponding **particle** — which means that you **don't** find **antibaryons** in ordinary matter.

The Number of Baryons in an Interaction is called the Baryon Number

The **baryon number** is the number of baryons. (A bit like **nucleon number** but including unusual baryons like Σ too.)
The **proton** and the **neutron** each have a baryon number **B = +1**. Antibaryons have a baryon number **B = –1**.
Other particles (i.e. things that aren't baryons) are given a baryon number **B = 0**.

Baryon number is a **quantum number** that must be **conserved** in any interaction — that means it can only take on a **certain set of values** (so you can't have 2.7981 baryons, or 1.991112 baryons... you get the idea).

When an **interaction** happens, the **baryon number** on either side of the interaction has to be the **same**.
You can use this fact to **predict** whether an **interaction** will **happen** — if the numbers don't match, it can't happen.

> The **total baryon number** in **any** particle interaction **never changes**.

Classification of Particles

Neutrons are Baryons that Decay into Protons

You saw on pages 5 and 9 that **beta decay** involves a **neutron** changing into a **proton**. This happens when there are many **more neutrons** than **protons** in a nucleus or when a **neutron** is **by itself**, **outside** of a nucleus. **Beta decay** is caused by the **weak interaction** (see page 14).

When a neutron decays, it forms a **proton**, an **electron** and an **antineutrino**:

$$n \rightarrow p + e^- + \bar{\nu}_e$$

Electrons and **antineutrinos** aren't baryons (they're **leptons**, as you'll see on the next page), so they have a baryon number $B = 0$. Neutrons and **protons** are baryons, so have a baryon number $B = 1$. This means that the **baryon numbers** on both sides are **equal** (to 1), so the interaction **can** happen.

The Mesons You Need to Know About are Pions and Kaons

The second type of hadron you need to know about is the **meson**.

1) **All mesons** are **unstable** and have **baryon number** $B = 0$ (because they're not baryons).

2) **Pions** (π-mesons) are the **lightest mesons**. You get **three versions** with different **electric charges** — π^+, π^0 and π^-. You get **loads** of pions in **high-energy particle collisions** like those studied at the **CERN** particle accelerator.

3) **Kaons** (**K**-mesons) are **heavier** and more **unstable** than **pions**. You get different ones like K^+ and K^0. Kaons have a very **short lifetime** and **decay** into **pions**.

4) Pions and kaons were **discovered** in **cosmic rays** — cosmic ray showers are a source of both particles. You can observe the tracks of these particles with a **cloud chamber** (see p.4).

5) Mesons **interact** with **baryons** via the **strong force**.

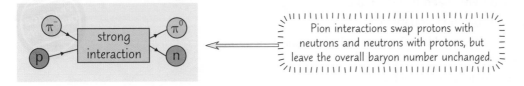

Pion interactions swap protons with neutrons and neutrons with protons, but leave the overall baryon number unchanged.

Summary of Hadron Properties

DON'T PANIC if you don't understand all this yet. For now, just **learn** these properties.

You'll need to work through to the end of page 15 to see how it **all fits together**.

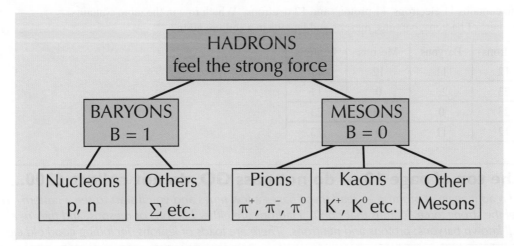

Classification of Particles

Leptons (e.g. Electrons and Neutrinos) Don't Feel the Strong Nuclear Force

1) **Leptons** are **fundamental particles** and they **don't** feel the **strong nuclear force**.
   They only really **interact** with other particles via the **weak interaction** (along with
   a bit of gravitational force and the electromagnetic force as well if they're charged).

2) **Electrons (e⁻)** are **stable** and very **familiar**, but — you guessed it — there are also **other leptons**,
   such as the **muon (μ⁻)**, that are just like **heavy electrons**.

3) **Muons** are **unstable**, and **decay** eventually into **ordinary electrons**.

4) The **electron** and **muon** leptons each come with their **own neutrino**, ν_e and ν_μ.

5) **Neutrinos** have **zero** or **almost zero mass**, and **zero electric charge** — so they don't do much.
   Neutrinos only take part in **weak interactions** (see p.14). In fact, a neutrino can
   pass right through the Earth without **anything** happening to it.

You Have to Count the Types of Lepton Separately

Like the baryon number, the **lepton number** is
just the number of **leptons**. **Each lepton** is given a
lepton number of **+1**, but the **electron** and **muon**
types of lepton have to be **counted separately**.
You get **different** lepton numbers, L_e and L_μ.

All the leptons and lepton-neutrinos have their
own **antiparticle** too — no surprises there. They
have the **opposite charge** and **lepton numbers**
to their matching particles. For example, the
antimuon μ^+ has charge = +1, $L_e = 0$ and $L_\mu = -1$.

Name	Symbol	Charge	L_e	L_μ
electron	e^-	−1	+1	0
electron-neutrino	ν_e	0	+1	0
muon	μ^-	−1	0	+1
muon-neutrino	ν_μ	0	0	+1

Warm-Up Questions

Q1 List the differences between a hadron and a lepton.

Q2 Which is the only stable baryon (probably)?

Q3 A particle collision at CERN produces 2 protons, 3 pions and 1 neutron.
What is the total baryon number of these particles?

Q4 Which two particles have lepton number $L_\mu = +1$?

Exam Questions

Q1 List all the decay products of the neutron.
Explain why this decay cannot be due to the strong interaction.   [3 marks]

Q2 Initially, the muon was incorrectly identified as a meson.
Explain why the muon is not a meson.   [3 marks]

Q3 A sodium atom contains 11 electrons, 11 protons and 12 neutrons. Which row in the table contains
the correct numbers of hadrons, baryons, mesons and leptons in a sodium atom?   [1 mark]

	Hadrons	Baryons	Mesons	Leptons
A	12	11	12	11
B	23	23	0	11
C	23	0	23	23
D	12	11	0	23

Go back to the top of page 10 — do not pass GO, do not collect £200...

*Do it. Go back and read it again. I promise — read these pages a few times and you'll start to see a pattern. There
are hadrons that feel the strong force, leptons that don't. Hadrons are either baryons or mesons, and they're all weird
except for those well-known baryons: protons and neutrons. There are loads of leptons, including good old electrons.*

Quarks

Quarks may sound like a bizarre concept, but they weren't just made up willy-nilly. Large teams of scientists and engineers all over the world worked for years to come up with the info on these pages.

Quarks are Fundamental Particles

Quarks are the **building blocks** for **hadrons** (baryons and mesons). Antiparticles of hadrons are made from **antiquarks**.

1) To make **protons** and **neutrons** you only need two types of quark — the **up** quark (**u**) and the **down** quark (**d**).

2) An extra one called the **strange** quark (**s**) lets you make more particles with a property called **strangeness**.

Strangeness is Only Conserved Some of the Time

1) **Strangeness**, like baryon number, is a **quantum number** (see p.10) — it can only take a certain set of values.

2) Strange particles, such as kaons, are **created** via the **strong** interaction but **decay** via the **weak** interaction.

3) Here's the catch — strangeness is **conserved** in the **strong interaction**, but **not** in the **weak interaction** (p.14).

4) That means strange particles are **always produced in pairs** (e.g. K+ and K−).
One has a strangeness of +1, and the other has a strangeness of −1, so the overall strangeness of 0 is **conserved**.

Quarks and Antiquarks have Opposite Properties

The **antiquarks** have **opposite properties** to the quarks — as you'd expect.

QUARKS

Name	Symbol	Charge	Baryon number	Strangeness
up	u	$+\frac{2}{3}$	$+\frac{1}{3}$	0
down	d	$-\frac{1}{3}$	$+\frac{1}{3}$	0
strange	s	$-\frac{1}{3}$	$+\frac{1}{3}$	−1

ANTIQUARKS

Name	Symbol	Charge	Baryon number	Strangeness
anti-up	$\bar{u}$	$-\frac{2}{3}$	$-\frac{1}{3}$	0
anti-down	$\bar{d}$	$+\frac{1}{3}$	$-\frac{1}{3}$	0
anti-strange	$\bar{s}$	$+\frac{1}{3}$	$-\frac{1}{3}$	+1

Baryons are Made from Three Quarks

Evidence for quarks came from **hitting protons** with **high-energy electrons**.
The way the **electrons scattered** showed that there were **three concentrations of charge** (quarks) **inside** the proton.

Proton = **uud**

Total charge
$= \frac{2}{3} + \frac{2}{3} - \frac{1}{3} = 1$
Baryon number
$= \frac{1}{3} + \frac{1}{3} + \frac{1}{3} = 1$

Antiproton = **ūūd̄**

Total charge
$= -\frac{2}{3} - \frac{2}{3} + \frac{1}{3} = -1$
Baryon number
$= -\frac{1}{3} - \frac{1}{3} - \frac{1}{3} = -1$

Neutron = **udd**

Total charge
$= \frac{2}{3} - \frac{1}{3} - \frac{1}{3} = 0$
Baryon number
$= \frac{1}{3} + \frac{1}{3} + \frac{1}{3} = 1$

Antineutron = **ūd̄d̄**

Total charge
$= -\frac{2}{3} + \frac{1}{3} + \frac{1}{3} = 0$
Baryon number
$= -\frac{1}{3} - \frac{1}{3} - \frac{1}{3} = -1$

Quarks

Mesons are a Quark and an Antiquark

Pions are just made from combinations of **up**, **down**, **anti-up** and **anti-down** quarks.
Kaons have **strangeness** so you need to put in **s** quarks as well (remember, the **s** quark has a strangeness of S = −1).

Before we move on, it's worth mentioning that the π⁻ meson is just the **antiparticle** of the π⁺ meson, the **K⁻** meson is the antiparticle of the **K⁺** meson, and the **antiparticle** of a π⁰ meson is **itself**. It all makes sense when you look at the quark compositions to the right...

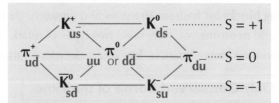

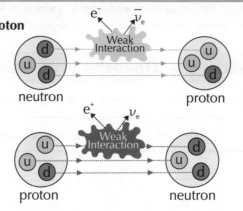

Physicists love patterns. Gaps in patterns like this predicted the existence of particles that were actually found later in experiments. Great stuff.

The Weak Interaction is something that Changes the Quark Type

In β⁻ decay a **neutron** is changed into a **proton** — in other words **udd** changes into **uud**. It means turning a **d** quark into a **u** quark. Only the weak interaction can do this.

Some unstable isotopes like **carbon-11** decay by β⁺ emission. In this case a **proton** changes to a **neutron**, so a **u** quark changes to a **d** quark and we get:

Four Properties are Conserved in Particle Interactions

Charge is Always Conserved

In **any** particle interaction, the **total charge** after the interaction must equal the total charge before the interaction.

Energy and momentum are also always conserved in particle interactions.

Baryon Number is Always Conserved

Just like with charge, in **any** particle interaction, the **baryon number** after the interaction must equal the baryon number before the interaction.

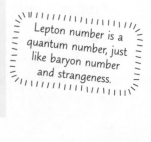

Dylan was committed to conserving strangeness.

Strangeness is Conserved in Strong Interactions

The **only** way to change the **type** of quark is with the **weak interaction**, so in strong interactions there has to be the same number of strange quarks at the beginning as at the end. In weak interactions, strangeness can change by −1, 0 or +1. The interaction $K^- + p \rightarrow n + \pi^0$ is fine for **charge** and **baryon number** but not for **strangeness** — so it won't happen. The negative kaon has an s quark in it.

Conservation of Lepton Number is a Bit More Complicated

The different types of lepton number have to be conserved separately.

1) For example, the interaction
   $\pi^- \rightarrow \mu^- + \bar{\nu}_\mu$ has $L_\mu = 0$ at the start and $L_\mu = 1 - 1 = 0$ at the end, so it's OK.
   Similarly, $n \rightarrow p + e^- + \bar{\nu}_e$ is fine. $L_e = 0$ at the start and $L_e = 1 - 1 = 0$ at the end.

2) On the other hand, the interaction $\nu_\mu + \mu^- \rightarrow e^- + \nu_e$ can't happen.
   At the start $L_\mu = 2$ and $L_e = 0$, but at the end $L_\mu = 0$ and $L_e = 2$.

Lepton number is a quantum number, just like baryon number and strangeness.

Quarks

There's No Such Thing as a Free Quark

What if you **blasted** a **proton** with **enough energy** — could you **separate out** the quarks? Nope.
Your energy just gets changed into more **quarks and antiquarks** — it's **pair production** again and
you just make **mesons**. It's not possible to get a quark by itself — this is called **quark confinement**.

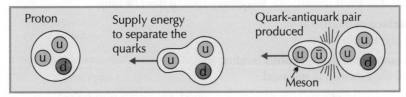

Simon was practising
quack confinement.

We're Still Searching for Particles

As time goes on, our knowledge and understanding of particle physics **changes**.

1) **New theories** are created to try to explain observations from experiments.
Sometimes, physicists hypothesise a new **particle** and the **properties** they expect it to have.
E.g. the **neutrino** was hypothesised due to observations of beta decay.

2) **Experiments** to try to find the existence of this new particle are then carried out. Results from different
experiments are **combined** to try to **confirm** the new particle. If it exists, the theory is **more likely** to be
correct and the scientific community start to accept it — it's **validated**.

3) It's not quite that simple though. Experiments in particle physics often need particles travelling at incredibly **high
speeds** (close to the speed of light). This can only be achieved using **particle accelerators**. These huge pieces of
equipment are very **expensive** to build and run. This means that **large groups** of scientists and engineers from all
over the **world** have to **collaborate** to be able to fund these experiments.

Example: Paul Dirac predicted the existence of **antimatter** in 1928. His theory was **validated** with the observation
of the **positron** and, over the years, more and more observations of antiparticles. Nowadays, it's **accepted** that
antimatter exists, but there are still **questions**. For example, there should have been **equal amounts** of matter
and antimatter created when the universe was formed, but **almost everything** we observe is made of **matter**.

Scientists are trying to figure out what happened to all the antimatter by studying the differences in behaviour of
matter and antimatter particles using the **Large Hadron Collider (LHC)** at **CERN**.
The LHC is a **17 mile long** particle accelerator costing around **£3 billion** to build and
£15 million per year to run. Some **10,000** scientists from **100** countries are involved.

ATLAS, just one of many experiments the LHC at CERN is used for, involves around 3000 scientists from 38 different countries.

Warm-Up Questions

Q1 What is a quark?

Q2 Kaons are produced by the strong interaction. Why must they be produced in pairs?

Q3 By how much can the strangeness change in a weak interaction?

Q4 Which type of particle is made from a quark and an antiquark?

Q5 Describe how a neutron is made up from quarks.

Q6 List six quantities that are conserved in strong particle interactions.

Exam Questions

Q1 a) Write down the quark composition of the π^-. [1 mark]

b) Explain how the charges of the quarks give rise to its charge. [1 mark]

Q2 Explain how the quark composition is changed in the β^- decay of the neutron. [2 marks]

Q3 Give two reasons why the reaction $p + p \rightarrow p + K^+$ does not happen. [2 marks]

A physical property called strangeness — how cool is that...

*True, there's a lot of information here, but this page really does tie up a lot of the stuff on the last few pages. Learn as
much as you can from this three-page spread, then go back to page 13, and work back through to here. Don't expect
to understand it all — but you'll definitely find it much easier to learn when you can see how all the bits fit together.*

The Photoelectric Effect

I think they should rename 'the photoelectric effect' as 'the piece-of-cake effect' — it's not easy, I just like cake.

Shining Light on a Metal can Release Electrons

If you shine **light** of a **high enough frequency** onto the **surface of a metal**, the metal will **emit electrons**. For **most** metals, this **frequency** falls in the **UV** range.

'Light' means any EM radiation — not just visible light.

1) **Free electrons** on the **surface** of the metal **absorb energy** from the light.

2) If an electron **absorbs enough** energy, the **bonds** holding it to the metal **break** and the electron is **released**.

3) This is called the **photoelectric effect** and the electrons emitted are called **photoelectrons**.

ultraviolet radiation

electrons

You don't need to know the details of any experiments on this, you just need to learn the three main conclusions:

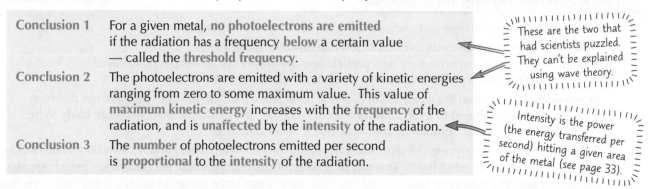

Conclusion 1   For a given metal, **no photoelectrons are emitted** if the radiation has a frequency **below** a certain value — called the **threshold frequency**.

Conclusion 2   The photoelectrons are emitted with a variety of kinetic energies ranging from zero to some maximum value. This value of **maximum kinetic energy** increases with the **frequency** of the radiation, and is **unaffected** by the **intensity** of the radiation.

Conclusion 3   The **number** of photoelectrons emitted per second is **proportional** to the **intensity** of the radiation.

These are the two that had scientists puzzled. They can't be explained using wave theory.

Intensity is the power (the energy transferred per second) hitting a given area of the metal (see page 33).

The Photoelectric Effect Couldn't be Explained by Wave Theory...

According to wave theory:

1) For a particular frequency of light, the **energy** carried is **proportional** to the **intensity** of the beam.

2) The energy carried by the light would be **spread evenly** over the wavefront.

3) **Each** free electron on the surface of the metal would gain a **bit of energy** from each incoming wave.

4) Gradually, each electron would gain **enough energy** to leave the metal.

SO... The **higher the intensity** of the wave, the **more energy** it should transfer to each electron — the kinetic energy should increase with **intensity**. There's **no explanation** for the **kinetic energy** depending only on the **frequency**.

There is also **no explanation** for the **threshold frequency**. According to **wave theory**, the electrons should be emitted **eventually**, no matter what the **frequency** is.

...But it Could be Explained by Einstein's Photon Model of Light

1) **Einstein** suggested that **EM waves** (and the energy they carry) **exist** in discrete packets — called **photons**.

2) The **energy carried** by one of these **photons** is:

$$E = hf = \frac{hc}{\lambda}$$

where h = Planck's constant = 6.63×10^{-34} Js and c = speed of light in a vacuum = 3.00×10^{8} ms^{-1}

You might have seen this formula before on page 6.

3) Einstein saw these photons of light as having a **one-on-one**, **particle-like** interaction with **an electron** in a **metal surface**. A photon would **transfer all** its **energy** to **one**, **specific electron**.

According to the photon model:

1) When light hits its surface, the metal is **bombarded** by photons.

2) If one of these photons **collides** with a free electron, the electron will gain energy equal to *hf*.

Before an electron can **leave** the surface of the metal, it needs enough energy to **break the bonds holding it there**. This energy is called the **work function** (which has the symbol ϕ (phi)) and its **value** depends on the **metal**.

The Photoelectric Effect

The **Photon Model** Explains the **Threshold Frequency**...

1) If the energy **gained** by an electron (on the surface of the metal) from a photon is **greater** than the **work function**, the electron is **emitted**.

2) If it **isn't**, the metal will heat up, but **no electrons** will be emitted.

3) Since, for **electrons** to be released, $hf \geq \phi$, the **threshold frequency** must be:

$$f = \frac{\phi}{h}$$

...and the **Maximum Kinetic Energy**

1) The **energy transferred** to an electron is hf.

2) The **kinetic energy** the electron will be carrying when it **leaves** the metal is hf **minus** any energy it's **lost** on the way out. Electrons **deeper** down in the metal lose more energy than the electrons on the **surface**, which explains the **range** of energies.

3) The **minimum** amount of energy it can lose is the **work function**, so the **maximum kinetic energy** of a photoelectron, $E_{k\,(max)}$, is given by the photoelectric equation:

$$hf = \phi + E_{k\,(max)} \quad \text{where} \quad E_{k\,(max)} = \frac{1}{2}mv_{max}^2$$

4) The **kinetic energy** of the electrons is **independent of the intensity** (the **number** of photons **per second** on an **area**, p.33), as they can **only absorb one photon** at a time. Increasing the **intensity** just means **more photons per second** on an **area** — each photon has the **same energy** as before.

The **Stopping Potential** Gives the **Maximum Kinetic Energy**

1) The **maximum kinetic energy** can be measured using the idea of **stopping potential**.

2) The **emitted electrons** are made to lose their energy by **doing work** against an applied **potential difference**.

3) The **stopping potential**, V_s, is the p.d. needed to stop the **fastest** moving electrons, with $E_{k\,(max)}$.

4) The **work done** by the p.d. in **stopping** the fastest electrons is equal to the **energy** they were carrying:

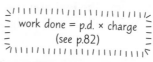
work done = p.d. × charge
(see p.82)

Work done = zero.

$$eV_s = E_{k\,(max)}$$

where e = charge on the electron = 1.60×10^{-19} C, V_s = stopping potential in V, and $E_{k\,(max)}$ is measured in J.

(see p.82)

Warm-Up Questions

Q1 Explain what the photoelectric effect is.

Q2 What three conclusions were drawn from experimentation on the photoelectric effect?

Q3 What is meant by the work function of a metal?

Q4 How is the maximum kinetic energy of a photoelectron related to the work function?

Q5 Explain what is meant by the stopping potential. Write down a formula relating stopping potential and $E_{k\,(max)}$.

PRACTICE QUESTIONS

Exam Questions

Q1 An isolated zinc plate with neutral charge is exposed to high-frequency ultraviolet light. State and explain the effect of the ultraviolet light on the charge of the plate. [2 marks]

Q2 Explain why photoelectric emission from a metal surface only occurs when the frequency of the incident radiation exceeds a certain threshold value. [2 marks]

I'm so glad we got that all cleared up...

The most important bits here are why wave theory doesn't explain the phenomenon of the photoelectric effect, and why the photon theory does. A good way to learn conceptual stuff like this is to try to explain it to someone else.

Energy Levels and Photon Emission

Quantum theory doesn't really make much sense — to anyone. It works though, so it's hard to argue with.

Electrons in Atoms Exist in Discrete Energy Levels

1) **Electrons** in an **atom** can **only exist** in certain **well-defined energy levels**. Each level is given a **number**, with **n = 1** representing the **ground state**.

2) Electrons can **move down** energy levels by **emitting** a **photon**.

3) Since these **transitions** are between **definite energy levels**, the **energy** of **each photon** emitted can **only** take a **certain allowed value**.

4) The diagram on the right shows the **energy levels** for **atomic hydrogen**.

5) The **energies involved** are **so tiny** that it makes sense to use a more **appropriate unit** than the **joule**. The **electronvolt (eV)** is defined as:

> The **kinetic energy carried** by an **electron** after it has been **accelerated** through a **potential difference** of **1 volt**.

> energy gained by electron (eV)
> = accelerating voltage (V)

> **1 eV = 1.60 × 10⁻¹⁹ J**

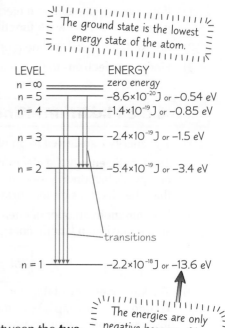

The ground state is the lowest energy state of the atom.

LEVEL	ENERGY
n = ∞	zero energy
n = 5	-8.6×10^{-20} J or -0.54 eV
n = 4	-1.4×10^{-19} J or -0.85 eV
n = 3	-2.4×10^{-19} J or -1.5 eV
n = 2	-5.4×10^{-19} J or -3.4 eV
n = 1	-2.2×10^{-18} J or -13.6 eV

transitions

The energies are only negative because of how "zero energy" is defined. Just one of those silly convention things — don't worry about it.

6) On the diagram, energies are labelled in **both units** for **comparison's** sake.

7) The **energy** carried by each **photon** is **equal** to the **difference in energies** between the **two levels**. The equation below shows a **transition** between a higher energy level n = 2 where the electrons have energy E_2 and a lower energy level n = 1 with electrons of energy E_1:

$$\Delta E = E_2 - E_1 = hf = \frac{hc}{\lambda}$$

8) Electrons can also **move up** energy levels if they **absorb a photon** with the **exact energy difference** between the two levels. The movement of an electron to a higher energy level is called **excitation**.

9) If an electron is **removed** from an atom, we say the atom is **ionised**. The energy of each **energy level** within an atom gives the amount of **energy** needed to **remove an electron** in that level from the atom. The **ionisation energy** of an atom is the amount of energy needed to completely remove an electron from the atom from the **ground state (n = 1)**.

Fluorescent Tubes use Excited Electrons to Produce Light

1) **Fluorescent tubes** contain **mercury vapour**, across which an initial **high voltage** is applied. This **high voltage** accelerates **fast-moving free electrons** that **ionise** some of the **mercury atoms**, producing **more** free electrons.

2) When this flow of free electrons **collides** with electrons in **other mercury atoms**, the electrons in the mercury atoms are **excited** to **higher energy levels**.

3) When these **excited electrons** return to their **ground states**, they emit **photons** in the **UV** range.

4) A **phosphor coating** on the **inside** of the tube **absorbs** these **photons**, exciting its **electrons** to **much higher orbits**. These electrons then **cascade** down the **energy levels**, emitting many **lower energy photons** in the form of **visible light**.

Fluorescent Tubes Produce Line Emission Spectra

1) If you **split** the light from a **fluorescent tube** with a **prism** or a **diffraction grating** (see pages 36-37), you get a **line spectrum**.

2) A line spectrum is seen as a **series** of **bright lines** against a **black background**.

3) Each **line** corresponds to a **particular wavelength** of light **emitted** by the source.

4) Since only certain photon energies are allowed, you only see the **wavelengths** corresponding to these energies.

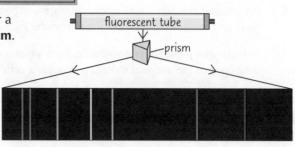

fluorescent tube

prism

Energy Levels and Photon Emission

Shining **White Light** through a **Cool Gas** gives an **Absorption Spectrum**

Continuous Spectra Contain All Possible Wavelengths

1) The **spectrum** of **white light** is **continuous**.

2) If you **split** the **light** up with a **prism**, the **colours** all **merge** into each other — there **aren't** any **gaps** in the spectrum.

3) **Hot things** emit a **continuous spectrum** in the visible and infrared.

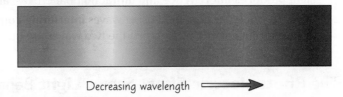

Decreasing wavelength ⟹

4) **All** the **wavelengths** are allowed because the electrons are **not confined** to **energy levels** in the object producing the **continuous spectrum**. The electrons are not bound to atoms and are **free**.

Cool Gases Remove Certain Wavelengths from the Continuous Spectrum

1) You get a **line absorption spectrum** when **light** with a **continuous spectrum** of **energy** (white light) passes through a cool gas.

2) At **low temperatures**, **most** of the **electrons** in the **gas atoms** will be in their **ground states**.

3) The electrons can only absorb **photons** with **energies** equal to the **difference** between **two energy levels**.

4) **Photons** of the **corresponding wavelengths** are **absorbed** by the **electrons** to **excite** them to **higher energy levels**.

5) These **wavelengths** are then **missing** from the **continuous spectrum** when it **comes out** the other side of the gas.

6) You see a **continuous spectrum** with **black lines** in it corresponding to the **absorbed wavelengths**.

7) If you **compare** the **absorption** and **emission** spectra of a **particular gas**, the **black lines** in the **absorption spectrum match up** to the **bright lines** in the **emission spectrum**.

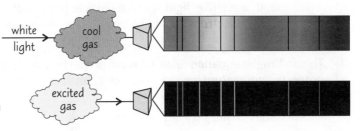

white light → cool gas

excited gas →

Warm-Up Questions

Q1 Describe line absorption and line emission spectra. How are these two types of spectra produced?

Q2 Use the size of the energy level transitions involved to explain how the coating on a fluorescent tube converts UV into visible light.

PRACTICE QUESTIONS

Exam Question

Q1 An electron is accelerated through a potential difference of 12.1 V.

a) How much kinetic energy has it gained in i) eV and ii) joules? [2 marks]

b) This electron hits a hydrogen atom in its ground state and excites it.

   i) Explain what is meant by excitation. [1 mark]

   ii) Using the energy values on the right, calculate which energy level the electron from the hydrogen atom is excited to. [1 mark]

   iii) Calculate the energies of the three photons that might be emitted as the electron returns to its ground state. [3 marks]

$n = 5$ — -0.54 eV
$n = 4$ — -0.85 eV
$n = 3$ — -1.5 eV
$n = 2$ — -3.4 eV
$n = 1$ — -13.6 eV

I can honestly say I've never got so excited that I've produced light...

This is heavy stuff. Quite interesting though, as I was just saying to Dom a moment ago. He's doing a psychology book. Psychology's probably quite interesting too — and easier. But it won't help you become an astrophysicist.

Wave-Particle Duality

Is it a wave? Is it a particle? No, it's a wave. No, it's a particle. No it's not, it's a wave. No, don't be daft, it's a particle.

Interference and Diffraction show Light as a Wave

1) Light produces **interference** and **diffraction** patterns — **alternating bands** of **dark** and **light**.

2) These can **only** be explained using **waves interfering constructively** (when two waves overlap in phase) or **interfering destructively** (when the two waves are out of phase). (See p.28.)

The Photoelectric Effect Shows Light Behaving as a Particle

1) **Einstein** explained the results of **photoelectricity experiments** (see p.16) by thinking of the **beam of light** as a series of **particle-like photons**.

2) If a **photon** of light is a **discrete** bundle of energy, then it can **interact** with an **electron** in a **one-to-one way**.

3) **All** the **energy** in the **photon** is **given** to one **electron**.

De Broglie Came Up with the Wave-Particle Duality Theory

1) Louis de Broglie made a **bold suggestion** in his **PhD thesis**:

> If **'wave-like'** light showed **particle properties** (photons), **'particles'** like **electrons** should be expected to show **wave-like properties**.

2) The **de Broglie equation** relates a **wave property** (**wavelength**, λ) to a **moving particle property** (**momentum**, mv). h = Planck's constant = 6.63×10^{-34} Js.

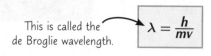

This is called the de Broglie wavelength.

$$\lambda = \frac{h}{mv}$$

I'm not impressed — this is just speculation. What do you think, Dad?

3) The **de Broglie wave** of a particle can be interpreted as a **'probability wave'**. (The probability of finding a particle at a point is directly proportional to the square of the amplitude of the wave at that point — but you don't need to know that for your exam.)

4) Many physicists at the time **weren't very impressed** — his ideas were just **speculation**. But later experiments **confirmed** the wave nature of electrons.

Electron Diffraction shows the Wave Nature of Electrons

1) **Diffraction patterns** are observed when **accelerated electrons** in a vacuum tube **interact** with the **spaces** in a graphite **crystal**.

2) This **confirms** that electrons show **wave-like** properties.

3) According to wave theory, the **spread** of the **lines** in the diffraction pattern **increases** if the **wavelength** of the wave is **greater**.

4) In electron diffraction experiments, a **smaller accelerating voltage**, i.e. **slower** electrons, gives more **widely-spaced** rings.

5) **Increase** the **electron speed** (and therefore the electron **momentum**) and the diffraction pattern circles **squash together** towards the **middle**. This fits in with the **de Broglie** equation above — if the **momentum** is **greater**, the **wavelength** is **shorter** and the **spread** of the lines is **smaller**.

> In general, λ for **electrons** accelerated in a **vacuum tube** is about the **same size** as **electromagnetic waves** in the **X-ray** part of the spectrum.

6) If particles with a **greater mass** (e.g. **neutrons**) were travelling at the **same speed** as the electrons, they would show a more **tightly-packed diffraction pattern**. That's because a neutron's **mass** (and therefore its **momentum**) is **much greater** than an electron's, and so a neutron has a **shorter de Broglie wavelength**.

Wave-Particle Duality

Particles Don't show Wave-Like Properties All the Time

You **only** get **diffraction** if a particle interacts with an object of about the **same size** as its **de Broglie wavelength**. A **tennis ball**, for example, with **mass 0.058 kg** and **speed 100 ms⁻¹** has a **de Broglie wavelength** of **10^{-34} m**. That's **10^{19} times smaller** than the **nucleus** of an **atom**! There's nothing that small for it to interact with.

> **Example:** An electron of mass 9.11×10^{-31} kg is fired from an electron gun at 7.00×10^{6} ms⁻¹ (to 3 s.f.). What size object will the electron need to interact with in order to diffract?
>
> Momentum of electron $= mv = (9.11 \times 10^{-31}) \times (7.00 \times 10^{6}) = 6.377 \times 10^{-24}$ kg ms⁻¹
>
> $\lambda = h/mv = 6.63 \times 10^{-34} / 6.377 \times 10^{-24} = 1.0396... \times 10^{-10} = \mathbf{1.04 \times 10^{-10}}$ **m (to 3 s.f.)**
>
> Only crystals with atom layer spacing around this size are likely to cause the diffraction of this electron.

Wave-Particle Duality Wasn't Accepted Straight Away

De Broglie first **hypothesised** wave-particle duality to explain **observations** of light acting as both a particle and a wave. But his theory **wasn't accepted** straight away. **Other scientists** had to **evaluate** de Broglie's theory (by a process known as **peer review**) before he **published** it, and then it was **tested with experiments**. Once enough evidence was found to back it up, the theory was accepted as **validated** by the scientific community.

Scientists' understanding of the nature of matter has changed over time through this process of **hypothesis and validation**. De Broglie's theory is **accepted** to be true — that is, until any new conflicting evidence comes along.

Warm-Up Questions

Q1 Which observations show light to have a 'wave-like' character?

Q2 Which observations show light to have a 'particle' character?

Q3 What happens to the de Broglie wavelength of a particle if its momentum increases? How does this affect the particle's diffraction pattern?

Q4 Particle A has a de Broglie wavelength of 8×10^{-10} m and particle B has a de Broglie wavelength of 2×10^{-10} m. If the particles are travelling at the same speed, which particle has the greater mass?

Q5 Which observations show electrons to have a 'wave-like' character?

Exam Questions

Q1 a) State what is meant by the wave-particle nature of electromagnetic radiation. [1 mark]

   b) Calculate the momentum of an electron with a de Broglie wavelength of 590 nm. [2 marks]

Q2 Electrons travelling at a speed of 3.50×10^{6} ms⁻¹ exhibit wave properties.

   a) Calculate the wavelength of these electrons. (Mass of an electron $= 9.11 \times 10^{-31}$ kg) [2 marks]

   b) Calculate the speed of protons with the same wavelength as these electrons. (Mass of a proton $= 1.67 \times 10^{-27}$ kg) [2 marks]

   c) Some electrons and protons were accelerated from rest by the same potential difference, giving them the same kinetic energy. Explain why they will have different wavelengths. [3 marks]

Don't hide your wave-particles under a bushel...

Right — I think we'll all agree that quantum physics is a wee bit strange when you come to think about it. What it's saying is that electrons and photons aren't really waves, and they aren't really particles — they're both... at the same time. It's what quantum physicists like to call a 'juxtaposition of states'. Well they would, wouldn't they...

Extra Exam Practice

Well you've made it through <u>Sections 1 and 2</u>, so now it's time to put that grey matter to work again. Once you're confident you can recall quark compositions in your sleep, you're ready for these exam style questions linking all of the physics you've covered in Sections 1 and 2.

- Have a look at this example of how to answer a tricky exam question.
- Then check how much you've understood from Sections 1 and 2 by having a go at the questions on the next page.

Once you've mastered all the sections, there are synoptic questions covering the whole course on page 268.

1 The equation below shows the decay of a kaon. A π^0 particle decays after 8.4×10^{-17} s.

$$K^+ \rightarrow \pi^0 + e^+ + X$$

1.1 Identify particle X by applying the conservation laws for particle interactions.

(3 marks)

1.2 Suggest why it may be difficult to directly detect any of the products of this K^+ decay.

(3 marks)

1.1

Apply the conservation laws for baryon number, lepton number and charge:

Baryon number: $0 \rightarrow 0 + 0 + X$

So particle X must have a baryon number of 0 since baryon number is conserved.

L_e: $0 \rightarrow 0 + -1 + X$ so particle X must have $L_e = 1$ to conserve electron lepton number.

L_μ: $0 \rightarrow 0 + 0 + X$ so particle X must have $L_\mu = 0$.

To calculate the charge of each particle, split up the particles into quarks:

The quark composition of K^+ is up, anti-strange ($u\bar{s}$), so its charge is:
$\frac{2}{3}e + \frac{1}{3}e = e$.

The quark composition of π^0 is up, anti-up ($u\bar{u}$) or down, anti-down ($d\bar{d}$), so its charge is either $\frac{2}{3}e - \frac{2}{3}e = 0$, or $-\frac{1}{3}e + \frac{1}{3}e = 0$.
Either way, the charge of π^0 is 0.

So for charge: $e \rightarrow 0 + e + X$ so particle X must have a charge of 0 in order to conserve charge.

Particle X has no charge, a baryon number and muon lepton number of 0 and an electron lepton number of 1.
A particle with these properties is an electron neutrino.

You'd get 1 mark for applying the conservation laws to the baryon and lepton numbers correctly, 1 mark for showing that particle X has zero charge, and 1 mark for saying that particle X is an electron neutrino.

1.2

A positron may be difficult to detect because it will be **annihilated** very quickly when it meets an electron. An electron neutrino may be hard to detect because it is neutral and virtually massless. The π^0 particle decays extremely quickly, after only 8.4×10^{-17} s, so it may decay before it can be detected.

You'd get 1 mark for saying the positron will be annihilated, 1 mark for saying the electron neutrino has no charge and (virtually) no mass, and 1 mark for saying that the pion may decay too fast to be detected.

Remember that kaons and pions are mesons, not baryons — this means that they have a baryon number of zero. The data sheet in the exam tells you which particles are baryons, mesons, or leptons.

Remember you need to count electron and muon lepton numbers separately, see page 12.

The charges of the different quarks are on the data sheet. All the values are equal and opposite for antiquarks.

It's easy to miss a particle when counting up each quantity. Be methodical and write everything down in a clear way so that you don't miss anything out.

This part pulls together a few different topics. Think about what you know about each particle that could make it hard to detect.

Make sure you use the correct scientific terminology. It shows the examiner you know what you're talking about.

Extra Exam Practice

2 A student is researching the properties of aluminium.

2.1 The student finds the emission and absorption line spectra for aluminium.
Explain what the line spectra indicate about the structure of an atom.

(2 marks)

2.2 **Figure 1** shows how the stopping potential of photoelectrons emitted from aluminium varies with the frequency of incident light.

Use data from **Figure 1** to determine the work function of aluminium.
($e = 1.60 \times 10^{-19}$ C)

(3 marks)

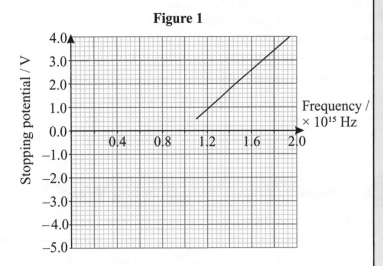

Figure 1

2.3 The student sets up an experiment in which electrons emitted from a sample of aluminium by the photoelectric effect are accelerated away from the sample by a potential difference. The sample is illuminated with light of frequency 2.10×10^{15} Hz. Determine the accelerating potential difference required for the emitted photoelectrons to have a minimum de Broglie wavelength of 415 pm.
($h = 6.63 \times 10^{-34}$ Js, $m_e = 9.11 \times 10^{-31}$ kg)

(5 marks)

3 Read the passage below and answer the following questions.

Neutrinos are fundamental particles that are difficult to detect. Neutrinos were first

theorised to exist in the 1930s, and discovered in 1956 by the Cowan-Reines neutrino

experiment. In the experiment a nuclear reactor was surrounded with water tanks.

Beta-minus decays inside the reactor produced antineutrinos which interacted with the

5 protons in water, creating positrons. Gamma rays produced by the annihilation of these

positrons and nearby electrons were then detected using a series of scintillators and

photomultiplier tubes. Photomultiplier tubes are very sensitive photon detectors that

make use of the photoelectric effect when photons hit a surface.

3.1 The interaction between an antineutrino and a proton (line 4) produces a second decay product besides a positron. Write a possible decay equation for this process. Explain your answer.

(3 marks)

3.2 Calculate the minimum frequency of the gamma rays produced (line 5).
(Rest energy of an electron = 0.511 MeV, $e = 1.60 \times 10^{-19}$ C, $h = 6.63 \times 10^{-34}$ Js)

(2 marks)

3.3 Photomultiplier tubes (line 7) can't detect photons with wavelengths longer than a certain value. Suggest why this is the case.

(2 marks)

Progressive Waves

Aaaah... playing with long springs and waggling ropes about. It's all good clean fun as my mate Richard used to say...

A **Wave** is the **Oscillation** of **Particles** or **Fields**

A **progressive** (moving) wave carries **energy** from one place to another **without transferring any material**.
A wave is caused by something making particles or fields oscillate (or vibrate) at a source.
These oscillations pass through the medium (or field) as the wave travels, carrying energy with it.

Here are some ways you can tell waves carry energy:

1) Electromagnetic waves cause things to **heat up**.
2) **X-rays** and **gamma rays** knock electrons out of their orbits, causing **ionisation**.
3) Loud **sounds** cause large oscillations of air particles which can make things **vibrate**.
4) **Wave power** can be used to **generate electricity**.
5) Since waves carry energy away, the **source** of the wave **loses energy**.

Alex loved wave power.

You Need to Know These **Bits** of a **Wave**

1) **Cycle** — one **complete vibration** of the wave.
2) **Displacement**, *x*, metres — how far a **point** on the wave has **moved** from its **undisturbed position.**
3) **Amplitude**, *A*, metres — **maximum magnitude** of **displacement**.
4) **Wavelength**, λ, metres — the **length** of **one whole wave cycle**, from **crest** to **crest** or **trough** to **trough**.

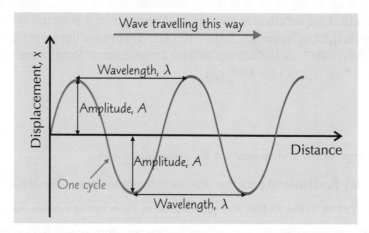

5) **Period**, *T*, seconds — the **time taken** for a **whole cycle** (vibration) to complete, or to pass a given point.
6) **Frequency**, *f*, hertz — the **number** of **cycles** (vibrations) **per second** passing a given **point**.
7) **Phase** — a measurement of the **position** of a certain **point** along the wave cycle.
8) **Phase difference** — the amount one wave lags behind another.

Phase and phase difference are measured in **angles** (in degrees or radians) or as **fractions of a cycle** (see p.28).

Waves Can Be **Reflected** and **Refracted**

Reflection — the wave is **bounced back** when it **hits a boundary**. E.g. you can see the reflection of light in mirrors. The reflection of water waves can be demonstrated in a ripple tank.

Refraction — the wave **changes direction** as it enters a **different medium**.
The change in direction is a result of the wave slowing down or speeding up.

The **Frequency** is the **Inverse** of the **Period**

$$\text{Frequency} = \frac{1}{\text{Period}} \qquad f = \frac{1}{T}$$

It's that simple.
Get the **units** straight: **1 Hz = 1 s⁻¹**.

Progressive Waves

The **Wave Equation** Links **Wave Speed**, **Frequency** and **Wavelength**

Wave speed can be measured just like the speed of anything else:

$$\text{Wave speed } (c) = \frac{\text{Distance travelled } (d)}{\text{Time taken } (t)}$$

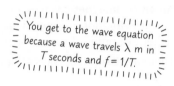
Remember, you're not measuring how fast a physical point (like one molecule of rope) moves. You're measuring how fast a point on the **wave pattern** moves.

From this you can get to the **wave equation**, which you've seen before on p.6.

$$\text{Speed of wave } (c) = \text{wavelength } (\lambda) \times \text{frequency } (f)$$

$$c = \lambda f$$

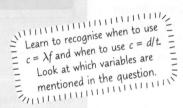
You get to the wave equation because a wave travels λ m in T seconds and $f = 1/T$.

Example: A wave has a wavelength of 420 m and travels at a speed of 125 ms^{-1}. Find the frequency of this wave.

Just rearrange the wave equation, to find f.

$$c = \lambda f \quad \text{so} \quad f = \frac{c}{\lambda} = \frac{125}{420} = 0.2976... = \mathbf{0.30\,Hz\ (to\ 2\ s.f.)}$$

The lowest no. of significant figures the question data is given to is 2 s.f., so give your answer to the same amount of significant figures.

Learn to recognise when to use $c = \lambda f$ and when to use $c = d/t$. Look at which variables are mentioned in the question.

You may have seen c used before as the **speed of light** in a vacuum. Light is a type of electromagnetic wave. All EM waves travel with a **constant speed** in a **vacuum** of $c = 3.00 \times 10^8$ ms^{-1}. The c used in the wave equation is the speed of the **wave in question** — it can take **any** value depending on the wave.

Warm-Up Questions

Q1 Does a wave carry matter **or** energy from one place to another?

Q2 Write down the relationship between the frequency of a wave and its time period.

Q3 Give the units of frequency, displacement and amplitude.

Q4 Write down the equation connecting c, λ and f.

Exam Questions

Q1 A buoy floating on the sea takes 6.0 seconds to rise and fall once (complete a full cycle). The difference in height between the buoy at its lowest and highest points is 1.2 m, and waves pass it at a speed of 3.0 ms^{-1}.

    a) Calculate the wavelength. [2 marks]

    b) State the amplitude of the waves. [1 mark]

Q2 Light travelling through a vacuum has a wavelength of 7.1×10^{-7} m. Calculate its frequency. [1 mark]

Q3 Which of the following statements is correct? [1 mark]

A	Progressive waves transfer energy by transferring material.
B	Progressive waves transfer energy by oscillating particles/fields.
C	The source of a progressive wave has a constant energy.
D	Light is faster than other EM waves in a vacuum.

Hope you haven't phased out...

This isn't too difficult to start you off — most of it you'll have done at GCSE anyway. But once again, it's a whole lot of definitions and a handy equation to remember, and you won't get far without learning them. Yada yada.

Longitudinal and Transverse Waves

There are different types of wave — the difference is easiest to see using a long spring. Try it — you'll have hours of fun.

Transverse Waves Vibrate at Right Angles to the Direction of Energy Transfer

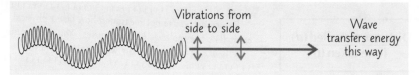

All **electromagnetic waves** are **transverse**. They travel as vibrating magnetic and electric **fields** — with vibrations **perpendicular** to the direction of **energy transfer**.
Other examples of transverse waves are **ripples** on water or waves on **strings**.

There are **two** main ways of **drawing** transverse waves:

① They can be shown as **graphs** of **displacement** against **distance** along the path of the wave.

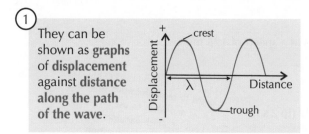

② Or, they can be shown as graphs of **displacement against time** for a point as the wave passes.

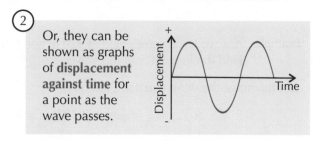

Both sorts of graph often give the **same shape**, so make sure you check out the label on the **x-axis**. Displacements **upwards** from the centre line are given a **+ sign**. Displacements downwards are given a **– sign**.

See p.50-51 for more on displacement-time graphs.

Longitudinal Waves Vibrate Along the Direction of Energy Transfer

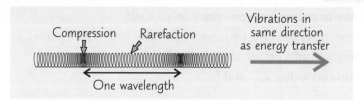

The most common example of a **longitudinal wave** is **sound**. A sound wave consists of alternate **compressions** and **rarefactions** of the **medium** it's travelling through. (That's why sound can't go through a vacuum.) Some types of earthquake shock waves are also longitudinal.

It's hard to **represent** longitudinal waves **graphically**. You'll usually see them plotted as **displacement** against **time**. These can be **confusing** though, because they look like a **transverse wave**.

A Polarised Wave Only Oscillates in One Direction

1) If you **shake a rope** to make a **wave** you can move your hand **up and down** or **side to side** or in a **mixture of** directions — it still makes a **transverse wave**.

2) But if you try to pass **waves in a rope** through a **vertical fence**, the wave will only get through if the **vibrations** are **vertical**. The fence filters out vibration in other directions. This is called **polarising** the wave.

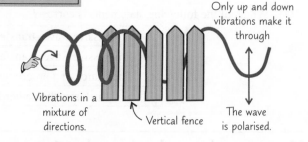

Polarisation **can only happen** for **transverse** waves.

Longitudinal and Transverse Waves

Polarisation is Evidence that Electromagnetic Waves are Transverse

In 1808, Etienne-Louis Malus discovered that light was **polarised** by reflection. Physicists at the time thought that light spread like sound, as a **longitudinal** wave, so they struggled to explain polarisation. In 1817, Young suggested light was a **transverse** wave consisting of vibrating electric and magnetic **fields** at right angles to the transfer of energy. This explained why light could be **polarised**.

Polarising Filters Only Transmit Vibrations in One Direction

1) Ordinary **light waves** are a mixture of **different directions** of **vibration**. (The things vibrating are electric and magnetic fields.) They can be **polarised** using a **polarising filter**.

2) If you have two polarising filters at **right angles** to each other, then **no** light will get through.

3) Light becomes **partially** polarised when reflected from some surfaces — some of it vibrates in the **same direction**.

4) If you view reflected partially polarised light through a polarising filter at the correct angle you can block out unwanted **glare**. **Polaroid sunglasses** make use of this effect.

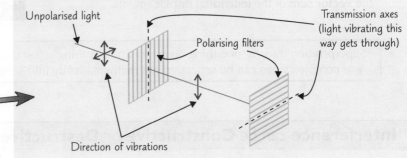

Unpolarised light

Polarising filters

Transmission axes (light vibrating this way gets through)

Direction of vibrations

Television and Radio Signals are Polarised

If you walk down the street and look up at the **TV aerials** on people's houses, you'll see that the **rods** (the sticky-out bits) on them are all **horizontal**. The reason for this is that **TV signals** are **polarised** by the orientation of the **rods** on the **broadcasting aerial**. To receive a strong signal, you have to **line up** the **rods** on the **receiving aerial** with the **rods** on the **transmitting aerial** — if they aren't aligned, the signal strength will be lower.

It's the **same** with **radio** — if you try **tuning a radio** and then **moving** the **aerial** around, your signal will **come and go** as the transmitting and receiving aerials go in and out of **alignment**.

The rods on this broadcasting aerial are horizontal.

Warm-Up Questions

Q1 Give an example of a transverse wave and a longitudinal wave.
Q2 What is a polarised wave?
Q3 How can you polarise light?
Q4 Why do you have to line up transmitting and receiving television aerials?

PRACTICE QUESTIONS

Exam Questions

Q1 Sunlight reflected from road surfaces mostly vibrates in one direction.

a) Explain how this is evidence that sunlight is made up of transverse waves. [2 marks]

b) Explain how Polaroid sunglasses help to reduce glare caused by reflections. [2 marks]

Q2 Explain why sound waves cannot be polarised. [2 marks]

So many waves — my arms are getting tired...

Right, there's lots to learn on these two pages, so I won't hold you up with chat. Don't panic though — a lot of this stuff will be familiar from GCSE, so it's not like you're starting from scratch. One last thing — I know television is on this page, but it doesn't mean you can tune in and call it revision — it won't help. Get the revision done, then take a break.

Superposition and Coherence

When two waves get together, it can be either really impressive or really disappointing.

Superposition Happens When Two or More Waves Pass Through Each Other

1) At the **instant** the waves **cross**, the **displacements** due to each wave **combine**. Then **each wave** goes on its merry way. You can **see** this if **two pulses** are sent **simultaneously** from each end of a rope.

2) The **principle of superposition** says that when two or more **waves cross**, the **resultant** displacement equals the **vector sum** of the **individual** displacements.

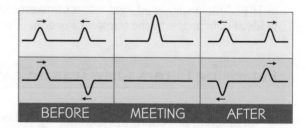

BEFORE   MEETING   AFTER

'Superposition' means 'one thing on top of another thing'. You can use the same idea in reverse — a complex wave can be separated out mathematically into several simple sine waves of various sizes.

Interference can be Constructive or Destructive

1) A **crest** plus a **crest** gives a **bigger crest**. A **trough** plus a **trough** gives a **bigger trough**. These are both examples of **constructive interference**.

2) A **crest** plus a **trough** of equal size gives... **nothing**. The two displacements **cancel each other out** completely. This is called **destructive interference**.

3) If the **crest** and the **trough** aren't the **same size**, then the destructive interference **isn't total**. For the interference to be **noticeable**, the two **amplitudes** should be **nearly equal**.

Graphically, you can superimpose waves by adding the individual displacements at each point along the x-axis, and then plotting them.

In Phase Means In Step — Two Points In Phase Interfere Constructively

1) Two points on a wave are **in phase** if they are both at the **same point** in the **wave cycle**. Points in phase have the **same displacement** and **velocity**.

   On the graph below, points **A** and **B** are **in phase**; points **A** and **C** are **out of phase**.

2) It's mathematically **handy** to show one **complete cycle** of a wave as an **angle of 360° (2π radians)**.

   To convert from degrees to radians, multiply by π/180°. To convert from radians to degrees, multiply by 180°/π.

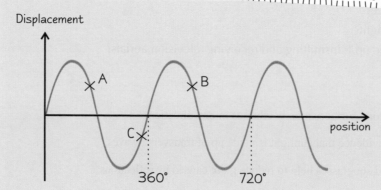

3) **Two points** with a **phase difference** of **zero** or a **multiple of 360°** (i.e. a **full cycle**) are **in phase**.

4) **Points** with a **phase difference of odd-number multiples of 180°** (π radians, or a **half cycle**) are **exactly out of phase**.

5) You can also talk about two **different waves** being **in phase**. **In practice** this happens because **both** waves came from the **same oscillator**. In **other** situations there will nearly always be a **phase difference** between two waves.

Superposition and Coherence

To Get Interference Patterns the Two Sources Must Be Coherent

Interference **still happens** when you're observing waves of **different wavelength** and **frequency** — but it happens in a **jumble**. In order to get clear **interference patterns**, the two or more sources must be **coherent** (and be **in phase**).

> *In exam questions, the 'fixed phase difference' is almost certainly going to be zero. The two sources will be in phase.*

> Two sources are **coherent** if they have the **same wavelength** and **frequency** and a **fixed phase difference** between them.

Constructive or Destructive Interference Depends on the Path Difference

1) Whether you get **constructive** or **destructive** interference at a **point** depends on how **much further one wave** has travelled than the **other wave** to get to that point.

2) The **amount** by which the path travelled by one wave is **longer** than the path travelled by the other wave is called the **path difference**.

3) At **any point an equal distance** from two sources that are **coherent** and **in phase**, you will get **constructive interference**. You also get constructive interference at any point where the **path difference** is a **whole number of wavelengths**. At these points the two waves are **in phase** and **reinforce** each other. But at points where the path difference is **half a wavelength**, **one and a half** wavelengths, **two and a half** wavelengths etc., the waves arrive **out of phase** and you get **destructive interference**.

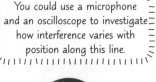

Diagram labels: Speakers, Amplifier, Loud — Path diff = λ, Quiet — Path difference = $\frac{\lambda}{2}$, Loud — No path difference, Quiet — Path difference = $\frac{\lambda}{2}$, Loud — Path diff = λ

Constructive interference occurs when:

> **path difference** $= n\lambda$ (where n is an integer)

Destructive interference occurs when:

> **path difference** $= \dfrac{(2n + 1)\lambda}{2} = (n + \frac{1}{2})\lambda$

> *You could use a microphone and an oscilloscope to investigate how interference varies with position along this line.*

Warm-Up Questions

Q1 Why does the principle of superposition deal with the **vector** sum of two displacements?

Q2 What happens when a crest meets a slightly smaller trough?

Q3 What is meant by the path difference of two waves?

Q4 If two points on a wave have a phase difference of 1440°, are they in phase?

PRACTICE QUESTIONS

Exam Questions

Q1 a) Two wave sources are coherent. Explain what this means. [2 marks]

b) Explain why you might have difficulty in observing interference patterns in an area affected by two waves from two sources even though the two sources are coherent. [1 mark]

Q2 Two points on a wave are exactly out of phase. Which row of the table correctly compares the two points? [1 mark]

	Phase Difference	Velocities	Displacements
A	180°	Equal	Opposite
B	180°	Opposite	Opposite
C	360°	Equal	Equal
D	360°	Opposite	Opposite

Learn this and you'll be in a super position to pass your exam...   ...I'll get my coat.

There are a few really crucial concepts here: a) interference can be constructive or destructive, b) constructive interference happens when the path difference is a whole number of wavelengths, c) the sources must be coherent.

Stationary Waves

Stationary waves are weird things — they move but they don't actually go anywhere.

Progressive Waves Reflected at a Boundary Can Create a Stationary Wave

> A stationary (standing) wave is the **superposition** of two progressive waves
> with the **same frequency** (**wavelength**), moving in **opposite directions**.

1) Unlike progressive waves, **no energy** is transmitted by a stationary wave.

2) You can demonstrate stationary waves by setting up a **driving oscillator** at one end of a **stretched string** with the other end fixed. The wave generated by the oscillator is **reflected** back and forth.

3) For most frequencies the resultant **pattern** is a **jumble**. However, if the oscillator happens to produce an **exact number of waves** in the time it takes for a wave to get to the **end** and **back again**, then the **original** and **reflected** waves **reinforce** each other.

4) At these **"resonant frequencies"** you get a **stationary wave** where the **pattern doesn't move** — it just sits there, bobbing up and down. Happy, at peace with the world...

A sitting wave.

Stationary Waves in Strings Form Oscillating "Loops" Separated by Nodes

Each particle vibrates at **right angles** to the string.
Nodes are where the **amplitude** of the vibration is **zero**. **Antinodes** are points of **maximum amplitude**.

At resonant frequencies, an **exact number** of **half wavelengths** fits onto the string:

First Harmonic

This stationary wave is vibrating at the **lowest possible** resonant frequency. It has one "loop" with a **node at each end**.

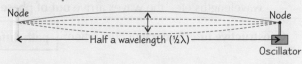

Second Harmonic

This is the **second harmonic**. It is **twice** the frequency of the **first harmonic**. There are two "loops" with a **node** in the **middle** and **one at each end**.

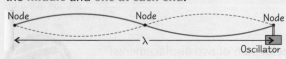

Third Harmonic

The **third harmonic** is **three times** the frequency of the first harmonic. **1½ wavelengths** fit on the string.

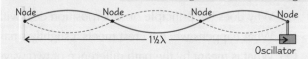

You can Demonstrate Stationary Waves with Microwaves and Sounds

Microwaves Reflected Off a Metal Plate Set Up a Stationary Wave

Microwave stationary wave apparatus
You can find the **nodes** and **antinodes** by moving the **probe** between the **transmitter** and **reflecting plate**.

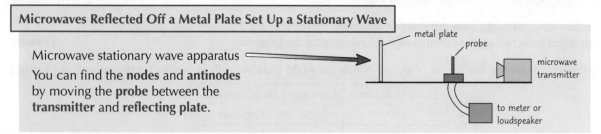

Powder Can Show Stationary Waves in a Tube of Air

Stationary **sound** waves are produced in the **glass tube**.
The lycopodium **powder** (don't worry, you don't need to know what that is) laid along the bottom of the tube is **shaken away** from the **antinodes** but left **undisturbed** at the **nodes**.

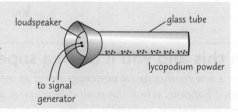

Stationary Waves

You Can Investigate **Factors** Affecting the **Resonant Frequencies** of a String

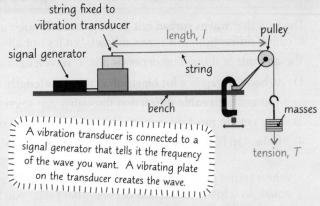

1) Start by measuring the mass (M) and length (L) of strings of different types using a **mass balance** and a ruler. Then find the **mass per unit length** of each string (μ) using:

$$\mu = \frac{M}{L}$$ The units of μ are kgm^{-1}

2) Set up the apparatus shown in the diagram with one of your strings. Record μ, measure and record the **length** (l) and work out the **tension** (T) using:

$$T = mg$$ where m is the total mass of the masses in kg

A vibration transducer is connected to a signal generator that tells it the frequency of the wave you want. A vibrating plate on the transducer creates the wave.

3) Turn on the **signal generator** and vary the frequency until you find the **first harmonic** — i.e. a stationary wave that has a **node** at each end and a single **antinode**. This is the **frequency of the first harmonic**, f.

Then investigate how the **length, tension** or **mass per unit length** of the string affects the **resonant frequency** by:

1) Keeping the string **type** (μ) and the **tension** (T) in it the same and altering the **length** (l). Do this by moving the **vibration transducer** towards or away from the pulley. Find the **first harmonic** again, and record f against l.

2) Keeping the string **type** (μ) and **length** (l) the same and **adding** or **removing masses** to change the **tension** (T). Find the first harmonic again and record f against T.

3) Keeping the **length** (l) and **tension** (T) the same, but using **different string** samples to vary μ. Find the first harmonic and record f against μ.

You can do all of this with a different harmonic — just remember to use the same one throughout the experiment so you're comparing the same resonant frequency.

You should find the following from your investigation:

1) The **longer** the string, the **lower** the resonant frequency — because the **half wavelength** at the resonant frequency is longer.

2) The **heavier** (i.e. the more mass per unit length) the string, the **lower** the resonant frequency — because waves travel more **slowly** down the string. For a given **length** a **lower** wave speed, **c**, makes a **lower** frequency, **f**.

3) The **looser** the string the **lower** the resonant frequency — because waves travel more **slowly** down a **loose** string.

The frequency of the first harmonic, f, is: $f = \frac{1}{2l}\sqrt{\frac{T}{\mu}}$ Where l is the string length in m, T is the tension in the string and μ is the mass per unit length of the string.

Warm-Up Questions

Q1 How do stationary waves form?

Q2 At four times the frequency of the first harmonic, how many half wavelengths would fit on a violin string?

Q3 Describe an experiment to investigate stationary waves in a column of air.

Q4 How does the displacement of a particle at one antinode compare to that of a particle at another antinode?

Exam Question

Q1 A stationary wave at the first harmonic frequency, 10 Hz (to 2 s.f.), is formed on a stretched string of length 1.2 m.

a) Calculate the wavelength of the wave. [2 marks]

b) The tension is doubled whilst all other factors remain constant. The frequency is adjusted to once more find the first harmonic of the string. Calculate the new frequency of the first harmonic. [3 marks]

c) Explain how the variation of amplitude along the string differs from that of a progressive wave. [2 marks]

Don't get tied up in knots...

Just remember that two progressive waves can combine to make a stationary wave. How many nodes there are shows what harmonic it is (e.g. 2 nodes = 1st harmonic), and you can change its frequency by changing the medium its in.

Diffraction

This page is essentially about shining light through small gaps and creating pretty patterns. Aaaahh look, a rainbow.

Waves Go **Round Corners** and **Spread** Out of **Gaps**

The way that **waves spread out** as they come through a **narrow gap** or go round obstacles is called **diffraction**. **All** waves diffract, but it's not always easy to observe.

The **amount** of diffraction depends on the **wavelength** of the wave compared with the **size of the gap**.

1) When the gap is **a lot bigger** than the **wavelength**, diffraction is **unnoticeable**.
2) You get **noticeable diffraction** through a gap **several** wavelengths wide.
3) You get the **most** diffraction when the gap is **the same** size as the **wavelength**.
4) If the gap is **smaller** than the wavelength, the waves are mostly just **reflected back**.

When sound passes through a doorway, the size of gap and the wavelength are usually roughly equal, so a lot of diffraction occurs. That's why you have no trouble hearing someone through an open door to the next room, even if the other person is out of your line of sight. The reason that you can't see him or her is that when light passes through the doorway, it is passing through a gap around a hundred million times bigger than its wavelength — the amount of diffraction is tiny. So to get noticeable diffraction with light, you must shine it through a very narrow slit.

Light Shone Through a **Narrow Slit** Can Form a **Diffraction Pattern**

To observe a clear **diffraction pattern** for light, you need to use a **monochromatic**, **coherent** light source. Monochromatic just means all the light has the same **wavelength** (and frequency) and so is the same **colour**. **Lasers** are a monochromatic and coherent light source.

Demonstrating Light Diffraction Patterns with a Laser

If the wavelength of light is about the **same size** as the aperture, you get a diffraction pattern.

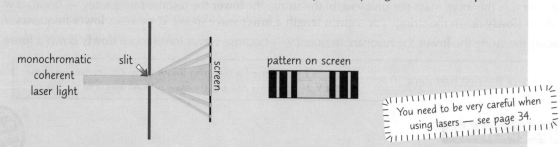

monochromatic coherent laser light | slit | screen | pattern on screen

You need to be very careful when using lasers — see page 34.

You'll see a **central bright fringe** (central maximum), with dark and bright fringes **alternating** on either side. The dark and bright fringes are caused by **destructive** and **constructive interference** of light waves (see p.28).

Diffracted **White Light** Creates **Spectra** of Colours

1) **White light** is actually a **mixture** of different colours, each with different **wavelengths**.

2) When white light is shone through a single narrow slit, all of the different wavelengths are **diffracted** by different amounts.

3) This means that **instead** of getting clear **fringes** (as you would with a **monochromatic** light source) you get **spectra** of colours.

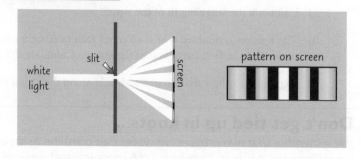

white light | slit | screen | pattern on screen

Diffraction

Intensity of Light Means Number of Photons

1) The central maximum in a single slit light diffraction pattern is the brightest part of the pattern.
2) This is because the intensity of light is highest in the centre.
3) Intensity is the power per unit area.
4) For monochromatic light, all photons have the same energy, so an increase in the intensity means an increase in the number of photons per second.
5) So there are more photons per unit area hitting the central maximum per second than the other bright fringes.

Fred wasn't sure about his fringe intensity.

See p.16 for the photon model of light.

The Width of the Central Maximum Varies with Wavelength and Slit Size

When light is shone through a single slit, there are **two** things which affect the **width** of the central maximum:

1) Increasing the slit width decreases the amount of diffraction. This means the central maximum is narrower, and the intensity of the central maximum is higher.
2) Increasing the wavelength increases the amount of diffraction. This means the central maximum is wider, and the intensity of the central maximum is lower.

Warm-Up Questions

Q1 What is diffraction?

Q2 Do all waves diffract?

Q3 a) Sketch the pattern produced when monochromatic light is shone through a narrow slit onto a screen.
   b) If the wavelength of the monochromatic light was decreased, what would happen to the central maximum?

Q4 What would you expect to see when white light is shone through a thin slit onto a screen?

Q5 What happens to the number of photons in a light beam if the intensity increases?

Exam Questions

Q1 A fire alarm can be heard from the next room through a doorway, even though it is not in the line of sight. Explain why this happens, with reference to the wavelengths of sound and light waves.

[3 marks]

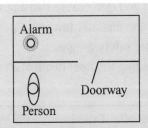

Q2 A student shines a laser beam through a narrow slit onto a screen.

a) State and explain one reason why using laser light produces a clearer diffraction pattern than other light sources.

[2 marks]

b) The student uses a narrower slit. Describe how this will affect the central maximum of the diffraction pattern. Explain your answer.

[3 marks]

Waves are just like me at the weekend — they like to spread out...

An important point to remember is that diffraction's only noticeable when the wavelength is roughly equal to the size of the gap the wave is going through. Different light sources give different patterns when diffracted, make sure you know this and can explain why it happens. Diffraction crops up again in physics — so make sure you really understand it.

Two-Source Interference

You know what happens with one light source, so now it's time to see what happens with two. I can hardly wait...

Demonstrating **Two-Source** Interference in **Water** and **Sound** is Easy

1) It's **easy** to demonstrate **two-source interference** for either **sound** or **water** because they've got **wavelengths** of a handy **size** that you can **measure**.

2) You need **coherent** sources, which means the **wavelength** and **frequency** have to be the **same**. The trick is to use the **same oscillator** to drive **both sources**. For **water**, one **vibrator drives two dippers**. For sound, **one oscillator** is connected to **two loudspeakers**. (See diagram on page 29.)

Demonstrating **Two-Source** Interference for **Light** is Harder

Young's Double-Slit Experiment

1) To see **two-source** interference with light, you can either use two separate, **coherent** light sources or you can shine a **laser** through **two slits**. Laser light is **coherent** and **monochromatic**.

2) Young's double-slit experiment shines a laser through two slits onto a **screen**.

3) The slits have to be about the **same size** as the **wavelength** of the laser light so that it is diffracted — then the light from the slits acts like two coherent point sources.

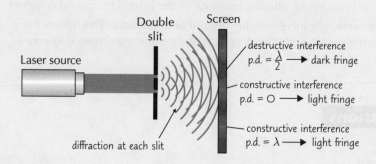

4) You get a pattern of light and dark **fringes**, depending on whether constructive or destructive **interference** is taking place. Thomas Young — the first person to do this experiment (with a lamp rather than a laser) — came up with an **equation** to **work out** the **wavelength** of the **light** from this experiment (see p.35).

Working with lasers is very **dangerous** because laser light is focused into a very direct, powerful beam of monochromatic light. If you looked at a laser beam **directly**, your eye's lens would focus it onto your retina, which would be **permanently damaged**.

To make sure you don't cause **damage** while using lasers, you should:

1) **Never** shine the laser **towards** a person.

2) Wear laser **safety goggles**.

3) Avoid shining the laser beam at a **reflective surface**.

4) Have a **warning sign** on display.

5) Turn the laser **off** when it's not needed.

You Can Do a Similar Experiment with Microwaves

To see interference patterns with **microwaves**, you can **replace** the laser and slits with two microwave **transmitter cones** attached to the **same** signal generator.

You also need to replace the screen with a microwave **receiver probe** (like the one used in the stationary waves experiment on page 30).

If you move the probe along the path of the green arrow, you'll get an **alternating pattern** of **strong** and **weak** signals — just like the light and dark fringes on the screen.

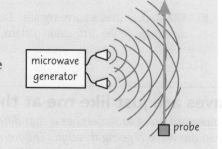

Two-Source Interference

Work Out the Wavelength with **Young's Double-Slit Formula**

1) The fringe spacing (*w*), wavelength (λ), spacing between slits (*s*) and the distance from slits to screen (*D*) are all related by **Young's double-slit formula**, which works for all waves.

$$\text{Fringe spacing, } w = \frac{\lambda D}{s}$$

'Fringe spacing' means the distance from the centre of one minimum to the centre of the next minimum or from the centre of one maximum to the centre of the next maximum.

Always check your fringe spacing.

2) Since the wavelength of light is so small you can see from the formula that a high ratio of *D* / *s* is needed to make the fringe spacing **big enough to see**.

3) Rearranging, you can use λ = *ws* / *D* to **calculate the wavelength** of light.

4) The fringes are **so tiny** that it's very hard to get an **accurate value of *w***. It's easier to measure across **several** fringes then **divide** by the number of **fringe widths** between them.

Young's Experiment was **Evidence** for the **Wave Nature** of EM Radiation

1) Towards the end of the **17th century**, two important **theories of light** were published — one by Isaac Newton and the other by a chap called Huygens. **Newton's** theory suggested that light was made up of tiny particles, which he called "**corpuscles**". And **Huygens** put forward a theory using **waves**.

2) The **corpuscular theory** could explain **reflection** and **refraction**, but **diffraction** and **interference** are both **uniquely** wave properties. If it could be **shown** that light showed interference patterns, that would help settle the argument once and for all.

3) **Young's** double-slit experiment (over 100 years later) provided the necessary evidence. It showed that light could both **diffract** (through the narrow slits) and **interfere** (to form the interference pattern on the screen).
Of course, this being Physics, nothing's ever simple — give it another 100 years or so and the debate would be raging again, (p.16).

Warm-Up Questions

Q1 In Young's experiment, why do you get a bright fringe at a point equidistant from both slits?

Q2 What does Young's experiment show about the nature of light?

Q3 Write down Young's double-slit formula.

PRACTICE QUESTIONS

Exam Questions

Q1 a) The diagram on the right shows two coherent light sources, S_1 and S_2, being shone on a screen. State the measurements you would need to take to calculate the wavelength of the light. [3 marks]

    b) S_1 and S_2 may be slits in a screen behind which there is a source of laser light, instead of being two separate sources. State two safety precautions you should take when using this set-up. Explain your answer. [2 marks]

screen

S_1

S_2

Q2 In an experiment to study sound interference, two loudspeakers are connected to an oscillator emitting sound at 1320 Hz and set up as shown in the diagram. They are 1.5 m apart and 7.3 m away from the line AC. A listener moving along the line hears minimum sound at A, maximum sound at B and minimum sound again at C. (You may assume that Young's double-slit formula can be used in this calculation).

Oscillator   1.5 m   7.3 m

A

B

C

    a) Calculate the wavelength of the sound waves if the speed of sound in air is taken to be 330 ms⁻¹. [1 mark]

    b) Calculate the separation of points A and C. [1 mark]

Learn this stuff — or you'll be playing ketchup...

A few things to learn here — some diffraction experiments, a formula and a little bit of history. Be careful when you're calculating the fringe width by averaging over several fringes. Don't just divide by the number of bright lines. Ten bright lines will only have nine fringe widths between them, not ten. It's an easy mistake to make, but you have been warned.

Diffraction Gratings

Ay... starting to get into some pretty funky stuff now. I like light experiments.

Interference Patterns Get **Sharper** When You Diffract Through **More Slits**

1) You can repeat **Young's double-slit** experiment (see p.34) with **more than two equally spaced** slits. You get basically the **same shaped** pattern as for two slits — but the **bright bands** are **brighter** and **narrower** and the **dark areas** between are **darker**.

2) When **monochromatic light** (one wavelength) is passed through a grating with **hundreds** of slits per millimetre, the interference pattern is **really sharp** because there are so **many beams reinforcing** the **pattern**.

3) Sharper fringes make for more **accurate** measurements.

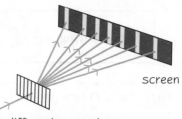

screen

diffraction grating

Monochromatic Light on a **Diffraction Grating** gives **Sharp Lines**

1) For **monochromatic** light, all the **maxima** are sharp lines. (It's different for white light — see page 32.)

2) There's a line of **maximum brightness** at the centre called the **zero order** line.

3) The lines just **either side** of the central one are called **first order lines**. The **next pair out** are called **second order** lines and so on.

4) For a grating with slits a distance **d** apart, the angle between the **incident beam** and **the nth order maximum** is given by:

$$d \sin \theta = n\lambda$$

5) So by observing **d**, **θ** and **n** you can **calculate the wavelength** of the light.

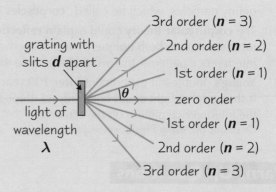

grating with slits **d** apart

light of wavelength **λ**

3rd order (**n** = 3)
2nd order (**n** = 2)
1st order (**n** = 1)
zero order
1st order (**n** = 1)
2nd order (**n** = 2)
3rd order (**n** = 3)

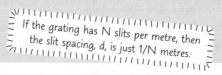

If the grating has N slits per metre, then the slit spacing, d, is just 1/N metres.

DERIVING THE EQUATION:

1) At **each slit**, the incoming waves are **diffracted**. These diffracted waves then **interfere** with each other to produce an **interference pattern**.

2) Consider the **first order maximum**. This happens at the **angle** when the waves from one slit line up with waves from the **next slit** that are **exactly one wavelength** behind.

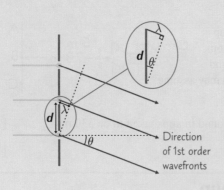

Direction of 1st order wavefronts

3) Call the **angle** between the **first order maximum** and the **incoming light** θ.

4) Now, look at the **triangle** highlighted in the diagram. The angle is **θ** (using basic geometry), **d** is the slit spacing and the **path difference** is λ.

5) So, for the first maximum, using trig:
$$d \sin \theta = \lambda$$

6) The other maxima occur when the path difference is 2λ, 3λ, 4λ, etc. So to make the equation **general**, just replace λ with **n**λ, where **n** is an integer — the **order** of the maximum.

Diffraction Gratings

You can Draw General Conclusions from $d \sin \theta = n\lambda$

1) If λ is bigger, $\sin \theta$ is bigger, and so θ is bigger. This means that the larger the wavelength, the more the pattern will spread out.

2) If d is bigger, $\sin \theta$ is smaller. This means that the coarser the grating, the less the pattern will spread out.

3) Values of $\sin \theta$ greater than 1 are impossible. So if for a certain n you get a result of more than 1 for $\sin \theta$ you know that that order doesn't exist.

Diffraction Gratings Help to Identify Elements and Calculate Atomic Spacing

1) White light is really a mixture of colours. If you diffract white light through a grating then the patterns due to different wavelengths within the white light are spread out by different amounts.

2) Each order in the pattern becomes a spectrum, with red on the outside and violet on the inside. The zero order maximum stays white because all the wavelengths just pass straight through.

3) Astronomers and chemists often need to study spectra to help identify elements. They use diffraction gratings rather than prisms because they're more accurate.

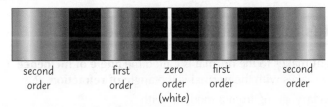

| second order | first order | zero order (white) | first order | second order |

4) The wavelength of X-rays is of a similar scale to the spacing between atoms in crystalline solids. This means that X-rays will form a diffraction pattern when directed at a thin crystal.

5) The crystal acts like a diffraction grating and the spacing between atoms (slit width) can be found from the diffraction pattern.

6) This is called X-ray crystallography — it was used to discover the structure of DNA.

Warm-Up Questions

Q1 How is the diffraction grating pattern for white light different from the pattern for laser light?

Q2 What difference does it make to the pattern if you use a finer grating?

Q3 What equation is used to find the angle between the nth order maximum and the incident beam for a diffraction grating?

Q4 Derive the equation you quoted in Q3.

Exam Questions

Q1 Yellow laser light of wavelength 6.0×10^{-7} m is transmitted through a diffraction grating of 4.0×10^5 lines per metre.

    a) Calculate the angle to the normal at which the first and second order bright lines are seen. [3 marks]

    b) State whether there is a fifth order line. Explain your answer. [1 mark]

Q2 Visible, monochromatic light is transmitted through a diffraction grating of 3.7×10^5 lines per metre. The first order maximum is at an angle of 14.2° to the incident beam. Calculate the wavelength of the incident light. [2 marks]

Ooooooooooooo — pretty patterns...

Derivation — ouch. At least it's not a bad one though. As long as you learn the diagram, it's just geometry and a bit of trig from there. Make sure you learn the equation — that way, you know what you're aiming for. As for the rest of the page, remember that the more slits you have, the sharper the image — and white light makes a pretty spectrum.

Refractive Index

The stuff on the next two pages explains why your legs look short in a swimming pool.

The **Refractive Index** of a Material Measures **How Much** It Slows Down Light

Light goes fastest in a **vacuum**. It **slows down** in other materials, because it **interacts** with the particles in them. The more **optically dense** a material is, the more light slows down when it enters it.

The **absolute refractive index** of a material, **n**, is a measure of **optical density**. It is found from the **ratio** between the **speed of light** in a **vacuum**, **c**, and the speed of light in that **material**, c_s.

$$n = \frac{c}{c_s}$$

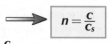
$c = 3.00 \times 10^8 \, ms^{-1}$

The **relative** refractive index **between two materials**, $_1n_2$, is the ratio of the speed of light **in material 1** to the speed of light **in material 2**.

$$_1n_2 = \frac{c_1}{c_2}$$

The speed of light in air is only a tiny bit smaller than c. So you can assume the refractive index of air is 1.

Combining the two equations gives:

$$_1n_2 = \frac{n_2}{n_1}$$

1) The **absolute refractive index** of a material is a **property** of that material only. A **relative refractive index** is a property of the **interface** between two materials. It's different for **every possible pair**.

2) Because you can assume $n_{air} = 1$, you can assume the refractive index for an **air to glass boundary** equals the **absolute refractive index** of the glass.

Snell's Law uses **Angles** to Calculate the Refractive Index

1) The **angle** the **incoming light** makes to the **normal** is called the **angle of incidence**, θ_1. The **angle** the **refracted ray** makes with the **normal** is the **angle of refraction**, θ_2.

2) The light is crossing a **boundary**, going from a medium with **refractive index** n_1 to a medium with refractive index n_2.

3) When light enters an **optically denser** medium it is refracted **towards** the normal.

4) **n**, θ_1 and θ_2 are related by **Snell's law**:

$$n_1 \sin \theta_1 = n_2 \sin \theta_2$$

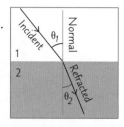

Light Leaving an **Optically Denser Material** is Refracted **Away** from the **Normal**

When light **goes from** an optically denser material into an optically **less dense** material (e.g. glass to air), interesting things can happen.

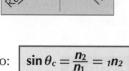

1) Shine a ray of light at a boundary going from refractive index n_1 to n_2, then gradually **increase** the angle of incidence.

2) The light is refracted away from the normal, so as you increase the angle of incidence, the angle of **refraction** gets closer and closer to **90°**.

3) Eventually θ_1 reaches a **critical angle** θ_c for which $\theta_2 = 90°$. The light is **refracted** along the **boundary**.

4) As $\sin 90° = 1$, Snell's law, $n_1 \sin \theta_1 = n_2 \sin \theta_2$, becomes $n_1 \sin \theta_c = n_2 \times 1$ so:

$$\sin \theta_c = \frac{n_2}{n_1} = {_1n_2}$$

5) At θ_1 **greater** than the **critical angle**, refraction is impossible. All the light is **reflected** back into the material — this is called **total internal reflection**.

Since sin can only take values between -1 and 1, total internal reflection can only happen if $\sin \theta_c < 1$ so $_1n_2 < 1$.

Optical Fibres Use **Total Internal Reflection**

An optical fibre is a very **thin flexible tube** of **glass** or **plastic** fibre that can carry **light signals** over long distances and round corners. You only need to know about **step-index** optical fibres.

1) Step-index optical fibres themselves have a **high refractive index** but are surrounded by **cladding** with a lower refractive index to allow **total internal reflection**. Cladding also protects the fibre from **scratches** which could let **light escape**.

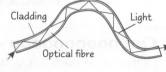
Cladding — Light — Optical fibre

2) Light is shone in at **one end** of the fibre. The fibre is so **narrow** that the light always **hits the boundary** between the fibre and cladding at an **angle bigger** than the **critical angle**.

3) So all the light is **totally internally reflected** from boundary to boundary until it reaches the other end.

Refractive Index

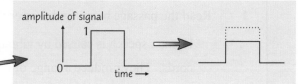

Dispersion and Absorption Cause Signal Degradation

A **signal** (a stream of pulses of light) travelling down an optical fibre can be **degraded** by **absorption** or by **dispersion**. **Signal degradation** can cause **information** to be **lost**.

Absorption Causes Loss in Amplitude

As the signal travels, some of its energy is lost through **absorption** by the **material** the fibre is made from. This energy loss results in the **amplitude** of the signal being **reduced**.

Dispersion Causes Pulse Broadening

There are two types of dispersion that can degrade a signal.

1) **Modal dispersion** — light rays enter the fibre at different angles, and so take different **paths**. The rays which take a **longer path** take longer to reach the other end than those that travel down the **middle** of the fibre. A **single-mode** fibre only lets light take **one path**, so it stops modal dispersion.

2) **Material dispersion** — light consists of different **wavelengths** that travel at different speeds in the fibre — this causes some light wavelengths to reach the end of the fibre faster than others. Using **monochromatic light** can stop material dispersion.

Both types of dispersion lead to **pulse broadening**. The signal sent down the fibre is broader at the other end. Broadened pulses can **overlap** each other and confuse the signal.

An **optical fibre repeater** can be used to **boost** and regenerate the signal every so often, which can **reduce** signal **degradation** caused by both **absorption** and **dispersion**.

Warm-Up Questions

PRACTICE QUESTIONS

Q1 Why does light go fastest in a vacuum and slow down in other media?

Q2 What is the formula for the critical angle for a ray of light at a water/air boundary?

Exam Questions

Q1 a) Light travels in diamond at 1.24×10^8 ms^{-1}. Calculate the refractive index of diamond. [1 mark]

   b) Calculate the angle of refraction if light strikes a facet of a diamond ring at an angle of 50° (to 2 s.f.) to the normal of the air/diamond boundary. [2 marks]

Q2 An adjustable underwater spotlight is placed on the floor of an aquarium tank. When the light points upwards at a steep angle a beam comes through the surface of the water into the air, and the tank is dimly lit. When the spotlight is placed at a shallower angle, no light comes up through the water surface, and the tank is brightly lit.

   a) Explain what is happening. [2 marks]

   b) It is found that the beam into the air disappears when the spotlight is pointed at any angle of less than 41.25° to the floor. Calculate the refractive index of water. [2 marks]

Q3 a) Explain the ways in which the cladding is designed to keep transmitted light inside an optical fibre. [2 marks]

   b) The cladding functions as expected, but there is still some information loss when a step-index optical fibre is used to transmit light signals over long distances.
   Discuss the potential causes of this loss of information and how the design and operation of the optical fibre could be altered to reduce information loss over long transmission distances. [6 marks]

I don't care about expensive things — all I care about is wave speed...

Physics examiners are always saying how candidates do worst in the waves bit of the exam. You'd think they'd have something more important to worry about — third world poverty, war, Posh & Becks... But no.

Extra Exam Practice

To answer exam questions on <u>Section 3</u>, you need to be able to link ideas from the section together.

- Have a look at this example of how to answer a tricky exam question.
- Then check how much you've understood from Section 3 by having a go at the questions on the next page.

1   Read the passage below and answer the following question.

Figure 1

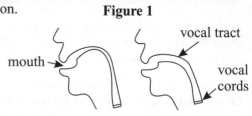

Human speech is caused by vibrations of the vocal cords. They produce a range of frequencies of sounds that can be varied by muscles tightening or loosening the vocal cords to alter their vibrations.

5   Tighter vocal cords produce a higher range of frequencies. The only frequencies of sound produced at the mouth are the frequencies of stationary waves in the vocal tract. These are called resonant frequencies. All other frequencies are absorbed in the vocal tract. The position of the vocal cords and the shape of the vocal tract can be altered, as shown in **Figure 1**.

10   For vowel sounds, the vocal tract can be modelled as a cylindrical tube with one open end (the mouth) and one closed end (the vocal cords), see **Figure 2**. A stationary wave in such a tube always has an antinode at the open end. The resonant

Figure 2

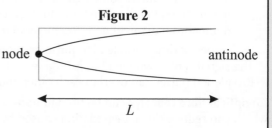

15   frequencies for stationary waves in such a tube are when a certain number of quarter wavelengths fit exactly in the tube. Resonant frequencies are equal to $f_n = \frac{nv}{4L}$, where v is the speed of sound in the vocal tract and n is the number of quarter wavelengths that fit into the tube, equal to a positive, odd whole number (1, 3, 5, etc). The frequency of sound determines pitch — a higher frequency sound produces a higher pitched noise.

Derive the equation for f_n on line 16. Use the equation and information from the passage to discuss the ways in which the pitch of a vowel sound can be altered by the vocal cords and vocal tract.

(6 marks)

Try using equations you know (e.g. $v = f\lambda$) that contain variables from the equation you're trying to derive.

This question can be split up into two parts, the derivation and the explanation, make sure you cover both parts to get all the marks.

1

Resonant frequencies happen when a certain number of quarter wavelengths, n, fit exactly in the tube (when n is a whole number).
So $L = \frac{n\lambda}{4}$, so $\lambda = \frac{4L}{n}$. $v = f\lambda$ so $f_n = \frac{v}{\lambda} = \frac{nv}{4L}$.

Resonant frequencies can only happen with a node at one end of the tube and an antinode at the other end. This only happens when n is odd, so **n must be an odd**, whole positive number: $f_n = \frac{nv}{4L}$, $n = 1, 3, 5...$

The range of frequencies produced depends on how tight/loose the vocal cords are, so the pitch of sounds produced is limited by the vocal cords. If the vocal cords vibrate faster the pitch of sound increases. The sounds that are heard also depend on the resonant frequencies of the vocal tract. The position of the vocal cords and the vocal tract shape **changes the overall length** of the vocal tract, e.g. in Figure 1 the vocal tract is longer in the first image than the second. If L increases, the resonant frequencies, and so the pitch, will decrease as $f_n = \frac{nv}{4L}$.

You may not have studied stationary sound waves in tubes of air, but you can apply what you know about stationary waves in general to this scenario.

Don't forget you need to show why n needs to be an odd number.

Figure 1 shows that the length of the vocal tract can be changed.

Extra Exam Practice

2   Two monochromatic rays of light of different colours are incident on a surface of glass. One ray is red and one ray is blue. The glass is surrounded by transparent material cladding, as shown in **Figure 3**. Both rays are directed into the glass at the same angle to the normal, θ, and meet at the boundary between the glass and the cladding.

Figure 3

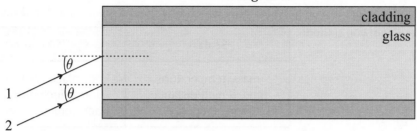

Information about the two rays of light is shown in **Table 1**.

Table 1

Colour	Frequency / $\times 10^{14}$ Hz	Refractive index of glass (n_g)	Refractive index of cladding (n_c)
Red	4.57	1.513	1.224
Blue	6.59	1.532	1.231

2.1   Use data from **Table 1** and Snell's law of refraction to determine which ray in **Figure 3** is blue light.

(3 marks)

2.2   The light rays enter the glass at an angle of $\theta = 15.0\,°$. Calculate the angle, ϕ, between the two rays of light when they meet at the boundary between the glass and the cladding.

(3 marks)

2.3   The rays reach the cladding 8.32 cm along the length of the cladding. Calculate the number of cycles that the red light goes through inside the glass before reaching the cladding.
($c = 3.00 \times 10^8$ ms⁻¹)

(4 marks)

2.4   Both rays fully reflect when they meet the boundary between the glass and the cladding.
The angle θ in **Figure 3** is slowly increased for both rays of light.
Determine which ray of light will begin to refract into the cladding first as θ is increased.

(4 marks)

2.5   The rays of light are shone through a small double slit and they diffract onto a screen ahead.
The red light is shone through one slit and the blue light is shone through the other.
Explain whether you would expect to see two-source interference demonstrated on the screen.

(2 marks)

2.6   The two light ray sources are replaced with a single source that produces both rays of light in **Table 1**. The light from the source is directed at a diffraction grating perpendicular to them with a slit spacing of 2.50×10^{-6} m. Determine the highest order maxima that could be seen for each colour of light.

(1 mark)

2.7   Explain the appearance of the central maximum and the first fringe on both sides of the central maximum. You do not need to include any calculations in your answer.

(2 marks)

Scalars and Vectors

Mechanics is one of those things that you either love or hate. I won't tell you which side of the fence I'm on.

Scalars Only Have Size, but Vectors Have Size and Direction

1) A **scalar** has **no direction** — it's **just an amount** of something, like the **mass** of a **sack of meaty dog food**.

2) A **vector** has magnitude (**size**) and **direction** — like the **speed and direction** of next door's **cat** running away.

3) **Force** and **velocity** are both **vectors** — you need to know **which way** they're going as well as **how big** they are.

4) Here are a few examples to get you started:

Scalars	Vectors
mass, temperature, time, length/distance, speed, energy	displacement, velocity, force (including weight), acceleration, momentum

There are Two Methods for Adding Vectors Together

Adding two or more vectors is called finding the **resultant** of them.
There are two ways of doing this you need to know about.

Scale Drawings

Start by making a **scale drawing** of the two vectors (tip-to-tail if they're not already), draw the **resultant vector** from the tail of the first to the tip of the last, and measure its **length** and **angle**.

Example: A man walks 3.0 m on a bearing of 055° then 4.0 m east. Find the magnitude and direction (to the nearest degree) of his displacement, *s*.

> The man's 'displacement' gives his position relative to his starting point.

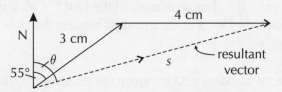

1 cm = 1 m
drawn to scale

Start by drawing a scale diagram for how far the man walked using a **ruler** and a **protractor**.

Then just **measure** the missing side with a ruler and the missing angle with a protractor:
s = 6.7 cm and θ = 75° (to the nearest degree)
So the man's displacement is **6.7 m**, on a bearing of **075°**.

> Don't forget to use the scale to convert back to metres at the end.

Pythagoras and Trigonometry

When two vectors are at **right angles** to each other, you can use maths to work it out without a scale drawing.

Example: Jemima goes for a walk. She walks 3 m north and 4 m east. She has walked 7 m but she isn't 7 m from her starting point. Find the magnitude and direction (to the nearest degree) of her displacement.

First, sketch the vectors **tip-to-tail**. Then draw a line from the **tail** of the first vector to the **tip** of the last vector to give the **resultant**:
Because the vectors are at right angles, you get the **magnitude** of the resultant using Pythagoras:
$R^2 = 3^2 + 4^2 = 25$
So $R = $ **5 m**

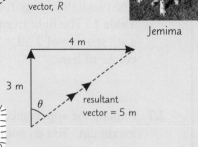

Jemima

Now find the **bearing** of Jemima's new position from her original position.

You use the triangle again, but this time you need to use trigonometry. You know the opposite and the adjacent sides, so you need to use:
$\tan θ = 4 / 3$
$θ = $ **053°**

> Trig's really useful in mechanics — so make sure you're completely okay with it. Remember SOH CAH TOA.

Scalars and Vectors

Sometimes you have to do it backwards.

It's Useful to Split a **Vector** into **Horizontal** and **Vertical Components**

This is the opposite of finding the resultant — you start from the resultant vector and split it into two **components** at right angles to each other. You're basically **working backwards** from the examples on the other page.

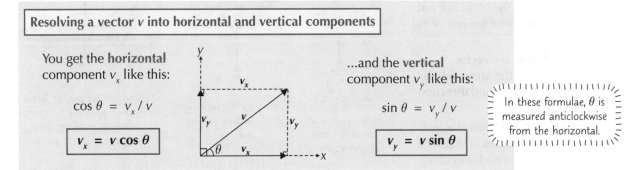

Resolving a vector *v* into horizontal and vertical components

You get the **horizontal** component v_x like this:

$$\cos \theta = v_x / v$$

$$v_x = v \cos \theta$$

...and the **vertical** component v_y like this:

$$\sin \theta = v_y / v$$

$$v_y = v \sin \theta$$

In these formulae, θ is measured anticlockwise from the horizontal.

Example: Charley's amazing floating home is travelling at a speed of 5.0 ms⁻¹ at an angle of 60° (to 2 s.f.) up from the horizontal. Find the vertical and horizontal components.

The **horizontal** component v_x is:
$v_x = v \cos \theta = 5 \cos 60° = $ **2.5 ms⁻¹**
The vertical component v_y is:
$v_y = v \sin \theta = 5 \sin 60° = $ **4.3 ms⁻¹ (to 2 s.f.)**

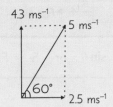

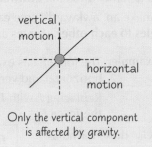
Charley's mobile home was the envy of all his friends.

Resolving is dead useful because the two components of a vector **don't affect each other**. This means you can deal with the two directions **completely separately**.

Only the vertical component is affected by gravity.

Warm-Up Questions

Q1 Explain the difference between a scalar quantity and a vector quantity.

Q2 Jemima is chasing a mechanised rabbit. She follows it for 50 m in a south-east direction. It then changes direction, and she follows it a further 80 m west before catching it. By drawing a scale diagram, show that when Jemima catches the rabbit her displacement is 57 m on a bearing of 232° (to the nearest degree).

Q3 Jemima has gone for a swim in a river which is flowing at 0.35 ms⁻¹. She swims at 0.18 ms⁻¹ at right angles to the current. Show that her resultant velocity is 0.39 ms⁻¹ (to 2 s.f.) at an angle of 27° (to 2 s.f.) to the current.

Exam Questions

Q1 The wind is creating a horizontal force of 20.0 N on a falling rock of weight 75 N.
Calculate the magnitude and direction of the resultant force. [2 marks]

Q2 A glider is travelling at a velocity of 20 ms⁻¹ (to 2 s.f.) at an angle of 15° below the horizontal.
Calculate the horizontal and vertical components of the glider's velocity. [2 marks]

Mum said my life was lacking direction, so I became a vector collector...

I always think that the hardest part of vector questions is getting the initial diagram right. Once you've worked out what's going on, they're all the same — they're a piece of cake taking a walk in the park. Easy as pie in a light breeze.

Forces

Remember the vector stuff from the last two pages... good, you're going to need it...

Free-Body Force Diagrams Show All Forces on a Single Body

1) **Free-body force** diagrams show a **single body** on its own.

2) The diagram should include all the **forces** that **act on** the body, but **not** the **forces it exerts** on the rest of the world.

3) Remember **forces** are **vector quantities** and so the **arrow labels** should show the **size** and **direction** of the forces.

4) If a body is in **equilibrium** (i.e. not accelerating) the **forces** acting on it will be **balanced** in each direction.

5) A body in equilibrium can be **at rest** or moving with a **constant velocity**.

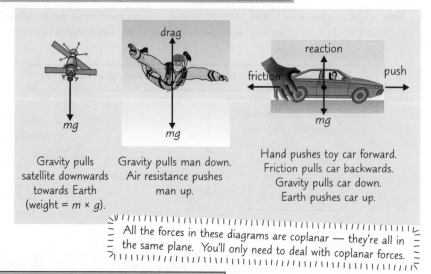

Gravity pulls satellite downwards towards Earth (weight = $m \times g$).

Gravity pulls man down. Air resistance pushes man up.

Hand pushes toy car forward. Friction pulls car backwards. Gravity pulls car down. Earth pushes car up.

All the forces in these diagrams are coplanar — they're all in the same plane. You'll only need to deal with coplanar forces.

Resolving a Force Means Splitting it into Components

1) Forces can be in **any direction**, so they're not always at right angles to each other. This is sometimes a bit **awkward** for **calculations**.

2) To make an 'awkward' force easier to deal with, you can think of it as **two separate forces**, acting at **right angles** to **each other**. Forces are **vectors**, so you can use the same method as on the previous page.

> **Example:** The force F has exactly the same effect as the horizontal and vertical forces, F_H and F_V.
>
> Replacing F with F_H and F_V is called **resolving the force F**.
>
> Use these formulas when resolving forces: $\dfrac{F_H}{F} = \cos\theta$ or $F_H = F\cos\theta$ and $\dfrac{F_V}{F} = \sin\theta$ or $F_V = F\sin\theta$

Things Get Tricky with 3 Forces

1) When you have **three** coplanar forces acting on a body in **equilibrium**, you can draw the forces as a triangle, forming a **closed loop** like these:

2) Be careful when you draw the triangles not to go into autopilot and draw F_3 as the sum of F_1 and F_2 — it has to be in the **opposite** direction to balance the other two forces.

3) If it's a right-angled triangle, you can use **Pythagoras** to find a missing force.

4) If not, you might have to **resolve the forces** in each direction.

> **Example:** 3 teams are taking part in the CGP Fun Day 3-Way Tug of War. If the knot is in equilibrium, find the size of force P.
>
> P has no vertical component, so you can ignore the vertical components of the other teams (as they must cancel each other out). Resolve the horizontal forces (take right as the positive direction):
>
> $(\cos 41° \times 1175) + (\cos 41° \times 1175) - P = 0$
>
> $P = 886.7... + 886.7... = \mathbf{1800\ N}$ **(to 2 s.f.)**
>
> You can check your answer by drawing a triangle with the three forces and seeing if it forms a closed loop:

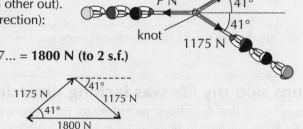

Forces

You Add Components Back Together to get the Resultant Force

1) If **two forces** act on an object, you find the **resultant** (total) **force** by adding the **vectors** together and creating a **closed triangle**, with the resultant force represented by the **third side**.

2) Forces are vectors (as you know), so you use **vector addition** — draw the forces as vector arrows put 'tip-to-tail'.

3) Then it's yet more trigonometry to find the **angle** and the **length** of the third side.

Example: Two dung beetles roll a dung ball along the ground at constant velocity. Beetle A applies a force of 0.50 N northwards while beetle B exerts a force of only 0.20 N eastwards. What is the resultant force on the dung ball?

The resultant force is **0.54 N (to 2 s.f.)** at an angle of **22° (to 2 s.f.)** from north.

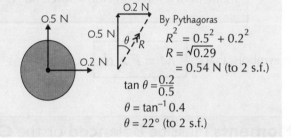

By Pythagoras
$$R^2 = 0.5^2 + 0.2^2$$
$$R = \sqrt{0.29}$$
$$= 0.54 \text{ N (to 2 s.f.)}$$

$$\tan \theta = \frac{0.2}{0.5}$$
$$\theta = \tan^{-1} 0.4$$
$$\theta = 22° \text{ (to 2 s.f.)}$$

Choose Sensible Axes for Resolving

Use directions that **make sense** for the situation you're dealing with. If you've got an object on a slope, choose your directions **along the slope** and **at right angles to it**. You can turn the paper to an angle if that helps.

Examiners like to call a slope an "inclined plane".

Always choose sensible axes

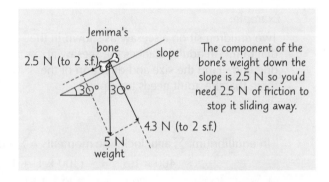

The component of the bone's weight down the slope is 2.5 N so you'd need 2.5 N of friction to stop it sliding away.

Warm-Up Questions

Q1 Sketch a free-body force diagram for an ice hockey puck moving across the ice (assuming no friction).

Q2 What are the horizontal and vertical components of the force F?

PRACTICE QUESTIONS

Exam Questions

Q1 A picture with a mass of 8.0 kg is suspended from a hook as shown in the diagram. Calculate the tension force, T, in the string. Use $g = 9.81 \text{ ms}^{-2}$.

[2 marks]

Q2 Two elephants pull a tree trunk as shown in the diagram. Calculate the resultant force on the tree trunk.

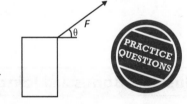

[2 marks]

Free-body force diagram — sounds like it comes with a dance mat...

Remember those F cos θ and F sin θ bits. Write them on bits of paper and stick them to your wall. Scrawl them on your pillow. Tattoo them on your brain. Whatever it takes — you just have to learn them.

Moments

This is not a time for jokes. There is not a moment to lose. Oh ho ho ho ho *bang*. (Ow.)

A **Moment** is the **Turning Effect** of a **Force**

The **moment** of a **force** depends on the **size** of the force and **how far** the force is applied from the **turning point**:

> moment of a force (in Nm) = force (in N) × **perpendicular distance from the point to the line of action of the force** (in m)

In symbols, that's: $M = F \times d$

The line of action of a force is a line along which it acts.

Moments Must be **Balanced** or the **Object** will **Turn**

The **principle of moments** states that for a body to be in **equilibrium**, the **sum of the clockwise moments** about any point **equals** the **sum of the anticlockwise moments** about the same point.

Example:

Two children sit on a seesaw as shown in the diagram. An adult balances the seesaw at one end. Find the size and direction of the force that the adult needs to apply.

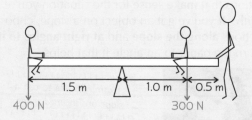

1.5 m · 1.0 m · 0.5 m
400 N · 300 N

In equilibrium, $\sum$ anticlockwise moments = $\sum$ clockwise moments

$$400 \times 1.5 = (300 \times 1) + 1.5F$$
$$600 = 300 + 1.5F$$

Final answer: $F = 200$ N downwards

$\sum$ means "the sum of"

Muscles, Bones and **Joints** Act as **Levers**

1) In a lever, an **effort force** (in this case from a muscle) acts against a **load force** (e.g. the weight of your arm) by means of a **rigid object** (the bone) rotating around a **pivot** (the joint).

2) You can use the **principle of moments** to answer lever questions:

Example:

Find the force, E, exerted by the biceps in holding a bag of gold still. The bag of gold weighs 100 N and the forearm weighs 20 N.

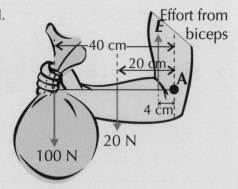

Effort from biceps
40 cm
20 cm
A
4 cm
20 N
100 N

Take moments about **A**.
In equilibrium:

$$\sum \text{anticlockwise moments} = \sum \text{clockwise moments}$$
$$(100 \times 0.4) + (20 \times 0.2) = 0.04E$$
$$40 + 4 = 0.04E$$

Final answer: $E = 1100$ N

Moments

A **Couple** is a **Pair** of **Coplanar Forces**

1) A couple is a **pair** of **forces** of **equal size** which act **parallel** to each other, but in **opposite directions**. The forces are **coplanar** (see page 44).

2) A couple doesn't cause any resultant linear force, but **does** produce a **turning effect** (i.e. a moment).

The **size** of this **moment** depends on the **size** of the **forces** and the **distance** between them.

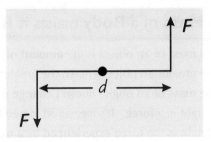

| moment of a couple (in Nm) = size of one of the forces (in N) × perpendicular distance between the lines of action of the forces (in m) |

Again, in symbols, that's: $M = F \times d$

Example:

A cyclist turns a sharp right corner by applying equal but opposite forces of 20 N to the ends of the handlebars.

The length of the handlebars is 0.6 m.
Calculate the moment applied to the handlebars.

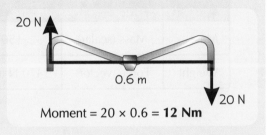

Moment = 20 × 0.6 = **12 Nm**

Warm-Up Questions

Q1 A force of 54 N acts at a perpendicular distance of 84 cm from a pivot. Calculate the moment of the force.

Q2 A girl of mass 40 kg sits 1.5 m from the middle of a seesaw.
Show that her brother, mass 50 kg, must sit 1.2 m from the middle if the seesaw is to balance.

Q3 What is meant by the word 'couple'?

Q4 A racing car driver uses both hands to apply equal and opposite forces of 65 N to the edge of a steering wheel with radius 20 cm. Calculate the moment of the forces.

Exam Questions

Q1 A driver is changing his flat tyre. The moment required to undo the nut is 60 Nm.
He uses a 0.40 m long double-ended wheel wrench.
Calculate the force that he must apply at each end of the wrench. [2 marks]

Q2 A diver of mass 60 kg stands on the end of a diving board 2.0 m from the pivot point.
Calculate the downward force exerted on the board by the retaining spring 30 cm from the pivot.

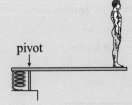

pivot

[2 marks]

It's all about balancing — just ask a tightrope walker...

They're always boring questions aren't they — seesaws or bicycles. It'd be nice if just once, they'd have a question on... I don't know, rotating knives or something. Just something unexpected. It'd make physics a lot more fun, I'm sure.

Mass, Weight and Centre of Mass

I'm sure you know all this 'mass' and 'weight' stuff from GCSE. But let's just make sure...

The Mass of a Body makes it Resist Changes in Motion

1) The **mass** of an object is the **amount of 'stuff'** (or **matter**) in it. It's measured in **kg**.
2) The greater an object's mass, the greater its **resistance** to a **change in velocity** (called its **inertia**).
3) The **mass** of an object **doesn't change** if the strength of the **gravitational field** changes.
4) Weight is a **force**. It's measured in **newtons** (N), like all forces.
5) Weight is the **force experienced by a mass** due to a **gravitational field**.
6) The weight of an object **does vary** according to the size of the **gravitational field** acting on it.

| **weight = mass × gravitational field strength ($W = mg$)** | where g = 9.81 Nkg^{-1} on Earth. |

This table shows Derek (the lion)'s
mass and weight on the Earth and the Moon.

Name	Quantity	Earth (g = 9.81 Nkg^{-1})	Moon (g = 1.6 Nkg^{-1})
Mass	Mass (scalar)	150 kg	150 kg
Weight	Force (vector)	1470 N (to 3 s.f.)	240 N (to 2 s.f.)

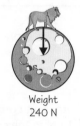

Weight
240 N

Weight
1470 N

Centre of Mass — Assume All the Mass is in One Place

1) The **centre of mass** of an object is the **single point** that you can consider
its **whole weight** to **act through** (whatever its orientation).
2) The object will always **balance** around this **point**, although in some cases the **centre of mass**
will **fall outside** the object.
3) The centre of mass of a **uniform, regular solid** (e.g. a sphere, a cube) is at its **centre**.

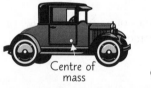

Centre of
mass

Centre of
mass

Centre of
mass

Find the Centre of Mass Either by Symmetry...

1) To find the centre of mass for a **regular** object you can just use **symmetry**.
2) The centre of mass of any regular shape is at its **centre** —
where the lines of symmetry will cross.
3) The centre of mass is **halfway** through the **thickness**
of the object at the point the lines meet.

The symmetry in this
picture shows the
centre of cuteness.

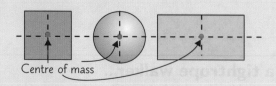

Centre of mass

Mass, Weight and Centre of Mass

... Or By **Experiment**

Experiment to find the Centre of Mass of an Irregular Object

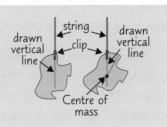

1) **Hang** the object freely from a point (e.g. one corner).
2) Draw a **vertical line** downwards from the point of suspension
   — use a plumb bob to get your line exactly vertical.
3) Hang the object from a different point.
4) Draw another vertical line down.
5) The centre of mass is where the two lines **cross**.

How **Stable** an Object is Depends on its **Centre of Mass** and Base Area

1) An object will topple over if a **vertical line** drawn **downwards** from its **centre of mass** (i.e. the line of action of its weight) falls **outside** its **base area**.

2) This is because a **resultant moment** (page 46) occurs, which provides a **turning force**.

3) An object will be nice and **stable** if it has a **low centre of mass** and a **wide base area**. This idea is used a lot in design, e.g. Formula 1® racing cars.

4) The higher the centre of mass and the smaller the base area, the less stable the object is. Think of unicyclists...

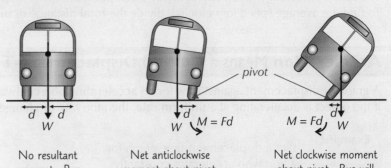

No resultant moment. Bus is stable and stationary.

Net anticlockwise moment about pivot. Bus will rotate to the left and right itself.

Net clockwise moment about pivot. Bus will rotate to the right and fall over.

Warm-Up Questions

Q1 What are the differences between mass and weight?

Q2 A lioness has a mass of 200 kg. What would be her mass and weight on the Earth (where $g = 9.81$ Nkg^{-1}) and on the Moon (where $g = 1.6$ Nkg^{-1})?

Q3 What is meant by the centre of mass of an object?

Q4 Why will an object topple if its centre of mass is not over the object's base?

Exam Question

Q1 a) Describe an experiment to find the centre of mass of an object of uniform density with a constant thickness and irregular cross-section. Identify one major source of uncertainty and suggest a way to reduce its effect on your result.　[5 marks]

b) Explain why you would not need to conduct this experiment for a regular, uniform solid.　[1 mark]

The centre of mass of this book should be round about page 154...

This is a really useful area of physics. To would-be nuclear physicists it might seem a little dull, but if you want to be an engineer — something a bit more useful (no offence Einstein) — then things like centre of mass are dead important things to understand. You know, for designing things like cars and submarines... yep, pretty useful I'd say.

Displacement-Time Graphs

Drawing graphs by hand — oh joy. You'd think examiners had never heard of the graphical calculator.
Ah well, until they manage to drag themselves out of the dark ages, you'll just have to grit your teeth and get on with it.

Displacement, Velocity, and Acceleration are All Linked

Displacement, velocity and acceleration are all **vector** quantities (page 42), so the direction matters.

> Speed — How fast something is moving, regardless of direction.
> Displacement (s) — How far an object's travelled from its starting point in a given direction.
> Velocity (v) — The rate of change of an object's displacement (its speed in a given direction).
> Acceleration (a) — The rate of change of an object's velocity.

You need to know these formulas for **velocity** and **acceleration**:

$$v = \frac{\Delta s}{\Delta t} \quad \text{and} \quad a = \frac{\Delta v}{\Delta t}$$

The triangle symbol is the Greek 'delta', and it means 'the change in'.

The speed (or velocity) of an object at any given point in time is known as its **instantaneous** speed (or velocity).
To find the **average** speed (or velocity), divide the **total** distance or displacement by the total time.

Acceleration Means a Curved Displacement-Time Graph

A graph of displacement against time for an **accelerating object** always produces a **curve**.
If the object is accelerating at a **uniform rate**, then the **rate of change** of the **gradient** will be constant.

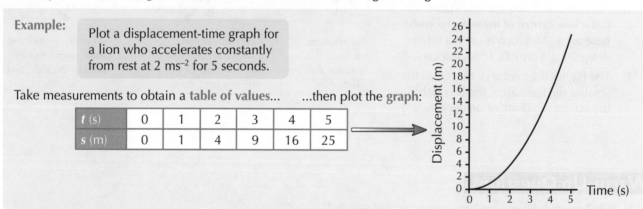

Example: Plot a displacement-time graph for a lion who accelerates constantly from rest at 2 ms⁻² for 5 seconds.

Take measurements to obtain a **table of values**... ...then plot the **graph**:

t (s)	0	1	2	3	4	5
s (m)	0	1	4	9	16	25

Different Accelerations Have Different Gradients

In the example above, if the lion has a **different acceleration** it'll change the **gradient** of the curve like this:

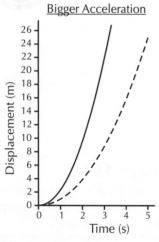

Bigger Acceleration

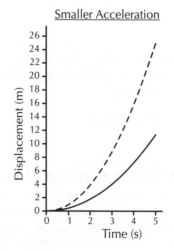

Smaller Acceleration

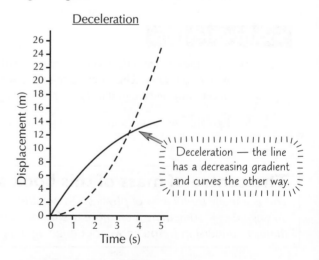

Deceleration

Deceleration — the line has a decreasing gradient and curves the other way.

Displacement-Time Graphs

The **Gradient** of a **Displacement-Time Graph** Tells You the Velocity

When the velocity is constant, the graph's a **straight line**.
As you saw on the previous page, velocity is defined as...

$$\text{velocity} = \frac{\text{change in displacement}}{\text{change in time}}$$

On the graph, this is $\dfrac{\text{change in } y\,(\Delta y)}{\text{change in } x\,(\Delta x)}$, i.e. the gradient.

So to get the velocity from a displacement-time graph, just find the gradient.

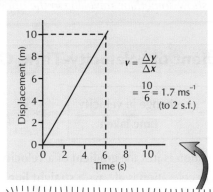

$$v = \frac{\Delta y}{\Delta x}$$
$$= \frac{10}{6} = 1.7 \text{ ms}^{-1}$$
(to 2 s.f.)

It's the Same with **Curved Graphs**

If the gradient **isn't constant** (i.e. if it's a curved line), it means the object is **accelerating**.

> To find the **instantaneous velocity** at a certain point you need to draw a **tangent** to the curve at that point and find its gradient.

To find the **average velocity** over a period of time, just divide the total change in displacement by the total change in time — it doesn't matter if the graph is curved or not.

Acceleration is $\dfrac{\text{change in velocity }(\Delta v)}{\text{change in time }(\Delta t)}$, so it is the rate of change of this gradient. If the gradient is constant (straight line) then there is no acceleration, and if it's changing (curved line) then there's acceleration or deceleration.

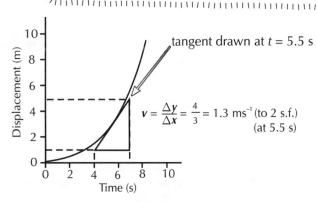

tangent drawn at $t = 5.5$ s

$$v = \frac{\Delta y}{\Delta x} = \frac{4}{3} = 1.3 \text{ ms}^{-1} \text{ (to 2 s.f.)}$$
(at 5.5 s)

Warm-Up Questions

Q1 What is given by the slope of a displacement-time graph?

Q2 Sketch a displacement-time graph to show: a) constant velocity, b) acceleration, c) deceleration

PRACTICE QUESTIONS

Exam Questions

Q1 Describe the motion of the cyclist as shown by the graph below.   [4 marks]

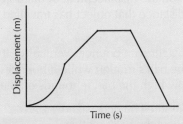

Q2 A baby crawls 5 m in 8 seconds at a constant velocity. She then rests for 5 seconds before crawling a further 3 m in 5 seconds. Finally, she makes her way back to her starting point in 10 seconds, travelling at a constant speed all the way.

a) Draw a displacement-time graph to show the baby's journey.   [4 marks]

b) Calculate her average velocity at all the different stages of her journey.   [2 marks]

Some curves are bigger than others...

Whether it's a straight line or a curve, the steeper it is, the greater the velocity. There's nothing difficult about these graphs — the problem is that it's easy to get them muddled up with velocity-time graphs (next page). Just think about the gradient — is it velocity or acceleration, is it changing (curve) or constant (straight line), is it 0 (horizontal line)...

Velocity-Time and Acceleration-Time Graphs

Speed-time graphs and velocity-time graphs are pretty similar. The big difference is that velocity-time graphs can have a negative part to show something travelling in the opposite direction:

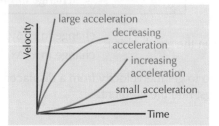

The **Gradient** of a **Velocity-Time Graph** Tells You the **Acceleration**

$$\text{acceleration} = \frac{\text{change in velocity}}{\text{time taken}}$$

likewise for a speed-time graph

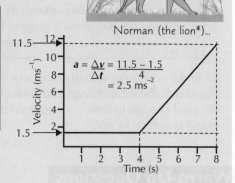

So the acceleration is just the **gradient** of a **velocity-time graph**.

1) **Uniform** acceleration is always a **straight line**.
   The **steeper** the **gradient**, the **greater** the **acceleration**.

2) A **curved** graph shows **changing** acceleration. **Increasing** gradient means **increasing acceleration**, and **decreasing** gradient means **decreasing acceleration** (or deceleration).

Example: A lion strolls along at 1.5 ms⁻¹ for 4 s and then accelerates uniformly at a rate of 2.5 ms⁻² for 4 s. Plot this information on a velocity-time graph.

So, for the first four seconds, the velocity is 1.5 ms⁻¹, then it increases by **2.5 ms⁻¹ every second**:

t (s)	v (ms⁻¹)
0 – 4	**1.5**
5	**4.0**
6	**6.5**
7	**9.0**
8	**11.5**

$$a = \frac{\Delta v}{\Delta t} = \frac{11.5 - 1.5}{4} = 2.5 \text{ ms}^{-2}$$

Norman (the lion*)...

You can see that the **gradient of the line** is **constant** between 4 s and 8 s and has a value of 2.5 ms⁻², representing the **acceleration of the lion**.

*Yes, I know — I just like lions, OK...

Displacement = **Area** Under **Velocity-Time Graph**

You know that: **distance travelled = average speed × time**

The **area under a velocity-time graph** tells you the displacement of the object. The magnitude of this displacement is the distance that object has travelled.

You can calculate areas using geometry or counting grid squares and multiplying the number by the value of each square.

Example: A ball is dropped from table-height so it bounces vertically. It bounces twice before someone catches it. The ball's motion while it bounces is shown on the *v-t* graph below. Calculate how high the ball rebounds on the first bounce.

Before you try and calculate anything, make sure you understand what each part of the graph is telling you about the ball's motion.

1) When the ball is first dropped, the velocity of the ball is **negative** — so downwards is the negative direction.

2) The points where the **ball hits the floor** are shown by the **vertical straight lines** on the graph — the ball's **speed** remains roughly the **same**, but its **direction** (and **velocity**) changes the instant it hits the floor.

3) The points where the ball's velocity is **zero** show where the ball reaches the **top of a bounce** before starting to fall downwards.

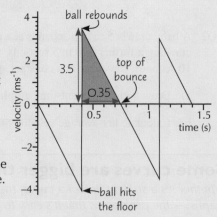

The height of the first bounce is the **area under the graph** between the time the ball first rebounds from the floor and the time it reaches the top of the bounce.

displacement = area under graph
= (3.5 × 0.35) ÷ 2 = 0.6125 = **0.61 m (to 2 s.f.)**

Velocity-Time and Acceleration-Time Graphs

Acceleration-Time Graphs are Useful Too

An **acceleration-time** (*a/t*) graph shows how an object's **acceleration** changes over time.

1) The **height** of the graph gives the object's **acceleration** at that time.
2) The **area** under the graph gives the object's **change in velocity**.
3) If *a* = 0, then the object is moving with **constant velocity**.
4) A negative acceleration is a **deceleration**.

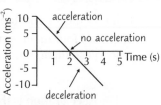

Example: The acceleration of a car in a drag race is shown in this acceleration-time graph.

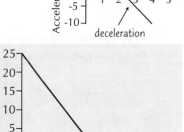

a) **After how many seconds does the car reach its maximum velocity?**
When the acceleration is 0, i.e. after **4 seconds**.

b) **If the car was stationary at *t* = 0 s, calculate its maximum velocity.**
(Change in) velocity = area under graph
$$= 0.5 \times 4 \times 25 = 50 \text{ ms}^{-1}$$

You Can Draw Displacement-Time and Velocity-Time Graphs Using ICT

Instead of gathering distance and time data using **traditional methods**, e.g. a stopwatch and ruler, you can be a bit more **high-tech**.

A fairly **standard** piece of kit you can use for motion experiments is an **ultrasound position detector**. This is a type of **data-logger** that automatically records the **distance** of an object from the sensor several times a second.

If you attach one of these detectors to a computer with **graph-drawing software**, you can get **real-time** displacement-time and velocity-time graphs.

The main advantages of data-loggers over traditional methods are:

1) The data is more accurate — you don't have to allow for human reaction times.
2) Automatic systems have a much higher sampling rate than humans — most ultrasound position detectors can take a reading ten times every second.
3) You can see the data displayed in real time.

Warm-Up Questions

Q1 How do you calculate acceleration from a velocity-time graph?
Q2 How do you calculate the displacement travelled from a velocity-time graph?
Q3 Sketch velocity-time graphs for constant velocity and constant acceleration.
Q4 Sketch velocity-time and acceleration-time graphs for a boy bouncing on a trampoline.
Q5 What does the area under an acceleration-time graph tell you?
Q6 Describe the main advantages of ICT over traditional methods for the collection and display of motion data.

Exam Question

Q1 A skier accelerates uniformly from rest at 2 ms⁻² down a straight slope for 5 seconds. He then reaches the bottom of the slope and continues along the flat ground, decelerating at 1 ms⁻² until he stops.

a) Sketch the velocity-time and acceleration-time graphs for his journey. [4 marks]

b) Use your *v-t* graph from part a) to find the distance travelled by the skier during the first 5 seconds. [2 marks]

Still awake — I'll give you five more minutes...

There's a really nice sunset outside my window. It's one of those ones that makes the whole landscape go pinky-yellowish. And that's about as much interest as I can muster on this topic. Normal service will be resumed on page 54.

Motion With Uniform Acceleration

Uniform Acceleration is Constant Acceleration

Acceleration could mean a change in speed or direction or both.

Uniform means **constant** here. It's nothing to do with what you wear.
There are **four main equations** that you use to solve problems involving **uniform acceleration**. You need to be able to **use them**, but you don't have to know how they're **derived** — we've just put it in to help you learn them.

1) **Acceleration is the rate of change of velocity.**
   From this definition you get:

   $$a = \frac{(v - u)}{t} \quad \text{so} \quad \boxed{v = u + at}$$

   where:
   u = initial velocity a = acceleration
   v = final velocity t = time taken

2) **s = average velocity × time**
   If acceleration is constant, the average velocity is just the average of the initial and final velocities, so:

   $$\boxed{s = \frac{(u + v)}{2} \times t} \quad s = \text{displacement}$$

3) Substitute the expression for v from equation 1 into equation 2 to give:

   $$s = \frac{(u + u + at) \times t}{2} = \frac{2ut + at^2}{2} \quad \boxed{s = ut + \tfrac{1}{2}at^2}$$

4) You can **derive** the fourth equation from equations **1** and **2**:

   Use equation **1** in the form:
   $$a = \frac{(v - u)}{t}$$

   Multiply both sides by s, where:
   $$s = \frac{(u + v)}{2} \times t$$

   This gives us:
   $$as = \frac{(v - u)}{t} \times \frac{(u + v)t}{2}$$

   The t's on the right cancel, so:
   $$2as = (v - u)(v + u)$$
   $$2as = v^2 - uv + uv - u^2$$

   so: $\boxed{v^2 = u^2 + 2as}$

Example: A tile falls from a roof 25 m high. Calculate its speed when it hits the ground and how long it takes to fall. Take $g = 9.81$ ms^{-2}.

First of all, write out what you know:

$s = 25$ m
$u = 0$ ms^{-1} since the tile's stationary to start with
$a = 9.81$ ms^{-2} due to gravity
$v = ?$ $t = ?$

Usually you take upwards as the positive direction. In this question it's probably easier to take downwards as positive, so you get $g = +9.81$ ms^{-2} instead of $g = -9.81$ ms^{-2}.

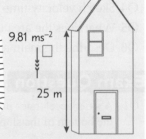

9.81 ms^{-2}

25 m

Then, choose an equation with only **one unknown quantity**.
So start with $v^2 = u^2 + 2as$
$v^2 = 0 + 2 \times 9.81 \times 25$
$v^2 = 490.5$
$v = 22$ ms^{-1} (to 2 s.f.)

Now, find t using:
$s = ut + \tfrac{1}{2}at^2$
$25 = 0 + \tfrac{1}{2} \times 9.81 \times t^2$
$t^2 = \frac{25}{4.9}$
$t = 2.3$ (to 2 s.f.)

Final answers:
$t = \mathbf{2.3}$ **s (to 2 s.f.)**
$v = \mathbf{22}$ **ms^{-1} (to 2 s.f.)**

Motion With Uniform Acceleration

Example: A car accelerates steadily from rest at a rate of 4.2 ms⁻² for 6.5 seconds.
   a)   Calculate the final speed.
   b)   Calculate the distance travelled in 6.5 seconds.

4.2 ms⁻²

Remember — always start by writing down what you know.

a) $a = 4.2$ ms⁻²   choose the right equation... $v = u + at$
   $u = 0$ ms⁻¹ $v = 0 + 4.2 \times 6.5$
   $t = 6.5$ s   **Final answer:** $v = 27.3$ ms⁻¹
   $v = ?$ $= \mathbf{27}$ **ms⁻¹ (to 2 s.f.)**

b) $s = ?$ you can use: $s = \dfrac{(u + v)t}{2}$ or: $s = ut + \tfrac{1}{2}at^2$
   $t = 6.5$ s
   $u = 0$ ms⁻¹
   $a = 4.2$ ms⁻² $s = \dfrac{(0 + 27.3) \times 6.5}{2}$ $s = 0 + \tfrac{1}{2} \times 4.2 \times (6.5)^2$
   $v = 27.3$ ms⁻¹

              Final answer: $s = \mathbf{89}$ **m (to 2 s.f.)** $s = \mathbf{89}$ **m (to 2 s.f.)**

Warm-Up Questions

Q1 Write out the four uniform acceleration equations.

Q2 A small steel ball is dropped from a height of 1.5 m. Calculate its speed as it hits the ground.

Exam Questions

Q1   A skydiver jumps from a helicopter hovering at a height of 1500 m from the ground.
   She accelerates due to gravity for 5.0 s.
   a)   Calculate her maximum vertical velocity. (Assume no air resistance.)   [2 marks]

   b)   Calculate how far she falls in this time.   [2 marks]

Q2   A motorcyclist slows down uniformly as he approaches a red light.
   He takes 3.2 seconds to come to a halt and travels 40 m (to 2 s.f.) in this time.
   a)   Calculate how fast he was initially travelling.   [2 marks]

   b)   Calculate his acceleration. (N.B. a negative value shows a deceleration.)   [2 marks]

Q3   A stream provides a constant acceleration of 6 ms⁻². A toy boat is pushed directly against the current
   and then released from a point 1.2 m upstream from a small waterfall. Just before it reaches the waterfall,
   it is travelling at a speed of 5 ms⁻¹.
   a)   Calculate the initial velocity of the boat.   [2 marks]

   b)   Calculate the maximum distance upstream from the waterfall the boat reaches.   [2 marks]

Constant acceleration — it'll end in tears...

*If a question talks about "uniform" or "constant" acceleration, it's a dead giveaway they want you to use one of these
equations. The tricky bit is working out which one to use — start every question by writing out what you know and
what you need to know. That makes it much easier to see which equation you need. To be sure. Arrr.*

Acceleration Due to Gravity

Ahhh acceleration due to gravity. The reason falling apples whack you on the head.

Free Fall is When There's Only Gravity and Nothing Else

Free fall is defined as the motion of an object undergoing an acceleration of '*g*'. You need to remember:

1) Acceleration is a **vector quantity** — and '*g*' acts **vertically downwards**.

2) The magnitude of '*g*' is usually taken as **9.81 ms⁻²**, though it varies slightly at different points on the Earth's surface.

3) The **only force** acting on an object in free fall is its **weight**.

4) Objects can have an initial velocity in any direction and still undergo **free fall** as long as the **force** providing the initial velocity is **no longer acting**.

All Objects in Free Fall Accelerate at the Same Rate

1) For over 1000 years the generally accepted theory was that heavier objects would fall towards the ground quicker than lighter objects. It was challenged a few times, but it was finally overturned when **Galileo** came on the scene.

2) The difference with Galileo was that he set up **systematic** and **rigorous experiments** to **test** his theories — just like in modern science. These experiments could be repeated and the results described **mathematically** and compared.

3) Galileo believed that all objects fall at the same rate. The problem in trying to prove it was that free-falling objects **fell too quickly** for him to be able to take any accurate measurements (he only had a water clock), and **air resistance** affects the rate at which objects fall.

4) Galileo measured the time a ball took to roll down a **smooth** groove in an inclined plane. He killed two birds with one stone by rolling it down a plane, which **slows** the ball's fall as well as reducing the effect of **air resistance**.

Another gravity experiment.

5) By rolling the ball along different fractions of the total length of the slope, he found that the distance the ball travelled was proportional to the square of the time taken. The ball was **accelerating** at a **constant rate**.

6) In the end it took **Newton** to bring it all together to show and explain why **all** free falling objects have the same acceleration. He showed **mathematically** that all objects are attracted towards the Earth due to a force he called **gravity**. Ah, good ol' Newton...

ball at rest at the top of the slope

smooth surface

accelerating ball

You Can Calculate *g* By Performing an Experiment...

PRACTICAL SKILLS

This is just one way of measuring *g*, there are loads of different experiments you could do — just make sure you know one method for your exams.

1) Set up the equipment shown in the diagram on the right.

2) Measure the height *h* from the bottom of the ball bearing to the trapdoor.

3) Flick the switch to simultaneously start the timer and disconnect the electromagnet, releasing the ball bearing.

4) The ball bearing falls, knocking the trapdoor down and breaking the circuit — which stops the timer. Record the time *t* shown on the timer.

5) Repeat this experiment three times and average the time taken to fall from this height. Repeat this experiment but drop the ball from several different heights.

6) You can then use these results to find *g* using a graph (see the next page).

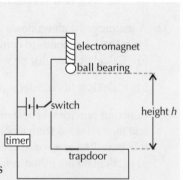

electromagnet

ball bearing

switch

timer

height *h*

trapdoor

- Using a small and heavy ball bearing means you can assume air resistance is so small you can ignore it.

- Having a computer automatically release and time the ball-bearing's fall can measure times with a smaller uncertainty than if you tried to drop the ball and time the fall using a stopwatch.

- The most significant source of error in this experiment will be in the measurement of *h*. Using a ruler, you'll have an uncertainty of about ±1 mm. This dwarfs any error from switch delay or air resistance.

Acceleration Due to Gravity

1) Use your data from the experiment on the last page to plot a graph of **height** (s) against the **time** it takes the ball to fall, **squared** (t^2). Then draw a **line of best fit**.

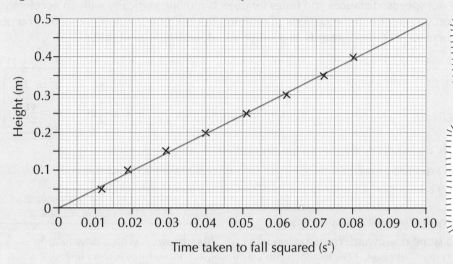

You could plot error bars on your data graph to find the error in your final value for g. See page 261 for more on error bars.

You can also measure g using light-gates. Drop a card (weighted at the bottom to keep it straight) between two light gates set to measure velocity and time, a fixed distance apart. Then you can find g using $a = \Delta v \div \Delta t$.

2) You know that with constant acceleration, $s = ut + \frac{1}{2}at^2$. If you drop the ball, initial speed $u = 0$, so $s = \frac{1}{2}at^2$.

3) Rearranging this gives $\frac{1}{2}a = \frac{s}{t^2}$, or $\frac{1}{2}g = \frac{s}{t^2}$ (remember the acceleration is all due to gravity).

4) So the gradient of the line of best fit, $\frac{\Delta s}{\Delta t^2}$, is equal to $\frac{1}{2}g$: $\quad g = 2 \times \frac{\Delta s}{\Delta t^2} = 2 \times \frac{0.44}{0.09} = \mathbf{9.8 \ ms^{-2}}$ (to 2 s.f.)

In the exam you might be asked to find g from a **displacement-time graph** (see page 51). The **gradient** of the graph will be velocity, so you can find g (which is an acceleration) by finding the change in gradient between two points on the graph (as $a = \Delta v \div \Delta t$).

Warm-Up Questions

Q1 What is meant by free fall?

Q2 How does the velocity of a free-falling object change with time?

Q3 What is the main reason Galileo's ideas became generally accepted in place of the old theory?

Q4 Describe an experiment that could be used to calculate the value of g.

Exam Question

Q1 In an experiment to determine the value of g, a small steel ball is dropped from a range of heights. The time it takes to reach the ground when dropped from each height is recorded.

a) Explain why using a steel ball is better than using a beach ball in this experiment. [1 mark]

b) State one random error that could arise from this experiment and suggest a way to remove it. [2 marks]

c) State one systematic error that could arise from this experiment and suggest a way to remove it. [2 marks]

d) A graph of the distance travelled by the ball against time taken squared is plotted. Show that the gradient of the graph is equal to half the value of g. [3 marks]

So it's this "Galileo" geezer who's to blame for my practicals...

Hmmm... I wonder what Galileo would be proudest of — insisting on the systematic, rigorous experimental method on which modern science hangs... or getting in a Queen song? Magnificoooooo...

Projectile Motion

Calculators at the ready — it's time to resolve more things into vertical and horizontal components.
It can be a bit tricky at first, but you'll soon get the hang of it. Chop chop, no time to lose.

You Can Just **Replace** *a* With **g** in the **Equations of Motion**

You need to be able to work out **speeds**, **distances** and **times** for objects moving vertically with an **acceleration** of g. As g is a **constant acceleration** you can use the **equations of motion**. But because g acts downwards, you need to be careful about directions, here we've taken **upwards as positive** and **downwards as negative**.

Case 1: No initial velocity (it's just falling)

Initial velocity $u = 0$
Acceleration $a = g = -9.81$ ms^{-2}. Hence the equations of motion become:

$$v = gt \qquad v^2 = 2gs$$
$$s = \tfrac{1}{2}gt^2 \qquad s = \tfrac{vt}{2}$$

Case 2: An initial velocity upwards (it's thrown up into the air)

The equations of motion are just as normal,
but with $a = g = -9.81$ ms^{-2}.

Sign Conventions — Learn Them:
g is always <u>downwards</u> so it's <u>usually negative</u>
t is <u>always positive</u>
u and v can be either <u>positive or negative</u>
s can be either <u>positive or negative</u>

Case 3: An initial velocity downwards (it's thrown down)

Example: Alex throws a stone downwards from the top of a cliff. She throws it with a downwards velocity of 2.0 ms^{-1}. It takes 3.0 s to reach the water below. How high is the cliff?

1) You know $u = -2.0$ ms^{-1}, $a = g = -9.81$ ms^{-2} and $t = 3.0$ s. You need to find s.

2) Use $s = ut + \tfrac{1}{2}gt^2 = (-2.0 \times 3.0) + \left(\tfrac{1}{2} \times -9.81 \times 3.0^2\right) = -50.145$ m. The cliff is **50 m (to 2 s.f.)** high.

s is negative because the stone ends up further down than it
started. Height is a scalar quantity, so is always positive.

You Have to Think of **Horizontal** and **Vertical** Motion **Separately**

Example: Sharon fires a scale model of a TV talent show presenter horizontally with a velocity of 100 ms^{-1} (to 3 s.f.) from 1.5 m above the ground. How long does it take to hit the ground, and how far does it travel horizontally? Assume the model acts as a particle, the ground is horizontal and there is no air resistance.

Think about the vertical motion first:

1) It's **constant acceleration** under gravity...

2) You know $u = 0$ (no vertical velocity at first),
$s = -1.5$ m and $a = g = -9.81$ ms^{-2}. You need to find t.

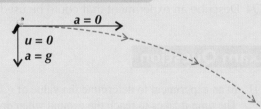

3) Use $s = \tfrac{1}{2}gt^2 \Rightarrow t = \sqrt{\tfrac{2s}{g}} = \sqrt{\tfrac{2 \times -1.5}{-9.81}} = 0.55300...$ s

4) So the model hits the ground after **0.55 seconds (to 2 s.f.)**.

Then do the horizontal motion:

1) The horizontal motion isn't affected by gravity or any other force, so it moves at a **constant speed**.

2) That means you can just use good old **speed = distance / time.**

Where v_H is the horizontal velocity, and
s_H is the horizontal distance travelled
(rather than the height fallen).

3) Now $v_H = 100$ ms^{-1}, $t = 0.55300...$ s and $a = 0$. You need to find s_H.

4) $s_H = v_H t = 100 \times 0.55300... = 55$ m (to 2 s.f.)

Projectile Motion

It's **Slightly Trickier** if it **Starts Off** at an **Angle**

If something's projected at an angle (like, say, a javelin) you start off with both horizontal and vertical velocity:

Method:
1) Resolve the initial velocity into horizontal and vertical components.
2) Use the vertical component to work out how long it's in the air and/or how high it goes.
3) Use the horizontal component to work out how far it goes horizontally while it's in the air.

Example: A cannonball is fired from ground height at an angle of exactly 40° with an initial velocity of 15 ms⁻¹. Calculate how far the cannonball travels before it hits the ground. Assume no air resistance.

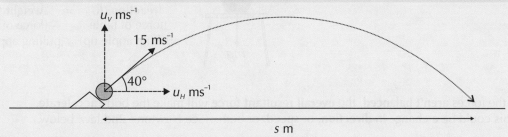

Resolve the velocity into horizontal and vertical components:

Horizontal component $u_H = \cos 40° \times 15 = 11.49... \text{ ms}^{-1}$

Vertical component $u_V = \sin 40° \times 15 = 9.64... \text{ ms}^{-1}$

Use the vertical component to work out how long the cannonball is in the air:

1) Halfway through the ball's flight, its v_V will be zero. $u_V = 9.64... \text{ ms}^{-1}$, $a = -9.81 \text{ ms}^{-2}$, $t = ?$,

   Use $v_V = u_V + at$: $0 = 9.64... + (-9.81 \times t) \Rightarrow t = \dfrac{9.64...}{9.81} = 0.98... \text{ s}$

2) So the time it takes to reach the ground again $= 2 \times 0.98... = 1.96... \text{ s}$

Use the horizontal component to work out how far it goes while it's in the air:

There's no horizontal acceleration, so $u_H = V_H = 11.49... \text{ ms}^{-1}$.

Distance = constant speed × time $= 11.49... \times 1.96... = 22.58... = \textbf{23 m (to 2 s.f.)}$

Warm-Up Questions

Q1 What is the initial vertical velocity for an object projected horizontally with a velocity of 5 ms⁻¹?

Q2 What is the initial horizontal velocity of an object projected at 45 degrees to the ground with a velocity of 25 ms⁻¹?

Exam Questions

Q1 Jason stands on a vertical cliff edge throwing stones into the sea below.
He throws a stone horizontally with a velocity of exactly 20 ms⁻¹, 560 m above sea level.

a) Calculate the time taken for the stone to hit the water from leaving Jason's hand.
Use $g = 9.81 \text{ ms}^{-2}$ and ignore air resistance. [2 marks]

b) Calculate the distance of the stone from the base of the cliff when it hits the water. [2 marks]

Q2 Robin fires an arrow into the air with a vertical velocity of exactly 30 ms⁻¹, and a horizontal velocity of exactly 20 ms⁻¹, from 1 m above the ground. Calculate the maximum height from the ground reached by his arrow to the nearest metre. Use $g = 9.81 \text{ ms}^{-2}$ and ignore air resistance. [3 marks]

All this physics makes me want to create projectile motions...

...by throwing my revision books out of the window. The maths on this page can be tricky, but take it step by step and all will be fine. Plus, the next page is all about Newton, and I must say he was a mighty clever chap.

Newton's Laws of Motion

You did most of this at GCSE, but that doesn't mean you can just skip over it now. You'll be kicking yourself if you forget this stuff in the exam — it's easy marks...

Newton's **1st Law** Says That a **Force** is Needed to Change Velocity

1) **Newton's 1st law of motion** states that the **velocity** of an object will **not change** unless a **resultant force** acts on it.

2) In plain English this means a body will stay still or move in a **straight line** at a **constant speed**, unless there's a **resultant force** acting on it.

An apple sitting on a table won't go anywhere because the forces on it are balanced.

| reaction (*R*) | = | weight (*mg*) |
| (force of table pushing apple up) | | (force of gravity pulling apple down) |

3) If the forces **aren't balanced**, the **overall resultant force** will make the body **accelerate**. This could be a change in **direction**, or **speed**, or both. (See Newton's 2nd law, below.)

Newton's **2nd Law** Says That **Acceleration** is **Proportional** to the Force

...which can be written as the well-known equation:

resultant force (N) = mass (kg) × acceleration (ms⁻²)

$$F = m \times a$$

Learn this — it crops up all over the place in Physics. And learn what it means too:

1) It says that the **more force** you have acting on a certain mass, the **more acceleration** you get.

2) It says that for a given force the **more mass** you have, the **less acceleration** you get.

3) There's more on this most excellent law on p.65.

REMEMBER:
1) The **resultant force** is the **vector sum** of all the forces.
2) The force is always measured in **newtons**.
3) The mass is always measured in **kilograms**.
4) The acceleration is always in the **same direction** as the resultant force and is measured in ms⁻².

Galileo said: **All Objects Fall** at the **Same Rate** (if You **Ignore Air Resistance**)

You need to understand **why** this is true. Newton's 2nd law explains it neatly — consider two balls dropped at the same time — ball **1** being heavy, and ball **2** being light. Then use Newton's 2nd law to find their acceleration.

mass = m_1
resultant force = F_1
acceleration = a_1

W_1

By Newton's Second Law:

$$F_1 = m_1 a_1$$

Ignoring air resistance, the only force acting on the ball is weight, given by $W_1 = m_1 g$ (where g = gravitational field strength = 9.81 Nkg⁻¹).

So: $F_1 = m_1 a_1 = W_1 = m_1 g$

So: $m_1 a_1 = m_1 g$, then m_1 cancels out to give: $a_1 = g$

mass = m_2
resultant force = F_2
acceleration = a_2

W_2

By Newton's Second Law:

$$F_2 = m_2 a_2$$

Ignoring air resistance, the only force acting on the ball is weight, given by $W_2 = m_2 g$ (where g = gravitational field strength = 9.81 Nkg⁻¹).

So: $F_2 = m_2 a_2 = W_2 = m_2 g$

So: $m_2 a_2 = m_2 g$, then m_2 cancels out to give: $a_2 = g$

...in other words, the **acceleration** is **independent of the mass**. It makes **no difference** whether the ball is **heavy or light**. And I've kindly **hammered home the point** by showing you two almost identical examples.

Newton's Laws of Motion

Newton's **3rd Law** Says Each Force has an **Equal, Opposite Reaction Force**

There are a few different ways of stating Newton's 3rd law, but the clearest way is:

> If an object A EXERTS a FORCE on object B, then
> object B exerts AN EQUAL BUT OPPOSITE FORCE on object A.

You'll also hear the law as "every action has an equal and opposite reaction". But this confuses people who wrongly think the forces are both applied to the same object. (If that were the case, you'd get a resultant force of zero and nothing would ever move anywhere...)

The two forces actually represent the **same interaction**, just seen from two **different perspectives**:

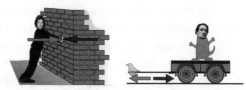

1) If you **push against a wall**, the wall will **push back** against you, **just as hard**. As soon as you stop pushing, so does the wall. Amazing...

2) If you **pull a cart**, whatever force **you exert** on the rope, the rope exerts the **exact opposite** pull on you (unless the rope's stretching).

3) When you go **swimming**, you push **back** against the water with your arms and legs, and the water pushes you **forwards** with an equal-sized force.

This looks like Newton's 3rd law...

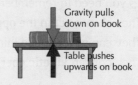

But it's <u>NOT</u>.

Gravity pulls down on book

Table pushes upwards on book

Newton's 3rd law applies in **all situations** and to all **types of force**. But the pairs of forces are always the **same type**, e.g. both gravitational or both electrical.

...because both forces are acting on the book, and they're not of the same type. They are two separate interactions. The forces are equal and opposite, resulting in zero acceleration, so this is showing Newton's 1st law.

Warm-Up Questions

Q1 State Newton's 1st, 2nd and 3rd laws of motion, and explain what they mean.

Q2 What are the two equal and opposite forces acting between an orbiting satellite and the Earth?

Exam Questions

Q1 A boat is moving across a river. The engines provide a force of 500 N at right angles to the flow of the river and the boat experiences a drag of 100 N in the opposite direction. The force on the boat due to the flow of the river is 300 N. The mass of the boat is 250 kg.

  a) Calculate the magnitude of the resultant force acting on the boat. [2 marks]

  b) Calculate the magnitude of the acceleration of the boat. [2 marks]

Q2 John's bike, which has a mass of m, breaks and he has to push it home. The bike has a constant acceleration a and a frictional force F opposes the motion. What force is John is using to push his bike? [1 mark]

A	ma
B	$ma + F$
C	$m(a - F)$
D	$ma - F$

Q3 Michael and Tom are both keen on diving. They notice that they seem to take the same time to drop from the diving board to the water. Use Newton's second law to explain why this is the case. (Assume no air resistance.) [3 marks]

Newton's three incredibly important laws of motion...

These laws may not really fill you with a huge amount of excitement (and I could hardly blame you if they don't)... but it was pretty fantastic at the time — suddenly people actually understood how forces work, and how they affect motion. I mean arguably it was one of the most important scientific discoveries ever...

Drag, Lift and Terminal Speed

If you jump out of a plane at 1500 m, you want to know that you're not going to be accelerating all the way.

Friction is a Force that Opposes Motion

There are two main types of friction — **dry friction** between **solid surfaces**
and **fluid friction** (known as **drag**, fluid resistance or air resistance).

Fluid Friction or Drag:

1) 'Fluid' is a word that means either a **liquid or a gas** — something that can **flow**.

2) The force depends on the thickness (or **viscosity**) of the fluid.

3) It **increases** as the **speed increases** (for simple situations it's directly
proportional, but you don't need to worry about the mathematical relationship).

4) It also depends on the **shape** of the object moving through it — the larger the
area pushing against the fluid, the greater the resistance force.

5) A **projectile** (see p. 58) is **slowed down** by air resistance. If you calculate how far a
projectile will travel without thinking about air resistance, your answer will be **too large**.

Things you need to remember about frictional forces:

1) They **always** act in the **opposite direction** to the **motion** of the object.

2) They can **never** speed things up or start something moving.

3) They convert **kinetic energy** into **heat** and **sound**.

Lift is Perpendicular to Fluid Flow

1) '**Lift**' is an **upwards force** on an
object moving through a fluid.

2) It happens when the shape of an object causes
the fluid flowing over it to **change direction**.

3) The force acts **perpendicular** to the
direction the fluid flows in.

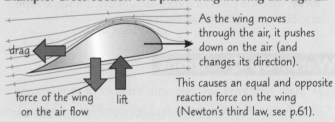

Example: Cross-section of a plane wing moving through air

drag

force of the wing
on the air flow   lift

As the wing moves
through the air, it pushes
down on the air (and
changes its direction).

This causes an equal and opposite
reaction force on the wing
(Newton's third law, see p.61).

Terminal Speed — When the Friction Force Equals the Driving Force

You will reach a **terminal (maximum) speed** at some point, if you have:

1) a **driving force** that stays the **same** all the time

2) a **frictional** or **drag force** (or collection of forces) that increases with speed

There are **three main stages** to reaching terminal speed:

Resultant Force

Driving Force

Resultant Force

Frictional Force   Driving Force

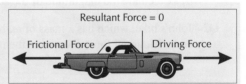

Resultant Force = 0

Frictional Force   Driving Force

The car **accelerates** from **rest**
using a constant driving force.

As the **speed increases**, the **frictional
forces increase** (because of things like
turbulence — you don't need the details).
This **reduces the resultant force** on the
car and hence **reduces its acceleration**.

Eventually the car reaches a speed at
which the **frictional forces are equal
to the driving force**. There is now **no
resultant force** and **no acceleration**,
so the car carries on at **constant speed**.

Different factors affect a vehicle's maximum speed

As you just saw, a vehicle reaches maximum speed when the driving force is equal to the frictional force.
So there are two main ways of increasing a vehicle's maximum speed:

1) **Increasing the driving force**, e.g. by increasing the engine size.

2) **Reducing the frictional force**, e.g. making the body more streamlined.

Drag, Lift and Terminal Speed

Things **Falling** through **Air** or **Water** Reach a **Terminal Speed** too

When something's falling through air, the weight of the object is a constant force accelerating the object downwards.
Air resistance is a frictional force opposing this motion, which increases with speed.
So before a parachutist opens the parachute, exactly the same thing happens as with the car example:

1) A skydiver leaves
   a plane and will
   accelerate until the
   air resistance equals
   his **weight**.

2) He will then be
   travelling at a
   terminal speed.

But... the terminal speed of a person in free fall is too great to land without dying a horrible death.
The **parachute increases** the **air resistance massively**, which slows him down to a lower terminal speed:

3) Before reaching the
   ground he will **open
   his parachute**, which
   immediately **increases
   the air resistance** so it
   is now **bigger** than his
   weight.

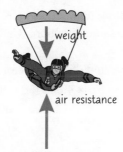

4) This **slows him down**
   until his speed has
   dropped enough for the
   air resistance to be **equal
   to his weight** again. This
   new terminal speed is
   small enough for him to
   land safely.

A *v-t* graph of the skydiver looks like this. He
reaches terminal speed twice during his fall —
the second one is much slower than the first.

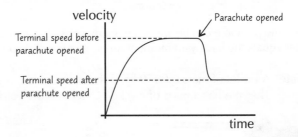

Warm-Up Questions

Q1 What forces limit the speed of a skier going down a slope?

Q2 What causes a lift force on a plane wing as it moves through air?

Q3 Suggest two ways in which the maximum speed of a car can be increased.

Q4 What conditions cause a terminal speed to be reached?

Exam Question

Q1 A space probe free-falls towards the surface of a planet.
The graph on the right shows the velocity of the probe as it falls.

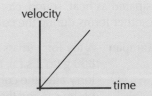

a) The planet does not have an atmosphere. Explain how you can tell this from the graph. [2 marks]

b) Sketch the velocity-time graph you would expect to see if the planet did have an atmosphere. [2 marks]

c) Explain the shape of the graph you have drawn. [3 marks]

You'll never understand this without going parachuting...*

*When you're doing questions about terminal velocity, remember the frictional forces reduce acceleration, not speed.
They usually don't slow an object down, apart from in the parachute example, where the skydiver is travelling faster just
before the parachute opens than the terminal velocity for the open parachute-skydiver combination.*

---

* No. 37 in a series of the 100 least convincing excuses for an interesting holiday.

Momentum and Impulse

These pages are about linear momentum — that's momentum in a straight line (not a circle).

Understanding **Momentum** Helps You Do **Calculations** on **Collisions**

The **momentum** of an object depends on two things — its **mass** and **velocity**.
The **product** of these two values is the momentum of the object.

| **momentum = mass × velocity** | or in symbols: | p (in kg ms^{-1}) = m (in kg) × v (in ms^{-1}) |

Remember, momentum is a vector quantity, so it has size and direction.

Momentum is Always **Conserved**

You might see momentum referred to as 'linear momentum'. The other kind is 'angular momentum', but you don't need to know about that for now.

1) Assuming **no external forces** act, momentum is always **conserved**.

2) This means the **total momentum** of two objects **before** they collide **equals** the total momentum **after** the collision.

3) This is really handy for working out the **velocity** of objects after a collision (as you do...):

Example: A skater of mass 75 kg and velocity 4.0 ms^{-1} collides with a stationary skater of mass 50 kg (to 2 s.f.). The two skaters join together and move off in the same direction. Calculate their velocity after impact.

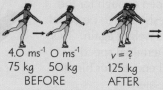

4.0 ms^{-1} 0 ms^{-1} v = ?
75 kg   50 kg   125 kg
BEFORE   AFTER

Before you start a momentum calculation, always draw a quick sketch.

Momentum of skaters before = Momentum of skaters after
$(75 × 4.0) + (50 × 0) = 125v$
$300 = 125v$
So v = **2.4 ms^{-1}**

4) The same principle can be applied in **explosions**. E.g. if you fire an **air rifle**, the **forward momentum** gained by the pellet **equals** the **backward momentum** of the rifle, and you feel the rifle recoiling into your shoulder.

Example: A bullet of mass 0.0050 kg is shot from a rifle at a speed of 200 ms^{-1}. The rifle has a mass of 4.0 kg. Calculate the velocity at which the rifle recoils.

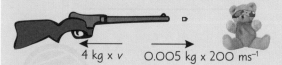

4 kg × v 0.005 kg × 200 ms^{-1}

Momentum before explosion = Momentum after explosion
$0 = (0.0050 × 200) + (4.0 × v)$
$0 = 1 + 4v$
v = **−0.25 ms^{-1}**

Collisions Can be **Elastic** or **Inelastic**

An **elastic collision** is one where **momentum** is **conserved** and **kinetic energy** is **conserved** — i.e. no energy is dissipated as heat, sound, etc. If a collision is **inelastic** it means that some of the kinetic energy is converted into other forms during the collision. But **momentum is always conserved**.

Example: A toy lorry (mass 2.0 kg) travelling at 3.0 ms^{-1} crashes into a smaller toy car (mass 800 g (to 2 s.f.)), travelling in the same direction at 2.0 ms^{-1}. The velocity of the lorry after the collision is 2.6 ms^{-1} in the same direction. Calculate the new velocity of the car and the total kinetic energy before and after the collision.

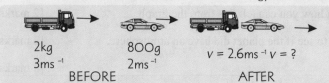

2kg   800g
3ms^{-1} 2ms^{-1}
BEFORE

v = 2.6ms^{-1} v = ?
AFTER

Momentum before collision = Momentum after collision
$(2 × 3) + (0.8 × 2) = (2 × 2.6) + (0.8v)$
$7.6 = 5.2 + 0.8v$
$2.4 = 0.8v$
v = **3 ms^{-1}**

Kinetic energy before = KE of lorry + KE of car
$= ½mv^2$ (lorry) + $½mv^2$ (car)
$= ½(2 × 3^2) + ½(0.8 × 2^2)$
$= 9 + 1.6$
$= $ **11 J (to 2 s.f.)**

Kinetic energy after $= ½(2 × 2.6^2) + ½(0.8 × 3^2)$
$= 6.76 + 3.6$
$= $ **10 J (to 2 s.f.)**

*The difference in the two values is the amount of kinetic energy dissipated as heat or sound, or in damaging the vehicles — so this is an **inelastic** collision.*

Momentum and Impulse

Newton's 2nd Law Says That Force is the Rate of Change in Momentum...

The **rate of change of momentum** of an object is **directly proportional** to the **resultant force** which acts on the object.

So: $\boxed{F = \dfrac{\Delta (mv)}{\Delta t}}$ or $\boxed{F\Delta t = \Delta (mv)}$ (where F is constant)

Remember that acceleration is equal to the rate of change of velocity (page 52),
so if mass is constant then this formula gives you that mechanics favourite, $F = m \times a$.

Impulse = Change in Momentum

1) Newton's second law says **force = rate of change of momentum**, or $F = (mv - mu) \div t$

2) **Rearranging** Newton's 2nd law gives: ⟹
   Where **impulse** is defined as **force × time**, Ft.
   The units of impulse are **newton seconds**, Ns.

   $$Ft = mv - mu$$
   so **impulse = change in momentum**

   Where v is the final velocity and u is the initial velocity.

3) **Impulse** is the **area under** a **force-time graph** — this is really handy for solving problems where the force changes.

   Example: The graph shows the resultant force acting on a toy car.
   If the car is initially at rest, what is its momentum after 3 seconds?

   Impulse = change in momentum = $mv - mu$. The **initial momentum** (mu) is
   zero because the toy car is stationary to begin with. So, **impulse = mv**.

   Impulse is the **area under the graph**, so to find the **momentum** of the car after
   3 seconds, you need to find the **area under the graph** between 0 and 3 seconds.

   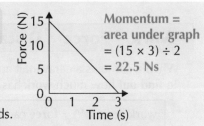
   Momentum =
   area under graph
   = $(15 \times 3) \div 2$
   = 22.5 Ns

4) The force of an impact is **increased** by **reducing**
   the impact time, e.g. the **less time** your foot
   is in contact with a football when kicking it,
   the **more force** you will kick it with (assuming
   the change in momentum is the same).

5) The **force** of an impact can be **reduced**
   by **increasing the time** of the impact,
   e.g. vehicle safety features.

6) In order to design vehicles **ethically**,
   manufacturers need to make sure the vehicles
   they produce are designed and fitted with
   features that help **protect people** in a crash.

- **Crumple zones** — the parts at the front and back
  of the car crumple up on impact. This causes the
  car to take longer to stop, increasing the impact
  time and decreasing the force on the passengers.

- **Seat belts** — these stretch slightly, increasing the
  time taken for the wearer to stop. This reduces
  the forces acting on the chest.

- **Air bags** — these also slow down passengers
  more gradually, and prevent them from hitting
  hard surfaces inside the car.

PRACTICE QUESTIONS

Warm-Up Questions

Q1 Give two examples of conservation of momentum in practice.

Q2 Describe what happens when a tiny object makes an elastic collision with a massive object, and why.

Q3 Describe how seat belts reduce the force acting on a car passenger in a collision.

Exam Questions

Q1 A ball of mass 0.60 kg moving at 5.0 ms⁻¹ collides with a larger stationary ball of mass 2.0 kg.
The smaller ball rebounds in the opposite direction at 2.4 ms⁻¹.

   a) Calculate the velocity of the larger ball immediately after the collision. [3 marks]

   b) State and explain whether this is an elastic or inelastic collision. Support your answer with calculations. [3 marks]

Q2 A toy train of mass 0.7 kg, travelling at 0.3 ms⁻¹, collides with a stationary toy carriage of mass 0.4 kg.
The two toys couple together. Calculate their new velocity. [3 marks]

Momentum'll never be an endangered species — it's always conserved...

*It seems odd to say that momentum's always conserved then tell you that impulse is the change in momentum. Impulse is just the change of momentum of one object, whereas conservation of momentum is talking about the **whole** system.*

Work and Power

As everyone knows, work in Physics isn't like normal work. It's harder. Work also has a specific meaning that's to do with movement and forces. You'll have seen this at GCSE — it just comes up in more detail for A level.

Work is Done Whenever Energy is Transferred

This table gives you some examples of **work being done** and the **energy changes** that happen.

1) Usually you need a force to move something because you're having to **overcome another force**.

2) The thing being moved has **kinetic energy** while it's **moving**.

3) The kinetic energy is transferred to **another form of energy** when the movement stops.

ACTIVITY	WORK DONE AGAINST	FINAL ENERGY FORM
Lifting up a box.	gravity	gravitational potential energy
Pushing a chair across a level floor.	friction	heat
Pushing two magnetic north poles together.	magnetic force	magnetic energy
Stretching a spring.	stiffness of spring	elastic potential energy

The word **'work'** in Physics means the **amount of energy transferred** from one form to another when a force causes a movement of some sort.

Work = Force × Distance

When a car tows a caravan, it applies a force to the caravan to move it to where it's wanted. To **find out** how much **work** has been **done**, you need to use the **equation**:

> **work done (W) = force causing motion (F) × distance moved (s), or W = Fs**
> ...where W is measured in joules (J), F is measured in newtons (N) and s is measured in metres (m).

Points to remember:

1) **Work** is the **energy** that's been **changed** from one form to another — it's not necessarily the **total** energy. E.g. moving a book from a low shelf to a higher one will increase its gravitational potential energy, but it had some potential energy to start with. Here, the **work done** would be the **increase** in potential energy, **not the total** potential energy.

2) Remember the distance needs to be measured in metres — if you have **distance in centimetres or kilometres**, you need to **convert** it to metres first.

3) The force **F** will be a **fixed** value in any calculations, either because it's **constant** or because it's the **average** force.

4) The equation assumes that the **direction of the force** is the **same** as the **direction of movement**.

5) The equation gives you the **definition** of the joule (symbol J): 'One joule is the work done when a force of 1 newton moves an object through a distance of 1 metre'.

The Force isn't Always in the Same Direction as the Movement

Sometimes the **direction of movement** is **different** from the **direction of the force**.

Example:

1) To calculate the work done in a situation like the one on the right, you need to consider the **horizontal** and **vertical components** of the **force**.

2) The only movement is in the horizontal direction. This means the vertical force is not causing any motion (and hence not doing any work) — it's just balancing out some of the weight, meaning there's a smaller reaction force.

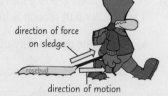
direction of force on sledge
rosebud
direction of motion

3) The horizontal force is causing the motion — so to calculate the work done, this is the only force you need to consider. Which means we get:

> **W = Fs cos θ**

Where θ is the **angle** between the **direction of the force** and the **direction of motion**. See page 44 for more on resolving forces.

F
θ
F cos θ
Direction of motion

Work and Power

The **Area** Under a **Force-Displacement Graph** Tells You the **Work Done**

1) For a **variable force**, you can't just use the formula **W = Fs** — nightmare.

2) Luckily, plotting a **graph** of **force against distance moved** lets you calculate the work done by just finding the **area under the graph**.

3) You might need to **split it up** into sections that make shapes you can work out the area for, e.g. trapeziums.

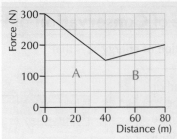

The graph shows the force exerted by Tibalt the circus monkey as he cycled up a hill.

Work done in section A:
$$40 \times \frac{300 + 150}{2} = 9000 \text{ J}$$

Work done in section B:
$$40 \times \frac{200 + 150}{2} = 7000 \text{ J}$$

Total work done = **16 000 J**

Power = Work Done per Second

Power means many things in everyday speech, but in Physics (of course!) it has a special meaning. Power is the **rate of doing work** — in other words it is the **amount of energy transferred** from one form to another **per second**. You **calculate power** from this equation:

> Power (P) = change in energy (or work done) (ΔW) / change in time (Δt), or $P = \dfrac{\Delta W}{\Delta t}$
>
> ...where P is measured in watts (W), ΔW is measured in joules (J) and Δt is measured in seconds (s).

The **watt** (symbol W) is defined as a **rate of energy transfer** equal to **1 joule per second** (Js^{-1}).

Power is also Force × Velocity

Sometimes, it's **easier** to use **this version** of the power equation:

1) You know $P = \Delta W / \Delta t$.

2) You also know $\Delta W = F\Delta s$, which gives $P = F\Delta s / \Delta t$.

3) But $v = \Delta s / \Delta t$, which you can substitute into the above equation to give:

$$P = Fv$$

 It's easier to use this if you're given speed in the question.

Warm-Up Questions

Q1 Write down the equation used to calculate work if the force and motion are in the same direction.

Q2 Write down the equation for work if the force is at an angle to the direction of motion.

Q3 What does the area under a force-distance graph represent?

Q4 Write down the equations relating a) power and work and b) power and speed.

Exam Questions

Q1 A traditional narrowboat is drawn by a horse walking along the towpath. The horse pulls the boat at a constant speed between two locks which are 1500 m apart. The tension in the rope is exactly 100 N (to 2 s.f.) at exactly 40° to the direction of motion.

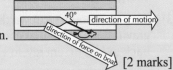

a) Calculate the work done on the boat. [2 marks]

b) The boat moves at 0.8 ms⁻¹. Calculate the power supplied to the boat in the direction of motion. [2 marks]

Q2 A motor is used to lift a 20 kg (to 2 s.f.) load a height of 3.0 m. (Take $g = 9.81 \text{ Nkg}^{-1}$.)

a) Calculate the work done in lifting the load. [2 marks]

b) The speed of the load during the lift is 0.25 ms⁻¹. Calculate the power delivered by the motor. [2 marks]

Work — there's just no getting away from it...

Loads of equations to learn. Well, that's what you came here for, after all. Can't beat a good bit of equation-learning, as I've heard you say quietly to yourself when you think no one's listening. Aha, can't fool me. Ahahahahahahahahaha.

Conservation of Energy and Efficiency

Energy can never be lost. I repeat — energy can never be lost. Which is basically what I'm about to take up two whole pages saying. But that's, of course, because you need to do exam questions on this as well as understand the principle.

Learn the **Principle** of **Conservation** of **Energy**

The **principle of conservation of energy** says that:

Energy **cannot be created** or **destroyed**. Energy **can be transferred** from one form to another but the total amount of energy in a closed system will not change.

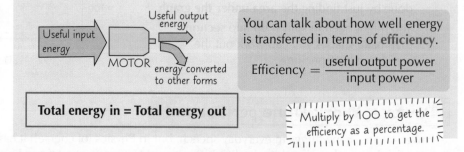

Total energy in = Total energy out

You can talk about how well energy is transferred in terms of **efficiency**.

$$\text{Efficiency} = \frac{\text{useful output power}}{\text{input power}}$$

Multiply by 100 to get the efficiency as a percentage.

You Need it for **Questions** about **Kinetic** and **Potential Energy**

The principle of conservation of energy nearly always comes up when you're doing questions about changes between kinetic and potential energy.

A quick reminder:

1) **Kinetic energy** is energy of anything **moving**, which you work out from $E_k = \frac{1}{2}mv^2$, where v is the velocity it's travelling at and m is its mass.

2) There are **different types of potential energy** — e.g. gravitational and elastic (see p.72).

3) **Gravitational potential energy** is the energy something gains if you lift it up. You work it out using: $\Delta E_p = mg\Delta h$, where m is the mass of the object, Δh is the height it is lifted and g is the gravitational field strength (9.81 Nkg^{-1} on Earth).

4) **Elastic strain energy** (elastic potential energy) is the energy you get in, say, a stretched rubber band or spring. You work this out using $E = \frac{1}{2}k\Delta l^2$, where Δl is the extension of the spring and k is the spring constant (p.70).

The energy you need to do things comes from your **food** — **chemical energy** inside the food is **converted** to other forms, e.g. **kinetic energy**. Be careful if you're trying to work out how much kinetic energy you can get from food though — a lot of the energy in food will actually be converted to other forms, e.g. **heat energy** to keep warm.

Examples: These pictures show you three **examples** of changes between kinetic and potential energy.

1) As Becky throws the **ball upwards**, **kinetic energy** is converted into **gravitational potential energy**. When it **comes down** again, that **gravitational potential** energy is **converted back** into **kinetic** energy.

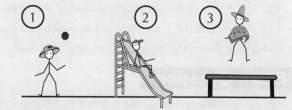

2) As Dominic goes **down the slide**, **gravitational potential energy** is converted to **kinetic energy**.

3) As Simon bounces upwards from the trampoline, **elastic potential energy** is converted to **kinetic energy**, to **gravitational potential energy**. As he comes back down again, that **gravitational potential** energy is **converted back** to **kinetic** energy, to **elastic potential** energy, and so on.

In **real life** there are also **frictional forces** — Simon would have to exert some **force** from his **muscles** to keep **jumping** to the **same height** above the trampoline each time. Each time Simon jumps, some kinetic energy is converted to heat energy due to air resistance. You're usually told to **ignore friction** in exam questions — this means you can **assume** that the **only forces** are those that provide the **potential or kinetic energy** (in this example that's **Simon's weight** and the **tension** in the springs and trampoline material). If you're ignoring friction, you can say that the **sum of the kinetic and potential energies is constant**.

4) In a **car crash**, a lot of kinetic energy is transferred in a **short space of time**. Car safety features are designed to transfer some of this energy into other forms — this reduces the amount of energy transferred to the car passengers and other road users to help protect them. For example, **crumple zones** (see page 71) absorb some of the car's kinetic energy by **deforming**, **seat belts** absorb some of the passengers' kinetic energy by **stretching**.

Conservation of Energy and Efficiency

Use Conservation of Energy to Solve Problems

You need to be able to **use** conservation of mechanical energy (change in potential energy = change in kinetic energy) to solve problems. The classic example is the **simple pendulum**.

In a simple pendulum, you assume that all the mass is in the **bob** at the end.

> **Example:** A simple pendulum has a mass of 720 g and a length of 50 cm (to 2 s.f.).
> It is pulled out to an angle of 30° (to 2 s.f.) from the vertical.
>
> a) Find the gravitational potential energy stored in the pendulum bob.

You can work out the increase in height, Δh, of the end of the pendulum using trig.

$$\text{Gravitational potential energy} = mg\Delta h$$
$$= 0.72 \times 9.81 \times (0.5 - 0.5\cos 30°)$$
$$= 0.473... \text{ J}$$
$$= \textbf{0.47 J (to 2 s.f.)}$$

> b) The pendulum is released. Find the maximum speed of the pendulum bob as it passes the vertical position.

To find the *maximum* speed, assume no air resistance, then $mg\Delta h = \frac{1}{2}mv^2$.

So $\frac{1}{2}mv^2 = 0.473...$

OR

Rearrange to find $v = \sqrt{\dfrac{2 \times 0.473...}{0.72}} = \textbf{1.1 ms}^{-1}$ **(to 2 s.f.)**

Cancel the *m*s and rearrange to give:
$$v^2 = 2g\Delta h$$
$$= 2 \times 9.81 \times (0.5 - 0.5\cos 30°)$$
$$= 1.31429...$$
$$v = \textbf{1.1 ms}^{-1} \textbf{ (to 2 s.f.)}$$

You could be asked to apply this stuff to just about any situation in the exam. **Roller coasters** are a bit of a favourite.

Warm-Up Questions

Q1 State the principle of conservation of energy.

Q2 What are the equations for calculating kinetic energy and gravitational potential energy?

Q3 Show that, if there's no air resistance and the mass of the string is negligible, the speed of a pendulum is independent of the mass of the bob.

Q4 An 1800 watt kettle transfers 1000 J per second to the water inside it. The rest is lost to other forms of energy. Calculate the efficiency of the kettle.

Exam Questions

Q1 A skateboarder is on a half-pipe. He lets the board run down one side of the ramp and up the other. The height of the ramp is 2 m. Take *g* as 9.81 Nkg^{-1}.

    a) Assume that there is no friction. Calculate his speed at the lowest point of the ramp.   [3 marks]

    b) How high will he rise up the other side?   [1 mark]

    c) Real ramps are not frictionless, so what must the skater do to reach the top on the other side?   [1 mark]

Q2 A 20.0 g rubber ball is released from a height of 8.0 m. (Assume that the effect of air resistance is negligible.)

    a) Find the kinetic energy of the ball just before it hits the ground.   [2 marks]

    b) The ball strikes the ground and rebounds to a height of 6.5 m. Calculate how much energy is converted to heat and sound in the impact with the ground.   [2 marks]

Energy is never lost — it just sometimes prefers the scenic route...

Right, done, on to the next question... remember to check your answers — I can't count the number of times I've forgotten to square the velocities or to multiply by the ½. I reckon it's definitely worth the extra minute to check.

Properties of Materials

Hooke's law applies to all materials, but only up to a point. For some materials that point is so tiny you wouldn't notice...

Density is Mass per Unit Volume

1) Density is a measure of the 'compactness' (for want of a better word) of a substance. It relates the mass of a substance to how much space it takes up.

$$\text{density} = \frac{\text{mass}}{\text{volume}} \qquad \rho = \frac{m}{v}$$

The **units** of **density** are **g cm⁻³** or **kg m⁻³**
(N.B. 1 g cm⁻³ = 1000 kg m⁻³)

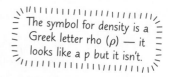
The symbol for density is a Greek letter rho (ρ) — it looks like a p but it isn't.

2) The density of an object depends on what it's made of. Density **doesn't vary** with **size or shape**.

3) The **average density** of an object determines whether it **floats** or **sinks** — a solid object will **float** on a fluid if it has a **lower density** than the **fluid**.

4) **Water** has a density of ρ = 1 g cm⁻³. So **1 cm³** of water has a mass of **1 g**.

Hooke's Law Says that Extension is Proportional to Force

If a **metal wire** is supported at the top and then a weight is attached to the bottom, the wire **stretches**. The weight pulls down with force **F**, producing an equal and opposite force at the support.

1) **Hooke's law** says that the extension of a stretched object, **ΔL**, is proportional to the load or force, **F**.

2) Hooke's law can be written:

$$F = k\Delta L$$

Where **k** is a constant (called the **stiffness** of an object) that depends on the object being stretched.

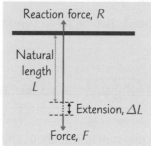

Reaction force, R

Natural length L

Extension, ΔL

Force, F

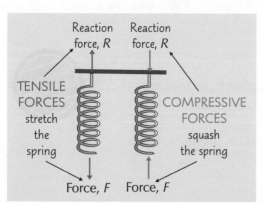

Reaction force, R   Reaction force, R

TENSILE FORCES stretch the spring

COMPRESSIVE FORCES squash the spring

Force, F   Force, F

The material will only deform (stretch, bend, twist etc.) if there's a pair of opposite forces acting on it.

3) **Springs** obey Hooke's Law — when you apply a **pair of opposite forces**, the **extension** (or **compression**) of a spring is **proportional** to the **force** applied.

4) For springs, **k** is usually called the **spring constant**.

5) Hooke's law works just as well for **compressive** forces as **tensile** forces. For a spring, **k** has the **same value** whether the forces are tensile or compressive (that's not true for all materials).

6) **Hooke's Law** doesn't just apply to metal **springs** and **wires** — most **other materials** obey it up to a point.

Hooke's Law Stops Working when the Force is Great Enough

There's a **limit** to the force you can apply for Hooke's law to stay true.

1) The graph shows force (or load) against extension for a **typical metal wire**.

2) The first part of the graph shows Hooke's law being obeyed — there's a **straight-line relationship** between **force** and **extension**.

3) When the force becomes great enough, the graph starts to **curve**. **Metals** generally obey Hooke's law up to the **limit of proportionality**, **P**.

4) The point marked **E** on the graph is called the **elastic limit**. If you increase the load past the elastic limit, the material will be **permanently stretched**. When all the force is removed, the material will be **longer** than at the start.

5) Be careful — there are some materials, like **rubber**, that only obey Hooke's law for **really small** extensions.

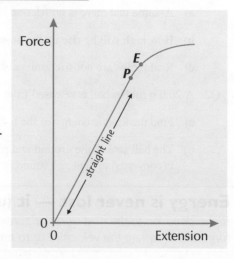

Force

E
P

straight line

0
0   Extension

Properties of Materials

A Stretch can be **Elastic** or **Plastic**

Elastic

If a deformation is elastic, the material returns to its original shape and size once the forces are removed.

1) When the material is put under tension, the atoms of the material are pulled apart from one another.

2) Atoms can move small distances relative to their equilibrium positions, without actually changing position in the material.

3) Once the load is removed, the atoms return to their equilibrium distance apart.

Elastic deformation happens as long as the elastic limit of the object isn't reached.

Plastic

If a deformation is **plastic**, the material is **permanently stretched**.

1) Some atoms in the material move position relative to one another.

2) When the load is removed, the **atoms don't return** to their original positions.

3) An object stretched **past its elastic limit** shows plastic deformation.

Life in plastic, it's fantastic.

Energy is Always **Conserved** When Stretching

There's more about elastic strain energy on the next two pages (plus some formulas — hurrah!).

When a material is **stretched**, **work** has to be done in stretching the material.

1) If a deformation is **elastic**, all the work done is **stored** as **elastic strain energy** in the material.

2) When the stretching force is removed, this **stored energy** is **transferred** to **other forms** — e.g. an elastic band is stretched and then fired across a room.

3) If a deformation is **plastic**, work is done to **separate atoms**, and energy is **not** stored as strain energy (it's mostly dissipated as heat).

4) This fact is used in **transport design** — **crumple zones** are designed to deform **plastically** in a **crash**. Some energy goes into **changing the shape** of the vehicle's **metal body** (and so less is transferred to the people inside).

Warm-Up Questions

Q1 Write down the formula for calculating density. Will a material with a density of 0.8 g cm^{-3} float on water?

Q2 State Hooke's law, and explain what is meant by the elastic limit of a material.

Q3 From studying the force-extension graph for a material as weights are suspended from it, how can you tell:

   a) if Hooke's law is being obeyed,   b) if the elastic limit has been reached?

Q4 What is plastic behaviour of a material under load?

Q5 Explain how crumple zones protect passengers during a car crash.

PRACTICE QUESTIONS

Exam Questions

Q1 A metal guitar string stretches 4.0 mm when a 10.0 N force is applied to it.

   a) If the string obeys Hooke's law, calculate how far the string will stretch with a 15 N force applied to it. [1 mark]

   b) Calculate the stiffness, k, for this string in Nm^{-1}. [2 marks]

   c) The string is now stretched beyond its elastic limit. Describe what effect this will have on the string. [1 mark]

Q2 A rubber band is 6.0 cm long. When it is loaded with 2.5 N, its length becomes 10.4 cm. Further loading increases the length to 16.2 cm when the force is 5.0 N.

   Does the rubber band obey Hooke's law when the force on it is 5.0 N? Justify your answer with a suitable calculation. [2 marks]

Sod's law — if you don't learn it, it'll be in the exam...

Hooke's law was discovered (unsurprisingly) by Robert Hooke 350 years ago. Three bonus facts about Mr Hooke — he was the first person to use the word 'cell' (in terms of biology, not prisons), he helped Christopher Wren with his designs for St. Paul's Cathedral, and finally no-one actually knows what he looked like. How sad. Poor old Hooke.

Stress and Strain

How much a material stretches for a particular applied force depends on its dimensions. If you want to compare it to another material, you need to use stress and strain instead. A stress-strain graph is the same for any sample of a particular material — the size of the sample doesn't matter.

A Stress Causes a Strain

A material subjected to a pair of **opposite forces** might **deform** (i.e. **change shape**).
If the forces **stretch** the material, they're **tensile**. If the forces **squash** the material, they're **compressive**.

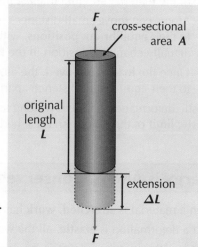

1) **Tensile stress** is defined as the **force applied**, **F**, divided by the **cross-sectional area**, **A**:

$$\text{stress} = \frac{F}{A}$$

The **units** of stress are **Nm⁻²** or pascals, **Pa**.

2) **Tensile strain** is defined as the **change in length** (i.e. the **extension**), divided by the **original length** of the material:

$$\text{strain} = \frac{\Delta L}{L}$$

Strain has **no units**, it's just a **ratio** and is usually written as a **number**. It can also be written as a **percentage**, e.g. extending a 0.5 m wire by 0.02 m would produce a strain of $(0.02 \div 0.5) \times 100 = 4\%$.

3) It doesn't matter whether the forces producing the **stress** and **strain** are **tensile** or **compressive** — the **same equations** apply. The only difference is that you tend to think of **tensile** forces as **positive**, and **compressive** forces as **negative**.

A Stress Big Enough to Break the Material is Called the Breaking Stress

As a greater and greater tensile **force** is applied to a material, the **stress** on it **increases**.

1) The effect of the **stress** is to start to **pull** the **atoms apart** from one another.

2) Eventually the stress becomes **so great** that atoms **separate completely**, and the **material breaks**. This is shown by point **B** on the graph. The stress at which this occurs is called the **breaking stress**.

3) The point marked **UTS** on the graph is called the **ultimate tensile stress**. This is the **maximum stress** that the material can withstand.

4) Both **UTS** and **B** depend on conditions e.g. **temperature**.

5) **Engineers** have to consider the **UTS** and **breaking stress** of materials when designing a **structure** — e.g. they need to make sure the stress on a material won't reach the UTS when the **conditions change**.

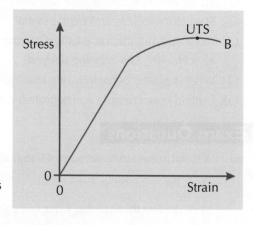

Elastic Strain Energy is the Area under a Force-Extension Graph

1) **Work** has to be done to **stretch** a material.

2) **Before** the **elastic limit** is reached, **all** this **work done** in stretching is **stored** as **elastic strain energy** in the material.

3) On a **graph** of **force against extension**, the elastic strain energy is given by the **area under the graph**.

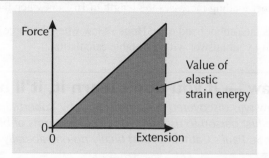

Stress and Strain

You can Calculate the Energy Stored in a Stretched Wire

Provided a material obeys Hooke's law, the **potential energy** stored inside it can be **calculated** quite easily.

1) The work done on the wire in stretching it is equal to the energy stored.

2) **Work done** equals **force × displacement**.

3) However, the **force** on the material **isn't constant**. It rises from zero up to force F.
To calculate the **work done**, use the **average force** between zero and F, i.e. $\frac{1}{2}F$.

$$\text{work done} = \frac{1}{2}F \times \Delta L$$

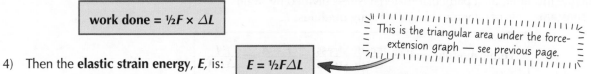
This is the triangular area under the force-extension graph — see previous page.

4) Then the **elastic strain energy**, E, is: $\boxed{E = \frac{1}{2}F\Delta L}$

5) Because Hooke's law is being obeyed, $F = k\Delta L$,
which means F can be replaced in the equation to give: $\boxed{E = \frac{1}{2}k\Delta L^2}$

> **Example:** A metal wire is 55.0 cm long. A force of 550 N is applied to the wire, and the wire stretches. The length of the stretched wire is 56.5 cm. Calculate the elastic strain energy stored in the wire.
>
> The extension of the wire is $\Delta L = 56.5$ cm $- 55.0$ cm $= 1.5$ cm $= 0.015$ m
> So the elastic strain energy $E = \frac{1}{2} \times F \times \Delta L$
> $= 1/2 \times 550 \times 0.015 = 4.125$ J $= \textbf{4.1 J (to 2 s.f.)}$

Warm-Up Questions

Q1 Write a definition for tensile stress.

Q2 Explain what is meant by the tensile strain on a material.

Q3 What is meant by the breaking stress of a material?

Q4 How can the elastic strain energy in a material under load be found from its force-extension graph?

Q5 The work done is usually calculated as force multiplied by displacement.
Explain why the work done in stretching a wire is $\frac{1}{2}F\Delta L$.

Exam Questions

Q1 A steel wire is 2.00 m long. When a 300 N (to 3 s.f.) force is applied to the wire, it stretches 4.0 mm. The wire has a circular cross-section with a diameter of 1.0 mm.

a) Calculate the tensile stress in the wire. [2 marks]

b) Calculate the tensile strain of the wire. [1 mark]

Q2 A copper wire (which obeys Hooke's law) is stretched by 3.0 mm when a force of 50.0 N is applied.

a) Calculate the stiffness for this wire in Nm^{-1}. [2 marks]

b) Calculate the value of the elastic strain energy in the stretched wire. [1 mark]

Q3 A pinball machine contains a spring which is used to fire a small, 12.0 g metal ball to start the game. The spring has a spring constant of 40.8 Nm^{-1}. It is compressed by 5.00 cm and then released to fire the ball.

Calculate the maximum possible kinetic energy of the ball. [3 marks]

UTS a laugh a minute, this stuff...

Here endeth the proper physics for this section — the rest of it's materials science (and I don't care what your exam boards say). It's all a bit "useful" for my liking. Calls itself a physics course... grumble... grumble... wasn't like this in my day... But to be fair — some of it's quite interesting, and there are some lovely graphs coming up on pages 75-77.

The Young Modulus

Busy chap, Thomas Young. He did this work on tensile stress as something of a sideline. Light was his main thing.
He proved that light behaved like a wave, explained how we see in colour and worked out what causes astigmatism.

The **Young Modulus** is Stress ÷ Strain

When you apply a **load** to stretch a material, it experiences a **tensile stress** and a **tensile strain**.

1) Up to the **limit of proportionality** (see p.70), the stress and strain of a material are proportional to each other.

2) So below this limit, for a particular material, stress divided by strain is a **constant**. This constant is called the **Young modulus**, **E**.

$$\text{Young modulus} = E = \frac{\text{tensile stress}}{\text{tensile strain}} = \frac{F \div A}{\Delta L \div L} = \frac{F\,L}{\Delta L\,A}$$

Where F = force in N, A = cross-sectional area in m², L = initial length in m and ΔL = extension in m.

3) The **units** of the Young modulus are the same as stress (Nm^{-2} or pascals), since strain has no units.

4) The Young modulus is a measure of the **stiffness** of a material. It is used by **engineers** to make sure the materials they are using can withstand sufficient forces.

To **Find** the Young Modulus, You need a **Very Long Wire**

PRACTICAL SKILLS

This is the experiment you're most likely to do in class:

wire fixed at one end   test wire   marker on wire   pulley

bench   ruler with mm markings   weights

"Okay, found one. Now what?"

Mum moment: if you're doing this experiment, wear safety goggles — if the wire snaps, it could get very messy...

1) The test wire should be thin, and as long as possible. The **longer and thinner** the wire, the more it **extends** for the same force — this reduces the uncertainty in your measurements.

2) First you need to find the **cross-sectional area** of the wire. Use a **micrometer** to measure the **diameter** of the wire in several places and take an **average** of your measurements. By assuming that the cross-section is **circular**, you can use the formula for the area of a circle:

$$\text{area of a circle} = \pi r^2$$

If the markings on your measuring equipment are quite far apart, you can often interpolate between them (e.g. if the marker is halfway between the markings for 24 mm and 25 mm you could record it as 24.5 mm). But it's better to use something with a finer scale if you can.

3) **Clamp** the wire to the bench (as shown in the diagram above) so you can hang **weights** off one end of it. Start with the **smallest weight** necessary to **straighten** the wire. (**Don't** include this weight in your final calculations.)

4) Measure the **distance** between the **fixed end of the wire** and the **marker** — this is your unstretched length.

5) Then if you increase the weight, the **wire stretches** and the **marker moves**.

6) **Increase** the **weight** in steps (e.g. 100 g intervals), recording the marker reading each time — the **extension** is the **difference** between this reading and the **unstretched length**.

To avoid random errors you should use a thin marker on the wire, and always look directly at the marker and ruler when measuring the extension.

7) You can use your results from this experiment to calculate the **stress** and **strain** of the wire and plot a stress-strain curve (see next page).

(The other standard way of measuring the Young modulus in the lab is using **Searle's apparatus**. This is a bit more accurate, but it's harder to do and the equipment's more complicated.)

The Young Modulus

Use a **Stress-Strain Graph** to Find **E**

You can plot a **graph** of **stress against strain** from your results.

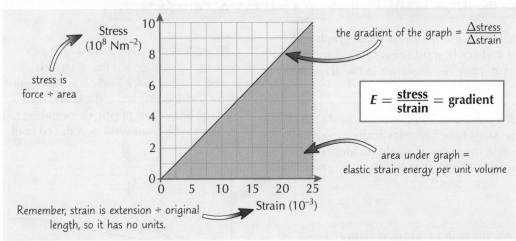

stress is force ÷ area

the gradient of the graph $= \dfrac{\Delta \text{stress}}{\Delta \text{strain}}$

$$E = \frac{\text{stress}}{\text{strain}} = \text{gradient}$$

area under graph = elastic strain energy per unit volume

Remember, strain is extension ÷ original length, so it has no units.

1) The **gradient** of the graph gives the Young modulus, **E**.

2) The **area under the graph** gives the **strain energy** (or energy stored) per unit volume, i.e. the energy stored per 1 m³ of wire.

3) The stress-strain graph is a **straight line** provided that Hooke's law is obeyed, so you can also calculate the energy per unit volume as:

energy per unit vol = ½ × stress × strain

Example: The stress-strain graph above is for a thin metal wire. Find the Young modulus of the wire from the graph.

E = change in stress ÷ change in strain = gradient

The gradient of the graph $= \dfrac{\Delta \text{stress}}{\Delta \text{strain}} = \dfrac{10 \times 10^{8}}{25 \times 10^{-3}}$

$= 4 \times 10^{10} \text{ Nm}^{-2}$

Warm-Up Questions

Q1 Define the Young modulus for a material. What are the units for the Young modulus?

Q2 Describe an experiment to find the Young modulus of a test wire. Explain why a thin test wire should be used.

Q3 What is given by the area contained under a stress-strain graph?

Exam Questions

Q1 A steel wire is stretched elastically. For a load of 80.0 N, the wire extends by 3.6 mm.
The original length of the wire was 2.50 m and its average diameter is 0.60 mm.
Calculate the value of the Young modulus for steel. [4 marks]

Q2 Two wires, A and B, are stretched elastically under a load of 50.0 N. The original length and the extension of both wires under this load are the same. The Young modulus of wire A is found to be 7.0×10^{10} Nm⁻². The cross-sectional area of wire B is half that of wire A. Calculate the Young modulus of wire B. [2 marks]

Q3 The Young modulus for copper is 1.3×10^{11} Nm⁻².

a) The stress on a copper wire is 2.6×10^{8} Nm⁻². Calculate the strain on the wire. [2 marks]

b) The load applied to the copper wire is 100 N (to 3 s.f.). Calculate the cross-sectional area of the wire. [2 marks]

c) Calculate the strain energy per unit volume for this loaded wire. [2 marks]

Learn that experiment — it's important...

Getting back to the good Dr Young... As if ground-breaking work in light, the physics of vision and materials science wasn't enough, he was also a well-respected physician, a linguist and an Egyptologist. He was one of the first to try to decipher the Rosetta stone (he didn't get it right, but nobody's perfect). Makes you feel kind of inferior, doesn't it...

Stress-Strain and Force-Extension Graphs

I hope the stresses and strains of this section aren't getting to you too much.
Don't worry, though — there's just these two pages to go before you're on to the electrifying world of electricity.

There are **Three Important Points** on a **Stress-Strain Graph**

In the exam you could be given a **stress-strain graph** and asked to **interpret** it. Luckily, most stress-strain graphs share **three** important points — as shown in the **diagram**.

Point **Y** is the **yield point** — here the material suddenly starts to **stretch** without any extra load. The **yield point** (or yield stress) is the **stress** at which a large amount of **plastic deformation** takes place with a **constant** or **reduced load**.

Point **E** is the **elastic limit** — at this point the material starts to behave **plastically**. From point E onwards, the material would **no longer** return to its **original shape** once the stress was removed.

Point **P** is the **limit of proportionality** — after this, the graph is no longer a straight line but starts to **bend**. At this point, the material **stops** obeying **Hooke's law**, but would still **return** to its **original shape** if the stress was removed.

Before point **P**, the graph is a **straight line** through the **origin**. This shows that the material is obeying **Hooke's law** (page 70). The **gradient** of the line is constant — it's the **Young modulus** (see pages 74-75).

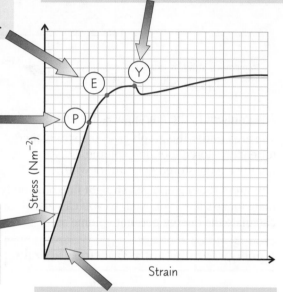

The **area** under the first part of the graph gives the **energy stored** in the **material per unit volume** (see page 75).

Stress-Strain Graphs for **Brittle** Materials **Don't Curve**

The graph shown below is typical of a **brittle** material.

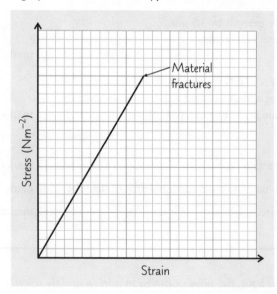

1) The graph starts the same as the one above — with a **straight line through the origin**. So brittle materials also obey **Hooke's law**.

2) However, when the **stress** reaches a certain point, the material suddenly **fractures** (breaks) — it **doesn't deform plastically**.

3) A **chocolate bar** is an example of a brittle material — you can break chunks of chocolate off the bar without the whole thing changing shape.

4) **Ceramics** (e.g. **glass** and **pottery**) are brittle too — they tend to shatter.

Stress-Strain and Force-Extension Graphs

Force-Extension Graphs Are Similar to Stress-Strain Graphs

1) Force-extension graphs look a lot like **stress-strain** graphs, but they show slightly different things.

2) Force-extension graphs are **specific** for the tested **object** and **depend on its dimensions**. Stress-strain graphs describe the **general behaviour** of a **material**, because stress and strain are **independent of the dimensions**.

3) You can plot a force-extension graph of what happens when you gradually **remove** a **force** from an object. The **unloading** line doesn't always match up with the **loading** line though.

You met force-extension graphs on page 70.

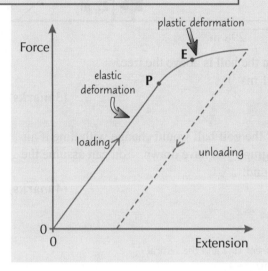

A force-extension graph for a metal wire

1) This graph is for a metal wire that has been stretched beyond its **limit of proportionality (P)** so the graph starts to **curve**.

2) When the load is **removed**, the **extension decreases**.

3) The unloading line is **parallel** to the loading line because the stiffness k is still the same (since the forces between the atoms are the same as they were during the loading).

4) But because the wire was stretched beyond its **elastic limit (E)** and deformed **plastically**, it has been **permanently stretched**. This means the unloading line doesn't go through the origin.

5) The **area** between the two lines is the **work done** to permanently deform the wire.

Of course, if you apply a big enough load to <u>fracture</u> the object, you can't draw an unloading line — you just get a force-extension graph like one of these graphs.

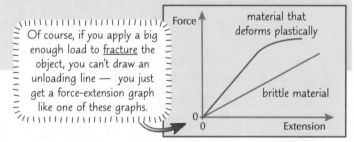

Warm-Up Questions

Q1 What is the difference between the limit of proportionality and the elastic limit?

Q2 Describe what happens at the yield point.

Q3 A metal wire is stretched beyond its elastic limit. Why does the unloading line on the force-extension graph for the wire not go through the origin?

Exam Questions

Q1 Hardened steel is a hard, brittle form of steel made by heating it up slowly and then quenching it in cold water.

a) State what is meant by the term brittle. [1 mark]

b) Sketch a stress-strain graph for hardened steel. [2 marks]

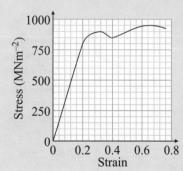

Q2 The diagram shows a stress-strain graph for a nylon thread.

a) State the yield stress for nylon. [1 mark]

b) Calculate how much energy per unit volume is stored in the thread when the limit of proportionality is reached. [2 marks]

c) The unloading curve is added to the stress-strain graph. Describe how the work done per unit volume to permanently deform the thread can be calculated. [2 marks]

My sister must be brittle — she's always snapping...

It's the end of the section on materials, but don't shed a tear — there's four more pages of extra practice coming up. You can always come back and re-read these pages too — it's a good idea, even if you can do all of the practice questions.

Extra Exam Practice

Phew — that's <u>Sections 4 and 5</u> all sewn up. Time to put it all into practice with a few mixed questions.

- Have a look at this example of how to answer a tricky exam question.
- Then check how much you've understood from Sections 4 and 5 by having a go at the questions on the next page.

---

1   A golf ball is struck off a tee at an angle of 42° to the horizontal. The ball has an initial velocity of 60.0 ms⁻¹, as shown in **Figure 1**.

Figure 1

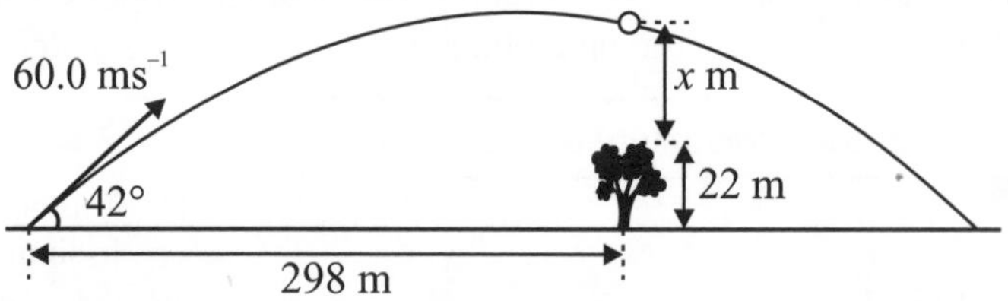

60.0 ms⁻¹

42°

298 m

x m

22 m

1.1   The golf ball flies directly over a tree. The tree is 22 m tall, and is a distance of 298 m from the tee. Calculate the vertical distance, x, between the ball and the tree when the ball is above the tree. Assume that no air resistance acts on the ball ($g = 9.81$ ms⁻²).

(3 marks)

1.2   Sketch a graph to show how the horizontal velocity of the golf ball would change with time if air resistance were considered. Explain the shape of the graph you have drawn. You can assume the golf ball is falling vertically by the time it hits the ground.

(4 marks)

1.1

Resolve the initial velocity into the horizontal component (u_h) and the vertical component (u_v): $u_h = 60\cos 42°$ ms⁻¹, $u_v = 60\sin 42°$ ms⁻¹

There is no air resistance, so the ball does not accelerate horizontally.

$v = \dfrac{\Delta s}{\Delta t}$, so the time taken for the ball to reach the tree is:

horizontal displacement ÷ horizontal velocity = $298 \div 60\cos 42° = 6.6833...$ s

The vertical motion of the ball is accelerating at a constant rate due to gravity:

Taking **upwards as positive**:

$s = ?$, $u = 60\sin 42°$ ms⁻¹, $a = -9.81$ ms⁻², $t = 6.6833...$ s

$s = ut + \dfrac{1}{2}at^2 = (60\sin 42° \times 6.6833...) + \left(\dfrac{1}{2} \times (-9.81) \times 6.6833...^2\right) = 49.2306...$ m

This is the vertical displacement of the ball at the point it passes over the tree. As the ball was at ground level when it was hit, this gives how high the ball is above the ground, so $x = 49.2306... - 22 = 27.2306...$ m $= 27$ m (to 2 s.f.).

You'd get 3 marks for the correct answer. If you got the answer wrong, you'd get 1 mark for calculating the time taken for the ball to reach the tree and 1 mark for calculating the vertical displacement of the ball at the tree.

Writing out all of the variables you know, as well as the variable you want to calculate, will often make it easier to choose a suitable equation for uniform acceleration.

You should bear in mind that s, u, v, and a can have negative or positive values, so you'll have to think about which direction you're taking as being positive at the start of the calculation.

1.2

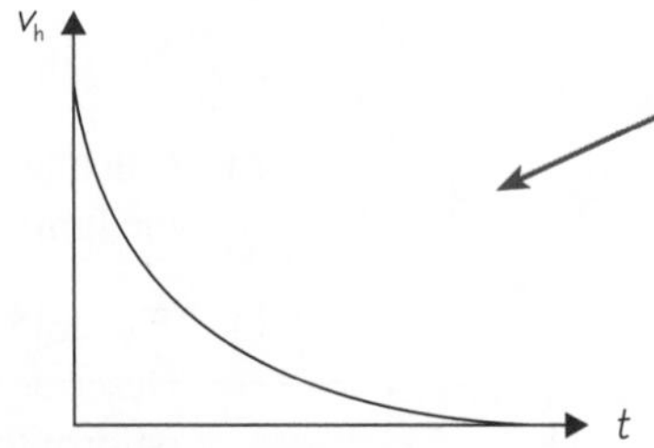

Air resistance provides a horizontal resultant force against the direction of motion. Newton's second law ($F = ma$) shows that this resultant force will cause the ball to decelerate, **so v_h decreases with time**. The ball's velocity is vertical by the time it hits the ground, **so v_h will decrease to zero.** The air resistance acting horizontally on the ball will decrease as v_h decreases. This means the horizontal deceleration of the ball will decrease with time. Deceleration is represented by the gradient of a v-t graph, **so the gradient of the graph decreases with time.**

v_h

t

Make sure you explain all the key features of the graph.

If you're asked to sketch a graph, you don't need to be accurate, but you do need to get the rough shape of the graph right.

Extra Exam Practice

2 A child has a toy gun that fires 1.2 g foam pellets. The toy works by compressing a spring. When the spring is released, the energy stored in the spring is transferred to the kinetic energy of the pellet with an efficiency of 92%. The child holds the gun still, before shooting a pellet out of the first floor window of his house and onto the lawn below, as shown in **Figure 2**. You may assume that the pellet does not experience any air resistance.

Figure 2

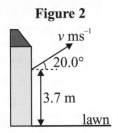

2.1 The spring in the toy has a spring constant of 275 Nm^{-1}. It is compressed by 4.0 cm before it is released. Show that the speed, v, of a pellet immediately after it has been pushed out of the gun is 18 ms^{-1}. You may assume that the spring obeys Hooke's law as it is compressed.

(3 marks)

2.2 The pellet applies a force of 4.1 N to the gun, causing the gun to recoil. Calculate the time over which this force is applied to the gun.

(2 marks)

2.3 Show that the time taken for the pellet to travel from the gun to the lawn is 1.7 s. ($g = 9.81$ ms^{-2})

(3 marks)

2.4 Calculate the speed and the angle from the horizontal at which the pellet hits the lawn.

(3 marks)

2.5 The child fires a second pellet. A wind exerts a force of 5.2×10^{-3} N on the pellet at an angle of 32° to the horizontal, as shown in **Figure 3**. Calculate the magnitude of the resultant force acting on the pellet during its flight.

(2 marks)

Figure 3

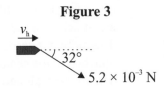

3 In an experiment, a motor is used to pull a 2.4 kg box up a rough ramp, as shown in **Figure 4**.

Figure 4

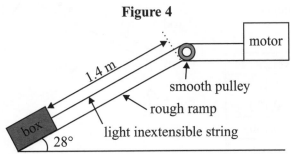

The box is pulled to the top of the ramp in 2.2 s. It accelerates at a constant rate of 14.6 ms^{-2} during this time. The frictional force, F, acting on the box as it moves is given by $F = \mu R$, where μ is the coefficient of friction of the ramp, and R is the normal contact force acting on the box. The ramp's coefficient of friction is 0.81.

3.1 Calculate the average output power of the motor during this time.

(4 marks)

3.2 The experiment is repeated, but this time, the motor is turned off when the box has travelled a distance of d m up the ramp. The box comes to a halt just as it reaches the top of the ramp. Calculate the value of d.

(4 marks)

Extra Exam Practice

In a second experiment, a light inextensible string is used to attach the same box to a mass. The string is passed over a pulley, and the mass is held at a height, h, above the ground, as shown in **Figure 5**. The box and the mass have weights of W_1 and W_2 respectively. $W_1 < W_2$, so when the mass is released, the box moves upwards and the mass moves downwards. They both move with an acceleration, a. You can assume that the pulley is frictionless and that air resistance is negligible.

3.3 Show that $a = \dfrac{(W_2 - W_1)g}{W_1 + W_2}$.

(3 marks)

Figure 5

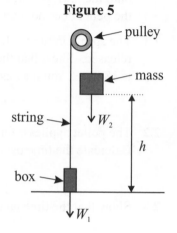

A motor is attached to the pulley when the mass is on the ground. The motor has an electrical power rating of 5.4 W and an efficiency of 78%. When it is switched on, the pulley is forced to spin, causing the box to be lowered to the ground (and the mass to be lifted) at a constant speed. $W_2 = 26.5$ N, and $h = 82$ cm.

3.4 Calculate how long the motor needs to be on for before the box hits the ground.

(4 marks)

4 A wooden mobile for a baby's crib is shown in **Figure 6**. The mobile is made up of four cylindrical rods that are attached to four sides of a central cube. Identical spheres, moons and stars are attached to each of the four rods using wire. The mobile is suspended by a piece of string that is attached to the centre of the top surface of the cube. The rods are all horizontal when the mobile is hung up by the piece of string. The components of the mobile are all made from wood with a uniform density of 0.55×10^3 kg m^{-3}.
Table 1 shows the weight of some of the mobile's components.

Figure 6

rod C

rod B

9.0 cm

4.0 cm

5.0 cm

rod A   7.0 cm

6.0 cm

rod D

Table 1

Component	Weight / N
Central cube	1.165
Rod A, rod D	0.120
Rod B, rod C	0.150
Moon	0.025
Wire	Negligible

4.1 Each sphere has a circumference of 9.2 cm. Show that the weight of a sphere is 0.071 N.

(3 marks)

4.2 Calculate the weight of one of the wooden stars.

(3 marks)

4.3 The piece of string that the mobile is suspended by has a diameter of 2.0 mm. The Young modulus of the string is 2.2 GPa. Calculate how much the string extends by when the mobile is hung up, as a percentage of the string's original length. You may assume that the string is cylindrical.

(3 marks)

Extra Exam Practice

5 A student is doing an experiment to determine the Young modulus of a wire. She uses the apparatus shown in **Figure 7**. Two identical wires are suspended from a rigid support. Each wire is attached to a metal frame, which are loosely connected by three cross supports. A spirit level is attached to one of the cross supports.

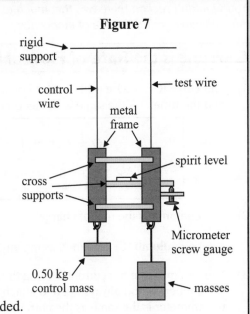

Figure 7

At the start of the experiment, both metal frames are loaded with a 0.50 kg mass, and the micrometer screw gauge is adjusted so that the spirit level lies horizontally. The reading on the micrometer, d_0, is recorded. Masses are then added one at a time to the metal frame of the test wire, whilst the control mass is kept constant. Each time an extra mass is added, the metal frame attached to the test wire moves down slightly, causing the spirit level to deviate from the horizontal. The micrometer is adjusted so that the spirit level is horizontal, and the reading on the micrometer, d, is recorded.

5.1 Explain how the apparatus in **Figure 7** reduces the effects of any thermal expansion of the wire during the experiment and the effects of any kinks in the wire. In your answer, you should include an explanation of how these would each affect the value obtained for the Young modulus if they were not accounted for.

(3 marks)

The student plots a stress-strain graph for the test wire, and labels point E (the elastic limit) and point P (the limit of proportionality). The lines of best fit are shown in **Figure 8**.

5.2 Describe how the student could have calculated the values of stress and strain for each set of results in order to plot them on the graph. State any extra equipment she would need.

(3 marks)

5.3 Describe what the elastic limit is. Suggest how the student could have estimated the position of point E from her experiment in order to plot it on her graph of results.

(3 marks)

5.4 Calculate the Young modulus of the test wire.

(1 mark)

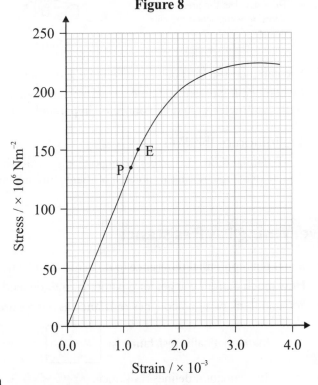

Figure 8

5.5 At the start of the experiment, the test wire had a length of 750 mm and a diameter of 0.40 mm. Calculate the total work done on the test wire to produce a strain of 0.11%.
You may assume that the volume of the test wire is constant throughout the experiment.

(3 marks)

Current, Potential Difference and Resistance

You wouldn't reckon there was that much to know about electricity... just plug something in, and bosh — electricity.
Ah well, never mind the age of innocence — here are all the gory details...

Current is the Rate of Flow of Charge

1) The **current** in a **wire** is like **water** flowing in a **pipe**. The **amount** of water that flows depends on the **flow rate** and the **time**. It's the same with electricity — **current is the rate of flow of charge**.

$$\Delta Q = I\Delta t \text{ or } I = \frac{\Delta Q}{\Delta t}$$

Where ΔQ is the charge in coulombs, I is the current in amperes and Δt is the time taken in seconds.

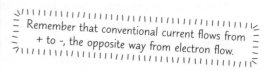
Remember that conventional current flows from + to -, the opposite way from electron flow.

2) The **coulomb** is the unit of **charge**.

> One **coulomb** (**C**) is defined as the **amount of charge** that passes in **1 second** if the **current** is **1 ampere** (**A**).

3) You can measure the current flowing through a part of a circuit using an **ammeter**. Remember — you always need to attach an ammeter in **series** (so that the current through the ammeter is the same as the current through the component — see page 92).

Potential Difference is the Energy per Unit Charge

1) To make electric charge flow through a conductor, you need to do work on it.

2) **Potential difference** (p.d.), or **voltage**, is defined as the **work done** (energy converted) **per unit charge moved**.

$$V = \frac{W}{Q}$$

W is the work done in joules.

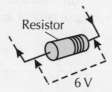

Back to the 'water analogy' again. The p.d. is like the pressure that's forcing water along the pipe.

Resistor

6 V

Here you do 6 J of work moving each coulomb of charge through the resistor, so the p.d. across it is 6 V. The energy gets converted to heat.

3) You can measure the potential difference across a component using a **voltmeter**.

4) Remember, the potential difference across components in parallel is **the same**, so the **voltmeter** should be connected in **parallel** with the component.

Definition of the Volt

The potential difference across a component is 1 volt when you convert 1 joule of energy moving 1 coulomb of charge through the component.

$$1\,V = 1\,JC^{-1}$$

Everything has Resistance

1) If you put a **potential difference** (p.d.) across an **electrical component**, a **current** will flow.

2) **How much** current you get for a particular **p.d.** depends on the **resistance** of the component.

3) You can think of a component's **resistance** as a **measure** of how **difficult** it is to get a **current** to **flow** through it.

Mathematically, **resistance** is: $R = \frac{V}{I}$

This equation **defines** resistance.

Unless told otherwise, you can assume voltmeters are infinitely resistant, and that ammeters have no resistance.

4) **Resistance** is measured in **ohms** (Ω).

> A component has a resistance of **1 Ω** if a **potential difference** of **1 V** makes a **current** of **1 A** flow through it.

Current, Potential Difference and Resistance

For an **Ohmic Conductor**, *R* is a **Constant**

1) A chap called **Ohm** did most of the early work on resistance.
He developed a rule to **predict** how the **current** would **change** as the applied
potential difference increased, for **certain types** of conductor.

2) The rule is now called **Ohm's law** and the conductors that **obey** it (mostly metals) are
called **ohmic conductors**.

Provided the **physical conditions**, such as **temperature**, remain **constant**, the **current**
through an ohmic conductor is **directly proportional** to the **potential difference** across it.

1) This graph shows what happens if you plot
current against voltage for an ohmic conductor.

2) As you can see it's a **straight-line** graph
— **doubling** the p.d. doubles the **current**.

3) What this means is that the **resistance** is
constant — *V* ÷ *I* is always a fixed value.

4) Often **factors** such as **light level** or **temperature** will have
a **significant effect** on resistance (the resistivity changes,
see page 86), so you need to remember that Ohm's law is
only true for **ohmic conductors** under **constant physical
conditions**, e.g. temperature.

5) Ohm's law is a **special case** — lots of components aren't
ohmic conductors and have characteristic current-voltage
(*I–V*) graphs of their very own (see pages 84-85).

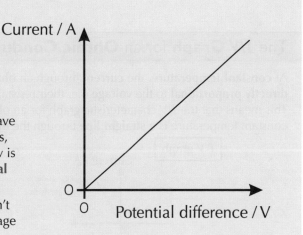

Warm-Up Questions

Q1 Describe in words how current and charge are related.

Q2 Define the coulomb.

Q3 Define potential difference.

Q4 Give the values of resistance that we assume voltmeters and ammeters to have.

Q5 Name one environmental factor likely to alter the resistance of a component.

Q6 What is special about an ohmic conductor?

Exam Questions

Q1 A battery delivers 4500 C of electric charge to a circuit in 10.0 minutes. Calculate the average current. [1 mark]

Q2 An electric motor runs off a 12 V d.c. supply.
Calculate how much electric charge will pass through the motor when it transfers 120 J of energy. [2 marks]

Q3 A current of 12 amps flows through an ohmic conductor when a potential difference of 2.0 V is applied across it.
Assume the temperature of the conductor remains constant.

a) Calculate the resistance of the conductor. [1 mark]

b) Calculate the current through the conductor when the potential difference across it is 35 V. [1 mark]

c) Sketch the *I-V* graph for the conductor when potential differences of up to 35 V are applied to it. [1 mark]

I can't even be bothered to make the current joke...

*Talking of currant jokes, I saw this bottle of wine the other day called 'raisin d'être' — 'raison d'être' of course meaning
'reason for living', but spelled slightly different to make 'raisin', meaning 'grape'. Ho ho. Chuckled all the way home.*

I/V Characteristics

Woohoo — real physics. This stuff's actually kind of interesting.

I/V Graphs Show how Resistance Varies

1) The term '*I/V characteristic*' refers to a **graph** of *I* **against** *V* which shows how the **current** (*I*) flowing through a **component changes** as the **potential difference** (*V*) across it is increased.

2) This **diagram** shows the type of **circuit** used to obtain a characteristic *I/V* graph for a component.

You could also be asked about a *V/I* **graphs**. They're pretty similar, but with *V* plotted against *I*. The **resistance** at a point on the graph is simply *V/I* at that point.

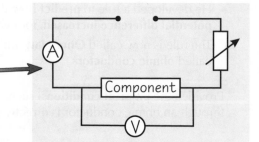

The I/V Graph for an Ohmic Conductor is a Straight Line through the Origin

At **constant temperature**, the **current** through an **ohmic conductor** (e.g. metals) is **directly proportional** to the **voltage** (i.e. their resistance is constant, see page 83). This means that the *I/V* characteristic graph for an ohmic conductor at a constant temperature is a **straight line** through the **origin**.

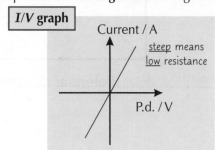

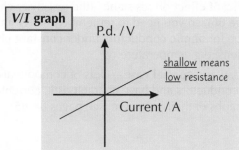

The I/V Characteristic for a Filament Lamp is a Curve

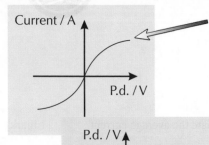

The *I/V* characteristic for a **filament lamp** is a **curve** that starts **steep** but gets **shallower** as the **voltage rises**.

The **filament** in a lamp is just a **coiled-up** length of **metal wire**, so you might think it should have the **same characteristic graph** as a **metallic conductor**. It doesn't because it **gets hot**. **Current** flowing through the lamp **increases** its **temperature**.

The **resistance** of a **metal increases** as the **temperature increases**.

The *V/I* graph for a filament lamp is a curve that starts shallow and gets steeper as the current and voltage increase.

Semiconductors are Used in Sensors

Semiconductors are **nowhere near** as good at **conducting** electricity as **metals**. This is because there are far, far **fewer charge carriers** available. However, if **energy** is supplied to the semiconductor, **more charge carriers** can be **released**. This means that they make **excellent sensors** for detecting **changes** in their **environment**.

You need to know about the **two** semiconductor components on the next page — **thermistors** and **diodes**.

I/V Characteristics

The **Resistance** of a **Thermistor** Depends on **Temperature**

1) A **thermistor** is a **resistor** with a **resistance** that depends on its **temperature**.

2) You only need to know about **NTC** thermistors — NTC stands for 'Negative Temperature Coefficient'.

3) This means that the **resistance decreases** as the **temperature goes up**.

The *I/V* characteristic graph for an NTC thermistor curves upwards.

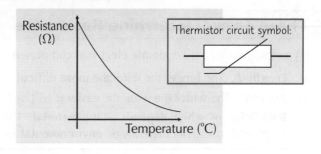

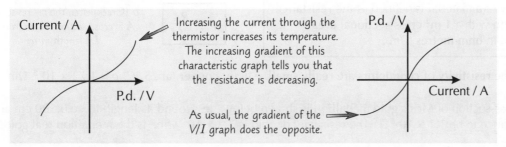

Increasing the current through the thermistor increases its temperature. The increasing gradient of this characteristic graph tells you that the resistance is decreasing.

As usual, the gradient of the *V/I* graph does the opposite.

Warming the thermistor gives more **electrons** enough **energy** to **escape** from their atoms. This means that there are **more charge carriers** available, so the resistance is lower.

Diodes Only Let **Current Flow** in **One Direction**

Diodes (including light emitting diodes (LEDs)) are designed to let **current flow** in **one direction** only. You don't need to be able to explain how they work, just what they do.

1) **Forward bias** is the **direction** in which the **current** is **allowed to flow**.

2) **Most** diodes require a **threshold voltage** of about **0.6 V** in the **forward direction** before they will conduct.

3) In **reverse bias**, the **resistance** of the diode is **very high** and the current that flows is **very tiny**.

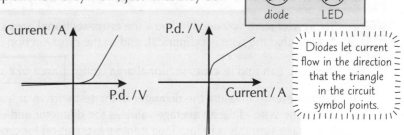

Diodes let current flow in the direction that the triangle in the circuit symbol points.

Warm-Up Questions

Q1 Sketch the circuit used to determine the *I/V* characteristics of a component.

Q2 Why does an *I/V* graph curve for a filament lamp?

Q3 Draw an *I/V* characteristic graph for a diode.

Exam Questions

Q1 a) Describe the shape of a current-voltage characteristic graph for a filament lamp. [1 mark]

   b) Explain the changes in the gradient of the graph as the current increases. [2 marks]

Q2 Explain, with reference to charge carriers, how an NTC thermistor connected in a circuit can be used as a temperature sensor. [3 marks]

You light up my world like an LED — with One Directional current...

Learn the graphs on these two pages, and check that you can explain them. Remember that a temperature increase causes an increase in resistance in a filament lamp, but a decrease in resistance in a thermistor.

Resistivity and Superconductivity

Resistance is all well and good, but it depends on the size of the thing doing the resisting. If you want to compare two materials, you need a quantity that doesn't depend on size. Enter 'resistivity'...

Three Things Determine Resistance

If you think about a nice, **simple electrical component**, like a **length of wire**, its **resistance** depends on:

1) **Length (l)**. The **longer** the wire, the **more difficult** it is to make a **current flow**.

2) **Area (A)**. The **wider** the wire, the **easier** it will be for the electrons to pass along it.

3) **Resistivity (ρ)**, which **depends** on the **material**. The **structure** may make it easy or difficult for charge to flow. In general, resistivity depends on **environmental factors** as well, like **temperature** and **light intensity**.

> The **resistivity** of a material is defined as the **resistance** of a **1 m length** with a **1 m² cross-sectional area**. It is measured in **ohm-metres** (Ωm).

$$\rho = \frac{RA}{l}$$

ρ (Greek letter 'rho') = resistivity,
A = cross-sectional area in m²,
l = length in m

Typical values for the **resistivity** of **conductors** are **really small**, e.g. for **copper** (at 25 °C) $\rho = 1.72 \times 10^{-8}$ Ωm.

Example: A cross-section of Mr T's gold medallion is shown below. Jess found its length to be 0.500 cm and its resistance to be 1.1×10^{-8} Ω. The resistivity of gold is 2.2×10^{-8} Ωm. Is the medallion real gold?

10 cm
10 cm

Convert all the lengths into metres.

The cross-sectional area of the medallion = 0.1 m × 0.1 m = 0.01 m². Length = l = 0.005 m

So the resistivity = $\rho = \frac{RA}{l} = \frac{(1.1 \times 10^{-8} \times 0.01)}{0.005} = \mathbf{2.2 \times 10^{-8} \, \Omega m}$

So Mr T's gold is the real deal.

To Find the Resistivity of a Wire you Need to Find its Resistance

Before you start, you need to know the **cross-sectional area** of the test wire. Assume that the wire is **cylindrical**, and so the cross-section is **circular**.

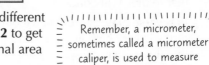

Then you can find its **cross-sectional area** using: **area of a circle = πr^2**

Use a **micrometer** to measure the **diameter** of the test wire in at least **three** different points along the wire. Take an **average** value as the diameter and divide by **2** to get the **radius** (make sure this is in m). Plug it into the equation for cross-sectional area and... **ta da**. Now you can get your teeth into the electricity bit...

> Remember, a micrometer, sometimes called a micrometer caliper, is used to measure very small distances.

1) The **test wire** should be **clamped** to a ruler with the circuit attached to the wire where the ruler reads zero.

2) Attach the **flying lead** to the test wire — the lead is just a wire with a crocodile clip at the end to allow connection to any point along the test wire.

3) Record the **length** of the test wire **connected** in the circuit, the **voltmeter reading** and the **ammeter reading**.

4) Use your readings to calculate the **resistance** of the length of wire, using: $R = \frac{V}{I}$

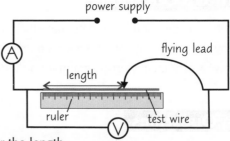

power supply

flying lead

length

ruler   test wire

5) Repeat this measurement and calculate an average resistance for the length.

6) Repeat for several **different** lengths, for example between 0.10 and 1.00 m.

7) Plot your results on a graph of **resistance** against **length**, and draw a **line of best fit** (see page 261).

> The **gradient** of the line of best fit is equal to $\frac{R}{l} = \frac{\rho}{A}$. So **multiply** the **gradient** of the line of best fit by the **cross-sectional area** of the wire to find the resistivity of the wire material.

8) The **resistivity** of a material depends on its **temperature**, so you can only find the resistivity of a material **at a certain temperature**. Current flowing in the test wire can cause its temperature to increase, which can lead to random errors and invalid results (see p.259). Try to keep the temperature of the test wire **constant**, e.g. by only having small currents flow through the wire.

Resistivity and Superconductivity

Superconductors Have Zero Resistivity

1) Normally, all materials have **some resistivity**
   — even really good conductors like silver and copper.

2) That resistance means that whenever electricity flows through them,
   they **heat up**, and some of the electrical energy is **wasted** as thermal energy (heat).

3) You can **lower** the resistivity of many materials like metals by **cooling them down**.

4) If you **cool** some materials (e.g. mercury) down to below a '**transition temperature**',
   their **resistivity disappears entirely** and they become a **superconductor**.

5) Without any resistance, **none** of the electrical energy is turned into heat, so **none** of it's
   wasted. That means you can start a current flowing in a circuit using a magnetic field,
   take away the magnet and the current would carry on flowing **forever**. Neat.

6) There's a catch, though. Most 'normal' conductors, e.g. metals, have transition temperatures
   below **10 kelvin (–263 °C)**. Getting things that cold is **hard**, and **really expensive**.

7) Solid-state physicists all over the world are trying to develop **room-temperature superconductors**.
   So far, they've managed to get some weird **metal oxide** things to superconduct at about **140 K (–133 °C)**,
   which is a much easier temperature to get down to. They've still got a long way to go though.

I couldn't find a conductor, so you'll have to make do with this instead.

Uses of Superconductors

Using superconducting wires you could make:

1) **Power cables** that transmit electricity without any **loss** of power.

2) Really **strong electromagnets** that **don't** need a constant power source
   (for use in medical applications and Maglev trains).

3) **Electronic circuits** that work really **fast**, because there's no resistance to slow them down.

Warm-Up Questions

Q1 What three factors does the resistance of a length of wire depend on?

Q2 What are the units for resistivity?

Q3 What happens to mercury when it's cooled to its transition temperature?

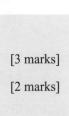

PRACTICE QUESTIONS

Exam Questions

Q1 Aluminium has a resistivity of 2.8×10^{-8} Ωm at 20 °C and a transition temperature of 1.2 K.

   a) Calculate the resistance of a pure aluminium wire of length 4.00 m and diameter 1.0 mm, at 20 °C.   [3 marks]

   b) The wire is cooled to a temperature of 1 K. What is its resistance now? Explain your answer.   [2 marks]

Q2 A student is trying to identify a piece of unknown thin metal wire using the table of resistivities
of common metals below. She measures the potential difference across and current through
different length pieces of the wire and calculates the resistance of each length of wire.

Metal	Resistivity at 20°C
Aluminium	2.82×10^{-8} Ωm
Silver	1.59×10^{-8} Ωm
Tungsten	5.6×10^{-8} Ωm

   a) Explain why she must keep the temperature
      of the wire constant at 20°C.   [2 marks]

   b) State one further measurement she must make
      and suggest an appropriate measuring instrument.   [2 marks]

   c) State one assumption that she must make about
      the wire in order to calculate the resistivity.   [1 mark]

Superconductors and Johnny Depp — just too cool to resist...

Superconducting electromagnets are used in magnetic resonance imaging (MRI) scanners in hospitals.
That way, the huge magnetic fields they need can be generated without using up a load of electricity. Great stuff...

Electrical Energy and Power

Power and energy are pretty familiar concepts — and here they are again. Same principles, just different equations.

Power is the Rate of Transfer of Energy

Power (*P*) is **defined** as the **rate** of **transfer** of **energy**.
It's measured in **watts** (*W*), where **1 watt** is equivalent to **1 joule per second**.

or $P = \dfrac{E}{t}$

There's a really simple formula for **power** in **electrical circuits**:

$$P = VI$$

This makes sense, since:

1) **Potential difference** (*V*) is defined as the **energy transferred** per **coulomb**.
2) **Current** (*I*) is defined as the **number** of **coulombs** transferred per **second**.
3) So **p.d.** × **current** is **energy transferred per second**, i.e. **power**.

He didn't know when, he didn't know where... but one day this PEt would get his revenge.

You know from the definition of **resistance** that: $V = IR$

Combining the **two equations** gives you loads of **different ways** to **calculate power**.

$$P = VI \qquad\qquad P = \dfrac{V^2}{R} \qquad\qquad P = I^2R$$

Obviously, which equation you should use depends on what **quantities** you're given in the **question**.

Phew... that's quite a few equations to learn and love. And as if they're not exciting enough, here are some examples to get your teeth into...

Example 1: A 24 W car headlamp is connected to a 12 V car battery.
Assume the wires connecting the lamp to the battery have negligible resistance.
a) How much energy will the lamp convert into light and heat energy in 2 hours?
b) Find the total resistance of the lamp.

a) Number of seconds in 2 hours = 2 × 60 × 60 = 7200 s
$E = P \times t = 24 \times 7200 = 172\,800\,\text{J} = \textbf{170 kJ (to 2 s.f.)}$

b) Rearrange the equation $P = \dfrac{V^2}{R}$, $R = \dfrac{V^2}{P} = \dfrac{12^2}{24} = \dfrac{144}{24} = \textbf{6}\,\boldsymbol{\Omega}$

Example 2: A robotic mutant Santa from the future converts 750 J of electrical energy into heat every second.
a) What is the power of the robotic mutant Santa?
b) All of the robotic mutant Santa's components are connected in series, with a total resistance of 30 Ω. What current flows through his wire veins?

a) Power = $\dfrac{E}{t} = \dfrac{750}{1} = \textbf{750 W}$

b) Rearrange the equation $P = I^2R$, $I = \sqrt{\dfrac{P}{R}} = \sqrt{\dfrac{750}{30}} = \sqrt{25} = \textbf{5 A}$

Electrical Energy and Power

Energy is Easy to Calculate if you Know the Power

Sometimes it's the **total energy** transferred that you're interested in. In this case you simply need to **multiply** the **power** by the **time**. So:

$$E = VIt$$ (or $E = \frac{V^2}{R}t$, or $E = I^2Rt$)

You've got to make sure that the time is in seconds.

Example:

Betty pops the kettle on to make a brew.
It takes 4.5 minutes for the kettle to boil the water inside it.
A current of 4.0 A flows through the kettle's heating element once it is connected to the mains (230 V).

How much energy does the kettle's heating element transfer to the water in the time it takes to boil?

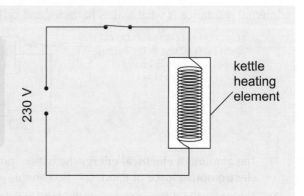

230 V — kettle heating element

Time the kettle takes to boil in seconds = 4.5 × 60 = 270 s.
You have the current, potential difference, and time taken, so use the equation $E = VIt$:

$E = 230 \times 4.0 \times 270 = 248\,400$ J = **250 kJ (to 2.s.f.)**

Warm-Up Questions

Q1 Power is measured in watts. What is 1 watt equivalent to?
Q2 What equation links power, voltage and resistance?
Q3 Write down the equation linking power, current and resistance.

PRACTICE QUESTIONS

Exam Questions

Q1 The circuit diagram for a mains-powered hair dryer is shown below.

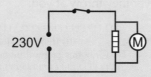

230V — M

  a) The heater has a power of 920 W in normal operation. Calculate the current in the heater. [1 mark]

  b) The motor has a resistance of 190 Ω.
    What current will flow through the motor when the hair dryer is in use? [1 mark]

  c) Show that the total power of the hair dryer in normal operation is about 1.2 kW. [2 marks]

Q2 A 12 V car battery supplies a current of 48 A for 2.0 seconds to the car's starter motor.
The total resistance of the connecting wires is 0.01 Ω.

  a) Calculate the energy transferred from the battery. [2 marks]

  b) Calculate the energy wasted as heat in the wires. [2 marks]

Ultimate cosmic powers...

Whenever you get equations in this book, you know you're gonna have to learn them. Fact of life.
I used to find it helped to stick big lists of equations all over my walls in the run-up to the exams. But as that's possibly the least cool wallpaper imaginable, I don't advise inviting your friends round till after the exams...

E.m.f. and Internal Resistance

There's resistance everywhere — inside batteries, in all the wires (although it's very small) and in the components themselves. I'm assuming the resistance of the wires is zero on the next two pages, but you can't always do this.

Batteries have **Resistance**

Remember, I'm assuming that the resistance of the wires in the circuit is zero.

Resistance comes from **electrons colliding** with **atoms** and **losing energy** to other forms.

In a **battery**, **chemical energy** is used to make **electrons move**. As they move, they collide with atoms inside the battery — so batteries **must** have resistance. This is called **internal resistance**.

Internal resistance is what makes **batteries** and **cells warm up** when they're used.

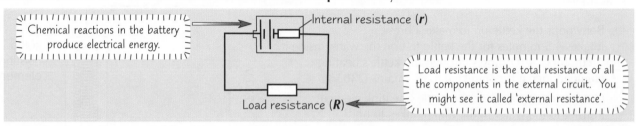

Chemical reactions in the battery produce electrical energy.

Internal resistance (**r**)

Load resistance is the total resistance of all the components in the external circuit. You might see it called 'external resistance'.

Load resistance (**R**)

1) The amount of **electrical energy** the battery produces for each **coulomb** of charge is called its **electromotive force** or **e.m.f.** (ε). Be careful — e.m.f. **isn't** actually a force. It's measured in **volts**.

$$\varepsilon = \frac{E}{Q}$$

2) The **potential difference** across the **load resistance** (**R**) is the **energy transferred** when **one coulomb** of charge flows through the **load resistance**. This potential difference is called the **terminal p.d.** (**V**).

3) If there was **no internal resistance**, the **terminal p.d.** would be the **same** as the **e.m.f.** However, in **real** power supplies, there's **always some energy lost** overcoming the internal resistance.

4) The **energy wasted per coulomb** overcoming the internal resistance is called the **lost volts** (**v**).

Conservation of energy tells us:

energy per coulomb supplied by the source	=	energy per coulomb transferred in load resistance	+	energy per coulomb wasted in internal resistance

There are Loads of **Calculations** with **E.m.f.** and **Internal Resistance**

Examiners can ask you to do **calculations** with **e.m.f.** and **internal resistance** in loads of **different** ways. You've got to be ready for whatever they throw at you.

$$\varepsilon = V + v \qquad \varepsilon = I(R + r)$$
$$V = \varepsilon - v \qquad V = \varepsilon - Ir$$

Learn these equations for the exam. Only this one will be on your formula sheet.

These are all basically the **same equation**, just written differently. If you're given enough information you can calculate the e.m.f. (ε), terminal p.d. (**V**), lost volts (**v**), current (**I**), load resistance (**R**) or internal resistance (**r**). Which equation you should use depends on what information you've got, and what you need to calculate.

You Can Work Out the **E.m.f.** of **Multiple** Cells in **Series** or **Parallel**

For cells **in series** in a circuit, you can calculate the **total e.m.f.** of the cells by **adding** their individual e.m.f.s.

$$\varepsilon_{total} = \varepsilon_1 + \varepsilon_2 + \varepsilon_3 + \dots$$

This makes sense if you think about it, because each charge goes through each of the cells and so gains e.m.f. (electrical energy) from each one.

See p.92 for all the rules for parallel and series circuits.

For identical cells **in parallel** in a circuit, the **total e.m.f.** of the combination of cells is the **same size** as the e.m.f. of each of the individual cells.

$$\varepsilon_{total} = \varepsilon_1 = \varepsilon_2 = \varepsilon_3 = \dots$$

This is because the current will split equally between identical cells. The charge only gains e.m.f. from the cells it travels through — so the overall e.m.f. in the circuit doesn't increase.

E.m.f. and Internal Resistance

Time for an Example E.m.f. Calculation Question...

Example Three identical cells with an e.m.f. of 2.0 V and an internal resistance of 0.20 Ω are connected in parallel in the circuit shown to the right. A current of 0.90 A is flowing through the circuit. Calculate the total p.d. across the cells.

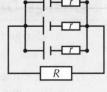

First calculate the lost volts, v, for 1 cell using $v = Ir$.

Since the current flowing through the circuit is split equally between each of the three cells, the current through one cell is $I/3$. So for 1 cell: $v = I/3 \times r = 0.90/3 \times 0.20 = 0.30 \times 0.20 = 0.06$ V

Then find the terminal p.d. across 1 cell using the equation: $V = \varepsilon - v = 2 - 0.06 = 1.94$

So the total p.d. across the cells combined = 1.94 = **1.9 V (to 2 s.f.)**

Investigate Internal Resistance and E.m.f. With This Circuit

1) **Vary** the **current** in the circuit by changing the value of the **load resistance** (R) using the variable resistor. **Measure** the **p.d.** (V) for several different values of **current** (I).

2) Record your data for V and I in a table, and **plot the results** in a graph of V against I.

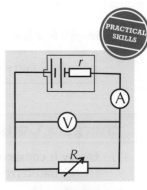

To find the **e.m.f.** and **internal resistance** of the cell, start with the equation: $\boxed{V = \varepsilon - Ir}$

1) Rearrange to give $V = -rI + \varepsilon$

2) Since ε and r are constants, that's just the equation of a **straight line**:

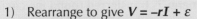
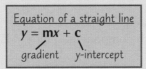

Equation of a straight line
$y = \mathbf{m}x + \mathbf{c}$
gradient   y-intercept

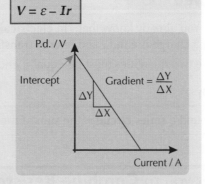

P.d. /V

Intercept   Gradient = $\frac{\Delta Y}{\Delta X}$

ΔY ΔX

Current / A

3) So the intercept on the vertical axis is ε.
4) And the gradient is $-r$.

Geoff didn't quite calculate the gradient correctly.

An **easier** way to **measure** the **e.m.f.** of a **power source** is by connecting a high-resistance **voltmeter** across its **terminals**. But, a **small current flows** through the **voltmeter**, so there must be some **lost volts** — this means you measure a value **very slightly less** than the **e.m.f.** (Although in practice the difference isn't usually significant.)

Warm-Up Questions

Q1 What causes internal resistance? Write down the equation linking e.m.f. and energy transferred.
Q2 What is the difference between e.m.f. and terminal p.d.?
Q3 Write the equation used to calculate the terminal p.d. of a power supply.

Exam Questions

Q1 A battery with an internal resistance of 0.80 Ω and an e.m.f. of 24 V powers a dentist's drill with resistance 4.0 Ω.

a) Calculate the current in the circuit when the drill is connected to the power supply. [2 marks]

b) Calculate the potential difference wasted overcoming the internal resistance. [1 mark]

Q2 A bulb of resistance R is powered by two cells connected in series each with internal resistance r and e.m.f. ε. Which expression represents the current flowing through each cell? [1 mark]

A $\frac{\varepsilon}{R+r}$ B $\frac{\varepsilon}{2(R+2r)}$ C $\frac{2\varepsilon}{R+2r}$ D $\frac{\varepsilon}{R+2r}$

Overcome your internal resistance for revision...

Make sure you know all your e.m.f. and internal resistance equations, they're an exam fave. A good way to get them learnt is to keep trying to get from one equation to another... pretty dull, but it definitely helps.

Conservation of Energy and Charge

There are some things in Physics that are so fundamental that you just have to accept them. Like the fact that there's loads of Maths in it. And that energy is conserved. And that Physicists get more homework than everyone else.

Charge Doesn't 'Leak Away' Anywhere — it's Conserved

1) As **charge flows** through a circuit, it **doesn't** get **used up** or **lost**.

2) This means that whatever **charge flows into** a junction will **flow out** again.

3) Since **current** is **rate of flow of charge**, it follows that whatever **current flows into** a junction is the same as the current **flowing out** of it.

> **Example:** *CHARGE FLOWING IN 1 SECOND*
>
> $Q_1 = 6\,C \Rightarrow I_1 = 6\,A$ ——————➤ $Q_2 = 2\,C \Rightarrow I_2 = 2\,A$
>
> $Q_3 = 4\,C \Rightarrow I_3 = 4\,A$
>
> $I_1 = I_2 + I_3$

Kirchhoff's first law says:

> The total **current entering a junction** = the total **current leaving it.**

Energy conservation is vital.

Energy is Conserved too

1) **Energy is conserved.** You already know that. In **electrical circuits**, **energy** is **transferred round** the circuit. Energy **transferred to** a charge is **e.m.f.**, and energy **transferred from** a charge is **potential difference**.

2) In a **closed loop**, these two quantities must be **equal** if energy is conserved (which it is).

Kirchhoff's second law says:

> The **total e.m.f.** around a **series circuit** = the **sum** of the **p.d.s** across each component. | (or $\varepsilon = \Sigma IR$ in symbols)

Exam Questions get you to Combine Resistors in Series and Parallel

A **typical exam question** will give you a **circuit** with bits of information missing, leaving you to fill in the gaps. Not the most fun... but on the plus side you get to ignore any internal resistance stuff (unless the question tells you otherwise)... hurrah. You need to remember the **following rules**:

Series Circuits:

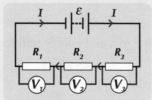

1) **same current** at **all points** of the circuit (since there are no junctions)

2) **e.m.f. split** between **components** (by Kirchhoff's 2nd law), so:
   $\varepsilon = V_1 + V_2 + V_3$

3) $V = IR$, so if I is constant:
   $IR_{total} = IR_1 + IR_2 + IR_3$

4) cancelling the Is gives:

> $$R_{total} = R_1 + R_2 + R_3$$

Parallel Circuits:

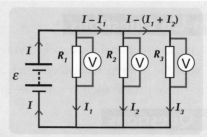

1) **current** is **split** at each **junction**, so: $I = I_1 + I_2 + I_3$

2) **same p.d.** across **all components** (three separate loops — within each loop the e.m.f. equals sum of individual p.d.s)

3) so, $V/R_{total} = V/R_1 + V/R_2 + V/R_3$

4) cancelling the Vs gives:

> $$\frac{1}{R_{total}} = \frac{1}{R_1} + \frac{1}{R_2} + \frac{1}{R_3}$$

$\varepsilon = V$ in this case, as we're ignoring internal resistance.

...and there's an example on the next page to make sure you know what to do with all that...

Conservation of Energy and Charge

Worked Exam Question

Example:

A battery of e.m.f. 16 V and negligible internal resistance is connected in a circuit as shown:

a)   Show that the group of resistors between X and Y could be replaced by a single resistor of resistance 15 Ω.

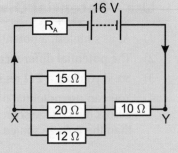

You can find the combined resistance of the 15 Ω, 20 Ω and 12 Ω resistors using:

$1/R = 1/R_1 + 1/R_2 + 1/R_3 = 1/15 + 1/20 + 1/12 = 1/5 \Rightarrow R = 5\,\Omega$

So overall resistance between X and Y can be found by $R = R_1 + R_2 = 5 + 10 = \mathbf{15\,\Omega}$

b)   If $R_A = 20\,\Omega$:
  i)   calculate the potential difference across R_A,

Careful — there are a few steps here. You need the p.d. across R_A, but you don't know the current through it. So start there: total resistance in circuit = 20 + 15 = 35 Ω, so current through R_A can be found using $I = V_{total}/R_{total}$: $I = 16/35$ A

then you can use $V = IR_A$ to find the p.d. across R_A: $V = 16/35 \times 20 = \mathbf{9\,V\ (to\ 1\ s.f.)}$

  ii)   calculate the current in the 15 Ω resistor.

You know the current flowing into the group of three resistors and out of it, but not through the individual branches. But you know that their combined resistance is 5 Ω (from part a) so you can work out the p.d. across the group:

$V = IR = 16/35 \times 5 = 16/7\,V$

The p.d. across the whole group is the same as the p.d. across each individual resistor, so you can use this to find the current through the 15 Ω resistor:

$I = V/R = (16/7)\,/\,15 = \mathbf{0.15\,A\ (to\ 2\ s.f.)}$

Warm-Up Questions

Q1 State the formulas used to combine resistors in series and in parallel.

Q2 Find the current through and potential difference across each of two 5 Ω resistors when they are placed in a circuit containing a 5 V battery, and are wired: a) in series, b) in parallel.

Exam Question

Q1 For the circuit on the right:

a) Calculate the total effective resistance of the three resistors in this combination.   [2 marks]

b) Calculate the main current, I_3.   [1 mark]

c) Calculate the potential difference across the 4.0 Ω resistor.   [1 mark]

d) Calculate the potential difference across the parallel pair of resistors.   [1 mark]

e) Using your answer from part d), calculate the currents I_1 and I_2.   [2 marks]

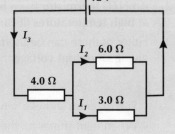

This is a very purple page — needs a bit of yellow I think...

V = IR is the formula you'll use most often in these questions. Make sure you know whether you're using it on the overall circuit, or just one specific component. It's amazingly easy to get muddled up — you've been warned.

The Potential Divider

I remember the days when potential dividers were pretty much the hardest thing they could throw at you. Then along came A level Physics. Hey ho. Anyway, in context this doesn't seem too hard now, so get stuck in.

Use a **Potential Divider** to get a **Fraction** of a **Source Voltage**

1) At its simplest, a **potential divider** is a circuit with a **voltage source** and a couple of **resistors** in series.

2) The **potential difference** across the voltage source (e.g. a battery) is **split** in the **ratio** of the **resistances** (p.92).

3) So, if you had a **2 Ω** resistor and a **3 Ω** resistor, you'd get **2/5** of the p.d. across the **2 Ω** resistor and **3/5** across the **3 Ω**.

4) You can use potential dividers to supply a potential difference, V_{out}, between **zero** and the potential difference across the voltage source. This can be useful, e.g. if you need a **varying** p.d. supply or one that is at a **lower p.d.** than the voltage source.

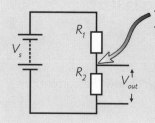

The voltage has **dropped** by V_1 (the voltage across R_1) by the time it gets to here. The **remaining voltage** that can be supplied, e.g. to another component, is V_{out}.

In the circuit shown, R_2 has $\dfrac{R_2}{R_1 + R_2}$ of the total resistance. So: $\boxed{V_{out} = \dfrac{R_2}{R_1 + R_2} V_s}$

E.g. if $V_s = 9\text{ V}$ and you want V_{out} to be 6 V, then you need:

$$\frac{R_2}{R_1 + R_2} = \frac{2}{3} \text{ which gives } R_2 = 2R_1$$

So you could have, say, $R_1 = 100\ \Omega$, $R_2 = 200\ \Omega$

5) This circuit is mainly used for **calibrating voltmeters**, which have a **very high resistance**.

6) If you put something with a **relatively low resistance** across R_2 though, you start to run into **problems**. You've **effectively** got **two resistors** in **parallel**, which will **always** have a **total** resistance **less** than R_2. That means that V_{out} will be **less** than you've calculated, and will depend on what's connected across R_2. Hrrumph.

Use a **Variable Resistor** to Vary the **Voltage**

If you replace R_1 with a **variable resistor**, you can change V_{out}. When $R_1 = 0$, $V_{out} = V_s$. As you increase R_1, V_{out} gets smaller.

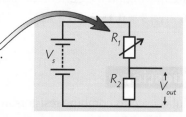

Add an **LDR** or **Thermistor** for a **Light** or **Temperature Sensor**

1) A **light-dependent resistor** (LDR) has a very **high resistance** in the **dark**, but a **lower resistance** in the **light**.

Circuit symbol for an LDR:

2) An **NTC thermistor** has a **high resistance** at **low temperatures**, but a much **lower resistance** at **high temperatures** (it varies in the opposite way to a normal resistor, only much more so).

3) Either of these can be used as one of the **resistors** in a **potential divider**, giving an **output voltage** that **varies** with the **light level** or **temperature**.

The diagram shows a sensor used to detect light levels.

When light shines on the LDR its resistance decreases, so V_{out} increases.

You can include LDRs and thermistors in circuits that control switches, e.g. to turn on a light or a heating system.

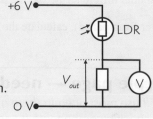

If you replace the LDR with a thermistor, V_{out} will increase with temperature.

+6 V

LDR

V_{out}

0 V

The Potential Divider

A **Potentiometer** uses a **Variable Resistor** to give a **Variable Voltage**

1) A **potentiometer** has a variable resistor replacing R_1 and R_2 of the potential divider, but it uses the **same idea** (it's even sometimes **called** a potential divider just to confuse things).

2) You move a **slider** or turn a knob to **adjust** the **relative sizes** of R_1 and R_2. That way you can vary V_{out} from **0 V** up to the source voltage.

3) This is dead handy when you want to be able to **change** a **voltage continuously**, like in the **volume control** of a stereo.

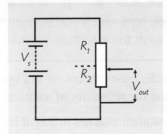

Example: Here, V_s is replaced by the input signal (e.g. from a CD player) and V_{out} is the output to the amplifier and loudspeaker.

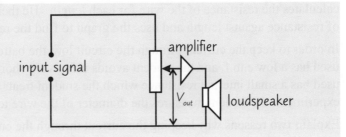

Warm-Up Questions

Q1 Look at the light sensor circuit on page 94.
How could you change the circuit so that it could be used to detect temperature changes?

Q2 The LDR in the circuit on page 94 has a resistance of 300 Ω when in light conditions, and 900 Ω in dark conditions. The fixed resistor has a value of 100 Ω. Show that V_{out} (light) = 1.5 V and V_{out} (dark) = 0.6 V.

Exam Questions

Q1 In the circuit on the right, all the resistors have the same value.
Calculate the p.d. between:

a) A and B. [1 mark]

b) A and C. [1 mark]

c) B and C. [1 mark]

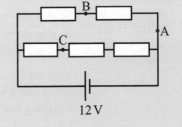

Q2 Look at the circuit on the right. All the resistances are given to 2 significant figures.

a) Calculate the p.d. between A and B as shown by a high resistance voltmeter placed between the two points. [1 mark]

b) A 40.0 Ω resistor is now placed between points A and B. Calculate the p.d. across AB and the current flowing through the 40.0 Ω resistor. [4 marks]

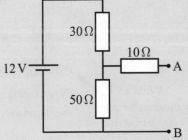

OI...YOU... [bang bang bang]... turn that potentiometer down...

You'll probably have to use a potentiometer in every experiment you do with electricity from now on in, so you'd better get used to them. I can't stand the things myself, but then lab and me don't mix — far too technical.

Extra Exam Practice

You've made it through <u>Section 6</u> — the last of the AS/Year 1 sections. If you understood it all and answered all the questions, then it's time for some extra exam-style questions on the whole section.

- Have a look at this example of how to answer a tricky exam question.
- Then check how much you've understood from Section 6 by having a go at the questions on the next page.

---

1   A student uses the circuit in **Figure 1** in an investigation to find the resistivity of a wire at room temperature.

Figure 1

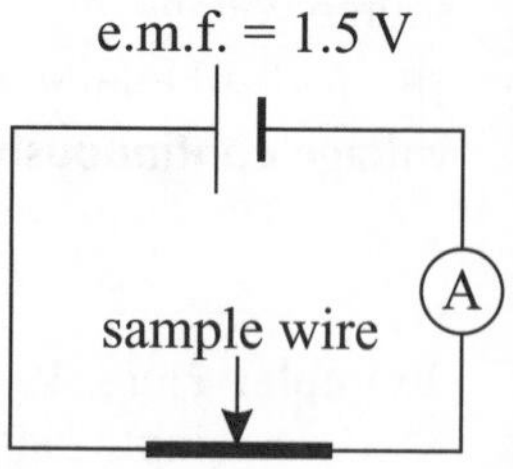

e.m.f. = 1.5 V

sample wire   (A)

The student attaches different lengths of the same wire into the test circuit. He measures the length of each piece of wire and the current through the circuit. He repeats this for a range of lengths of the wire and calculates the resistance of the wire for each length. He then plots a graph of resistance against length and uses the graph to find the resistivity.

In order to keep the current through the circuit low, the battery used has a low e.m.f. and the student avoids using very short lengths of wire. The battery used has a small internal resistance which the student treats as negligible. Before the experiment, the student measures the diameter of the wire to be 0.80 mm ± 1.0%.

1.1   Explain **two** reasons why keeping the current through the circuit low will improve the results.

(4 marks)

1.2   For a length of 21.0 cm ± 0.50%, the reading on the ammeter is 0.75 A ± 0.50%. Calculate the resistivity of the wire. Include the percentage uncertainty in the resistivity. You can assume that the uncertainty in the potential difference across the wire is negligible.

(2 marks)

Think about the effects that increasing the current would have, and try to link that to the values being measured.

1.1

A low current minimises heating of the wire, which would increase the wire's resistance. Resistivity depends on resistance, $\rho = \dfrac{RA}{l}$, and so temperature, so the results will be more accurate if the temperature is controlled.

A low current also means that the lost volts (v) due to the internal resistance of the battery (r) are low because $v = Ir$. $V = \varepsilon - v$ so the terminal p.d. (V) can be assumed to equal the e.m.f. of 1.5 V at low currents. $R = V \div I$ so having an accurate value of V gives an accurate value for R, and hence the resistivity calculated will be more accurate.

You'd get 1 mark for saying a low current stops the wire heating up, 1 mark for saying that it keeps the terminal p.d. close to 1.5 V, and 1 mark each (up to 2) for explaining how each of these effects improve the results.

1.2

Write an equation for ρ in terms of what's been given in the question, then you can easily see which values have uncertainties.

Combine $\rho = \dfrac{RA}{l}$, $R = \dfrac{V}{I}$ and $A = \pi r^2 = \pi \left(\dfrac{d}{2}\right)^2 = \dfrac{\pi d^2}{4}$

Divide the diameter by 2 to get the radius.

$\rho = \dfrac{V\pi d^2}{4Il} = \dfrac{1.5 \times \pi \times (0.80 \times 10^{-3})^2}{4 \times 0.75 \times 0.210} = 4.787\ldots \times 10^{-6} = \mathbf{4.8 \times 10^{-6}}$ Ωm (to 2 s.f.)

The least number of significant figures given in the question is 2, so leave your final answer to 2 s.f.

$\rho = \dfrac{V\pi d^2}{4Il}$ so the total uncertainty is the combined uncertainty of I, l and d^2.

When raising to a power, multiply the percentage uncertainty by the power. The uncertainty in d^2 is 2 × the percentage uncertainty in d: 2 × 1.0 = 2.0%

When multiplying or dividing two or more values with uncertainties, add the uncertainties. The uncertainty in ρ is given by adding the percentage uncertainties in I, l and d^2: 0.50 + 0.50 + 2.0 = 3.0%

So $\rho = 4.8 \times 10^{-6}$ Ωm ± 3.0% (to 2 s.f.)

You'd get 1 mark for the correct value of ρ and 1 mark for the correct uncertainty.

There's more on combining uncertainties on page 260.

Extra Exam Practice

2   A student is investigating the electronic systems inside a car.

2.1 The main purpose of a car battery is to start the engine. To start the engine a very large current is supplied to the starter motor for a short amount of time. The starter motor will not start the engine unless a minimum potential difference, *V*, is applied across it. Most car batteries have an e.m.f. rated at approximately this minimum value, *V*. Explain why a car battery must have a very low internal resistance in order to start the car.

(2 marks)

2.2 Describe an experiment that the student could carry out to investigate the internal resistance of a car battery. In your answer you should include an explanation of how the student can ensure valid and accurate results.

(6 marks)

A student is designing a circuit that keeps a car's rear window glass mist-free when the temperature outside is low. **Figure 2** shows a simplified circuit that the student uses to model the five heating wires that are embedded in the glass. The heating wires get hotter the more current that flows through them. **Figure 3** shows how the resistance of the thermistor changes with the outside temperature. The resistance of resistor R_1 is 2.50 Ω.

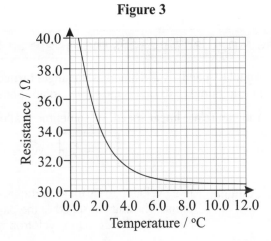

Figure 2

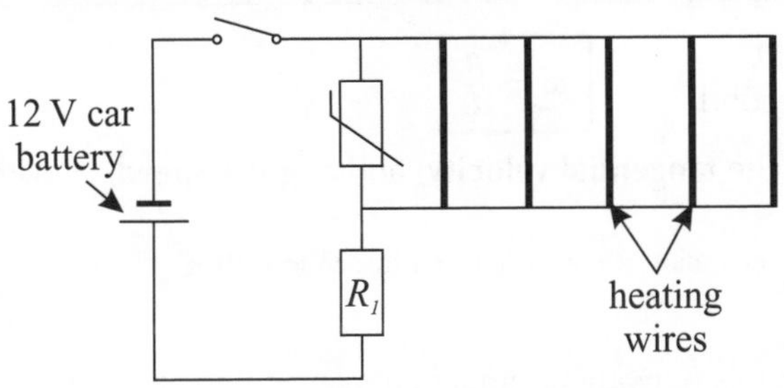

Figure 3

2.3 Explain how a drop in temperature causes the rear window glass to heat up.

(2 marks)

2.4 Each wire has a diameter of 0.102 mm and a length of 1.25 m. The resistivity of each wire is 3.86×10^{-8} Ωm. Show that the resistance of each of the heater wires is 5.90 Ω.

(1 mark)

2.5 Calculate the current through each heater wire when the temperature is 1.0 °C.

(3 marks)

2.6 The student designs a second circuit in which the five heating wires are attached as shown in **Figure 4**. Calculate the current through the heater wires when the outside temperature is 1.0 °C.

(2 marks)

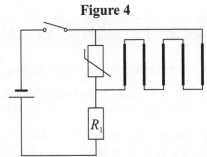

Figure 4

2.7 Determine which design would heat the rear window faster at 1.0 °C.

(2 marks)

Circular Motion

*It's probably worth putting a bookmark in here — this stuff is needed **all over** the place.*

Angles can be Expressed in Radians

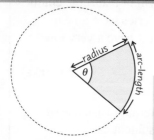

The angle in **radians**, θ, is defined as the **arc-length** divided by the radius of the circle.

For a **complete circle** (360°), the arc-length is just the circumference of the circle ($2\pi r$). Dividing this by the radius (**r**) gives 2π. So there are **2π radians** in a complete circle.

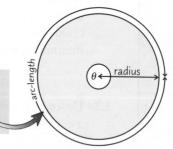

Some common angles:

45° $\frac{\pi}{4}$ rad   90° $\frac{\pi}{2}$ rad   180° π rad

To convert from degrees to radians, multiply by $\frac{\pi}{180}$.
To convert from radians to degrees, multiply by $\frac{180}{\pi}$.
1 radian $\approx 57°$.

The Angular Speed is the Angle an Object Rotates Through per Second

1) **Angular speed**, ω, is defined as the **angle turned**, θ, per unit **time** t. Its unit is rad s^{-1} — radians per second.

$$\omega = \frac{\theta}{t}$$

2) You can relate **linear speed**, v, (sometimes called the **tangential velocity**) and **angular speed**, ω, with:

$$\omega = \frac{v}{r}$$

Where r is the radius of the circle being turned in metres.

Example: In a cyclotron, a beam of particles spirals outwards from a central point. The angular speed of the particles remains constant. The beam of particles in the cyclotron rotates through 360° in 35 μs.

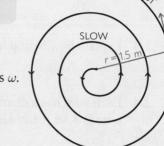

a) Explain why the linear speed of the particles increases as they spiral outwards, even though their angular speed is constant.

Linear speed depends on r, the radius of the circle being turned as well as ω. So, as r increases, so does v, even though ω remains constant.

b) Calculate the linear speed of a particle at a point 1.5 m from the centre of rotation.

First, calculate the angular speed:

$$\omega = \frac{\theta}{t} = \frac{2\pi}{35 \times 10^{-6}} = 1.7951... \times 10^{5}\,\text{rad s}^{-1}$$

Then substitute ω into $v = \omega r$:

$$v = \omega r = 1.7951... \times 10^{5} \times 1.5 = 2.6927... \times 10^{5}\,\text{ms}^{-1}$$
$$v = 2.7 \times 10^{5}\,\text{ms}^{-1}\ \text{(to 2 s.f.)}$$

You can find out more about cyclotrons on p. 143.

Circular Motion has a Frequency and Period

1) The frequency, f, is the number of complete **revolutions per second** (rev s^{-1} or hertz, Hz).

2) The period, T, is the **time taken** for a complete revolution (in seconds). Frequency and period are **linked** by the equation:

$$f = \frac{1}{T}$$

3) For a complete circle, an object turns through **2π radians** in a time T, so frequency and period are related to ω by:

$$\omega = \frac{2\pi}{T} = 2\pi f$$

ω = angular speed in rad s^{-1}
f = frequency in rev s^{-1} or Hz
T = period in s

Circular Motion

Objects Travelling in Circles are **Accelerating** Since Their **Velocity is Changing**

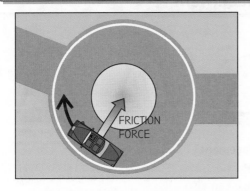

1) Even if the car shown is going at a **constant speed**, its **velocity** is changing since its **direction** is changing.

2) Since acceleration is defined as the **rate of change of velocity**, the car is accelerating even though it isn't going any faster.

3) This acceleration is called the **centripetal acceleration** and is always directed towards the **centre of the circle**.

There are two formulas for centripetal acceleration:

$$a = \frac{v^2}{r}$$

$$a = \omega^2 r$$

a = centripetal acceleration in ms^{-2}
v = linear speed in ms^{-1}
ω = angular speed in rad s^{-1}
r = radius in m

The **Centripetal Acceleration** is produced by a **Centripetal Force**

From Newton's laws, if there's a **centripetal acceleration**, there must be a **centripetal force** acting towards the **centre of the circle**.

Since $F = ma$, the centripetal force must be:

$$F = \frac{mv^2}{r} = m\omega^2 r$$

The centripetal force is what keeps the object moving in a circle — remove the force and the object would fly off at a tangent.

Men cowered from the force of the centripede.

Warm-Up Questions

Q1 How many radians are there in a complete circle?

Q2 How is angular speed defined and what is the relationship between angular speed and linear speed?

Q3 Define the period and frequency of circular motion. What is the relationship between period and angular speed?

Q4 Explain why an object travelling at a constant speed in a circular path is accelerating.

Q5 Write equations for centripetal acceleration, a, and centripetal force, F, for an object travelling at a linear speed, v, in a circular path with a radius r.

Q6 In which direction does the centripetal force act, and what happens when this force is removed?

Exam Questions

Q1 a) Calculate the angular speed at which the Earth orbits the Sun. (1 year = 3.2×10^7 s) [2 marks]

b) Calculate the Earth's linear speed. (Assume radius of orbit = 1.5×10^{11} m) [1 mark]

c) Calculate the centripetal force needed to keep the Earth in its orbit. (*Mass of Earth = 5.98 × 10²⁴ kg*) [2 marks]

d) State what is providing this force. [1 mark]

Q2 A bucket full of water, tied to a rope, is being swung around in a vertical circle (so it is upside down at the top of the swing). The radius of the circle is 1.00 m.

a) By considering the acceleration due to gravity at the top of the swing, calculate the minimum frequency with which the bucket can be swung without any water falling out. [3 marks]

b) The bucket is now swung with a constant angular speed of 5.00 rad s^{-1}. Calculate the tension in the rope when the bucket is at the top of the swing if the total mass of the bucket and water is 10.0 kg. [3 marks]

I'm spinnin' around, move out of my way...

"Centripetal" just means "centre-seeking". The centripetal force is what actually causes circular motion. What you feel when you're spinning, though, is the reaction (centrifugal) force. Don't get the two mixed up.

Simple Harmonic Motion

Something simple at last — I like the sound of this. And colourful graphs too — you're in for a treat here.

SHM is Defined in terms of Acceleration and Displacement

1) An object moving with **simple harmonic motion** (SHM) **oscillates** to and fro, either side of a **midpoint**.

2) The distance of the object from the midpoint is called its **displacement**.

3) There is always a **restoring force** pulling or pushing the object back **towards** the **midpoint**.

4) The **size** of the **restoring force** is directly proportional to the **displacement** — i.e. if the displacement doubles, the restoring force doubles too.

5) As the restoring force causes **acceleration** towards the midpoint, we can also say the **acceleration** is directly **proportional** to **displacement**.

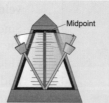

Midpoint

Small displacement, therefore small force.

Large displacement, therefore large force.

There's a negative sign as the acceleration is opposing the displacement.

Condition for SHM: an oscillation in which the **acceleration** of an object is **directly proportional** to its **displacement** from the **midpoint**, and is directed **towards the midpoint**.

$a \propto -x$

The Restoring Force Makes the Object Exchange E_p and E_k

1) The **type** of **potential energy** (E_p) depends on **what it is** that's providing the **restoring force**. This will be **gravitational** E_p for pendulums and **elastic** E_p (elastic stored energy) for masses on springs moving horizontally.

2) As the object moves **towards the midpoint**, the restoring force **does work** on the object and so **transfers** some E_p to E_k. When the object is moving **away from the midpoint**, all that E_k is transferred **back to** E_p again.

3) At the **midpoint**, the object's E_p is **zero** and its E_k is **maximum**.

4) At the **maximum displacement** (the **amplitude**) on both sides of the midpoint, the object's E_k is **zero** and its E_p is at its **maximum**.

5) The **sum** of the **potential** and **kinetic** energy is called the **mechanical energy** and **stays constant** (as long as the motion isn't damped — see p. 104).

6) The **energy transfer** for one complete cycle of oscillation is: E_p to E_k to E_p to E_k to E_p … and then the process repeats…

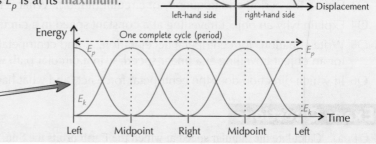

Energy

$E_p + E_k$

E_p

E_k

Displacement

left-hand side   right-hand side

Energy

One complete cycle (period)

E_p E_p

E_k E_k

Time

Left   Midpoint   Right   Midpoint   Left

You can Draw Graphs to Show Displacement, Velocity and Acceleration

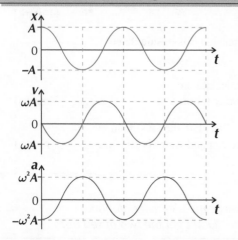

Displacement, x, varies as a cosine with a maximum value, A (the amplitude).

The equations for these graphs are on the next page. You can use a data logger to plot these graphs for a simple oscillator, e.g. a pendulum.

Velocity, v, is the gradient of the **displacement**-time graph. It has a maximum value of ωA (where ω is the angular frequency of the oscillation — see next page) and is a **quarter of a cycle** in front of the **displacement**.

Acceleration, a, is the gradient of the **velocity**-time graph. It has a maximum value of $\omega^2 A$, and is in **antiphase** with the **displacement**.

The velocity-time graph is derived from the gradient of the displacement-time graph because $v = \dfrac{\Delta x}{\Delta t}$. Similarly, $a = \dfrac{\Delta v}{\Delta t}$.

Simple Harmonic Motion

The **Frequency** and **Period** Don't Depend on the **Amplitude**

1) From **maximum positive displacement** (e.g. maximum displacement to the right) to **maximum negative displacement** (e.g. maximum displacement to the left) and **back again** is called a **cycle** of oscillation.

2) The **frequency**, f, of the SHM is the number of cycles per second (measured in Hz).

3) The **period**, T, is the **time** taken for a complete cycle (in seconds).

4) The **angular frequency**, ω, is $2\pi f$. The formulas for ω are the same as for **angular speed** in circular motion.

> In SHM, the **frequency** and **period** are independent of the **amplitude** (i.e. constant for a given oscillation). So a **pendulum clock** will keep ticking in **regular** time **intervals** even if its swing becomes very **small**.

Learn the SHM Equations

You'll be given these formulas in the exam, so just make sure you know what they mean and how to use them.

1) For an object to be moving with SHM, the **acceleration**, a, is directly proportional to the **displacement**, x.

2) The **constant of proportionality** depends on ω, and the acceleration is always in the **opposite direction** from the displacement (so there's a minus sign in the equation).

This is the defining equation of SHM: $\boxed{a = -\omega^2 x}$ Maximum acceleration: $\boxed{a_{max} = \omega^2 A}$

Don't forget, A is the maximum displacement — it's not acceleration.

3) The **velocity** is **positive** if the object's moving in one direction, and **negative** if it's moving in the **opposite** direction — that's why there's a ± sign.

$$\boxed{v = \pm\,\omega\sqrt{A^2 - x^2}}$$ $\boxed{\textbf{Maximum speed} = \omega A}$

4) The **displacement** varies with time according to the equation on the right. To use this equation you need to start timing when the pendulum is at its **maximum displacement** — i.e. when $t = 0$, $x = A$.

$$\boxed{x = A\cos(\omega t)}$$

Helene was investigating swinging as a form of simple harmonic motion.

Warm-Up Questions

Q1 Write down the defining equation of SHM.

Q2 Sketch graphs to show how the displacement, velocity and acceleration for an object in SHM each vary with time. Explain how the velocity and acceleration graphs can be derived from the displacement-time graph.

Q3 Given the amplitude and the frequency, how would you work out the maximum acceleration?

Q4 What is the equation for the velocity of an object moving with SHM? Why does the equation include a ± sign?

PRACTICE QUESTIONS

Exam Questions

Q1 a) Describe the condition necessary for an object to be moving with simple harmonic motion. [2 marks]
   b) Explain why the motion of a ball bouncing off the ground is not simple harmonic motion. [1 mark]

Q2 Describe how the total energy, the kinetic energy and the elastic potential energy of a mass-spring system undergoing simple harmonic motion varies as the displacement of the mass varies. [4 marks]

Q3 A pendulum is pulled a distance 0.05 m from its midpoint and released.
   It oscillates with simple harmonic motion with a frequency of 1.5 Hz. Calculate:
   a) its maximum speed [2 marks]
   b) its displacement 0.1 s after it is released [2 marks]
   c) the time it takes to fall to 0.01 m from the midpoint after it is released [2 marks]

Q4 Two pendulums, C and D are oscillating with simple harmonic motion. Pendulum C has the same maximum displacement, A, as pendulum D, but twice the angular speed, ω. Which option correctly describes the maximum acceleration of pendulum C with respect to pendulum D?
   A half   B the same   C double   D quadruple   [1 mark]

"Simple" harmonic motion — hmmm, I'm not convinced...

The basic concept of SHM is simple enough (no pun intended). Make sure you can remember the shapes of all the graphs on page 100. You're given the formulas on this page in the exam, but make sure you're comfortable using them.

Simple Harmonic Oscillators

There are a couple more equations to learn on this page I'm afraid. The experiment described at the bottom of the page shows where they come from, though, so that should help you remember them.

A **Mass** on a **Spring** is a **Simple Harmonic Oscillator (SHO)**

1) When the mass is **pushed to the left** or **pulled to the right** of the **equilibrium position**, there's a **force** exerted on it. The size of this force (in N) is:

$$F = -kx$$

where k is the **spring constant** (stiffness) of the spring in Nm^{-1} and x is the **displacement** in m.

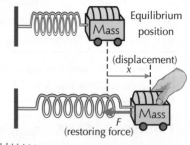

Equilibrium position

(displacement) x

F (restoring force)

2) After a bit of jiggery-pokery involving Newton's second law and some of the ideas on the previous page, you get the **formula for the period of a mass oscillating on a spring**:

$$T = 2\pi\sqrt{\frac{m}{k}}$$

T = period of oscillation in seconds
m = mass in kg
k = spring constant in Nm^{-1}

A simple theory of how atoms in a lattice (i.e. a solid) behave can be worked out by considering them as masses oscillating on springs. So there you go.

You Can **Check the Formula Experimentally**

PRACTICAL SKILLS

1) Set up the equipment as shown in the diagram.

2) **Pull** the masses down a set amount, this will be your initial **amplitude**. Let the masses go.

3) The masses will now oscillate with **simple harmonic motion**.

4) The **position sensor** measures the **displacement** of the mass over **time**.

5) Connect the position sensor to a computer and create a **displacement-time** graph. Read off the period T from the graph.

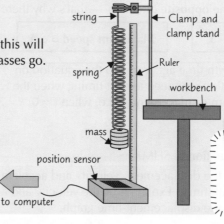

string — Clamp and clamp stand

spring

Ruler

workbench

mass

position sensor

to computer

You could also measure the period of an oscillation using a stop watch. It's sensible to measure the time taken for e.g. five oscillations, then divide by the number of oscillations to get an average, as it'll reduce the random error in your result.

Because the spring in this experiment is hung vertically, the potential energy is both elastic and gravitational. For the horizontal spring system shown above, the potential energy is just elastic.

You Can Use This Set Up to **Investigate Factors** Which Affect the **Period**

1) Change the **mass, m,** by loading more **masses** onto the spring.

2) Change the **spring stiffness constant, k,** by using different combinations of springs.

3) Change the **amplitude, A,** by pulling the masses down by different distances.

$k \rightarrow 2k \rightarrow 3k$

$\frac{1}{2}k$

$\frac{1}{3}k$

You'll get the following **results**:

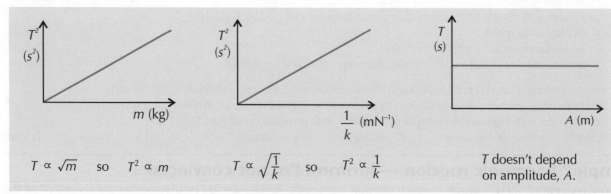

$T \propto \sqrt{m}$ so $T^2 \propto m$

$T \propto \sqrt{\frac{1}{k}}$ so $T^2 \propto \frac{1}{k}$

T doesn't depend on amplitude, A.

Simple Harmonic Oscillators

The **Simple Pendulum** is the **Classic Example** of an **SHO**

PRACTICAL SKILLS

1) Attach a **pendulum** to an **angle sensor** connected to a **computer**.

2) **Displace** the pendulum from its rest position by a small angle (less than 10°) and let it go. The pendulum will oscillate with **simple harmonic motion**.

3) The angle sensor measures how the bob's **displacement** from the **rest** position varies with **time**.

4) Use the computer to plot a **displacement-time** graph and read off the **period**, *T*, from it. Make sure you calculate the average period over **several oscillations** to reduce the **percentage uncertainty** in your measurement (see page 260).

5) Change the **mass** of the pendulum bob, *m*, the **amplitude** of displacement, *A*, and the **length** of the rod, *l*, independently to see how they affect the **period**, *T*.

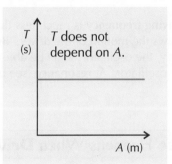

> You can also do this experiment by hanging the pendulum from a clamp and timing the oscillations using a stop watch.
> Use the clamp stand as a reference point so it's easy to tell when the pendulum has reached the mid-point of its oscillation.

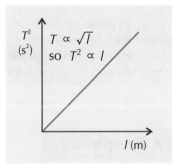

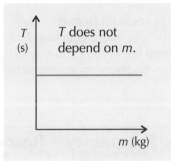

Bob hung around waiting for the experiment to start.

The **formula for the period of a pendulum** is:
(The derivation's quite hard, so you don't need to know it.)
This formula only works for small angles of oscillation — up to about 10° from the equilibrium point.

$$T = 2\pi\sqrt{\frac{l}{g}}$$

T = period of oscillation in seconds
l = length of pendulum (between pivot and centre of mass of bob) in m
g = gravitational field strength in Nkg^{-1}

Warm-Up Questions

Q1 Write down the formula for calculating the period of a mass-spring system.

Q2 Describe an experiment to find how changing the mass in a mass-spring system affects its period of oscillation.

Q3 For a mass-spring system, what graphs could you plot to find out how the period depends on:
a) the mass, b) the spring constant, and c) the amplitude? What would they look like?

Q4 Write down the formula for calculating the period of a simple pendulum displaced by a small angle.

PRACTICE QUESTIONS

Exam Questions

Q1 A spring of original length 0.10 m is suspended from a stand and clamp.
A mass of 0.10 kg is attached to the bottom and the spring extends to a total length of 0.20 m.

a) Calculate the spring constant of the spring in Nm^{-1}. (*g* = 9.81 Nkg^{-1}) [2 marks]

b) The mass is pulled down a further 2.0 cm and then released. Assuming the mass oscillates with simple harmonic motion, calculate the period of the subsequent oscillations. [1 mark]

c) Calculate the mass needed to make the period of oscillation twice as long. [2 marks]

Q2 Two pendulums of different lengths were released from rest at the top of their swing.
It took exactly the same time for the shorter pendulum to make five complete oscillations
as it took the longer pendulum to make three complete oscillations. The shorter pendulum
had a length of 0.20 m. Show that the length of the longer one was 0.56 m. [3 marks]

Go on — SHO the examiners what you're made of...

The most important things to remember on these pages are those two period equations. You'll be given them in your exam, but you need to know what they mean and be happy using them. So go and practise using them for a bit.

Free and Forced Vibrations

Resonance... tricky little beast. The Millennium Bridge was supposed to be a feat of British engineering, but it suffered from a severe case of the wobbles caused by resonance. How was it sorted out? By damping, of course — read on...

Free Vibrations — No Transfer of Energy To or From the Surroundings

1) If you stretch and release a mass on a spring, it oscillates at its **resonant frequency**.

2) If **no energy's transferred** to or from the surroundings, it will **keep** oscillating with the **same amplitude forever**.

3) In practice this **never happens**, but a spring vibrating in air is called a **free vibration** anyway.

Forced Vibrations Happen When There's an External Driving Force

1) A system can be **forced** to vibrate by a periodic **external force**.

2) The frequency of this force is called the **driving frequency**.

> If the **driving frequency** is much **less than** the **resonant frequency** then the two are **in phase** — the oscillator just follows the motion of the driver. But, if the **driving frequency** is much **greater than** the **resonant frequency**, the oscillator won't be able to keep up — you end up with the driver completely **out of phase** with the oscillator. At **resonance** (see below) the **phase difference** between the driver and oscillator is **90°**.

Resonance Happens When Driving Frequency = Resonant Frequency

When the **driving frequency** approaches the **resonant frequency**, the system gains more and more energy from the driving force and so vibrates with a **rapidly increasing amplitude**. When this happens the system is **resonating**.

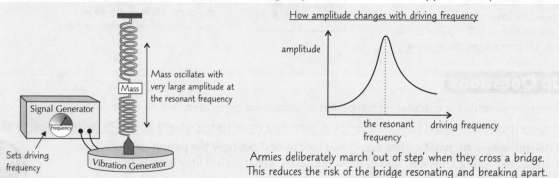

Mass oscillates with very large amplitude at the resonant frequency

How amplitude changes with driving frequency

amplitude

the resonant frequency — driving frequency

Signal Generator — Sets driving frequency

Vibration Generator

Armies deliberately march 'out of step' when they cross a bridge. This reduces the risk of the bridge resonating and breaking apart.

Examples of resonance:

a) organ pipe

The column of air resonates, setting up a stationary wave (p.28) in the pipe.

b) swing

A swing resonates if it's driven by someone pushing it at its resonant frequency.

c) glass smashing

A glass resonates when driven by a sound wave at the right frequency.

d) radio

A radio is tuned so the electric circuit resonates at the same frequency as radio broadcasts.

Damping Happens When Energy is Lost To the Surroundings

1) In practice, **any** oscillating system **loses energy** to its surroundings.

2) This is usually down to **frictional forces** like air resistance.

3) These are called **damping forces**.

4) Systems are often **deliberately damped** to **stop** them oscillating or to **minimise** the effect of **resonance**.

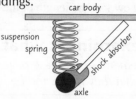

car body

suspension spring

shock absorber

axle

Shock absorbers in a car suspension provide a damping force by squashing oil through a hole when compressed.

Section 7 — Further Mechanics

Free and Forced Vibrations

Different Amounts of Damping have Different Effects

1) The **degree** of damping can vary from **light** damping (where the damping force is small) to **overdamping**.

2) Damping **reduces** the **amplitude** of the oscillation over time. The **heavier** the damping, the **quicker** the amplitude is reduced to zero.

3) **Critical damping** reduces the amplitude (i.e. stops the system oscillating) in the **shortest possible time**.

4) Car **suspension systems** and moving coil **meters** are critically damped so that they **don't oscillate** but return to equilibrium as quickly as possible.

5) Systems with **even heavier damping** are **overdamped**. They take **longer** to return to equilibrium than a critically damped system.

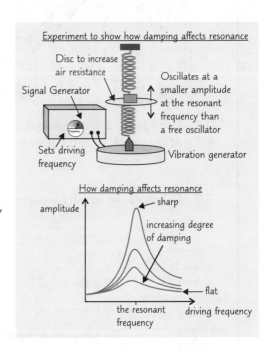

Plastic deformation of ductile materials **reduces** the **amplitude** of oscillations in the same way as damping. As the material changes shape, it **absorbs energy**, so the oscillation will be smaller.

Damping Affects Resonance too

1) **Lightly damped** systems have a **very sharp** resonance peak. Their amplitude only increases dramatically when the **driving frequency** is **very close** to the **resonant frequency**.

2) **Heavily damped** systems have a **flatter response**. Their amplitude doesn't increase very much near the resonant frequency and they aren't as **sensitive** to the driving frequency.

3) Structures are **damped** to avoid being **damaged** by resonance. Taipei 101 is a very tall skyscraper which uses a **giant pendulum** to damp oscillations caused by strong winds.

4) Damping can also be used to **improve performance**. For example, loudspeakers in a room create sound waves in the air. These reflect off of the walls of the room, and at certain frequencies **stationary sound waves** are created between the walls of the room. This causes **resonance** and can affect the quality of the sound — some frequencies are louder than they should be. Places like recording studios use **soundproofing** on their walls which absorb the sound energy and **convert** it into heat energy.

Warm-Up Questions

Q1 What is a free vibration? What is a forced vibration?

Q2 Draw diagrams to show how a damped system oscillates with time when the system is lightly damped and when the system is critically damped.

Q3 Explain how damping is used to improve sound quality in enclosed spaces.

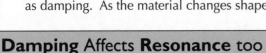

Exam Questions

Q1 a) Describe resonance. [2 marks]
    b) Sketch a graph to show how the amplitude of a lightly damped system varies with driving frequency. [2 marks]
    c) On the graph, show how the amplitude of the system varies with driving frequency when it is heavily damped. [1 mark]

Q2 a) Describe critical damping. [1 mark]
    b) State one situation where critical damping is used. [1 mark]

A-Level Physics — it can really put a damper on your social life...

Resonance can be really useful (radios, oboes, swings — yay) or very, very bad...

Extra Exam Practice

Well that's <u>Section 7</u> settled. These questions will test you can apply it all together to unfamiliar contexts.

- Have a look at this example of how to answer a tricky exam question.
- Then check how much you've understood from Section 7 by having a go at the questions on the next page.

When you're comfortable with the content in all of the sections, try tackling the synoptic questions on p.268-275. They'll test your knowledge of the whole course, so they're great practice for the exam.

1 **Figure 1** shows a wrecking ball that is used to demolish old buildings. The wrecking ball starts at a small angle of θ, and swings towards the building. The edge of the building is at the centre of the wrecking ball's swing. **Figure 2** shows a graph of how the velocity, v, of the wrecking ball varies with its displacement, x, from the point of impact with the building.

Figure 1

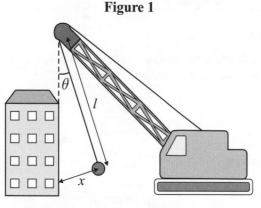

Figure 2

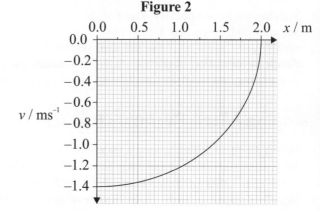

1.1 Use **Figure 2** to calculate the maximum magnitude of the acceleration of the wrecking ball before it hits the building.

(3 marks)

1.2 Calculate the length l as shown in **Figure 1**. ($g = 9.81$ ms^{-2})

(2 marks)

It'd be an easy mistake to try to read the maximum gradient off the graph. But Figure 2 isn't a v-t graph, so the gradient isn't acceleration.

Maximum speed has no direction, so it's always positive. The graph shows velocity, so you can ignore the minus sign.

Always look back to see if you've done some of the work already — ω was calculated in 1.1.

1.1

The wrecking ball acts like a simple pendulum — a simple harmonic oscillator.

The maximum acceleration formula for a simple harmonic oscillator is $a_{max} = \omega^2 A$.

The maximum displacement, $A = 2.0$ m (from the graph). ◄

Maximum speed $= \omega A$, so $\omega =$ maximum speed $\div A$

From the graph, **maximum speed = 1.4 ms^{-1}**, so $\omega = 1.4 \div 2.0 = 0.7$ rad s^{-1}. ◄

Maximum acceleration $= \omega^2 A = 0.7^2 \times 2.0 = 0.98$ ms^{-2}.

You'd get 3 marks for the correct answer. If you got the answer wrong, you'd still get 1 mark for reading A off the graph and 1 mark for calculating ω correctly.

1.2

The formula for the period of a simple pendulum is $T = 2\pi\sqrt{\dfrac{l}{g}}$, so $T^2 = \dfrac{4\pi^2 l}{g}$ and $l = \dfrac{gT^2}{4\pi^2}$.

$T = \dfrac{1}{f}$ and $\omega = 2\pi f$, so $T = \dfrac{2\pi}{\omega} = \dfrac{2\pi}{0.7} = 8.9759...$ s and $g = 9.81$ ms^{-2}.

$l = \dfrac{gT^2}{4\pi^2} = \dfrac{9.81 \times 8.9759...^2}{4\pi^2} = 20.0204...$ m $=$ **20 m (to 2 s.f.)** ◄

You'd get 2 marks for the correct answer, but if you got it wrong, you'd still get 1 mark for calculating the period of oscillation correctly.

You've been asked to use Figure 2, so think about the quantities that you can read off the graph.

You could've also calculated ω by reading a coordinate off the graph (x, v), and plugging them into the formula $v = \pm\omega\sqrt{A^2 - x^2}$.

Round your final answer to the lowest number of s.f. given in the question. In this case it's 2, but don't round until the end.

Extra Exam Practice

2 A stunt aeroplane at an air show flies in a vertical circle at a constant linear speed. The diameter of the circle is 185 m. **Figure 3** shows the positions of the pilot at four different points along the plane's circular path.

Figure 3

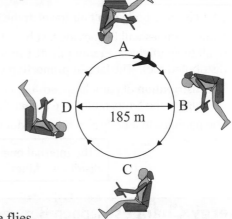

2.1 At the top of the circle (point A), the force on the pilot from the seat is 0.00 N. Calculate the linear speed of the aeroplane at point A.

(2 marks)

2.2 At point D, the plane is moving vertically upwards. The seat applies a non-zero overall force on the pilot at this point. Without further calculation, state and explain the direction of this force.

(4 marks)

At another part of the air show, a remote-controlled plane flies alternately through a series of high and low hoops. The plane travels with a constant horizontal velocity of 75 ms⁻¹, and has a vertical velocity that can be described by simple harmonic motion. The vertical separation of the hoops is 24 m and the horizontal separation is 56 m.

2.3 Calculate the magnitude of the resultant velocity of the plane at the midpoint of a vertical oscillation.

(4 marks)

The final low hoop is only 19 m below the high hoops. The horizontal separation is still 56 m.

To pass safely through the final hoop, the horizontal velocity of the plane is increased whilst maintaining the same oscillating vertical motion.

2.4 Calculate the new average horizontal velocity between the final two hoops.

(2 marks)

3 A loudspeaker is a device that converts electrical energy into sound energy. An alternating current with frequency f forces a loudspeaker cone to vibrate back and forth at the same frequency. This forces air molecules to vibrate, causing a sound wave of frequency f. The loudness of the sound produced will depend on the amplitude of the sound wave, and the pitch depends on its frequency. A higher amplitude means a louder sound and a higher frequency means a higher pitched sound.

3.1 A loudspeaker cone has a mass of 42 g. The back and forth movement of the loudspeaker cone can be modelled as a mass oscillating on a spring. At time t, the cone is at a distance of 2.4 mm from the midpoint of an oscillation. The cone is oscillating at 25 Hz. Calculate the magnitude of the restoring force acting on the cone at time t.

(3 marks)

Figure 4

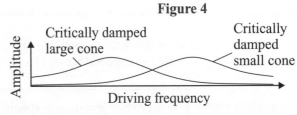

Many loudspeaker units use two cones to produce sounds. The large cone has a low resonant frequency and the small cone has a high resonant frequency. A filter ensures that the small cone produces the high frequency sounds and the large cone produces the low frequency sounds. Both cones are usually critically damped. **Figure 4** shows how the amplitude of vibration of two different cones varies with the driving frequency of a fixed amplitude signal.

3.2 Explain why the quality of the sound of a loudspeaker unit is improved by using critical damping and by using different-sized cones.

(6 marks)

Thermal Energy Transfer

Thermal physics is really all about energy transfer to and from particles.

Internal Energy Depends on the Kinetic and Potential Energy of Particles

The **particles** in a body **don't** all **travel** at the **same speed**.

1) Some particles will be moving **fast** but others much more **slowly**. The speeds of all the particles are **randomly distributed** (so **kinetic energy** is randomly distributed too). The **largest proportion** will travel at about the **average speed**.

2) The **distribution** of particle speeds depends on the **temperature** of the body. The **higher** the temperature, the **higher** the **average kinetic energy** of the particles.

3) The particles in a body also have **randomly distributed potential energies** that depend on their **relative positions**.

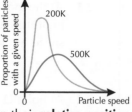

> The **internal energy** of a body is the **sum** of the randomly distributed **kinetic** and **potential energies** of **all** its particles.

Energy Changes Happen Between Particles

A **system** is just a group of bodies considered as a whole. A **closed system is** one which doesn't allow any **transfer of matter** in or out. For a closed system, the total internal energy is **constant**, as long as it's **not** heated or cooled, and **no work** is done.

1) Energy is **constantly transferred** between particles within a system, through **collisions between particles**. But the **total combined energy** of all the particles **doesn't change** during these collisions.

2) However, the **internal energy** of the system can be **increased** by **heating** it, or by **doing work** to transfer energy to the system (e.g. changing its shape).

3) The **opposite** is also true — the internal energy can be **reduced** by **cooling** the system, or by doing work to **remove energy** from the system.

4) In such a change, the **average kinetic** and/or **potential energy** of the particles will **change** as a result of energy being **transferred to** or **from** the system.

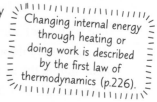

Changing internal energy through heating or doing work is described by the first law of thermodynamics (p.226).

A Change of State Means a Change of Internal Energy

1) When a substance **changes state** (between solid, liquid or gas), its **internal energy** changes but its **kinetic energy** (and temperature) **stays the same**. This is because the **potential energy** of the particles is altered — not their kinetic energy.

2) As a liquid turns into a gas (for example, boiling water becoming steam) its **potential energy increases** even though the water molecules in both states are at **100 °C**.

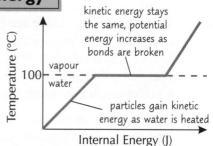

kinetic energy stays the same, potential energy increases as bonds are broken

particles gain kinetic energy as water is heated

Specific Heat Capacity is how much Energy it Takes to Heat Something

When you heat something, its particles get more **kinetic energy** and its **temperature** rises.

> The **specific heat capacity** (c) of a substance is the amount of **energy** needed to **raise** the **temperature** of **1 kg** of the substance by **1 K** (or 1°C).

or put another way: **energy change = mass × specific heat capacity × change in temperature**

in symbols: $Q = mc\Delta\theta$ ← ΔT or Δt is sometimes used instead of $\Delta\theta$ for the change in temperature.

Q is the energy change in J, m is the mass in kg and $\Delta\theta$ is the temperature change in K or °C.
Units of c are J kg^{-1} K^{-1} or J kg^{-1} °C^{-1}.

Thermal Energy Transfer

Find Specific Heat Capacity using a Continuous-Flow Calorimeter

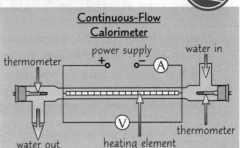

Continuous-Flow Calorimeter

Continuous-flow heating is when a **fluid** flows continuously over a **heating element**. As it flows, **energy** is **transferred** to the fluid.

1) Set up the experiment shown and let water flow at a **steady rate** until the water out is at a **constant temperature**.

2) Record the **flow rate** of the water and the duration of the experiment, t, (to find the mass of water). You also need to measure the **temperature difference**, $\Delta\theta$, (of the water from the point that it flows in to the point that it flows out) between the thermometers. Also record the **current**, I, and **potential difference**, V.

3) The **energy supplied** to the water is $Q = mc\Delta\theta + H$, where H is the **heat lost** to the surroundings.

4) **Repeat** the experiment **changing** only the **p.d. of the power supply** and the **flow rate** (mass) so $\Delta\theta$ remains **constant**. You should now have an equation for each experiment: $Q_1 = m_1c\Delta\theta + H$ and $Q_2 = m_2c\Delta\theta + H$.

5) The values of c, $\Delta\theta$ and H are the same, so $Q_2 - Q_1 = (m_2 - m_1)c\Delta\theta$. Rearranging gives: $c = \dfrac{Q_2 - Q_1}{(m_2 - m_1)\Delta\theta}$.

6) Q is just the **electrical energy** supplied over time t in each case, so you can use $Q = VIt$ to find Q_1 and Q_2, and therefore c, the **specific heat capacity** of water.

Specific Latent Heat is the Energy Needed to Change State

To **melt** a **solid** or **boil or evaporate** a **liquid**, you need **energy** to **break the bonds** that hold the particles in place. The **energy** needed for this is called **latent heat**. The **larger** the **mass** of the substance, the **more energy** it takes to **change** its **state**. That's why the **specific latent heat** is defined per kg:

> The **specific latent heat** (l) of **fusion** or **vaporisation** is the quantity of **thermal energy** required to **change the state** of **1 kg** of a substance.

So: | energy change = mass of substance changed × specific latent heat | or: | $Q = ml$

Where Q is the energy change in J and m is the mass in kg. The units of l are J kg^{-1}.

You'll usually see the latent heat of vaporisation (boiling or condensing) written l_v and the latent heat of fusion (melting or freezing) written l_f.

Warm-Up Questions

Q1 Give the definition of internal energy.

Q2 Define specific heat capacity and specific latent heat.

Q3 Show that the thermal energy needed to heat 2 kg of water from 20 °C to 50 °C is ~250 kJ (c_{water} = 4180 J kg^{-1} K^{-1}).

Exam Questions

Q1 A 2.0 kg metal cylinder is heated uniformly from 4.5 °C to 12.7 °C in 3 minutes. The electric heater supplies electrical energy at a rate of 90 Js^{-1}. Assuming that heat losses are negligible, calculate the specific heat capacity of the metal. State a correct unit for your answer. [4 marks]

Q2 A kettle transfers energy at a rate of 3.00×10^3 Js^{-1}.

a) If the kettle contains 0.500 kg of water at 20.0 °C, calculate how long it will take the water to reach 100.0 °C and then boil dry, assuming the kettle remains switched on throughout and no energy is lost to the surroundings. (l_v(water) = 2260 kJkg^{-1}, c_{water} = 4180 J kg^{-1} K^{-1}) [5 marks]

b) Which of the following statements is true about the energy of the particles in the water during this process?

A The temperature of the water increases steadily throughout the time found in part a).

B At the point of boiling, only the potential energy of the water particles is changing.

C Once the water starts boiling, the kinetic energy of the water particles starts increasing.

D Both the kinetic and potential energy of the water particles are continually increasing throughout the time found in part a). [1 mark]

My specific eat capacity — 24 pies...

This stuff's a bit dull, but hey... make sure you're comfortable using those equations. Interesting(ish) fact for the day — the huge difference in specific heat capacity between the land and the sea is one of the causes of monsoons in Asia.

Gas Laws

Laws for gases? What ever next... I give it about 5 minutes before the no-win no-fee lawyers start calling you.

There's an **Absolute Scale** of **Temperature**

There is a **lowest possible temperature** called **absolute zero***. Absolute zero is given a value of **zero kelvins**, written **0 K**, on the absolute temperature scale.

At **0 K** all particles have the **minimum** possible **kinetic energy** — everything pretty much stops. At higher temperatures, particles have more energy. In fact, with the **Kelvin scale**, a particle's **energy** is **proportional** to its **temperature** (see page 116).

1) The Kelvin scale is named after Lord Kelvin who first suggested it.
2) A change of **1 K** equals a change of **1 °C**.
3) To change from degrees Celsius into kelvins you **add 273** (or 273.15 if you need to be really precise).

$$K = C + 273$$

All equations in **thermal physics** use temperatures measured in kelvins.

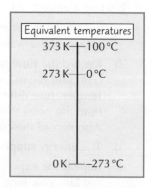

Equivalent temperatures

373 K — 100 °C

273 K — 0 °C

0 K — −273 °C

It's true. −273.15 °C is the lowest temperature theoretically possible. Weird, huh. You'd kinda think there wouldn't be a minimum, but there is.

There are **Three Gas Laws**

The three gas laws were each worked out **independently** by **careful experiment**.
Each of the gas laws applies to a **fixed mass** of gas.

Boyle's Law: pV = constant

At a **constant temperature** the **pressure p** and **volume V** of a gas are **inversely proportional**.

E.g. if you **reduce** the volume of a gas, its particles will be **closer together** and will **collide** with each other and the container more often, so the pressure **increases**.

A (theoretical) gas that obeys Boyle's law at all temperatures is called an **ideal gas**.

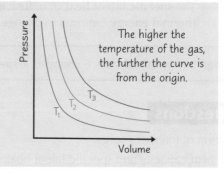

The higher the temperature of the gas, the further the curve is from the origin.

Pressure

T_1 T_2 T_3

Volume

Charles's Law: V/T = constant

At constant pressure, the volume V of a gas is directly proportional to its absolute temperature T.

When you heat a gas the particles gain kinetic energy (page 108). At a constant pressure, this means they move more quickly and further apart, and so the volume of the gas increases.

Ideal gases obey this law and the pressure law as well.

'Ello, 'ello...

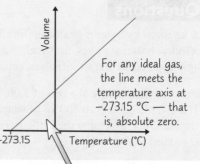

Volume

For any ideal gas, the line meets the temperature axis at −273.15 °C — that is, absolute zero.

−273.15   Temperature (°C)

The Pressure Law: p/T = constant

At constant volume, the pressure p of a gas is directly proportional to its absolute temperature T.

If you heat a gas, the particles gain kinetic energy. This means they move faster. If the volume doesn't change, the particles will collide with each other and their container more often and at higher speed, increasing the pressure inside the container.

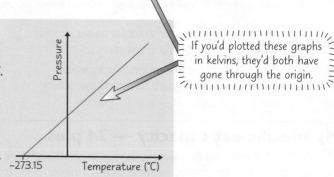

Pressure

−273.15   Temperature (°C)

If you'd plotted these graphs in kelvins, they'd both have gone through the origin.

Gas Laws

Investigate the Gas Laws with these Experiments

Experiment to investigate Boyle's Law

You can investigate the effect of **pressure** on **volume** by setting up the experiment shown. The **oil** traps a pocket of air in a sealed **tube** with **fixed dimensions**. A **tyre pump** is used to **increase** the pressure on the oil and the **Bourdon gauge** records the **pressure**. As the pressure increases, more oil will be pushed into the tube, the **oil level** will **rise**, and the air will **compress**. The volume occupied by air in the tube will **reduce**.

Measure the volume of air when the system is at **atmospheric pressure**, then gradually increase the pressure, keeping the **temperature constant**. Note down both the pressure and the volume of air as it changes. Multiplying these together at any point should give the **same value**.

If you plot a **graph** of p against $\frac{1}{V}$ you should get a **straight line**.

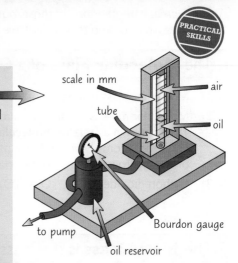

Experiment to investigate Charles's Law

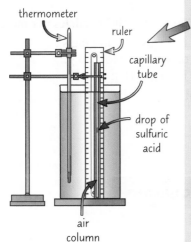

You can investigate the effect of **temperature** on **volume** by setting up the experiment shown. A **capillary tube** is **sealed** at the bottom and contains a drop of **concentrated sulfuric acid** halfway up the tube — this traps a **column of air** between the bottom of the tube and the acid drop. The beaker is filled with **near-boiling water**, and the **length** of the trapped column of air increases. As the water cools, the length of the air column **decreases**.

Regularly record the **temperature** of the water and the air column **length** as the water cools. **Repeat** with fresh near-boiling water twice more, letting the tube adjust to the new temperature between each repeat. Record the length at the **same temperatures** each time and take an **average** of the three results.

If you plot your **average results** on a graph of **length** against **temperature** and draw a line of best fit, you will get a **straight line**. This shows that the length of the air column is **proportional** to the temperature. The volume of the column of air is equal to the volume of a cylinder, which is proportional to its length ($V = \pi r^2 l$), so the **volume** is also proportional to the temperature. This agrees with **Charles' law**.

Warm-Up Questions

Q1 Give the value of absolute zero in kelvins and degrees Celsius.

Q2 State Boyle's law, Charles's law and the pressure law.

Q3 The pressure of a gas is 100 000 Pa and its temperature is 27 °C. The gas is heated — its volume stays fixed but the pressure rises to 150 000 Pa. Show that its new temperature is 177 °C.

Q4 Describe an experiment to demonstrate the effect of temperature on the volume of a gas when pressure is constant.

Exam Questions

Q1 An unknown solution boils at 107.89 °C. Calculate its boiling temperature in kelvins. [1 mark]

Q2 A gas expands from 2.42 m³ to 6.43 m³. The final temperature of the gas is 293 K.
Calculate the initial temperature of the gas, assuming the pressure remains constant. [2 marks]

Q3 a) Describe an experiment to investigate the effect of pressure on the volume
of a gas when temperature is constant. Include a description of your method
and the relationship you would expect to see. [4 marks]

b) A parcel of air has a volume of 0.460 m³ at 1.03×10^5 Pa. Calculate its volume at 3.41×10^5 Pa.
Assume that the temperature does not change. [2 marks]

Don't feel under pressure — take some time to chill out...

Three laws, two practicals, one thing to do — learn it all. Learning laws probably isn't your favourite way to spend your time (unless you want to be a lawyer) but it'll stop a nasty question from slowing you down in the exams.

Ideal Gas Equation

Aaahh... great... another one of those 'our equation doesn't work properly with real gases, so we'll invent an ideal gas that it does work for and they'll think we're dead clever' situations. Hmm. Physicists, eh...

The **Molecular Mass** of a **Gas** is the Mass of **One Molecule** of that Gas

1) Molecular mass is the **sum** of the **masses** of **all the atoms** that make up a **molecule**.

2) Molecular mass is usually given relative to the mass of a **carbon-12** atom. This is known as **relative molecular mass**. Carbon-12 has a relative mass of **12**. Hydrogen atoms have a relative mass of 1, but hydrogen molecules are made up of **two** hydrogen atoms, so the relative **molecular mass** of hydrogen is **2**.

3) Carbon dioxide ($^{12}_{6}C + ^{16}_{8}O + ^{16}_{8}O$) has a relative molecular mass of 12 + 16 + 16 = 44.

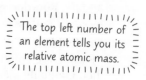
The top left number of an element tells you its relative atomic mass.

The **Molar Mass** is the Mass of **One Mole** of a **Gas**

1) At a fixed **pressure** and **temperature**, a fixed volume of gas will contain the **same amount** of gas molecules, **no matter** what the gas is. This leads to a unit called a **mole**.

2) **One mole** of any **gas** contains the same number of particles. This number is called **Avogadro's constant** — it has the symbol N_A and is equal to **6.02 × 10²³ particles per mole**.

3) The **molar mass** of a substance is the mass that **1 mole** of that substance would have (usually in **grams**). It is **equal** to the **relative molecular mass** of that substance. So the molar mass of helium ($^4_2$He) is 4 g and the molar mass of an oxygen molecule, which consists of 2 oxygen atoms, is 16 g + 16 g = 32 g.

4) The **number of moles** in a substance is usually given by *n*, and its units are 'mol'. The number of molecules in a mass of gas is given by the number of moles, *n*, **multiplied by** Avogadro's constant. So the number of molecules, $N = nN_A$.

If you **Combine** All Three Gas Laws you get the **Ideal Gas Equation**

1) Remember the gas laws from page 110? **Combining all three** of them gives the equation:
$$\frac{pV}{T} = \text{constant}$$

2) The constant in the equation depends on the amount of gas used. The amount of **gas** can be **measured** in **moles**, *n*.

(Pretty obvious... if you have more gas it takes up more space.)

3) The constant then becomes *nR*, where *R* is called the **molar gas constant**. Its value is **8.31 J mol⁻¹ K⁻¹**. Plugging this into the equation gives:

$$\frac{pV}{T} = nR \text{ or rearranging, } pV = nRT \text{ — the ideal gas equation}$$

This equation works well (i.e., a real gas approximates to an ideal gas) for gases at **low pressures** and fairly **high temperatures**.

Ideal gases obey Boyle's, Charles's and the pressure laws.

Boltzmann's Constant *k* is like a **Gas Constant** for **One Particle** of Gas

1) **Boltzmann's constant**, *k*, is equivalent to R/N_A (molar gas constant / Avogadro's constant) — you can think of Boltzmann's constant as the **gas constant** for **one particle of gas**, while *R* is the gas constant for **one mole of gas**.

2) The value of Boltzmann's constant is **1.38 × 10⁻²³ JK⁻¹**.

3) If you combine $N = nN_A$ and $k = R/N_A$ you'll see that $Nk = nR$ — which can be substituted into the ideal gas equation:

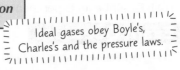
$pV = NkT$ — the equation of state

The equation $pV = NkT$ is called the equation of state of an ideal gas.

Ideal Gas Equation

Work is Done to Change the Volume of a Gas at Constant Pressure

1) For a gas to **expand** or **contract** at **constant pressure**,
work must be **done** — i.e. there must be a transfer of energy.

2) This normally involves the **transfer** of **heat energy** — e.g. if you **heat** a gas-filled balloon, it will **expand**.
Remove the heat source and it will **contract** back to its **original size**
as the heat is transferred back to its surroundings.

3) The **work done** in **changing** the **volume** of a gas at a constant pressure is given by: $\boxed{\text{work done} = p\Delta V}$
where **p** is **pressure** and ΔV is change in **volume**.

> **Example:** A gas cylinder is heated so that its volume increases from 0.320 m³ to 0.875 m³.
> Assuming the pressure remains constant at 1.15×10^5 Pa,
> calculate the energy transferred to the gas.
>
> energy transferred = work done, so use:
> $$W = p\Delta V$$
> $$= (1.150 \times 10^5) \times (0.875 - 0.320)$$
> $$= 63\ 825 = \mathbf{63\ 800\ J\ (to\ 3\ s.f.)}$$
>
> The area under a graph of pressure against volume shows
> the energy transferred to change the volume of the gas.

Warm-Up Questions

Q1 What is meant by molecular mass and relative molecular mass?

Q2 What is the molar mass of carbon-12 ($^{12}_6$C)?

Q3 How many atoms are there in one mole of krypton?

Q4 What is the ideal gas equation?

Q5 What is the equation of state of an ideal gas?

Q6 Show that the work done when a gas expands from 3.4 m³ to 9.3 m³ at 1.0×10^{15} Pa is 5.9×10^{15} J.

Exam Questions

Q1 The mass of one mole of nitrogen gas is 0.028 kg.

   a) A flask contains 0.014 kg of nitrogen gas. Calculate the number of:
     i) moles of nitrogen gas in the flask.   [1 mark]
     ii) nitrogen molecules in the flask.   [1 mark]

   b) The flask has a volume of 0.0130 m³ and its temperature is 27.2 °C.
     Calculate the pressure of the gas inside it. ($R = 8.31$ J mol⁻¹ K⁻¹)   [2 marks]

   c) Explain what would happen to the pressure inside the flask if the number
     of molecules of nitrogen in the flask were halved.   [2 marks]

Q2 A large helium balloon has a volume of 10.0 m³ at ground level.
The temperature of the gas in the balloon is 293 K and the pressure is 1.00×10^5 Pa.
The balloon is released and rises to a height where its volume becomes 25.0 m³ and
its temperature is 261 K. Calculate the pressure inside the balloon at its new height.   [3 marks]

Q3 470 kJ of work (to 3 significant figures) is done to increase the volume of a gas to 10.3 m³.
Calculate the original volume of the gas assuming a constant pressure of 1.12×10^5 Pa.   [2 marks]

Ideal revision equation: marks = (pages read × questions answered)²...

*All this might sound a bit theoretical, but most gases you'll meet in the everyday world come fairly close to being 'ideal'.
They only stop obeying these laws well when the pressure's too high or they're getting close to their condensation point.*

The Pressure of an Ideal Gas

Kinetic theory tries to explain the gas laws. It basically models a gas as a series of hard balls that obey Newton's laws.

You Need to be Able to **Derive** the **Pressure** of an **Ideal Gas**

Start by **Deriving** the **Pressure** on **One Wall** of a Box — in the *x* direction

Imagine a cubic box with sides of length *l* containing *N* particles each of mass *m*.

This isn't an easy page. Work through it properly and make sure you understand it.

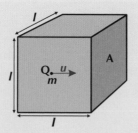

1) Say particle **Q** moves directly towards **wall A** with velocity *u*. Its **momentum** approaching the wall is *mu*. It strikes wall **A**. Assuming the **collisions** are perfectly **elastic**, it rebounds and heads back in the opposite direction with momentum −*mu*. So the **change in momentum** is −*mu* − *mu* = −2*mu*.

2) Assuming **Q** suffers no collisions with other particles, the **time between collisions** of **Q** and wall **A** is 2*l* ÷ *u*. The number of **collisions per second** is therefore *u* ÷ 2*l*.

Gases under pressure can be udderly delightful.

3) This gives the **rate of change of momentum** as −2*mu* × *u* ÷ 2*l*.

4) Force equals the rate of change of momentum (Newton's second law), so the **force exerted by the wall** on this one particle = −2*mu²* ÷ 2*l* = −*mu²* ÷ *l*.

5) Particle **Q** is only one of many in the cube. Each particle will have a different velocity u_1, u_2 etc. towards **A**.

   The total force, *F*, of all these particles on wall **A** is:

   $$F = \frac{m(u_1^2 + u_2^2 + ...)}{l}$$

   *This force is now positive as we're talking about the force **on** the wall.*

6) You can define a quantity called the **mean square speed**, $\overline{u^2}$ as:

   $$\overline{u^2} = \frac{u_1^2 + u_2^2 + ...}{N}$$

7) If you put that into the equation above, you get:

   $$F = \frac{Nm\overline{u^2}}{l}$$

8) So, the pressure of the gas on end **A** is given by: where *V* = volume of the cube

   $$\text{pressure, } p = \frac{force}{area} = \frac{Nm\overline{u^2} \div l}{l^2} = \frac{Nm\overline{u^2}}{l^3} = \frac{Nm\overline{u^2}}{V}$$

...Then for the **General Equation** you need to think about **All 3 Directions** — *x*, *y* and *z*

A gas particle can move in **three dimensions** (i.e. the *x*, *y* and *z* directions).

1) You can calculate its **speed**, *c*, from Pythagoras' theorem in three dimensions:
   $c^2 = u^2 + v^2 + w^2$ where *u*, *v* and *w* are the components of the particle's velocity in the *x*, *y* and *z* directions.

2) If you treat all *N* particles in the same way, this gives an **overall** mean square speed of: $\overline{c^2} = \overline{u^2} + \overline{v^2} + \overline{w^2}$

3) Since the particles move **randomly**: $\overline{u^2} = \overline{v^2} = \overline{w^2}$ so $\overline{c^2} = 3\overline{u^2}$ and so $\overline{u^2} = \frac{\overline{c^2}}{3}$.

4) You can substitute this into the equation for pressure that you derived above to give:

   $$pV = \frac{1}{3}Nm\overline{c^2}$$

The Pressure of an Ideal Gas

A Useful Quantity is the **Root Mean Square Speed** or c_{rms}

As you saw on the previous page, it often helps to think about the motion of a **typical particle** in kinetic theory.

1) $\overline{c^2}$ is the **mean square speed** and has **units** m^2s^{-2}.

2) $\overline{c^2}$ is the average of the **square speeds** of **all** the particles, so the square root of it gives you the typical speed.

3) This is called the **root mean square speed** or, usually, the **r.m.s. speed**. It's often written as c_{rms}.
   The **unit** is the same as any speed — ms^{-1}.

$$r.m.s.\ speed = \sqrt{mean\ square\ speed} = \sqrt{\overline{c^2}} = c_{rms}$$

4) So you can write the equation on the previous page as:

$$pV = \tfrac{1}{3}Nm(c_{rms})^2$$

Lots of **Simplifying Assumptions** are Used in **Kinetic Theory**

In **kinetic theory**, physicists picture gas particles moving at **high speed** in **random directions**.
To get **equations** like the one you just derived though, some **simplifying assumptions** are needed:

1) The molecules continually move about randomly.
2) The motion of the molecules follows Newton's laws.
3) Collisions between molecules themselves or at the walls of a container are perfectly elastic.
4) Except for during collisions, the molecules always move in straight lines.
5) Any forces that act during collisions last for much less time than the time between collisions.

A **gas obeying** these **assumptions** is called an **ideal** gas. Ideal gases also follow the three **gas laws**, and have an **internal energy** (p.108) that is dependent only on the kinetic energy of their particles.
(The **potential energy = 0 J** as there are no forces between them except when they are **colliding**.)
Real gases behave like ideal gases as long as the **pressure isn't too big** and the **temperature** is **reasonably high** (compared with their boiling point), so they're useful assumptions.

Warm-Up Questions

Q1 What is the change in momentum when a gas particle hits a wall of its container head-on?
Q2 What is the force exerted on the wall by this one particle? What is the total force exerted on the wall?
Q3 What is the pressure exerted on this wall? What is the total pressure on the container?
Q4 What is 'root mean square speed'? How would you find it?
Q5 Give three of the assumptions made about ideal gas behaviour.

Exam Question

Q1 Some helium gas is contained in a flask of volume 7.00×10^{-5} m³. Each helium atom has a mass of 6.65×10^{-27} kg, and there are 2.17×10^{22} atoms present. The pressure of the gas is 1.03×10^5 Pa.

a) Calculate the mean square speed of the atoms. [2 marks]

b) Calculate the r.m.s. speed of a typical helium atom in the flask. [1 mark]

c) If the absolute temperature of the gas is doubled, calculate the new r.m.s. speed of its atoms. [2 marks]

Help — these pages are de-riving me crazy...

Make sure you know the derivation inside out and back to front — it's not easy, so you might want to go through it a few times, but it is worth it. Remember — mean square speed is the average of the squared speeds — i.e. square all the speeds, then find the average. Don't make the mistake of finding the average speed first and then squaring. No, no no...

Kinetic Energy and the Development of Theories

If, like me, you've spent this whole section wondering just how such spiffing physics came to be, you're in luck.

Average Kinetic Energy is Proportional to Absolute Temperature

There are **two equations** for the **product pV** of a gas — the ideal gas equation (page 112), and the equation involving the mean square speed of the particles (page 115). You can **equate these** to get three expressions for the **average kinetic energy**.

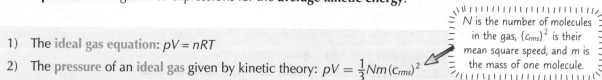

N is the number of molecules in the gas, $(c_{rms})^2$ is their mean square speed, and m is the mass of one molecule.

1) The ideal gas equation: $pV = nRT$

2) The pressure of an ideal gas given by kinetic theory: $pV = \frac{1}{3}Nm(c_{rms})^2$

3) Equating these two gives: $\frac{1}{3}Nm(c_{rms})^2 = nRT$

4) Multiplying by 3/2 gives: $\frac{3}{2} \times \frac{1}{3}Nm(c_{rms})^2 = \frac{3nRT}{2}$, so: $\boxed{\frac{1}{2}m(c_{rms})^2 = \frac{3}{2}\frac{nRT}{N}}$

5) $\frac{1}{2}m(c_{rms})^2$ is the average kinetic energy of a particle.

6) You can substitute Nk for nR, where k is the Boltzmann constant (see page 112) to show that the average kinetic energy of a particle is directly proportional to T (absolute temperature). $\boxed{\frac{1}{2}m(c_{rms})^2 = \frac{3}{2}kT}$

   You can use $\frac{3}{2}kT$ as an approximation for the average kinetic energy of the molecules in any substance.

7) Finally, the Boltzmann constant is equivalent to R/N_A (see p.112), so you can substitute this for k in the equation above, to get: $\boxed{\frac{1}{2}m(c_{rms})^2 = \frac{3}{2}\frac{RT}{N_A}}$

The Gas Laws are Empirical, Kinetic Theory is Theoretical

1) **Empirical laws** are based on **observations** and **evidence**.
   This means that they can **predict what will happen** but they **don't explain why**.

2) For example, the **gas laws** (page 110) and the **ideal gas** equation (page 112) are all based on **observations** of how a gas responds to changes in its environment. They were discovered by scientists making **direct observations** of the gases' **properties** and can be **proven** with **simple experiments**.

3) **Kinetic theory** (pages 114-115) is based on **theory** — the clue is in the name.
   This means it's based on **assumptions** and **derivations** from **knowledge** and **theories** we already had.

Our Understanding of Gases has Developed over Thousands of Years

Our knowledge and understanding of gases has **changed significantly** over time. The gas laws in this section (see p.110) were developed by lots of different scientists over **thousands of years**.

1) **Ancient Greek** and **Roman philosophers** including **Democritus** had ideas about gases **2000 years ago**, some of which were quite close to what we now know to be true.

2) **Robert Boyle** discovered the relationship between **pressure** and **volume** at a constant temperature in **1662** — this is Boyle's law (page 110).

3) This was followed by **Charles's law** (p.110) in **1787** when **Jacques Charles** discovered that the **volume** of a gas is proportional to **temperature** at a constant pressure.

4) The **pressure law** (p.110) was discovered by **Guillaume Amontons** in **1699**, who noticed that at a constant volume, **temperature** is proportional to **pressure**. It was then **re-discovered** much later by **Joseph Louis Gay-Lussac** in **1809**.

5) In the **18th century** a physicist called **Daniel Bernoulli** explained Boyle's Law by assuming that gases were made up of tiny particles — the beginnings of **kinetic theory**. But it took another couple of hundred years before kinetic theory became widely accepted.

6) **Robert Brown** discovered **Brownian motion** in **1827**, which helped support kinetic theory — see next page.

Thanks for calling the scientific community, please hold while we validate your ideas for 2000 years.

Kinetic Energy and the Development of Theories

Scientific **Ideas Aren't** Accepted **Immediately**

You might have thought that when Bernoulli published his work on kinetic theory (see previous page) everyone would **immediately agree** with it. Not so. The scientific community **only** accepts new ideas when they can be **independently validated** — that is, other people can reach the **same conclusions**. Otherwise anyone could make up **any old nonsense**.

In the case of kinetic theory, most physicists thought it was just a **useful hypothetical model** and atoms **didn't really exist**. It wasn't until the **1900s**, when Einstein was able to use kinetic theory to make predictions for Brownian motion, that **atomic** and **kinetic theory** became **widely accepted**.

I hereby postulate that the Moon is made of cheese.

Brownian Motion Supports **Kinetic Theory**

1) In 1827, botanist Robert Brown noticed that pollen grains in water moved with a **zigzag**, **random motion**.

2) This type of movement of any particles suspended in a fluid is known as **Brownian motion**. It **supports** the **kinetic particle theory** of the different states of matter. It says that the random motion is a result of **collisions** with **fast, randomly-moving** particles in the fluid.

3) You can see this when **large, heavy** particles (e.g. smoke) are moved with Brownian motion by **smaller, lighter** particles (e.g. air) travelling at **high speeds** — it is why smoke particles in air appear to **move around randomly** when you observe them in the lab.

4) This is **evidence** that the air is made up of **tiny atoms** or **molecules** moving **really quickly**.

5) So Brownian motion really helped the idea that everything is made from atoms **gain acceptance** from the **scientific community**.

A strong Brownian motion generator (with biscuits)

Warm-Up Questions

Q1 Give an equation linking absolute temperature and average kinetic energy.

Q2 What happens to the average kinetic energy of a particle if the temperature of a gas doubles?

Q3 Discuss the differences between theories and empirical laws.

Q4 Describe how our knowledge and understanding of the behaviour of gases has evolved over time.

Exam Questions

Q1 The mass of one mole of nitrogen molecules is 2.80×10^{-2} kg. There are 6.02×10^{23} molecules in one mole. Calculate the typical speed of a nitrogen molecule at 308 K. $k = 1.38 \times 10^{-23}$ JK^{-1}. [4 marks]

Q2 Some air freshener is sprayed at one end of a room. The room is 8.19 m long and the temperature is 21.2 °C.

a) Assuming the average air freshener molecule moves at 395 ms^{-1}, calculate how long it would take for a particle to travel directly to the other end of the room. [1 mark]

b) The perfume from the air freshener only slowly diffuses from one end of the room to the other. Explain why this takes much longer than suggested by your answer to part a). Include reference to Brownian motion in your answer. [3 marks]

Make your own Brownian motion — mix some greenian and redian motion...

This topic has it all. Lovely little equations, a couple of handy definitions, a brief historical interlude and even a cuppa. Ooh, don't mind if I do. Mine's white with two sugars please. And have you got any of those little jammy biscuits? Ta. Right, you'd best get learning this now. Make sure you can handle the equations — don't get caught out in the exam.

Extra Exam Practice

Hasta la vista <u>Section 8</u>... almost — here's a mix of questions from this section for you to have a crack at.

- Have a look at this example of how to answer a tricky exam question.
- Then check how much you've understood from Section 8 by having a go at the questions on the next page.

1   A student is carrying out an experiment to find the value of absolute zero in °C. The apparatus he uses is shown in **Figure 1**. When the air in the sealed syringe is heated using the electric heater, the plunger moves until the pressure inside the syringe is the same as the air pressure outside the syringe. The student initially measures the air's volume (V) and temperature (T). He finds the initial temperature is 20 °C. The student then heats the air by 10 °C, turns off the heater and waits for the plunger to stop moving, before recording V and T again. This process is repeated until $T = 70$ °C.

Figure 1

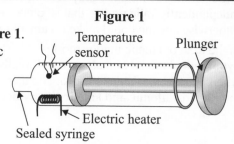

The student repeats the experiment at a low pressure, by placing the entire apparatus in a bell jar and reducing the pressure outside of the syringe. **Table 1** shows the value of absolute zero calculated from the results of each experiment.

Table 1

Experiment	Experimental value of absolute zero
Using air at atmospheric pressure	$-325\,(\pm 45)$ °C
Using air at a low pressure	$-283\,(\pm 28)$ °C

Explain how the student could have used his measurements to calculate experimental values for absolute zero, and discuss the validity of the results obtained. Compare the accuracy of the two values, and use your knowledge of kinetic theory to suggest why they may differ from each other.

(6 marks)

The question asks you to explain the experimental method, so you'll need to link your description to scientific theory.

If a question asks you to discuss, make sure you give points outlining both sides of the argument.

It's a good idea to say what the actual value of absolute zero is, as it allows you to quantify any statements you make about the accuracy of the results.

1

The experiment uses a fixed mass of gas at a constant pressure, so the **gas should obey Charles's Law.** This states that the volume of a gas (V) is directly proportional to its temperature in kelvin (T), so at absolute zero ($T = 0$ K), $V = 0$ cm³. The student could have plotted a graph of V (cm³) against T (°C). He could then have drawn a **line of best fit** through the points and **extrapolated** this line backwards to find the temperature at which the volume is 0 cm³.

A valid result answers the original question. Charles's law only applies when the number of moles of gas and the pressure are constant. The student controls these variables by using a sealed syringe, and allowing the gas pressure to equilibrate with the surroundings before measuring its volume, so **the experimental data is valid.** However, to obtain a value for absolute zero, the student has to make a large extrapolation, using experimental data that covers a much smaller temperature range. **This makes the values of absolute zero less valid**, as the relationship between V and T cannot be assumed to hold to very low temperatures.

Absolute zero is −273 °C. This value lies within the range of uncertainty of the low pressure experiment, but not that of the experiment conducted at atmospheric pressure. The low pressure experiment is therefore more accurate (it gives a value closer to the true value). **Kinetic theory explains absolute zero in terms of an ideal gas.** It's assumed that there are no forces acting between particles of an ideal gas except during collisions. Boyle's law states that at lower pressures, a set number of particles at the same temperature will occupy a larger volume. This means they will be further apart, so the forces between them will be smaller. The air in the low pressure experiment will therefore behave more like an ideal gas than at atmospheric pressure, so its value of absolute zero is more accurate.

You could also sketch a graph to help illustrate your written answer.

If you're asked about validity, you should comment on the control variables of the experiment, as well as any assumptions that may have been made.

Make sure you clearly link your answer to the question.

Extra Exam Practice

2 A fixed mass of crushed ice is placed in a funnel. At the point at which the ice begins to melt, an electric heater is placed in the ice and turned on, and the funnel is placed over a measuring cylinder. After 500.0 s, the mass of water in the measuring cylinder is measured. The experiment is carried out twice with the same initial mass of ice, but with the heater set to a different power each time. Both experiments were carried out in a laboratory at room temperature (20.0 °C). The results of the experiment are shown in **Table 2**.

Table 2

Experiment	Power of heater (W)	Operating temperature of heater (°C)	Time the heater was on for (s)	Mass of ice collected in measuring cylinder (g)
1	36.0	150.0	500.0	76.3
2	50.0	210.0	500.0	97.3

2.1 The rate of heat transfer between the ice and the room is directly proportional to the difference in temperature between them. Use the results in **Table 2** and your knowledge of thermal energy transfers to calculate an experimental value for the latent heat of fusion of water.

(3 marks)

If the heater is not sealed properly, water can leak inside. If the heater is then switched on, it will rapidly heat the water to form water vapour. This rapidly increases the pressure in the heater, which could cause it to explode.

2.2 In a previous experiment, 0.21 mg of water leaked into a cavity in the heater. The volume of the cavity is 0.10 cm³. Calculate the maximum additional internal pressure that the water could exert on the heater when the heater is used in experiment 1. (The relative molecular mass of water is 18. $R = 8.31 \, \text{J} \, \text{mol}^{-1} \text{kg}^{-1}$.)

(2 marks)

2.3 Calculate the root mean square speed of the molecules of water vapour at this maximum pressure.

(2 marks)

2.4 Explain why the root mean square speed of the vapour particles will be slower than the speed calculated in **2.3**.

(3 marks)

2.5 Using the kinetic theory of gases, explain why the heater is more likely to explode in experiment 2 than in experiment 1, if the same mass of water had initially leaked inside the heater and the heater was then turned on.

(4 marks)

3 A waitress warms a pot of milk for a coffee by passing steam through it. The steam condenses in the milk to form hot water and cools, transferring thermal energy to the milk.

3.1 The steam has a temperature of 100.0 °C. Calculate the mass of steam needed to warm 225 g of milk from 7.5 °C to 80.0 °C. The specific heat capacity of milk is $3.93 \times 10^3 \, \text{J} \, \text{kg}^{-1} \text{K}^{-1}$. The specific heat capacity of water is $4.20 \times 10^3 \, \text{J} \, \text{kg}^{-1} \text{K}^{-1}$. The latent heat of vaporisation of water is $2.26 \times 10^6 \, \text{J} \, \text{kg}^{-1}$. You may assume there is no heat transferred to the surroundings.

(3 marks)

3.2 The waitress sprinkles some cocoa powder on top of the coffee. Describe the motion of the cocoa particles on the surface of the coffee, and explain how this will change as the coffee cools.

(3 marks)

Gravitational Fields

*Gravity's all about masses **attracting** each other. If the Earth didn't have a **gravitational field**, apples wouldn't fall to the ground and you'd probably be floating off into space instead of sitting here reading this page...*

A **Gravitational Field** is a **Force Field**

1) A **force field** is a **region** where an object will experience a **non-contact force**.

2) Force fields cause **interactions** between objects or particles — e.g. between **static** or **moving charges** (p. 126), or in the case of gravity, between **masses**.

3) Any object with mass will **experience an attractive force** if you put it in the **gravitational field** of another object.

Tides are caused by gravitational fields.

4) Only objects with a **large** mass, such as stars and planets, have a significant effect. E.g. the effects of the gravitational fields of the **Moon** and the **Sun** are noticeable here on Earth — they're the main cause of our **tides**.

You can Draw **Lines of Force** to Show the **Field** Around an Object

Force fields can be represented as **vectors**, showing the **direction** of the force they would exert on an object placed in that field. **Gravitational field lines** (or "**lines of force**") are arrows showing the **direction of the force** that masses would feel in a gravitational field. Simply look at the direction the arrows are pointing to find the direction of the force — easy.

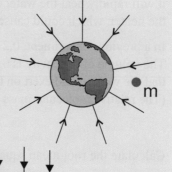

1) If you put a small mass, ***m***, anywhere in the Earth's gravitational field, it will always be attracted **towards** the Earth.

2) The Earth's gravitational field is **radial** — the lines of force meet at the centre of the Earth.

3) If you move mass *m* further away from the Earth — where the **lines** of force are **further apart** — the **force** it experiences **decreases**.

4) The small mass, *m*, has a gravitational field of its own. This doesn't have a noticeable effect on the Earth though, because the Earth is so much **more massive**.

5) Close to the Earth's surface, the field is (almost) uniform — the **field lines** are (almost) **parallel** and **equally spaced**.

You can **Calculate Forces** Using **Newton's Law of Gravitation**

The **force** experienced by an object in a gravitational field is always **attractive**. It's a **vector** which depends on the **masses** involved and the **distances** between them. It's easy to work this out for **point masses** — or objects which behave as if all their mass is concentrated at the centre, e.g. uniform spheres. You just put the numbers into this equation...

Newton's Law of Gravitation:

$$F = \frac{Gm_1m_2}{r^2}$$

F is the magnitude of the gravitational force between masses m_1 and m_2.
G is the gravitational constant — 6.67×10^{-11} Nm^2kg^{-2}.
r is the distance (in metres) between the centres of the two masses.

The diagram shows the force acting on m_1 due to m_2. (The force on m_2 due to m_1 is equal but in the opposite direction.)

The law of gravitation is an **inverse square law** so:

1) If the distance *r* between the masses **increases** then the force *F* will **decrease**.

$$F \propto \frac{1}{r^2}$$

If you're trying to estimate the gravitational force between objects, remember their distance has a bigger impact than their mass.

2) If the **distance doubles** then the **force** will be one **quarter** the strength of the original force.

Gravitational Fields

The **Field Strength** is the **Force per Unit Mass**

Gravitational field strength, *g*, is the **force per unit mass**. Its value depends on **where you are** in the field.
There's a really simple equation for working it out:

$$g = \frac{F}{m}$$

g has units of newtons per kilogram (Nkg^{-1})

The **value** of *g* at the **Earth's surface** is approximately **9.81 Nkg^{-1}** (or 9.81 ms^{-2}).

1) *F* is the force experienced by a mass *m* when it's placed in the gravitational field.
   Divide *F* by *m* and you get the force per unit mass.

2) *g* is a vector quantity, always pointing towards the centre of the mass whose field you're describing.

3) Since the gravitational field is almost uniform at the Earth's surface, you can assume
   g is a constant (as long as you don't go too high above the Earth's surface).

4) *g* is just the acceleration of a mass in a gravitational field. It's often called the acceleration due to gravity.

In a **Radial Field**, *g* is **Inversely Proportional** to *r*²

Point masses have **radial** gravitational fields (see previous page).
The **magnitude** of *g* depends on the distance *r* from the point mass *M*.

$$g = \frac{GM}{r^2}$$

where *g* is the gravitational field strength (Nkg^{-1}),
G is the gravitational constant (6.67 × 10^{-11} Nm^{2}kg^{-2}),
M is a point mass (kg)
and *r* is the distance from the centre (m).

And it's an **inverse square law** again — as *r* increases, *g* decreases.

If you plot a graph of *g* against *r* for the **Earth**, you get a curve like this.

It shows that *g* is greatest at the surface of the Earth, but decreases rapidly
as *r* increases and you move further away from the centre of the Earth.

R$_E$ is the **radius** of the Earth.

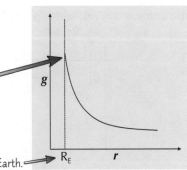

Warm-Up Questions

Q1 What is a force field?

Q2 Draw the gravitational field lines for a uniform spherical mass.

Q3 Draw the direction of the force acting on the Moon caused by the Earth. Assume they're both uniform spheres.

Q4 Write down Newton's law of gravitation.

Q5 Sketch a graph of distance from mass (*r*) against gravitational field strength (*g*) for a point mass.

Exam Questions

Q1 The Earth's radius is approximately 6400 km. The mass of the Sun is 1.99 × 10^{30} kg.
The average distance from the Earth to the Sun is 1.5 × 10^{11} m.

a) Estimate the mass of the Earth (*use g = 9.81 Nkg^{-1} at the Earth's surface*). [2 marks]

b) Estimate the force of gravitational attraction between the Sun and the Earth. [2 marks]

Q2 The Moon has a mass of 7.35 × 10^{22} kg and a radius of 1740 km.
Calculate the force acting on a 25 kg mass on the Moon's surface. [2 marks]

Q3 Two planets, A and B, have gravitational fields such that an object placed three quarters of the way along from A to
B will experience no net force due to gravity. Which option correctly describes the mass, M$_B$ of planet B, in terms of
the mass of planet A, M$_A$? Assume no other gravitational fields are present.

A $\frac{1}{9}$ M$_A$ B $\frac{9}{16}$ M$_A$ C $\frac{1}{3}$ M$_A$ D $\frac{3}{4}$ M$_A$ [1 mark]

If you're really stuck, put 'Inverse Square Law'...

Clever chap, Newton, but famously tetchy. He got into fights with other physicists, mainly over planetary motion and calculus... the usual playground squabbles. Then he spent the rest of his life trying to turn scrap metal into gold. Weird.

Gravitational Potential

Gravitational potential is all to do with the energy something has based on where it is in a gravitational field.

Gravitational Potential is Potential Energy per Unit Mass

The **gravitational potential**, **V**, at a point is the **gravitational potential energy** that a **unit mass** at that point would have. For example, if a **1 kg** mass has **−62.5 MJ of potential energy** at a point **Z**, then the **gravitational potential at Z is −62.5 MJkg⁻¹**. The reason the potential energy is **negative** is covered below.

In a **radial field** (like the Earth's), the equation for gravitational potential is:

$$V = -\frac{GM}{r}$$

V is gravitational potential (Jkg⁻¹), *G* is the gravitational constant, *M* is the mass of the object causing the gravitational field (kg), and *r* is the distance from the centre of the object (m).

Gravitational potential is **negative** on the **surface** of the mass and **increases with distance** from the mass. You can think of this **negative energy** as being caused by you having to **do work against** the **gravitational field** to move an object out of it. This means that the gravitational potential at an **infinite distance** from the mass will be **zero**. **Gravitational potential energy** is also negative — you might have worked out positive values in the past (from *mgh*) but this is just the **gain** in potential energy. Potential energy becomes **less negative** as the object moves upwards.

Gravitational field strength, *g*, can be calculated from the amount the **gravitational potential**, *V*, varies with **distance**, *r*.

$$g = \frac{-\Delta V}{\Delta r}$$

You can see this relationship by plotting graphs of *V* against *r* and *g* against *r*:

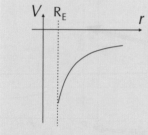

If you find the **gradient** of this graph at a particular **point**, you get the value of *g* at that point.

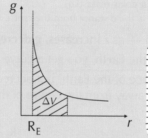

If you find the **area** under this graph it gives you the change in gravitational potential, Δ*V*.

Remember you can estimate the area below this curve by counting squares (if it's plotted on squared paper) or by splitting it into trapeziums and adding together the areas of each trapezium.

To Escape a Gravitational Field, a Mass Must Travel at the Escape Velocity

The **escape velocity** is defined as the velocity at which an object's **kinetic energy** is **equal** to minus its **gravitational potential energy**. This means the **total energy** is **zero**. The formula for it is:

$$v = \sqrt{\frac{2GM}{r}}$$

v is escape velocity (ms⁻¹)

Deriving Escape Velocity

1) First, **multiply** *V* (the gravitational potential energy per unit mass) by a mass *m* to get the **gravitational potential energy**.

2) Then, as you know total energy is zero: $\frac{1}{2}mv^2 - \frac{GMm}{r} = 0$ so $\frac{1}{2}mv^2 = \frac{GMm}{r}$

3) **Cancel** out *m*: $\frac{1}{2}v^2 = \frac{GM}{r}$

4) **Rearrange** for velocity, *v*: $v^2 = \frac{2GM}{r} \longrightarrow v = \sqrt{\frac{2GM}{r}}$

The escape velocity is the same for all masses in the same gravitational field.

Example: Find the escape velocity from the Earth's surface. Mass of Earth = 5.98 × 10²⁴ kg, radius of Earth = 6.37 × 10⁶ m and *G* = 6.67 × 10⁻¹¹ Nm²kg⁻². Simply substitute in the given values:

$$v = \sqrt{\frac{2GM}{r}} = \sqrt{\frac{2 \times 6.67 \times 10^{-11} \times 5.98 \times 10^{24}}{6.37 \times 10^6}} = 11\,190.7... = \mathbf{11\,200\ ms^{-1}}\ \textbf{(to 3 s.f.)}$$

This means you'd have to throw a ball upwards at 11.2 km/s for it to fully escape Earth's pull. That's probably faster than you can manage.

Gravitational Potential

Gravitational Potential Difference is the Energy Needed to Move a Unit Mass

Two points at different distances from a mass will have **different** gravitational potentials (because gravitational potential increases with distance) — this means that there is a **gravitational potential difference** between these two points.

When you **move** an object you do **work** against the force of **gravity** — the **amount of energy** you need depends on the **mass** of the object and the **gravitational potential difference** you move it through:

$$\Delta W = m\Delta V$$

where ΔW is the work done (J), m is the mass of the object (kg) and ΔV is the gravitational potential difference (Jkg^{-1}).

A short derivation of this is on p. 129.

Equipotentials Show All Points of Equal Potential in a Field

1) **Equipotentials** are **lines** (in 2D) and **surfaces** (in 3D) that join all of the points with the **same potential**, V.

2) This means as you travel along an equipotential, your potential doesn't change — you **don't lose or gain energy**.

3) This means that for the journey the **gravitational potential difference**, $\Delta V = 0$.

4) As $\Delta W = m\Delta V$, this means that the amount of **work done** is also **zero**.

5) For a uniform spherical mass (you can usually assume the Earth's one) the equipotentials are **spherical surfaces**.

6) **Equipotentials** and **field lines** are **perpendicular**.

Equipotentials of −60, −50 and −40 $MJkg^{-1}$ around Earth.

Warm-Up Questions

Q1 What is gravitational potential? Write an equation for it.

Q2 Write down the equation linking gravitational field strength and gravitational potential.

Q3 What quantity does the gradient of a tangent to the curve of a V-r graph represent?

Q4 Describe how you would find the change in gravitational potential between two points in a gravitational field from a graph of g against r for the field.

Q5 Write down the equation for escape velocity.

Q6 What is an equipotential surface?

Exam Question

$G = 6.67 \times 10^{-11}\ Nm^2kg^{-2}$

Q1 A 300 kg probe is sent to the asteroid Juno to collect rock samples before returning to Earth. Juno has a mass of 2.67×10^{19} kg.

a) The gravitational potential, V, at the surface of the asteroid is -1.52×10^4 Jkg^{-1}. At a point 1.54 km above the surface, V is -1.50×10^4 Jkg^{-1}. Calculate the value of g at the surface of the asteroid, assuming it is constant across this range. [2 marks]

b) Calculate the radius of the asteroid Juno. [2 marks]

c) Calculate the speed at which an object would need to be launched from the surface of Juno for it to fully escape Juno's gravitational field. [1 mark]

d) Calculate the work done by the probe as it travels from the surface to a point 2020 m above the surface. [3 marks]

With enough work you have the potential for brilliance...

So quite a lot of new stuff here, but hopefully you can see how everything links together. It's all to do with energy — you do work to change your gravitational potential energy or you do none and merrily travel along an equipotential. Just remember the few simple formulas and once you've got the basic info like radius and mass, you're set.

Orbits and Gravity

Any object travelling with a circular or elliptical path around something is said to be in orbit.

The **Period** and **Radius** of an **Orbit** are Related

Any object undergoing **circular motion** (e.g. a satellite) is kept in its path by a **centripetal force**. What causes this force depends on the object — in the case of satellites it's the **gravitational attraction** of the mass they're orbiting. This means that, in this case the centripetal force is the gravitational force.

The force acting on an object in circular motion (p. 99) is given by:

$$F = \frac{mv^2}{r}$$

The force of attraction due to gravity between two objects with masses m and M (p. 120) is given by:

$$F = \frac{GMm}{r^2}$$

Make the two equations equal each other and rearrange to find the speed, v, of a satellite in a gravitational field:

$$\frac{mv^2}{r} = \frac{GMm}{r^2} \Rightarrow v^2 = \frac{GMmr}{r^2 m} \Rightarrow v = \sqrt{\frac{GM}{r}}$$

So the speed of a satellite is inversely proportional to the square root of its orbital radius, or $v \propto \frac{1}{\sqrt{r}}$.

The time taken for a satellite to make one orbit is called the orbital period, T.
Remember, speed $= \frac{\text{distance}}{\text{time}}$, and the distance for a circular orbit is $2\pi r$, so $v = \frac{2\pi r}{T}$. Rearrange for T:

$$v = \frac{2\pi r}{T} \Rightarrow T = \frac{2\pi r}{v}$$

Then substitute the expression for v found above and rearrange:

$$T = \frac{2\pi r}{v} = \frac{2\pi r}{\left(\sqrt{\frac{GM}{r}}\right)} = \frac{2\pi r \sqrt{r}}{\sqrt{GM}}$$

To make it a bit easier to deal with, square both sides:

$$T^2 = \frac{2^2 \pi^2 r^2 r}{GM} = \frac{4\pi^2 r^3}{GM}$$

This leads to the relationship: $\boxed{T^2 \propto r^3 \text{ (Period squared is proportional to the radius cubed)}}$

You Can **Solve Problems** About **Orbital Radius** and **Period**

Example: Planets A and B are orbiting the same star. Planet A has an orbital radius of 8.0×10^{10} m and a period of 18 hours. Planet B has an orbital radius of 1.0×10^{12} m. Calculate the orbital period of planet B in hours.

As $T^2 \propto r^3$, this means $\frac{T^2}{r^3} = $ constant. So $\frac{T_A^2}{r_A^3} = \frac{T_B^2}{r_B^3}$ so $T_B^2 = \frac{T_A^2 r_B^3}{r_A^3}$

$$T_B = \sqrt{\frac{T_A^2 r_B^3}{r_A^3}} = \sqrt{\frac{(18 \times 60 \times 60)^2 \times (1.0 \times 10^{12})^3}{(8.0 \times 10^{10})^3}}$$

$$= \sqrt{8.20125 \times 10^{12}} = 2\,863\,782.46480... \text{ s}$$

$2\,863\,782.46480... \div 3600 = 795.4851...$ hours = **800 hours (to 2 s.f.)**

Orbits and Gravity

The **Energy** of an **Orbiting Satellite** is **Constant**

An orbiting **satellite** has **kinetic** and **potential energy** — its **total energy** (i.e. kinetic + potential) is always **constant**.

1) In a **circular orbit**, a satellite's **speed** and **distance** above the mass it's orbiting are **constant**. This means that its **kinetic energy** and **potential energy** are also both **constant**.

2) In an **elliptical orbit**, a satellite will **speed up** as its **height decreases** (and slow down as its height increases). This means that its **kinetic energy increases** as its **potential energy decreases** (and vice versa), so the **total energy** remains **constant**.

When calculating gravitational potential, remember that r is from the centre of the orbit, not the height above the surface.

Geostationary Satellites Orbit the Earth once in **24 hours**

1) A **synchronous** orbit is one where the **orbital period** of the orbiting object is the **same** as the **rotational period** of the orbited object.

2) **Geostationary** satellites are a type of synchronous orbit — they're always above the **same point on Earth**.

3) To do this they must always be **directly above** the **equator** — i.e. their **plane** of orbit follows the Earth's equator.

4) A geostationary satellite travels at the **same angular speed as the Earth** turns below it.

5) Their orbit takes exactly **one day**.

6) Their **orbital radius** is about **42 000 km** — about 36 000 km above the **surface** of Earth.

7) These satellites are really useful for sending TV and telephone signals — the satellite is **stationary** relative to a certain point on the **Earth**, so you don't have to alter the angle of your receiver (or transmitter) to keep up.

Low Orbit Satellites Orbit Below 2000 km **Above** the **Earth's Surface**

1) **Low orbiting satellites** are defined as any satellites which orbit between **180-2000 km** above Earth.

2) Satellites designed for low earth orbits are **cheaper** to launch and require less powerful **transmitters** as they're closer to Earth.

3) This makes them useful for **communications**. However, their proximity to Earth and relatively **high orbital speed** means you need multiple satellites **working together** to maintain constant coverage.

4) Low orbit satellites are close enough to see the Earth's surface in a **high level** of detail. **Imaging** satellites are usually placed in this type of orbit and are used for things like **spying** and monitoring the **weather**.

5) Their orbits usually lie in a **plane** that includes the **north** and **south pole**.

6) Each orbit is over a **new** part of the Earth's surface as the Earth rotates underneath — so the **whole** of the Earth can be scanned.

Warm-Up Questions

Q1 Derive the relationship between the period and radius of an orbit.

Q2 The International Space Station orbits the Earth with velocity v. If another vehicle docks with it, increasing its mass, what difference, if any, does this make to the speed or radius of the orbit?

Q3 Compare the advantages and disadvantages of geostationary and low orbit satellites.

Exam Questions

Q1 Which of the following correctly describes a satellite's new velocity compared to its original velocity, v_o, if its orbital radius is doubled.

    A $0.25\,v_o$ B $0.64\,v_o$ C $0.71\,v_o$ D $2.0\,v_o$ [1 mark]

Q2 A satellite has an orbital period of 3 hours around a planet. The velocity of the satellite is then halved. Calculate the new orbital period.   [4 marks]

All this talk of orbits is putting my head in a spin...

When I hear the word 'satellite' I just think of man-made ones, e.g. for phones or TV, and tend to forget that moons are satellites too — don't make the same mistake. You're probably best off learning all the stuff about satellites and their orbits too, including the advantages of different types — just knowing what they are won't get you too far in the exam.

Electric Fields

Electric fields can be attractive or repulsive, so they're different from gravitational ones. It's all to do with charge.

There is an **Electric Field** around a **Charged Object**

Any object with **charge** has an **electric field** around it — the region where it can attract or repel other charges.

1) Electric charge, Q, is measured in **coulombs** (C) and can be either positive or negative.
2) **Oppositely** charged particles **attract** each other. **Like** charges **repel**.
3) If a **charged object** is placed in an electric field, then it will experience a **force**.
4) If the charged object is a **sphere**, you can assume all of its **charge** is at its **centre**.
5) Just like with gravitational fields, **electric fields** can be represented by **field lines**.

Electric fields are force fields (p. 120) where charged objects will experience a non-contact force.

You can **Calculate Forces** using **Coulomb's Law**

Coulomb's law gives the force of attraction or repulsion between two **point charges** in a **vacuum**:

$$F = \frac{1}{4\pi\varepsilon_0}\frac{Q_1 Q_2}{r^2}$$

ε_0 ("epsilon-nought") is the **permittivity of free space** and is equal to 8.85×10^{-12} Fm^{-1},
Q_1 and Q_2 are the **charges**,
r is the **distance** between Q_1 and Q_2.

This unit is a 'farad per metre' — see p.132.

1) The force on Q_1 is always **equal** and **opposite** to the force on Q_2 — the **direction** depends on the charges.

If the charges are **opposite** then the force is **attractive**.
F will be **negative**.

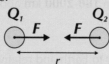

If Q_1 and Q_2 are **alike** then the force is **repulsive**.
F will be **positive**.

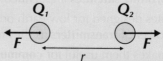

2) Coulomb's law is an **inverse square law**.
The **further apart** the charges, the **weaker** the force between them.

3) If the point charges aren't in a vacuum, then the size of the force F also depends on the **permittivity**, ε, of the material between them. **Air** can be treated as a **vacuum** when using Coulomb's law.

Mr Allan liked to explain Coulomb's law using prairie dogs.

Electric Field Strength is Force per Unit Charge

Electric field strength, E, is defined as the **force per unit positive charge**.
It's the force that a charge of +1 C would experience if it was placed in the electric field.

F is the force on a 'test' charge Q

$$E = \frac{F}{Q}$$

where E is **electric field strength** (NC^{-1}), F is the **force** (N) and Q is the **charge** (C).

1) E is a **vector** pointing in the **direction** that a **positive charge** would **move**.
2) The units of E are **newtons per coulomb** (NC^{-1}).
3) Field strength depends on **where you are** in the field.
4) A **point charge** — or any body that behaves as if all its charge is concentrated at the centre — has a **radial** field.

The electric field lines around a charged sphere would look the same as for a point charge.

For a positive Q, the small positive 'test' charge q would be **repelled**, so the field lines point away from Q.

For a negative Q, the small positive charge q would be **attracted**, so the field lines point **towards** Q.

Section 9 — Gravitational and Electric Fields

Electric Fields

In a **Radial Field, *E*** is **Inversely Proportional** to *r²*

1) In a **radial field**, the electric field strength, **E**, depends on the distance **r** from the point charge **Q**:

$$E = \frac{1}{4\pi\varepsilon_0}\frac{Q}{r^2}$$

where *E* is the **electric field strength** (NC⁻¹),
ε_0 is the **permittivity of free space** (8.85×10^{-12} Fm⁻¹), *Q* is the **point charge** (C) and *r* is the **distance** from the point charge (m).

2) It's another **inverse square law**.

3) Field strength **decreases** as you go **further away** from *Q* — on a diagram, the **field lines** get **further apart**.

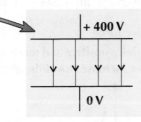

$$E \propto \frac{1}{r^2}$$

In a **Uniform Field, *E*** is **Inversely Proportional** to *d*

A **uniform field** can be produced by connecting two **parallel plates** to the opposite poles of a battery. The field strength, **E**, is the **same** at **all points** between the two plates.

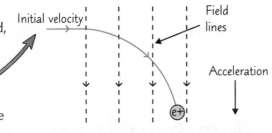

$$E = \frac{V}{d}$$

where *E* is the **electric field strength** (Vm⁻¹ or NC⁻¹), *V* is the **potential difference** between the plates (V) and *d* is the distance between them (m)

Uniform electric fields can be used to determine whether a particle is **charged** or not. The **path** of a charged particle moving through an electric field will **bend** — the **direction** depends on whether it's a positive or negative charge.

1) A charged particle that enters an electric field at **right angles** to the field feels a **constant force parallel** to the electric **field lines**.

2) If the particle is **positively** charged then the force acts on it in the **same direction** as the field lines. If it's **negatively** charged, the force is in the **opposite** direction to the field lines.

3) This causes the particle to **accelerate** at right angles to the particle's original **motion** — and so it follows a **curved** path (a **parabola**).

4) In a **3D** situation, the **motion** is the **same** (a parabola) as there are no other significant forces acting on the charged particle.

Warm-Up Questions

Q1 Write down Coulomb's law.

Q2 Sketch a radial electric field and a uniform electric field. How would you find *E* for each?

Q3 Sketch the path of an electron entering a uniform electric field at right angles to the field lines.

Exam Questions

Q1 An alpha particle (charge +2*e*) was deflected while passing through thin gold foil. The alpha particle passed within 5.0×10^{-12} m of a gold nucleus (charge +79*e*). What was the magnitude and direction of the electrostatic force experienced by the alpha particle? ($e = 1.60 \times 10^{-19}$ C) [4 marks]

Q2 a) Two parallel plates are connected to a 1500 V dc supply, and separated by an air gap of 4.5 mm. What is the electric field strength between the plates? State the direction of the field. [2 marks]

b) The plates are now pulled further apart so that the distance between them is doubled. The electric field strength remains the same. What is the new voltage between the plates? [1 mark]

Electric fields — one way to roast beef...

At least you get a choice here — uniform or radial, positive or negative, attractive or repulsive, chocolate or strawberry...

Electric Potential and Work Done

Some more about potential energy and doing work — but this time it's charges instead of masses.

Absolute Electric Potential is Potential Energy per Unit Charge

All points in an **electric field** have an **absolute electric potential**, *V*. This is the electric **potential energy** that a **unit positive charge** (+ 1 C) would have at that point. The **absolute electric potential** of a point depends on **how far** it is from the **charge** creating the **electric field** and the **size** of that charge.

In a **radial field**, **absolute electric potential** is given by:

$$V = \frac{1}{4\pi\varepsilon_0}\frac{Q}{r}$$

where *V* is absolute electric potential (V),
Q is the size of the charge (C)
and *r* is the distance from the charge (m).

1) The **sign** of *V* depends on the charge *Q* — i.e. *V* is **positive** when *Q* is positive and the force is **repulsive**, and **negative** when *Q* is negative and the force is **attractive**.

2) The **absolute magnitude** of *V* is **greatest** on the **surface of the charge**, and **decreases** as the **distance** from the charge **increases** — *V* will be **zero** at an **infinite distance** from the charge.

Repulsive force

V is initially **positive** and tends to **zero** as *r* increases towards **infinity**.

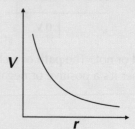

Attractive force

V is initially **negative** and tends to **zero** as *r* increases towards **infinity**.

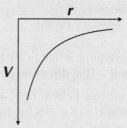

You can also find ΔV between two points from the **area** under a graph of *E* (see p.127) against *r*.

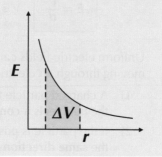

The **gradient** of a **tangent** to either graph gives the **field strength** at that point:

$$E = \frac{\Delta V}{\Delta r}$$

Electric Potential Difference is the Energy Needed to Move a Unit Charge

If **two points** in an **electric field** have different potential, then there is an **electric potential difference** between them. To **move a charge** across a **potential difference** (i.e. from one electric potential to another) you need to use **energy**.

The **amount of energy** you need (or the **work done**) depends on the **size** of the **charge** you're moving and the size of the **potential difference** you want to move it across:

$$Fd = Q\Delta V \quad \text{or} \quad \Delta W = Q\Delta V$$

where *F* is the force on the charge (N), *d* is the distance that the charge moves (m), *Q* is the charge being moved (C), ΔV is the electric potential difference (V) and ΔW is the work done (J).

Deriving the Formula for Work Done

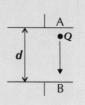

There are two parallel plates with a potential difference of ΔV across them, creating a **uniform electric field**.

1) The field strength is given by $E = \frac{F}{Q} = \frac{\Delta V}{d}$ (see p.126 and 127).

2) This rearranges to give the formula above, $Fd = Q\Delta V$.

3) To move a charge *Q* from A to B, the **work done** = force × distance moved = *Fd*. So $\Delta W = Fd$.

4) So the **work done** in moving a charge *Q* through a potential difference of ΔV is given by $\Delta W = Q\Delta V$.

Electric Potential and Work Done

You Can Also Derive Work Done for a Gravitational Field

At the **Earth's surface** the gravitational field is **uniform**.

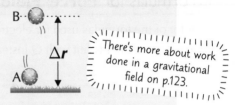

The field strength is $g = \dfrac{-\Delta V}{\Delta r} = \dfrac{F}{m}$

↗ *g in a uniform field*

↖ *g as force per unit mass*

which rearranges to give $m\Delta V = -F\Delta r$

F is negative because you're working against gravity

There's more about work done in a gravitational field on p.123.

1) To throw a ball m from A to B, the **work done** = **force** × **distance moved** = $m\Delta V$

2) So the energy needed to move a mass m against a gravitational potential difference is given by $m\Delta V$.

Equipotentials Show All Points of Equal Potential in a Field

1) Just like in **gravitational fields**, you find **equipotentials** (p.123) in electric fields too.

2) For a **point charge**, the equipotentials are **spherical surfaces**. Between **parallel plates**, the equipotentials are **flat planes**.

3) Remember, **no work** is done when you travel **along** an equipotential — an electric charge can travel along an equipotential without any **energy** being transferred.

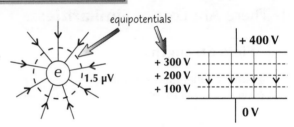

equipotentials

+ 400 V
+ 300 V
+ 200 V
+ 100 V
0 V

Warm-Up Questions

Q1 What is meant by 'absolute electric potential'? What value would it have at infinity?

Q2 How would you find the absolute electric potential in a radial field?

Q3 Sketch a graph of absolute electric potential against distance for an attractive and a repulsive charge.

Q4 What quantity does the area under the curve of a graph of E against r represent?

Q5 What is 'potential difference'?

Q6 Define the term 'equipotential'.

Q7 What shapes are the equipotentials in the electric field of a point charge?

PRACTICE QUESTIONS

Exam Questions

Q1 Calculate the absolute electric potential at a point 6.0×10^{-10} m from an electron.
($e = 1.60 \times 10^{-19}$ C, $\varepsilon_0 = 8.85 \times 10^{-12}$ Fm^{-1}) [2 marks]

Q2 Show how the formula for uniform electric field strength can be derived from $W = Q\Delta V$. [2 marks]

Q3 Two parallel charged plates form a uniform electric field, as shown in the diagram.

a) Calculate the work done in moving the electron from A to C. [1 mark]

b) Explain why no work is done if the electron moves from A to B. [1 mark]

+ 400 V
20 mm   A ---- B + 300 V
         30 mm
         C ---- + 100 V
0 V

I prefer gravitational fields — electric fields are repulsive...

Revising fields is a bit like a buy-one-get-one-free sale — you learn all about gravitational fields and they throw electric fields in for free. You just have to remember to change your ms for Qs and your Gs for 1/4πε₀s... okay, so it's not quite a BOGOF sale. Maybe more like a buy-one-get-one-half-price sale... anyway, you get the point — go learn some stuff.

Comparing Electric and Gravitational Fields

You might have thought a lot of the formulas from the last topic looked familiar —
electric and gravitational fields are more similar than you might think...

Formulas for **Force**, **Field Strength** and **Potential** All Have the Same Layout

A lot of the formulas used for electric fields are the same as those used for
gravitational fields but with Q instead of m (or M) and $\frac{1}{4\pi\varepsilon_0}$ instead of G.

	Gravitational Fields	Electric Fields
Force due to	$F = \dfrac{Gm_1m_2}{r^2}$	$F = \dfrac{1}{4\pi\varepsilon_0}\dfrac{Q_1Q_2}{r^2}$
Field strength	$g = \dfrac{GM}{r^2}$	$E = \dfrac{1}{4\pi\varepsilon_0}\dfrac{Q}{r^2}$
Potential	$V = -\dfrac{GM}{r}$	$V = \dfrac{1}{4\pi\varepsilon_0}\dfrac{Q}{r}$

Both have **inverse-square**
relationships with r.

There Are Lots of **Similarities**...

Field Strengths

Gravitational field strength, g, is
force per unit mass.

$$g = \frac{F}{m}$$

Electric field strength, E, is
force per unit positive charge.

$$E = \frac{F}{Q}$$

Field Lines

The gravitational
field lines for a point
mass point towards
the centre of mass.

The electric field lines
for a negative point
charge point towards
the centre of charge.

The gravitational field lines near the
surface of a large object are parallel lines.

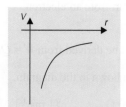

The electric field lines for a uniform field
between two parallel plates are parallel lines.

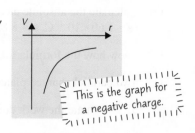

Potential

Gravitational potential, V,
is potential energy per unit
mass and is zero at infinity.

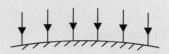

Absolute electric potential,
V, is potential energy per
unit positive charge and is
zero at infinity.

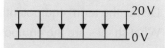

This is the graph for
a negative charge.

Equipotentials

The equipotentials for a **uniform spherical mass** and a **point charge** both form a **spherical surface**.

Work Done

Work done to move a unit mass
through a gravitational potential.

$$\Delta W = m\Delta V$$

Work done to move a unit charge
through an electric potential.

$$\Delta W = Q\Delta V$$

Comparing Electric and Gravitational Fields

... And One Important **Difference**

Although gravitational and electric fields are similar, they're not the same. The main thing to keep in mind is that gravitational forces are **always attractive**, whereas electric forces can be **attractive** or **repulsive**.

Comparing **Forces** at **Subatomic Levels**

When you get down to the subatomic level of electrons, protons and neutrons, the distances between particles becomes **tiny**. As both the gravitational and electrostatic forces have an **inverse square** relationship with **distance**, you'd expect these forces to be huge.

1) However, **gravity** at this level can pretty much be ignored. This is because although they're close together, all of the particles have incredibly **small masses** — the gravitational force at these distances is much **weaker** than the electrostatic force.

2) Thankfully, the nucleus doesn't break apart from all of this electrostatic **repulsion** — there are **other forces** at work (page 8).

Despite being small, Lola wouldn't be ignored.

Example: Two protons in a nucleus are 3.00 fm apart. Calculate the gravitational and electrostatic forces between them. $m_p = 1.67 \times 10^{-27}$ kg, $Q_{proton} = 1.6 \times 10^{-19}$ C, $\varepsilon_0 = 8.85 \times 10^{-12}$ Fm^{-1} and $G = 6.67 \times 10^{-11}$ m^{3}kg^{-1}s^{-2}.

Gravitational:

$$F = \frac{Gm_1m_2}{r^2} = \frac{6.67 \times 10^{-11} \times (1.67 \times 10^{-27})^2}{(3.00 \times 10^{-15})^2}$$

$$F = 2.066... = \mathbf{2.07 \times 10^{-35} \ N}$$

Electrostatic:

$$F = \frac{1}{4\pi\varepsilon_0}\frac{Q_1Q_2}{r^2} = \frac{(1.60 \times 10^{-19})^2}{4\pi \times 8.85 \times 10^{-12} \times (3.00 \times 10^{-15})^2}$$

$$F = 25.57... = \mathbf{25.6 \ N}$$

So here, the force on the protons due to electrostatic repulsion is **10^{36} times bigger** *than the force on the protons due to gravity.*

Warm-Up Questions

Q1 Write down the equations for the forces due to electric and gravitational fields. Comment on their relationship with distance.

Q2 Draw field lines to show the gravitational field for a point mass and the electric field for a negative point charge.

Q3 Draw the graphs of gravitational potential against distance and absolute electric potential against distance for a negative charge.

Q4 What are the values of gravitational and electric potential at infinity?

Q5 What do the equipotentials for a uniform spherical mass look like? How do they compare to the equipotentials of a point charge?

Q6 State one difference between gravitational and electric fields.

PRACTICE QUESTIONS

Exam Question

$e = 1.60 \times 10^{-19} C$, $m_e = 9.11 \times 10^{-31}$ kg, $\varepsilon_0 = 8.85 \times 10^{-12}$ Fm^{-1} and $G = 6.67 \times 10^{-11}$ Nm^{2}kg^{-2}

Q1 Two electrons are 8.00×10^{-10} m apart.

a) Compare the magnitude and direction of the gravitational and electric forces between them, supporting your comments with calculations. [4 marks]

b) Use your answer to a) to explain why gravitational forces can be ignored at a subatomic level. [1 mark]

Double the physics, double the fun — right?

Or maybe not, but it makes it a bit easier to remember all of this stuff. Get cracking and start learning all of this information, especially the stuff on subatomic particles, then reward yourself with a break before doing any more work.

Capacitors

Capacitors are things that store electrical charge — like a charge bucket. The capacitance of one of these things tells you how much charge the bucket can hold. Sounds simple enough... ha... ha, ha, ha...

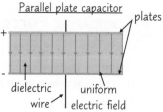

Capacitors Build Up Charge on Plates

1) A capacitor is an electrical component made up of two **conducting plates** separated by a **gap** or a **dielectric** (an insulating material, see below).

2) When a capacitor is connected to a **power source**, **positive** and **negative** charge build up on **opposite** plates, creating a uniform **electric field** between them (p.127).

3) The amount of **charge per unit potential difference** (voltage) stored by a capacitor is called its **capacitance**.

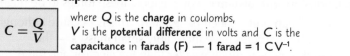

$$C = \frac{Q}{V}$$

where Q is the **charge** in coulombs, V is the **potential difference** in volts and C is the **capacitance** in **farads (F)** — 1 farad = 1 CV^{-1}.

Parallel plate capacitor

plates

dielectric wire   uniform electric field

4) A farad is a **huge** unit so you'll usually see capacitances expressed in terms of:

$$\mu F — \text{microfarads} \ (\times 10^{-6}) \quad nF — \text{nanofarads} \ (\times 10^{-9}) \quad pF — \text{picofarads} \ (\times 10^{-12})$$

You Can Increase Capacitance Using Dielectrics

1) **Permittivity** is a measure of how difficult it is to generate an **electric field** in a certain material.

2) The **relative permittivity** is the ratio of the permittivity of a material to the permittivity of free space:

$$\varepsilon_r = \frac{\varepsilon_1}{\varepsilon_0}$$

Where ε_r is the relative permittivity of material 1, ε_1 is the permittivity of material 1 in Fm^{-1}, ε_0 is the permittivity of free space.

3) Relative permittivity is sometimes also called the **dielectric constant**.

No charge is applied

1) Imagine a dielectric is made up of lots of polar molecules — they have a positive end and a negative end.

2) When no charge is stored by the capacitor, there is no electric field — so these molecules point in a bunch of random directions.

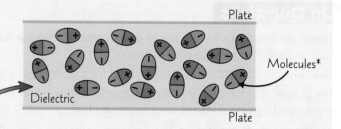

Plate

Molecules*

Dielectric

Plate

*Not to scale.

Charge is applied

1) When a charge is applied to a capacitor, an electric field is generated.

2) The negative ends of the molecules are attracted to the positively charged plate and vice versa.

3) This causes all of the molecules to rotate and align themselves with the electric field.

4) The molecules each have their own electric field, which in this alignment now opposes the applied electric field of the capacitor. The larger the permittivity, the larger this opposing field is.

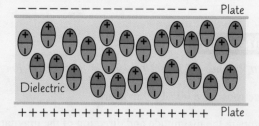

Plate

Dielectric

Plate

5) This reduces the overall electric field, which reduces the potential difference needed to charge the capacitor — so the capacitance increases.

You can calculate the capacitance of a capacitor using the **dimensions** of the capacitor and the **permittivity** of the **dielectric**:

$$C = \frac{A \varepsilon_0 \varepsilon_r}{d}$$

Where A is the **area** of the plates (m^2), ε_0 is the permittivity of **free space** (Fm^{-1}), ε_r is the **relative permittivity** of the dielectric and d is the **separation** of the plates (m).

Capacitors

Capacitors **Store Energy**

1) When **charge** builds up on the plates of a **capacitor**, **electrical energy** is **stored** by the capacitor.

2) You can find the **energy stored** in a capacitor from the **area** under a **graph** of **charge stored** against **potential difference** across the capacitor.

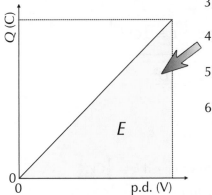

3) The potential difference across the capacitor is directly **proportional** to the charge stored on it, so the graph will be a **straight line** through the origin.

4) On this graph, the **energy stored** is given by the **yellow triangle**.

5) The greater the **capacitance**, the more **energy** is stored by the capacitor for a given potential difference.

6) **Area of a triangle = ½ × base × height** so the energy stored by the capacitor is:

$$E = \tfrac{1}{2}QV$$

Where E is the **energy stored** (J), Q is the **charge** on the capacitor (C) and V is the **potential difference** (V).

Samantha had heard there was energy stored on plates.

The gradient of a Q-V graph effectively gives the capacitance.

Warm-Up Questions

Q1 Define capacitance.

Q2 What is the relationship between charge, potential difference and capacitance?

Q3 What is the dielectric constant of a material also known as?

Q4 Describe and explain what happens to the molecules in a dielectric when they're exposed to an electric field.

Q5 Write down the formula for capacitance involving plate area, plate separation and permittivity.

Q6 How would you find the energy stored by a capacitor for a given potential difference from a graph of charge against potential difference?

Q7 Write down an equation that relates the energy stored in a capacitor to the charge it stores and the potential difference between its plates.

Exam Questions

Q1 The potential difference of a test circuit was measured as a capacitor was charged. The graph below was plotted from the recorded data.

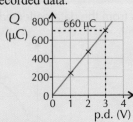

a) Explain what is meant by the term 'capacitance'. [1 mark]

b) Calculate the capacitance of the capacitor. [2 marks]

Q2 A capacitor with capacitance 137 pF is charged until it stores a charge of 2.47 nC and is then disconnected. It has a dielectric with a relative permittivity of 3.1. The dielectric is removed, so there is now a vacuum between the plates, but nothing else is changed. Calculate the change in potential difference across the capacitor. [4 marks]

Q3 A 8.0 μF capacitor is fully charged from a 12 V supply. Calculate the energy stored by the capacitor. [3 marks]

Capacitance — fun, it's not...

Capacitors are really useful in the real world. Pick an appliance, any appliance, and it'll probably have a capacitor or several. If I'm being honest, though, the only saving grace of these pages for me is that girl eating a plate...

Charging and Discharging

Charging and discharging — pushing electrons onto a capacitor, then letting them scamper off again.

There are **Three** Expressions for the **Energy Stored** by a Capacitor

When you charge a capacitor, you store energy on it. Starting from the energy equation on page 133, you can find two more.

$$E = \frac{1}{2}QV$$

$C = \frac{Q}{V}$, so $Q = CV$. Substitute this into the equation above and you get: $\boxed{E = \frac{1}{2}CV^2}$

$C = \frac{Q}{V}$, so $V = \frac{Q}{C}$. Substitute this into the first equation and you get: $\boxed{E = \frac{1}{2}\frac{Q^2}{C}}$

Example: A 900 µF capacitor is charged up to a potential difference of 240 V. Calculate the energy stored by the capacitor.

First, choose the best equation to use — you've been given V and C, so you need $E = \frac{1}{2}CV^2$.

Substitute the values in: $E = \frac{1}{2} \times (9 \times 10^{-4}) \times 240^2 = 25.92 = $ **30 J (to 1 s.f.)**

You can **Investigate** What Happens When you **Charge** a **Capacitor**

1) Set up the test circuit shown in the circuit diagram.

2) Close the switch to connect the **uncharged** capacitor to the dc power supply.

3) Let the capacitor **charge** whilst the **data logger** records both the **potential difference** (from the voltmeter) and the **current** (from the ammeter) over time.

4) When the current through the ammeter is **zero**, the capacitor is fully charged.

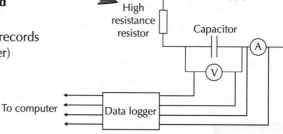

You Can Plot Graphs of **Current**, **Potential Difference** and **Charge** Against **Time**

You should be able to plot the following graphs from the data collected from this experiment:

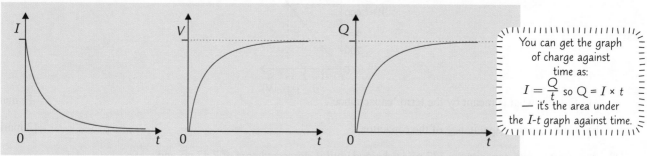

You can get the graph of charge against time as: $I = \frac{Q}{t}$ so $Q = I \times t$ — it's the area under the I-t graph against time.

Once a capacitor begins charging:

1) As soon as the switch closes, current starts to flow. The electrons flow onto the plate connected to the **negative terminal** of the dc power supply, so a **negative charge** builds up.

2) This build-up of negative charge **repels** electrons off the plate connected to the **positive terminal** of the power supply, making that plate positive. These electrons are attracted to the positive terminal of the power supply.

3) An **equal** but **opposite** charge builds up on each plate, causing a **potential difference** between the plates. Remember that **no charge** can flow **between** the plates because they're **separated** by an **insulator** (a vacuum, gap or dielectric).

4) As **charge** builds up on the plates, **electrostatic repulsion** makes it **harder** and **harder** for more electrons to be deposited. When the p.d. across the **capacitor** is equal to the p.d. across the **power supply**, the **current** falls to **zero**.

Charging and Discharging

To **Discharge** a Capacitor, **Remove** the **Power Supply** and **Close** the **Switch**

1) **Remove the power supply** from the test circuit on page 134 and close the **switch** to complete the circuit.

2) Let the capacitor **discharge** whilst the data logger records **potential difference** and **current** over time.

3) When the **current** through the ammeter and the **potential difference** across the plates are **zero**, the capacitor is fully discharged.

You can then plot graphs of current, potential difference and charge against time once more.

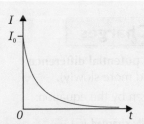 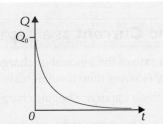 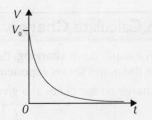

1) The current flows in the opposite direction from the charging current.

2) As the potential difference decreases, the current decreases as well.

3) When a capacitor is discharging, the amount of charge on and potential difference between the plates falls exponentially with time. That means it always takes the same length of time for the charge or potential difference to halve, no matter what value it starts at — like radioactive decay (see p.162).

4) The same is true for the amount of current flowing around the circuit.

Warm-Up Questions

Q1 Write down the three formulas for calculating the energy stored by a capacitor.

Q2 Describe how you could investigate how the potential difference across a charging capacitor varies with time.

Q3 Sketch graphs to show the variation of the current round the circuit and potential difference across the plates of a capacitor with time for: a) charging a capacitor, b) discharging a capacitor.

Q4 Explain the shape of the Q-t graph for a charging capacitor.

Exam Questions

Q1 A 250 µF capacitor is fully charged to 1.5 µC and then discharged through a fixed resistor.

a) Calculate the energy stored by the capacitor when it is fully charged. [1 mark]

b) Calculate the voltage of the battery used to charge the capacitor. [2 marks]

c) Sketch the graph of charge against time as the capacitor discharges. [1 mark]

Q2 The graph of current against time for a charging capacitor is shown on the right. Explain the shape of the graph. [1 mark]

Q3 The charge stored on a capacitor is kept constant while the potential difference across the plates is increased by a factor of two. Which of the following statements is true? [1 mark]

A The capacitance of the capacitor will increase.   B The energy stored by the capacitor will half.
C The energy stored by the capacitor will quadruple.   D The energy stored by the capacitor will remain the same.

An analogy — consider the lowly bike pump...

A good way to think of the charging process is like pumping air into a bike tyre. To start with, the air goes in easily, but as the pressure in the tyre increases, it gets harder and harder to squeeze any more air in. The tyre's 'full' when the pressure of the air in the tyre equals the pressure of the pump. The analogy works just as well for discharging...

More Charging and Discharging

Even more charging and discharging — now it's time for some fun exponential relationships.

The **Time Taken** to **Charge** or **Discharge** Depends on **Two Factors**

The **time** it takes to charge or discharge a capacitor depends on:

1) The **capacitance** of the capacitor (**C**). This affects the amount of **charge** that can be transferred at a given **potential difference**.

2) The **resistance** of the circuit (**R**). This affects the **current** in the circuit.

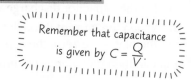
Remember that capacitance is given by $C = \frac{Q}{V}$.

You can Calculate **Charge**, **P.d.** and **Current** as a Capacitor **Charges**

1) When a capacitor is **charging**, the **growth rate** of the amount of **charge** on and **potential difference** across the plates shows **exponential decay** (so over time they increase more and more slowly).

2) The charge on the plates at a given time after a capacitor begins charging is given by the equation:

$$Q = Q_0\left(1 - e^{\frac{-t}{RC}}\right)$$

where Q_o is the **charge** of the capacitor when it's **fully charged** (C), t is **time since** charging began (s), R is the resistance (Ω) and C is the capacitance (F).

3) The potential difference between the plates at a given time is given by:

$$V = V_0\left(1 - e^{\frac{-t}{RC}}\right)$$

4) The **charging current** is different however, as it decreases exponentially — the formula to calculate the charging current at a given time is:

$$I = I_0 e^{\frac{-t}{RC}}$$

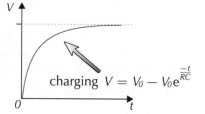
charging $V = V_0 - V_0 e^{\frac{-t}{RC}}$

You can do the Same for a **Discharging Capacitor**

1) Because the amount of **charge** left on the plates falls **exponentially with time** as a capacitor discharges, it always takes the **same length of time** for the charge to **halve**, no matter **how much charge** you start with.

2) The charge left on the plates at a given time after a capacitor begins discharging from being fully charged is given by the equation:

$$Q = Q_0 e^{\frac{-t}{RC}}$$

3) As the **potential difference** and **current** also decrease **exponentially** as a capacitor discharges, the formulas for calculating the current or potential difference at a certain time are similar:

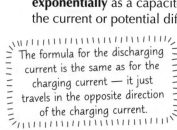
The formula for the discharging current is the same as for the charging current — it just travels in the opposite direction of the charging current.

$$I = I_0 e^{\frac{-t}{RC}}$$

$$V = V_0 e^{\frac{-t}{RC}}$$

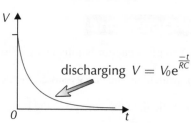
discharging $V = V_0 e^{\frac{-t}{RC}}$

Time Constant $\tau = RC$

τ is the Greek letter 'tau'

If $t = \tau = RC$ is put into the **discharging** equations above, then $Q = Q_0 e^{-1}$, $V = V_0 e^{-1}$ and $I = I_0 e^{-1}$.

So when $t = \tau$: $\dfrac{Q}{Q_0} = \dfrac{1}{e} \approx \dfrac{1}{2.718} \approx 0.37$

1) τ, the time constant, is the time taken for the charge, potential difference or current of a discharging capacitor to fall to 37% of its value when fully charged.

2) It's also the time taken for the charge or potential difference of a charging capacitor to rise to 63% of its value when fully charged.

3) So the larger the resistance in series with the capacitor, the longer it takes to charge or discharge.

4) In practice, the time taken for a capacitor to charge or discharge fully is taken to be about 5RC.

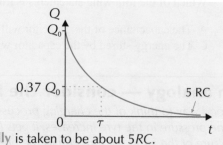

More Charging and Discharging

You Can **Find** the **Time Constant** from **Log-Linear** Graphs

Instead of using $\tau = RC$, you can create **log-linear graphs** from data (p.266) to find the time constant. Here **charge** is used, but this works for potential difference and current as well.

1) Starting from the equation for Q on a discharging capacitor, take the **natural log** of both sides and rearrange:

$$Q = Q_0 e^{\frac{-t}{RC}} \text{ becomes } \boxed{\ln(Q) = \left(\frac{-1}{RC}\right)t + \ln(Q_0)}$$

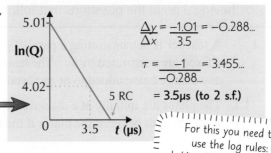

$$\frac{\Delta y}{\Delta x} = \frac{-1.01}{3.5} = -0.288...$$

$$\tau = \frac{-1}{-0.288...} = 3.455...$$

$$= 3.5\mu s \text{ (to 2 s.f.)}$$

2) The equation is now in the form of $y = mx + c$ (p.91). This means if you plotted a graph of **ln(Q)** against time, **t**, you would get a **straight line**.

3) The **gradient** of this line would be $\frac{-1}{RC}$ or $\frac{-1}{\tau}$ and the y-intercept would be $\ln(Q_0)$.

4) To get the time constant from the graph, you **divide –1 by the gradient** of the line.

For this you need to use the log rules:
$\ln(A \times B) = \ln(A) + \ln(B)$
and $\ln(e^A) = A$

Time to Halve, $T_{\frac{1}{2}} = 0.69RC$

The 'time to halve' is the time taken for the **charge**, **current** or **potential difference** of a **discharging** capacitor to reach **half** of the value it was when it was **fully charged**.

$$\boxed{T_{\frac{1}{2}} = 0.69RC}$$

Where $T_{\frac{1}{2}}$ is the time to halve (s), R is the resistance in the circuit (Ω) and C is the capacitance of the capacitor (F).

Example: Find the time taken for the charge of a capacitor to drop to half of its initial value.

We're looking for the time when $Q = \frac{1}{2}Q_0$ so $Q = \frac{1}{2}Q_0 = Q_0 e^{\frac{-t}{RC}} \implies \frac{1}{2} = e^{\frac{-t}{RC}}$

Take the natural log of both sides: $\ln\left(\frac{1}{2}\right) = \ln\left(e^{\frac{-t}{RC}}\right) \implies \ln(1) - \ln(2) = \frac{-t}{RC}$

For this you need to use another log rule: $\ln(A \div B) = \ln(A) - \ln(B)$.

Rearrange to get $t = \ln(2)RC$. $\ln(2) = 0.693...$ so $t = $ **0.69RC (to 2 s.f.)**

Warm-Up Questions

Q1 What two factors affect how quickly a capacitor charges?
Q2 Write down the formula for calculating potential difference at a given time for a charging capacitor.
Q3 Write down the formula for calculating charge at a given time for a discharging capacitor.
Q4 Describe how you would calculate the time constant from a plot of ln(V) against t.
Q5 Write down the formula for the 'time to halve'.

Exam Questions

Q1 A 250 µF capacitor is fully charged from a 6.0 V battery and then discharged through a 1.0 kΩ resistor.

a) Calculate the time taken for the charge on the capacitor to fall to 37% of its original value. [2 marks]

b) Calculate the percentage of the total charge remaining on the capacitor after 0.7s. [2 marks]

c) The charging voltage is increased to 12 V. Explain the effect this has on the total charge stored on the capacitor, the capacitance of the capacitor and the time taken to fully charge the capacitor. [3 marks]

Q2 A fully charged 320 µF capacitor is discharged through a 1.6 kΩ resistor.
Calculate the time taken for its voltage to drop to half of its value when it was fully charged. [2 marks]

I'll spare you a log cabin joke...

That's a lot of maths. You're given the formulas for charge in the exam though, so remember how these compare to potential difference and current and life will become much simpler. Best swat up on your log skills too — they're pretty tricky and you need them to create those nice straight line plots to get the time constant from.

Extra Exam Practice

Exam questions might mix together different parts of a section to really keep you on your toes, so here are some questions mixing parts of <u>Sections 9 and 10</u> for you to practice.

- Have a look at this example of how to answer a tricky exam question.
- Then check how much you've understood from Sections 9 and 10 by having a go at the questions that follow.

There's a load of synoptic questions covering the entire course on page 268. Take a look at these when you're confident with all the sections separately.

1 A teacher is demonstrating a parallel plate capacitor. The capacitor consists of two metal plates of a fixed area separated by air. The teacher is able to change the distance between the plates without any charge being added to or removed from the capacitor.

1.1 The plates are initially at a distance of x from each other. Explain what happens to the electric field strength between the plates if the teacher increases the separation of the plates to $4x$.

(2 marks)

1.2 Describe the change in energy stored by the capacitor as the separation of plates is quadrupled, and explain how this change in energy takes place.

(2 marks)

Because the electric field is between two parallel plates, it is a uniform field, see p.127.

1.1

Electric field, $E = \dfrac{V}{d}$

Combining $C = \dfrac{Q}{V}$ and $C = \dfrac{A\varepsilon_0\varepsilon_r}{d}$ gives:

$V = \dfrac{Qd}{A\varepsilon_0\varepsilon_r}$

$E = \dfrac{V}{d} = \dfrac{Qd}{dA\varepsilon_0\varepsilon_r} = \dfrac{Q}{A\varepsilon_0\varepsilon_r}$

In the equation $E = \dfrac{V}{d}$, there are two variables that E is dependant on. You need to find an equation for E in which d is the only variable, so you can see exactly how E varies with d.

Q and A remain constant as the distance is increased, so E is independent of d and **the electric field strength remains the same if the distance is quadrupled**.

Make sure you include a conclusion so that you've answered the question fully.

You'd get 1 mark for stating that the electric field strength doesn't change, and 1 mark for a correct explanation.

1.2

When comparing quantities you need to say by what factor one is bigger than the other. Just saying that the energy stored has increased might not be enough to get the marks.

$E = \frac{1}{2}QV$ and from part 1.1, $V = \dfrac{Qd}{A\varepsilon_0\varepsilon_r}$. If the distance quadruples, the voltage **quadruples**, therefore the energy stored by the capacitor **quadruples**.

The teacher does work to separate the plates. The teacher applies a force over a distance to overcome the force of attraction between the plates. This work done transfers energy to the capacitor.

There are two parts to this question — explaining the change in energy, and how this energy is transferred. Be sure to answer both parts.

You'd get 1 mark for showing that the energy quadruples and 1 mark for saying that the energy transfer is due to the work done as the teacher applies a force to overcome the attraction between the plates.

2 **Figure 1** shows an electron and a proton whose centres are separated by a distance of 1.00×10^{-10} m. Point P is at the midpoint between the centres of the two particles.

Figure 1

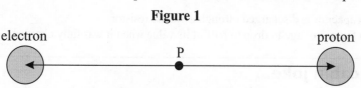

electron   P   proton

2.1 Explain why the absolute electric potential is 0 V at point P.

(2 marks)

Extra Exam Practice

2.2 Calculate the magnitude and direction of the electric field strength at point P.
($e = 1.60 \times 10^{-19}$ C, $\varepsilon_0 = 8.85 \times 10^{-12}$ Fm^{-1})

(3 marks)

2.3 Calculate the minimum kinetic energy that the electron must have if it is to escape the proton's electric field. Ignore any gravitational effects of the electron and proton.

(2 marks)

2.4 Explain why the gravitational effects of the electron and proton can be ignored in part 2.3. Include calculations to support your answer.
($G = 6.67 \times 10^{-11}$ Nm^{2}kg^{-2}, $m_e = 9.11 \times 10^{-31}$ kg, $m_p = 1.67 \times 10^{-27}$ kg)

(2 marks)

3 A hollow conducting sphere has a radius of 12.8 cm and is mounted on an insulated rod as shown in **Figure 2**. A hollow conducting sphere can be considered as a capacitor. The potential difference across the capacitor is the same as the potential difference between the dome and the Earth. The charge stored by the capacitor is equal to the charge on the surface of the dome.

Figure 2

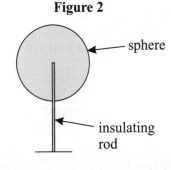

sphere

insulating rod

3.1 Calculate the capacitance of the sphere in **Figure 2**.
($\varepsilon_0 = 8.85 \times 10^{-12}$ Fm^{-1})

(2 marks)

3.2 The sphere is surrounded by a second hollow sphere of a conducting material. Both spheres are connected to a circuit as shown in **Figure 3**.

The capacitance of the two spheres is now 8.43×10^{-11} F. When the capacitor is fully charged, it has a total charge of 5.60×10^{-8} C. The resistance of the circuit is 10.0 MΩ.

The capacitor is initially uncharged. Calculate the energy stored in the capacitor after it has been charging for 1.15 ms.

Figure 3

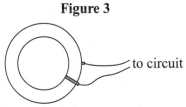

to circuit

(2 marks)

3.3 When a dielectric material is placed between the two spheres, the potential difference between the spheres decreases. Describe the properties of a dielectric material and explain how this results in a reduced potential difference.

(3 marks)

4 Data about two planets is shown in **Table 1**.

4.1 Calculate the mass of planet 1 in terms of M.

(3 marks)

Table 1

Planet	Radius	g at surface of planet	Mass
1	$5r$	$2g$	—
2	r	g	M

4.2 In the absence of any other bodies, the gravitational potential at a point between the two planets, which is 3.10×10^{10} m from the centre of planet 1, is $V = -\dfrac{GM}{6.65 \times 10^8}$, where V is in Jkg^{-1}, G is in Nm^{2}kg^{-2} and M is in kg. Calculate the distance between the centres of the two planets.

(3 marks)

Magnetic Fields

Magnetic fields — making pretty patterns with iron filings before spending an age trying to pick them off the magnet.

A **Magnetic Field** is a **Region** Where a **Force** is Exerted on **Magnetic Materials**

1) Magnetic fields can be represented by **field lines** (also called flux lines).

2) Field lines go from the **north** to the **south pole** of a magnet.

3) The **closer** together the lines, the **stronger** the field.

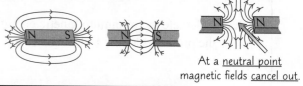

At a <u>neutral point</u> magnetic fields <u>cancel out</u>.

There is a **Magnetic Field** Around a **Wire** Carrying **Electric Current**

When **current** flows in a **wire** or any other long straight conductor, a **magnetic field** is induced around the wire.

1) The **field lines** are **concentric circles** centred on the wire.

2) The **direction** of a magnetic **field** around a current-carrying wire can be worked out with the **right-hand rule**.

3) If you loop the wire into a **coil**, the field is **doughnut-shaped**, while a coil with length (a **solenoid**) forms a **field** like a **bar magnet**.

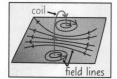

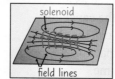

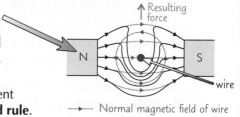

RIGHT-HAND RULE

1) Stick your <u>right thumb</u> up, like you're hitching a lift.
2) Your <u>thumb</u> points in the direction of <u>conventional current</u>...
3) ...your curled <u>fingers</u> point in the direction of the <u>field</u>.

A **Wire** Carrying a **Current** in a **Magnetic Field** will **Experience** a **Force**

1) If you put a **current-carrying wire** into an **external** magnetic field (e.g. between two magnets), the field around the wire and the field from the magnets are **added together**. This causes a **resultant field** — lines **closer together** show where the magnetic field is **stronger**. These bunched lines cause a 'pushing' **force** on the wire.

2) The direction of the force is always **perpendicular** to both the current direction and the magnetic field — it's given by **Fleming's left-hand rule**.

3) If the current is **parallel** to the field lines the size of the force is **0 N** — there is **no component** of the magnetic field perpendicular to the current.

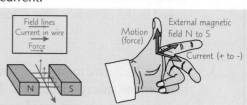

- - - -▶ Normal magnetic field of wire
- - - -▶ Normal magnetic field of magnets
——▶ Resultant magnetic field of magnets

Fleming's Left-Hand Rule

The First finger points in the direction of the external uniform magnetic Field, the seCond finger points in the direction of the conventional Current. Then your thuMb points in the direction of the force (in which Motion takes place).

The **Force** on a Wire is **Proportional** to the **Flux Density**

1) The **force** on a **current-carrying** wire at a **right angle** to an external magnetic field is proportional to the **magnetic flux density**, **B**. Magnetic flux density is sometimes called the **strength** of the magnetic field.

2) **Magnetic flux density**, **B**, is **defined** as:

> The **force** on **one metre** of wire carrying a **current** of **one amp** at **right angles** to the **magnetic field**.

3) When current is at 90° to the magnetic field, the size of the **force**, **F** is proportional to the **current**, **I**, the **length of wire** in the field, **l**, as well as the **flux density**, **B**. This gives the equation:

$$F = BIl$$

4) **Flux density** is a **vector** quantity with both a **direction** and **magnitude**. It's measured in **teslas**, **T**:

$$1 \text{ tesla} = \frac{Wb}{m^2}$$

It helps to think of flux density as the number of flux lines (measured in webers (Wb), see p.144) per unit area.

Magnetic Fields

Use a **Top Pan Balance** to **Investigate** Flux Density

You can use the set-up shown to investigate the relationship between the **force on a wire**, the **length of wire perpendicular** to a magnetic field, the **current** through it and **flux density** ($F = BIl$).

1) A **square hoop** of metal wire is positioned so that the **top** of the hoop, **length l**, passes through the magnetic field, **perpendicular** to it. When a current flows, the **length of wire** in the magnetic field will experience a downwards **force** (Fleming's left-hand rule).

2) The power supply should be connected to a **variable resistor** so that you can **alter** the **current**. Zero the digital balance when there is **no** current through the wire so that the mass reading is due to the electromagnetic force only. Turn on the power supply.

3) Note the **mass** and the **current**. Use the variable resistor to **change** the current and record the new mass — do this for a **large range** of currents. Repeat this until you have 3 mass readings for each current. Calculate the **mean** for each mass reading.

4) Convert your mass readings into **force** using $F = mg$. **Plot** the data on a graph of **force F** against **current I**. Draw a line of best fit.

5) Because $F = BIl$, the **gradient** of your graph is equal to $B \times l$. Measure the gradient, then divide by length l to **get a value for B**.

6) Alternatively, you could vary the **length of wire** perpendicular to the magnetic field by using **different sized hoops**. You could also keep current and wire length the same and instead vary the **magnetic field** by changing the **strength** of the magnets.

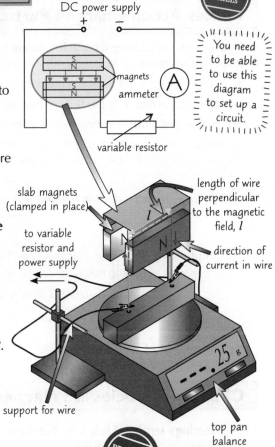

DC power supply

magnets
ammeter

You need to be able to use this diagram to set up a circuit.

variable resistor

slab magnets (clamped in place)

to variable resistor and power supply

length of wire perpendicular to the magnetic field, l

direction of current in wire

support for wire

top pan balance

Warm-Up Questions

Q1 Sketch the magnetic field lines around a long, straight, current-carrying wire. Show the directions of the current and the magnetic field.

Q2 Write the rule that relates the directions of force, current and B field. What is this rule called?

Q3 A copper bar can roll freely on two copper supports, as shown in the diagram. When current is applied in the direction shown, which way will the bar roll?

Q4 What is magnetic flux density? What are its units?

Q5 Describe an experiment using a top pan balance to investigate the force on a wire carrying current that is flowing perpendicular to a magnetic field.

magnets with poles on their largest faces

copper bar

Exam Questions

Q1 A wire carrying a current of 3.00 A runs perpendicular to a magnetic field of strength 2.00×10^{-5} T. 4.00 cm of the wire is within the field.

a) Calculate the magnitude of the force on the wire. [2 marks]

b) The wire is rotated so that it runs parallel to the magnetic field. Give the new force on the wire. Explain your answer. [2 marks]

Q2 A student plots a graph of force against wire length for a current carrying wire in a magnetic field. The current-carrying wire is perpendicular to the field. Which of the following statements is true?

    A The flux density is the gradient of the best fit line.

    B The force is inversely proportional to the wire length.

    C The force is proportional to the wire length.

    D The flux density is the y-intercept of the best fit line.

[1 mark]

Left hand rule. Left hand rule. LEFT HAND RULE. *LEFT HAND RULE.*

Fleming's left hand rule is the key to this section — so make sure you know how to use it and understand what it all means. Remember that the direction of the magnetic field is from N to S, and that the current is from +ve to −ve — this is as important as using the correct hand. You need to get those right or it'll all go to pot...

Charged Particles in a Magnetic Field

Magnetic fields don't just exert a force on current-carrying wires — they have the same effect on all charged particles.

Forces Act on Charged Particles in Magnetic Fields

A **force** acts on a charged particle **moving** in a **magnetic field**. This is why a **current-carrying wire** experiences a force in a magnetic field (page 140) — electric current in a wire is the **flow** of **negatively charged electrons**.

- The force on a current-carrying wire in a magnetic field that is **perpendicular** to the current is given by $F = BIl$.
- Electric current, I, is the flow of charge, Q, per unit time, t. So $I = \frac{Q}{t}$.
- A **charged** particle which moves a distance l in time t has a velocity, $v = \frac{l}{t}$. So $l = vt$.

Putting all these equations together gives the force acting on a single charged particle moving through a magnetic field, where its velocity is perpendicular to the magnetic field:

$$F = BIl = B\frac{Q}{\cancel{t}}v\cancel{t} \longrightarrow \boxed{F = BQv}$$

where F = force in N,
B = magnetic flux density in T,
Q = charge on the particle in C,
v = velocity of the particle in ms^{-1}

In many exam questions, Q is the magnitude of the charge on the electron, which is 1.60×10^{-19} C.

> **Example:** An electron travels at a velocity of 2.00×10^4 ms^{-1} perpendicular to a uniform magnetic field with a magnetic flux density of 2.00 T. What is the magnitude of the force acting on the electron?
>
> Just use the equation $F = BQv$ and put the correct numbers in:
>
> $F = BQV = 2.00 \times (1.60 \times 10^{-19}) \times (2.00 \times 10^4) = \mathbf{6.40 \times 10^{-15}\ N}$

Charged Particles in a Magnetic Field are Deflected in a Circular Path

1) **Fleming's left-hand rule** says that the force on a **moving charge** in a magnetic field is always **perpendicular** to its **direction of travel**.

2) Mathematically, that is the condition for **circular** motion.

3) To use Fleming's left-hand rule for charged particles, use your **second finger** (normally current) as the **direction of motion** for a **positive** charge.

4) If the particle carries a **negative** charge (e.g. an **electron**) point your **second finger** in the **opposite direction** to its motion.

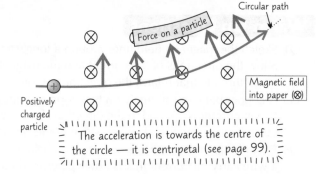

Circular path

Force on a particle

Magnetic field into paper (⊗)

Positively charged particle

The acceleration is towards the centre of the circle — it is centripetal (see page 99).

5) The **force** due to the magnetic field ($F = BQv$) experienced by a particle travelling through a magnetic field is **independent** of the particle's **mass**, but the **centripetal acceleration** it experiences **will depend** on the **mass** — from Newton's 2nd law of motion.

- The particle's acceleration will be $a = \frac{v^2}{r}$.
- Combining this with **Newton's 2nd law**, $F = ma$, gives the force on a particle in a circular orbit $F = \frac{mv^2}{r}$ (see page 99).

The **radius** of the circular path followed by a charged particle in a magnetic field can be found by **combining** the equations for the force on a charged particle in a **magnetic field** and for the force on a particle in a **circular orbit**:

$$F = \frac{mv^2}{r} \quad \text{and} \quad F = BQv \quad \text{so} \quad \frac{mv^2}{r} = BQv$$
$$\text{which gives you } r = \frac{mv}{BQ}$$

This means:

- The radius **increases** (i.e. the particle is **deflected less**) if the **mass** or **velocity** of the particle **increases**.
- The radius **decreases** (i.e. the particle is **deflected more**) if the **strength** of the **magnetic field** or the **charge** on the particle **increases**.

Charged Particles in a Magnetic Field

Cyclotrons Make Use of Circular Deflection

1) Circular deflection is used in particle accelerators such as **cyclotrons**.

2) Cyclotrons have many uses, for example in **medicine**. Cyclotrons are used to produce **radioactive tracers** or high-energy beams of radiation for use in **radiotherapy**.

3) A **cyclotron** is made up of two hollow **semicircular electrodes** with a uniform magnetic field applied perpendicular to the plane of the electrodes, and an **alternating** potential difference applied between the electrodes:

This is not a cyclotron.

- Charged particles are **fired** into one of the electrodes. The magnetic field makes them follow a (semi)circular path and then **leave** the electrode.

- An applied potential difference between the electrodes **accelerates** the particles across the gap until they enter the next electrode.

- Because the particle's speed is **slightly higher**, it will follow a circular path with a **larger** radius (see page 98) before leaving the electrode again.

- The potential difference is **reversed** so the particle is **accelerated again** before entering the next electrode. This process repeats as the particle **spirals outwards**, increasing in speed, before eventually **exiting** the cyclotron.

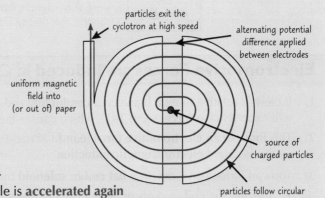

particles exit the cyclotron at high speed

alternating potential difference applied between electrodes

uniform magnetic field into (or out of) paper

source of charged particles

particles follow circular paths with increasing radius in the electrodes

Warm-Up Questions

Q1 What is the equation for the force acting on a single charged particle that is moving through a magnetic field perpendicular to the field lines? Why is the particle deflected in a circular path?

Q2 Give the hand rule for working out the direction of motion of a positively charged particle in a magnetic field.

Q3 What happens to the radius of the circular path of a charged particle in a magnetic field if the velocity of the particle increases?

Q4 Describe how a cyclotron works.

Exam Questions

Q1 An electron is travelling through a uniform magnetic field of flux density 1.10 T. A force of 4.91×10^{-15} N is acting on the electron. Calculate the velocity of the electron perpendicular to the field. [2 marks]

Q2 State the direction of force acting on a negative particle in a power transmission line moving from east to west in a uniform magnetic field that acts vertically downwards. [1 mark]

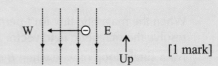

Q3 a) Show that the radius of the circular path followed by charged a particle in a magnetic field is equal to the product of the mass and the velocity of the particle divided by the product of magnetic flux density and the charge of the particle. [2 marks]

b) An electron is travelling in a circular path of radius 3.52×10^{-2} m in a magnetic field of flux density 0.00510 T. Calculate the velocity of the electron. *Mass of an electron $= 9.11 \times 10^{-31}$ kg* [1 mark]

A Cyclotrons' Legacy — a load of very dizzy and rather queasy electrons...

So how do all those poor particles know which way they should be turning without getting dizzy, I hear you cry. We can only assume that they make excellent use of Fleming's left hand rule. But if the particle is negative, remember to point your second finger in the opposite direction to its motion. Got all that? Good.

Electromagnetic Induction

So it turns out that if you waggle a bit of metal around near a magnet you can make your own electricity — don't ever let anybody tell you that physics isn't seriously cool. Chemistry's got nothing on this.

Think of the **Magnetic Flux** as the Total **Number** of **Field Lines**

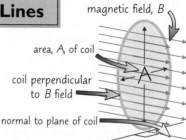

magnetic field, B

1) **Magnetic flux density**, *B*, is a measure of the **strength** of a magnetic field. It helps to think of it as the **number** of field lines **per unit area**.

2) The total **magnetic flux**, *Φ*, passing through an **area**, *A*, perpendicular to a **magnetic field**, *B*, is defined as:

$$\Phi = BA$$

where *Φ* is magnetic flux (Wb), *B* is magnetic flux density (T) and *A* is area (m²).

area, A, of coil

coil perpendicular to B field

normal to plane of coil

Electromotive Forces are **Induced** in Conductors when they **Cut** Magnetic Flux

1) If there is relative motion between a **conducting rod** and a magnetic field, the **electrons in the rod** will experience a **force** (see p.142), which causes them to **accumulate** at one end of the rod.

2) This **induces** an **electromotive force** (**e.m.f.**) across the ends of the rod — this is called **electromagnetic induction**.

motion

B-field

3) You can induce an e.m.f. in a **flat coil** or **solenoid** by:
   - **moving the coil** towards or away from the poles of a magnet.
   - **moving a magnet** towards or away from the coil.

4) In either case, the e.m.f. is caused by the **magnetic field** (or '**magnetic flux**') that passes through the coil **changing**.

5) If the coil is part of a **complete circuit**, an **induced current** will flow through it.

magnet moves this way

current

N

magnet moves this way

current

N

Remember e.m.f. is a voltage — check your Year 1 notes.

More Turns in a **Coil of Wire** Mean a **Bigger e.m.f.** will be **Induced**

1) When you move a **coil** in a magnetic field, the size of the e.m.f. induced depends on the **magnetic flux** passing through the coil, *Φ*, and the **number of turns** in the coil that **cut the flux**, *N*. The product of these is called the **flux linkage**. For a coil with *N* turns, perpendicular to a field with flux density *B*, the flux linkage is given by:

$$N\Phi = BAN$$

The unit of both flux linkage and *Φ* is the **weber, Wb**.

2) The rate of change in flux linkage tells you how **strong** the **electromotive force** will be in **volts**:

> A **change** in **flux linkage** of **one weber per second** will induce an **electromotive force** of **1 volt** in a loop of wire.

Flux linkage is sometimes given in "weber-turns" or "Wb turns"

Use **Trig** if the Magnetic Flux **Isn't Perpendicular** to the **Area**

When the magnetic flux **isn't perpendicular** to the area you're interested in, you need to use **trig** to resolve the **magnetic field vector** into components that are **parallel** and **perpendicular** to the area.

For a **single loop** of wire when *B* is **not perpendicular** to **area**, you can find the **magnetic flux** using this equation:

$$\Phi = BA\cos\theta$$

where *θ* is the angle between the field and the normal to the plane of the loop.

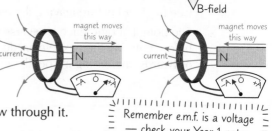

Top-down view

single loop of wire

uniform magnetic field

θ

normal to plane of coil

3D view

Pulling the coil out of field B would induce an e.m.f. — see next page.

For a **coil** with *N* turns the **flux linkage** is:

$$N\Phi = BAN\cos\theta$$

Remember SOH CAH TOA: cos θ = adjacent ÷ hypotenuse

Electromagnetic Induction

The **Angle** of a Coil in a *B* Field Affects the **Induced E.M.F.**

1) You can investigate the effect of **angle** to the **flux lines** on **effective magnetic flux linkage** using this apparatus.

2) The stretched metal spring acts as a solenoid and is connected to an **alternating** power supply (so the **flux** through the search coil is **constantly changing**). The search coil should have a **known area** and a **set number of loops** of fine wire. It is connected to an **oscilloscope** (see p.148) to record the induced e.m.f. in the coil.

3) Set up the oscilloscope so that it only shows the **amplitude** of the e.m.f. as a **vertical line** (i.e. turn off the time base).

4) Position the search coil so that it is about **halfway** along the solenoid. Orientate the search coil so that it is **parallel** to the **solenoid** (and its area is **perpendicular** to the **field**), then **record** the induced e.m.f. in the search coil from the amplitude of the oscilloscope trace.

5) **Rotate** the search coil so its **angle** to the solenoid changes by **10°**. Record the induced e.m.f. and **repeat** until you have rotated the search coil by **90°**.

6) You'll find that as you turn the search coil, the induced e.m.f. **decreases**. This is because the search coil is cutting **fewer** flux lines as the **component** of the magnetic field **perpendicular** to the area of the coil **gets lower**, so the **total magnetic flux passing** through the search coil is **lower**. This means that the magnetic flux linkage experienced by the coil is lower.

7) Plot a **graph** of **induced e.m.f.** against θ. The induced e.m.f. should be **maximum** at **0°**, and a **zero** at **90°**.

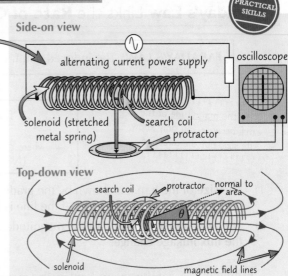

Warm-Up Questions

Q1 Describe the three ways an e.m.f. can be induced in a conductor in a magnetic field.

Q2 What is the difference between magnetic flux density, magnetic flux and magnetic flux linkage?

Q3 A coil consists of *N* turns, each of area *A* in magnetic field *B*. State the equation to calculate its flux linkage if:
   a) the normal to the plane of the coil is perpendicular to a uniform magnetic field.
   b) the normal to the plane of the coil is at an angle to a uniform magnetic field.

Q4 Describe an experiment you could carry out to investigate how the magnetic flux density experienced by a search coil in a magnetic field changes when you vary the angle of it relative to the field.

Exam Questions

Q1 The magnetic flux density of a uniform magnetic field is 2.00×10^{-3} T.

   a) Calculate the magnetic flux passing through an area of 0.230 m^2 at right angles to the field lines. [1 mark]
   b) A coil of area 0.230 m^2 with 151 turns is placed in the field at right angles to the field lines. Calculate the magnetic flux linkage in the coil. [1 mark]
   c) Over a period of 2.50 seconds the magnetic field is reduced uniformly to 1.50×10^{-3} T. Calculate the e.m.f induced across the ends of the coil. [3 marks]

Q2 A 0.010 m^2 coil of 550 turns is perpendicular to a magnetic field of strength 0.92 T generated.

   a) Calculate the magnetic flux linkage in the coil. [1 mark]
   b) The coil is rotated until the normal to the plane of the coil is at 90° to the magnetic field. The movement is uniform and takes 0.5 s. Calculate the e.m.f. induced by this movement. [2 marks]

Q3 The graph shows how the flux through a coil varies over time. Sketch a graph to show how the induced e.m.f. in the coil varies over this same time period. [3 marks]

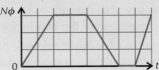

Beware — physics can induce extreme confusion...

Make sure you know the difference between flux and flux linkage, and that you can calculate both. Although I'd love to NΦ all tricky stuff, there's simply nothing else to do but learn it. And if you didn't get the flux-tastic pun in that last sentence, you haven't learnt the equations well enough — back to the start with you, don't stop until you're laughing.

Induction Laws and Alternators

Congratulations, your application has been accepted. Now you must be inducted into our laws. And our alternators.

Faraday's Law Links the Rate of Change of Flux Linkage with E.M.F.

> **FARADAY'S LAW:** The **induced e.m.f.** is **directly proportional** to the **rate of change of flux linkage**.

It can be written as:

$$\varepsilon = \frac{\text{flux linkage change}}{\text{time taken}} = N\frac{\Delta\Phi}{\Delta t}$$

where ε is the **magnitude** of induced e.m.f.
($N = 1$ if it's just a loop, not a coil)

It's the <u>magnitude</u> of the e.m.f. because you only know its size, not the direction.

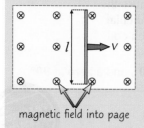

e.m.f. = gradient

$N\Delta\Phi$ = area

1) The **size** of the e.m.f. is shown by the **gradient** of a graph of flux linkage ($N\Phi$) against time. If the line is flat the gradient is 0 and no e.m.f. is induced.

2) The **area under** the graph of the magnitude of the e.m.f. against time gives the **flux linkage change**.

Example: A conducting rod of length l moves through a perpendicular uniform magnetic field, B, at a constant velocity, v. Show that the magnitude of the e.m.f. induced in the rod is equal to Blv.

magnetic field into page

Distance travelled, $s = v\Delta t$ (distance = speed × time)

Area of flux it cuts, $A = lv\Delta t$

Total magnetic flux cut through, $\Delta\phi = BA = Blv\Delta t$

Faraday's law gives $\varepsilon = \frac{\Delta(N\phi)}{\Delta t} = \frac{\Delta\phi}{\Delta t}$ (since $N = 1$)

So induced e.m.f., $\varepsilon = \frac{\Delta\phi}{\Delta t} = \frac{Blv\Delta t}{\Delta t} = \boldsymbol{Blv}$

You might be asked to find the e.m.f. induced on something more interesting than a rod, e.g. the Earth's magnetic field across the wingspan of a plane. Just think of it as a moving rod and use the equation as usual.

The Direction of the Induced E.M.F. and Current are given by Lenz's Law...

> **LENZ'S LAW:** The induced e.m.f. is always in such a direction as to oppose the change that caused it.

1) **Lenz's law** and **Faraday's law** can be **combined** to give one formula that works for both:

$$\varepsilon = \frac{-\text{flux linkage change}}{\text{time taken}} = -N\frac{\Delta\Phi}{\Delta t}$$

where ε is the induced e.m.f.

Kevin's lenses always acted in the opposite direction.

2) The **minus sign** shows the direction of the **induced e.m.f.**

3) The idea that an induced e.m.f. will **oppose** the change that caused it agrees with the principle of the **conservation of energy** — the **energy used** to pull a conductor through a magnetic field, against the **resistance** caused by magnetic **attraction**, is what **produces** the **induced current**.

4) **Lenz's law** can be used to find the **direction** of an **induced e.m.f.** and **current** in a conductor travelling at right angles to a magnetic field.

- **Lenz's law** says that the induced e.m.f. will produce a force that **opposes** the motion of the conductor — in other words a resistance.

- Using Fleming's left-hand rule (see p.140), point your thumb in the direction of the force of resistance — which is in the **opposite direction** to the motion of the conductor.

- Point your **first finger** in the direction of the field. Your **second finger** will now give you the direction of the induced e.m.f..

- If the conductor is **connected** as part of a **circuit**, a current will be induced in the **same direction** as the induced e.m.f..

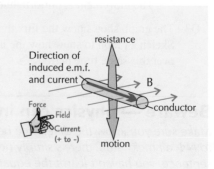

resistance

Direction of induced e.m.f. and current

Force

Field

Current (+ to -)

B

conductor

motion

Induction Laws and Alternators

An **Alternator** is a **Generator** of **Alternating Current**

1) **Generators**, or dynamos, **convert** kinetic energy into **electrical energy** — they **induce** an electric **current** by **rotating** a **coil** in a magnetic field.

2) The diagram shows a simple **alternator** — a generator of **ac**. It has **slip rings** and **brushes** to connect the coil to an external circuit.

3) The output **voltage** and **current** change direction with every **half rotation** of the coil, producing **alternating current** (**ac**).

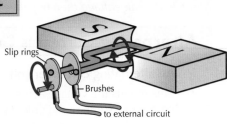

Flux Linkage and Induced Voltage are 90° Out of Phase

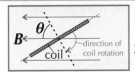

1) The amount of flux cut by the coil (**flux linkage**) is: (θ is the angle between the normal to the coil and the flux lines)

$$N\Phi = BAN \cos \theta$$ See page 144.

2) As the coil rotates θ changes, so the **flux linkage** varies **sinusoidally** between $+BAN$ and $-BAN$.

3) How fast θ changes depends on the angular speed, ω, of the coil (see page 98), $\theta = \omega t$. So you can write:

$$\text{flux linkage} = N\Phi = BAN \cos \omega t$$

4) The **induced e.m.f.**, ε, depends on the **rate of change** of **flux linkage** (Faraday's law), so it also varies **sinusoidally**. The equation for the e.m.f. at time t is:

$$\varepsilon = BAN \omega \sin \omega t$$

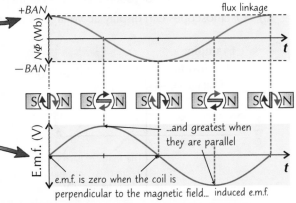

...and greatest when they are parallel

e.m.f. is zero when the coil is perpendicular to the magnetic field... induced e.m.f.

Example: A rectangular coil with 30.0 turns, each with an area of 0.200 m², is rotated as shown at 20.0 rad s⁻¹ in a uniform 1.50 mT magnetic field. Calculate the maximum e.m.f. induced in the coil.

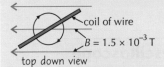

$\varepsilon = BAN \omega \sin \omega t$. So, ε will be greatest when $\sin \omega t = \pm 1$, which gives $\varepsilon = 1.50 \times 10^{-3} \times 0.200 \times 30.0 \times 20.0 \times \pm 1$ = ± 0.180 V

rad stands for radians — see page 98.

Warm-Up Questions

Q1 State Faraday's law and Lenz's law.

Q2 Describe how to find the direction of an induced e.m.f. in a copper bar moving at right angles to a magnetic field.

Q3 Show that flux linkage and induced e.m.f. are 90° out of phase in an alternator.

Exam Questions

Q1 An aeroplane with a wingspan of 33.9 m flies at a speed of 148 ms⁻¹ perpendicular to the Earth's magnetic field, as shown. The Earth's magnetic field at the aeroplane's location is 6.00×10^{-5} T.

a) Calculate the induced e.m.f. between the wing tips. [3 marks]

b) Copy and complete the diagram to show the direction of the induced e.m.f. between the wing-tips. [1 mark]

Q2 A 0.0105 m² coil of 521 turns is rotated on an axis that is perpendicular to a magnetic field of 0.900 T.

a) Find the flux linkage when the angle between its normal and the magnetic field is 60.0°. [1 mark]

b) Calculate the peak e.m.f. induced when the coil is rotated at an angular speed of 40π rad s⁻¹. [3 marks]

Alternators and laws of induction? They generatorly don't phase me...

Bless my soul — there are so many Greek letters on this page it looks like Hercules had a few too many and spewed the alphabet all over everywhere. Go from zero to (physics) hero and learn what they all mean, then find your way through all the equations too. Then when you get into the exam you'll easily be able to go the distance — just like that.

Alternating Currents

Oh alternating current, you're just no good for me. You're up then you're down, you're in then you're out, you're positive at peak voltage then negative in a trough. I should know that you're always going to cha-a-aange...

Alternating Current is Constantly Changing

1) An **alternating current** or voltage is one that changes direction with time.

2) This means the voltage across a resistance goes up and down in a **regular pattern** — some of the time it's positive and some of the time it's negative.

3) You can use an **oscilloscope** to **display** the **voltage** of an alternating current (and **direct current** too). Oscilloscopes are just like really **fancy voltmeters** — the **vertical height** of the trace at any point shows the **input voltage** at that point.

4) The oscilloscope screen has a **grid** on it — you can select how many **volts per division** you want the y-axis scale to represent using the Y-gain control dial, e.g. 5 V per division.

5) An alternating current (ac) source gives a regularly repeating **sinusoidal waveform**. A direct current (dc) source is always at the same voltage, so you get a **horizontal line** (see below).

6) Oscilloscopes can display ac voltage as a **vertical line** and dc voltage as a **dot** if you **turn off** the time base.

alternating currants

Example:

A **sinusoidal alternating voltage** signal.

Voltage / V
0 V
Time / s
The width of each square represents 1 ms and the height 2 V.

Oscilloscope settings:
Y-gain = 2 V per division,
time base = 1 ms per division.

A sinusoidal alternating voltage with the **time base** turned **off**.

The height of each square represents 2 V.

Oscilloscope settings:
Y-gain = 2 V per division,
time base turned off.

A **direct current** supply.

Oscilloscope settings:
Y-gain = 2 V per division,
time base = 1 ms per division.

Find the rms, Peak and Peak-to-Peak Voltages using an Oscilloscope

1) There are three basic pieces of information you can get from an ac oscilloscope trace — the **time period**, T, the **peak voltage**, V_0, and the **peak-to-peak voltage**.

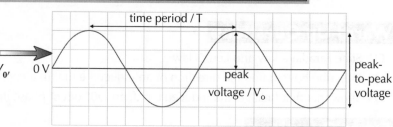

time period / T
0 V
peak voltage / V_0
peak-to-peak voltage

2) An ac supply with a peak voltage of 2 V will be **below** 2 V **most of the time**. That means it **won't** have as high a **power output** as a 2 V **dc** supply. To compare them properly, you need to calculate the **root mean square** (rms) **voltage**.

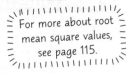
For more about root mean square values, see page 115.

3) For a sine wave, you can calculate the rms voltage (V_{rms}) by **dividing** the **peak voltage**, V_0, by $\sqrt{2}$. You do the same to calculate the rms current I_{rms}:

$$V_{rms} = \frac{V_0}{\sqrt{2}}$$
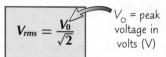
V_0 = peak voltage in volts (V)

$$I_{rms} = \frac{I_0}{\sqrt{2}}$$
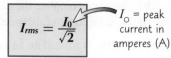
I_0 = peak current in amperes (A)

To work out the **average power** for an ac supply, just use the **rms values** of voltage and current: **average power** = $I_{rms} \times V_{rms}$

4) Measuring the distance **between** successive **peaks** along the **time axis** (the horizontal axis) gives you the **time period** (as long as you know the time base setting). You can use this to calculate the **frequency**:

$$\text{frequency} = \frac{1}{\text{time period}}, \text{ or } f = \frac{1}{T}$$

Alternating Currents

You'll Need to Use those **Equations** to **Answer Questions**

Example: A light is powered by a sinusoidal ac power supply with a peak voltage of 2.12 V and a root mean square current of 0.40 A.

a) Calculate the root mean square voltage of the power supply.

$$V_{rms} = \frac{V_0}{\sqrt{2}} = \frac{2.12}{\sqrt{2}} = 1.499... = \mathbf{1.50\ V}\ \textbf{(to 3 s.f.)}$$

b) Calculate the power of the power supply.

$$\text{Power} = I_{rms} \times V_{rms} = 1.499... \times 0.40 = 0.5996... = \mathbf{0.60\ W}\ \textbf{(to 2 s.f.)}$$

Mains Electricity is an **Alternating Current**

The UK's mains electricity supply is **around 230 V**, although this does vary a little.
This is an **alternating** supply, so the value of 230 V stated is actually the **rms value**.

Example: Calculate the peak-to-peak voltage of the UK mains electricity supply.

Just rearrange $V_{rms} = \frac{V_0}{\sqrt{2}}$ into $V_0 = \sqrt{2}\,V_{rms}$:

$$V_0 = \sqrt{2} \times V_{rms} = \sqrt{2} \times 230 = 325.26...\ \text{V}$$
$$= 330\ \text{(to s.f.)}$$

$$V_{peak\text{-}to\text{-}peak} = 2 \times V_0 = 650.53...$$
$$= \mathbf{650\ V}\ \textbf{(to 2 s.f.)}$$

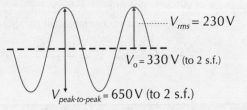

$V_{rms} = 230\,\text{V}$

$V_0 = 330\,\text{V}$ (to 2 s.f.)

$V_{peak\text{-}to\text{-}peak} = 650\,\text{V}$ (to 2 s.f.)

Warm-Up Questions

Q1 What is an alternating current?

Q2 Describe the waveform of the voltage in an alternating current.

Q3 Write down the equations for calculating root mean square voltage and root mean square current from peak voltage and peak current.

Q4 The frequency of UK mains alternating current is 50 Hz. Show that its time period is 0.02s.

PRACTICE QUESTIONS

Exam Questions

Q1 Two students are trying to use an oscilloscope to display an alternating current.

a) One student sets up her power supply and connects it to the oscilloscope. She sees a vertical line in the middle of the screen. What setting must she adjust to display a sinusoidal wave form? [1 mark]

b) Another student sets up his power supply and connects it to the oscilloscope. He sees a flat horizontal line at 7 V. Explain what he has done wrong. [1 mark]

Q2 a) The peak current in an ac circuit is 9.13 A. Calculate the root mean square current. [1 mark]

b) The root mean square voltage of the same alternating supply is 119 V. Calculate the peak-to-peak voltage. [2 marks]

Careful on your surfboard — these currents keep changing direction...

If it helps, have a quick daydream about a summer beach holiday. Ah, the sand, waves, ice cream, torrential rain, wind, woolly hats, waterproof trousers, hypothermia and then the roaring fire... I love Cornwall in August. But you can't enjoy any of that until you've done your exams, so you might as well do a good job and learn all this alternating current stuff.

Transformers

Turns out electromagnetic induction is quite useful in the real world — remember that place?

Transformers Work by Electromagnetic Induction

iron core

magnetic field in the iron core

primary coil

secondary coil

1) **Transformers** are devices that make use of electromagnetic induction to **change** the size of the **voltage** for an **alternating current**.

2) An alternating current flowing in the **primary** (or input) **coil** produces **magnetic flux**.

3) The changing **magnetic field** is passed through the **iron core** to the **secondary** (or output) coil, where it **induces** an alternating **voltage** of the same frequency as the input voltage.

4) From Faraday's law, the **induced** e.m.f.s in both the **primary** and **secondary** coils can be calculated:

Primary coil

$$V_p = N_p \frac{\Delta \Phi}{\Delta t}$$

Secondary coil

$$V_s = N_s \frac{\Delta \Phi}{\Delta t}$$

(where N is the number of turns in a coil)

These can be combined to give the **transformer equation** for an **ideal** transformer:

$$\frac{N_s}{N_p} = \frac{V_s}{V_p}$$

(where N is the number of turns in a coil)

5) **Step-up** transformers **increase** the **voltage** by having **more turns** on the **secondary** coil than the primary. **Step-down** transformers **reduce** the voltage by having **fewer** turns on the secondary coil.

Example: What is the output voltage for a transformer with a primary coil of 120 turns, a secondary coil of 350 turns and an input voltage of 230 V?

$$\frac{N_s}{N_p} = \frac{V_s}{V_p} \implies V_s = \frac{V_p \times N_s}{N_p} = V_s = \frac{230 \times 350}{120} = 670.83... = \mathbf{670 \text{ V}} \text{ (to 2 s.f.)}$$

Transformers are Not 100% Efficient

You can put the two ideal transformer equations together to give:
$$\frac{V_p}{V_s} = \frac{N_p}{N_s} = \frac{I_s}{I_p}$$

1) If a transformer was **100% efficient**, the **power in** would **equal** the **power out**.

2) Power is current × voltage. This means that for an **ideal transformer:** $\boxed{I_p V_p = I_s V_s}$ or $\boxed{\frac{I_s}{I_p} = \frac{V_p}{V_s}}$

3) However, in practice there will be **small losses** of **power** from the transformer, mostly due to **eddy currents** in the transformer's iron **core**

4) Eddy currents are looping currents induced by the changing magnetic flux in the core. They create a **magnetic field** that **acts against** the field that induced them, reducing the field strength. They also dissipate energy by **generating heat**.

5) The effect of eddy currents can be reduced by **laminating** the core with layers of **insulation**.

6) Heat is also generated by **resistance** in the coils — to minimise this, **thick copper wire** is used, which has a **low resistance**.

7) The **efficiency** of a transformer is simply the **ratio** of **power out** to **power in**, so: (this gives the efficiency as a **decimal** — multiply by 100 to get a **percentage**). $\boxed{\text{efficiency} = \frac{I_s V_s}{I_p V_p}}$

Example: a) A transformer has an input current of 173 A and doubles the input voltage to give an output voltage of 35 600 V. Calculate the maximum possible current output by the transformer.

$$V_p = 35\,600 \div 2 = 17\,800 \text{ V}$$

$$I_p V_p = I_s V_s \text{ so } I_s = \frac{I_p \times V_p}{V_s} = \frac{173 \times 17\,800}{35\,600} = \mathbf{86.5 \text{ A}}$$

You could also work this out by realising that if the voltage doubles, the current must halve, as they are inversely proportional.

b) The efficiency of another transformer is 0.871. It decreases an initial voltage of 11 560 V to 7851 V and I_p is 195 A. Calculate the current output by the transformer.

$$\text{efficiency} = \frac{I_s V_s}{I_p V_p} \text{ so } I_s = \frac{\text{efficiency} \times I_p \times V_p}{V_s} = \frac{0.871 \times 195 \times 11560}{7851}$$

$$= 250.083... = \mathbf{250 \text{ A}} \text{ (to 3 s.f.)}$$

Transformers

Transformers are an Important Part of the National Grid...

1) **Electricity** from power stations is sent round the country in the **national grid** at the **lowest** possible current, because the **power losses** due to the **resistance** of the cables is equal to $P = I^2R$ — so if you double the transmitted current, you **quadruple** the power lost.

2) Since **power** = **current** × **voltage**, a **low current** means a **high voltage**.

3) **Transformers** allow us to **step up** the voltage to around **400 000 V** for **transmission** through the national grid, and then **reduce** it again to **230 V** for domestic use.

... robots in disguise

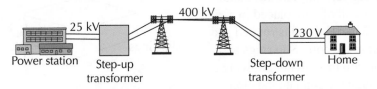

Power station   Step-up transformer   Step-down transformer   Home

25 kV   400 kV   230 V

...and You Need to be Able to Work Out the Power Wasted in Transmission

Example: A current of 1330 A is used to transmit 1340 MW of power through 147 km of cables.
The resistance of the transmission wire is 0.130 Ω per kilometre.
Calculate the power wasted.

Total resistance = 0.130 × 147 = 19.11 Ω

Power lost = I^2R = 1330^2 × 19.11 = 3.3803... × 10^7 = **3.38 × 10^7 W (to 3 s.f.)**

Warm-Up Questions

Q1 Draw a diagram of a simple transformer.

Q2 State the transformer equation.

Q3 What is meant by a step-down transformer?

Q4 Describe how eddy currents are formed in a transformer and explain why they reduce a transformer's efficiency.

Q5 Why is electricity transmitted across the national grid at as low a current as possible?

PRACTICE QUESTIONS

Exam Questions

Q1   A simple transformer with 158 turns in the primary coil has an input voltage of 9.30 V.

    a)   Calculate the number of turns needed in the secondary coil to step up the voltage to 45.0 V.   [1 mark]

    b)   The input current for the transformer is 1.50 A.
Assuming the transformer is ideal, calculate the output current.   [2 marks]

    c)   Calculate the actual efficiency of the transformer given that the power output is measured as 10.8 W.   [1 mark]

    d)   Describe a change that could be made to the transformer to improve its efficiency
by reducing the effect of eddy currents.   [1 mark]

Q2   A substation receives 943 kW of electricity from a power station through wires
with a total resistance 132 Ω. The input current was 15.6 A
Calculate the electrical power originally transmitted from the power station.   [2 marks]

Arrrrrrrrrgggggggghhhhhhhh...

Breathe a sigh of relief, pat yourself on the back and make a brew — well done, you've revised everything in the section. That was pretty nasty stuff (the section, not your tea), but don't let all of those equations get you down — once you've learnt the main ones and can use them blindfolded, move onto the next two pages for some extra practice...

Extra Exam Practice

Section 11 is a tough section — don't worry, it's nearly finished. As they say, practice makes perfect, so have a go at these practice questions that mix together different pages from all of Section 11.

- Have a look at this example of how to answer a tricky exam question.
- Then check how much you've understood from Section 11 by having a go at the questions on the next page.

---

1 **Figure 1** shows an alternator which is used to produce an alternating current. The alternator consists of a circular coil of wire placed in a uniform magnetic field. The coil is rotated and an e.m.f. is induced in the coil. Slip rings and brushes connect the coil to a circuit, allowing a current to flow through the coil and the circuit. One slip ring is attached to one end of the coil. The other slip ring is attached to the other end of the coil. Each brush is in contact with one of the slip rings. The coil of wire has exactly 5 turns, each with a radius of 5.00 cm. At $t = 0$ s, the normal to the coil of wire is parallel with the magnetic field lines between the two magnets.

Figure 1

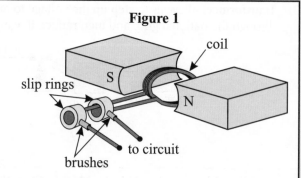

1.1 The coil rotates with an angular frequency of 91.8π rads^{-1}. At $t = 7.60$ s the magnetic flux linkage in the coil is 4.80×10^{-3} Wb. Calculate the maximum e.m.f. induced in the circuit by the alternator.

(3 marks)

1.2 Explain how the set-up in **Figure 1** results in an alternating current rather than a direct current in the circuit.

(2 marks)

You'll need the magnetic field strength, B, later on to calculate ε.

Make sure your calculator is in radians mode when doing these calculations, as the angular frequency is given in radians per second.

1.1

First find B using $N\Phi = BAN \cos \theta = BAN \cos \omega t$

$B = \dfrac{N\Phi}{AN \cos \omega t}$

A is the coil's area (a circle): $A = \pi r^2 = \pi \times (5.00 \times 10^{-2})^2 = 2.5 \times 10^{-3}\pi$

$B = \dfrac{4.80 \times 10^{-3}}{2.5 \times 10^{-3}\pi \times 5 \times \cos(91.8\pi \times 7.60)} = 0.228...$ T

$\varepsilon = BAN \omega \sin \omega t$ and the maximum value that $\sin(\omega t)$ can be is ± 1, so ε is maximum when $\varepsilon = BAN \omega \times \pm 1 = 0.228... \times 2.5 \times 10^{-3}\pi \times 5 \times 91.8\pi \times \pm 1$
$= \pm 2.583... = \pm 2.58$ V (to 3 s.f.)

You'd get 3 marks for the correct answer, otherwise you'd get 1 mark for correctly calculating the magnetic field strength B and 1 mark for stating that ε is a maximum when $\sin(\omega t) = \pm 1$.

θ is the same as ωt because ω is the angle rotated per second.

You can leave this answer in a multiple of π for now to avoid rounding errors.

ε is a sinusoidal function so it has a maximum value when $\sin(\omega t) = \pm 1$.

1.2

If you can't see this straight away, you could use Fleming's Left-Hand Rule to work it out.

As the coil rotates, the direction of motion of one side of the coil will change from upwards to downwards, and the other side will change from downwards to upwards. This happens each half turn. **When the direction of motion changes, the direction of the induced e.m.f. changes, which causes the direction of the current in the coil to switch direction.** The slip rings and brushes ensure that each end of the coil is attached to a different end of the circuit, **so the current through the circuit also changes direction with each half turn.**

You'd get 1 mark for explaining why the current in the coil changes direction, and 1 mark for explaining how the slip rings and brushes make sure the current through the circuit also changes direction.

Make sure you fully answer the question — you'll need to explain the purpose of the slip rings and brushes to explain how an alternating current is produced in the circuit.

Extra Exam Practice

2 A cyclotron is used in a research facility to accelerate alpha particles. An alpha particle is made up of two protons and two neutrons. The cyclotron consists of two semicircular hollow electrodes as shown in **Figure 2**, each with a radius of 55.0 cm. A uniform magnetic field of strength 0.365 T is applied perpendicular to the plane of the electrodes. An alternating potential difference is applied between the electrodes.

Figure 2

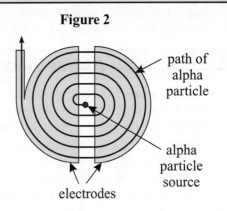

path of alpha particle

alpha particle source

electrodes

2.1 Calculate the maximum speed of an alpha particle that can be contained by the cyclotron.
($e = 1.60 \times 10^{-19}$ C, $m_p = m_n = 1.67 \times 10^{-27}$ kg)

(3 marks)

2.2 The research facility uses a transformer to increase the potential difference supplied to the cyclotron from the mains electricity. The mains electricity has a voltage of 238 V and the voltage required by the cyclotron is 1020 V. The transformer runs with an efficiency of 85.0%. The rms input current to the transformer is 11.8 A. Calculate the maximum current in the secondary coil.

(2 marks)

2.3 The transformer core is replaced with a laminated core.
Explain the effect this has on the path of the alpha particles.

(4 marks)

3 Read the passage below and answer the following questions.

Figure 3 shows a wire being moved downwards between two pairs of magnets. Each magnet has a square face with

5   dimensions 5.5 cm × 5.5 cm and there is a uniform magnetic field strength of

Figure 3

circuit

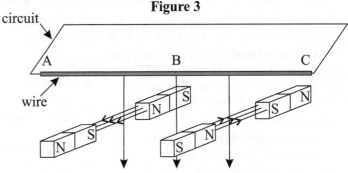

wire

155 mT between each pair. The wire is connected in a closed circuit with no battery. A voltmeter is connected in parallel across points A and B. The wire is moved

10   downwards at a constant velocity of 1.2 ms⁻¹, which causes a charge to build up at point B and the voltmeter to display a reading.

A battery is then connected in the circuit so a current flows from points A to C. The wire is moved back to the position shown in **Figure 3** and then dropped between the magnets.

3.1 State and explain whether the build up of charge at point B is positive or negative (line 10).

(3 marks)

3.2 Calculate the maximum reading on the voltmeter (line 11). You can assume that the magnetic flux density outside of the area between the magnets is negligible, and that there are no energy losses.

(3 marks)

3.3 Suggest and explain what happens to the motion of the wire when it is dropped through the magnets (line 13). You may ignore the effects of any induced e.m.f. in the wire.

(2 marks)

Rutherford Scattering and Atomic Structure

You'll be learning about the 'nuclear model' of the atom shortly. But first it's time for a trip back in time to see how scientists came up with it. And it's got a bit to do with plum puddings.

Scientists Thought **Atoms** Were Like a **Plum Pudding**

1) The idea of **atoms** has been around since the time of the Ancient Greeks in the 5th Century BC. A man called Democritus proposed that all matter was made up of little, **identical lumps** called 'atomos'.

2) Much later, in 1804, a scientist called John Dalton put forward a hypothesis that agreed with Democritus — that matter was made up of tiny spheres ('atoms') that couldn't be broken up. He reckoned that each **element** was made up of a **different** type of 'atom'.

James fancied doing a bit of nuclear physics

3) Nearly 100 years later, J. J. Thomson discovered that **electrons** could be removed from atoms. So Dalton's theory wasn't quite right (atoms could be broken up).

4) Thomson suggested that atoms were **spheres** of **positive charge** with tiny negative electrons stuck in them like fruit in a **plum pudding**.

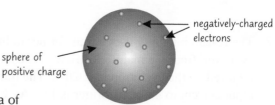

negatively-charged electrons

sphere of positive charge

5) Until this point though, nobody had proposed the idea of the **nucleus**. Rutherford was the first to suggest atoms did not have **uniformly** distributed **charge** and **density**.

Rutherford Scattering Showed the Existence of a **Nucleus**

1) In 1909, Rutherford and Marsden tried firing a beam of **alpha particles** (see p.158) at thin gold foil.

2) A circular detector screen surrounding the gold foil and the alpha source was used to detect alpha particles deflected by any angle.

3) They expected that the positively-charged alpha particles would be **deflected** by the electrons by a very **small amount** if the plum pudding model was true.

alpha source   gold foil   circular detector screen surrounds the source and foil

alpha particle beam   any deflection can be detected

4) Instead, most of the alpha particles just went **straight through** the foil, while a small number were deflected by a **large angle**.

5) Some were even deflected by more than **90°**, sending them back the way they came — this was confusing at the time and called for a change to the **model** of the atom.

The results of Rutherford scattering suggested that atoms must have a small, positively-charged nucleus at the centre:

1) Most of the atom must be empty space because most of the alpha particles passed straight through the foil.

2) The nucleus must have a large positive charge, as some positively-charged alpha particles were repelled and deflected by a large angle.

3) The nucleus must be small as very few alpha particles were deflected back.

4) Most of the mass must be in the nucleus, since the fast alpha particles (with high momentum) are deflected by the nucleus.

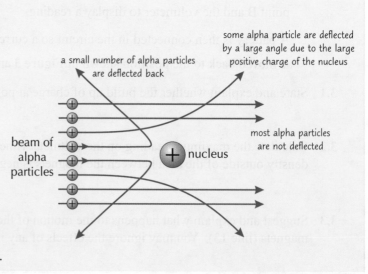

some alpha particle are deflected by a large angle due to the large positive charge of the nucleus

a small number of alpha particles are deflected back

beam of alpha particles

nucleus

most alpha particles are not deflected

Rutherford Scattering and Atomic Structure

You can **Estimate** the **Closest Approach** of a **Scattered Particle**

1) When you fire an alpha particle at a gold nucleus, you know its **initial kinetic energy**.

2) An alpha particle that 'bounces back' and is deflected through 180° will have reversed direction a short distance from the nucleus. It does this at the point where its **electric potential energy** (see p.128) **equals** its **initial kinetic energy**.

3) It's just conservation of energy — and you can use it to find how close the particle can get to the nucleus.

4) Using a form of Coulomb's law (p.126) to find the electric potential energy:

$$E_k = E_{elec} = \frac{Q_{gold}Q_{alpha}}{4\pi\varepsilon_0 r}$$

where $\varepsilon_0 = 8.85 \times 10^{-12}$ Fm^{-1} is the permittivity of free space (p.126) and r is the distance from the centre of the nucleus (m)

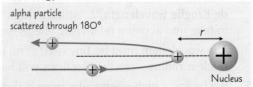
alpha particle scattered through 180°

Nucleus

5) To find the charge of a nucleus you need to know the atom's **proton number**, Z — that tells you how many protons are in the nucleus (surprisingly). A proton has a charge of **+e** (where e is the size of the charge on an electron), so the charge of a nucleus must be **+Ze**.

6) The **distance of closest approach** is an **estimate** of **nuclear radius** — it gives a **maximum** value for it. However, electron diffraction (next page) gives much more accurate values for nuclear radii.

> **Example:** An alpha particle with an initial kinetic energy of 6.0 MeV is fired at a gold nucleus. Estimate the radius of the nucleus by finding the closest approach of the alpha particle to the nucleus.
>
> Initial particle energy = 6.0 MeV = 6.0×10^6 eV
> Convert this energy into joules: $(6.0 \times 10^6) \times (1.60 \times 10^{-19}) = 9.6 \times 10^{-13}$ J
> You know that this equals the electric potential energy at the distance of closest approach:
>
> $$\frac{Q_{gold}Q_{alpha}}{4\pi\varepsilon_0 r} = 9.6 \times 10^{-13}$$
> $$r = \frac{Q_{gold}Q_{alpha}}{(9.6 \times 10^{-13}) \times 4\pi\varepsilon_0} = \frac{(79 \times 1.60 \times 10^{-19}) \times (2 \times 1.60 \times 10^{-19})}{4\pi \times (9.6 \times 10^{-13}) \times 8.85 \times 10^{-12}}$$
>
> A gold nucleus has 79 protons and an alpha particle is made up of two protons and two neutrons.
>
> $r = 3.788... \times 10^{-14} = \mathbf{3.8 \times 10^{-14}}$ **m** (to 2 s.f.)

Warm-Up Questions

Q1 Describe the plum pudding model of the atom.

Q2 Describe Rutherford scattering and explain how the results from the experiment showed that a nucleus is both small and positively charged.

Q3 Describe how you could estimate the nuclear radius of an atom.

PRACTICE QUESTIONS

Exam Question

$\varepsilon_0 = 8.85 \times 10^{-12}$ Fm^{-1}, $e = 1.60 \times 10^{-19}$ C, $Z_{gold} = 79$

Q1 A beam of alpha particles is directed onto a very thin gold film. Each alpha particle has a kinetic energy of 4.8 MeV.

a) Explain why the majority of alpha particles are not scattered. [2 marks]

b) Explain how alpha particles are scattered by atomic nuclei. [3 marks]

c) Calculate the distance of closest approach for an alpha particle that has been deflected by 180°. [2 marks]

d) What is the kinetic energy of the alpha particle at the distance of closest approach? [1 mark]

Alpha scattering — It's positively repulsive...

Scattering is a key idea you need to understand for questions about atomic size and structure. Just one experiment managed to change how we view the atom, proving the old-fashioned 'plum pudding' model to be wrong. We now know the atom is mostly made of empty space, and it contains a small nucleus with a large positive charge.

Nuclear Radius and Density

The tiny nucleus — such a weird place, but one that you need to become ultra familiar with. Lucky you...

You Can Use **Electron Diffraction** to **Estimate Nuclear Radius**

1) **Electrons** are a type of particle called a **lepton**. Leptons **don't interact** with the **strong nuclear force** (whereas neutrons and alpha particles do). Because of this, electron diffraction is an **accurate** method for estimating the **nuclear radius**.

2) Like other particles, electrons show **wave-particle duality** (see p.20) — so **electron beams** can be diffracted.

3) A beam of moving electrons has an associated **de Broglie wavelength**, λ, which at high speeds (where you have to take into account relativistic effects (see p.254)) is approximately:

$$\lambda \simeq \frac{hc}{E}$$

E is electron energy (J), h is the Planck constant and c is the speed of light in a vacuum

4) The wavelength must be **tiny** (~10^{-15} m) to investigate the nuclear **radius** — so the electrons will have a very **high** energy.

5) If a beam of **high-energy electrons** is directed onto a thin film of material in front of a screen, a **diffraction pattern** will be seen on the screen.

6) The first minimum appears where:

$$\sin\theta \approx \frac{1.22\lambda}{2R}$$

R is the radius of the nucleus it has been scattered by.

7) Using measurements from this diffraction pattern, you can rearrange the above equation to find the **radius** of the nucleus.

> **Example:** A beam of 300 MeV electrons is fired at a piece of thin foil, and produces a diffraction pattern on a fluorescent screen. The first minimum of the diffraction pattern is at an angle of 30° from the straight-through position. Estimate the radius of the nuclei the electrons were diffracted by.
>
> $E = 300$ MeV $= (3.00 \times 10^8) \times (1.60 \times 10^{-19}) = 4.8 \times 10^{-11}$ J
>
> $\lambda = \dfrac{hc}{E} = \dfrac{6.63 \times 10^{-34} \times 3.00 \times 10^8}{4.8 \times 10^{-11}} = 4.143... \times 10^{-15}$ m
>
> $R \approx \dfrac{1.22\lambda}{2\sin\theta} = \dfrac{1.22 \times 4.143... \times 10^{-15}}{2\sin(30)} = 5.055... \times 10^{-15}$ m $= $ **5 fm (to 1 s.f.)**

Intensity Varies With **Diffraction Angle**

1) The diffraction pattern is very similar to that of a light source shining through a **circular aperture** — a **central bright** maximum (circle) containing the majority of the incident electrons, surrounded by other **dimmer** rings (maxima).

2) The **intensity** of the maxima **decreases** as the **angle of diffraction** increases. The graph shows the **relative intensity** of electrons in each maximum. (You might also see a **logarithmic plot** of this graph, where the **difference** in the **peak heights** is less pronounced).

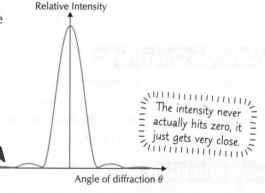

Relative Intensity

Angle of diffraction θ

The intensity never actually hits zero, it just gets very close.

The **Nuclear Radius** is Very **Small** in Comparison to the **Atomic Radius**

By **probing atoms** using scattering and diffraction methods, we know that:

1) The **radius of an atom** is about 0.05 nm (5×10^{-11} m)

2) The radius of the smallest **nucleus** is about 1 fm (1×10^{-15} m — pronounced 'femtometres').

So **nuclei** are really **tiny** compared with the size of the **whole atom**.

*Imagine a Ferris wheel is the size of an atom. If you put a **grain of rice** in the centre, this would be the size of the atom's **nucleus**.*

Make sure you know that the typical radius of a nucleus is ≈ 1×10^{-15} m.

Nuclear Radius and Density

The **Nucleus** is **Made Up** of **Nucleons**

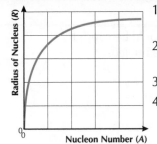

1) The **particles** that make up the nucleus (i.e. **protons** and **neutrons**) are called **nucleons**.

2) The **number of nucleons** in an atom is called the **nucleon** (or mass) **number, A**.

3) As **more nucleons** are added to the nucleus, it gets **bigger**.

4) And as we all know by now, you can measure the size of a nucleus by firing particles at it (see previous page).

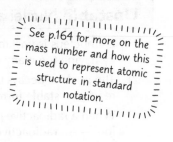

See p.164 for more on the mass number and how this is used to represent atomic structure in standard notation.

Nuclear Radius is **Proportional** to the **Cube Root** of the **Nucleon Number**

1) When data from nuclear radii experiments is plotted on a **graph** of **nuclear radius** R against the **cube root** of the **nucleon number** $A^{1/3}$, the line of best fit gives a **straight line**.

2) This shows a **linear relationship** between R and $A^{1/3}$. As the nucleon number increases, the radius of the nucleus increases proportionally to the cube root of A.

3) This relationship can be written as: $R \propto A^{1/3}$.

4) You can make this into an equation by introducing a constant, R_0, giving:

$$R = R_0 A^{1/3}$$ Where R_0 is roughly 1.4 fm.

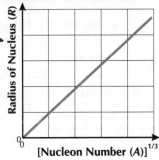

The **Density** of **Nuclear** Matter is **Enormous**

1) The **volume** that each nucleon (i.e. a **proton** or a **neutron**) takes up in a nucleus is about the **same**.

2) Because protons and neutrons have nearly the **same mass** (we'll call it $m_{nucleon}$), it means that all nuclei have a **similar density** (ρ), which you can quickly prove:

$$\rho = \frac{\text{mass}}{\text{volume}} = \frac{A \times m_{nucleon}}{\frac{4}{3}\pi R^3} = \frac{A \times m_{nucleon}}{\frac{4}{3}\pi (R_0 A^{\frac{1}{3}})^3} = \frac{3 m_{nucleon}}{4\pi R_0^3} = \text{constant}$$

3) If you substitute the constants into this formula, you'll get that nuclear density is around 1.45×10^{17} kgm^{-3}.

4) Nuclear matter is **no ordinary** stuff. Its density is **enormous** — much larger than **atomic density**. This suggests that an atom contains lots of **empty space**, with **most** of its **mass** being in a **small nucleus**.

Warm-Up Questions

Q1 What order of magnitude is the radius of a typical nucleus?

Q2 Write down the formula relating nuclear radius and nucleon number.

PRACTICE QUESTIONS

Exam Questions

Q1 High-energy electrons with a de Broglie wavelength of 3.00 fm are diffracted by a carbon-12 nucleus (radius = 2.7×10^{-15} m).

a) Estimate the angle at which the first minimum appears on the electron beam's diffraction pattern. [2 marks]

b) Sketch a graph of relative intensity against angle of diffraction for the electrons. [2 marks]

Q2 Show that the density of a carbon-12 nucleus and the density of a gold nucleus are roughly the same. [4 marks]
(R_0 = 1.4 fm, carbon-12 nucleus mass = 2.00×10^{-26} kg and A = 12, gold nucleus mass = 3.27×10^{-25} kg and A = 197)

Time to fill all that empty space in your head...

Thankfully this isn't too tricky — just a couple of formulas and a graph to learn. Cover these pages, scribble down what you can remember and see how you've done. Then read again any bits you missed — not too fun, but it works.

Radioactive Emissions

Now it's time to see the big consequences of when a tiny nucleus starts to break down.

Unstable Nuclei are Radioactive

1) If a nucleus is **unstable**, it will **break down** to **become** more stable. Its **instability** could be caused by having **too many neutrons**, **not enough neutrons**, or just **too much energy** in the nucleus.

2) The nucleus **decays** by **releasing energy** and/or **particles**, until it reaches a **stable form** — this is called **radioactive decay**.

3) When a radioactive particle **hits** an **atom** it can **knock off electrons**, creating an **ion** — so, **radioactive emissions** are also known as **ionising radiation**.

4) An individual radioactive decay is **random** — it can't be predicted.

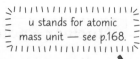

u stands for atomic mass unit — see p.168.

There are Four Types of Nuclear Radiation

Radiation	Symbol	Constituent	Relative Charge	Mass (u)
Alpha	α	A helium nucleus — 2 protons & 2 neutrons	+2	4
Beta-minus (Beta)	β or β⁻	Electron	-1	(negligible)
Beta-plus	β⁺	Positron	+1	(negligible)
Gamma	γ	Short-wavelength, high-frequency electromagnetic wave	0	0

You Can Use Penetrating Power to Investigate Radiation Types

Different types of radiation have different **penetrating powers**, and so can be stopped by different types of **material**:

1) Record the **background radiation** count rate when no source is present (p.160).

2) Place an **unknown** source near to a **Geiger counter** and record the count rate.

3) Place a sheet of **paper** between the source and the Geiger counter. Record the count rate.

4) Repeat step two, replacing the paper with a **3 mm** thick sheet of **aluminium.**

Depending on when the count rate **significantly decreased**, you can calculate what **kind of radiation** the source was emitting. For example, if **paper** has **no effect** and **aluminium** causes a significant (but not complete) **reduction** in count rate, the source must be emitting **beta** and **gamma** radiation.

Radiation	Symbol	Ionising	Speed	Penetrating power	Affected by magnetic field?
Alpha	α	Strongly	Slow	Absorbed by paper or a few cm of air	Yes
Beta-minus (Beta)	β or β⁻	Weakly	Fast	Absorbed by ~3 mm of aluminium	Yes
Beta-plus	β⁺	Annihilated by electron — so virtually zero range			
Gamma	γ	Very weakly	Speed of light	Absorbed by many cm of lead, or several m of concrete.	No

You Can Control How Thick Material Is Using Radiation

1) When creating **sheets of material** like paper, foil or steel, ionising radiation can be used to control its **thickness**.

2) The material is flattened as it is fed through **rollers**.

3) A radioactive **source** is placed on one side of the material, and a radioactive **detector** on the other. The **thicker** the material, the **more** radiation it **absorbs** and **prevents** from reaching the detector.

4) If **too much** radiation is being absorbed, the rollers move **closer** together to make the material **thinner**. If too **little** radiation is being absorbed, they move further **apart**.

Radioactive Emissions

Alpha and Beta Particles have Different Ionising Properties

What a radioactive source can be used for often depends on its **ionising properties**.

1) **Alpha** particles are **strongly positive** — so they can **easily pull electrons** off atoms.

2) Ionising an atom **transfers** some of the **energy** from the **alpha particle** to the **atom**. The alpha particle **quickly ionises** many atoms (about 10 000 ionisations per mm in air for each alpha particle) and **loses** all its **energy**. This makes alpha-sources suitable for use in **smoke alarms** because they allow **current** to flow, but won't **travel very far**.

3) Although alpha particles can't penetrate your skin, sources of alpha particles are **dangerous** if they are **ingested**. They quickly **ionise body tissue** in a small area, causing lots of **damage**.

4) The **beta**-minus particle has **lower mass** and **charge** than the alpha particle, but a **higher speed**. This means it can still **knock electrons** off atoms. Each **beta** particle will ionise about 100 atoms per mm in air, **losing energy** at each interaction.

5) This **lower number of interactions** means that beta radiation causes much **less damage** to body tissue.

6) **Beta radiation** is commonly used for controlling the **thickness** of a **material** (see previous page).

Gamma Rays Are Used In Medicine

Gamma radiation is even more **weakly ionising** than beta radiation, so will do even **less damage** to body tissue. This means it can be used in medicine:

1) **Radioactive tracers** are used to help **diagnose** patients without the need for **surgery**. A radioactive source with a **short half-life** to prevent prolonged radiation exposure is either eaten or injected into the patient. A **detector**, e.g. a PET scanner, is then used to detect the emitted gamma rays.

2) Gamma rays can be used in the **treatment** of **cancerous tumours** — damaging cells and sometimes curing patients of cancer. Radiation **damages all cells** though — cancerous or not, and so sometimes a **rotating beam** of gamma rays is used. This **lessens** the damage done to surrounding tissue, whilst giving a high dose of radiation to the tumour at the centre of rotation.

3) Damage to other, healthy cells is not completely prevented however and treatment can cause patients to suffer **side effects** — such as tiredness and reddening or soreness of the skin.

4) Exposure to gamma radiation can also cause **long term** side effects like **infertility** for certain treatments.

5) As well as patients, the risks towards **medical staff** giving these treatments must be kept as low as possible. **Exposure time** to radioactive sources is kept to a minimum, and generally staff leave the room (which is itself **shielded**) during treatment.

Eric and his mates knew the importance of a shield.

Simply put, radiation use in medicine has **benefits** and **risks**. The key is trying to use methods which **reduce** the risks (shielding, rotating beams etc.) while still giving you the results you want. It's all one big balancing act.

Warm-Up Questions

Q1 What makes a nucleus radioactive?

Q2 Name three types of nuclear radiation and give three properties of each.

Q3 Describe how radiation can be used to control the thickness of steel sheets during manufacture.

Q4 Suggest why alpha sources are not used in medical treatments.

PRACTICE QUESTIONS

Exam Questions

Q1 Briefly describe an absorption experiment to distinguish between alpha, beta and gamma radiation. You may wish to include a sketch in your answer. [4 marks]

Q2 Gamma rays are often used in medicine. State one example of where they are used and describe one benefit and one risk of using gamma rays in this way. [3 marks]

Radioactive emissions — as easy as α, β, γ...

You need to learn the different types of radiation and their properties. Remember that alpha particles are by far the most ionising and so cause more damage if they get inside your body than the same dose of any other radiation — which is one reason we don't use alpha sources as medical tracers. Learn this all really well, then go and have a brew.

Investigations of Radioactive Emissions

Radiation is all around us... Not quite as catchy as the original, but it is true at least...

We're **Surrounded** by **Background Radiation**

Put a Geiger counter anywhere and the counter will click — it's detecting **background radiation**.

When you take a reading from a **radioactive source**, you need to measure the **background radiation** separately and **subtract** it from your measurement.

There are many **sources** of background radiation:

1) **The air**: Radioactive **radon gas** is released from **rocks**. It emits alpha radiation. The concentration of this gas in the atmosphere varies a lot from place to place, but it's usually the largest contributor to the background radiation.

2) **The ground and buildings**: **All rock** contains radioactive isotopes.

3) **Cosmic radiation**: Cosmic rays are particles (mostly high-energy protons) from **space**. When they collide with particles in the upper atmosphere, they produce nuclear radiation.

4) **Living things**: All plants and animals contain **carbon**, and some of this will be radioactive **carbon-14**. They also contain other radioactive materials such as potassium-40.

5) **Man-made radiation**: In most areas, radiation from **medical** or **industrial** sources makes up a tiny, tiny fraction of the background radiation.

The **Intensity** of **Gamma Radiation** Obeys the **Inverse Square Law**

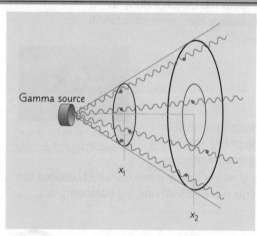

Gamma source

x_1

x_2

1) A **gamma source** will **emit** gamma **radiation** in **all directions**.

2) This radiation **spreads out** as you get **further away** from the source.

3) This means the amount of **radiation per unit area** (the **intensity**) will **decrease** the further you get from the source.

4) If you took a reading of **intensity**, I, at a **distance**, x, from the source you would find that it **decreases** by the **square of the distance** from the source.

5) This can be written as the equation:

$$I = \frac{k}{x^2}$$ where k is a constant

6) This **relationship** can be **proved** by taking **measurements of intensity** at different distances from a gamma source, using a **Geiger counter** (see next page).

7) If the **distance** from the source is **doubled**, the **intensity** is found to **fall to a quarter** — which **verifies** the inverse square law.

Consider the **Inverse Square Law** When Working With **Radioactive Sources**

1) Using a radioactive source becomes **significantly** more dangerous the closer you get to the source. This is why you should always hold a source **away from your body** when transporting it through the lab.

2) Long handling **tongs** should also be used to minimise the radiation absorbed by the body.

3) For those not working directly with radioactive sources, it's best to just keep as **far away** as possible.

Will thought the roof would be far enough away to be safe.

Investigations of Radioactive Emissions

You Can **Investigate** the **Inverse Square Law**

1) Set up the equipment as shown in the **diagram**, leaving out the **source** at first.

2) Turn on the Geiger counter and take a reading of the **background radiation count rate** (in counts per sec). Do this **3** times and take an **average**.

3) Place the **tube** of the Geiger counter so it is lined up with the **start** of the rule.

4) Carefully place the radioactive source at a **distance** *d* from the tube.

5) **Record** the count rate at that distance. Do this **3** times and take an **average**.

6) Move the source so the **distance** between it and the Geiger counter doubles (2*d*).

7) Repeat steps 5 and 6 for distances of 3*d*, 4*d* etc.

8) Once the experiment is finished, put away your source **immediately** — you don't want to be exposed to more radiation than you need to be.

9) **Correct** your data for **background radiation** (previous page). Then plot a graph of **corrected count rate** against **distance** of the counter from the source. You should see that as the distance doubles, the corrected count rate drops to a quarter of its starting value, supporting the **inverse square law**.

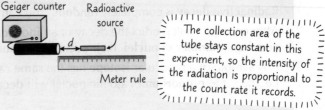

Geiger counter — Radioactive source — *d* — Meter rule

The collection area of the tube stays constant in this experiment, so the intensity of the radiation is proportional to the count rate it records.

*You could also plot a graph of the relative intensity for each distance — both graphs will give you the **same curve**.*

Warm-Up Questions

Q1 Give three sources of background radiation.

Q2 What is usually the largest contributor to background radiation?

Q3 Write down the equation that links intensity and distance from the source for gamma radiation.

Q4 Explain why handling tongs are used to handle radioactive sources, with reference to the inverse square law.

Q5 Briefly describe an experiment you could do to demonstrate the inverse square law for the intensity of gamma radiation.

Q6 Sketch a graph of the relative intensity against distance for a radioactive gamma source.

Exam Question

Q1 The count rate detected by a Geiger counter, 10.0 cm from a gamma source, is 240 counts per second (cps) (to 3 s.f.). If the source is removed, there is a count rate of 60 counts per minute (to 2 s.f.).

   a) Estimate the counts per second at a distance of 20.0 cm from the source, to the nearest cps.   **[2 marks]**

   b) Estimate the counts per second at a distance of 35.0 cm from the source, to the nearest cps.   **[1 mark]**

Q2 A Geiger counter is moved gradually away from a gamma source, and the graph of the corrected count rate per second against distance shown to the right is plotted. Calculate the distance from the source to the Geiger counter at point A.   **[2 marks]**

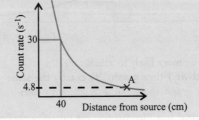

Inverse square laws aren't very funny...

True, there's nothing particularly fascinating on these pages, but they're also not too difficult — mostly just banging on about this inverse square law and how you can show it. But we don't go on about anything unless it's important, so even though the equation is given in the exam, make sure you are happy sticking numbers in and using it.

Exponential Law of Decay

Oooh look — some more maths. Good.

Every Isotope Decays at a Different Rate

1) **Radioactive decay** is completely **random**. You **can't predict which** atom's nucleus will decay **when**.

2) Although you can't predict the decay of an **individual nucleus**, if you take a **very large number of nuclei**, their **overall behaviour** shows a **pattern**.

3) Any sample of a particular **isotope** has the **same rate of decay**, i.e. the same **proportion** of atomic nuclei will **decay** in a **given time**.

> *Isotopes of an element have the same number of protons, but different numbers of neutrons in their nuclei.*

The Rate of Decay is Measured by the Decay Constant

The **activity** of a sample — the **number** of nuclei (N) that **decay each second** — is **proportional** to the **size of the sample**. For a **given isotope**, a sample **twice** as big would give **twice** the **number of decays** per second. Activity is measured in **becquerels** (Bq). 1 Bq = 1 decay per second.

The **decay constant** (λ) is the probability of a given nucleus decaying per second. The **bigger** the value of λ, the faster the rate of decay. Its unit is **s^{-1}**.

> If you get given a molar mass you'll need to calculate the number of moles (p.112). Then, no. atoms = no. moles × Avogadro's constant, $N_A = 6.02 \times 10^{23}$ mol^{-1}.

$$\boxed{\text{activity = decay constant} \times \text{number of nuclei} \quad \text{or} \quad A = \lambda N}$$

Activity is the rate of change of N, so:

$$\boxed{\frac{\Delta N}{\Delta t} = -\lambda N}$$

There's a negative because the number of atoms left is always decreasing.

> You could model this equation with a spreadsheet — see p.266.

You Need to Learn the Definition of Half-Life

> The **half-life** ($T_{1/2}$) of an **isotope** is the **average time** it takes for the **number of unstable nuclei** to **halve**.

Measuring the **number of unstable nuclei** isn't the easiest job in the world. **In practice**, half-life isn't measured by counting nuclei, but by measuring the **time it takes** the **activity** to **halve**.

The **longer** the **half-life** of an isotope, the **longer** it stays **radioactive**.

The Number of Undecayed Particles Decreases Exponentially

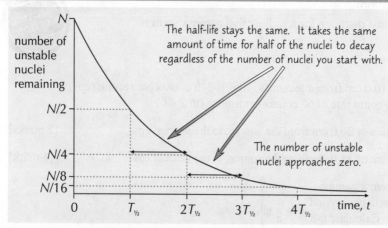

The half-life stays the same. It takes the same amount of time for half of the nuclei to decay regardless of the number of nuclei you start with.

The number of unstable nuclei approaches zero.

> When you're **measuring** the **activity** and **half-life** of a **source**, you've got to **remember background radiation**. The **background radiation** needs to be **subtracted** from the activity readings to give the **source activity**.

You'd be **more likely** to actually meet a **count rate (activity)-time graph**. It's **exactly the same shape** as the graph above, but with **different y-axes**.

Plotting the natural log ('ln' button on your calculator) of the **number** of radioactive **atoms** (or the activity) against **time** gives a **straight-line** graph (see p.266). The gradient is the negative decay constant. You can use this to **calculate half-life** (next page).

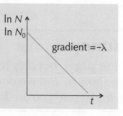

gradient = $-\lambda$

How to find the half-life of an isotope:

1) Read off the value of count rate (activity) or the particles when $t = 0$.

2) Go to **half** the original value.

3) Draw a horizontal line to the curve, then a vertical line down to the x-axis.

4) Read off the half-life where the line crosses the x-axis.

5) Check the units carefully.

6) It's always a good idea to **check** your answer. Repeat steps 1–4 for a quarter the original value. Divide your answer by two. This will also give you the half-life. Check that you get the same answer both ways.

Exponential Law of Decay

You Need to Know the Equations for Half-Life and Decay...

1) The number of radioactive nuclei decaying per second (**activity**) is proportional to the number of nuclei remaining.

2) The **half-life** can be **calculated** using the equation:

$$T_{\frac{1}{2}} = \frac{\ln 2}{\lambda} \approx \frac{0.693}{\lambda}$$

(where ln is the natural log)

3) The **number of unstable nuclei** remaining, N, depends on the **number originally present**, N_0. The **number remaining** can be calculated using the equation:

$$N = N_0 e^{-\lambda t}$$

Here t = time, measured in seconds.

4) As a sample decays, its activity goes down — there's an equation for that too:

$$A = A_0 e^{-\lambda t}$$

Different Half-Lives have Different Uses

Radioactive substances are extremely useful. You can use them for all sorts — to **date** organic material, diagnose **medical problems**, **sterilise** food, and in **smoke alarms**. Knowledge about half-lives can be used for:

1) **Radioactive dating of objects** — the radioactive isotope **carbon-14** is used in **radioactive dating**. Living plants take in carbon dioxide from the atmosphere as part of **photosynthesis**, including the **radioactive isotope carbon-14**. When they die, the **activity** of carbon-14 in the plant starts to **fall**, with a **half-life** of around **5730 years**. Archaeological finds made from once living material (like wood) can be tested to find the **current amount** of carbon-14 in them, and date them.

2) **Medical diagnosis** — radioactive tracers (p.159) are used to help diagnose patients. Technetium-99m is suitable for this use because it emits **γ-radiation**, has a **half-life of 6 hours** (long enough for data to be recorded, but short enough to limit the radiation to an acceptable level) and **decays** to a **much more stable isotope**.

Long Half-Lives can be Dangerous

As well as being useful, radioactive substances can be **dangerous** too (p.159). This is an even bigger problem if the substances stay radioactive for a **long time**. Some isotopes found in waste products of nuclear power generation have incredibly **long half-lives**. This means that we must **plan ahead** about how nuclear waste **will be stored** — e.g. in water tanks or **sealed underground** — to prevent **damage** to the **environment** or **people** not only now but years into the **future** too (p.167).

Warm-Up Questions

Q1 Define radioactive activity and state the two formulas for calculating it. What unit is it measured in?

Q2 Define what is meant by the decay constant.

Q3 What is meant by the term 'half-life'?

Q4 Sketch a general radioactive decay graph showing the activity of a sample against time and describe how it could be used to find the half-life.

Q5 Describe how radioactive dating works.

Exam Questions

Q1 Explain what is meant by the random nature of radioactive decay. [1 mark]

Q2 A reading of 750 Bq is taken from a pure radioactive source. The radioactive source initially contains 8.3×10^{-20} moles (to 2 s.f.), and background activity in the lab is measured as 50 Bq (to 2 s.f.).

   a) Determine the half-life of this sample. ($N_A = 6.02 \times 10^{23}\ mol^{-1}$) [5 marks]

   b) Approximately how many atoms of the radioactive source will there be after 300 seconds? [1 mark]

Q3 Explain the implications of the half-life of highly radioactive nuclear waste on its safe disposal and storage. [2 marks]

Radioactivity is a random process — just like revision shouldn't be...

Remember the shape of that graph — whether it's count rate, activity or number of atoms plotted against time, the shape's always the same. Then it's just lots of mathsy stuff — make sure you really practise using all of those equations.

Nuclear Decay

The stuff on these pages covers the most important facts about nuclear decay that you're just going to have to make sure you know inside out. I'd be very surprised if you didn't get a question about it in your exam...

Atomic Structure can be Represented Using Standard Notation

STANDARD NOTATION:

The **proton number** or **atomic number** (*Z*) — there are six protons in a carbon atom.

$^{12}_{6}C$

The **nucleon number** or **mass number** (*A*) — there are a total of 12 protons and neutrons in a carbon-12 atom.

The symbol for the element carbon.

Atoms with the **same number of protons** but **different numbers of neutrons** are called **isotopes**. The following examples are all isotopes of carbon:

$^{12}_{6}C$, $^{13}_{6}C$, $^{14}_{6}C$.

Some Nuclei are More Stable than Others

The nucleus is under the **influence** of the **strong nuclear force holding** it **together** and the **electromagnetic force pushing** the **protons apart** (p.8). It's a very **delicate balance**, and it's easy for a nucleus to become **unstable**. You can get a stability graph by plotting **Z** (atomic number) against **N** (number of neutrons).

A nucleus will be **unstable** if it has:

1) **too many neutrons**

2) **too few neutrons**

3) **too many nucleons** altogether, i.e. it's **too heavy**

4) **too much energy**

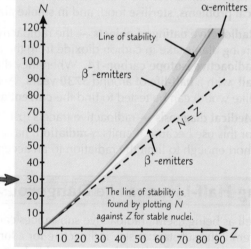

The line of stability is found by plotting *N* against *Z* for stable nuclei.

α Emission Happens in Heavy Nuclei

When an alpha particle is **emitted**:

The **proton number decreases by two**, and the **nucleon number decreases by four**.

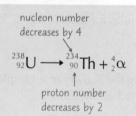

nucleon number decreases by 4

$^{238}_{92}U \longrightarrow ^{234}_{90}Th + ^{4}_{2}\alpha$

proton number decreases by 2

1) **Alpha emission** only happens in **very heavy** atoms, like **uranium** and **radium**.

2) The **nuclei** of these atoms are **too massive** to be stable.

β⁻ Emission Happens in Neutron Rich Nuclei

1) **Beta-minus** (usually just called beta) decay is the emission of an **electron** from the **nucleus** along with an **antineutrino**.

2) Beta decay happens in isotopes that are **"neutron rich"** (i.e. have many more **neutrons** than **protons** in their nucleus).

3) When a nucleus ejects a beta particle, one of the **neutrons** in the nucleus is **changed** into a **proton**.

In **beta-plus emission**, a proton gets **changed** into a **neutron**. The proton number decreases by **one**, and the nucleon number stays the same.

When a **beta-minus** particle is **emitted**:

The **proton number increases by one**, and the **nucleon number stays the same**.

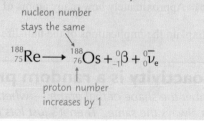

nucleon number stays the same

$^{188}_{75}Re \longrightarrow ^{188}_{76}Os + ^{0}_{-1}\beta + ^{0}_{0}\overline{\nu}_{e}$

proton number increases by 1

Nuclear Decay

γ **Radiation** is Emitted from **Nuclei** with **Too Much Energy**

1) After alpha or beta decay, the **nucleus** often has **excess energy** — it's **excited**. This energy is **lost** by emitting a **gamma ray**.

2) During **gamma emission**, there is **no change** to the nuclear **constituents** — the nucleus just **loses excess energy**.

3) **Another way** that gamma radiation is produced is when a nucleus **captures** one of its own orbiting **electrons**.

4) **Electron capture** causes a **proton** to **change** into a **neutron**. This makes the **nucleus unstable** and it **emits** gamma radiation.

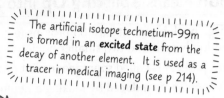

The artificial isotope technetium-99m is formed in an **excited state** from the decay of another element. It is used as a tracer in medical imaging (see p 214).

$$p + e \rightarrow n + \nu_e + \gamma$$

You Can Draw **Energy Level Diagrams** for **Nuclear Reactions**

Just like for electron energy transitions (p.18), you can draw **energy level diagrams** for these radioactive processes.

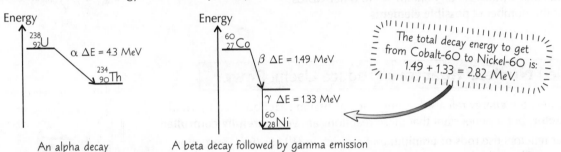

The total decay energy to get from Cobalt-60 to Nickel-60 is: 1.49 + 1.33 = 2.82 MeV.

An alpha decay

A beta decay followed by gamma emission

There are **Conservation Rules** in **Nuclear Reactions**

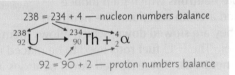

In every nuclear reaction **energy, momentum, charge** and **nucleon number** must be conserved.

$238 = 234 + 4$ — nucleon numbers balance

$$^{238}_{92}U \longrightarrow ^{234}_{90}Th + ^4_2\alpha$$

$92 = 90 + 2$ — proton numbers balance

Eugene was all about balance.

PRACTICE QUESTIONS

Warm-Up Questions

Q1 Sketch a graph of N against Z, marking on the line of stability and the regions where beta-minus and alpha decays occur.

Q2 What can make a nucleus unstable?

Q3 Describe the changes that happen in the nucleus during alpha, beta-minus, beta-plus and gamma decay.

Q4 What is the isotope technetium-99m used for?

Q5 List the circumstances in which gamma radiation may be emitted.

Q6 Draw an energy level diagram for a nucleus $^{14}_6C$ that undergoes beta decay and releases 0.16 MeV of energy.

Exam Questions

Q1 Radium-226 undergoes alpha decay to radon, releasing 4.78 MeV of energy.

a) Complete the balanced nuclear equation for this reaction. $^{226}_{88}Ra \rightarrow Rn$ [2 marks]

b) Draw an energy level diagram showing this transition. [1 mark]

Q2 Potassium-40 ($Z = 19$, $A = 40$) undergoes beta decay to calcium. Write a balanced nuclear equation for this reaction. [3 marks]

Nuclear decay — it can be enough to make you unstable...

Unstable nuclei will decay, and energy, momentum, proton number and nucleon number are conserved when they do. Make sure you learn how to draw and read those level diagrams — you could be asked about them in your exam.

Nuclear Fission and Fusion

Nuclear power provides shed-loads of energy whilst not creating as many greenhouse gases as traditional fossil fuels.

Fission Means Splitting Up into Smaller Parts

1) **Large nuclei**, with at least 83 protons (e.g. uranium), are **unstable** and some can randomly **split** into two **smaller** nuclei — this is called **nuclear fission**.

2) This process is called **spontaneous** if it just happens **by itself**, or **induced** if we **encourage** it to happen.

3) Fission can be **induced** by making a neutron enter a ^{235}U nucleus, causing it to become very unstable. Only **low energy** neutrons (called **thermal neutrons**) can be captured in this way.

4) **Energy is released** during nuclear fission because the new, smaller nuclei have a **higher binding energy per nucleon** (see p. 168).

5) The **larger** the nucleus, the more **unstable** it will be — so large nuclei are **more likely** to **spontaneously fission**.

6) This means that spontaneous fission **limits** the **number of nucleons** that a nucleus can contain — in other words, it **limits** the number of **possible elements**.

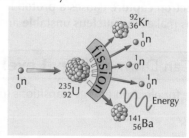

Controlled Nuclear Reactors Produce Useful Power

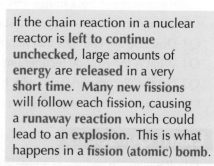

We can **harness** the **energy** released during nuclear **fission reactions** in a **thermal nuclear reactor**, but it's important that these reactions are very **carefully controlled**.

1) Nuclear reactors use **rods of uranium** that are rich in ^{235}U as 'fuel' for fission reactions. (The rods also contain a lot of ^{238}U, but that doesn't undergo fission.) These are placed into the reactor **remotely** which keeps workers as far away from the radiation as possible (p.160).

2) These **fission** reactions produce more **neutrons** which then **induce** other nuclei to fission — this is called a **chain reaction**. The **neutrons** will only cause a chain reaction if they are **slowed down**, which allows them to be **captured** by the uranium nuclei. The ^{235}U **fuel rods** need to be placed in a **moderator** (for example, **water**) to further **slow down** and/or absorb **neutrons**. These slowed down neutrons are called **thermal neutrons**.

3) This happens through **elastic collisions** (kinetic energy is conserved) with **nuclei** of the moderator material. Collisions with particles of a **similar mass** are more **efficient** at slowing neutrons down. **Water** is often used as a moderator because it contains **hydrogen**, which fits this condition.

4) You want the chain reaction to continue on its own at a **steady rate**, where **one** fission follows another. The amount of 'fuel' you need to do this is called the **critical mass** — any less than the critical mass (**sub-critical mass**) and the reaction will just peter out. Nuclear reactors use a **supercritical** mass of fuel (where several new fissions normally follow each fission) and **control the rate of fission** using **control rods**.

5) Control rods control the **chain reaction** by **limiting** the number of **neutrons** in the reactor. These **absorb neutrons** so that the **rate of fission** is controlled. **Control rods** are made up of a material that **absorbs neutrons** (e.g. boron), and they can be inserted by varying amounts to control the reaction rate. In an **emergency**, the reactor will be **shut down** automatically by the **release of the control rods** into the reactor, which will stop the reaction as quickly as possible.

6) **Coolant** is sent around the reactor to **remove heat** produced in the fission — often the coolant is the **same water** that is being used in the reactor as a **moderator**. The **heat** from the reactor can then be used to make **steam** for powering **electricity-generating turbines**.

7) The nuclear reactor is surrounded by a thick **concrete case**, which acts as **shielding**. This prevents **radiation escaping** and reaching the people working in the power station.

If the chain reaction in a nuclear reactor is **left to continue unchecked**, large amounts of **energy** are **released** in a very **short time**. **Many new fissions** will follow each fission, causing a **runaway reaction** which could lead to an **explosion**. This is what happens in a **fission (atomic) bomb**.

Before a new power plant is built, it has to be decided whether the benefits of nuclear power outweigh the risks (e.g. power plant meltdowns). Shielding and control rods help to reduce the risks involved with using nuclear power. It will never be risk-free but there are lots of measures in place to make it as safe as possible. A good understanding of nuclear physics can help society to make informed decisions about how electricity should be generated.

Nuclear Fission and Fusion

Waste Products of Fission Must be Stored Carefully

1) Although nuclear fission produces **lots** of **energy** and creates less **greenhouse gases** than burning fossil fuels, there are still lots of dangerous waste products.

2) The **waste products** of **nuclear fission** usually have a **larger proportion of neutrons** than nuclei of a similar atomic number — this makes them **unstable** and **radioactive**.

3) The products can be used for **practical applications** such as **tracers** in medical diagnosis (see p.214).

4) However, they may be **highly radioactive** and so their **handling** and **storage** needs **great care**.

5) When material is removed from the reactor, it is initially **very hot**, so is placed in **cooling ponds** until the **temperature falls** to a safe level.

6) This is done **remotely** — just like the handling of **fuel** — to limit the radiation workers are exposed to.

7) The radioactive waste is then **stored** in **sealed containers** until its **activity has fallen** sufficiently. Areas for storage are chosen where there will be **minimal impact** on animals and the environment — and any **people** that live nearby are **consulted** about the decision to store nuclear waste near them.

Fusion Means Joining Nuclei Together

1) **Two light nuclei** can **combine** to create a larger nucleus — this is called **nuclear fusion**.

2) A lot of **energy** is released during nuclear fusion because the new, heavier nuclei have a **much higher binding energy per nucleon** (see p.168).

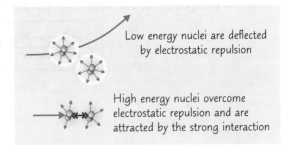

In the Sun, **hydrogen nuclei** fuse in a series of reactions to form **helium**.

e.g. $^2_1H + ^1_1H \rightarrow ^3_2He +$ energy

Nuclei Need Lots of Energy to Fuse

1) All nuclei are **positively charged** — so there will be an **electrostatic** (or Coulomb) **force** of **repulsion** between them.

2) Nuclei can only **fuse** if they **overcome** this electrostatic force and get **close** enough for the attractive force of the **strong interaction** to hold them both together.

3) About **1 MeV** of kinetic energy is **needed** to make nuclei fuse together — and that's **a lot of energy**.

Low energy nuclei are deflected by electrostatic repulsion

High energy nuclei overcome electrostatic repulsion and are attracted by the strong interaction

Warm-Up Questions

Q1 What is the difference between spontaneous and induced fission and how can fission be induced in ^{235}U?

Q2 Describe and explain the roles of the moderator, coolant and shielding in a nuclear reactor, giving examples of the materials commonly used for them and the reasons for choosing these materials.

Q3 Why must the waste products of nuclear fission be handled remotely and disposed of very carefully?

Q4 Why is a lot of energy required for nuclear fusion to occur?

Exam Questions

Q1 Nuclear reactors use carefully controlled chain reactions to produce energy.

a) Explain what is meant by the expressions 'chain reaction' and 'critical mass' in terms of nuclear fission. [3 marks]

b) State one feature of a nuclear reactor whose role is to control the rate of fission and describe how it works. Include an example of a suitable material for the feature you have chosen. [3 marks]

c) Explain what happens in a nuclear reactor during an emergency shut-down. [2 marks]

Q2 State two advantages and two disadvantages of using nuclear fission to produce electricity. [4 marks]

If anyone asks, I've gone fission... that joke never gets old...

So many words... But all of them pretty important. You already knew fission created loads of energy, but now you have to learn all the grizzly details about how reactors actually work and what to do with all the waste they produce.

Binding Energy

Turn off the radio and close the door, 'cos you're going to need to concentrate hard on this stuff about binding energy...

The **Mass Defect** is **Equivalent** to the **Binding Energy**

1) The **mass** of a **nucleus** is **less than** the mass of its **constituent parts** — the difference is called the **mass defect**.

2) Einstein's equation, $E = mc^2$, says that mass and energy are **equivalent**. It applies to **all** energy changes.

3) So, as nucleons join together, the total mass **decreases** — this 'lost' mass is **converted** into energy and **released**.

4) The amount of **energy released** is **equivalent** to the **mass defect**.

5) If you **pulled** the nucleus completely **apart**, the **energy** you'd have to use to do it would be the **same** the energy **released** when the nucleus formed.

> The energy needed to **separate** all of the nucleons in a nucleus is called the **binding energy** (measured in **MeV**), and it is **equivalent** to the **mass defect**.

Example: Estimate the binding energy in eV of the nucleus of a lithium atom, ^6_3Li, given that its mass defect is 0.0343 u.

1) Convert the mass defect into kg.
Mass defect = $0.0343 \times (1.661 \times 10^{-27}) = 5.697... \times 10^{-29}$

2) Use $E = mc^2$ to calculate the binding energy.
$E = (5.697... \times 10^{-29}) \times (3.00 \times 10^8)^2 = 5.127... \times 10^{-12}$ J
$= (5.127... \times 10^{-12}) \div (1.60 \times 10^{-13})$
$= 32.0...$ MeV = **32.0 MeV (to 3 s.f.)**

Atomic mass is usually given in atomic mass units (u) where 1 u = 1.661×10^{-27} kg

1 MeV = 1.60×10^{-13} J

6) A mass defect of **1 u** is equivalent to about **931.5 MeV** of binding energy.

$$\frac{\text{binding energy}}{\text{mass defect}} \approx 931.5 \text{ MeVu}^{-1}$$

Captain Skip didn't believe in ghosts, marmalade and that things could be bound without rope.

You could get 1 u equivalent to 931.75 MeV using the numbers on this page. The value of 931.5 MeV is found from using more precise values of u, c and e.

The **Average Binding Energy Per Nucleon** is at a **Maximum** around **A = 50**

A useful way of **comparing** the binding energies of different nuclei is to look at the average **binding energy per nucleon**.

$$\text{Average binding energy per nucleon (in MeV)} = \frac{\text{Binding energy } (B)}{\text{Nucleon number } (A)}$$

So, the binding energy per nucleon for ^6_3Li (in the example above) is $32 \div 6 = 5.3$ MeV.

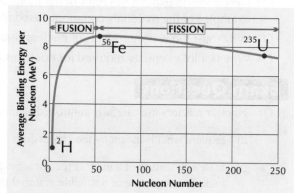

1) A **graph** of **average binding energy per nucleon** against **nucleon number**, for all elements, shows a **curve**. **High** average binding energy per nucleon means that **more energy** is needed to **remove** nucleons from the nucleus.

2) In other words, the **most stable** nuclei occur around the **maximum point** on the graph — which is at **nucleon number 56** (i.e. **iron, Fe**).

3) **Combining small nuclei** is called nuclear **fusion** (see p.167) — this **increases** the **average binding energy per nucleon** dramatically, which means a lot of **energy is released** during nuclear fusion.

4) **Fission** is when **large nuclei** are **split in two** (see p.166) — the **nucleon numbers** of the two **new nuclei** are **smaller** than the original nucleus, which means there is an **increase** in the average binding energy per nucleon. So, energy is also **released** during nuclear fission (but not as much energy per nucleon as in nuclear fusion).

Binding Energy

The **Change** in **Average Binding Energy** Gives the **Energy Released**

The average **binding energy per nucleon graph** can be used to **estimate** the **energy released** from nuclear reactions.

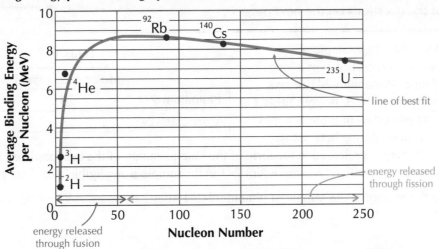

Fusion

1) ^{4}He nuclei have **4 nucleons**, so the **binding energy** of ^{4}He $= 4 \times 6.8 = $ **27.2 MeV**.

2) The binding energy of ^{2}H and ^{3}H $= (2 \times 1.1) + (3 \times 2.6) = $ **10.0 MeV**.

3) So if ^{2}H and ^{3}H nuclei were **fused** together to form ^{4}He (and a neutron), the **energy released** would be $27.2 - 10.0 = 17.2 = $ **17 MeV (to 2 s.f.)**.

Fission

1) The binding energy of ^{235}U $= 235 \times 7.4 = $ 1739 MeV.

2) The binding energy of ^{92}Rb and ^{140}Cs $= (92 \times 8.8) + (140 \times 8.2) = $ 1957.6 MeV.

3) So if a ^{235}U nucleus splits into ^{92}Rb and ^{140}Cs (plus a few neutrons) during nuclear fission, the energy released would be $= 1957.6 - 1739 = 218.6 = $ 220 MeV (to 2 s.f.)

Warm-Up Questions

Q1 State the formula relating energy to mass and the speed of a light in a vacuum.

Q2 What is the binding energy of a nucleus?

Q3 What is the binding energy in MeV equivalent to a mass defect of 1 u?

Q4 What is meant by the binding energy per nucleon?

Q5 Sketch a graph of average binding energy per nucleon against nucleon number, labelling the regions where fusion and fission occur and the element with the highest average binding energy per nucleon.

Q6 How would you calculate the energy released by a fission reaction, given the masses of the products and reactants?

Exam Questions

Q1 The mass defect of a uranium-235 nucleus is 1.864557 u.

a) Calculate the binding energy, in joules, of a uranium-235 nucleus. *(1 MeV = 1.60 × 10^{-13} J)* [2 marks]

b) Calculate the average binding energy (in MeV) per nucleon for uranium-235. [1 mark]

Q2 The following equation shows a nuclear reaction between two deuterium ($^2_1$H) nuclei, to form helium-3 ($^3_2$He):

$$^2_1\text{H} + ^2_1\text{H} \rightarrow ^3_2\text{He} + ^1_0\text{n} + \text{energy}$$

a) State what type of nuclear reaction this is. [1 mark]

b) The binding energy per nucleon is 0 MeV for a neutron, approximately 1.11 MeV for a $^2_1$H nucleus, and approximately 2.58 MeV for a $^3_2$He nucleus. Use these values to estimate the energy released by this reaction. [3 marks]

A mass defect of 1 u is equivalent to a binding energy of 931.5 MeV...

Remember this useful little fact, and it'll save loads of time in the exam — because you won't have to fiddle around with converting atomic mass from u to kg and binding energy from J to MeV. What more could you possibly want...

Extra Exam Practice

Section 12 is done — before moving on to your optional module, have a final practice of Nuclear Physics.

- Have a look at this example of how to answer a tricky exam question.
- Then check how much you've understood from Section 12 by having a go at the questions on the next page.

Don't forget, there's also a section of synoptic questions covering the whole course on page 268.

---

1 The activity of a 250 g sample of plutonium-241 is recorded over a long period of time. Plutonium-241 decays into americium-241 by β^- decay. **Table 1** shows some properties of these isotopes. Energy is released during beta decay.

Table 1

	Molar mass / gmol^{-1}	Half-life / s
Plutonium-241	241	4.5×10^8
Americium-241	241	1.4×10^{10}

Some of the energy is released in the form of the kinetic energy of the beta particle. For this question, assume the activity of americium-241 in the sample is negligible after 2.00 years.

1.1 Calculate the activity of the sample of plutonium-241 after 2.00 years. ($N_A = 6.02 \times 10^{23}$)

(3 marks)

1.2 After 2.00 years, 1.82×10^{19} eV of the energy released by the sample is transferred to the kinetic energy of the beta particles every second. Calculate the average speed of the emitted beta particles. ($e = 1.60 \times 10^{-19}$ C, $m_e = 9.11 \times 10^{-31}$ kg).

(2 marks)

1.3 Suggest and explain why the assumption stated about americium-241 is justified.

(3 marks)

1.1

You'll need to use $A = A_o e^{-\lambda t}$. $A_o = \lambda N$, but you're not given N or λ, so you'll need formulas for each of them.

$N = n \times N_A = \dfrac{\text{mass}}{\text{molar mass}} \times N_A = \dfrac{250}{241} \times 6.02 \times 10^{23} = \mathbf{6.244... \times 10^{23}}$

$A_o = \lambda N = \dfrac{\ln 2}{T_{1/2}} \times N = \dfrac{\ln 2}{4.5 \times 10^8} \times 6.244... \times 10^{23} = 9.619... \times 10^{14}$ Bq

$A = A_o e^{-\lambda t} = 9.619... \times 10^{14} \times e^{-(\ln 2 \div 4.5 \times 10^8) \times 2.00 \times 365 \times 24 \times 60 \times 60}$

$= 8.728... \times 10^{14} = 8.7 \times 10^{14}$ Bq (to 2 s.f.)

Don't round any answers until the very end. You can use your calculator memory function to save long values and recall them in later calculations.

You'd get 3 marks for the correct answer, otherwise you'd get 1 mark for correctly calculating N and 1 mark for correctly calculating the initial activity of the sample.

1.2

Remember to convert the time to seconds.

Remember, activity is decays per second, and one beta particle is released per decay.

The average kinetic energy of each beta particle is equal to the total energy transferred every second to the kinetic energy of the beta particles divided by the number of beta particles released per second:

average kinetic energy $= \dfrac{1.82 \times 10^{19}}{8.728... \times 10^{14}} = 20\,851.2141$ eV

$20\,851.2141 \times 1.60 \times 10^{-19} = \mathbf{3.336... \times 10^{-15}}$ J

$E_k = \dfrac{1}{2} m_e v^2$, so $v = \sqrt{\dfrac{2E_k}{m_e}} = \sqrt{\dfrac{2 \times 3.336... \times 10^{-15}}{9.11 \times 10^{-31}}}$

$= 8.558... \times 10^7 = 8.6 \times 10^7$ ms^{-1} (to 2 s.f.)

The energy given in the question is in eV — don't forget you need to convert this into joules to use the formula for E_k.

You'd get 2 marks for the correct answer, otherwise you'd get 1 mark for calculating the average kinetic energy of each beta particle in eV.

You'd get 1 mark for comparing N for both isotopes, 1 mark for comparing λ for both isotopes, and 1 mark for explaining why this means A for americium is much smaller than for plutonium.

1.3

After 2 years the plutonium's activity is $\dfrac{A}{A_o} \approx \dfrac{8.7}{9.6} \approx 90\%$ of its original value. So only 10% of the sample is now americium and so N for americium is **smaller than** for plutonium. Americium has a much **longer half-life** than plutonium, so λ is smaller. $A = \lambda N$ and since λ and N for americium are both small compared to plutonium, the activity is very small in comparison.

You have to show that americium's activity is negligible compared to plutonium's, so you need to make comparisons to plutonium-241.

Extra Exam Practice

2 Nuclear fission and fusion can be used to produce large amounts of energy.

2.1 Use the concept of mass defect to explain how fission and fusion release energy.
Your answer should include a graph sketch and a discussion of under what conditions energy can and cannot be released by fusion and fission.

(6 marks)

2.2 A fast neutron reactor is a nuclear fission reactor in which neutrons do not have to be slowed down in order to be absorbed by the fuel. In a fast neutron reactor, a neutron with a kinetic energy of 11.5 MeV is absorbed by a stationary uranium-235 nucleus, and the following decay occurs:

$$^{235}_{92}U + ^{1}_{0}n \rightarrow ^{141}_{56}Ba + ^{92}_{36}Kr + 3^{1}_{0}n$$

During this particular fission reaction, 4.20% of the energy released is in the form of the kinetic energy of the emitted neutrons. Calculate the average kinetic energy of an emitted neutron in eV.
Mass of U-235 = 235.044 u, mass of Ba-141 = 140.914 u, mass of Kr-92 = 91.926 u.
(1 u is equivalent to 931.5 MeV, m_n = 1.00867 u)

(4 marks)

2.3 Explain how the design of a fast neutron reactor would differ from a thermal neutron reactor.

(1 mark)

3 Nuclear radius (R) is difficult to measure as the nucleus is too small for visible light to interact with. It has been determined by experiments to be related to nucleon number (A) by $R = R_0 A^{1/3}$.

A scientist carries out two experiments to investigate the nuclear radius of silver ($A = 107$, $Z = 47$).
Figure 1 shows the results of a diffraction experiment in which electrons with a de Broglie wavelength of 4.10 fm are fired at a thin sheet of silver foil. **Figure 2** shows the results of an alpha scattering experiment in which alpha particles are accelerated to a fixed kinetic energy and fired at a sheet of silver foil. The number of alpha particles deflected between the angles 60° to 80°, N_α, is recorded by a detector as the kinetic energy is gradually increased.

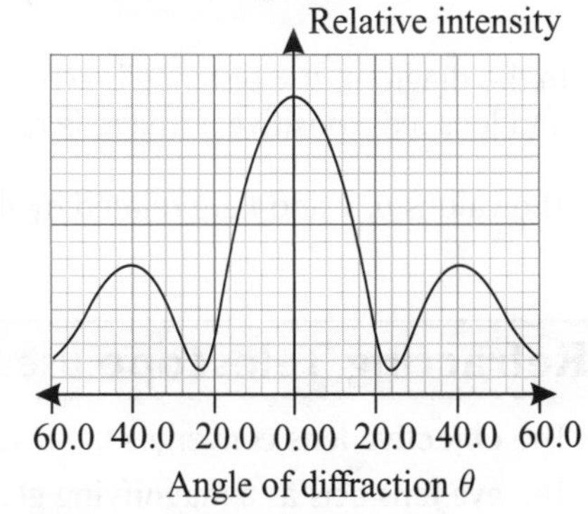

3.1 For waves diffracting around a spherical object, the first minimum is found at $\sin\theta \approx \dfrac{1.22\lambda}{2R}$.
Use **Figure 1** to calculate an estimate of R_0.

(3 marks)

Figure 1

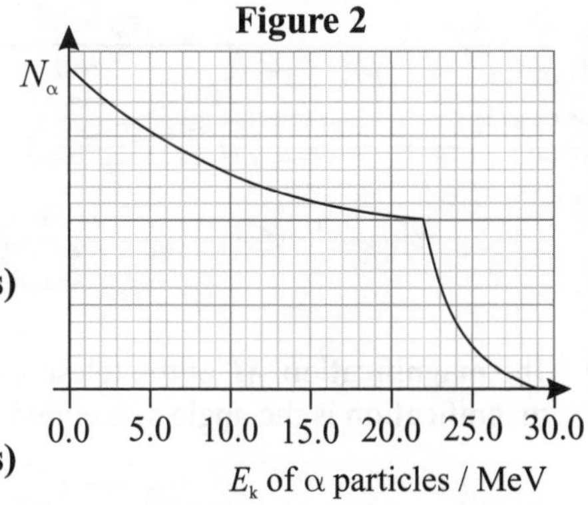

The nucleus is held together by the attractive strong nuclear force which, at very small separations, overcomes the repulsive electrostatic force between protons.

3.2 Suggest a reason for the change in the shape of **Figure 2** at E_k = 22.0 MeV.

(2 marks)

3.3 Use **Figure 2** to calculate an estimate of R_0.
($e = 1.60 \times 10^{-19}$ C, $\varepsilon = 8.85 \times 10^{-12}$ Fm^{-1})

(3 marks)

Figure 2

3.4 R_0 is usually stated as being between 1.2 and 1.5 fm.
Explain why it is difficult to assess the accuracy of the results in 3.1 and 3.3.

(1 mark)

Optical Telescopes

Some optical telescopes use lenses (no, really), so first, here's a bit of lens theory...

Converging Lenses Bring Light Rays Together

1) **Lenses** change the **direction** of light rays by **refraction**.

2) Rays **parallel** to the **principal axis** of the lens converge onto a point called the **principal focus**. Parallel rays that **aren't** parallel to the principal axis converge somewhere else on the **focal plane** (see diagram).

3) The **focal length**, f, is the distance between the **lens axis** and the **focal plane**.

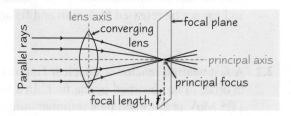

Images can be Real or Virtual

1) A **real image** is formed when light rays from an object are made to **pass through** another point in space. The light rays are **actually there**, and the image can be **captured** on a **screen**.

2) A **virtual image** is formed when light rays from an object **appear** to have come from another point in space. The light rays **aren't really where the image appears to be**, so the image **can't** be captured on a screen.

3) Converging lenses can form both **real** and **virtual** images, depending on where the object is. If the object is **further** than the **focal length** away from the lens, the image is **real**. If the object's **closer**, the image is **virtual**.

4) To work out where an image will appear, you can draw a **ray diagram**. Draw **two rays** from the same point on the object (the top is best) one **parallel** to the principal axis that passes through the **principal focus**, and one passing through the **centre** of the lens that **doesn't get refracted** (bent). The image will form where the **two rays meet** if the image is real, or where the two rays appear to have **come from** if the image is virtual:

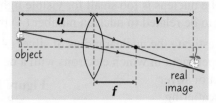
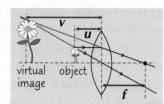

If an object sits on the principal axis, so will the image.

In the diagram, u = distance between object and lens axis, v = distance between image and lens axis (**positive** if image is **real**, **negative** if image is **virtual**), f = focal length.

5) The values u, v and f are related by the **lens equation**: ⟹ $\boxed{\frac{1}{f} = \frac{1}{u} + \frac{1}{v}}$

A Refracting Telescope uses Two Converging Lenses

1) The **objective lens** converges the rays from the object to form a **real image**.

2) The **eye lens** acts as a **magnifying glass** on this real image to form a **magnified virtual image**.

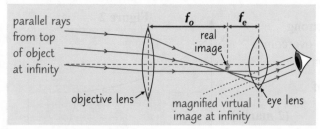

3) If you assume the object is at infinity, then the rays from it are **parallel**, and the real image is formed on the **focal plane**.

4) A **telescope** (in normal adjustment) is set up so that the **principal focus** of the **objective** lens is in the **same position** as the principal focus of the **eye** lens, so the **final magnified image** appears to be at **infinity**.

5) The **magnification**, M, of the telescope can be calculated in terms of angles, or the focal length. The **angular magnification** is the **angle** subtended by the **image** θ_i over the **angle** subtended by the **object** θ_o at the eye:

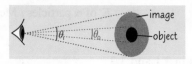

$\boxed{M = \frac{\theta_i}{\theta_o}}$

or in terms of **focal length** (with the telescope in normal adjustment as shown above): $\boxed{M = \frac{f_o}{f_e}}$

A large magnification is needed — so $f_o > f_e$

Optical Telescopes

A **Reflecting Telescope** use **Two Mirrors** and a **Converging Lens**

1) A **parabolic concave mirror** (the **primary mirror**) converges parallel rays from an object, forming a **real image**.

2) An **eye lens magnifies** the image as before.

3) The principle focus of the mirror (where the image is formed) is **in front** of the mirror, so an arrangement needs to be devised where the observer doesn't **block out** the light.

4) A set-up called the **Cassegrain arrangement**, which uses a **convex secondary mirror**, is a common solution to this problem.

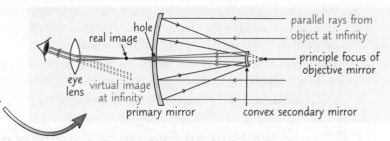

The **Resolving Power** of a Telescope — How Much **Detail** You Can See

1) The **resolving power** of a telescope is just a **measure** of how much **detail** you can see. It's dependent on the **minimum angular resolution** — the **smallest** angular **separation** at which the instrument can **distinguish two points**. The **smaller** the minimum angular resolution, the **better** the resolving power.

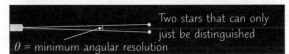

Two stars that can only just be distinguished

θ = minimum angular resolution

About half of the stars that we see in the night sky are actually collections of two or more stars. Our eyes see them as a single star since the angle between them is too small to resolve.

2) Resolution is limited by diffraction. If a beam of light passes through a circular **aperture**, then a **diffraction pattern** is formed. The central circle is called the **Airy disc** (see p. 250 for an example of the pattern).

3) **Two** light sources can **just** be distinguished if the **centre** of the **Airy disc** from one source is at **least as far away** as the **first minimum** of the other source. This led to the **Rayleigh criterion**:

$$\theta \approx \frac{\lambda}{D}$$

where θ is the **minimum angular resolution** in **radians**, λ is the **wavelength** of the light in **metres** and D is the **diameter** of the **aperture** in **metres**.

4) For **telescopes**, D is the diameter of the **objective lens** or the **objective mirror**. So **very large** lenses or mirrors are needed to see **fine detail**.

There are **Big Problems** with **Refracting Telescopes**

1) Glass refracts **different colours** of light by **different amounts** and so the image for each colour is in a slightly **different position**. This **blurs** the image and is called **chromatic aberration**.

2) Any **bubbles** and **impurities** in the glass **absorb** some of the light, which means that **very faint** objects **aren't seen**. Building large lenses that are of a **sufficiently good quality** is **difficult** and **expensive**.

glass lens bends blue light more than red

white object | blue image | red image

3) **Large lenses** are very **heavy** and can only be **supported** from their **edges**, so their **shape** can become **distorted**.

4) For a **large magnification**, the **objective lens** needs to have a **very long focal length**. This means that refracting telescopes have to be **very long**, leading to very **large** and **expensive buildings** needed to house them.

Reflecting Telescopes are **Better** than Refractors but Still Have **Problems**

1) **Large mirrors** of **good quality** are much **cheaper** to build than large lenses. They can also be **supported** from **underneath** so they don't **distort** as much as lenses.

2) Mirrors don't suffer from **chromatic aberration** (see above) but can have **spherical aberration**:

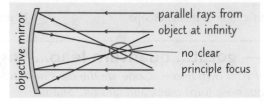

parallel rays from object at infinity

no clear principle focus

If the **shape** of the mirror isn't quite **parabolic**, parallel rays reflecting off different parts of the mirror do not all **converge** onto the same point.

When the **Hubble Space Telescope** was first launched it suffered from **spherical aberration**. They had to find a way round the problem before it could be used.

Optical Telescopes

Charge-Coupled Devices (CCDs) are Very Sensitive Image Detectors

1) CCDs are **silicon chips** about the size of a postage stamp, divided up into a grid of millions of **identical pixels**.

2) When photons hit the silicon in a pixel, they cause **electrons** to be released. These electrons alter the charge on each pixel — this charge can be measured and used to create a **digital signal**.

3) This signal describes not only **where** the light hits, but its **brightness/intensity** too, as the charge on each pixel will vary depending on how many photons hit it. This allows a **digital image** of an object to be created.

4) CCDs are used in **lots** of places — **digital cameras**, barcode scanners and giant astronomical **telescopes**.

CCDs and the Human Eye can be Compared as Image Detectors

1) **Quantum Efficiency** — Quantum efficiency is the proportion of the incident photons that are detected. For a CCD it's typically 80% or more. The quantum efficiency of the eye is of the order of 1%, so CCDs detect far more of the light that falls on them than the eye does.

2) **Detectable Light Spectrum** — The eye can only detect visible light, whereas CCDs can detect infrared, visible and UV light.

3) **Resolution** — If you were to project the whole visual field of an eye onto a screen, you'd need over 500 megapixels for the eye not to see any pixelation. CCDs on the other hand have of the order of 50 megapixels, so it seems like the eye captures more detail than a CCD. However, what's also important is how far apart different parts of the object being viewed need to be in order for them to be distinguishable — this is called spatial resolution. The minimum resolvable distance of the human eye is around 100 μm, whereas CCDs can have a spatial resolution of around 10 μm. So CCDs are better for capturing fine detail.

The numbers here are a bit rough and ready — it's hard to measure things like quantum efficiency for the eye, and CCDs come with a range of different specifications. You may be asked about these figures in the exam, so make sure you learn them, but remember they're only a rough guide.

4) **Convenience** — The human eye doesn't need any extra equipment, and looking down a telescope is simpler than setting up a CCD, but CCDs produce digital images which can be stored, copied, and shared globally.

Warm-Up Questions

Q1 Define the focal length and principal focus of a converging lens.

Q2 Draw ray diagrams to show how an image is formed in a refracting telescope in normal adjustment and a reflecting (Cassegrain) telescope.

Q3 Explain resolving power and state the Rayleigh criterion.

Q4 What does quantum efficiency mean? Estimate the quantum efficiency of a CCD.

Q5 Give two reasons why you would use a telescope with a CCD to collect data instead of one without a CCD.

Exam Questions

Q1 a) A telescope has a dish diameter of 1.6 m. It is being used to detect light with wavelength 620 nm from two stars. Calculate the minimum angular separation of the two stars in order for them to be distinguishable by the telescope. [1 mark]

   b) If the dish of the telescope is made smaller, explain what happens to its resolving power. [1 mark]

Q2 An objective lens with a focal length of 5.0 m and an eye lens with a focal length of 0.10 m are used in a refracting telescope.

   a) Calculate how far apart the lenses should be placed for the telescope to be in normal adjustment. [1 mark]

   b) Define angular magnification and calculate the angular magnification of this telescope. [2 marks]

CCDs were a quantum leap for astronomy — get it... quantum leap... *sigh*

With CCDs, you can get all the images you want from the comfort of your own home. Gone are the days of standing on a hill with a telescope and a flask hoping the sky clears before your nose turns black and falls off. Shame.

Non-Optical Telescopes

Some telescopes don't use visible light — they use radio waves, IR, UV or X-rays instead — read on to learn more...

Radio Telescopes are Similar to Optical Telescopes in Some Ways

1) The most obvious feature of a radio telescope is its **parabolic dish**.
   This works in exactly the same way as the **objective mirror** of an **optical reflecting** telescope.

2) An **antenna** is used as a detector at the **focal point** instead of an eye or camera
   in an optical telescope, but there is **no equivalent** to the **eye lens**.

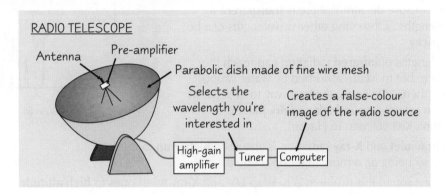

RADIO TELESCOPE

Antenna Pre-amplifier

Parabolic dish made of fine wire mesh

High-gain amplifier — Tuner — Computer

Selects the wavelength you're interested in

Creates a false-colour image of the radio source

3) Most radio telescopes are **manoeuvrable**, allowing the source of the waves to be **tracked** (in the same way as optical telescopes). The telescope moves with the source, stopping it 'slipping out of view' as the Earth rotates.

Radio Waves have a Much Longer Wavelength than Light...

1) The **wavelengths** of **radio waves** are about a **million times longer** than the wavelengths of **light**.

2) The **resolving power** of a telescope is dependent on the **Rayleigh criterion** (see p.173), which is $\theta \approx \lambda/D$.

3) So for a radio telescope to have the **same resolving power** as an optical telescope, its
   dish would need to be a **million times bigger** (about the size of the UK for a decent
   one). The **resolving power** of a radio telescope is **worse** than the **unaided eye**.

Radio astronomers get around this by linking lots of telescopes together.

Using some nifty computer programming, their data can be combined to form a single image. This is equivalent to one huge dish the size of the separation of the telescopes.

Resolutions thousands of times better than optical telescopes can be achieved this way.

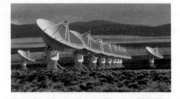

...so Radio Telescopes aren't as Fiddly to Make as Optical Reflectors

1) Instead of a **polished mirror**, a **wire mesh** can be used since the long wavelength radio waves don't notice the gaps. This makes their **construction** much **easier** and **cheaper** than optical reflectors.

2) The **shape** of the dish has to have a **precision** of about $\lambda/20$ to avoid **spherical aberration** (see page 173). So the dish does not have to be **anywhere near as perfect** as a mirror.

3) However, unlike an optical telescope, a radio telescope has to **scan across** the radio source to **build up** the **image**.

Non-Optical Telescopes

The **Atmosphere Blocks** Certain **EM Wavelengths**

1) One of the big problems with doing astronomy on Earth is trying to look through the atmosphere.

2) Our atmosphere only lets **certain wavelengths** of **electromagnetic radiation** through and is **opaque** to all the others. The graph shows how the **transparency** of the atmosphere varies with **wavelength**.

3) We can use **optical** and **radio** telescopes on the surface of the Earth because the atmosphere is **transparent** to these wavelengths. Observing other wavelengths can be a bit more tricky.

4) A few wavelengths of **infrared** radiation can reach the Earth's surface, but most are absorbed by water vapour in the atmosphere. On Earth, the best way to observe IR radiation is to set up shop in **high** and **dry** places, like the Mauna Kea volcano in Hawaii.

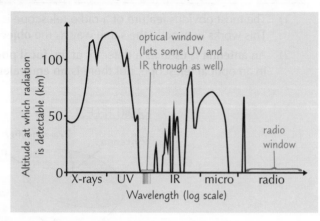

5) But most **ultraviolet** and **X-ray** radiation is absorbed **higher up** in the atmosphere, so being on a mountain doesn't help.

6) One way to get round this problem is to strap UV and X-ray telescopes to **high altitude weather balloons** or **aeroplanes**. They can take the telescope high enough into the atmosphere to detect the radiation.

7) The ideal situation is to get your telescope **above the atmosphere** altogether, by launching it into **space** and setting it in orbit around the Earth.

IR and **UV** Telescopes have a **Very Similar Structure** to **Optical** Telescopes

1) Infrared and ultraviolet telescopes are very similar to optical reflecting telescopes. They use the same **parabolic mirror** set-up to focus the radiation onto a detector.

2) In both cases, **CCDs** (see p.174) or **special photographic paper** are used as the radiation detectors, just as in optical telescopes.

3) The **longer** the **wavelength** of the radiation, the **less** it's affected by imperfections in the mirror (see previous page). So the mirrors in **infrared** telescopes **don't** need to be as perfectly shaped as in optical telescopes. But the mirrors in **UV** telescopes have to be even **more** precisely made.

IR telescopes have the added problem that they produce their **own** infrared radiation due to their **temperature**. They need to be **cooled** to very low temperatures using liquid helium, or refrigeration units.

X-ray Telescopes have a **Different Structure** from Other Telescopes

1) X-rays don't reflect off surfaces in the same way as most other EM radiation. Usually X-ray radiation is either **absorbed** by a material or it **passes straight through** it.

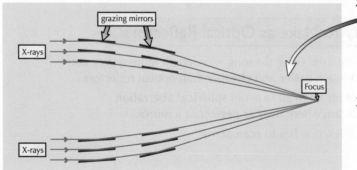

2) X-rays **do** reflect if they just **graze** a mirror's surface though. By having a series of **nested mirrors**, you can gradually alter the direction of X-rays enough to bring them to a **focus** on a detector. This type of telescope is called a **grazing telescope**.

3) The X-rays can be detected using a modified **Geiger counter** or a **fine wire mesh**. Newer X-ray telescopes such as the XMM-Newton telescope use highly sensitive X-ray **CCD** cameras.

Non-Optical Telescopes

Different Telescopes have Different **Resolving** and **Collecting Powers**

The RESOLVING POWER of a telescope is limited by two main factors:

1) The **Rayleigh criterion** (see page 173):
This depends on the **wavelength** of the radiation and the **diameter** of the objective mirror or dish.
So, for the **same size** of dish, a UV telescope has a much better resolving power than a radio telescope.

2) The quality of the **detector**:
Just like in digital cameras, the resolving power of a telescope is limited by the resolution of the detector. That can be how many **pixels** there are on a CCD, or for a wire mesh X-ray detector, how **fine** the wire mesh is.

The COLLECTING POWER of a telescope is proportional to its **collecting area**.

1) A **bigger dish** or **mirror** collects **more energy** from an object in a given time.
This gives a **more intense image**, so the telescope can observe **fainter** objects.

2) The **collecting power** (energy collected per second) is proportional to the area:

The bigger the dish, the greater the collecting power. Mmm....

$$\text{Power} \propto \text{Diameter}^2$$

3) For a **radio**, **optical**, **UV** or **IR** telescope, this is the area of the objective mirror or dish.

4) For **X-ray** telescopes, it's the area of the **opening** through which X-rays can enter the telescope.
In general, X-ray telescopes have a much **smaller collecting power** than other types of telescope.

Warm-Up Questions

PRACTICE QUESTIONS

Q1 Why do radio telescopes tend to have poor resolving powers?

Q2 Why is it easier to make a parabolic dish for a radio telescope than it is to make a parabolic mirror for an optical telescope?

Q3 Why don't astronomers install UV and X-ray telescopes on the top of mountains?

Exam Questions

Q1 Describe and explain the differences in resolving and collecting powers of a radio telescope and a UV telescope with the same surface area, given that their detectors have the same resolution. [4 marks]

Q2 In 1983, the IRAS satellite observed the entire sky in infrared wavelengths. The satellite was kept at a temperature of 2 K by a reservoir of liquid helium which cooled the satellite by evaporation.

    a) Explain why the satellite needed to be kept at such a low temperature. [2 marks]

    b) Some infrared telescopes are on the surface of the Earth.
    State the typical location of this type of telescope [1 mark]

Q3 a) Many X-ray and UV telescopes are housed on satellites that orbit high above the Earth's atmosphere.
    Where else are X-ray and UV telescopes positioned? Explain why this is necessary. [2 marks]

    b) Describe and explain the major differences between the mirrors in X-ray and UV telescopes. [3 marks]

Q4 a) State how the collecting power of a telescope is related to its objective diameter. [1 mark]

    b) The Arecibo radio telescope has a dish diameter of 300 m (to 2 s.f.). The Lovell radio telescope has a dish diameter of 76 m. Calculate the ratio of their collecting powers. [2 marks]

Power is proportional to diameter²? Bring on the cakes...

If you can't observe the radiation you want to from Earth, just strap your telescope to a rocket and blast it into space. Sounds easy enough till you remember it's going to be reeeally hard to repair if anything goes wrong.

Distances and Magnitude

There are a couple of ways to classify stars — the first is by luminosity, using the magnitude scale.

The **Luminosity** of a Star is the **Total Energy** Emitted **per Second**

1) Stars can be **classified** according to their luminosity — that is, the **total** amount of energy emitted in the form of electromagnetic radiation **each second** (see p.180).

2) The **Sun's** luminosity is about 4×10^{26} W (luminosity is measured in watts, since it's a sort of power). The **most luminous** stars have a luminosity about a **million** times that of the Sun.

3) The **intensity**, I, of an object that we observe is the power **received** from it per unit area **at Earth**. This is the effective **brightness** of an object.

Apparent Magnitude, m, is Based on how **Bright** things **Appear** from **Earth**

1) The **brightness** of a star in the night sky depends on **two** things — its **luminosity** and its **distance from us** (if you ignore weather and light pollution, etc.). So the **brightest** stars will either be **close** to us or have a **high luminosity**.

2) An Ancient Greek called **Hipparchus** invented a system where the very **brightest** stars were given an **apparent magnitude** of **1** and the **dimmest** visible stars an apparent magnitude of **6**, with other levels catering for the stars in between.

3) In the 19th century, the scale was redefined using a strict **logarithmic** scale:

> A **magnitude 1** star has an **intensity 100 times** greater than a **magnitude 6** star.

This means a difference of **one magnitude** corresponds to a difference in **intensity** of $100^{1/5}$ **times**. So a magnitude 1 star is about **2.51 times brighter** than a magnitude 2 star.

4) At the same time, the range was **extended** in **both directions** with the very brightest objects in the sky having **negative apparent magnitude**.

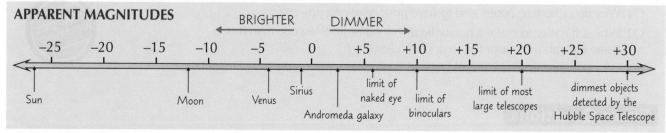

APPARENT MAGNITUDES
BRIGHTER DIMMER
−25 −20 −15 −10 −5 0 +5 +10 +15 +20 +25 +30

Sun — Moon — Venus — Sirius — Andromeda galaxy — limit of naked eye — limit of binoculars — limit of most large telescopes — dimmest objects detected by the Hubble Space Telescope

5) You can calculate the **brightness** (or intensity) **ratio** between **two stars** using:

*Brightness is a **subjective** scale of measurement. This means that two different people could measure the brightness of the same object as different values — it depends on the person.*

$$\frac{I_2}{I_1} \approx 2.51^{m_1 - m_2}$$

where I_1 is the **intensity** of **star 1**, I_2 is the **intensity** of **star 2**, m_1 is the apparent magnitude of **star 1** and m_2 is the apparent magnitude of **star 2**.

The **Distance** to **Nearby Stars** can be Measured in **Parsecs**

1) Imagine you're in a **moving car**. You see that (stationary) objects in the **foreground** seem to be **moving faster** than objects in the **distance**. This **apparent change in position** is called **parallax**.

2) Parallax is measured in terms of the **angle of parallax**. The **greater** the **angle**, the **nearer** the object is to you.

3) The distance to **nearby stars** can be calculated by observing how they **move relative** to **very distant stars** when the Earth is in **different parts** of its **orbit**. This gives a **unit** of distance called a **parsec (pc)**.

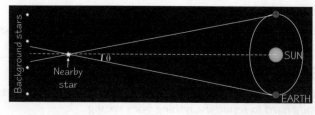

A star is exactly **one parsec (pc)** away from Earth if the **angle of parallax**, θ, is:

$$\theta = 1\,\text{arcsecond} = \left(\frac{1}{3600}\right)^{\circ}$$

1 parsec = 3.08×10^{16} m.

Distances and Magnitude

Absolute Magnitude, *M*, is based only on the Luminosity of the Star

1) The **absolute magnitude** of a star or galaxy, *M*, does not depend on its distance from Earth. It is defined as what its apparent magnitude **would be** if it were **10 parsecs** away from Earth.

2) The relationship between *M* and *m* is given by the formula:

$$m - M = 5\log\left(\frac{d}{10}\right)$$

where *d* is the distance in parsecs

If you know the absolute magnitude of a star, you can use this equation to calculate its **distance** from Earth. This is really handy, since the distance to most stars is **too big** to measure using parallax (see previous page).

This method uses objects like **type 1a supernovae** that are known as **standard candles**. Standard candles are objects that you can calculate the luminosity of **directly**. So, if you find a type 1a supernova within a galaxy, you can work out how far that galaxy is from us. This is how the **Hubble constant** was worked out (see p.192).

Distances in the Solar System can be Measured in Astronomical Units (AU)

The **parsec** is only one measurement used in **astrophysics** — luckily the others you need to know are much **simpler**.

1) From the time of **Copernicus** (in the 1500s) onwards, astronomers could work out the **distances** between the **planets** and the Sun **relative** to the Earth, using **astronomical units** (AU). But they couldn't work out the **actual distances**.

> One astronomical unit (AU) is defined as the mean distance between the Earth and the Sun.

2) The **size** of the AU (1.50×10^{11} m) wasn't known until 1769 — when it was carefully **measured** during a **transit of Venus** (when Venus passed between the Earth and the Sun).

Another Measure of Distance is the Light-Year (ly)

1) All **electromagnetic waves** travel at the **speed of light**, *c*, in a vacuum ($c = 3.00 \times 10^8$ ms⁻¹).

> The **distance** that electromagnetic waves travel through a vacuum in **one year** is called a **light-year** (ly).

2) If we see the light from a star that is, say, **10 light-years away** then we are actually seeing it as it was **10 years ago**. The further away the object is, the further **back in time** we are actually seeing it.

3) **1 ly** is equivalent to about **9.46×10^{15} m**, and 1pc is equal to about **3.26 ly**.

Warm-Up Questions

Q1 What is the relationship between apparent magnitude and intensity?
Q2 What is the equation that links apparent magnitude, absolute magnitude and distance?
Q3 Give three units of distance used in astrophysics. Explain the meaning of each one.

Exam Questions

Q1 Define the absolute magnitude of a star. [2 marks]

Q2 Calculate the absolute magnitude of the Sun given that the Sun's apparent magnitude is –27.
(1 pc $= 2.1 \times 10^5$ AU) [3 marks]

Q3 The star Sirius has an apparent magnitude of –1.46 and an absolute magnitude of +1.4.
The star Canopus has an apparent magnitude of –0.72 and an absolute magnitude of –5.5.

a) State which of the two stars appears brighter from Earth. [1 mark]

b) Calculate the distance from Earth to the furthest star. [3 marks]

Learn all this and you'll look like the brightest in class...

The magnitude scale is a pretty weird system, but like with a lot of astronomy, the old ways have stuck. Remember — the lower the number, the brighter the object. The definition of absolute magnitude is a bit random as well — I mean, why ten parsecs? Ours not to reason why, ours but to... erm... learn it. (Doesn't have quite the same ring does it.)

Stars as Black Bodies

Now they're telling us the Sun's black. Who writes this stuff?

A **Black Body** is a **Perfect Absorber** and **Emitter**

1) Objects emit **electromagnetic radiation** due to their **temperature**. At everyday temperatures this radiation lies mostly in the **infrared** part of the spectrum (which we can't see) — but heat something up enough and it will start to **glow**.

2) **Pure black** surfaces emit radiation **strongly** and in a **well-defined way**. We call it **black body radiation**.

3) A black body is defined as:

> A body that absorbs all wavelengths of electromagnetic radiation (that's why it's called a black body) and can emit all wavelengths of electromagnetic radiation.

4) The graph of **intensity** against **wavelength** for black body radiation varies with **temperature**, as shown in the graph:

5) To a reasonably good approximation **stars** behave as **black bodies** and their black body radiation produces their **continuous spectrum**.

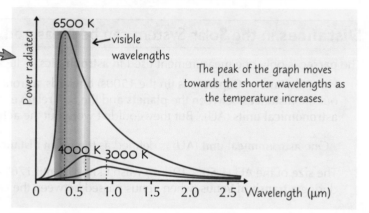

The peak of the graph moves towards the shorter wavelengths as the temperature increases.

The **Peak Wavelength** gives the **Temperature**

1) For each temperature, there is a **peak** in the black body curve at a wavelength called the **peak wavelength**, λ_{max}.

2) λ_{max} is related to the **temperature** by **Wien's displacement law**:

$$\lambda_{max}T = \text{constant} = 2.9 \times 10^{-3} \text{ mK}$$

where T is the temperature in kelvin and mK is a metre-kelvin.

The **Power Output** of a Star Depends on its **Temperature** and **Surface Area**

1) The **power output** of a star (its **luminosity**) is the **total energy** it emits **per second** and is related to the **temperature** of the star and its **surface area**. You might see it shown as *P* or *L*.

2) The power output is proportional to the **fourth power** of the star's **temperature** and is **directly proportional** to the **surface area**. This is **Stefan's law**:

$$P = \sigma AT^4$$

where *P* is the power output of the star (in W), *A* is its surface area (in m²), *T* is its surface temperature (in K) and σ (a little Greek "sigma") is Stefan's constant.

3) Measurements give Stefan's constant as $\sigma = 5.67 \times 10^{-8} \text{ Wm}^{-2}\text{K}^{-4}$.

4) From **Earth**, we can measure the **intensity** of the radiation received from the star. The intensity is the **power** of radiation **per square metre**, so as the radiation spreads out and becomes **diluted**, the intensity **decreases**. If the energy has been emitted from a **point** or a **sphere** (like a star, for example) then it obeys the **inverse square law**:

$$I = \frac{P}{4\pi d^2}$$

where *P* is the power output of the star (in W), and *d* is the distance from the star (in m).

Stars as Black Bodies

You Can Put the Equations Together to Solve Problems

Example: The star Sirius B has a surface area of 4.1×10^{13} m^2 and produces a black body spectrum with a peak wavelength of 115 nm. The intensity of the light from Sirius B when it reaches Earth is 1.12×10^{-11} Wm^{-2}. How many years does the light from Sirius B take to reach Earth? ($\sigma = 5.67 \times 10^{-8}$ Wm^{-2}K^{-4})

First, find the **temperature of Sirius B:**

$$\lambda_{max}T = 2.9 \times 10^{-3} \text{ mK, so } T = 2.9 \times 10^{-3} \div \lambda_{max} = 2.9 \times 10^{-3} \div 115 \times 10^{-9} = 25\,217.39... \text{ K}$$

Now, you can use **Stefan's law** to find the **luminosity:**

$$P = \sigma AT^4 = (5.67 \times 10^{-8}) \times (4.1 \times 10^{13}) \times 25\,217.39...^4 = 9.400... \times 10^{23} \text{ W}$$

Then use $I = \dfrac{P}{4\pi d^2}$ to find the **distance of Sirius B from Earth:**

Remember, $c = 3.00 \times 10^8$ ms^{-1}.

$$d = \sqrt{\frac{P}{4\pi I}} = \sqrt{\frac{9.400... \times 10^{23}}{4\pi \times 1.12 \times 10^{-11}}} = 8.17... \times 10^{16}$$

Use $c = d \div t$ to find the **time taken** $t = d \div c = 8.17... \times 10^{16} \div 3.00 \times 10^8 = 272\,426\,013.226... $ s
Finally, convert this to years: $272\,426\,013.226... \div (60 \times 60 \times 24 \times 365) = 8.638... = \textbf{8.6 years (to 2 s.f.)}$

It's Hard to get Accurate Measurements

1) **Wien's displacement law**, **Stefan's law** and the **inverse square law** can all be used to work out various **properties** of stars. This needs very **careful measurements**, but our **atmosphere** mucks up the results.

2) It only lets through **certain wavelengths** of **electromagnetic radiation** — **visible** light, most **radio** waves, **very near infrared** and a bit of **UV**. It's **opaque** to the rest.

3) And then there are things like **dust** and **man-made light pollution** to contend with. Observatories are placed at **high altitudes**, well away from **cities**, and in **low-humidity** climates to minimise the problem. The best solution, though, is to send up **satellites** that can take measurements **above** the atmosphere.

4) Our **detectors** don't do us any favours either. The **measuring devices** that astronomers use aren't perfect since their **sensitivity** depends on the **wavelength**.

5) For example, **glass absorbs UV** light but is **transparent** to **visible light**, so any instruments that use glass affect UV readings straight off.

6) All you can do about this is choose the best materials for what you want to measure, and then **calibrate** your instruments really carefully.

Warm-Up Questions

Q1 What is Wien's displacement law and what is it used for?
Q2 What is the relationship between luminosity, surface area and temperature?
Q3 Why are accurate measurements of black body radiation difficult on the Earth's surface?

PRACTICE QUESTIONS

Exam Questions

Q1 A star, X, has a surface temperature of 4000 K and the same power output as the Sun (3.9×10^{26} W). The Sun has a surface temperature of 6000 K.

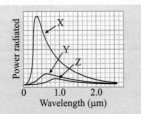

a) State which radiation curve represents this star — X, Y or Z. Explain your answer. [2 marks]

b) State whether star X or the Sun is larger. Explain your answer. [2 marks]

Q2 The star Procyon A, which has a luminosity of 2.3×10^{27} W, produces a black body spectrum with a peak wavelength of 436 nm.

Calculate the surface area of Procyon A. [3 marks]

Astronomy — theories, a bit of guesswork and a whole load of calibration...

Astronomy isn't the most exact of sciences, I'm afraid. The Hubble Space Telescope's improved things a lot, but try to get a look at some actual observational data. Then look at the error bars — they'll generally be about the size of a house.

Spectral Classes and the H-R Diagram

As well as classifying stars by luminosity (the magnitude scale, p.178), they can be classified by colour.

The **Balmer Series** is a Set of Lines in the **Spectrum** of **Hydrogen**

1) The lines in **emission** and **absorption spectra** occur because electrons in an atom can only exist at certain well-defined **energy levels**.

2) In **atomic hydrogen**, the electron is usually in the **ground state** ($n = 1$), but there are lots of energy levels ($n = 2$ to $n = \infty$ — called excitation levels) that the electron **could** exist in if it was given more energy.

The wavelengths corresponding to the **visible bit** of hydrogen's spectrum are caused by electrons moving from **higher energy levels** to the **first excitation level** ($n = 2$). This leads to a series of **lines** called the **Balmer series**.

The **Strengths** of the **Spectral Lines** Show the **Temperature** of a Star

1) For a **hydrogen absorption line** to occur in the **visible** part of a star's spectrum, electrons in the hydrogen atoms already need to be in the $n = 2$ state.

2) This happens at **high temperatures**, where **collisions** between the atoms give the electrons extra energy.

3) If the temperature is **too high**, though, the majority of the electrons will reach the $n = 3$ level (or above) instead, which means there won't be so many Balmer transitions.

4) So the **intensity** of the Balmer lines depends on the **temperature** of the star.

5) For a particular intensity of the Balmer lines, **two temperatures** are possible. Astronomers get around this by looking at the **absorption lines** of other atoms and molecules as well.

The **Relative Strength** of Absorption Lines gives the **Spectral Class**

Well... quite.

1) For historical reasons the stars are classified into **spectral classes**:

| **O** (hottest), **B**, **A**, **F**, **G**, **K** and **M** | Use a **mnemonic** to remember the order. The standard one is the rather non-PC **'Oh Be A Fine Girl, Kiss Me'**. |

2) The graph shows how the **intensity** of the visible spectral lines changes with **temperature**:

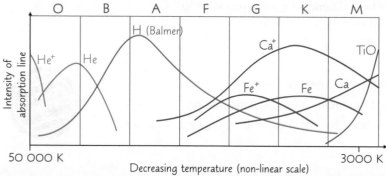

— Helium lines — Metal lines
— Hydrogen lines — Molecular bands

A quick note on the temperature axis: These diagrams, and the H-R diagram (next page), tend to be drawn with spectral class along the horizontal axis. The relationship between spectral class and temperature isn't linear or logarithmic.

THE VISIBLE SPECTRAL CHARACTERISTICS OF SPECTRAL CLASSES

O Blue stars: temperature **25 000 – 50 000 K**. The strongest spectral lines are **helium ion** and **helium atom** absorptions, since these need a really high temperature. They have weak **hydrogen Balmer** lines too.

B Blue stars: **11 000 – 25 000 K**. These spectra show strong **helium atom** and **hydrogen** absorptions.

A Blue-white stars: **7500 – 11 000 K**. Visible spectra are governed by the strongest Balmer **hydrogen** lines, but there are also some **metal ion** absorptions.

F White stars: **6000 – 7500 K**. These spectra have strong **metal ion** absorptions.

G Yellow-white stars: **5000 – 6000 K**. These have both **metal ion** and **metal atom** absorptions.

K Orange stars: **3500 – 5000 K**. At this temperature, most spectral lines are from neutral **metal atoms**.

M Red stars: **< 3500 K**. **Molecular band** absorptions from compounds like **titanium oxide** are present in the spectra of these stars, since they're cool enough for molecules to form.

Spectral Classes and the H-R Diagram

Absolute Magnitude vs Temperature/Spectral Class — the H-R diagram

1) Independently, Hertzsprung and Russell noticed that a plot of **absolute magnitude** (see p.179) against **temperature** (or **spectral class**) didn't just throw up a random collection of stars but showed **distinct areas**.

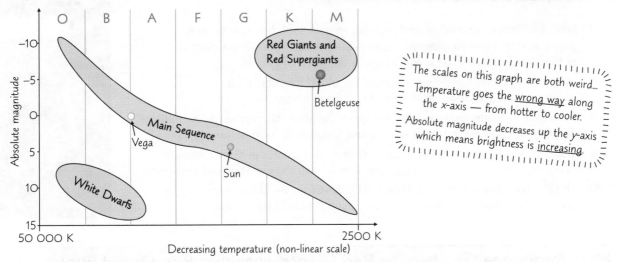

The scales on this graph are both weird... Temperature goes the <u>wrong way</u> along the x-axis — from hotter to cooler. Absolute magnitude decreases up the y-axis which means brightness is <u>increasing</u>.

2) The **long, diagonal band** is called the **main sequence**. Main sequence stars are in their long-lived **stable phase** where they are fusing **hydrogen** into **helium**. The Sun is a main sequence star.

3) Stars that have a **high luminosity** and a relatively **low surface temperature** must have a **huge** surface area because of Stefan's law (page 180). These stars are called **red giants** and **red supergiants** and are found in the **top-right** corner of the H-R diagram. These are stars that have **moved off** the main sequence and fusion reactions other than hydrogen to helium are also happening in them.

4) Stars that have a **low luminosity** but a **high temperature** must be very **small**, again because of Stefan's law. These stars are called **white dwarfs** and are about the size of the Earth. They lie in the **bottom-left** corner of the H-R diagram. White dwarfs are stars at the **end** of their lives, where all of their fusion reactions have stopped and they are just **slowly cooling down**.

Warm-Up Questions

Q1 Why does hydrogen have to be at a particular temperature before Balmer absorption lines are seen?

Q2 List the spectral classes in order of decreasing temperature and outline their spectral characteristics.

Q3 What is an H-R diagram and what are the three main groups of stars that emerge when the diagram is plotted?

Exam Questions

Q1 The spectral classes of stars can be identified by examining the lines in their absorption spectra.

   a) Explain how temperature affects the strength of the Balmer lines in stellar absorption spectra. [3 marks]

   b) State the two spectral classes of star in which strong Balmer lines are observed. [2 marks]

   c) Describe the visible spectral characteristics and temperature of a star in class F. [3 marks]

Q2 The spectra of M stars have absorption bands corresponding to energy levels of molecules.
Explain why this only occurs in the lowest temperature stars. [1 mark]

Q3 Draw the basic features of an H-R diagram, indicating where you would find main sequence stars, red giants and white dwarfs. Plot where you would find our Sun. [5 marks]

'Ospital Bound — A Furious Girl Kicked Me...

Spectral classes are another example of astronomers sticking with tradition. The classes used to be ordered alphabetically by the strength of the Balmer lines. When astronomers realised this didn't quite work, they just fiddled around with the old classes rather than coming up with a sensible new system. Just to make life difficult for people like you and me.

Stellar Evolution

Stars go through several different stages in their lives and move around the H-R diagram as they go (see p.183).
What happens to them depends on their mass — who said size doesn't matter?...

Stars Begin as Clouds of Dust and Gas

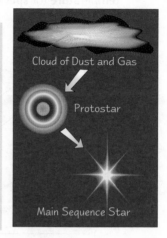

Cloud of Dust and Gas

Protostar

Main Sequence Star

1) Stars are born in a **cloud** of **dust** and **gas**, most of which was left when previous stars blew themselves apart in **supernovae**. The denser clumps of the cloud **contract** (very slowly) under the force of **gravity**.

2) When these clumps get dense enough, the cloud fragments into regions called **protostars**, that continue to contract and **heat up**.

3) Eventually the **temperature** at the centre of the protostar reaches a **few million degrees**, and **hydrogen nuclei** start to **fuse** together to form helium (see p.167).

4) This releases an **enormous** amount of **energy** and creates enough radiation **pressure** (along with the star's gas pressure) to stop the **gravitational collapse**.

5) The star has now reached the MAIN SEQUENCE and will stay there, relatively **unchanged**, while it fuses hydrogen into helium.

Main Sequence Stars become Red Giants when they Run Out of Fuel

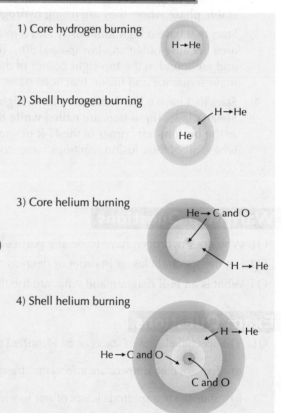

1) Core hydrogen burning

H→He

2) Shell hydrogen burning

H→He

He

3) Core helium burning

He→C and O

H → He

4) Shell helium burning

H → He

He→C and O

C and O

1) Stars spend most of their lives as MAIN SEQUENCE stars. The pressure produced from hydrogen fusion in their core **balances** the **gravitational force** trying to compress them. This stage is called **core hydrogen burning**.

2) When all the **hydrogen** in the **core** has fused into helium, nuclear fusion **stops**, and with it the **outward pressure stops**. The helium core **contracts** and **heats up** under the **weight** of the star. The outer layers **expand** and **cool**, and the star becomes a RED GIANT.

The material **surrounding** the core still has **plenty of hydrogen**. **Heat** from the contracting helium **core** raises the **temperature** of this material enough for the hydrogen to **fuse**. This is called **shell hydrogen burning**. (Very low-mass stars stop at this point. They use up their fuel and slowly fade away...)

3) The helium core continues to contract until, eventually, it gets **hot** enough and **dense** enough for **helium** to **fuse** into **carbon** and **oxygen**. This is called **core helium burning**. This releases a **huge** amount of energy, which **pushes** the **outer layers** of the star further outwards.

4) When the **helium** runs out, the carbon-oxygen core **contracts again** and heats a **shell** around it so that helium can fuse in this region — **shell helium burning**.

Low Mass Stars (like the Sun) Eject their Shells, leaving behind a White Dwarf

1) In low-mass stars, the **carbon-oxygen core isn't hot enough** for any further **fusion** and so it continues to **contract** under its own **weight**. Once the core has shrunk to about **Earth-size**, **electrons** exert enough pressure (**electron degeneracy pressure**) to stop it collapsing any more (fret not — you don't have to know how).

2) The **helium shell** becomes more and more **unstable** as the core contracts. The star **pulsates** and **ejects** its outer layers into space as a **planetary nebula**, leaving behind the dense core.

3) The star is now a very **hot, dense solid** called a WHITE DWARF, which will simply **cool down** and **fade away**.

Stellar Evolution

As Stars Age Their **Position** On The H-R Diagram **Changes**

1) **Where** a star is on a Hertzsprung-Russell diagram changes as it **evolves**.

2) Our Sun won't stay in the **main sequence** forever — its position on the diagram will drift to the **top-right** as it becomes a red giant. It will be **colder** and appear **brighter** than it was on the main sequence.

3) Once it has run out of helium to burn in its core, it will then become a **white dwarf** and its position will move to the **bottom-left** of the diagram. It will be **hotter** but will also be **dimmer** than it was on the main sequence.

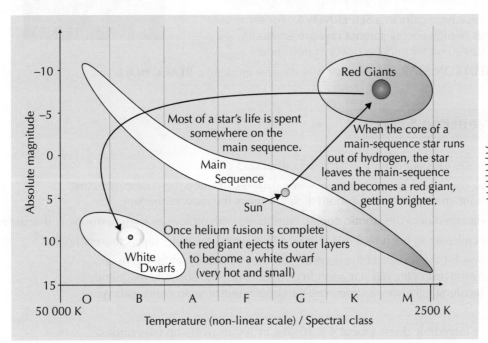

Most of a star's life is spent somewhere on the main sequence.

When the core of a main-sequence star runs out of hydrogen, the star leaves the main-sequence and becomes a red giant, getting brighter.

Once helium fusion is complete the red giant ejects its outer layers to become a white dwarf (very hot and small)

Star formation, from a cloud of gas to the main sequence, happens off this side of the H-R diagram.

Warm-Up Questions

Q1 What is a protostar?

Q2 Describe fully the four stages of fuel burning in a low mass star.

Q3 Describe what is meant by a white dwarf and explain how it is formed.

Q4 Describe the transitions the Sun will undertake in the rest of its lifetime.

Q5 Draw these transitions on a Hertzsprung-Russell diagram.

Exam Questions

Q1 Describe briefly how main sequence stars are formed. [3 marks]

Q2 A low mass star is on the main sequence.

a) Describe what happens to the star just after it runs out of hydrogen fuel to fuse within its core. [2 marks]

b) State the name of the type of star it has now become. [1 mark]

c) State the name of the type of star it will become when it runs out of fuel completely. [1 mark]

Our Sun will one day fade away...

But don't worry, that's not for a few billion years. Make sure you can describe the lifetime of a star like our Sun — all the way from a cloud of dust to a cooling white dwarf. Then make sure you're happy drawing it on a HR diagram too.

Stellar Evolution

High Mass Stars go out with a Bit of a Bang...

1) Even though stars with a **large mass** have a **lot of fuel**, they use it up **more quickly** and don't spend so long as main sequence stars.

2) When they are **red giants** the **'core burning to shell burning'** process can continue beyond the fusion of helium, building up layers in an **onion-like structure** to become **red supergiants**. For **really massive** stars this can go all the way up to **iron**.

3) Nuclear fusion **beyond iron** isn't **energetically favourable**, though, so once an iron core is formed then very quickly it's goodbye star.

4) The star explodes cataclysmically in a **SUPERNOVA**. For some very massive stars, **bursts** of high energy **gamma rays** are emitted. The gamma burst can go on for minutes or very rarely, hours.

5) Left behind is a **NEUTRON STAR** or (if the star was massive enough) a **BLACK HOLE**.

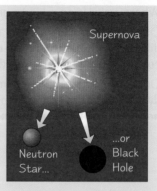

...Leaving Behind Neutron Stars...

1) When the core of a star runs out of fuel, it starts to **contract**.

2) If the star is **massive enough**, **electron degeneracy** (see p.184) can't **stop** the core contracting. This happens when the mass of the core is more than **1.4 times** the mass of the **Sun**.

3) The electrons get **squashed** onto the atomic **nuclei**, combining with protons to form **neutrons** and **neutrinos**.

4) The core suddenly collapses to become a **NEUTRON STAR**, which the outer layers then **fall** onto.

5) When the outer layers **hit** the surface of the **neutron star** they **rebound**, setting up huge **shockwaves**, ripping the rest of the old star apart in a **supernova**. The absolute magnitude rapidly increases, meaning light from a supernova can briefly outshine an **entire galaxy**.

---

1) Neutron stars are incredibly dense (about 4×10^{17} kg m^{-3}) stars made up of neutrons.

2) They're very small, typically about 20 km across, and they can rotate very fast (up to 600 times a second).

3) Some neutron stars emit radio waves in two beams as they rotate. These beams sometimes sweep past the Earth and can be observed as radio pulses rather like the flashes of a lighthouse. These rotating neutron stars are called PULSARS.

...Or Black Holes

1) If the **core** of the star remaining after a supernova is more than **3 times** the **Sun's mass**, the **neutrons** can't withstand the gravitational forces.

2) There are **no known mechanisms** left to stop the core collapsing to an **infinitely dense** point called a **singularity**. At that point, the **laws of physics** break down completely. This is called a **black hole**.

3) Up to a certain distance away (called the **Schwarzschild radius**) the gravitational pull is **so strong** that nothing, not even **light**, can escape its grasp. The **boundary** of this region is called the **event horizon**.

> The **Schwarzschild radius** is the **distance** at which the **escape velocity** is the **speed of light**

An object moving at the **escape velocity** has **just enough kinetic energy** to overcome the black hole's gravitational field.

From Newton's law of gravitation we get $\frac{1}{2}mv^2 = \frac{GMm}{r}$

Dividing through by m and making r the subject gives: $r = \frac{2GM}{v^2}$

By replacing v with the speed of light, c, you get the Schwarzschild radius, R_s.

This is a bit of a fudge that happens to give the right answer — we've used Newtonian physics when really general relativity (and some very hard maths) is needed.

$$R_s = \frac{2GM}{c^2}$$

M = mass of black hole,
$G = 6.67 \times 10^{-11}$ Nm^{2}kg^{-2}
and c is the speed of light in a vacuum

Stellar Evolution

Learn the **Light Curve** for **Type 1a Supernovae**

The defining characteristic of a supernova is a **rapid**, **massive increase** in **brightness**.

1) Different types of supernovae have characteristic **light curves**
   — a plot of **absolute magnitude** M against **time** since the supernova began.

2) Type I light curves have two defining features:
   - A **sharp initial peak**
   - Then a **gradually decreasing** curve.

You don't need to know the light-curve for a type II supernova.

1) A subset of Type I supernovae, called Type 1a, are really important because they always happen in the same way, with a star of the same mass.

2) This means that every Type 1a supernova has the same absolute magnitude curve so it can be used as a standard candle (p.179). They are so bright that distances up to 1000 Mpc can be measured.

3) You need to know what the light curve for a type 1a supernova looks like:

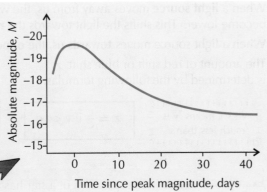

The Amount of **Energy** Released in a Supernova is **Huge**

1) In a type 1a supernova, around **10^{44} J** of energy is released.

2) This is roughly the **same** as the energy output of the Sun over its **entire lifetime**.

3) Other types of supernova may release **much more** energy than this.

4) Some supernovae release **bursts** of **high energy gamma rays**.

If a supernova was **too close** to Earth and it's energy was directed towards us — it could destroy the ozone layer, leading to possible mass **extinction**.

Warm-Up Questions

Q1 What is a neutron star?

Q2 What is a pulsar?

Q3 What core condition has to be fulfilled for a star to become a black hole at the end of its life?

Q4 Sketch the light curve of a typical Type 1a supernova.

Q5 How much energy is released by a Type 1a supernova?
How does this compare to the total energy released by the Sun in its lifetime?

Exam Questions

Q1 a) What is meant by the Schwarzschild radius of a black hole? [2 marks]

   b) Calculate the Schwarzschild radius for a black hole that has a mass of 6.0×10^{30} kg. [2 marks]

Q2 a) A star with a core twice the mass of our Sun runs out of fuel.
Describe the process through which it creates a supernova. [3 marks]

   b) Very massive stars sometimes emit burst of gamma rays as they turn into supernovae.
Explain why these types of supernova might be dangerous to life on Earth. [2 marks]

Live fast — die young...

The more massive a star, the more spectacular its life cycle. The most massive stars burn up the hydrogen in their core so quickly that they only live for a fraction of the Sun's lifetime — but when they go, they do it in style.

The Doppler Effect and Red Shift

Everyone's heard of the Big Bang theory — well here's some evidence for it.

The Doppler Effect — the Motion of a Wave's Source Affects its Wavelength

1) You'll have experienced the Doppler effect **loads of times** with **sound waves**.

2) Imagine an ambulance driving past you. As it moves **towards you** its siren sounds **higher-pitched**, but as it **moves away**, its **pitch** is **lower**. This change in **frequency** and **wavelength** is called the **Doppler shift**.

3) The frequency and the wavelength **change** because the waves **bunch together** in **front** of the source and **stretch out behind** it. The **amount** of stretching or bunching together depends on the **velocity** of the **source**.

4) When a **light source** moves **away** from us, the wavelengths of its light become **longer** and the frequencies become lower. This shifts the light towards the **red** end of the spectrum and is called **red shift**.

5) When a light source moves **towards** us, the **opposite** happens and the light undergoes **blue shift**.

6) The amount of red shift or blue shift, **z**, is determined by the following formulas:

v << c means "v is much less than c"

$$z = \frac{v}{c} \text{ if } v << c$$

$$z = \frac{\Delta f}{f} = -\frac{\Delta \lambda}{\lambda}$$

λ is the emitted wavelength, f is the emitted frequency $\Delta \lambda = \lambda_{emitted} - \lambda_{observed}$, $\Delta f = f_{emitted} - f_{observed}$ v is the recessional velocity (how fast the source is moving away from the observer) c is the speed of light.

Example: A line in the spectrum of a star has a wavelength of 410 nm. On Earth we observe the wavelength of the line to be 365 nm. Calculate the Doppler shift observed, along with the velocity of the star relative to Earth.

First, calculate the change in wavelength:

$\Delta \lambda = \lambda_{emitted} - \lambda_{observed} = 410 \text{ nm} - 365 \text{ nm} = 45 \text{ nm}$

Then use: $z = -\frac{\Delta \lambda}{\lambda} = -\frac{45}{410} = -0.109... = \textbf{−0.11 (to 2 s.f.)}$

This means that

$\frac{v}{c} = -0.109...$ so $v = -0.109...c$

$= -0.109... \times 3.00 \times 10^8 = -3.29... \times 10^7 \text{ ms}^{-1} = \textbf{−3.3} \times \textbf{10}^7 \textbf{ms}^{-1} \textbf{ (to 2 s.f.)}$

As the wavelength is getting shorter (and the velocity is negative), the light is being blue-shifted. So the star is moving towards Earth.

Velocity has a direction, and here it's defined as positive if the source is moving away from the observer (red shift) and negative if it is moving towards the observer (blue shift).

The Red Shift of Galaxies is Strong Evidence for the HBB

1) The **spectra** from **galaxies** (apart from a few very close ones) all show **red shift** — the **characteristic spectral lines** of the elements are all at a **longer wavelength** than you would expect. This shows they're all **moving apart**.

2) The way cosmologists tend to look at this stuff, the galaxies aren't actually moving **through space** away from us. Instead, **space itself** is expanding and the light waves are being **stretched** along with it. This is called **cosmological red shift** to distinguish it from **red shift** produced by sources that **are** moving through space.

Hot big bang — the ultimate firework display?

3) The same formula works for both types of red shift as long as *v* is **much less** than *c*. If *v* is close to the speed of light, you need to use a nasty, relativistic formula instead (you don't need to know that one).

4) Hubble realised that the **speed** that **galaxies moved away** from us depended on **how far** they were away. This led to the idea that the universe started out **very hot** and **very dense** and is currently **expanding**.

THE HOT BIG BANG THEORY (HBB): the universe started off **very hot** and **very dense** (perhaps as an **infinitely hot**, **infinitely dense** singularity) and has been **expanding** ever since.

The Doppler Effect and Red Shift

Doppler Shift is Used to Study Spectroscopic Binary Stars

1) About half of the stars we observe are actually **two stars** that orbit each other. Many of them are too far away from us to be **resolved** with **telescopes** but the **lines** in their **spectra** show a binary star system. These are called **spectroscopic binary stars**.

2) By observing how the **absorption lines** in the spectrum change with **time** the **orbital period** can be calculated:

> For simplicity, think about only one absorption line from the spectrum:
>
> a) Both stars are moving at right angles to our line of sight, so there's no Doppler shift.
>
> b) Both stars are moving along our line of sight. Star A shows maximum blueshift. Star B shows maximum redshift.
>
>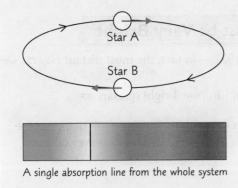
>
>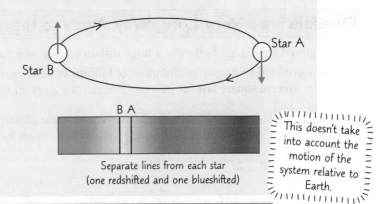
>
> A single absorption line from the whole system
>
> Separate lines from each star (one redshifted and one blueshifted)
>
> This doesn't take into account the motion of the system relative to Earth.

> As the stars orbit each other, the separation between the lines goes from zero [at a)] up to the maximum separation [at b)] and back to zero again in half a period.

3) Astronomers have used a similar method to find **extrasolar planets** (p. 191).

Warm-Up Questions

Q1 What is the Doppler effect?

Q2 Write down the formula for the red shift and blue shift of light.

Q3 Explain what is meant by the Hot Big Bang. How does Doppler shift support the idea of a Hot Big Bang?

Q4 Explain how the spectra of binary stars can be used to calculate their period of orbit.

Exam Questions

Q1 The spectra of two objects have been taken. What can you deduce from each of the following?

  a) The absorption lines from object A have been shifted towards the blue end of the spectrum. [1 mark]

  b) The absorption lines from object B oscillate back and forth on the spectrum with a period of two weeks. [2 marks]

Q2 The observed wavelength of the hydrogen alpha line of a distant object's spectrum is 667.83 nm. In the laboratory, the wavelength of the same line is measured as 656.28 nm.

  a) Calculate the amount of red or blue shift of the spectral line. [1 mark]

  b) Calculate the velocity of the object relative to Earth. State and explain whether it is moving towards or away from Earth. [2 marks]

Neeeee-Owwww — like my Doppler shift impression?

Doppler shift is one of the lovely parts of astrophysics that you can actually see in your daily life (without a big ol' telescope anyway...). The basics of it are pretty simple, but to get all of the marks you've got to be able to explain how its used in astrophysics — to study binary stars or to support the Hot Big Bang. Get that down and you're laughing.

Quasars and Exoplanets

The Doppler effect is handy in explaining quasars and detecting exoplanets too. Read on.

Quasars — Quasi-Stellar Objects

1) **Quasars** were discovered in the late 1950s and were first thought to be **stars in our galaxy**.

2) The puzzling thing was that their spectra were **nothing like** normal stars. They sometimes shot out **jets** of material, and many of them were very active **radio sources**.

3) The 'stars' produced a **continuous spectrum** that was nothing like a black body radiation curve and instead of absorption lines, there were **emission lines** of elements that astronomers **had not seen before**.

4) However, these lines looked strangely familiar and in 1963 Maarten Schmidt realised that they were simply the **Balmer series** of hydrogen (see p.182) but **red shifted** enormously.

Quasars are a **Very Long Way Away** so they must be **Very Bright**

This **huge red shift** suggests they're a **huge distance away** (see page 192) — in fact, the **most distant** objects seen.

The measured red shifts give us distances of **billions of light years**.

Using the **inverse square law** for intensity (see p.180) gives an idea of just how **bright** quasars are:

> **Example** A quasar has the same intensity as a star 20 000 ly away with the same power output as the Sun (4×10^{26} W). Its red shift gives a distance of 1×10^{10} ly. Calculate its power output.
>
> $$P \propto Id^2$$
>
> $$\Rightarrow \frac{P_{quasar}}{P_{star}} = \frac{I_{quasar}}{I_{star}} \frac{d_{quasar}^{\,2}}{d_{star}^{\,2}} = \frac{d_{quasar}^{\,2}}{d_{star}^{\,2}}$$
>
> $I_{quasar} = I_{star}$ so they cancel out of the equation.
>
> $$\Rightarrow P_{quasar} = P_{star}\frac{d_{quasar}^{\,2}}{d_{star}^{\,2}} = 4 \times 10^{26} \times \frac{1 \times 10^{20}}{4 \times 10^8} = \mathbf{1 \times 10^{38}\ W}$$
>
> That's bright — about **10 times** the **luminosity** of the **entire Milky Way galaxy**!

1) There's very good evidence to suggest that quasars are only about the size of the Solar System.

2) Let me run that past you again. **That's the power of a trillion Suns from something the size of the Solar System.**

3) These numbers caused a lot of controversy in the astrophysics community — they seemed crazy. Many astrophysicists thought there must be a more reasonable explanation. But then evidence for the distance of quasars came when sensitive CCD equipment detected the fuzzy cloud of a galaxy around a quasar.

4) The current consensus is that a quasar is a very powerful galactic nucleus, containing a huge active black hole (one which is currently taking in matter) at the centre of a distant galaxy. This supermassive black hole has a mass of about 10^6 times the mass of the Sun.

   (Almost all galaxies are thought to have these 'supermassive' black holes at their centres, but most aren't active).

5) This black hole is surrounded by a doughnut shaped mass of whirling gas falling into it, which produces the light. In the same way as a pulsar (see p.186), magnetic fields produce jets of radiation streaming out from the poles. The black hole must consume the mass of about 10 Suns per year to produce the energy observed.

Exoplanets Are Hard To Find

Red shift can also be used to discover other objects like **exoplanets**. An exoplanet (sometimes called an **extrasolar** planet) is any 'planet' not in our solar system — this is because the word **planet** is usually reserved for only things within our solar system, orbiting the **Sun**. They're pretty hard to find though, because:

1) They're orbiting **stars** which are much **brighter** than them. Most exoplanets cannot be seen as the bright light from the stars or other objects they're orbiting drowns out any light from the exoplanet.

2) They're **too small** to distinguish from nearby stars (the subtended angle is too small for the resolving power of most telescopes — see p.173.)

Only a few of the largest and hottest exoplanets that are furthest away from their stars can be **seen directly** using specially built telescopes.

Quasars and Exoplanets

One Method To **Find Exoplanets** is To Use **Doppler Shift**

Sometimes called the **radial velocity method**, the Doppler shift method measures how much the emissions from stars have been red or blue shifted (similar to binary stars on p.189).

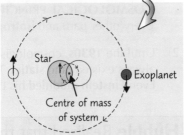
This is sometimes called Doppler spectroscopy.

1) An exoplanet orbiting a star has a small effect on the star's orbit. It causes **tiny variations** (a **wobble**) in the star's **orbit**.

2) This is because the star and the exoplanet are actually orbiting around the **centre of mass** between them — but as the star is so much bigger than the exoplanet, the centre is much closer to the centre of the star.

3) This wobble causes **tiny red** and **blue shifts** in the star's emissions which can be **detected** on Earth and can suggest the presence of an exoplanet.

4) From this, the **minimum mass** of the exoplanet can also be calculated.

5) There are however problems with this method, as the movement needs to be **aligned** with the observer's line of sight — if the planet orbits the star perpendicular to the line of sight then there won't be any detectable shift in the light from the star.

Star
Exoplanet
Centre of mass of system

Another is the **Transit Method**

The **transit** method measures the **change** in **apparent magnitude** as an exoplanet travels in front of a star.

1) As the **exoplanet** crosses in front of the star, some of the light from the star is **blocked** from Earth's view.

2) This leads to a **dip** in the **light curve** observed on Earth.

3) From this, the **radius** of the exoplanet can be found.

4) However, the **chances** of the planet's path being perfectly lined up so that it crosses the line of sight between the star and the Earth is **incredibly low**. This means you can only **confirm** observed exoplanets, not **rule out** the locations of any.

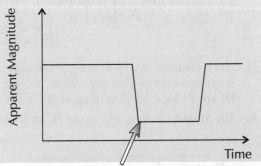

The dip caused by the exoplanet blocking some of the light from the star.

Warm-Up Questions

Q1 Define an exoplanet.

Q2 Explain two reasons why exoplanets are hard to observe.

Q3 Describe the radial velocity method for observing exoplanets.

Q4 Explain why you cannot use either of the methods above to rule out the presence of exoplanets around a star.

PRACTICE QUESTIONS

Exam Questions

Q1 a) State one piece of evidence that suggests quasars are a very long distance away. [1 mark]

b) Use the concept of the inverse square law to suggest why quasars must be very bright. [2 marks]

c) Describe the main features of a quasar according to the current theory. [2 marks]

Q2 A scientist is confirming the existence of an exoplanet using the transit method.

a) Describe and explain how the transit method can detect exoplanets. [3 marks]

b) Draw the typical light curve for the transit. [2 marks]

Long ago, in a galaxy far, far away — there was a radio-loud, supermassive black hole with a highly luminous arc...

Quasars are really weird. There's still some disagreement in the astrophysics community about what they even are. Then you get onto exoplanets — we at least know what they are, but they're really hard to find. Make sure you understand both methods used when trying to find exoplanets and make sure you can draw that light curve.

The Big Bang Model of the Universe

Right, we're moving on to the BIG picture now — we all like a bit of cosmology...

The **Universe** is **The Same** in **Every Direction**

When you read that all the **galaxies** in the universe are **moving away** from the **Earth** (see p. 188 and below), it's easy to imagine that the Earth is at the **centre of the universe**, or that there's something really **special** about it. **Earth** is special to us because we **live here** — but on a **universal scale**, it's just like any other lump of rock.

1) The **demotion** of **Earth** from anything special is taken to its logical conclusion with the **cosmological principle**...

> **COSMOLOGICAL PRINCIPLE:** on a **large scale** the universe is **homogeneous** (every part is the same as every other part) and **isotropic** (everything looks the same in every direction) — so it doesn't have a **centre**.

2) Until the **1930s**, cosmologists believed that the universe was **infinite** in both **space** and **time** (that is, it had always existed) and **static**. This seemed the **only way** that it could be **stable** using **Newton's law** of gravitation. Even **Einstein modified** his theory of **general relativity** to make it consistent with the **Steady-State universe**.

Hubble Realised that the **Universe** is **Expanding**

1) The **spectra** from **galaxies** (apart from a few very close ones) all show **red shift**. The amount of **red shift** gives the **recessional velocity** — how fast the galaxy is moving away (see page 188).

2) A plot of **recessional velocity** against **distance** (found using standard candles — see p.179) showed that they were **proportional**, which suggests that the universe is **expanding**. This gives rise to **Hubble's law**:

$$v = H_0 d$$

v = recessional velocity in **kms^{-1}**,
d = distance in **Mpc** and
H_0 = Hubble's constant in **kms^{-1}Mpc^{-1}**.

Remember $z = \dfrac{v}{c}$ for v<<c.

3) Since distance is very difficult to measure, astronomers used to **disagree** greatly on the value of H_0, with measurements ranging from 50 to 100 km s^{-1} Mpc^{-1}. It's now generally accepted that H_0 lies **between 65 and 80 km s^{-1} Mpc^{-1}** and most agree it's in the **mid to low 70s**. You'll be given a value to use in the exam.

4) The **SI unit** for H_0 is s^{-1}. To get H_0 in SI units, you need v in ms^{-1} and d in m (1 Mpc = 3.08 × 10^{22} m).

The **Expanding Universe** gives rise to the **Hot Big Bang Model**

1) The universe is **expanding** and **cooling down** (because it's a closed system). So further back in time it must have been **smaller** and **hotter**. If you trace time back **far enough**, you get a **Hot Big Bang** (see page 188).

2) Since the universe is **expanding uniformly** away from **us** it seems as though we're at the **centre** of the universe, but this is an **illusion**. You would observe the **same thing** at **any point** in the universe.

The **Age** and **Observable Size** of the **Universe** Depend on H_0

1) If the universe has been **expanding** at the **same rate** for its whole life, the **age** of the universe is $t = 1/H_0$ (time = distance/speed). This is only an estimate though — see below.

2) Unfortunately, since no one knows the **exact value** of H_0 we can only guess the universe's age. If H_0 = 75 kms^{-1}Mpc^{-1}, then the age of the universe ≈ 1/(2.4 × 10^{-18} s^{-1}) = 4.1 × 10^{17} s = **13 billion years**.

3) The **absolute size** of the universe is **unknown** but there is a limit on the size of the **observable universe**. This is simply a **sphere** (with the Earth at its centre) with a **radius** equal to the **maximum distance** that **light** can travel during its **age**. So if H_0 = 75 kms^{-1}Mpc^{-1} then this sphere will have a radius of **13 billion light years**. Taking into account the **expansion** of the universe, the radius of the sphere of the observable universe is thought to be more like 46-47 billion light years.

THE RATE OF EXPANSION HASN'T BEEN CONSTANT

1) All the mass in the universe is attracted together by gravity. This attraction tends to slow down the rate of expansion of the universe. It's thought that the expansion was decelerating until about 5 billion years ago.

2) But in the late 90s, astronomers found evidence that the expansion is now accelerating. Cosmologists are trying to explain this acceleration using dark energy — a type of energy that fills the whole of space. There's lots of speculation about what dark energy even is — no-one knows for sure. This leads to lots of new theories and mathematical models being proposed to try and explain the accelerating universe.

The Big Bang Model of the Universe

Cosmic Microwave Background Radiation — More Evidence for the HBB

1) The Hot Big Bang model predicts that loads of **electromagnetic radiation** was produced in the **very early universe**. This radiation should **still** be observed today (it hasn't had anywhere else to go).

2) Because the universe has **expanded**, the wavelengths of this cosmic background radiation have been **stretched** and are now in the **microwave** region.

3) This was picked up **accidentally** by Penzias and Wilson in the 1960s.

Properties of the Cosmic Microwave Background Radiation (CMBR)

1) In the late 1980s a satellite called the **Cosmic Background Explorer** (**COBE**) was sent up to have a **detailed look** at the radiation.

2) It found a **perfect black body spectrum** corresponding to a **temperature** of **2.73 K** (see page 180).

3) The radiation is largely **isotropic** and **homogeneous**, which confirms the cosmological principle (see page 192).

4) There are **very tiny fluctuations** in temperature, which were at the limit of COBE's detection. These are due to tiny energy-density variations in the early universe, and are needed for the initial 'seeding' of galaxy formation.

5) The background radiation also shows a **Doppler shift**, indicating the Earth's motion through space. It turns out that the **Milky Way** is rushing towards an unknown mass (the **Great Attractor**) at over a **million miles an hour**.

Another Bit of Evidence is the **Amount** of **Helium** in the Universe

1) The HBB model also explained the **large abundances of hydrogen and helium** in the universe (around 74% of the universe is hydrogen and 24% is helium).

2) The early universe had been very hot, so at some point it must have been hot enough for **hydrogen fusion** to happen. By studying how much **helium** there is **compared** to **hydrogen**, we can work out a **time frame** for this fusion. Together with the theory of the synthesis of the **heavier elements** in stars, the **relative abundances** of all of the elements can be accounted for.

Warm-Up Questions

Q1 State the cosmological principle.

Q2 What is Hubble's law? How can it be used to find the age of the universe?

Q3 What is the cosmic background radiation?

Q4 How do the relative amounts of hydrogen and helium in the universe provide evidence for the HBB model?

Exam Questions

Q1 a) State Hubble's law, explaining the meanings of all the symbols. [2 marks]

    b) State the implications of Hubble's law for the nature of the universe. [2 marks]

    c) Assume $H_0 = +50$ kms^{-1}Mpc^{-1} (*1 Mpc = 3.08 × 10^{22} m*).

      i) Calculate H_0 in SI units. [2 marks]

      ii) Calculate an estimate of the age of the universe, and hence the size of the observable universe. [3 marks]

Q2 a) A certain object has a red shift of 0.37. Estimate the speed the object is moving away from us and the distance (in light years) that the object is away from us. (*Take $H_0 = 2.4 × 10^{-18}$ s^{-1}, 1 ly = 9.46 × 10^{15} m*). [3 marks]

    b) Explain why this distance is only an estimate. [1 mark]

Q3 Describe the main features of the cosmic background radiation and explain why its discovery was considered strong evidence for the Hot Big Bang model of the universe. [6 marks]

My brother was a Great Attractor — everyone fell for him...

The simple Big Bang model doesn't actually work — not quite, anyway. There are loads of little things that don't quite add up. Modern cosmologists are trying to improve the model using a period of very rapid expansion called inflation.

Physics of the Eye

The eye uses lenses, rods and cones to allow you to see all the things around you.

The Eyes Contain **Converging Lenses**

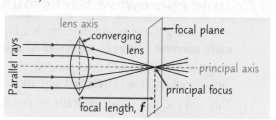

1) **Lenses** change the **direction** of light rays by **refraction**.

2) Rays **parallel** to the **principal axis** of the lens **converge** (are brought together) onto a point called the **principal focus**.

3) The **focal length**, *f*, is the distance between the **lens axis** and the **principal focus**.

4) The **eye** has a **converging lens** which focuses incoming light to form an image on the **retina**, which is then **interpreted** by the **brain**.

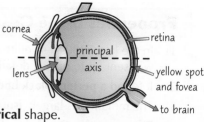

5) The **cornea** is a **transparent** 'window' with a **convex** shape, and a **high refractive index**. The cornea does most of the eye's focusing.

6) The **lens** acts as a **fine focus** and is controlled by muscles which release tension in the lens when **contracted**. The lens then takes on a **fat**, more **spherical** shape. When the muscles **relax**, the lens is pulled into a **thin, flatter** shape. This changes the **focal length** of the eye.

7) The **retina** is where images are formed. It contains **light-sensitive cells** called **rods** and **cones** (see below). The **yellow spot** is a particularly sensitive region of the retina. In the centre of the yellow spot is the **fovea**. This is the part of the retina with the highest concentration of **cones**.

You can use the **Lens Equation** for **Eyes**

The **lens equation** for **thin lenses** can be applied to the whole eye:

$$\frac{1}{f} = \frac{1}{u} + \frac{1}{v}$$

where *f* is the focal length (m), *u* is the object distance (m) and *v* is the image distance (m).

You can also calculate the **power** of a lens, which tells you the lens' ability to **bend light**. The higher the power, the more the lens will **refract** light.

$$P = \frac{1}{f}$$

where *P* is the power of the lens in dioptres (D).

The **Eye** is an **Optical Refracting System**

1) The **far point** is the **furthest distance** that the eye can focus comfortably. For normally sighted people that's **infinity**. When your eyes are focusing at the far point, they're **'unaccommodated'**.

2) The **near point** is the **closest distance** that the eye can focus on. For young people it's about 9 cm.

3) You can **add together** the **powers** of the cornea, lens and other eye parts. That means you can think of the eye as a **single converging lens** of power **59 D** at the far point. This gives a **focal length** of **1.7 cm**.

4) When looking at nearer objects, the eye's power **increases**, as the lens changes shape and the **focal length decreases** — but the distance between the lens and the image, *v*, stays the same at 1.7 cm.

Power ≈ 67 D, *f* = 1.5 cm

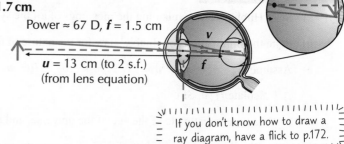

u = 13 cm (to 2 s.f.) (from lens equation)

If you don't know how to draw a ray diagram, have a flick to p.172.

The **Retina** has **Rods** and **Cones**

1) **Rods** and **cones** are cells at the back of the **retina** that respond to **light**. They're known as **photoreceptors**. Light travels **through the retina** to the rods and cones at the back.

2) Rods and cones all contain chemical **pigments** that **bleach** when **light** falls on them. This bleaching stimulates (or activates) the cell to send signals to the **brain** via the **optic nerve**.

3) The cells are **reset** (i.e. unbleached) by enzymes using **vitamin A** from the blood.

4) There's only **one** type of **rod** but there are **three** types of **cone**, which are sensitive to **red**, **green** and **blue** light.

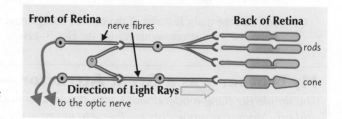

Front of Retina   nerve fibres   Back of Retina

rods

Direction of Light Rays to the optic nerve   cone

Physics of the Eye

The **Cones** let you See in **Full Colour**

1) The red, green and blue **cones** each absorb a **range of wavelengths**.

2) The eye is **less responsive** to blue light than to red or green, so blues often look dimmer.

3) The brain receives signals from the three types of cone and interprets their **weighted relative strengths** as **colour**...

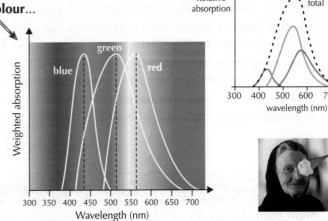

Yellow light produces almost equal responses from the red and green cones. Yellow light can therefore be 'faked' by combining red and green light of almost equal intensity — the electrical signal from the retina will be the same and the brain interprets it as 'yellow'.

4) **Any** colour can be produced by **combining** different intensities of **red**, **green** and **blue** light. Colour televisions work like this.

You Need Good **Spatial Resolution** to See **Details**

1) Two objects can only be distinguished from each other if there's **at least one rod** or **cone between** the light from each of them. Otherwise the brain can't **resolve** the two objects and it 'sees' them as one.

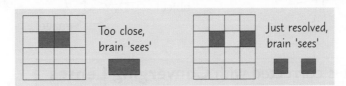

2) **Spatial resolution** is **best** at a certain spot on the retina, called the yellow spot — the **cones** are very **densely packed** here and each cone always has its **own nerve fibre**. There are **no rods in the yellow spot**, though. This means that in **dim light**, when **cones don't work**, resolution is best slightly off the direct line of sight, where the **rods** are more **densely packed**.

3) Away from the yellow spot, resolution is much worse. The light-sensitive cells are **not** as **densely packed** and the rods **share nerve fibres** — there are up to 600 rods per fibre at the edges of the retina.

Warm-Up Questions

Q1 Briefly describe how the three types of cone cells combine to let you see in colour.

Q2 Sketch a graph showing how the different types of cone cell in the retina respond to different wavelengths of light.

Exam Question

Q1 The power of an unaccommodated eye is 60 D (to 2 s.f.).

a) Calculate the image distance, *v*, when the eye focuses at infinity. [2 marks]

b) The eye then focuses on an object 30 cm away (to 2 s.f.).
Draw a ray diagram showing the eye focusing on the image, labelling the image and object distances. [2 marks]

c) Calculate the extra power that the lens must produce for the eye to focus on the object. [2 marks]

The eyes are the window on the soul...

Or so they said in the 16th century. Sadly, that won't get you far with a question about the power of eye lenses.

Defects of Vision

Plenty of people don't have perfect vision, and need auxiliary lenses to correct their sight.

Real is Positive, Virtual is Negative

Lenses can produce **real** or **virtual** images, and you need to follow the "**real** is **positive**, **virtual** is **negative**" rule.

1) A **real image** is formed when light rays from an object are made to **pass through** another point in space. The light rays are **actually there**, and the image can be **captured** on a **screen**.

2) A **virtual image** is formed when light rays from an object **appear** to have come from another point in space. The light rays **aren't really where the image appears to be**, so the image **can't** be captured on a screen.

3) **Converging lenses** can form both **real** and **virtual** images, depending on where the **object** is. So converging lenses can have **positive or negative** focal lengths.

4) **Diverging lenses** create a **virtual image**. They have a **negative focal length**.

5) The **linear magnification**, *m*, of a lens is:

$$m = \frac{\text{size of image}}{\text{size of object}} = \frac{v}{u}$$

where v is image distance (m) and u is object distance (m)

Myopia is Corrected with Diverging Lenses

1) **Short-sighted** (myopic) people are unable to focus on distant objects — this happens if their **far point** is **closer** than infinity (see p.194).

2) Myopia occurs when the **cornea** and **lens** are too **powerful** or the **eyeball** is too **long**.

3) The focusing system is **too powerful** and images of distant objects are brought into focus in **front** of the retina.

4) A lens of **negative power** is needed to correct this defect — so a **diverging** lens is placed in front of the eye.

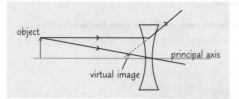

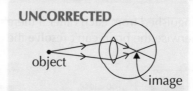

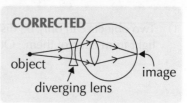

Hypermetropia is corrected with Converging Lenses

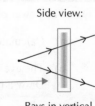
Long-sightedness is common among young children whose lenses have grown quicker than their eyeballs.

1) **Long-sighted** (hypermetropic) people are unable to focus clearly on near objects. This happens if their **near point** is **further** away than normal (25 cm or more).

2) Long sight occurs because the **cornea** and **lens** are too **weak** or the **eyeball** is too **short**.

3) The focusing system is **too weak** and images of near objects are brought into focus **behind** the retina.

4) A lens of **positive power** is needed to correct the defect — so a **converging** lens is placed in front of the eye.

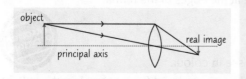

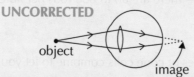

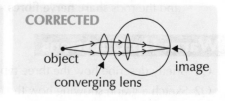

Astigmatism is Corrected with Cylindrical Lenses

1) **Astigmatism** is caused by an irregularly shaped **cornea** or **lens** which has **different focal lengths** for different **planes**. For instance, when **vertical lines** are in focus, **horizontal** lines might not be.

2) The condition is corrected with **cylindrical lenses**.

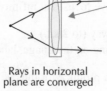
Top view:

Rays in horizontal plane are converged

An optician's prescription gives the **angle** of this axis to the **horizontal**, and how curved the cylindrical lens needs to be (the degree of astigmatism).

Side view:

Rays in vertical plane are unaffected

3) A cylindrical lens **prescription** has the **power** needed to correct for the long or short-sightedness, the power needed to **correct** the astigmatism and the **angle** to the **horizontal** of the **plane** that **doesn't** need correcting for astigmatism (shown by the **axis** in the **diagram**).

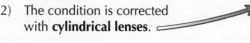

Section 13: Option B — Medical Physics

Defects of Vision

Choosing a **Lens** to Correct for **Short Sight** Depends on the **Far Point**

1) To correct for **short sight**, a **diverging** lens is chosen which has its **principal focus** at the eye's **faulty far point**.

2) The **principal focus** is the point that rays from a distant object **appear** to have come from.

3) The lens must have a **negative focal length** which is the same as the **distance to the eye's far point**. This means that objects at **infinity**, which were out of focus, now seem to be in focus at the far point.

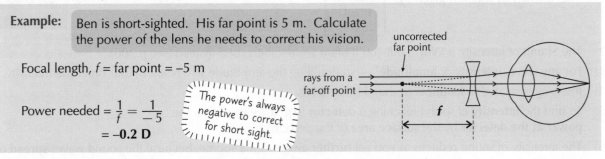

Example: Ben is short-sighted. His far point is 5 m. Calculate the power of the lens he needs to correct his vision.

Focal length, f = far point = −5 m

Power needed = $\frac{1}{f} = \frac{1}{-5}$

$= -0.2$ D

The power's always negative to correct for short sight.

Calculations Involving **Long Sight** Use the **Lens Equation**

1) People with these conditions have a near point which is too far away. An 'acceptable' near point is 25 cm.

2) A **converging lens** is used to produce a **virtual image** of objects 0.25 m away **at the eye's near point**. This means that close objects, which were out of focus, now seem to be in focus at the near point.

3) You can work out the **focal length**, and hence the **power** of lens needed, using the **lens equation**.

Example: Mavis can't read her book — her near point is 5 m. What power of lens does she need?

$u = 0.25$ m, $v = -5$ m

$\frac{1}{f} = \frac{1}{u} + \frac{1}{v} = \frac{1}{0.25} + \frac{1}{-5}$

$\frac{1}{f} = 3.8$ and $P = \frac{1}{f}$ so $P = $ **3.8 D**

The power's always positive to correct for long sight.

assume this distance is negligible

Warm-Up Questions

Q1 Write down the equation for calculating the linear magnification of a lens.

Q2 Define the terms myopia, hypermetropia and astigmatism.

Q3 What type of auxiliary lenses are used to correct each of these conditions?

Exam Questions

Q1 A man with short sight has a far point of 4.0 m.
Calculate the power of auxiliary lens needed to correct his far point. [3 marks]

Q2 A girl has a near point of 2.0 m.
Calculate the power of lens required to correct her near point to 25 cm. [3 marks]

Q3 Claire suffers from astigmatism.

a) State the type of lenses that are used to correct astigmatism. [1 mark]

b) State what information the optician includes in a prescription for lenses which correct astigmatism. [2 marks]

You can't fly fighter planes if you wear glasses...

There's a hidden bonus to having dodgy eyes — in the exam, you can take your specs off (discreetly) and have a look at the lenses to remind yourself what type is needed to correct short sight, long sight, or whatever it is you have. Cunning.

Physics of the Ear

Ears are pretty amazing — they convert sound into electrical energy, using some tiny bones and lots of even tinier hairs.

The **Intensity** of **Sound** is **Power** per **Unit Area**

The **intensity** of a sound wave is defined as the amount of sound **energy** that passes **per second per unit area** (perpendicular to the direction of the wave). That's **power per unit area**.

Felicity thought her waves were sound.

1) The intensity of sound is given by:

$$I = \frac{P}{A}$$

2) The SI unit of intensity is Wm^{-2}, but you'll often see decibels used instead (see p.200).

3) For any wave, **intensity ∝ amplitude²** — so doubling the amplitude will result in four times the intensity.

4) Intensity is related to **loudness** of sound (see p.200).

5) To find the **intensity** of sound reaching a **detector** (e.g. the ear), divide the **power at the detector** by the **surface area** of the detector.

6) The intensity of sound **reduces** as you get **further** away from a source, because the sound waves **spread out**. You can work out the **intensity** of sound at a **distance** from a source by assuming the sound spreads out **equally** in all directions. So A is the surface area of a **sphere** with a **radius** equal to the **distance** from the source.

> **Example:** A fire alarm sounds with a power of 4.5 W. Calculate the intensity of sound a person standing 3.0 m away would hear, assuming the sound waves spread equally in all directions.
>
> Surface area of a sphere = $4\pi r^2$ so $A = 4\pi \times 3.0^2 = 36\pi$
>
> Intensity = $I = \frac{P}{A} = \frac{4.5}{36\pi} = 0.03978...Wm^{-2} = \mathbf{0.040\ Wm^{-2}}$ **(to 2 s.f.)**

The **Ear** has **Three Main Sections**

The ear consists of three sections:

1) The **outer** ear (**pinna** and **auditory canal**).

2) The **middle** ear (**ossicles** and **Eustachian tube**).

3) The **inner** ear (**semicircular canals**, **cochlea** and **auditory nerve**).

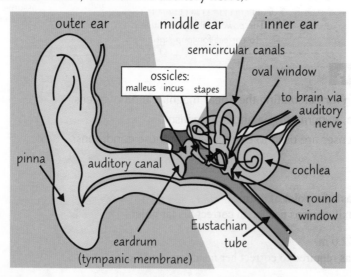

1) The **tympanic membrane** (eardrum) separates the **outer** and **middle** ears.

2) Although separated, the **outer** and **middle** ears both contain **air** at **atmospheric pressure**, apart from slight pressure variations due to sound waves. This pressure is maintained by **yawning** and **swallowing** — the middle ear is opened up to the outside via the **Eustachian tube** (which is connected to the throat).

3) The **oval** and **round windows** separate the **middle** and **inner** ears.

4) The **inner ear** is filled with fluid called **perilymph** (or **endolymph** in the **cochlear duct**). This fluid allows **vibrations** to pass to the basilar membrane in the **cochlea**.

5) The **semicircular canals** are involved with **maintaining balance**.

Physics of the Ear

The Ear acts as a Transducer, converting Sound Energy...

1) The **pinna** (external ear) acts like a funnel, channelling sound waves into the auditory canal. The sound energy is now **concentrated** onto a **smaller area**, which increases its **intensity**.

2) The sound waves consist of **variations** in **air pressure**, which make the **tympanic membrane** (eardrum) **vibrate**.

3) The tympanic membrane is connected to the **malleus** — one of the **three tiny bones** (**ossicles**) in the middle ear. The malleus then passes the **vibrations** of the eardrum on to the **incus** and the **stapes** (which is connected to the **oval window**).

4) As well as **transmitting vibrations**, the ossicles have **two** other functions — **amplifying** the sound signal and **reducing** the **energy reflected back** from the inner ear.

5) The **oval window** has a much **smaller area** than the **tympanic membrane**. Together with the **increased force** produced by the ossicles, this results in **greater pressure variations** at the oval window.

6) The **oval window** transmits vibrations to the **fluid** in the **inner ear**.

7) As the sound wave travels **through** the ear, its **amplitude decreases**, but its **frequency** remains the **same**.

...into Electrical Energy

1) Pressure waves in the fluid of the **cochlea** make the **basilar membrane** vibrate. Different regions of this membrane have different **natural frequencies**, from 20 000 Hz near the middle ear to 20 Hz at the other end.

2) When a sound wave of a particular **frequency** enters the inner ear, one part of the basilar membrane **resonates** and so vibrates with a **large amplitude**.

3) **Hair cells** attached to the basilar membrane trigger **nerve impulses** at this point of greatest vibration.

4) These **electrical impulses** are sent, via the **auditory nerve**, to the **brain**, where they are interpreted as **sounds**.

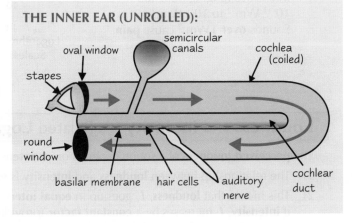

THE INNER EAR (UNROLLED):

Warm-Up Questions

Q1 What is meant by the 'intensity' of sound? What is the formula for intensity?

Q2 Sketch a diagram of the ear, labelling the structures within it.

Q3 Describe the function of the ossicles.

Q4 Explain why the relative sizes of the oval window and tympanic membrane are important.

Exam Question

Q1 The ear is designed to transduce sound energy into electrical energy.

a) State the function of the pinna. [1 mark]

b) Describe how sound energy is transmitted through the middle ear. [3 marks]

c) The surface area of the tympanic membrane is around 14 times the area of the oval window. Show that this increases the amplitude of vibrations in the ear by a factor of approximately 3.7. [3 marks]

d) Describe how pressure waves in the cochlea are converted to electrical impulses. [2 marks]

e) Explain how the ear is able to encode the frequency of a sound in the information sent to the brain. [2 marks]

Ears are like essays — they have a beginning, middle and end...

Or outer, middle and inner, if we're being technical. Learn what vibrates where, and you'll be fine.

Intensity and Loudness

The ear's sensitivity depends on the frequency and intensity of sounds, and deteriorates as you get older.

Humans can Hear a Limited Range of Frequencies

1) Young people can hear frequencies ranging from about **20 Hz** (low pitch) up to **20 000 Hz** (high pitch). As you get older, the upper limit decreases.

2) Our ability to **discriminate between frequencies** depends on how **high** that frequency is. For example, between 60 and 1000 Hz, you can hear frequencies 3 Hz apart as **different pitches**. At **higher** frequencies, a **greater difference** is needed for frequencies to be distinguished. Above 10 000 Hz, pitch can hardly be discriminated at all.

3) The **loudness** of sound you hear depends on the **intensity** and **frequency** of the sound waves.

4) The **weakest intensity** you can hear depends on the **frequency** of the sound wave.

5) The ear is **most sensitive** at around **3000 Hz**. For any given intensity, sounds of this frequency will be **loudest**.

6) Humans can hear sounds at intensities ranging from about 10^{-12} Wm^{-2} to 100 Wm^{-2}. Sounds **over 1 Wm^{-2}** cause **pain**.

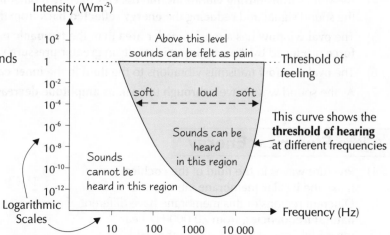

Loudness and Intensity are Related Logarithmically

The **perceived loudness** of a sound depends on its **intensity** (and its frequency — see above).

1) The relationship between **loudness** and **intensity** is **logarithmic**.

2) This means that **loudness**, **L**, goes up in **equal intervals** if **intensity**, **I**, increases by a **constant factor** (provided the frequency of the sound doesn't change).

$$\Delta L \propto \log\left(\frac{I_2}{I_1}\right)$$

ΔL is increase in loudness
I_1 is the original intensity
I_2 is the new intensity

3) E.g. if you **double** the intensity, **double it again** and so on, the **loudness** keeps going up in **equal steps**.

The Decibel Scale is used for Measuring Relative Intensity

1) You can often measure loudness using a **decibel meter**. The **decibel scale** is a **logarithmic scale** which actually measures **intensity level** — how intense the sound is **compared** to the human **threshold of hearing**.

2) The **intensity level**, **IL**, of a sound of intensity **I** is defined as:

3) **I$_0$** is the **threshold of hearing** (the **lowest intensity** of sound that can be heard) at a frequency of **1000 Hz**.

$$IL = 10\log\left(\frac{I}{I_0}\right)$$

I = intensity
I_0 = threshold of hearing

4) The value of **I$_0$** is **1.0 × 10^{-12} Wm^{-2}**.

5) The units of **IL** are **decibels** (dB). Intensity level can be given in **bels** (one decibel is a tenth of a bel) but decibels are usually a more convenient size.

A logarithmic scale is used as the range from the threshold of hearing to the threshold of pain is so large.

The dBA Scale is an Adjusted Decibel Scale

1) The **perceived loudness** of a sound depends on its **frequency** as well as its intensity. Two different frequencies with the **same loudness** will have **different intensity levels** on the dB scale.

2) The **dBA** scale is an **adjusted decibel scale** which is designed to take into account the **ear's response** to **different frequencies**.

3) On the **dBA scale**, sounds of the **same intensity level** have the **same loudness** for the average human ear.

Intensity and Loudness

You can Generate Curves of Equal Loudness

1) Start by generating a **control frequency** of **1000 Hz** at a particular **intensity level**.

2) Generate another sound at a different frequency. Vary the volume of this sound until it appears to have the **same loudness** as the 1000 Hz frequency. Measure the **intensity level** at this volume.

3) Repeat this for several different frequencies, and plot the resulting curve on a graph.

4) Change the **intensity level** of the **control frequency** and repeat steps two and three.

5) If you measure **intensity level** in **decibels**, then the **loudness** of the sound is given in **phons**.

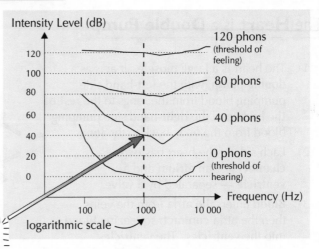

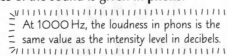

At 1000 Hz, the loudness in phons is the same value as the intensity level in decibels.

Hearing Deteriorates with Age and Exposure to Excessive Noise

1) As you get **older**, your hearing deteriorates **generally**, but **higher frequencies** are affected **most**.

2) Your ears can be damaged by **excessive noise**. This results in general hearing loss, but frequencies around **4000 Hz** are usually worst affected.

3) People who've worked with very **noisy machinery** have most hearing loss at the **particular frequencies** of the noise causing the damage.

4) **Equal loudness curves** can show hearing loss.

5) For a person with hearing loss, **higher intensity levels** are needed for the **same loudness**, when compared to a normal ear. A **peak** in the curve shows damage at a **particular** range of **frequencies**.

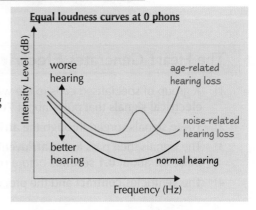

Equal loudness curves at 0 phons

Warm-Up Questions

Q1 Define the threshold of hearing and sketch a graph that shows how it depends on frequency.

Q2 What is the dB scale? How is the dBA scale different?

Q3 How are curves of equal loudness generated?

Exam Questions

Q1 A siren, which can be regarded as a point source, emits sound waves at a frequency of 3000 Hz (to 2 s.f.). The intensity of the sound is 0.94 Wm^{-2} at a distance of 10 m (to 2 s.f.).

a) State the accepted value of the threshold of hearing at 1000 Hz, I_0, in Wm^{-2}. [1 mark]

b) Calculate the intensity level of the sound of the siren. [1 mark]

c) Explain why the siren uses a frequency of 3000 Hz. [1 mark]

Q2 The diagram shows an equal loudness curve for a person suffering hearing loss and a person with normal hearing. The patient believes his hearing may have been damaged by working with noisy machinery. Does his equal loudness curve support this? Explain your answer.

[3 marks]

Saved by the decibel....

It's medical fact that prolonged loud noise damages your hearing, so you should really demand ear protection before you agree to do the housework — some vacuum cleaners are louder than 85 dBA — the 'safe' limit for regular exposure.

Electrocardiography (ECG)

You don't need to know about the structure of the heart or how it actually generates electrical signals for your exam, but you should probably understand the basics before you jump into electrocardiographs.

The **Heart** is a **Double Pump**

1) The heart is a **large muscle**. It acts as a **double pump**, with the **left**-hand side pumping blood from the **lungs** to the **rest of the body** and the **right**-hand side pumping blood from the **body** back to the **lungs**.

2) Each side of the heart has **two chambers** — an **atrium** and a **ventricle** — separated by a **valve**.

3) **Blood** enters the atria from the veins, then the atria **contract**, squeezing blood into the **ventricles**. The **ventricles** then **contract**, squeezing the blood **out** of the heart into the **arteries**.

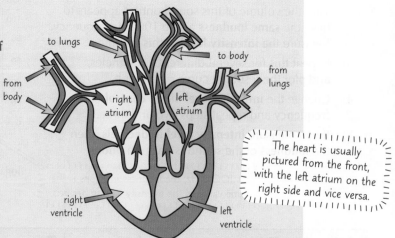

The heart is usually pictured from the front, with the left atrium on the right side and vice versa.

The Heart Generates **Electrical Signals**

1) A group of specialised cells in the wall of the right atrium produce **electrical signals** that pulse about **70 times a minute**.

2) These signals spread through the **atria** and make them **contract**.

3) The signals then pass to the **atrioventricular node**, which **delays** the pulse for about **0.1 seconds** before passing it on to the **ventricles**.

4) The ventricles **contract** and the process repeats.

Lucy's heart went a bit out of control when she saw Josh.

The Heart can be **Monitored** by an **Electrocardiograph**

1) The electrical signals of the heart can be detected **weakly** on the surface of the body. A machine called an **electrocardiograph** detects these signals and produces an **ECG** — an **electrocardiogram.**

2) An ECG is a plot of the **potential difference** between electrodes **against time**. They're used to find out about the **condition** of the heart being examined.

Obtaining an ECG

1) When obtaining an ECG, **electrodes** are placed on the body and the difference in potential difference between the sites is measured.

2) The signal is heavily **attenuated** (absorbed and weakened) by the body and needs to be **amplified** by a **high impedance** amplifier.

3) Electrodes are placed on the chest, which is close to the heart, and the limbs, where the **arteries** are **close** to the **surface**. The right leg is **never** used since it is too far away from the heart.

4) In order to reduce the electrical resistance at the point of contact, **hairs** and dead skin cells are **removed** (e.g. using sandpaper), a **conductive gel** is used and the electrodes are **securely attached**.

5) To reduce unwanted signals, the patient should also remain **relaxed** and **still** during the procedure, and the leads used should be shielded from any possible **interference** from ac sources in the area.

Electrocardiography (ECG)

An **Electrocardiogram** Has **Three** Distinct Waves

A normal ECG across one heart beat has a set pattern, split into **three parts**.

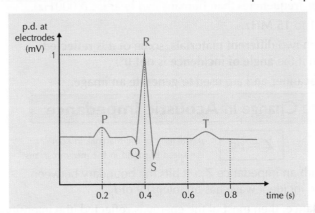

Martin loved distinct waves.

1) **P wave** — this is where a generated signal causes the **atria** to **contract**.

2) **QRS wave** — (about 0.2 seconds later) this is when the **ventricles** are **contracting**. This signal is much greater than the P wave which causes the atria to contract.

3) **T wave** — (another 0.2 seconds later) this corresponds to the **relaxation** of the **ventricles** as they prepare for another heartbeat.

Warm-Up Questions

Q1 What is an electrocardiograph?

Q2 How many standard ways are there to place electrodes for an ECG?

Q3 What does attenuation mean?

Q4 Why are electrodes never placed on the right leg?

Q5 Why should electrocardiograph leads be shielded if there are sources of ac current nearby?

Exam Questions

Q1 A patient has an ECG taken, part of which is shown.

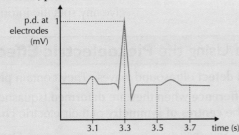

a) State the times that the P, QRS and T wave peaks occur. [1 mark]

b) State which wave corresponds to the atria contracting. [1 mark]

Q2 a) A problem is found on the QRS wave of a patient's ECG.
State the area of the heart which could be causing this. [1 mark]

b) The problem arose from intermittent electrical resistance between the electrode and the patient's skin.
Suggest one measure which could be taken to prevent this. [1 mark]

Be still my contracting atria...

If you rely on the cast of Casualty to get your heart beating faster, console yourself that it's all very educational.
Listen out for the machine that goes 'bip, bip, bip' , and look for the P waves, QRS waves and T waves on the screen.
If there aren't enough waves, the brave docs have to start shouting 'clear' and waving defibrillators around.

Ultrasound Imaging

Ultrasound imaging is a kind of non-invasive diagnostic technique used to avoid having to open you up.

Ultrasound has a **Higher Frequency** than **Humans** can **Hear**

1) Ultrasound waves are **longitudinal** waves with **higher frequencies** than humans can hear (>20 000 Hz).

2) For **medical** purposes, frequencies are usually from **1** to **15 MHz**.

3) When an ultrasound wave meets a **boundary** between two **different materials**, some of it is **reflected** and some of it passes through (undergoing **refraction** if the **angle of incidence** is **not 0°**).

4) The **reflected waves** are detected by the **ultrasound scanner** and are used to **generate an image**.

The Amount of **Reflection** depends on the Change in **Acoustic Impedance**

1) The **acoustic impedance**, Z, of a medium is defined as: Z has units of $kgm^{-2}s^{-1}$.

$$Z = \rho c$$

ρ = density of the material, in kgm^{-3}
c = speed of sound in the medium, in ms^{-1}

2) Say an ultrasound wave travels through a material with an impedance Z_1. It hits the boundary between this material and another with an impedance Z_2. The incident wave has an intensity of I_i.

3) If the two materials have a **large difference** in **impedance**, then **most** of the energy is **reflected** (the intensity of the reflected wave I_r will be high). If the impedance of the two materials is the **same** then there is **no reflection**.

4) The **fraction** of wave **intensity** that is reflected is given by:

5) Ultrasound waves undergo **attenuation** (they are **absorbed** and **scattered**) when they travel through a material. The larger the impedance of a material, the greater the attenuation of the ultrasound moving through the material.

$$\frac{I_r}{I_i} = \left(\frac{Z_2 - Z_1}{Z_2 + Z_1}\right)^2$$

where I_r is the intensity of the reflected wave.

There are **Advantages** and **Disadvantages** to **Ultrasound Imaging**

ADVANTAGES:

1) There are no known hazards — in particular, no exposure to ionising radiation (p.159).

2) It's good for imaging soft tissues, since you can obtain real-time images — X-ray fluoroscopy (p.210) can achieve this, but involves a huge dose of radiation.

3) Ultrasound devices are relatively cheap and portable.

4) The scan is a quick procedure (10-15 minutes) and the patient can move during the scan.

DISADVANTAGES:

1) Ultrasound doesn't penetrate bone — so it can't be used to detect fractures or examine the brain.

2) Ultrasound cannot pass through air spaces in the body (due to the mismatch in impedance) — so it can't produce images from behind the lungs.

3) The resolution is poor (about 10 times worse than X-rays), so you can't see fine detail.

4) Ultrasound can detect solid masses, but can't give any specific information as to what they are.

Ultrasound Images are **Produced** Using the **Piezoelectric Effect**

1) **Transducers** are used in imaging to **send** and **detect** ultrasound waves. They contain **piezoelectric crystals**.

2) **Piezoelectric crystals** produce a **potential difference** when they are **deformed** (squashed or stretched) — the rearrangement in structure displaces the **centres of symmetry** of their electric **charges**.

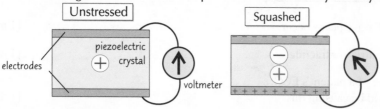
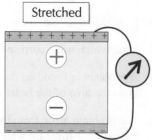

3) When you **apply a p.d.** across a piezoelectric crystal, the crystal **deforms**. If the p.d. is **alternating**, then the crystal **vibrates** at the **same frequency**.

4) A piezoelectric crystal can act as a **receiver** of **ultrasound**, converting **sound waves** into **alternating voltages**, and also as a **transmitter**, converting **alternating voltages** into **sound waves**.

5) Ultrasound devices use **lead zirconate titanate** (**PZT**) crystals. The **thickness** of the crystal is **half the wavelength** of the ultrasound that it produces. Ultrasound of this frequency will make the crystal **resonate** (like air in an open pipe — see p.104) and produce a large signal.

6) The PZT crystal is **heavily damped**, to produce **short pulses** and **increase** the **resolution** of the device.

Ultrasound Imaging

You need a **Coupling Medium** between the **Transducer** and the **Body**

1) **Soft tissue** has a very different **acoustic impedance** from **air** (as does the transducer), so almost all the ultrasound **energy** is **reflected** from the surface of the body if there is air between the **transducer** and the **body**.

2) To avoid this, you need a **coupling medium** between the transducer and the body — this **displaces** the **air** and has an impedance much closer to that of body tissue. The use of **coupling media** is an example of **impedance matching**.

3) The coupling medium is usually an **oil** or **gel** that is smeared onto the skin.

The **A-Scan** is a **Range Measuring** System

1) The **amplitude scan** (**A-Scan**) sends a short **pulse** of ultrasound into the body simultaneously with an **electron beam** sweeping across a cathode ray oscilloscope (**CRO**) screen.

2) The scanner receives **reflected** ultrasound pulses that appear as **vertical deflections** on the CRO screen. **Weaker** pulses (that have travelled further in the body and **arrive later**) are **amplified** more to avoid the loss of valuable data — this process is called **time-gain compensation** (**TGC**).

3) The **horizontal positions** of the reflected pulses indicate the **time** the 'echo' took to return, and are used to work out **distances** between structures in the body (e.g. the **diameter** of a **baby's head** in the uterus).

4) A **stream** of pulses can produce the appearance of a **steady image** on the screen, although modern CROs can store a digital image after just one exposure.

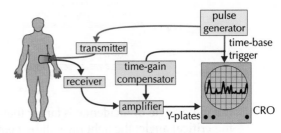

In a **B-Scan**, the **Brightness** Varies

1) In a **brightness scan** (**B-Scan**), the electron beam sweeps **down** the screen rather than across.

2) The amplitude of the reflected pulses is displayed as the **brightness** of the spot.

3) You can use a **linear array** of transducers to produce a **two-dimensional** image — for example of a foetus in a womb.

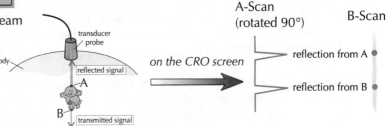

Warm-Up Questions

Q1 State the equation for acoustic impedance.
Q2 How are ultrasound waves produced and received in an ultrasound transducer?
Q3 What are the two types of ultrasound scan, and what are they both used for?

Exam Questions

Q1 a) Calculate what fraction of intensity is reflected when ultrasound waves pass from air to soft tissue.
Use $Z_{air} = 0.430 \times 10^3$ kgm⁻²s⁻¹, $Z_{tissue} = 1630 \times 10^3$ kgm⁻²s⁻¹. [2 marks]

b) Calculate the ratio between the intensity of the ultrasound that enters the body when a coupling gel is used ($Z_{gel} = 1500 \times 10^3$ kgm⁻²s⁻¹) and when none is used. Give your answer to the nearest power of ten. [4 marks]

Q2 The acoustic impedance of a certain soft tissue is 1.63×10^6 kgm⁻²s⁻¹ and its density is 1.09×10^3 kgm⁻³. Calculate the velocity the ultrasound waves travel at in this medium. [2 marks]

Q3 State one advantage and one disadvantage of using ultrasound as a medical imaging technique. [2 marks]

Ultrasound — Mancunian for 'très bien'

You can use ultrasound to make images in cases where other techniques would do too much damage — like to check the development of a baby in the womb. You have to know what you're looking for though, or it just looks like a blob.

Endoscopy

Phew, that ultrasound stuff wasn't exactly a walk in the park — luckily, endoscopes are easier to understand...

Optical Fibres Use Total Internal Reflection to Transmit Light

1) **Optical fibres** are a bit like electric wires — but instead of carrying current they **transmit light**.

2) A typical optical fibre consists of a **glass core** (about 5 μm to 50 μm in diameter) **surrounded** by a **cladding**, which has a slightly **lower refractive index**.

3) The **difference** in refractive index means that light travelling along the fibre will be **reflected** at the **cladding-core interface**. If the light ray's **angle of incidence** is **less than or equal** to a **critical angle**, some light will be **lost** out of the fibre.

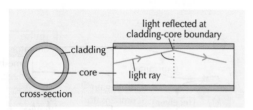

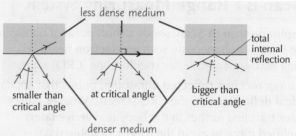

4) But if the **angle of incidence** is **larger** than the **critical angle**, the light ray will be **completely reflected** inside the fibre.

5) This phenomenon is called **total internal reflection** and means that the ray **zigzags** its way along the fibre — so long as the fibre isn't too curved.

The Critical Angle for an Optical Fibre can be Worked Out

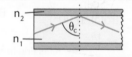

1) The **critical angle**, θ_c, depends on the **refractive index** of the **core**, n_1, and **cladding**, n_2, in an optical fibre.

2) You can work out this value using the formula: $\boxed{\sin\theta_c = \dfrac{n_2}{n_1}}$

Example: An optical fibre consists of a core with a refractive index of 1.5 and cladding with a refractive index of 1.4. Calculate the critical angle at the core-cladding boundary, and determine whether total internal reflection would occur if the incident angle was 70°.

$$\theta_c = \sin^{-1}\left(\frac{n_2}{n_1}\right) = \sin^{-1}\left(\frac{1.4}{1.5}\right) = 68.96...° = \textbf{69° (to 2 s.f.)}$$

70° > 69°, so total internal reflection would occur.

Lots of Optical Fibres can be Bundled Together

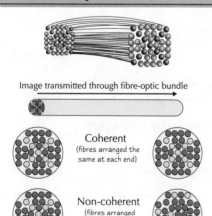

Image transmitted through fibre-optic bundle

Coherent
(fibres arranged the same at each end)

Non-coherent
(fibres arranged differently at each end)

1) An **image** can be transmitted along a **bundle** of optical fibres.

2) This can only happen if the **relative positions** of fibres in a bundle are the **same** at each end (otherwise the image would be jumbled up) — a fibre-optic bundle in this arrangement is said to be **coherent**.

3) The **resolution** (i.e. how much detail can be seen) depends on the **thickness** of the fibres. The thinner the fibres, the **more detail** that can be resolved — but thin fibres are more **expensive** to make.

4) Images can be **magnified** by making the diameters of the fibres get **gradually larger** along the length of the bundle.

5) If the relative **position** of the fibres **does not** remain the same between each end the bundle of fibres is said to be **non-coherent**.

6) **Non-coherent bundles** are much easier and **cheaper** to make. They **can't** transmit an **image** but they can be used to get **light** to hard-to-reach places — kind of like a flexible **torch**.

Endoscopy

Endoscopes Use Optical Fibres to Create an Image

1) An **endoscope** consists of a **long tube** containing **two bundles** of fibres — a **non-coherent** bundle to carry **light** to the area of interest and a **coherent** bundle to carry an **image** back to the eyepiece.

2) Endoscopes are widely used by surgeons to examine inside the body.

3) An **objective lens** is placed at the **distal** end (**furthest from the eye**) of the **coherent** bundle to form an image, which is then transmitted by the fibres to the **proximal** end (**closest to the eye**) where it can be **viewed** through an **eyepiece**.

4) The **endoscope tube** can also contain a **water channel**, for cleaning the objective lens, a **tool aperture** to perform **keyhole surgery** and a CO_2 **channel** which allows CO_2 to be pumped into the area in front of the endoscope, making more room in the body.

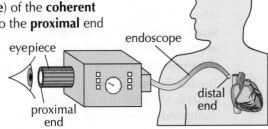

Endoscopes are Used in Keyhole Surgery

1) **Traditional** surgery needs a **large cut** to be made in the body so that there's **room** for the surgeons to get in and perform an **operation**.

2) This means that there's a **large risk of infection** to the exposed tissues and that permanent **damage** could be done to the patient's **body**.

3) New techniques in **minimally invasive surgery** (MIS or **keyhole surgery**) mean that only a **few small holes** need to be cut into the body.

4) An **endoscope** can be used in keyhole surgery to show the surgeon an **image** of the area of interest. **Surgical instruments** are passed through the endoscope tube, or through additional **small holes** in the body, so that the **operation** can be carried out.

5) **Common procedures** include the removal of the **gall bladder**, investigation of the **middle ear**, and removal of abnormal polyps in the **colon** so that they can be investigated for **cancer**.

6) **Recovery times** tend to be **quicker** for keyhole surgery, so the **patient** can usually **return home** on the **same day** — which makes it much **cheaper** for the hospital and **nicer** for the patient.

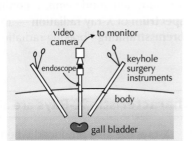

Warm-Up Questions

Q1 What conditions must be satisfied for total internal reflection to occur?
Q2 Describe the difference between a coherent and a non-coherent bundle of fibres.
Q3 Describe the main features of an endoscope.
Q4 How have endoscopes revolutionised some surgical procedures?

Exam Questions

Q1 A beam of light is transmitted through an optical fibre. The refractive index of the fibre's core is 1.35 and the refractive index of its cladding is 1.30.

a) Determine the critical angle for the core-cladding boundary. [2 marks]

b) Explain why the angle of incidence of the beam of light should be kept at or above the critical angle. [2 marks]

Q2 Coherent fibre-optic bundles can be used to transmit images. Describe the main features of the structure of a coherent fibre-optic bundle, and explain why each feature is important for the bundle's function. [4 marks]

If you ask me, physics is a whole bundle of non-coherentness...

If this is all getting too much, and your brain is as fried as a pork chipolata, just remember the wise words of revision wisdom from the great Spike Milligan — Ying tong, ying tong, ying tong, ying tong, ying tong, iddly-I-po, iddly-I-po...

X-Ray Production

Now it's time to make some X-rays by firing electrons at some metal.

X-Rays are Produced by Bombarding Tungsten with High Energy Electrons

1) In an X-ray tube, **electrons** are emitted from a **heated filament** and **accelerated** through a high **potential difference** (the **tube voltage**) towards a **tungsten anode**.

2) When the **electrons** smash into the **tungsten anode**, they **decelerate** and some of their **kinetic energy** is converted into **electromagnetic energy**, as **X-ray photons**.

3) The **maximum energy** of the X-ray photons is equal to the **potential difference** of the X-ray tube multiplied by the **charge** of an electron. So, if a potential difference of 50 kV is used in the tube, the maximum X-ray energy will be 50 keV.

4) The tungsten anode emits a **continuous spectrum** of **X-ray radiation** — this is called **bremsstrahlung** ('braking radiation').

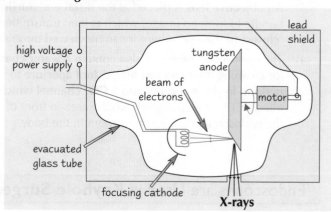

Characteristic X-Rays are also Produced

1) X-rays are also produced when beam electrons **knock out** other electrons from the **inner shells** of the **tungsten atoms**.

2) Electrons in the atoms' **outer shells** move into the **vacancies** in the **lower energy levels**, and **release energy** in the form of **X-ray photons**.

3) The energies of these X-rays are **known** for a given metal as they relate to the energy between electron shells in tungsten — so they're called **characteristic X-rays**.

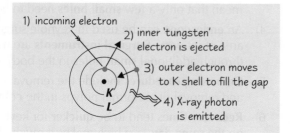

1) incoming electron
2) inner 'tungsten' electron is ejected
3) outer electron moves to K shell to fill the gap
4) X-ray photon is emitted

Combining Both gives the Energy Spectrum of X-Rays Produced

When you combine the **continuous** spectrum from **bremsstrahlung** and the **characteristic** spectrum you see **line spectra** superimposed on a **continuous spectrum**.

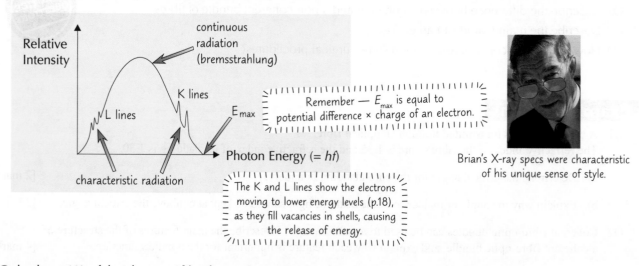

Relative Intensity

continuous radiation (bremsstrahlung)

K lines

L lines

E_{max}

Photon Energy (= hf)

characteristic radiation

Remember — E_{max} is equal to potential difference × charge of an electron.

The K and L lines show the electrons moving to lower energy levels (p.18), as they fill vacancies in shells, causing the release of energy.

Brian's X-ray specs were characteristic of his unique sense of style.

Only about **1%** of the electrons' **kinetic energy** is converted into **X-rays**. The rest is converted into **heat**, so, to avoid overheating, the tungsten anode is **rotated** at about 3000 rpm. It's also **mounted** on **copper** — this **conducts** the heat away effectively.

X-Ray Production

Beam Intensity and Photon Energy can be Varied

The **intensity** of the X-ray beam is the **energy per second per unit area** passing through a surface (at right angles). There are two ways to increase the **intensity** of the X-ray beam:

1) Increase the **tube voltage**. This gives the electrons **more kinetic energy**. Higher energy electrons can **knock out** electrons from shells **deeper** within the tungsten atoms — giving more 'spikes' on the graphs. Individual **X-ray photons** also have **higher maximum energies**.
   Intensity is approximately **proportional** to **voltage squared**.

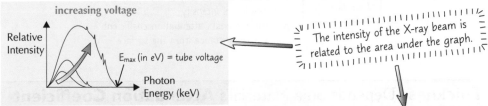

The intensity of the X-ray beam is related to the area under the graph.

2) Increase the **current** supplied to the filament. This liberates **more electrons per second**, which then produce **more X-ray photons per second**. Individual **photons** have the **same energy** as before.
   Intensity is approximately **proportional** to **current**.

Radiographers try to Produce a Sharp Image and Minimise the Radiation Dose

Medical X-rays are a compromise between producing really sharp, clear images, whilst keeping the amount of radiation the patient is exposed to as low as possible. To do this, radiographers:

1) Put the **detection plate close** to the patient and the **X-ray tube far** away from the patient to **increase image sharpness**.

2) Make sure the patient **keeps still** — if they move around, the image will be blurred.

3) Put a **lead grid** between the patient and film to **stop** scattered radiation '**fogging**' the film and **reducing contrast**.

4) Use an **intensifying screen** next to the film surface. This consists of crystals that **fluoresce** — they **absorb X-rays** and re-emit the energy as **visible light**, which helps to develop the photograph quickly. A shorter exposure time is needed, keeping the patient's radiation dose lower.

Warm-Up Questions

Q1 Draw a diagram of an X-ray tube and explain how a typical X-ray spectrum is produced.

Q2 State two methods used to avoid overheating of the anode.

Q3 Give two ways in which the intensity of an X-ray beam can be increased.

Q4 What measures can be taken to produce a high quality X-ray image while reducing the patient's radiation dose?

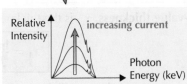

Exam Question

Magnitude of the charge on an electron (e) = 1.60 × 10⁻¹⁹ C.

Q1 An X-ray tube is connected to a potential difference of 30 kV.

   a) Sketch a graph of relative intensity against photon energy (in eV) for the resulting X-ray spectrum, and indicate its main features. [3 marks]

   b) Calculate the maximum energy of the X-ray photons produced. Give your answer in joules. [2 marks]

   c) Sketch how the graph in (a) would change if the tube voltage were increased. [2 marks]

Situation vacant — electron needed for low energy position...

I have a question — why, when something could have a nice, simple name like 'braking radiation', do scientists insist on giving it a much fancier one? 'Bremsstrahlung' just sounds baffling — well, unless you speak German of course.

X-Ray Imaging Techniques

So, you know how X-rays are produced and what the radiographer does — but why, I hear you cry, do some bits of you (i.e. your bones) show up nicely in an X-ray image, while others fade into the background? Attenuation, that's why...

X-Rays are Attenuated when they Pass Through Matter

When X-rays pass through matter (e.g. a patient's body), they are **absorbed** and **scattered**. The intensity of the X-ray beam **decreases** (attenuates) **exponentially** with the **distance from** the **surface**, according to the material's **attenuation coefficient**.

$$I = I_0 e^{-\mu x}$$

Where I is the intensity of the X-ray beam,
I_O is the initial intensity,
μ is the material's attenuation coefficient
and x is the distance from the surface.

Half-value Thickness Depends on a Material's Attenuation Coefficient

1) **Half-value thickness**, $x_{\frac{1}{2}}$, is the thickness of material required to **reduce** the **intensity** to **half** its **original value**.

$$x_{\frac{1}{2}} = \frac{\ln 2}{\mu}$$

Where μ is the material's linear attenuation coefficient.

2) The **mass attenuation coefficient**, μ_m, describes how the intensity of an X-ray beam decreases **per unit mass**. For a material of **density** ρ, it is given by:

$$\mu_m = \frac{\mu}{\rho}$$

X-Rays are Absorbed More by Bone than Soft Tissue

1) X-rays are **attenuated** by **absorption** and **scattering**. How much **energy is absorbed** by a **material** depends on its **atomic number**.

2) So tissues containing atoms with **different atomic numbers** (e.g. **soft tissue** and **bone**) will **contrast** in the X-ray image.

3) If the tissues in the region of interest have similar attenuation coefficients then artificial **contrast media** can be used — e.g. **barium meal**.

4) **Barium** has a **high atomic number**, so it shows up clearly in X-ray images and can be followed as it moves along the patient's digestive tract.

Bones show up brightly in X-ray images because they absorb more X-rays than the surrounding soft tissue.

CT Scans use X-Rays to Produce High-Quality Images

1) **Computed tomography** (CT) scans produce an image of a **two-dimensional slice** through the body.

2) A narrow **X-ray beam** consisting of a single wavelength (**monochromatic**) **rotates** around the body and is picked up by thousands of **detectors**. The detectors feed the signal to a **computer**.

3) The computer works out how much attenuation has been caused by each part of the body and produces a very **high quality** image.

4) However, the machines are **expensive** and the scans involve a **high radiation dose** for the patient.

Fluoroscopy is used to Create Moving Images

1) **Moving images** can be created using a **fluorescent screen** and an **image intensifier**. This is useful for **imaging organs** as they **work**.

2) **X-rays** pass through the patient and hit the **fluorescent screen**, which **emits light**.

3) The **light** causes **electrons** to be emitted from the **photocathode**.

4) The **electrons** travel through the **glass tube** towards the **fluorescent viewing screen**, where they form an image. Electrodes in the glass tube **focus** the **image** onto the screen.

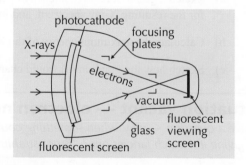

X-Ray Imaging Techniques

Flat Panel (FTP) Detectors can be used Instead of Photographic Detection

Flat Panel detectors are a **digital** method of X-ray imaging. X-rays are fired at the patient, who has a FTP detector behind them. The X-rays hit the detector and an **image** is created.

1) X-ray photons excite **scintillator** material in the detector. This produces **light** with intensity proportional to the energy of the incident X-ray photon.

2) **Photodiode pixels** in the detector generate a **voltage** when light hits them. The voltage is **proportional** the intensity of the light.

3) **Thin-film transistors** — one for every pixel — are then used to read the **digital signal**. A **digital image** of inside the patient is then created.

FTP Detectors have many Advantages over Photographic Detection

1) They are more **light-weight** and compact, making them much more convenient as they can be **moved** around a hospital or positioned around an immobile patient.

2) They have a **higher resolution** so can detect finer details.

3) There is **less distortion** of the final image.

4) The digital read out can easily be **copied**, stored or **shared**.

5) They require a **lower exposure** to produce **clear images**.

There are Advantages and Disadvantages to X-Ray Imaging

ADVANTAGES:

1) Good **resolution** and provides clear imaging of **bones**.

2) CT scans are **much quicker** than MR scans (p.212).

3) **Cheaper** than MR scanners.

DISADVANTAGES:

1) X-rays are a form of ionising radiation — which can damage cells and in rare cases lead to the development of cancer.

2) Investigating soft tissue with fluoroscopy requires a larger dose of radiation.

3) Generally unsuitable for pregnant women.

Warm-Up Questions

Q1 Write down the formula which relates the intensity of X-rays at a given point, initial intensity, distance and the attenuation constant.

Q2 State the formula for calculating the half-value thickness of a material.

Q3 Explain how fluoroscopy allows you to see a real-time image.

Q4 State two advantages of using a Flat Panel detector.

Exam Questions

Q1 The half-value thickness for aluminium is 3 mm for 30 keV X-ray photons.

    a) State what is meant by the term 'half-value thickness'. [1 mark]

    b) Calculate the thickness of aluminium needed to reduce the intensity of a homogeneous beam of X-rays at 30 keV to 1% of its initial value. [3 marks]

Q2 a) A patient is going in for a CT scan. Describe briefly how a CT scan works. [3 marks]

    b) State one negative aspect of CT scanners. [1 mark]

There's more than just the bare bones of X-ray imaging here...

I'm afraid you've got to get into the mathsy details of how an X-ray works. Practise using those equations and make some lists weighing up the advantages and disadvantages of using things like CT scanners and fluoroscopy.

Magnetic Resonance (MR) Imaging

Magnetic Resonance (MR) imaging is another form of non-invasive diagnostic imaging — enjoy.

Magnetic Resonance can be used to Create Images

1) The MR machine contains a huge **superconducting** magnet which the patient lies in the centre of. This magnet produces a **uniform magnetic field**. The magnet needs to be **cooled** by liquid helium — this is partly why the scanner is so expensive.

Tom and Taylor thought it was never too early to start learning physics.

2) The uniform magnetic field generated by the machine has an effect on the **protons** (hydrogen nuclei) in the patient's body. **Protons** (and neutrons) possess a quantum property called **spin**, which makes them behave like **tiny magnets**.

3) Initially, all of the protons are orientated **randomly**, but in a uniform magnetic field the protons align themselves with the **magnetic field lines**.

4) Protons in **parallel alignment** point in the **same direction** as the external **magnetic field**. **Antiparallel** alignment means the protons point in the **opposite** direction to the field.

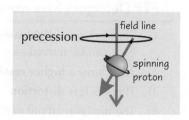

5) As the protons spin, they **precess** (**wobble**) about the magnetic **field lines**.

6) This wobble has an **angular frequency** (p.101) called the **precession frequency**, which is proportional to the magnetic **field strength**.

7) By using smaller electromagnets, smaller magnetic fields can be **superimposed** onto the main one, creating a **gradient** of **magnetic field strength** across the patient. This means the protons in different sections of the body will have **different precession frequencies** and will absorb **different frequencies of radiation** (see below).

Radio Waves at the Precession Frequency Excite the Protons

1) Radio frequency (RF) **coils** are used to transmit **pulses** of **radio waves** at the same **frequency** as the **precession frequency**, allowing the protons to **absorb** their energy and become **excited,** causing them to change their **spin state** (**flip** their alignment).

2) **Protons** in different **sections** of the body have different **precession frequencies** (due to the **gradient** of the field) and will absorb **different** RF waves.

3) The RF coils can transmit pulses of **different frequencies** to **excite** protons in successive **small regions** of the body.

4) When the radio waves are switched **off**, the protons **relax** and **re-emit** electromagnetic energy at their **precession frequency**. This is the **MR signal**.

5) As the computer knows the **positions** in the body **relating** to each precession **frequency**, it can then generate an **image** of a **2D cross-section** through the body, or build up a 3D image, by measuring various quantities of the MR signal like amplitude, frequency and phase.

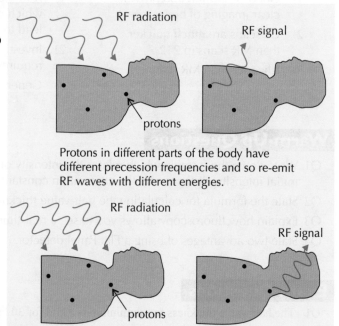

Protons in different parts of the body have different precession frequencies and so re-emit RF waves with different energies.

Contrast can be Controlled by Varying the Pulses of Radio Waves

1) Radio waves are applied in **pulses**. Each short pulse **excites** the hydrogen nuclei and then allows them to **relax** and emit a signal. The response of **different tissue types** can be enhanced by varying the **time between pulses**.

2) Tissues consisting of **large molecules** such as **fat** are best imaged using **rapidly repeated pulses**. This technique is used to image the internal **structure** of the body.

3) Allowing **more time** between pulses enhances the response of **watery** substances. This is used for **diseased** areas.

Magnetic Resonance (MR) Imaging

MR scans have Advantages and Disadvantages

ADVANTAGES:

1) There are **no** known **side effects**.
2) An image can be made for any slice in any **orientation** of the body from a single scan.
3) High quality images can be obtained for **soft tissue** such as the **brain**.
4) **Contrast** can be **weighted** in order to investigate different situations.
5) MR imaging can give **real-time** images.

DISADVANTAGES:

1) The imaging of bones is very poor.
2) Some people suffer from claustrophobia in the scanner.
3) Scans can be noisy and take a long time.
4) MR imaging can't usually be used on people with pacemakers or some metal implants — the strong magnetic fields would be very harmful.
5) Scanners cost millions of pounds.

Comparing MR, CT Scans and Ultrasound

You need to be able to **compare** imaging techniques — ultrasound (p.204-205), X-rays (p.208-211) and MR scans — and talk about their **convenience**, **safety** and **resolution**.

	Ultrasound	X-Rays	MR
Safety	No known side effects	Uses ionising radiation	No known side effects
Image Resolution for Bones	Can't penetrate	Very good	Poor
Image Resolution for Soft Tissue	Poor	Good	Very good
Convenience	Quick, cheap and portable	Quick, becoming more portable	Expensive and large

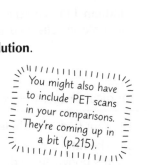

You might also have to include PET scans in your comparisons. They're coming up in a bit (p.215).

Warm-Up Questions

Q1 Describe what is meant by precession frequency.

Q2 Describe how using a magnetic field gradient can produce a cross-section of a patient.

Q3 What method is used to investigate diseased areas using radio frequency pulses?

Q4 State which imaging method would be best out of ultrasound, X-rays and an MR scan, when trying to take an image of a fracture in a bone.

PRACTICE QUESTIONS

Exam Questions

Q1 Outline how an MR scanner is used to produce an image of a section of a patient's body. The quality of your written answer will be assessed in this question. **[6 marks]**

Q2 State two advantages and two disadvantages of using MR scanners as an imaging technique. **[4 marks]**

All those radio waves have given me a headache...

OK, so these aren't the easiest of pages. Make sure you really understand how MR scanners work — it took me a long time to get my head around it. At least now you know why people sit in vats of baked beans to raise money for their local hospital to buy an MR scanner though... well, maybe not the beans part, best leave that to A-level psychology.

Medical Uses of Radiation

Radiation can be incredibly useful in medicine, but any use of ionising radiation carries some risk.

Medical Tracers are Used to Diagnose the Function of Organs

Medical tracers are **radioactive substances** that are used to show tissue or **organ function**. Other types of imaging, e.g. **X-rays** (p.210), only show the **structure** of organs — medical tracers show **structure and function**.

Medical tracers usually consist of a **radioactive isotope** — e.g. **technetium-99m, iodine-131** or **indium-111** — bound to a **substance** that is **used** by the **body** — e.g. **glucose** or **water**. The tracer is **injected** into or **swallowed** by the patient and then **moves** through the **body** to the region of interest. **Where** the tracer goes depends on the **substance** the isotope is bound to — i.e. it goes anywhere that the substance would **normally go**, and is used how that substance is **normally used**. The **radiation emitted** is **recorded** (e.g. by a **gamma camera** or **PET scanner**, see p.215) and an **image** of inside the patient produced.

You need to know about three of the main radioactive isotopes used in medical tracing:

1) **Technetium-99m** is a **widely** used isotope, due to its effective half-life — **long enough** that γ radiation can still be **detected** once it reaches the **organ** and **short enough** that the patient isn't **exposed** to radiation for too long.

2) Iodine is naturally used by the **thyroid**, so **iodine-131** is used to detect and treat problems in the thyroid.

3) **Indium-111** is used to label **antibodies** and **blood cells**, to detect **infections**.

	Physical half-life	Radiation emitted	Energy of gamma radiation emitted
Technetium-99m	6 hours	Gamma	140 keV
Iodine-131	8 days	Beta and gamma	360 keV
Indium-111	2.8 days	Gamma	170 or 250 keV

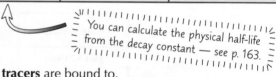

You can calculate the physical half-life from the decay constant — see p. 163.

Medical Tracers Have An Effective Half-Life

1) Your body **metabolises** (uses up) the substances that **medical tracers** are bound to.

2) The **rate** at which it manages to do this — the rate of excretion — affects how long emissions from the body can be detected for. You can think of this rate in the form of a **biological half-life**, T_B.

3) When combined with the **physical half-life**, T_P (which only depends on the decay constant, p.162) you get an **effective half-life**, T_E, for the tracer.

$$\frac{1}{T_E} = \frac{1}{T_B} + \frac{1}{T_P}$$

Technetium-99m is Generated with Molybdenum

Technetium-99m has a physical half-life which is **too short** for it to be practically transported. Instead, hospitals have **Molybdenum-Technetium generators** delivered. Molybdenum has a much longer half-life — **66 hours**, making it much better for transport.

1) Inside the generator, the molybdenum has been combined with **aluminium oxide**, which it bonds strongly with.

2) Molybdenum then **decays**, producing Technetium-99m which does not bond as strongly with aluminium oxide.

3) A **saline solution** is placed into the generator, washing out any technetium-99m. This solution can then be injected into patients, or combined with a substance to make a specific **tracer**.

Gamma Cameras Detect Gamma Radiation

The γ-rays emitted by **radiotracers** injected into a patient's body are detected using a **gamma camera**. **Gamma cameras** (like the one shown on the right) consist of **five** main parts:

1) **Lead shield** — **stops radiation** from **other sources** entering the camera.

2) **Lead collimator** — a **piece of lead** with thousands of **vertical holes** in it — only γ-rays **parallel** to the holes can **pass through**.

3) **Sodium iodide crystal** — emits a **flash of light** (**scintillates**) whenever a **γ-ray** hits it.

4) **Photomultiplier tubes** — turn the flashes of **light** into **pulses of electricity**. Each tube contains a **photocathode** that releases an electron by the **photoelectric effect** when hit by a photon. Each electron is then **multiplied** into a **cascade** of electrons.

5) **Electronic circuit** — **collects** the **signals** from the photomultiplier tubes and sends them to a **computer** for processing into an **image**.

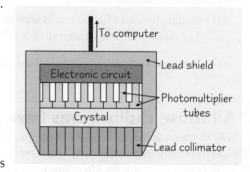

To computer
Lead shield
Electronic circuit
Photomultiplier tubes
Crystal
Lead collimator

Medical Uses of Radiation

PET Scanning Involves Positron/Electron Annihilation

1) The patient is injected with a substance used by the body, e.g. glucose, containing a **positron-emitting** radiotracer with a **short half-life**, e.g. ^{13}N, ^{15}O, ^{18}F.

2) The patient is left for a time to allow the radiotracer to **move through the body** to the organs.

3) **Positrons** emitted by the radioisotope collide with **electrons** in the organs, causing them to **annihilate**, emitting **high-energy gamma rays** in the process.

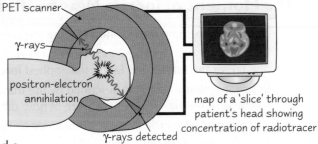

PET scanner

γ-rays

positron-electron
annihilation

γ-rays detected

map of a 'slice' through
patient's head showing
concentration of radiotracer

4) **Detectors** around the body record these **gamma rays**, and a computer builds up a **map of the radioactivity** in the body.

5) The main advantage of PET scans is that the **distribution of radioactivity** matches up with **metabolic activity**. This is because **more** of the radioactive glucose (or whatever) injected into the patient is taken up and **used** by cells that are **doing more work** (cells with an **increased metabolism**, in other words).

6) Another advantage is that **brain activity** can be investigated, whereas some other non-invasive methods cannot **penetrate** the **skull**. It can also give information about the **malignancy** of tumours and whether a tumour is **spreading**.

7) There are **disadvantages** too — **ionising radiation** is used which could **damage** the patient's cells. Scans take a **long time** and require the patient to stay **still**, which can be **uncomfortable** and **claustrophobic**. The machine itself is **expensive** and very **large**, so patients have to **travel** to their nearest hospital which has a PET scanner, which could be **inconvenient** for them.

Radiation Can Also Be Used to Treat Cancer

Ionising radiation **damages cells** — usually a bad thing, but in some cases this property can be helpful.

1) **High energy X-rays** are fired at tumours from outside of the patient's body. This means that surrounding **healthy cells** are also **damaged** — which can lead to **mutations** and even a higher risk of **future cancers**.

2) To **limit** the radiation patients are exposed to, carefully **focussed beams** are controlled by computers to ensure the majority of the radiation is hitting the tumour. **Shielding** is also sometimes used, and the X-ray beam may be **rotated** around the patient to minimise the radiation dose to healthy tissue.

3) Radioactive treatments can also be placed **inside** a patient. Implants containing **beta-emitters** are placed next to or inside of the tumour. Beta radiation is ionising, so damages the cells in the tumour, but has a **short range** so the damage to healthy tissue is **limited**.

Warm-Up Questions

Q1 List 3 radioactive isotopes which are used in medical tracers. State the energies of the gamma radiation they emit.

Q2 Which of the three isotopes is primarily used to investigate problems in the thyroid?

Q3 Explain what an effective half-life is and why it must be used when evaluating medical tracers.

Q4 Explain how technetium-99m is generated in hospitals.

Q5 Describe how gamma cameras work.

Q6 Apart from radioactive tracers, what else can nuclear radiation be used for?

Exam Questions

Q1 If technetium-99m has a biological half-life of 24 hours, calculate its effective half-life. [2 marks]

Q2 Discuss the advantages and disadvantages of PET scanners. [4 marks]

Q3 A patient has a small, cancerous tumour. Explain how and why beta-emitters could be used to internally treat it. [2 marks]

Gamma cameras — for energetic selfies...

Woo-hoo! Finally, at the end of the section. Doesn't mean you can run off and enjoy yourself just yet though — there's some extra exam practice for Medical Physics on page 256 for you to have a go at. Aren't you lucky...

Inertia and Kinetic Energy

The moment of inertia — it sounds weird but it's a fairly simple concept. It's just the rotational equivalent of mass.

The **Moment of Inertia** Measures **Resistance** to **Rotation**

1) To make something **start** or **stop moving** requires a **force** to be applied.

2) **Inertia** is a measure of how much an object **resists** a change in velocity
(the **larger** the **inertia**, the **larger** the applied **force** needed to change its velocity by a given amount).

3) In **linear** systems, inertia is described by the **mass** of an object, but for **rotating objects** it's described by the **moment of inertia**. This is a measure of how difficult it is to rotate an object, or to change its rotational speed.

4) The **moment of inertia** measures **resistance** to **rotation**, and depends on **mass** and its **distance** from the **axis of rotation** (the point or line around which the object is rotating).

Moment of Inertia Depends on How the **Mass** is **Distributed**

1) For a particle (**point mass**), the moment of inertia is simply:

$$I = mr^2$$ where I is moment of inertia (kgm^2), m is the mass of the particle (kg) and r is the distance from the axis of rotation (m).

2) For an **extended object**, like a rod, the moment of inertia is calculated by **adding** up the **individual** moments of inertia of **each point mass** that makes up the object.

$$I = \Sigma mr^2$$

3) This means that the moment of inertia changes depending on the **mass** and how it is **distributed** about the **axis of rotation**. For example, a **hollow** object will have a different moment of inertia to a **solid** one with the same mass.

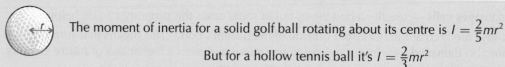

The moment of inertia for a solid golf ball rotating about its centre is $I = \frac{2}{5}mr^2$

But for a hollow tennis ball it's $I = \frac{2}{3}mr^2$

The moment of inertia for a solid wheel rotating about its centre is $I = \frac{1}{2}mr^2$

But for a hollow ring or circular hoop it's $I = mr^2$

You don't need to learn specific moments of inertia for different shapes — they'll be given in the exam.

The mass is concentrated further from the centre, so its moment of inertia is greater, per unit mass.

4) Similarly, an object rotated about its **centre** will have a different moment of inertia if it is rotated about a point near its **edge**.

You Can **Combine Moments of Inertia**

You can **add together** the individual moments of inertia of different objects to find the moment of inertia of the whole system. You'll usually be able to model individual objects as point masses.

Example: a)   Calculate the moment of inertia of a 750 g bike wheel, which has a radius of 31.1 cm. The moment of inertia for a hollow cylinder (a bike wheel) is $I = mr^2$.

$$I = 0.75 \times 0.311^2 = 0.0725... = \textbf{0.073 kgm}^2 \text{ (to 2 s.f.)}$$

b)   A 20.0 g reflector is attached to the wheel 6.0 cm in from the outer edge. Assuming the reflector behaves like a point mass, calculate the new moment of inertia of the wheel.

A bicycle wheel can be modelled as a hollow cylinder or a circular hoop — the moment of inertia is the same.

$I = \Sigma mr^2$, so $I_{new} = I_{initial} + mr^2$ *This is the MOI of the reflector.*

$r = 31.1 - 6.0 = 25.1$ cm $= 0.251$ m and $m = 0.0200$ kg

$$I_{new} = 0.0725... + 0.0200 \times 0.251^2 = 0.0738...$$
$$= \textbf{0.074 kgm}^2 \text{ (to 2 s.f.)}$$

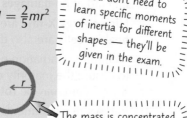

r = 31.1 cm

6.0 cm

Inertia and Kinetic Energy

An Object's Rotational Kinetic Energy Depends on its Moment of Inertia

Just like you can find the **kinetic energy** of an object with **linear** motion, you can find the kinetic energy of a **rotating object**:

$$E_k = \tfrac{1}{2}I\omega^2$$

where I is moment of inertia (kgm²), and ω is the angular speed (rad s⁻¹)

The moment of inertia, I, is like the rotational equivalent of linear mass, m. This means $\tfrac{1}{2}mv^2$ can be rewritten using I and ω to get rotational kinetic energy.

Example: A dancer adds a 60.0 g mass to each end of her twirling baton. The baton rod is uniform, 70 cm long (to 2 s.f.) and has a mass of 150 g. Assume the added masses act as point masses. Calculate the rotational kinetic energy of the baton as she spins it about its centre at an angular speed of 1.1 rad s⁻¹ (to 2 s.f.). The moment of inertia for a rod of length L about its centre is $I = \tfrac{1}{12}mL^2$.

First, calculate the overall moment of inertia for the object.

$$I = I_{rod} + \Sigma mr^2 = \tfrac{1}{12}mL^2 + 2 \times \left[m \times \left(\tfrac{L}{2}\right)^2\right]$$

There are 2 masses, each a distance of L/2 from the baton's centre.

$$= \tfrac{1}{12} \times 0.15 \times 0.7^2 + 2 \times [0.06 \times 0.35^2] = 0.0208...\,\text{kgm}^2$$

Then substitute this value into the formula for kinetic energy:

$$E_k = \tfrac{1}{2}I\omega^2 = \tfrac{1}{2} \times 0.0208... \times 1.1^2 = 0.0125...$$

axis of rotation

So the rotational kinetic energy of the baton is **0.013 J (to 2 s.f.)**

Warm-Up Questions

Q1 What is the moment of inertia?

Q2 What is the formula for calculating the moment of inertia of a point mass?

Q3 Describe how you get the moment of inertia for an extended object.

Q4 State the formula for calculating rotational kinetic energy.

PRACTICE QUESTIONS

Exam Questions

Q1 Calculate the moment of inertia for a 30 g point mass 80 cm from the axis of rotation. [1 mark]

Q2 A child jumps onto the edge of a 130 kg roundabout. The moment of inertia of the roundabout with the child is 531 kgm². Assuming the child is a point mass, calculate the mass of the child. The radius of the roundabout is 2.5 m and the moment of inertia for a solid disc is $I = \tfrac{1}{2}mr^2$. [3 marks]

Q3 A hollow 500 g ball with a 10 cm radius rolls down a slope with an angular velocity of 1.5 rad s⁻¹. $I = \tfrac{2}{3}mr^2$ for a hollow sphere.

a) Calculate the moment of inertia for the ball. [1 mark]

b) Calculate the rotational kinetic energy of the ball. [2 marks]

c) The ball is replaced with a solid ball of the same mass and radius, travelling at the same angular velocity. Calculate the ratio of the solid ball's kinetic energy to the kinetic energy of the hollow ball. $I = \tfrac{2}{5}mr^2$ for a solid sphere. [2 marks]

I'll give you a moment to let this sink in...

It sounds tricky, but really the moment of inertia is pretty simple. You want to make something spin about a point, but it's putting up a bit of a fight. You'll be given any formulas you need in the exam, but make sure you are comfortable using them and you know how to work out the new moment of inertia if a point mass is added to the system.

Rotational Motion

All you could ever want to know about how to describe rotating objects... almost.

Angular Displacement is Measured in Radians

You need to be familiar with each of these terms to do with rotational motion:

1) **Angular displacement** is the **angle** through which a point has been rotated.

2) **Angular velocity** is a **vector** quantity describing the **angle** a point rotates through **per second**.

$$\omega = \frac{\Delta\theta}{\Delta t}$$

where ω is angular velocity (rad s^{-1}), θ is angular displacement (rad) and t is time (s).

3) **Angular speed** is just the **magnitude** of the angular velocity.

4) **Angular acceleration** is the **rate of change** of **angular velocity**.

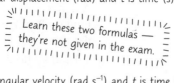
Learn these two formulas — they're not given in the exam.

$$\alpha = \frac{\Delta\omega}{\Delta t}$$

where α is angular acceleration (rad s^{-2}), ω is angular velocity (rad s^{-1}) and t is time (s).

Equations of Motion for Uniform Angular Acceleration

The **equations of motion** for uniform (constant) linear acceleration that you already know can be **rewritten** using the substitutions in the table to get the **equations of motion** for objects **rotating** with **uniform angular** acceleration.

	Linear	Rotational
Displacement	s	θ
Velocity	v	ω
Acceleration	a	α

$$\omega_2 = \omega_1 + \alpha t \qquad \omega_2^2 = \omega_1^2 + 2\alpha\theta$$

$$\theta = \omega_1 t + \tfrac{1}{2}\alpha t^2 \qquad \theta = \tfrac{1}{2}(\omega_1 + \omega_2)t$$

where ω_1 is initial angular velocity and ω_2 is final angular velocity

> **Example:** A figure skater initially at rest begins to spin with uniform angular acceleration. After 2.5 revolutions, she has an angular velocity of 4.9 rad s^{-1}. Calculate her angular acceleration.
>
> First, see what variables you have to tell you which equation to use.
>
> $\alpha = ?$, $\omega_1 = 0$, $\omega_2 = 4.9$ rad s^{-1}, $\theta = 2.5$ revolutions — so you should use $\omega_2^2 = \omega_1^2 + 2\alpha\theta$.
>
> Next, make sure all values are in the correct units.
>
> $\theta = 2.5$ revolutions $= 2.5 \times 2\pi = 15.7...$ radians
>
> Rearrange the formula for α and substitute in the given values.
>
> $\alpha = \dfrac{\omega_2^2 - \omega_1^2}{2\theta} = \dfrac{4.9^2 - 0}{2 \times 15.7...} = 0.764... = \mathbf{0.76 \ rad \ s^{-2}}$ **(to 2 s.f.)**
>
> *Angular displacement might be given in revolutions, and angular velocity in revs min^{-1} or revs s^{-1}. So make sure you always convert to radians for displacement and rad s^{-1} for velocity.*

Angular Velocity is the Gradient of an Angular Displacement-Time Graph

When you plot **angular displacement** against **time** for a **constant** angular acceleration, you get a curve showing that **displacement** is **proportional** to t^2.

When the angular acceleration is **not constant**, the displacement is no longer proportional to t^2.

The gradient of a tangent to the curve gives the angular velocity at that point.

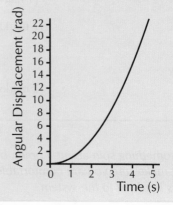

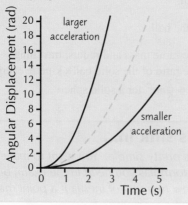

larger acceleration

smaller acceleration

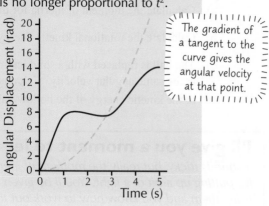

Rotational Motion

Angular Acceleration is the Gradient of an Angular Velocity-Time Graph

When you plot angular velocity against time for a constant angular acceleration, you get a straight line.

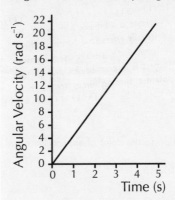

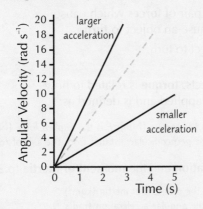

When the angular acceleration is not constant, the graph has a changing gradient.

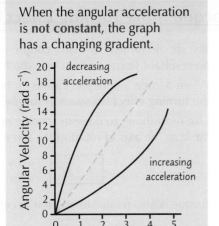

1) For **uniform** angular acceleration, to find the acceleration, you simply find the **gradient** of the **angular velocity-time** graph.

2) For **non-uniform** angular acceleration, to find the acceleration at a **given point**, you find the **gradient** of the **tangent** to the curve at that point.

3) The **area** under the curve between two points gives the **angular displacement** travelled in that time period.

4) A **negative** gradient would show **deceleration**.

Warm-Up Questions

Q1 What is angular velocity? State the formula for calculating it.

Q2 What is the formula for calculating angular acceleration?

Q3 How do you find angular velocity from an angular displacement-time graph?

Q4 What does the gradient of an angular velocity-time graph describe?

Q5 What does the area under an angular velocity-time graph describe?

Exam Questions

Q1 Calculate the angular velocity of Earth spinning about its axis. [1 mark]

Q2 An object is spinning at 30.0 revs min⁻¹ at a time t. If it has a constant angular acceleration of 1.57 rad s⁻², calculate its angular velocity 5.00 seconds after time t. [3 marks]

Q3 Sketch a graph of angular displacement against time for an object with constant angular acceleration. [2 marks]

Q4 The graph shows the angular velocity against time for a spinning object.

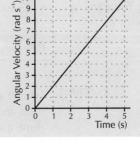

   a) State whether the object's angular acceleration is increasing, decreasing or constant. [1 mark]

   b) Calculate the angular acceleration of the object. [1 mark]

   c) Calculate the angular displacement for the object for the interval 2-5 seconds. [1 mark]

All this spinning in circles makes my head hurt — or maybe it's the maths...

They look pretty horrible, but actually the equations on these pages are pretty much the same as the equations of motion that you're used to — only someone's come along and replaced some letters with Greek ones. The only thing that might catch you out is not remembering to convert your angular displacement into radians per second, so beware.

Torque, Work and Power

Again, lots of similarities here between the regular force, work and power that you know. It's just a case of changing those formulas to describe stuff that's rotating instead of moving in a straight line.

Torque is the Turning Effect of a Force

1) You should remember that a **couple** is a pair of **forces** which cause **no resultant** linear motion, but which cause an object to **turn**.

2) When a force (or couple) causes an object to turn, the **turning effect** is known as **torque**.

3) Like most things to do with rotating objects, **torque** is related to how **far** from the **axis of rotation** the **force** is applied and is defined as:

> *A torque is a bit like a moment, but it usually refers to a turning object. 'Moment' is generally used when an object is in equilibrium, and all the potential turning forces are balanced.*

$$T = Fr$$

where T is the torque (Nm), F is the applied force (N) and r is the perpendicular distance from the axis of rotation to the point of applied force (m).

4) Torque is also related to **angular acceleration** and the **moment of inertia** (p.216).

$$T = I\alpha$$

where I is the moment of inertia (kgm^2) and α is the angular acceleration (rad s^{-2}).

Example: Four 100 g (to 2 s.f.) masses are suspended from the axle of a wheel, as shown in the diagram. The perpendicular distance from the point of the applied weight to the centre of the axis of rotation is 0.15 m. When the masses are released, the wheel spins with an angular acceleration of 1.3 rad s^{-2}. Calculate the moment of inertia of the wheel. Friction is negligible.

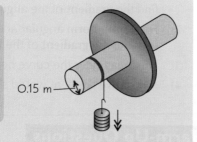

0.15 m

$T = Fr = mgr = 4 \times 0.10 \times 9.81 \times 0.15$
$\qquad = 0.5886 \text{ Nm}$

$T = I\alpha$ so $I = T \div \alpha = 0.5886 \div 1.3$
$\qquad = 0.452... = \textbf{0.45 kgm}^2 \textbf{ (to 2 s.f.)}$

Torque is also Related to Work and Power

When you rotate an object, you have to do **work** to make it move. Work in a linear system is the **force** multiplied by the **distance**. This can be rewritten for a rotating system using **torque** and **angular displacement** (p.218).

$$W = T\theta$$

where W is the work (J), T is the torque (Nm) and θ is the angular displacement (rad).

Power is the amount of **work done** in a **given time**.
You can use $\omega = \frac{\Delta\theta}{\Delta t}$ to derive an equation for power from the equation for work shown above.

$$P = T\omega$$

where P is the power (W), T is the torque (Nm) and ω is the angular velocity (rad s^{-1}).

Liz had just about had enough of work for the minute.

Example: Louise applies a torque of 0.2 Nm to turn a doorknob 90° with an angular speed of 3.1 rad s^{-1}. Calculate the work done and the power exerted by Louise to turn the doorknob.

The doorknob is turned 90° = $90 \times \frac{\pi}{180} = \frac{\pi}{2}$ radians.

So $W = T\theta = 0.2 \times \frac{\pi}{2} = 0.314... = \textbf{0.3 J (to 1 s.f.)}$

Power = $T\omega = 0.2 \times 3.1 = 0.62 = \textbf{0.6 W (to 1 s.f.)}$

Torque, Work and Power

In Mechanical Systems There is Frictional Torque

In real-world applications, **friction** has to be taken into account. Machines with rotating parts will experience an opposing **frictional torque**. Some of the **power** of the machine has to be used to overcome this frictional torque.

> **Example:** A cog has a moment of inertia of 0.0040 kgm² and a diameter of 20.0 cm. A force of 0.070 N acts at the edge of the cog in the direction of the motion of the cog at that point, causing it to accelerate. Find the power needed to overcome the frictional torque at the point that the cog has an angular velocity of 120 revs min⁻¹, if the angular acceleration at that instant is 1.25 rad s⁻².

1) First calculate the net torque on the cog: $T_{net} = T_{applied} - T_{frictional} = I\alpha = 0.0040 \times 1.25 = 0.0050$ Nm

2) Then calculate the applied torque: $T_{applied} = Fr = 0.070 \times 0.100 = 0.0070$ Nm

3) Rearrange the equation for net torque to find the frictional torque:

   $T_{frictional} = T_{applied} - T_{net} = 0.0070 - 0.0050 = 0.0020$ Nm

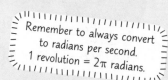
Remember to always convert to radians per second. 1 revolution = 2π radians.

4) Finally, calculate the power needed to overcome friction using $P = T\omega$:

   $P = T\omega = 0.0020 \times \left(\frac{120 \times 2\pi}{60}\right) = 0.0251... = \mathbf{0.025\ W\ (to\ 2\ s.f.)}$

> **Example:** A wheel has four 0.10 kg masses suspended from it. The four masses are released. Just before they hit the ground, the masses have velocity 1.70 ms⁻¹ and the wheel has 0.73 J of rotational kinetic energy, having turned through 0.90 radians. There is 0.10 Nm of frictional torque acting upon the system. Calculate the height at which the masses were initially suspended above the ground.

Energy is always conserved, so the gravitational potential energy lost by the masses is equal to the total kinetic energy gained by the masses and the wheel, plus the work done to overcome frictional torque.

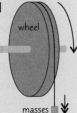
wheel

$E_P = E_K + W$ so $mgh = \frac{1}{2}mv^2 + E_{Krotational} + T\theta$ The total KE is the linear KE of the masses, plus the rotational KE of the wheel.

$mgh = \frac{1}{2} \times 0.40 \times 1.70^2 + 0.73 + 0.10 \times 0.90 = 1.398$

$g = 9.81$ ms⁻²

So $h = \frac{1.398}{0.40 \times 9.81} = 0.356... = \mathbf{0.36\ m\ (to\ 2\ s.f.)}$

masses

Warm-Up Questions

Q1 Define torque. State the two formulas for calculating torque.

Q2 What is the formula for calculating the work done turning an object?

Q3 State the formula which relates power, torque and angular velocity.

Q4 What is frictional torque?

PRACTICE QUESTIONS

Exam Questions

Q1 A force of 1 N is applied at the edge of a wheel to make it spin. If the diameter of the wheel is 0.1 m, calculate the torque applied to the wheel. [1 mark]

Q2 A constant force of 140 N is applied at the edge of a park roundabout. The force acts perpendicular to the roundabout's radius of 2.5 m, causing it to complete a full spin. The roundabout has moment of inertia 500 kgm². Assume there is no frictional torque.

    a) Calculate the angular acceleration of the roundabout. [2 marks]

    b) Calculate the work done to move the roundabout one full spin. [2 marks]

Q3 Without friction, a torque of 0.45 Nm would be needed to rotate an object at an angular velocity of 3.0 rad s⁻¹. A total torque of 0.50 Nm is applied, in order to overcome friction and rotate the object at the required angular velocity. Calculate how much power is lost in overcoming frictional torque. [2 marks]

Don't torque to me about work — I had to write all this...

Thankfully, most of the equations on these two pages are given to you in the exam — yippee. I know they're not too difficult, but you should still spend some time practising using them. And make sure you understand all of the symbols.

Flywheels

Flywheels are things you've probably not heard much about, but which are used in lots of ingenious ways.

Flywheels **Store Energy**

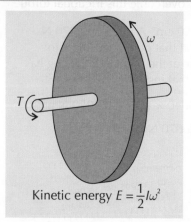

Kinetic energy $E = \frac{1}{2}I\omega^2$

1) A flywheel is a **heavy** wheel with a high **moment of inertia** (p.216) in order to resist changes to its rotational motion.

2) This means that **once** it is spinning, it's hard to make it **stop** spinning (it has a high **angular momentum**).

3) It is 'charged' as it is spun, turning the inputted **torque** (p. 220) into **rotational kinetic energy** (p.217).

4) **Just enough** power is continuously input to overcome **frictional torque**, keeping the flywheel fully charged.

5) When **extra energy** is needed in a machine, the flywheel decelerates, transferring some of its **kinetic energy** to another part of the machine.

6) Flywheels designed to store as much **energy** as possible are called **flywheel batteries**.

Energy Stored is Affected by **Mass, Shape** and **Angular Speed**

Rotational kinetic energy is related to the **moment of inertia** and the square of the **angular speed**, which means these both affect how much **energy** a flywheel can store.

To **increase** the energy a flywheel can store, you should make it:

1) **Heavier** — the moment of inertia, and so the kinetic energy stored, is **directly proportional** to the mass. So the heavier the flywheel is, the better.

2) **Spin faster** — the **energy stored** increases with **angular speed squared**, so increasing the speed the flywheel spins at greatly increases the amount of energy it can store.

3) **Spoked** — compared to a solid wheel, a **spoked wheel** of the same mass stores almost **twice** as much energy (assuming everything else is kept constant).

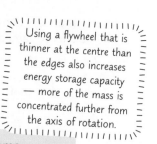

Using a flywheel that is thinner at the centre than the edges also increases energy storage capacity — more of the mass is concentrated further from the axis of rotation.

However, there is a **limit** to how much you can increase these factors before they become impractical — you don't want a giant, heavy wheel taking up half of your machine. And if you increase the **angular velocity**, the **centrifugal force** can increase to a point where it starts **breaking** the flywheel **apart**. Modern flywheels are generally made out of **carbon fibre** to stop this — although it is **lighter** than steel, it is far **stronger** and so the wheel can be spun much **faster**.

A Flywheel's **Energy** is also Affected by **Friction**

Even though a flywheel is very efficient at storing energy, it still loses some to **air resistance** and **friction** between the wheel and the **bearings** which it spins on. To combat this, modern flywheels can be:

1) **Lubricated** to reduce friction between the bearings and the wheel.

2) **Levitated** with **superconducting magnets** so there is **no** contact between the bearings and the wheel.

3) Operated in **vacuums** or inside **sealed cylinders** to reduce the drag from **air resistance**.

Flywheels **Smooth Torque** and **Angular Velocity**

1) In systems where the **force supplied** to the system can **vary**, e.g. if an engine only kicks in intermittently, flywheels are used to keep the **angular velocity** of any rotating components **constant**.

2) Flywheels use each spurt of power to **charge up**, then they deliver the stored energy **smoothly** to the rest of the system, instead of in bursts.

3) They are also used when the **force** that the system has to **exert** can **vary**. If at any time the **load torque** is **too high**, then the flywheel **decelerates**, releasing some of its energy to **top-up** the system.

4) When the engine torque is **higher** than the load torque, the flywheel **accelerates** and **stores** the spare energy until it is needed.

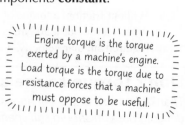

Engine torque is the torque exerted by a machine's engine. Load torque is the torque due to resistance forces that a machine must oppose to be useful.

Flywheels

Flywheels are used in many Different Systems

Flywheels are used in lots of everyday things, with some of the most common examples being:

1) **Potter's wheels** — A potter's wheel is controlled by a foot pedal, making it hard to apply a **constant force** to it. A flywheel is used to keep the speed of the wheel constant in order to make ceramic pots.

2) **Regenerative braking** — In regular cars, when the brakes are applied, friction causes the wheels to slow down, generating lots of heat. However, in some electric vehicles like cars and buses, when the brakes are hit, a **flywheel** is engaged. The flywheel then **charges up** with the energy being lost. When the vehicle is ready to accelerate, the flywheel uses its energy to turn the vehicle's wheels faster, before being disengaged until it's needed again.

3) **Power grids** — When lots of **electricity** is used in an area, the electricity grid sometimes cannot meet that **demand**. Flywheels can be used to provide the **extra energy** needed whilst **backup power stations** are started up.

4) **Wind turbines** — Flywheels can be used to store excess power on windy days or during off-peak times, and to give power on days without wind.

5) **Riveting machines** — An electric motor charges up a flywheel, which then **rapidly transfers** a **burst** of **power** as the machine **presses down** on the rivet and fixes two sheets of material together. This is useful as it stops rapid changes of power going through the motor, which could cause it to **stall**, and means a **less powerful** motor can be used.

Flywheels have Advantages and Disadvantages

ADVANTAGES
1) They are very **efficient**.
2) They last a **long time** without degrading.
3) The **recharge time** is **short**.
4) They can react and **discharge quickly**.
5) They are **environmentally friendly** (they don't rely on chemicals to store energy).

DISADVANTAGES
1) They are much **larger** and **heavier** than other storage methods (e.g. batteries).
2) They pose a safety risk as the wheel could **break apart** at high speeds. **Protective casing** to protect against this results in **extra weight**.
3) Energy can be lost through **friction**.
4) If used in **moving objects**, they can **oppose changes in direction**, which can cause problems for **vehicles**.

This feature can also be an advantage as it improves the vehicle's stability.

Warm-Up Questions

Q1 What is a flywheel?
Q2 How does a flywheel store energy?
Q3 What three properties affect how much energy can be stored in a flywheel?
Q4 How can energy loss through friction be reduced?
Q5 Give two advantages and disadvantages of flywheels.

PRACTICE QUESTIONS

Exam Questions

Q1 Taylor buys a new car with regenerative braking that uses a flywheel.

a) Explain how regenerative braking works in Taylor's car. [3 marks]

b) Give another use for flywheels. [1 mark]

Q2 An engineer is trying to improve a solid flywheel battery and decides to double the mass of the flywheel. Explain what effect this would have on the energy the flywheel could store and suggest one disadvantage of doing this. Suggest another improvement the engineer could make to increase the energy stored by the flywheel battery. [4 marks]

Time flies when you're doing physics...

Flywheels are pretty nifty things, used in loads of places you wouldn't even imagine. Make sure you understand and can explain how they work. Then get a few examples of their uses stored in your brain too for good measure.

Angular Momentum

Surprisingly, angular momentum is a lot like regular momentum. Who'd have thought it?

Angular Momentum Relates Moment of Inertia and Angular Velocity

You already know that **linear momentum** is equal to mass × velocity.
You can replace **mass** with the **moment of inertia**, and **linear velocity**
with **angular velocity**, and you get the formula for **angular momentum**:

$$\text{angular momentum} = I\omega$$

where I is the moment of inertia (kgm^2),
ω is the angular velocity (rad s^{-1})
and angular momentum has units Nms.

Billy thinks his dad misunderstood when he asked him to explain angular momentum.

Angular Momentum is Always Conserved

When **no external forces** are applied (torque, friction, etc.), the total angular
momentum of a system remains constant. It's useful to write this as:

$$I_{\text{initial}}\omega_{\text{initial}} = I_{\text{final}}\omega_{\text{final}}$$

This is the law of conservation of angular momentum.

This can be seen if you put two objects with **different moments of inertia** or **angular velocities** together.

> **Example:** A disc has a moment of inertia I and is rotating at an angular velocity of 4 rad s^{-1}.
> A second identical disc that is not spinning is placed on top of the spinning disc, where
> it is held in place and begins to spin. Calculate the angular velocity of the combined
> discs as they spin together at the same speed. Frictional losses are negligible.
>
> Before the discs are put together, angular momentum $= I_1\omega_1 + I_2\omega_2$
>
> Once they are put together, angular momentum $= (I_1 + I_2)\omega$
>
> You can then equate these: $I_1\omega_1 + I_2\omega_2 = (I_1 + I_2)\omega$
>
> So $\omega = \dfrac{I_1\omega_1 + I_2\omega_2}{(I_1 + I_2)}$
>
> The discs are identical, so $I_1 = I_2$ and the equation becomes:
>
> $\omega = \dfrac{I \times 4 + I \times 0}{2I} = \dfrac{4}{2} = \mathbf{2\ rad\ s^{-1}}$

Another common example is an **ice skater** doing a spin. At the start of the spin, her arms are out
away from her body. She then pulls her arms **closer** towards her, and begins to **spin faster**. This
is due to the **conservation of angular momentum** — as she pulls in her arms, she decreases her
moment of inertia, so her **angular velocity** must increase in order to conserve angular momentum.

> **Example:** An ice skater is spinning with her arms out at an angular velocity of 13 rad s^{-1}.
> With her arms out, her moment of inertia is 3.5 kgm^2. She then tucks in her
> arms, changing her moment of inertia to 1.2 kg m^2. Calculate her angular
> velocity in revolutions per second as she spins with her arms tucked in.
>
> You can write the conservation of angular momentum as:
>
> $I_{\text{initial}}\omega_{\text{initial}} = I_{\text{final}}\omega_{\text{final}}$
>
> $\omega_{\text{final}} = \dfrac{I_{\text{initial}}\omega_{\text{initial}}}{I_{\text{final}}} = \dfrac{3.5 \times 13}{1.2} = 37.91...\ \text{rad s}^{-1}$
>
> $37.91... \div 2\pi = 6.03... = \mathbf{6.0\ revolutions\ per\ second\ (to\ 2\ s.f.)}$

Angular Momentum

Angular **Impulse** is the **Change** in **Angular Momentum**

You can write the equation of angular impulse as:

$$\text{Angular impulse} = \Delta(I\omega)$$ The units are Nms.

However, if the torque (p.220) on the system is constant, this can also be written as:

$$\Delta(I\omega) = T\Delta t$$ where T is torque (Nm) and Δt is the time the torque is applied for (s).

Example: A spanner, initially at rest, has a constant torque of 0.3 Nm applied to it for 2 seconds. Calculate the angular impulse acting on the spanner and the angular velocity of the spanner at the end of the 2 seconds. The moment of inertia of the spanner is 0.2 kgm^2.

The equation for angular impulse is: $\Delta(I\omega) = T\Delta t$

This can also be written as: $I\omega_{final} - I\omega_{initial} = T\Delta t$

Which can then be rearranged to give: $\omega_{final} = \dfrac{T\Delta t + I\omega_{initial}}{I} = \dfrac{0.3 \times 2 + 0.2 \times 0}{0.2}$

$$= \textbf{3 rad s}^{-1}$$

Luke, Chris and Ben were regretting their impulse buy of matching suits.

Warm-Up Questions

Q1 Write down the formula for angular momentum.

Q2 What is angular impulse?

Q3 State the formula for angular impulse when the torque isn't constant.

Q4 State the formula relating angular impulse, constant torque and time.

PRACTICE QUESTIONS

Exam Questions

Q1 A ball with a moment of inertia of 0.04 kgm^2 is rolling with an angular velocity of 4 rad s^{-1}.
Calculate its angular momentum.

[1 mark]

Q2 Using ideas about angular momentum, explain why divers tuck
themselves into a ball to complete fast spins.

[3 marks]

Q3 A clutch in a car brings together two rotating shafts. The engine shaft has a moment of inertia
of 0.10 kgm^2 and spins at 3000 rpm (to 2 s.f.). The second shaft has a moment of inertia of 0.15 kgm^2
and an angular velocity of 2000 rpm (to 2 s.f.) in the same direction as the first shaft.
Calculate the angular velocity of the system once the two shafts are brought together.

[3 marks]

Q4 A bike wheel is spinning at an angular velocity of 2.2 rad s^{-1}. A constant torque is applied for 4.0 s
until the angular velocity of the wheel is 24 rad s^{-1}. The wheel has a moment of inertia of 0.20 kgm^2.

a) Calculate the angular impulse applied to the bike wheel over the
four seconds during which the torque is applied.

[1 mark]

b) Calculate the size of the torque applied to the wheel.

[1 mark]

I have the impulse to take a break...

All in all, these last two pages haven't been too bad. Mostly just a few equations you've already seen dressed up to look like fancy new ones. Go back over these pages before looking back over the whole of the section so far. Make sure you're set with how to describe rotating things, then have a well-earned break. The joys of thermodynamics await.

The First Law of Thermodynamics

Ah, thermodynamics — it's all about the wonders of heat energy. The first law tells you how adding heat energy can be used to do work or to ramp up the internal energy of the gas particles in your system. Which is surprisingly useful...

The First Law of Thermodynamics Describes Energy Conservation

1) The **first law of thermodynamics** describes how **energy** is **conserved** in a **system** through heating, cooling and doing work.

2) A **system** is a **volume** of space filled with **gas**.

3) Systems can be either **open** or **closed**.

4) **Open systems** allow gas to **flow** in, out or through them, e.g. water vapour leaving a boiling kettle.

5) **Closed systems don't** allow gas to **enter** or **escape**, e.g. gas in a balloon.

After baked beans, Sgt. Gray was an open system.

The First Law Links Heat, Work and Internal Energy

1) The first law of thermodynamics can be written as:

$$Q = \Delta U + W$$

2) Q is the **energy transferred** to the system by **heating**. If energy is transferred **away** from the system, this will be **negative**.

3) ΔU is the **increase** in **internal energy**. Internal energy is the **sum** of the **potential** and **kinetic energies** of all of the particles in a system (see p.108 for more).

4) W is the **work done by** the system (the work the **gas** is **doing**), e.g. gas in a cylinder expanding and moving a piston. If work is done **on** the gas, e.g. by **compressing** it, then the value of W will be **negative**.

Example: A cylinder is sealed by a moveable piston. The gas in the cylinder is heated with 60 J of heat to move the piston. The internal energy of the gas increases by 5 J.

a) Calculate the work done by the gas to move the piston.

As heat is being inputted and the gas is doing work, both Q and W are positive. $Q = \Delta U + W$, so $W = Q - \Delta U = 60 - 5 = $ **55 J** of work is done by the gas to move the piston.

b) Now the piston does 60 J of work on the gas to compress it. No heat is lost. Calculate the change in the internal energy of the gas.

$Q = \Delta U + W = 0$, so $\Delta U = -W$. Work is done **on** the gas, so $W = -60$ J. $\Delta U = -W = $ **60 J** — the internal energy of the gas increases by 60 J.

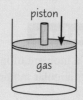

You Can Use Ideal Gas Assumptions

1) You need to know how to **apply** the first law to changes in **closed systems**. These are also known as **non-flow processes** because the gas doesn't go anywhere.

2) To do this, you have to assume that the gas in a system is an **ideal gas**.

3) This means you **assume** that **internal energy** is only dependent on the **temperature** — as the **temperature increases**, the internal energy **increases**.

4) You also assume **work done** causes a **change in volume**.

5) You can use the **ideal gas law** (p.112):

$$pV = nRT$$

p is the pressure (Pa),
V is the volume of the system (m³),
n is the number of moles of gas,
R is the molar gas constant, 8.31 JK⁻¹mol⁻¹,
T is the absolute temperature (K)

0 K ≈ −273 °C

6) For a change in a closed system, n is constant, so $\dfrac{pV}{T} = $ **constant**. You could also write this as:

$$\frac{p_1 V_1}{T_1} = \frac{p_2 V_2}{T_2}$$

This form is really handy to remember for thermodynamics questions.

The First Law of Thermodynamics

Isothermal Changes Happen at a Constant Temperature

1) The **internal energy** of a gas, U, only depends on the **temperature**. The temperature during an isothermal change remains **constant**, which means that for an **isothermal** process:

$$\Delta U = 0$$

2) Using the first law of thermodynamics, $Q = 0 + W$, which means that: $\longrightarrow$

$$Q = W$$

> That means the amount of **work** a system **does** will be **equal** to the amount of **heat energy supplied** (here Q and W will both be **positive**). It also means that any work done **on** the system will cause the system to **lose** that amount of **heat energy** (Q and W will both be **negative**).

3) Using the **ideal gas law** (see p.112), you can see that a constant temperature T means that:

$$pV = \text{constant} \quad \text{and} \quad p_1V_1 = p_2V_2$$

In Adiabatic Processes Q = 0

1) An **adiabatic** process is one where **no heat** is **lost** or **gained** by the system: $Q = 0$.

2) Using the first law, if $Q = 0$ then $\Delta U = -W$. This means that any change in the **internal energy** of the system is **caused** by **work** done by/on the system. E.g. if work is done by the system (it expands), W will be positive, and so the **internal energy** of the system will **decrease**.

3) As internal energy only depends on **temperature**, this means a **change** in **temperature** occurs.

4) The maths behind this process is pretty hard, but thankfully you just need to know that for an adiabatic change:

$$pV^\gamma = \text{constant} \quad \text{and} \quad p_1V_1^\gamma = p_2V_2^\gamma$$

> γ is the adiabatic constant, which depends on the type of gas in the system. For a monatomic gas, $\gamma = \frac{5}{3}$.

> **Example:** A container full of helium (a monatomic gas) is sealed by a moveable piston (so gas cannot escape). The container is cylindrical, with a radius of 20 cm and a height of 60 cm. The initial pressure inside the container is 1.2×10^5 Pa. The piston moves downwards by 15 cm, adiabatically compressing the gas. Calculate the pressure inside the container after the piston has moved.

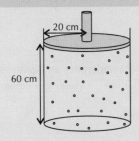
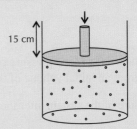

1) The volume of a cylinder is given by $V = \pi r^2 h$. As the gas is compressed, **r** stays **constant** so the change in volume **only** depends on the **change in height**.

2) This means you can rearrange $p_1V_1^\gamma = p_2V_2^\gamma$ to give:

> Helium is monatomic so $\gamma = \frac{5}{3}$.

$$p_2 = \frac{p_1V_1^\gamma}{V_2^\gamma} = p_1\left(\frac{h_1}{h_2}\right)^\gamma = (1.2 \times 10^5) \times \left(\frac{60}{45}\right)^{\frac{5}{3}} = 193\,826.1...$$

So the final pressure inside the container is **1.9×10^5 Pa (to 2 s.f.)**.

> Don't worry if you didn't spot that you could do it this way — you'd still get all of the marks if you calculated each volume separately and then substituted them into the equation for p_2.

The First Law of Thermodynamics

$W = p\Delta V$ for Changes at a **Constant Pressure**

1) For processes where the **pressure doesn't change**, you can calculate work done by using:

$$W = p\Delta V$$

W is the work done by a system (J),
p is the pressure of the system (Pa),
ΔV is the change in the volume of the system (m³)

2) You can easily see where this equation comes from. Work = force × distance, $W = F\Delta x$. Pressure = force ÷ area, so force is pressure times area, $F = pA$. Substituting pA for F in the work done equation gives you $W = pA\Delta x$. $A\Delta x$ is simply the change in volume, which gives $W = p\Delta V$.

3) For an expansion, the change in volume and work done **by the** system are **positive**. For a compression, both are **negative**.

4) From the ideal gas law (see page 112), if p is constant then:
$$\frac{V_1}{T_1} = \frac{V_2}{T_2}$$
(where T is the absolute temperature (see p.110)).

To maintain a constant pressure, a change in temperature must cause a change in volume. (E.g. heating a gas will cause it to expand.)

Processes at a **Constant Volume** do **No Work**

1) In changes where the **volume** of the system is kept **constant**, the **work done** is **zero**. $\boxed{W = 0}$

2) From the first law, if $W = 0$, then: $\boxed{Q = \Delta U}$

3) This means that by transferring **heat energy** to the system, you only increase the **internal energy** U of the system.

4) You can also see this by using $pV = nRT$ for a system. If V is **constant** and you increase the **pressure**, only the **temperature** increases, which will increase the internal energy.

Remember that for an ideal gas the internal energy only depends on the temperature.

Warm-Up Questions

Q1 Define an open and a closed system.

Q2 Give the equation for the first law of thermodynamics and the meanings of the symbols used.

Q3 Write down the ideal gas equation.

Q4 What is an isothermal process?

Q5 What is an adiabatic process?

Q6 State the rule relating pressure and volume for an adiabatic process. Define gamma.

Q7 How would you calculate the work done in a non-flow process that occurs at a constant pressure?

Q8 How much work is done in a non-flow process where the volume doesn't change?

PRACTICE QUESTIONS

Exam Questions

Q1 A system containing 0.82 moles of gas at a pressure of 1.2×10^4 Pa undergoes an isothermal compression. The system is compressed from an initial volume of 0.40 m³ to 0.30 m³. (Molar gas constant, $R = 8.31$ JK⁻¹mol⁻¹)

    a) Calculate the new pressure of the system after the compression. [2 marks]

    b) Calculate the temperature of the system. [2 marks]

Q2 A closed system at 300 K has a pressure of 1.1×10^4 Pa. 3000 J of heat is transferred to the system while the pressure is kept constant. The internal energy of the system increases by 300 J. The volume of the system after this heat transfer is 0.360 m³. Calculate the final temperature of the gas. [4 marks]

Q3 A closed system undergoes three thermodynamic processes. From 0-3 s, it is heated at a constant volume. The volume of the system is then increased isothermally from 3-8 s, before being left to compress adiabatically from 8-15 s. Explain whether the temperature is increasing, decreasing or constant for each stage. [5 marks]

If only keeping your belly volume constant in real-life took no work...

Whew, that's a lot to take in. Make sure you know the definitions of all the symbols in the first law — and know when they're negative and when they're not. Then get your head around all the different processes a system can undergo.

p-V Diagrams

p-V diagrams are really useful as all of the non-flow processes you've just met can be plotted on them. You can use them to calculate work done for any process and they're super handy once you get to the section about engines...

You can use *p-V* Diagrams to Represent **Non-flow Processes**

1) As well as using equations, all of the different **non-flow** processes (see page 227-228) that can happen to a system can be **represented** on a *p-V* diagram — a graph of pressure against volume.

2) An **arrow** is put on a *p-V* curve to show the **direction** the change is happening in.

3) The **area under a line** on a *p-V* diagram represents the **work done** during that process.

4) You need to be able to **estimate** the **work done** from a given *p-V* diagram. You can estimate area by **counting squares** (like in the example below) or by using the **trapezium rule**.

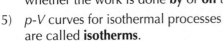

'The trapezium rule' sounds pretty fancy, but all it means is estimating the area of the curve by splitting it into trapeziums. Calculate the area of each trapezium and then add them all together. The more trapeziums you create, the more accurate your answer will be.

p-V Curves for **Isothermal** Processes are Called **Isotherms**

1) A *p-V* diagram for an **isothermal process** (p.227) will be a smooth curve — remember $p_1V_1 = p_2V_2$.

2) The *p-V* diagram for an isothermal **compression** is shown on the right. The **arrow** shows the direction the change happens in *(V decreases and p increases)*.

3) A *p-V* diagram for an **isothermal expansion** at the same **temperature** will look almost **identical** to the compression *p-V* diagram. The only difference would be that the **arrow** would point in the **other direction** (as *V* would increase and *p* would decrease).

4) The **area under the curve** (shaded in blue) is the **magnitude** of the **work done** during the process. (Remember, the sign will depend on whether the work is done **by** or **on** the system.)

5) *p-V* curves for isothermal processes are called **isotherms**.

6) The **position** of an isotherm on a *p-V* diagram depends on the **temperature** the process happens at. The **higher** the temperature of the system, the **further** from the **origin** the isotherm will be.

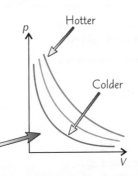

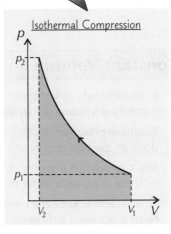

Isothermal Compression

Example: The *p-V* diagram below shows the isothermal expansion of a system. Calculate the work done by the system as it expands between pressures A and B.

The work done is equal to the **area** under the graph.

You can estimate the area by counting the **total number** of **squares** under the curve. To find the work done between A and B, go across from the vertical axis to the curve and find the value of *V* at each of those points. Then find the area under the graph between these two values of *V*.

First find out how much energy each square is worth:

1) The height of each square represents $(1 \times 10^5) \div 10 = 1 \times 10^4$ Pa.

2) The width of each square represents $(1 \times 10^{-2}) \div 5 = 0.002$ m³.

3) $W = p\Delta V$, so work done represented by each square is $0.002 \times 1 \times 10^4 = 20$ J.

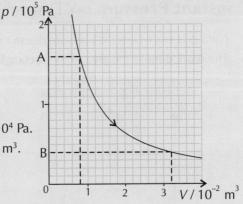

Next count the number of squares under the curve and multiply it by the work per square.

The number of squares under the line between the values of *V* that correspond to pressures A and B is around 89.

So about $89 \times 20 \approx$ **1780 J** of work is done between pressures A and B.

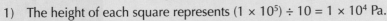

p-V Diagrams

p-V Diagrams for **Adiabatic** Processes are Similar to **Isotherms**

1) The *p-V* curves for **adiabatic** processes (p.227) are similar to those for **isothermal** processes, but they have a **steeper gradient**.

2) The graph below shows how an **isothermal** and **adiabatic compression** between two volumes would look if they had the **same initial temperature**.

3) The **area** under the **adiabatic curve** is **larger** than the area under the **isothermal curve**, so **more work** is done to **compress gas adiabatically** than isothermally.

4) The gas does **less work** if it **expands adiabatically instead** of isothermally.

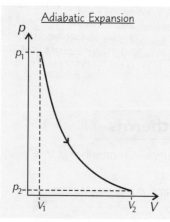

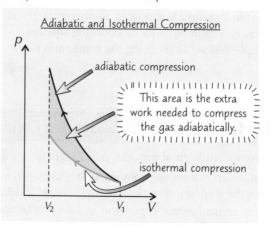

Constant Volume *p-V* Diagrams are **Straight Vertical Lines**

1) Unsurprisingly, *p-V* diagrams for changes with a **constant volume** are **straight vertical lines**.

2) For these processes (p.228), there is **no work** done as the volume doesn't change.

3) You can see this from the *p-V* diagram — there is no **area** under the line.

4) As a system is kept at a constant volume but **heated** between temperatures T_1 and T_2, its pressure will **increase**. If it is **cooled** at a constant volume, the pressure will **decrease**.

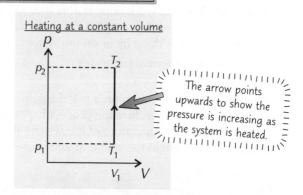

Constant Pressure *p-V* Diagrams are **Straight Horizontal Lines**

1) For a process where the pressure doesn't change, the *p-V* diagram is a **horizontal straight** line.

2) The **work done** is the **area** of the **rectangle** under the graph — work done $W = p\Delta V$.

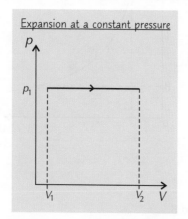

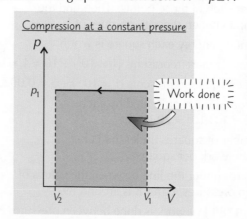

Louise worked best when she was under constant pressure.

p-V Diagrams

Cyclic Processes Create a Loop on a p-V Diagram

1) A system can undergo **different processes one after another** which form a **cycle** (loop). They start at a certain **pressure** and **volume** and return to them at the end of each **cycle**.

2) To find the **net work** of the cyclic process, you find the **difference** between the **work** done **by** a system and the work done **to** the system. This equals the **area of the loop** created by the cyclic process.

| Work done per cycle = Area of loop |

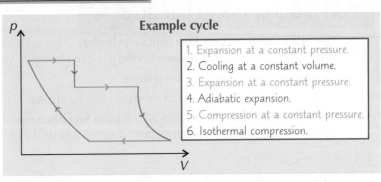

Example cycle

1. Expansion at a constant pressure.
2. Cooling at a constant volume.
3. Expansion at a constant pressure.
4. Adiabatic expansion.
5. Compression at a constant pressure.
6. Isothermal compression.

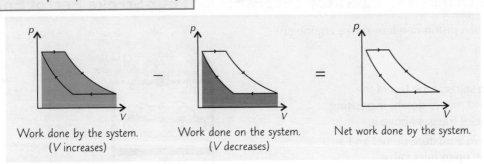

Work done by the system. (*V* increases)

Work done on the system. (*V* decreases)

Net work done by the system.

The operation of an engine is one example of a cyclic process (see p.232).

Warm-Up Questions

Q1 How would you calculate work done from a *p-V* diagram showing an adiabatic expansion between two volumes?

Q2 What are the *p-V* curves for isothermal processes called?

Q3 Sketch the *p-V* diagrams for a change where the pressure is constant and a change where the volume is constant.

Q4 What is a cyclic process?

Q5 How would you calculate the work done for one cycle of a cyclic process from a *p-V* diagram?

PRACTICE QUESTIONS

Exam Questions

Q1 A system undergoes a cyclic process made up of four stages, A, B, C and D, described below.
Stage A: heated at a constant volume, V_1. Stage B: expansion at a constant pressure until the system reaches a volume of V_2. Stage C: adiabatic expansion. Stage D: isothermal compression until it reaches volume V_1.
Draw the *p-V* diagram for this cycle, labelling stages A, B, C and D. [4 marks]

Q2 The *p-V* diagram on the right is for a cyclic process where the system undergoes an isothermal expansion, an isothermal compression, and an expansion and compression at a constant pressure.

a) Calculate the work done during the expansion at a constant pressure. [1 mark]

b) Estimate the net work done by the process per cycle. [3 marks]

c) Explain whether the net work done per cycle would increase, decrease or stay the same if the system was adiabatically expanded instead of isothermally expanded to 4×10^6 Pa. No other changes are made to the cycle processes. [2 marks]

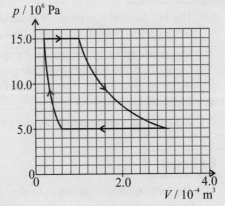

$p / 10^6$ Pa

15.0

10.0

5.0

0

2.0

4.0

$V / 10^{-4}$ m^3

Become a cyclic process — reread the last three pages...

Seriously, this stuff is really helpful for understanding what's actually happening to a system. Go back and make sure you've got it all in your head. The big things to remember are what each line looks like and how to calculate the work done by each process. Then have a good practice at actually drawing the graphs and calculating the work from them.

Four-Stroke Engines

Ever wondered how a car engine actually works? Well, now you get to find out...

Fuel is Burnt Every Four Strokes

1) **Internal combustion engines** contain **cylinders** filled with air. The air in these cylinders is trapped by tight-fitting **pistons** (so the gas can't escape), which move up and down.

2) The **gas** inside a cylinder is the **system**.

3) Each time a piston moves up or down is called a **stroke**.

4) **Four-stroke engines** are engines which **burn fuel once** every **four strokes** of a piston. (Two-stroke engines burn it every two strokes etc.)

Bailey thought that four strokes wasn't nearly enough.

You Need to Understand Indicator Diagrams for Four-Stroke Petrol Engines

The four strokes of a piston in a four-stroke engine are:

Induction

1) The **piston** starts at the **top** of the cylinder and moves **down, increasing** the **volume** of the gas above it.

2) This sucks in a mixture of fuel and air through the **open inlet valve**.

3) The **pressure** of the gas in the cylinder remains **constant, just below** atmospheric pressure.

Compression

1) The inlet valve is **closed**.

2) The piston moves back **up** the cylinder and does work on the gas, **increasing** the **pressure**.

3) **Just before** the piston is at the end of this stroke, the **spark plug** creates a spark which **ignites** the **air-fuel mixture**.

4) The **temperature** and **pressure** suddenly increase at an almost **constant volume**.

Expansion

1) The hot air-fuel gas mixture **expands** and does work on the piston, moving it **downwards**.

2) The **work done** by the gas as it **expands** is **more** than the **work done** to **compress** the gas, as it is now at a higher temperature. There is a **net output of work**.

3) **Just before** the piston is at the bottom of the stroke, the **exhaust valve** opens and the **pressure** reduces.

Exhaust

1) The **piston** moves **up** the cylinder, and the burnt gas leaves through the **exhaust valve**.

2) The pressure remains almost **constant, just above** atmospheric pressure.

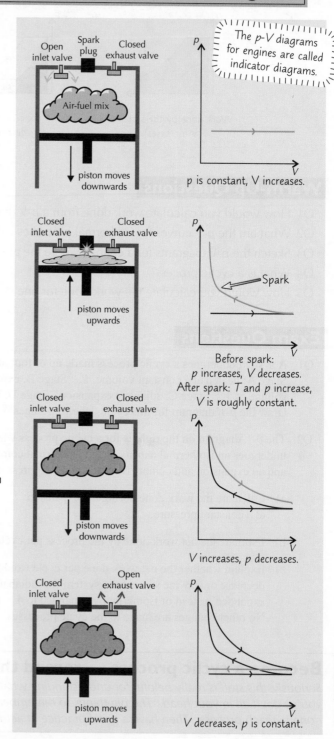

The p-V diagrams for engines are called indicator diagrams.

p is constant, V increases.

Before spark: p increases, V decreases. After spark: T and p increase, V is roughly constant.

V increases, p decreases.

V decreases, p is constant.

Four-Stroke Engines

Four-Stroke **Diesel Engines** Use **Compressed Air** to **Ignite Fuel**

1) Whilst four-stroke diesel engines undergo the same four strokes, they work slightly differently to four-stroke petrol engines.

2) The induction stroke: here only air is pulled into the cylinder, not an air-fuel mixture.

3) The compression stroke: the air is compressed so it reaches a temperature high enough to ignite diesel fuel. Just before the end of the stroke, diesel is sprayed into the cylinder through a fuel injector and ignites.

4) The expansion and exhaust strokes are then the same as for a petrol engine.

5) The indicator diagram for a diesel engine is also slightly different — there is no sharp peak at the start of the expansion stroke — as you can see in the diagram on the right.

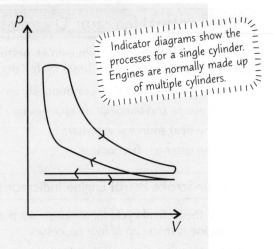

Indicator diagrams show the processes for a single cylinder. Engines are normally made up of multiple cylinders.

Warm-Up Questions

Q1 What is meant by the term 'four-stroke engine'?

Q2 Name the four strokes of a four-stroke engine.

Q3 What is the function of the inlet valve in a four-stroke petrol engine?

Q4 What is the function of the spark plug in a four-stroke petrol engine?

Q5 Explain why there is a net output of work by a four-stroke engine.

Q6 Sketch the indicator diagram for a four-stroke diesel engine.

Exam Questions

Q1 The sketched indicator diagram below shows the pressure and volume changes for the first two strokes in the cycle of a four-stroke petrol engine.

a) Describe what happens during the two strokes shown by the indicator diagram. [4 marks]

b) Complete the indicator diagram to show a complete cycle of a four-stroke engine. [2 marks]

c) Mark a cross at the point on the p-V diagram where the spark plug ignites the gas in the engine cycle. [1 mark]

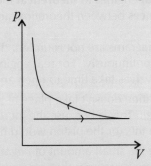

Q2 Describe the differences between how a four-stroke petrol engine and a four-stroke diesel engine operate. [3 marks]

Show examiners you're a bright spark...

Four-stroke engines have four different strokes — sorted. Unfortunately, you have to delve a bit deeper to get all the marks. Learn each of the four strokes and make sure you can describe what happens in them. Then make sure you know what the indicator diagrams look like for both petrol and diesel engines, and what each line shows.

Using Indicator Diagrams

By comparing an ideal p-V diagram to a real one for an engine, you can see how well it's performing.
You can find out all kinds of things, like how much friction there is and how much power the engine actually produces.

Theoretical Indicator Diagrams Assume Perfect Conditions

The **theoretical cycle** for a four-stroke **petrol engine** is called the **Otto cycle**. The theoretical cycle for a four-stroke **diesel engine** is called the **diesel cycle**. Both of these **theoretical models** make the following **assumptions**:

1) The **same gas** is taken **continuously** around the cycle. The gas is **pure air**, with an adiabatic constant $\gamma = 1.4$.
2) Pressure and temperature changes can be **instantaneous**.
3) The **heat source** is **external**.
4) The engine is **frictionless**.

Four-Stroke Petrol Engine Indicator Diagrams

The **theoretical cycle** for a four-stroke **petrol engine** is made up of four processes:

A First, it is assumed that the gas is compressed **adiabatically** (p.227), so no heat is transferred.
B Heat is supplied whilst the **volume** is kept **constant**.
C The gas is allowed to cool **adiabatically**.
D The system is cooled at a **constant volume**.

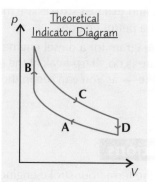

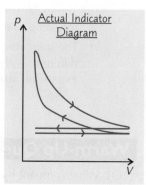

Four-Stroke Diesel Engine Indicator Diagrams

The four processes in the **theoretical cycle** for a four-stroke **diesel engine** are:

A The gas is **adiabatically** compressed.
B Then heat is supplied, but this time **pressure** is kept **constant**.
C The gas is allowed to cool **adiabatically**.
D Then the system is cooled at a **constant volume**.

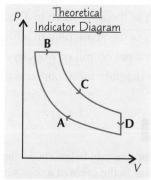

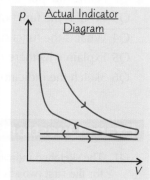

You Can Compare Theoretical Diagrams to Real Engines

Engineers **compare** indicator diagrams of **real** engines to **theoretical** models in order to see how well they are **performing**. The main **differences** between theoretical and real-life diagrams are:

1) The corners of theoretical indicator diagrams are not rounded. This is because it is assumed that the same air is used continuously. For real engines, these corners are rounded as the inlet and exhaust valves take time to open and close.

2) In a real four-stroke petrol engine, heating doesn't take place at a constant volume (process B on the petrol engine indicator diagram above). This is because the increase in pressure and temperature would have to be instantaneous to do this (or the piston would have to pause for a moment).

3) The theoretical model doesn't include the small amount of negative work caused by the loop between the exhaust and the induction lines because it assumes the same air cycles around the system continuously.

4) Engines have an internal heat source (the burning air-fuel mixture), not an external one. This means the temperature rise is not as large as in the theoretical model because the fuel used to heat the gas is never completely burned in the cylinder, so you can never get the maximum energy out of it. This means that theoretical engines can achieve higher pressures (and so have a higher peak).

5) Energy is needed to overcome friction caused by the moving parts of a real engine, so the net work done will always be less than for a theoretical engine. This means that the area inside the loop is smaller for real four-stroke engines.

Using Indicator Diagrams

You Can Calculate Engine Power from Indicator Diagrams

1) You know that the **area** of a **loop** for a cyclic process gives the work done (p.231). For engines, the small amount of **negative work** (see previous page) is **negligible**, so the **net work done** by an engine cylinder for one cycle is the **area** of the **loop** on the indicator diagram.

2) The **indicated power** is the **net work done** by the **engine cylinder** in **one second** (work done in one cycle × number of cycles per second).

3) If an engine has more than one cylinder, multiply the **cylinder's** indicated power by the **number of cylinders** to get the **engine's indicated power**.

> **Indicated power = (area of p-V loop) × (number of cycles per second) × (number of cylinders)**

Friction Reduces the Output Power of an Engine

1) **Friction** occurs between **moving parts** of an engine, e.g. between the **piston** and the **cylinder**, at the **bearings** and when the **valves** are opened or closed.

2) **Work** needs to be done to **overcome friction** in the engine. The power needed to do this is called the **friction power**. This means that the **brake power** (or **output** power) of the engine is **less** than the **indicated power** that was calculated for the engine.

> **friction power = indicated power − brake power**

3) The **output** (or **brake**) **power** can be calculated using the equation from p.220:

$$P = T\omega$$

where T is the engine torque (Nm) and ω is the angular velocity (rad s^{-1}) of the crankshaft.

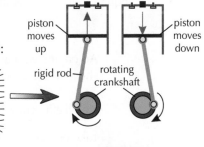
An engine crankshaft just converts the up/down motion of the piston in a cylinder into rotational motion (p.218).

piston moves up / piston moves down / rigid rod / rotating crankshaft

PRACTICE QUESTIONS

Warm-Up Questions

Q1 Sketch the theoretical p-V diagrams for four-stroke petrol and diesel engines. Explain what processes are represented by them.

Q2 Why are the corners of real-life four-stroke engine indicator diagrams rounded?

Q3 Where does the negative work in an indicator diagram come from?

Q4 Describe and explain any other differences between theoretical and real-life indicator diagrams for four-stroke engines.

Exam Questions

Q1 A four-stroke petrol engine operates at 29 cycles per second. The engine has eight identical cylinders. The area of a p-V loop on an indicator diagram for one cylinder is 120 J.

a) Calculate the indicated power of the engine. [1 mark]

b) The angular velocity of the engine's crankshaft is 58π rad s^{-1} and the engine torque is 130 Nm. Calculate the friction power of the engine. [2 marks]

Q2 Indicator diagrams for two real, single-cylinder engines with identical cylinders are shown on the right. The cylinders are powered by crankshafts with the same angular velocity and both engines have the same friction power. Use these indicator diagrams to compare the torque of engine A and engine B. [3 marks]

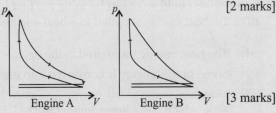
Engine A / Engine B

Assuming I can sing, in theory, I'm a world-famous rock star...

Unfortunately, theoretical models are generally too good to be true. Still, you have to know them. Learn the theoretical diagrams for petrol and diesel engines and the reasons why the real-life versions are different. Then make sure you know the equations for calculating the indicated, friction and output power and get some practice actually using them.

Engine Efficiency

Efficiency is how much bang for your buck (or work for your energy) your engine is giving you.

There are **Three Types** of **Engine Efficiency** You Need to Know...

All **efficiencies** are just a measure of how much of the input power is **transferred usefully**. An engine's **input power** is the amount of **heat energy** per unit time it could **potentially** gain from **burning fuel**. The **calorific value** of the fuel tells you how much **energy** the fuel has **stored** in it per unit volume. So the **input power** is the rate fuel is supplied multiplied by its calorific value.

> **input power = calorific value × fuel flow rate**

You might be given the calorific value in terms of energy per unit mass. If this happens, you'll need the flow rate to be in terms of mass per second rather than volume per second.

There are three kinds of **engine efficiency** you need to know:

1) The **mechanical efficiency** of an engine is affected by the amount of energy lost through **moving parts** (for example, through friction).

$$\text{mechanical efficiency} = \frac{\text{brake power}}{\text{indicated power}}$$

2) **Thermal efficiency** describes how well **heat** energy is **transferred** into **work**.

$$\text{thermal efficiency} = \frac{\text{indicated power}}{\text{input power}}$$

3) The equation for the **overall efficiency** is:

$$\text{overall efficiency} = \frac{\text{brake power}}{\text{input power}}$$

> **Example:** An engine with an overall efficiency of 36% has an input power of 123 kW. The indicator diagram shows the engine has an indicated power of 53 kW. Calculate the mechanical efficiency of the engine.
>
> $\text{overall efficiency} = \dfrac{\text{brake power}}{\text{input power}}$ so $\text{brake power} = \text{overall efficiency} \times \text{input power}$
>
> $\text{brake power} = 0.36 \times 123\,000 = 44\,280 \text{ W}$
>
> $\text{mechanical efficiency} = \dfrac{\text{brake power}}{\text{indicated power}} = \dfrac{44\,280}{53\,000} = 0.835... = \textbf{84\% (to 2 s.f.)}$

The **Second Law of Thermodynamics** — No Engine is **100% Efficient**

1) **Heat engines** convert **heat** energy into **work**. No engine can transfer **all** the heat energy it is supplied with into useful work though — some heat always ends up **increasing** the **temperature** of the **engine**.

2) If the engine temperature reaches that of the **heat source**, then no heat **flows** and no **work** is done. This means that **no** heat engine can operate by using only the **first law of thermodynamics** (p.226).

3) Engines also have to obey the **second law of thermodynamics**: that heat engines **must** operate between a **heat source** and a **heat sink** (a region which **absorbs** heat from the engine).

The **Second** Law of Thermodynamics

If an engine **could** work just by using the **first law** of thermodynamics, theoretically **all** of the heat energy supplied to a heat engine could be transferred into **useful work**.

1) The heat energy transferred to the engine from the **heat source** is Q_H.

2) Some of this energy is **converted** into **useful work**, W.

3) However, some of this energy (Q_C) must be **transferred** to a **heat sink**, which has a **lower temperature** (T_C) than the heat **source**.

4) This means engines can **never** be **100%** efficient.

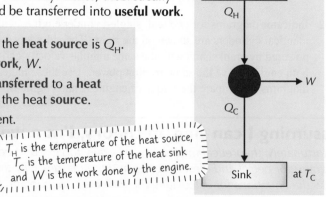

T_H is the temperature of the heat source, T_C is the temperature of the heat sink and W is the work done by the engine.

Engine Efficiency

You Can Use the Second Law to Calculate **Efficiency**

You can calculate the **efficiency** of a heat engine using this equation:

$$\text{efficiency} = \frac{W}{Q_H} = \frac{Q_H - Q_C}{Q_H}$$

Q_H is the heat transferred from the heat source (J),
Q_C is the heat transferred to the heat sink (J),
W is work output of the engine (J)

By assuming **perfect conditions**, you can also calculate the **maximum theoretical efficiency**:

$$\text{maximum theoretical efficiency} = \frac{T_H - T_C}{T_H}$$

T_H is the temperature of the heat source (K),
T_C is the temperature of the heat sink (K)

Real heat engine's efficiencies are **lower** than their theoretical maximum for multiple reasons:

1) There are **frictional** forces inside the engine (p.235).
2) **Fuel** doesn't burn **entirely**.
3) Energy is needed to **move internal components** of the engine.

Waste Heat is Reused in **CHP Plants**

1) To **maximise** the efficiency of an engine, as much as possible of the inputted heat energy must be transferred usefully.
2) Engines are very **inefficient** — there is usually a lot of **waste heat** from heat engines, which is transferred to the **surrounding area** and lost.
3) **Combined heat and power** (CHP) plants try to limit **energy waste** by using this waste heat for other purposes — e.g. heating houses and businesses nearby.
4) For example, the Markinch Biomass CHP plant was recently built in Fife, Scotland. It generates **electricity** which it supplies to a **local papermaker** and the National Grid. The excess **heat** is then used to create **steam** to dry paper in the **paper mill**.

Warm-Up Questions

Q1 State the equation for calculating the input power of an engine.
Q2 What are the equations for calculating overall, thermal and mechanical efficiency?
Q3 Why can heat engines never be 100% efficient?
Q4 Draw a diagram to show the second law of thermodynamics being applied to a heat engine.
Q5 Name a system which tries to maximise the work done from the heat input of an engine.

Exam Questions

Q1 Petrol has a calorific value of 44.8 MJkg^{-1}. A petrol engine burns petrol at a rate of 2.8 g per second. The brake power of the engine is 44.7 kW. Calculate the overall efficiency of the engine. [3 marks]

Q2 A heat engine has 1000 J of energy transferred to it from a heat source at 1200 K. The engine is also in contact with a heat sink at a temperature of 290 K. The engine transfers 550 J of the supplied energy to the heat sink.

a) Calculate the maximum theoretical efficiency of the engine. [2 marks]

b) Calculate the efficiency of the engine. [2 marks]

c) Suggest one reason for the difference between the efficiencies calculated in a) and b). [1 mark]

The second law of thermodynamics — not an excuse to do less work...

First things first, learn that diagram. Not only do you need to know it, but it'll help you remember all of the efficiency stuff that goes with it. Then get to learning and practising the equations for overall, thermal and mechanical efficiency. Then it's just a case of remembering ways that useful work out can be maximised to make an efficient engine.

Reversed Heat Engines

Normal heat engines do work, so reversed heat engines have work done to them.

Refrigerators and Heat Pumps are Reversed Heat Engines

1) **Reversed** heat engines operate between **hot** and **cold reservoirs** like other engines.

2) The big difference is the direction of energy transfer — **heat energy** is taken **from** the **cold** reservoir and transferred **to** the **hot** reservoir. For reversed heat engines, we call these reservoirs **spaces** (instead of **sources** and **sinks**).

3) Heat naturally flows from **hotter to colder** spaces. To transfer heat from a **colder** space to a **hotter** space, **work** (*W*) must be done.

4) **Heat pumps** and **refrigerators** are both reversed heat engines, but they have **different functions**.

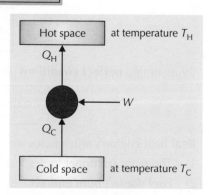

Refrigerators

1) A refrigerator aims to **extract** as much heat energy from the **cold space** as possible for each joule of **work done**.

2) The **cold space** is the **inside** of the refrigerator, whilst the **hot space** is the **room** the refrigerator is in.

3) Refrigerators keep enclosed spaces cool that can be used to store **perishable food** fresh for longer.

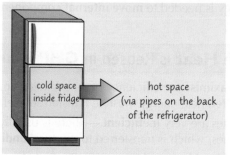

Heat Pumps

1) A **heat pump** aims to **pump** as much heat as possible into the **hot** space **per joule of work done**.

2) Here, the **cold space** is usually the **outdoors** and the **hot space** is the **inside** of a **house**.

3) They are used to **heat rooms** and **water** in homes.

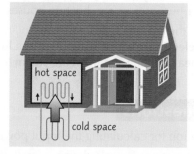

Coefficient of Performance (COP) Describes How Well Work is Converted

1) Heat engines are judged on how well they can **transfer heat** based on the **amount of work done** on them.

2) The **coefficient of performance** is a measure of how well this **work** is **converted** into **heat transfer**. E.g. a heat pump with a coefficient of performance of **4** transfers **4 J** of energy for every **1 J** of **work** done.

3) It can be thought of like **efficiency** (see page 236), but it's not called that as the **coefficient of performance** can be **above 1**.

You Can Calculate the Coefficient of Performance (COP) for Refrigerators

As it's the **heat removed** from the **cold** space that's important for a refrigerator, its **coefficient of performance** is:

$$COP_{ref} = \frac{Q_C}{W} = \frac{Q_C}{Q_H - Q_C}$$

Q_H is the heat transferred to the hot space (J),
Q_C is the heat transferred from the cold space (J),
W is work done (J)

If it is running at the **maximum theoretical** efficiency, the coefficient of performance becomes:

$$COP_{ref} = \frac{T_C}{T_H - T_C}$$

T_H is the temperature of the hot space (K),
T_C is the temperature of the cold space (K)

Reversed Heat Engines

Coefficient of Performance (COP) is Similar for a Heat Pump

As it's the heat transferred to the hot space that's important for a heat pump, its **coefficient of performance** is:

$$COP_{hp} = \frac{Q_H}{W} = \frac{Q_H}{Q_H - Q_C}$$

The **maximum theoretical coefficient of performance** is:

$$COP_{hp} = \frac{T_H}{T_H - T_C}$$

Dave's heat pump performance wasn't much cop...

> **Example:** A house installs a heat pump to keep its rooms at 23 °C by pumping heat in from the outside. In theory, how much does the coefficient of performance change if the outside temperature rises from 2 °C to 10°C?

If the outside temperature is 2 °C, the theoretical coefficient of performance is:

$$COP_{hp} = \frac{T_H}{T_H - T_C} = \frac{296}{296 - 275} = \frac{296}{21} = 14.09...$$

If the outside temperature is 10 °C, the theoretical coefficient of performance is:

$$COP_{hp} = \frac{T_H}{T_H - T_C} = \frac{296}{296 - 283} = \frac{296}{13} = 22.76...$$

So the coefficient of performance increases by:

$$22.76... - 14.09... = 8.67... = \mathbf{8.7 \ (to \ 2 \ s.f.)}$$

Remember to convert to Kelvin for calculating the coefficient of performance. O K ≈ −273 °C

Warm-Up Questions

Q1 Describe how reversed heat engines work.

Q2 Give two examples of reversed heat engines.

Q3 What is the function of a refrigerator, and how does it differ from the function of a heat pump?

Q4 What is a coefficient of performance of a reversed heat engine?

Q5 State the equations for the coefficient of performance for a refrigerator and a heat pump.

Q6 State the maximum theoretical coefficient of performance for a heat pump.

Exam Questions

Q1 In one hour, a refrigerator extracts 5.66 MJ of heat energy from the cold space in the fridge and transfers it to the air surrounding the fridge. An input of 2.02 MJ of work is needed for this energy transfer to take place.

   a) Calculate the amount of heat energy leaving the refrigerator. [1 mark]

   b) Calculate the coefficient of performance for this refrigerator. [1 mark]

Q2 a) A heat pump is used to warm a room to 25 °C by transferring heat energy from outside the house to inside. The outside temperature is 3.0 °C.
   Calculate the maximum theoretical coefficient of performance. (0 °C = 273 K) [1 mark]

   b) The heat pump has an actual coefficient of performance of 3.5. It pumps 4.10 MJ of energy into the room. Show that 1.2 MJ of work is done to transfer this energy to the room. [2 marks]

It's the end of the section — don't COP out now...

So a fridge is just an engine turned on its head. Good to know. Although the diagram and equations are pretty similar to the ones you've already seen before, don't get lazy now. Practise using them and make sure you learn the maximum theoretical coefficients of performance — you won't be given them. Then have a go at the extra practice on page 257.

Specific Charge of the Electron

e/m$_e$ was known for quite a long time before anyone came up with a way to measure e or m$_e$ separately.

Cathode Ray is an Old-Fashioned name for a Beam of Electrons

1) The phrase '**cathode ray**' was first used in 1876, to describe the **glow** that appears on the wall of a **discharge tube** like the one in the diagram, when a **potential difference** is applied across the terminals.

2) The **rays** seemed to come from the **cathode** (hence their name) and there was a lot of argument about **what** the rays were made of.

3) **J. J. Thomson** ended the debate in 1897, when he demonstrated (see next page) that cathode rays:

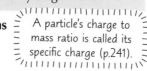

High voltage

Cathode rays — Glass glows where cathode rays hit

Cathode — Anode

Evacuated glass tube

Cathode rays were used in TV and computer screens before LCD, plasma and LED screens came along.

- have **energy**, **momentum** and **mass**,
- have a **negative charge**,
- have the **same properties**, no matter **what gas** is in the tube and what the **cathode** is made of,
- have a **charge to mass ratio** much **bigger** than that of **hydrogen** ions. So they either have a **tiny mass**, or a much higher charge — Thomson assumed they had the same size charge as hydrogen ions.

Thomson concluded that **all atoms** contain these 'cathode ray particles', or **electrons** as they were soon known. He had discovered the **first subatomic particle**.

A particle's charge to mass ratio is called its specific charge (p.241).

Electron Beams are Produced by Thermionic Emission

1) When you **heat** a **metal**, its **free electrons** gain a load of **kinetic energy**.

2) Give them **enough energy** and they'll **break free** from the surface of the metal — this is called **thermionic emission**. (Try breaking the word down — think of it as '**therm**' [to do with heat] + '**ionic**' [to do with charge] + '**emission**' [giving off] — so it's 'giving off charged particles when you heat something'.)

3) Once they've been emitted, the electrons can be **accelerated** by an **electric field** in an **electron gun**:

- A **heating coil** heats the metal cathode. The electrons that are emitted are **accelerated** towards the **cylindrical anode** by the electric field set up by the high voltage.

- Some electrons pass through a **little hole** in the **anode**, making a narrow electron beam. The electrons in the beam move at a **constant velocity** because there's **no field** beyond the anode — i.e. there's **no force**.

High voltage

Heater -ve +ve

Evacuated glass tube

Electron beam

Cylindrical anode with hole in it

Hot cathode Electrons emitted from cathode Electrons attracted towards anode

The Electronvolt is Defined Using Accelerated Charges

1) The **work done** on a particle with charge **Q** when it's **accelerated** through a p.d. of **V** volts is **QV** joules. This just comes from the definition of the **volt** (JC^{-1}). This energy is converted into the **kinetic energy** of the particle.

$$\text{work done} = \tfrac{1}{2}mv^2 = eV$$

2) If you replace **Q** in the equation with the magnitude of the charge of a **single electron**, **e**, you get:

3) From this you can define a new **unit of energy** called the **electronvolt (eV)**:

> 1 electronvolt is the **kinetic energy carried** by an **electron** after it has been **accelerated** through a **potential difference** of **1 volt**.

The unit MeV is the mega-electronvolt (equal to 1.6×10^{-13} J) and GeV is the giga-electronvolt (1.6×10^{-10} J).

4) So, the **energy gained**, in **electronvolts**, by an electron accelerated through a potential difference is:

> **energy gained by electron (eV) = accelerating voltage (V)**
> **(work done)**

Conversion factor: $1 \text{ eV} = 1.6 \times 10^{-19}$ J

Specific Charge of the Electron

Thomson Measured the Specific Charge of the Electron

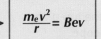
specific charge = $\frac{e}{m_e}$

1) The **specific charge** of a charged particle is just its **charge** per unit **mass**.
2) There are a **few different ways** of measuring it, and you need to know about **one** of them. This isn't the method that Thomson used, but that's not important.

Measuring the Specific Charge of an Electron:

Check out Section 11 — Magnetic Fields if you're having trouble with this experiment.

1) Electrons are charged particles, so they can be deflected by an **electric** or a **magnetic field**. This method uses a magnetic field in a piece of apparatus called a **fine beam tube**.

2) When the beam of electrons from the **electron gun** (see previous page) passes through the low-pressure gas, hydrogen atoms along its path **absorb energy**. As the electrons in these **excited hydrogen atoms** fall back to the ground state, they **emit light**. The electron beam is seen as a **glowing trace** through the gas.

3) Two circular **magnetic field coils** either side generate a **uniform magnetic field** inside the tube.

4) The electron beam is initially fired at **right angles** to the **magnetic field**, so the beam curves round in a **circle**.

magnetic field coils
electron gun
electron beam
glass bulb containing hydrogen at low pressure

5) This means that the **magnetic force** on the electron (see p.142) is acting as a **centripetal force** (see p.99). So the radius of the circle is given by:

$$\frac{m_e v^2}{r} = Bev$$

Where m_e is the mass of an electron, e is the magnitude of the charge on an electron, B is the magnetic field strength, v is the velocity of the electron and r is the radius of the circle.

6) You can **rearrange** this equation to give v in terms of B, e, m_e and r.

Then you can substitute that expression into $\frac{1}{2} m_e v^2 = eV$ and tidy it all up a bit to get:

$$\frac{e}{m_e} = \frac{2V}{B^2 r^2}$$

Where V is the accelerating potential.

You can **measure** all the quantities on the **right-hand side** of the equation using the **fine beam tube**, leaving you with the **specific charge**, e/m_e. It turns out that e/m_e (1.76×10^{11} Ckg⁻¹) is about **1800 times greater** than the **specific charge** of a hydrogen ion or proton (9.58×10^7 Ckg⁻¹). And the **mass** of a **proton** is about **1800 times greater** than the **mass** of an **electron**. **Thomson was right** — electrons and protons do have the **same size charge**.

Warm-Up Questions

Q1 What is meant by thermionic emission? Describe how this is relevant to cathode ray tube televisions.
Q2 Sketch a labelled diagram of an electron gun that could be used to accelerate electrons.
Q3 What was Thomson's main conclusion following his measurement of e/m_e for electrons?
Q4 How does the specific charge of the electron compare with the specific charge of the proton?

PRACTICE QUESTIONS

Exam Questions

Q1 An electron of mass 9.11×10^{-31} kg and charge -1.60×10^{-19} C is accelerated from rest through a potential difference of 1.00 kV.
a) State its energy in eV. [1 mark]
b) Calculate its energy in joules. [1 mark]
c) Calculate its speed in ms⁻¹ and express this as a percentage of the speed of light (3.00×10^8 ms⁻¹). [3 marks]

Q2 Explain the main features of an experiment to determine the specific charge of the electron. The quality of your written answer will be assessed in this question. [5 marks]

New Olympic event — the electronvault...

Electronvolts are really handy units — they crop up all over the rest of this book, particularly in nuclear and particle physics. They save you having to mess around with a load of nasty powers of ten. Cathode ray tubes (CRTs) used to be in every TV and computer monitor, but now you'll probably only find them in museums (or in my flat...).

Millikan's Oil-Drop Experiment

Thomson had already found the specific charge of the electron in 1897 — now it was down to Robert Millikan, experimenter extraordinaire, to find the absolute charge...

Millikan's Experiment used Stokes' Law

1) Before you start thinking about Millikan's experiment, you need a bit of **extra theory**.

2) When you drop an object into a fluid, like air, it experiences a **viscous drag** force. This force acts in the **opposite direction** to the velocity of the object, and is due to the **viscosity** of the fluid.

3) You can calculate this viscous force on a spherical object using **Stokes' law**:

$$F = 6\pi\eta rv$$

where η is the viscosity of the fluid, r is the radius of the
object and v is the velocity of the object.

Millikan's Experiment — the Basic Set-Up

1) An **atomiser** created a **fine mist** of oil drops that were **charged** by **friction** as they left the atomiser (positively if they lost electrons, negatively if they gained electrons).

2) Some of the drops fell through a **hole** in the top plate and could be viewed through the **microscope**. (The eyepiece carried a **scale** to measure distances — and so **velocities** — accurately.)

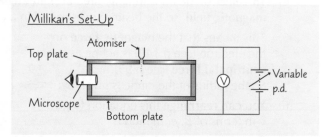

Millikan's Set-Up

Atomiser

Top plate

Microscope

Bottom plate

Variable p.d.

3) When he was ready, Millikan could apply a **potential difference** between the two plates, producing a **field** that exerted a **force** on the charged drops. By **adjusting** the p.d., he could vary the strength of the field.

4) To give you a feel for the **size** of the apparatus, Millikan's plates were circular, with a diameter of about the width of this page. They were separated by about 1.5 cm.

Before the Field is Switched on, there's only Gravity and the Viscous Force

1) With the electric field turned off, the forces acting on each oil drop are:

    a) the weight of the drop — acting downwards

    b) the viscous force from the air — acting upwards

Millikan had to take account of things like upthrust as well, but you don't have to worry about that — keep it simple.

2) The drop will reach **terminal velocity** (i.e. it will stop accelerating) when these two forces are equal. So, from Stokes' law (see above):

$$mg = 6\pi\eta rv$$

3) Since the **mass** of the drop is the **volume** of the drop multiplied by the **density**, ρ, of the oil, this can be rewritten as:

$$\frac{4}{3}\pi r^3 \rho g = 6\pi\eta rv \text{ so } r^2 = \frac{9\eta v}{2\rho g}$$

Millikan measured η and ρ in separate experiments, so he could now calculate r — ready to be used when he **switched on** the electric field...

field switched off

field switched on

Millikan's Oil-Drop Experiment

Then he **Turned On** the **Electric Field...**

1) The field introduced a **third major factor** — an **electric force** on the drop.

2) Millikan adjusted the applied p.d. until the drop was **stationary**. Since the **viscous force** is proportional to the **velocity** of the object, once the drop stopped moving, the viscous force **disappeared**.

3) Now the only two forces acting on the oil drop were:

   a) the **weight** of the drop — acting downwards
   b) the force due to the **uniform electric field** — acting upwards

4) The **electric force** is given by: $F = \dfrac{QV}{d}$ where Q is the charge on the oil drop, V is the p.d. between the plates and d is the distance between the plates.

5) Since the drop is **stationary**, this electric force must be equal to the weight, so: $\dfrac{QV}{d} = mg = \dfrac{4}{3}\pi r^3 \rho g$

   See p. 126-129 for more on electric fields.

   The first part of the experiment gave a value for r, so the **only unknown** in this equation is Q.

6) So Millikan could find the **charge on the drop**, and repeated the experiment for hundreds of drops. The charge on any drop was always a **whole number multiple** of -1.60×10^{-19} C.

These Results Suggested that **Charge** was **Quantised**

1) This result was **really significant**. Millikan concluded that charge can **never exist** in **smaller** quantities than 1.60×10^{-19} C. He assumed that this was the **charge** carried by an **electron**.

2) Later experiments confirmed that **both** these things are true.

> Charge is "**quantised**". It exists in "packets" of size **1.60×10^{-19} C** — the **fundamental unit of charge**. This is the size of the charge carried by **one electron**.

3) This meant that the mass of an electron could be calculated exactly, proving that it was the lightest particle ever discovered (at the time).

Warm-Up Questions

Q1 Write down the equation for Stokes' law, defining any variables.
Q2 List the forces that act on the oil drop in Millikan's experiment:
   a) with the drop drifting downwards at terminal velocity but with no applied electric field,
   b) when the drop is stationary, with an electric field applied.
Q3 Briefly explain the significance of Millikan's oil-drop experiment in the context of quantum physics.

Exam Question

Q1 An oil drop of mass 1.63×10^{-14} kg is held stationary in the space between two charged plates 3.00 cm apart. The potential difference between the plates is 4995 V. The density of the oil used is 885 kgm^{-3}.

   a) Describe the relative magnitude and direction of the forces acting on the oil drop. [2 marks]
   b) Calculate the charge on the oil drop using g = 9.81 Nkg^{-1}. Give your answer in terms of e, the charge on an electron. [3 marks]

   The electric field is switched off and the oil drop falls towards the bottom plate.

   c) Explain why the oil drop reaches terminal velocity as it falls. [3 marks]
   d) Calculate the terminal velocity of the oil drop using $\eta = 1.84 \times 10^{-5}$ kgm^{-1}s^{-1}. [3 marks]

So next time you've got a yen for 1.59×10^{-19} coulombs — tough...

This was a huge leap. Along with the photoelectric effect (see p.247), this experiment marked the beginning of quantum physics. The world was no longer ruled by smooth curves — charge now jumped from one allowed step to the next...

Light — Particles vs Waves

Newton was quite a bright chap really, but even he could make mistakes — and this was his biggest one. The trouble with being Isaac Newton is that everyone just assumes you're right...

Newton had his Corpuscular Theory and Thought Light was Particles

1) In 1671, Newton published his **theory of colour**. In it he suggested that **light** was made up of **tiny particles** that he called '**corpuscles**'.

2) One of his major arguments was that light was known to travel in **straight lines**, yet waves were known to **bend** in the shadow of an **obstacle** (diffraction). Experiments weren't **accurate enough** then to detect the diffraction of light. Light was known to **reflect** and **refract**, but that was it.

3) His theory was based on the principles of his **laws of motion** — that all particles, including his 'corpuscles', will 'naturally' travel in **straight lines**.

4) Newton believed that **reflection** was due to a force that **pushed** the particles away from the surface — just like a ball bouncing back off a wall.

5) He thought **refraction** occurred because the corpuscles travelled **faster** in a **denser** medium like glass.

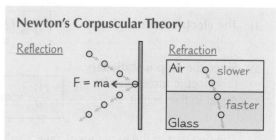

Newton's Corpuscular Theory

Huygens thought Light was a Wave

1) The idea that light might be a **wave** had existed for some time before it was formalised by Huygens in 1678 — not long after Newton first publicly stated his belief that light was a particle.

2) Huygens developed a **general model** of the propagation of **waves** in what is now known as **Huygens' principle**:

> **HUYGENS' PRINCIPLE:** Every point on a wavefront may be considered to be a **point source** of **secondary wavelets** that spread out in the forward direction at the speed of the wave. The **new wavefront** is the surface that is **tangential** to all of these **secondary wavelets**.

This diagram shows how this works:

3) By applying his theory to **light**, he found that he could explain **reflection** and **refraction** easily.

Huygens predicted that light should **slow down** when it entered a **denser medium**, rather than speed up.

4) Huygens also predicted that light should **diffract** around tiny objects and that two coherent light sources should **interfere** with each other.

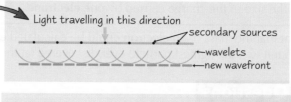

Light travelling in this direction — secondary sources — wavelets — new wavefront

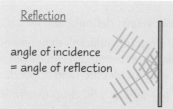

Reflection — angle of incidence = angle of reflection

Refraction

Scientists of the Period Preferred Newton's Theory

Newton's corpuscular theory was much more popular because:

- Imagining light as a stream of particles explained **reflection** and **refraction** in a way that more intuitively fitted in with the existing understanding of physics. It couldn't explain **diffraction**, but the equipment of the time wasn't capable of demonstrating diffraction in light.

- There was **no experimental evidence** to support Huygens' theory that light was a wave until Young's interference experiments more than 100 years later.

- Scientists thought **double refraction** (a polarisation effect, where shining light through certain crystals makes two images instead of one) couldn't be explained by thinking of light as a wave. Newton's corpuscular theory explained it in terms of the corpuscles having '**sides**'.

- Over time, Newton's **reputation** grew as his ideas on maths, gravity, forces and motion **revolutionised physics**. By the time of Thomas Young a century later, he was a figure scientists didn't want to disagree with.

Huygens

Newton

Light — Particles vs Waves

Young Proved Huygens Right with his Double-Slit Experiment

1) **Diffraction** and **interference** (p.34) are both uniquely **wave** properties. If it could be shown that **light** showed **interference** patterns, that would help decide once and for all between corpuscular theory and wave theory.

2) The problem with this was getting two **coherent** light sources, as **light** is emitted in **random bursts**.

3) In 1802, Thomas Young solved this problem by using only **one point source of light** (a light source behind a narrow slit). In front of this was a **screen** with **two narrow slits** in it. Light spreading out by **diffraction** from the slits was equivalent to **two coherent point sources**.

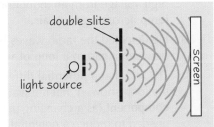

4) In the area on the screen where light from the two slits **overlapped**, bright and dark '**fringes**' were formed. This was **proof** that light could both **diffract** (through the narrow slits) and **interfere** (to form the interference pattern on the screen) — **Huygens** was right all along.

- Even then, Huygens' and Young's ideas weren't widely accepted. Newton's work had **revolutionised physics**, and by this point he was an established historical figure who other scientists didn't want to contradict.

- Huygens had proposed that light was a **longitudinal wave** (like sound), but this couldn't explain **double refraction**.

- It took more than a decade before Young (at about the same time as the French scientist **Fresnel**) realised that **transverse waves** could explain the behaviour of light. Following this, other scientists soon started **agreeing** with Huygens that light was a wave.

Fizeau Measured the Speed of Light

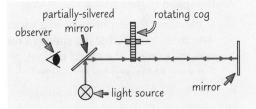

1) In the mid 1800s, a French physicist called Hippolyte Fizeau measured the **speed of light** by passing a **beam** of light through the gap between two **cog teeth** to a **reflector** about 9 km away. The cog was rotated at exactly the right speed so that the reflected beam was **blocked** by the next cog tooth.

2) Using the **frequency of rotation** and the **number of gaps**, Fizeau was able to calculate the **time taken** for the light to travel to the reflector and back to the cog.

3) So Fizeau could use the time taken and the **distance travelled** to calculate the speed of light.

This **estimate** of the speed of light was **really significant** because **Maxwell** was able to use this value to support his theory that **light** is an electromagnetic wave...

Maxwell Predicted EM Waves and their Speed

1) In the second half of the 19th century, James Clerk Maxwell was trying to unite the ideas of magnetism and electricity. He created a **mathematical model** of magnetic and electric fields. This model said that a change to these fields would create an **electromagnetic** (EM) **wave**, radiating out from the source of the disturbance. Maxwell's prediction came before any experimental evidence for the existence of EM waves. He predicted that there would be a **spectrum** of EM waves, travelling at the same speed with different **frequencies**.

2) Maxwell showed theoretically that **all electromagnetic waves** should travel at the same speed in a vacuum, **c**:

Maxwell calculated the **speed of electromagnetic waves** in a vacuum using:

$$c = \frac{1}{\sqrt{\mu_0 \varepsilon_0}} = 2.998... \times 10^8 \text{ ms}^{-1}$$

c is the speed of the wave in ms^{-1}, μ_0 is the permeability of free space $(4\pi \times 10^{-7} \text{ Hm}^{-1})$, and ε_0 is the permittivity of free space $(8.85 \times 10^{-12} \text{ Fm}^{-1})$.

You can think of ε_0 as relating the electric field strength to the charge on the object producing it. You can think of μ_0 as relating the magnetic flux density produced by a wire to the current flowing through it.

3) Maxwell's value of c was very close to the value measured by Fizeau. So this provided strong evidence that **light**, as well as ultraviolet and infrared radiation beyond the visible spectrum, is an **electromagnetic wave**.

4) Maxwell was proved right by modern measurements of the speed of light and by the discovery of **radio waves** and other **EM waves**.

Light — Particles vs Waves

Heinrich Hertz Discovered Radio Waves...

1) In 1887, **Heinrich Hertz** produced and detected **radio waves** using electric sparks.

2) He showed that radio waves were produced when a high voltage from an induction coil caused sparks to **jump** across a **gap of air**.

3) He detected the radio waves by watching for sparks between a gap in a **loop of wire**.

4) The fact that a **potential difference** was induced in the loop showed that the waves had a **magnetic component** (as a changing magnetic field is needed to induce a potential difference, see p.144).

5) Hertz later went on to show that radio waves could be reflected, refracted, diffracted and polarised, and show interference.

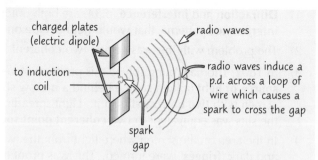

charged plates (electric dipole)

radio waves

to induction coil

radio waves induce a p.d. across a loop of wire which causes a spark to cross the gap

spark gap

You can show that radio waves have an electric component by replacing the wire loop with a second dipole parallel to the first. The radio waves will create an alternating current in the second dipole.

...and Measured their Speed

Hertz set up stationary radio waves (see page 30) at a fixed resonant frequency to measure their speed.

1) He found the wavelength λ by measuring the **distance** between the **nodes**.

2) Using the **frequency**, Hertz was able to calculate the **speed** of the radio waves (using $v = f\lambda$).

3) Conducting the experiment in a **vacuum**, Hertz was able to show that the **speed** of **radio waves** was the **same** as the **speed of light**, and matched the speed **Maxwell** had predicted all electromagnetic waves would travel at.

4) This helped confirm that radio waves, like light, are **electromagnetic waves**.

5) So light as a wave was the accepted theory up until the very end of the 19th century, when the **photoelectric effect** was discovered. Then the particle theory had to be resurrected, and it was all up in the air again...

detector

node   node   node   node

1½ λ

radio wave transmitter   reflecting sheet

By moving the detector horizontally between the transmitter and the reflecting sheet, Hertz could locate the nodes and measure the distance between them.

Warm-Up Questions

Q1 What was the main argument that Newton used to support his corpuscular theory of light?

Q2 What part does diffraction play in Young's double-slit experiment?

Q3 Sketch a diagram showing an experiment to demonstrate Young's fringes for white light in a laboratory.

Q4 What do μ_0 and ε_0 refer to in Maxwell's speed of light calculation?

Q5 Describe an experiment you could do to investigate the speed of electromagnetic waves using stationary waves.

PRACTICE QUESTIONS

Exam Questions

Q1 a) Describe Newton's corpuscular theory of light. [2 marks]

b) Explain why Newton's corpuscular theory was more widely accepted than Huygens' wave theory. [4 marks]

Q2 Explain how the work of Young, Fizeau, Maxwell and Hertz provided evidence to support the wave theory of light. Include descriptions of the experimental evidence they produced in your answer. [4 marks]

This isn't a light debate — the physics is so heavy it Hertz... (sorry)

Now then young 'un, these three pages might look like one huge-ens history lesson but there's still a new ton of fizeaucs for you to slit down and learn on the double. Don't waver, but if you're wondering how to boost your marks to the max — well, you have to learn it particle-ularly thoroughly so the full corpus(cle) is stored behind your fringe.

The Photoelectric Effect and the Photon Model

You did the photoelectric effect in the first year of A-Level, so it should be familiar. You need it again though, so here it is...

High Frequency Light can Release Electrons from Metals

If you shine **light** of a **high enough frequency** onto the **surface of a metal**,
the metal will **emit electrons**. For **most** metals, this **frequency** falls in the **UV** range.

1) **Free electrons** on the **surface** of the metal can sometimes **absorb energy** from the light.

2) If an electron **absorbs enough** energy, the **bonds** holding it to the metal can be **broken** and the electron **released**.

3) This is called the **photoelectric effect** and the electrons emitted are called **photoelectrons**.

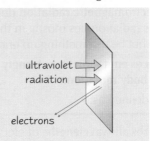

ultraviolet radiation

electrons

You don't need to know the details of any experiments on this
— you just need to learn the three main conclusions:

Conclusion 1

For a given metal, **no photoelectrons are emitted** if the radiation has a frequency **below** a certain value — called the **threshold frequency**.

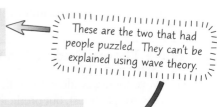

These are the two that had people puzzled. They can't be explained using wave theory.

Conclusion 2

The photoelectrons are emitted with a variety of kinetic energies ranging from zero to some maximum value. This value of **maximum kinetic energy** increases with the **frequency** of the radiation, and is **unaffected** by the **intensity** of the radiation.

Conclusion 3

The **number** of photoelectrons emitted per second is **directly proportional** to the **intensity** of the radiation.

Remember that Wave Theory Can't Explain the Photoelectric Effect

According to wave theory:

1) For a particular frequency of light, the **energy** carried is **proportional** to the **intensity** of the beam.

2) The energy carried by the light would be **spread evenly** over the wavefront.

3) **Each** free electron on the surface of the metal would gain a **bit of energy** from each incoming wave.

4) Gradually, each electron would gain **enough energy** to be able to leave the metal.

Theory and practice — two very different things.

SO... The **higher the intensity** of the wave, the **more energy** it should transfer to each electron
— so the kinetic energy should increase with **intensity**.
There's **no explanation** for the **kinetic energy** depending only on the **frequency**.

There is **no explanation** for the **threshold frequency**. According to wave theory, electrons
should be emitted eventually, no matter what the frequency is.

The Photoelectric Effect and the Photon Model

The **Ultraviolet Catastrophe** was about **Black-Body Radiation**

A bit of background, then we'll crack on with something else wave theory couldn't explain...

A **Black Body** is a **Perfect Absorber** and **Emitter**

1) Objects emit **electromagnetic radiation** due to their **temperature**. At everyday temperatures this radiation lies mostly in the **infrared** part of the spectrum (which we can't see) — but heat something up enough and it will start to **glow**.

2) **Pure black** surfaces emit radiation **strongly** and in a **well-defined way**. We call it **black body radiation**.

3) A black body is defined as:

> A body that **absorbs all wavelengths** of electromagnetic radiation (that's why it's called a **black** body) and can **emit all wavelengths** of electromagnetic radiation.

4) The graph of **intensity** against **wavelength** for black body radiation shows that power radiated varies with wavelength.

5) But wave theory **couldn't explain** all of this graph — catastrophe!

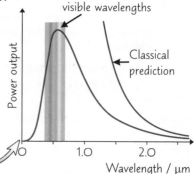

Radiation graph for a very hot black body (e.g. a star).

Wave Theory Predicted an **Infinitely High Peak**

1) Wave theory could explain the slope of the black body radiation graph at long wavelengths (low frequencies), but predicted an **infinitely high** peak towards the ultraviolet region.

2) This was the **ultraviolet catastrophe** — wave theory, then widely accepted, had predicted something that was **impossible**, and nobody could work out how to adapt the theory to explain it.

3) It wasn't until **Einstein** built on **Max Planck's** interpretation of radiation in terms of **quanta** and came up with the **photon model of light** that physics was able to **explain** black body curves — even though Planck wasn't actually trying to solve the ultraviolet catastrophe at the time.

Einstein came up with the **Photon Model of Light**...

1) When Max Planck was investigating **black body radiation** he suggested that **EM waves** can **only** be released in **discrete packets**, or **quanta**.

2) The **energy carried** by one of these **wave-packets** had to be:

$$E = hf = \frac{hc}{\lambda}$$

where h = Planck's constant = 6.63×10^{-34} Js
and c = speed of light in a vacuum = 3.00×10^8 ms^{-1}

Quanta is the plural of quantum.

Popular new model at the physicists' fashion show.

3) **Einstein** went **further** by suggesting that **EM waves** (and the energy they carry) can only **exist** in discrete packets. He called these wave-packets **photons**.

4) He saw these photons of light as having a **one-on-one**, **particle-like** interaction with **an electron** in a **metal surface**. It would **transfer all** its **energy** to that **one, specific electron**.

... which **Explained** the **Photoelectric Effect** Nicely

1) According to the photon model, when light hits a metal surface, the metal is bombarded by photons.

2) If one of these photons collides with a free electron, the electron will gain energy equal to hf. If hf is greater than the work function (see below), the electron can be emitted.

3) Each electron only absorbs one photon at a time, so all the energy the electron needs to be emitted must come from a single photon.

Before an electron can **leave** the surface of the metal, it needs enough energy to **break the bonds holding it there**. This energy is called the **work function** (symbol ϕ) and its **value** depends on the **metal**.

The Photoelectric Effect and the Photon Model

The **Photon Model** Explains the Photoelectric Effect's **Threshold Frequency...**

1) If the energy **gained** from a photon is **greater** than the **work function**, the electron can be **emitted**.

2) If the energy **isn't** greater than the work function, the metal will heat up, but **no electrons** will be emitted.

3) The threshold frequency is the **minimum frequency** a photon can have and still cause a photoelectron to be emitted. The **energy** of a photon at the threshold frequency is equal to the **work function**.

... and the **Maximum Kinetic Energy**

1) The **energy transferred** to an electron by a photon depends on the photon's **frequency**.

2) The **kinetic energy** the electron will be carrying when it **leaves** the metal is the energy it gained from the **photon minus** any energy it's **lost** on the way out.

3) Electrons from deeper down in the metal lose more energy than electrons on the **surface**, so the photoelectrons have a **range** of energies. Photoelectrons have a **maximum kinetic energy** — electrons have this energy when they are on the surface of the metal and the only energy lost is in escaping from the material (i.e. the **work function**).

4) The **kinetic energy** of the photoelectrons is **independent of intensity**, as they **only absorb one photon** at a time. However, increasing the intensity increases the **number** of photons hitting the metal, so increases the number of photoelectrons emitted.

> Einstein's work was hugely significant:
>
> - He'd demonstrated that light is a stream of particles called **photons**, and that photons are the **smallest possible** unit of electromagnetic radiation — a **quantum**.
>
> - As well as winning him the **Nobel Prize** in 1921, Einstein's photon model opened up a whole **new branch** of physics called **quantum theory**.

Warm-Up Questions

Q1 Explain how light can eject electrons from a metal.

Q2 What is a black body?

Q3 What was Max Planck's suggestion about electromagnetic radiation?

Q4 Briefly describe Einstein's photon model and its significance to physics.

Exam Questions

Q1 a) State the two results of experiments investigating the photoelectric effect that contradicted wave theory, and describe what physicists would have expected to observe instead if wave theory was correct. [4 marks]

   b) Explain these two results in terms of the photon model of electromagnetic radiation. [4 marks]

Q2 Explain the 'ultraviolet catastrophe' and its implications for wave theory. [3 marks]

Avoid ultraviolet catastrophes — don't play with black-lights...

So as it turns out, everybody was equally right because light is a wave AND a particle. Or maybe everybody was equally wrong... Anyway — learn why the wave theory can't explain the photoelectric effect, and how photon theory does — then tell someone else to make sure you've learnt it all. Then go and make yourself a nice cup of tea.

Wave-Particle Duality

If you're not very good at making decisions, consider a career as an electron. Wave? Particle? I dunno, let's be both.

Light Behaves as a Wave in Interference and Diffraction

1) Light produces **interference** and **diffraction** patterns — **alternating bands** of **dark** and **light**.

2) These can **only** be explained using **waves interfering constructively** (when two waves overlap in phase) or **interfering destructively** (when two waves are out of phase).

Give us a wave.

Light Behaves as a Particle in the Photoelectric Effect

1) **Einstein** explained the results of **photoelectricity experiments** (see p. 247) by thinking of the **beam of light** as a series of **particle-like "photons"**.

2) If a **photon** of light is a **discrete** bundle of energy, then it can **interact** with an **electron** in a **one-to-one way**.

3) **All** the **energy** in the **photon** is **given** to one **electron**.

Neither the **wave theory** nor the **particle theory** describe what light actually **is**. They're just two different **models** that help to explain the way light behaves.

De Broglie came up with the Wave-Particle Duality Theory

1) Louis de Broglie made a **bold suggestion** in his **PhD thesis**:

> If **"wave-like"** light showed **particle properties** (photons), **"particles"** like **electrons** should be expected to show **wave-like properties**.

2) The **de Broglie equation** relates a **wave property** (**wavelength, λ**) to a **moving particle property** (**momentum, p**). h = Planck's constant = 6.63×10^{-34} Js.

$$p = \frac{h}{\lambda}$$

Remember that momentum (p) is just mass × velocity.

3) The **de Broglie wave** of a particle can be interpreted as a **"probability wave"**. The **probability** of finding a particle at a point is **directly** proportional to the **square of the wave's amplitude** at that point.

4) Many physicists at the time **weren't very impressed** — his ideas were just **speculation**. But later experiments **confirmed** the wave nature of electrons.

Electron Diffraction shows the Wave Nature of Electrons

1) De Broglie's suggestions prompted a lot of experiments to try to show that **electrons** can have **wave-like** properties. In **1927**, Davisson and Germer succeeded in **diffracting electrons**.

2) They saw **diffraction patterns** when **accelerated electrons** in a vacuum tube **interacted** with the **spaces** in a graphite **crystal**.

3) According to wave theory, the **spread** of the **lines** in the diffraction pattern **increases** if the **wavelength** of the wave **increases**.

4) In electron diffraction experiments, a **small accelerating voltage**, i.e. **slow** electrons, gives **widely spaced** rings.

5) **Increase** the **electron speed** and the diffraction pattern circles **squash together** towards the **middle**. This fits in with the **de Broglie** equation above — if the **velocity** is **higher**, the **wavelength** is **shorter** and the **spread** of the lines is **smaller**.

Electron diffraction patterns look like this.

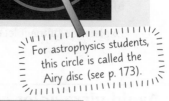

For astrophysics students, this circle is called the Airy disc (see p. 173).

In general, λ for **electrons** accelerated in a **vacuum tube** is about the **same** size as λ for **electromagnetic waves** in the **X-ray** part of the spectrum.

6) The de Broglie wavelength of an electron (λ) is related to the **accelerating voltage** (V) by:

$$\lambda = \frac{h}{\sqrt{2meV}}$$

where e is the charge on the electron and m is its mass

Wave-Particle Duality

Particles Don't Show Wave-Like Properties All the Time

You **only** get **diffraction** if a particle interacts with an object of about the **same size** as its **de Broglie wavelength**.
A **tennis ball**, for example, with **mass 0.058 kg** and **speed 100 ms⁻¹** has a **de Broglie wavelength** of 10^{-34} m.
That's **10^{19} times smaller** than the **nucleus** of an **atom**! There's nothing that small for it to interact with.

Example: An electron of mass 9.11×10^{-31} kg is fired from an electron gun at 7.00×10^6 ms⁻¹.
What size object will the electron need to interact with in order to diffract?
What anode voltage will emit electrons with this wavelength?

Only crystals with atom layer spacing around this size will diffract this electron.

$p = mv = 6.377 \times 10^{-24}$ kg ms⁻¹ $\lambda = h/p = 6.63 \times 10^{-34} \div 6.377 \times 10^{-24} = 1.039... \times 10^{-10}$ m
So the electron must interact with an object with a size of around **1.04×10^{-10} m (to 3 s.f.)** to diffract.

Calculate the anode voltage needed to emit electrons with this
wavelength using the formula at the bottom of the previous page: $\lambda = \dfrac{h}{\sqrt{2meV}}$ so $V = \dfrac{h^2}{2me\lambda^2} = \mathbf{139\ V}$ **(to 3 s.f.)**

A **shorter wavelength** gives **less diffraction**. This is important in **microscopes**, where diffraction **blurs out details**.
The **tiny** wavelength of electrons means an **electron microscope** can resolve **finer detail** than a **light** microscope.

Electron Microscopes use Electrons Instead of Light

1) A **stream of electrons** is accelerated towards the sample using a **positive electric potential** — an **electron gun**.

2) To **resolve detail** around the size of an **atom**, the **electron wavelength** needs to be similar to the **diameter** of an **atom (0.1 nm)** or smaller. From the equation on the previous page this means an **anode voltage** of **at least 150 V**.

3) The **stream of electrons** from the electron gun is confined into a thin **beam** using a **magnetic lens** (made of electromagnet coils that bend the path of electrons — it's called a lens as it acts like a glass lens does for light).

4) The beam is focused onto the sample and any interactions are transformed into an **image**.
The sort of image you get depends on the **type of microscope** you're using:

A **transmission electron microscope** (**TEM**) works a bit like an old-fashioned **slide** projector, but uses electrons instead of light. A **very thin** specimen is used and the parts of the beam that pass through the specimen are projected onto a **screen** to form an image.	A scanning tunnelling microscope (STM) is a different kind of microscope that uses principles of quantum mechanics. A very fine probe is moved over the surface of the sample and a voltage is applied between the probe and the surface. Electrons "tunnel" from the probe to the surface, resulting in a weak electrical current. The smaller the distance between the probe and the surface, the greater the current. By scanning the probe over the surface and measuring the current, you can produce an image of the surface of the sample.

Warm-Up Questions

Q1 What name is normally given to "particles" of light?
Q2 What observation showed that electrons could behave as waves?
Q3 What is the advantage of an electron microscope over a light microscope?

PRACTICE QUESTIONS

Exam Questions

Use $h = 6.63 \times 10^{-34}$ Js, $e = 1.60 \times 10^{-19}$ C, $m_e = 9.11 \times 10^{-31}$ kg.

Q1   An electron is accelerated from rest through a p.d. of 515 V.
   a)   Calculate:
      i)   the velocity of the electron,   ii)   its de Broglie wavelength.   [4 marks]
   b)   In which region of the electromagnetic spectrum does this fall?   [1 mark]

Q2   a)   Describe how a transmission electron microscope (TEM)
          uses a beam of electrons to produce an image.   [3 marks]
      b)   Show that an anode voltage of at least 150 V is needed for a TEM to resolve detail
          around the size of an atom (0.100 nm).   [3 marks]

Wave-Particle duelity — pistols at dawn...

You're getting into the weird bits of quantum physics now — light isn't a wave, and it isn't a particle: it's both... at the same time. And if you think that's confusing, just wait till you get onto relativity — not that I want to put you off.

The Speed of Light and Relativity

First — a bit of a history lesson. Then a really good bit about trains.

Michelson and Morley tried to find the Absolute Speed of the Earth

1) During the 19th century, most physicists believed in the idea of **absolute motion**. They thought everything, including light, moved relative to a **fixed background** — something called the **ether**.

2) **Michelson** and **Morley** tried to measure the **absolute speed** of the **Earth** through the ether using a piece of apparatus called an **interferometer**.

3) They expected the motion of the Earth to affect the **speed of light** they measured in **certain directions**. According to Newton, the speed of light measured in a **lab** moving parallel to the light would be ($c + v$) or ($c - v$), where v is the speed of the lab. By measuring the speed of light **parallel** and **perpendicular** to the motion of the Earth, Michelson and Morley hoped to find v, the absolute speed of the Earth.

They used an Interferometer to Measure the Speed of the Earth

The interferometer was basically **two mirrors** and a **partial reflector** (a beam-splitter). When you shine light at a partial reflector, some of the light is **transmitted** and the rest is **reflected**, making **two separate beams**.

The mirrors were at **right angles** to each other, and an **equal distance**, **L**, from the beam-splitter.

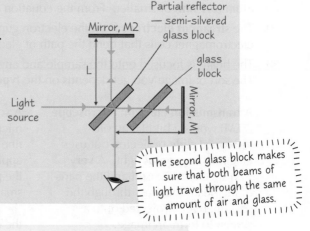

The Michelson-Morley Interferometer

1) **Monochromatic light** is sent towards the **partial reflector**.
2) The light is split into **two beams** travelling at **right angles** to each other.
3) The beams are reflected at **mirrors M1** and **M2**.
4) When the reflected beams meet back at the partial reflector, they form an **interference pattern**.
5) This interference pattern is **recorded** by the observer.
6) Then the whole interferometer is **rotated** through **90°** and the experiment **repeated**.

The second glass block makes sure that both beams of light travel through the same amount of air and glass.

EXPECTED OUTCOME

According to Newton's laws, light moving parallel to the motion of the Earth should take longer to travel to the mirror and back than light travelling at right angles to the Earth's motion. So rotating the apparatus should have changed the travel time for the two beams. This would cause a tiny shift in the interference pattern.

They Didn't get the Result they were Expecting

They **repeated** the experiment **over** and **over** again — at different **times of day** and at different points in the **year**. Taking into account any **experimental errors**, there was **absolutely no shift** in the interference pattern.

The time taken by each beam to travel to each mirror was **unaffected** by rotating the apparatus.

So, Newton's laws **didn't work** in this situation.

Most scientists were really puzzled by this "null result". Eventually, the following **conclusions** were drawn:

a) It's **impossible** to detect **absolute motion** — the ether doesn't exist.

b) The **speed of light** has the **same value** for all observers.

The Speed of Light and Relativity

Anything Moving with a **Constant Velocity** is in an **Inertial Frame**

The **invariance** of the speed of light (see previous page) is one of the cornerstones of special relativity.

The other is based on the concept of an **inertial frame of reference**. A reference frame is just a **space** that we decide to use to describe the **position of an object** — you can think of a reference frame as a **set of coordinates**.

> An **inertial reference frame** is one in which **Newton's 1st law** is obeyed. (Newton's 1st law says that objects won't accelerate unless they're acted on by an external force.)

1) Imagine sitting in a carriage of a train **waiting at a station**. You put a **marble** on the table. The marble **doesn't move**, since there aren't any horizontal **forces** acting on it. **Newton's 1st law** applies, so it's an **inertial frame**.

2) You'll get the **same result** if the carriage moves at a **steady speed** (as long as the track is **smooth, straight and level**) — another inertial frame.

3) As the train **accelerates** out of the station, the marble **moves** without any force being applied. Newton's 1st law **doesn't apply**. The accelerating carriage **isn't an inertial frame**.

4) **Rotating** or **accelerating** reference frames **aren't** inertial. In most cases, though, you can think of the **Earth** as an inertial frame — it's near enough.

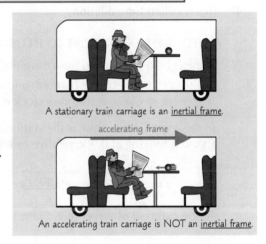

A stationary train carriage is an <u>inertial frame</u>.

An accelerating train carriage is NOT an <u>inertial frame</u>.

Einstein's **Postulates** of **Special Relativity**

Einstein's theory of **special relativity** only works in **inertial frames** and is based on **two postulates** (assumptions):

> 1) **Physical laws have the same form in all inertial frames.**
>
> 2) **The speed of light in free space is invariant.**

1) The first postulate says that if we do **any physics experiment** in any inertial frame we'll always get the **same result**. That means it's **impossible** to use the result of **any experiment** to work out if you're in a **stationary reference frame** or one moving at a **constant velocity**.

2) The second postulate says that the **speed of light** (in a vacuum) always has the **same value**. It isn't affected by the **movement** of the **person measuring it** or by the movement of the **light source**.

Warm-Up Questions

Q1 Draw a labelled diagram showing the apparatus used by Michelson and Morley to determine the absolute speed of the Earth. Include the light source, mirrors, partial reflector, glass block and the position of the observer.

Q2 State the postulates of Einstein's theory of special relativity.

Q3 Explain why a carriage on a rotating Ferris wheel is not an inertial frame.

Exam Questions

Q1 In the Michelson-Morley interferometer experiment, interference fringes were observed. When the apparatus was rotated through 90 degrees the expected result was not observed.
a) State the result that was expected. [1 mark]
b) Describe the conclusions that were eventually drawn from these observations. [2 marks]

Q2 a) Using a suitable example, explain what is meant by an inertial reference frame. [2 marks]
b) Explain what is meant by the invariance of the speed of light. [2 marks]

The speed of light is always the same — whatever your reference frame...

Michelson and Morley showed that Newton's laws didn't always work. This was a huge deal. Newton's laws of motion had been treated like gospel by the physics community since the 17th century. Then along came Herr Einstein...

Special Relativity

Special relativity ONLY WORKS IN INERTIAL FRAMES — it doesn't work in an accelerating frame.

A **Moving Clock** Runs **Slow**

1) Time runs at **different speeds** for two observers **moving relative** to each other.

2) A **stationary** observer measures the interval between two events as t_0, the **proper time**.

3) An observer moving at a **constant velocity**, v, will measure a **longer** interval, t, between the two events. t is given by the equation:
   The bottom part of this equation is called the **Lorentz factor**.

$$t = \frac{t_0}{\sqrt{1 - \frac{v^2}{c^2}}}$$

4) This is called **time dilation**.

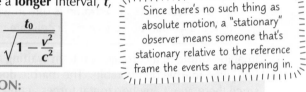
Since there's no such thing as absolute motion, a "stationary" observer means someone that's stationary relative to the reference frame the events are happening in.

A THOUGHT EXPERIMENT TO ILLUSTRATE TIME DILATION:

Anne is on a high-speed train travelling at 0.90c. She switches on a torch for exactly 2 seconds.

Claire is standing on the platform and sees the same event, but records a longer time.
It appears to Claire that Anne's clock is running slow.

In this experiment, **Anne** is the **stationary observer**, so she measures the **proper time**, t_0.
Claire is **moving** at 0.90c **relative** to the events, and so measures a time t given by:

$$t = \frac{t_0}{\sqrt{1 - \frac{v^2}{c^2}}} = \frac{2}{\sqrt{1 - \frac{(0.90c)^2}{c^2}}} = \frac{2}{\sqrt{1 - 0.90^2}} = 4.5883... = \textbf{4.6 s (to 2 s.f.)}$$

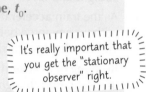
It's really important that you get the "stationary observer" right.

To the **external observer** (e.g. Claire) **moving clocks** run **slowly**.

There's **Proof** of **Time Dilation** from **Muon Decay**

1) **Muons** are **particles** created in the **upper atmosphere** that move towards the ground at speeds close to **c**.

2) In the laboratory (**at rest**) they have a **half-life** of less than **2 μs**. From this half-life, you would expect most muons to **decay** between the top of the atmosphere and the Earth's surface, but that **doesn't happen**.

Experiment to Measure Muon Decay

1) Measure the **speed**, v, of the muons (this is about 0.99c).

2) Place a **detector** (MR1) at **high altitude** and measure the muon count rate.

3) Use another detector (MR2) to measure the count rate at **ground level**.

4) **Compare** the two figures.

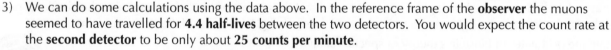
muons moving with velocity, v
MR1
d
MR2

Here are some typical results:
MR1 = 500 per minute   MR2 = 325 per minute   Distance between detectors (d) = 2000 m
Time as measured by an observer = d/v = 6.73 μs   Half-life of muons at rest = 1.53 μs

3) We can do some calculations using the data above. In the reference frame of the **observer** the muons seemed to have travelled for **4.4 half-lives** between the two detectors. You would expect the count rate at the **second detector** to be only about **25 counts per minute**.

4) However, in a **muon's reference frame**, travelling at 0.99c, the time taken for the journey is just $t_0 = 0.95$ μs. From the point of view of the muons, the time elapsed is **less** than their **half-life**. But from the point of view of the **observer**, it appears that the half-life of the muons has been **extended**.

A **Moving Rod** Looks **Shorter**

1) A **rod** moving in the **same direction** as its **length** looks **shorter** to an external observer.

2) A **stationary** observer measures the length of an object as l_0. An observer moving at a **constant velocity**, v, will measure a **shorter** length, l. l is given by the equation: This is called **length contraction**.

$$l = l_0 \sqrt{1 - \frac{v^2}{c^2}}$$

A LENGTH CONTRACTION THOUGHT EXPERIMENT:

Anne (still in the train moving at 0.90c) measures the length of her carriage as 25 m.
Claire, on the platform, measures the length of the carriage as it moves past her.

Length measured by Claire, $l = l_0 \sqrt{1 - \frac{v^2}{c^2}} = 25\sqrt{1 - \frac{(0.90c)^2}{c^2}} = 25\sqrt{1 - 0.90^2} = 10.897... = \textbf{11 m (2 s.f.)}$

Special Relativity

The **Mass** and **Energy** of an Object **Increase** with **Speed**

1) The **faster** an object **moves**, the **more massive** it gets.

2) An object with rest mass m_0 moving at a **velocity** v has a **relativistic mass** m given by the equation:

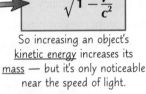

$$m = \frac{m_0}{\sqrt{1 - \frac{v^2}{c^2}}}$$

3) As the relative speed of an object approaches c, the mass approaches **infinity**. So, in practice, no massive object can accelerate to a speed **greater than** or **equal to** the speed of light.

So increasing an object's <u>kinetic energy</u> increases its <u>mass</u> — but it's only noticeable near the speed of light.

4) Einstein extended his idea of **relativistic mass** to write down the most famous equation in physics: ➡ $E = mc^2$
This means that **mass** and **energy** are **equivalent**.

5) This equation says that **mass** can be **converted** into **energy** and vice versa. Or, alternatively, **any energy** you supply to an object **increases** its **mass** — it's just that the increase is usually **too small** to measure.

6) The **total energy** of a relativistic object is given by this equation:

$$E = \frac{m_0 c^2}{\sqrt{1 - \frac{v^2}{c^2}}}$$

Equating this with $E = mc^2$ and cancelling the c^2's gives the formula for relativistic mass.

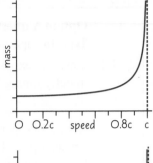

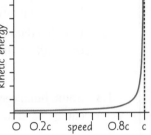

Bertozzi Demonstrated that Mass **Increases** with Speed

1) In the 1960s **Bertozzi** used **linear particle accelerators** to accelerate pulses of electrons to a range of energies from 0.5 MeV to 15 MeV. The particles were **smashed** into an **aluminium disc** a set distance away.

2) The **time** taken by electrons of each energy to reach the aluminium disc was measured so that their speeds could be calculated. As the energy of the electrons was **increased**, the **speed** of the electron's didn't increase as you would expect from $E = \frac{1}{2}mv^2$, but instead tailed off towards a **maximum value** approaching 3×10^8 ms^{-1} (c). This showed that as the **energy** increased, the **mass increased** (as the velocity didn't increase past c).

3) Bertozzi used the **heat** generated by these collisions at each energy to calculate the **kinetic energy** of the particles immediately before impact.

Bertozzi found that plotting a graph of kinetic energy against **speed** gave a **curve** that **closely matched** that predicted by **Einstein's formula**. This was the **first direct evidence** for special relativity.

Warm-Up Questions

Q1 State the equations for time dilation and length contraction, carefully defining each symbol.

Q2 Using the results from the muon experiment (page 254), show that the time elapsed in the reference frame of the muon is 0.95 µs.

Q3 A particle accelerated to near the speed of light gains a very large quantity of energy. Sketch a graph and describe how the mass and the energy of the particle change as its speed increases.

Q4 Describe an experiment that provides evidence that mass increases with speed.

PRACTICE QUESTIONS

Exam Questions

Q1 A subatomic particle has a half-life of 20.0 ns when at rest. If a beam of these particles is moving at $0.995c$ relative to an observer, calculate the half-life of these particles in the frame of reference of the observer. [3 marks]

Q2 Describe a thought experiment to illustrate time dilation. [4 marks]

Q3 For a proton ($m_0 = 1.67 \times 10^{-27}$ kg) travelling at 2.80×10^8 ms^{-1} calculate:
   a) the relativistic mass, [2 marks]
   b) the total energy. [1 mark]

Have you ever noticed how time dilates when you're revising physics...

In a moving frame, time stretches out, lengths get shorter and masses get bigger. One of the trickiest bits is remembering which observer's which — t_0, m_0 and l_0 are the values you'd measure if the object was at rest.

Extra Exam Practice

Time to test your knowledge of <u>Section 13</u>. Fortunately for you, these are the optional modules, so you will only need to answer the question for the option you're studying. Happy days.

1   **Option A question:** Astronomers have classified supernovae into different types. Type 1a supernovae happen in binary star systems.

    1.1   State and explain **two** properties of type 1a supernovae that make them useful in determining how far away distant galaxies are from Earth.

                                                (2 marks)

     A type 1a supernova has an absolute magnitude of -19.0 and an apparent magnitude of $+15.0$. An absorption line in the observed spectra of light from the supernova has a wavelength of 645.6 nm. When the equivalent absorption line is measured in a laboratory, it has a wavelength of 636.0 nm.

    1.2   Use this data to estimate the age of the universe in seconds.
          $(c = 3.00 \times 10^8 \text{ ms}^{-1}, 1 \text{ parsec} = 3.08 \times 10^{16} \text{ m})$

                                                (3 marks)

    1.3   Some binary systems can be identified using a telescope. Explain how this and **one** other method can be used to determine whether a system is binary, and discuss the limitations of each method.

                                                (6 marks)

2   **Option B question:** A pulmonary embolism is a blood clot in the blood vessels of the lungs. Different procedures can be used to diagnose it.

     In one procedure, an iodine-based contrast medium is injected into the patient's blood. This enables an X-ray image of the blood flow in the lungs to be produced. **Figure 1** shows the relationship between the mass attenuation coefficient, μ_m, and the potential difference supplied to the X-ray tube for iodine and lung tissue.

Figure 1

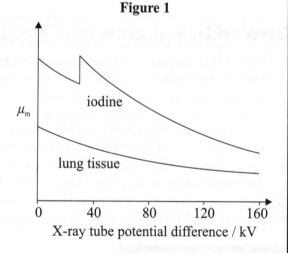

    2.1   Suggest and explain the X-ray tube potential difference that would produce the best image of blood flow in the lungs.

                            (3 marks)

     A V/Q scan can also be used to help diagnose a pulmonary embolism. The procedure involves using two medical tracers to compare the air and blood flow in the lungs. The patient is first asked to breathe in a gas containing xenon-133 (Xe-133). Less than 15% of the gas is absorbed into the body. Technetium-99m (Tc-99m) is then injected into their bloodstream. Their physical and effective half-lives in this procedure are shown in **Table 1**.

Table 1

Half-life	Xe-133	Tc-99m
Physical	5.2 days	6.0 hours
Effective	30 s	4.8 hours

    2.2   Use the data in **Table 1** to compare the biological half-life of Xe-133 and Tc-99m. Suggest a reason for this difference.

                                                (2 marks)

     The lungs are made up of thousands of tubes filled with air and millions of tiny air sacs. Each air sac is surrounded by tissue that contains blood vessels supplying the air sacs with blood. The acoustic impedance of air is 400 kg ms^{-2}. The acoustic impedance of lung tissue is $1.8 \times 10^5 \text{ kg ms}^{-2}$.

    2.3   Suggest why the structure of the lungs may make it difficult to image the lungs using an ultrasound scan. Justify your answer with a calculation.

                                                (2 marks)

Extra Exam Practice

3   **Option C question:** Four-stroke petrol engines are internal combustion engines that are frequently used in vehicles. A petrol engine has four cylinders. Each cylinder has a compression ratio of $8:1$. The compression ratio is the ratio of maximum to minimum volume of the compression chamber in the cylinder ($V_{max}:V_{min}$) during the compression stroke.

3.1   The gas in the cylinder of a four-stroke petrol engine can be assumed to undergo adiabatic compression during the compression stroke of its cycle. Calculate the adiabatic constant of the gas in the cylinder, γ, if the gas pressure in the cylinder goes from 1.0×10^5 Pa to 1.8×10^6 Pa in one compression stroke.

(2 marks)

The crankshaft in a car transforms the linear motion produced by the pistons in the cylinders to rotational motion. It spins at a rate of 2400 revolutions per minute (rpm).

3.2   The crankshaft has an angular momentum of $13.07 \ \text{kg} \, \text{m}^2 \text{s}^{-1}$.
Determine the rotational kinetic energy of the crankshaft.

(2 marks)

3.3   The torque exerted on the crankshaft by the engine is 340 Nm. The friction power of the engine is 21 400 W. Determine the mechanical efficiency of the engine.

(3 marks)

3.4   Explain how the indicated power and thermal efficiency of the engine would change if:

- The engine contained 6 cylinders instead of 4 cylinders.
- The compression chamber had the same volume at the start of each compression stroke, but the compression ratio of the cylinders was $10:1$ instead of $8:1$.

Assume all other factors of the engine remain unchanged.

(6 marks)

4   **Option D question:** An electron has a charge of -1.60×10^{-19} C and a specific charge of $1.76 \times 10^{11} \ \text{C} \text{kg}^{-1}$. A muon has the same charge as an electron but a different specific charge.

4.1   In an experiment, a horizontal beam of low-speed muons travels through a vacuum between two charged parallel plates. **Figure 2** is a side-on view of the setup, and shows that the beam is not deflected when the distance between plates is 2.50 mm and the potential difference between them is 28.8 pV. Calculate the magnitude of the specific charge of a muon. ($g = 9.81 \ \text{ms}^{-2}$)

(2 marks)

Figure 2

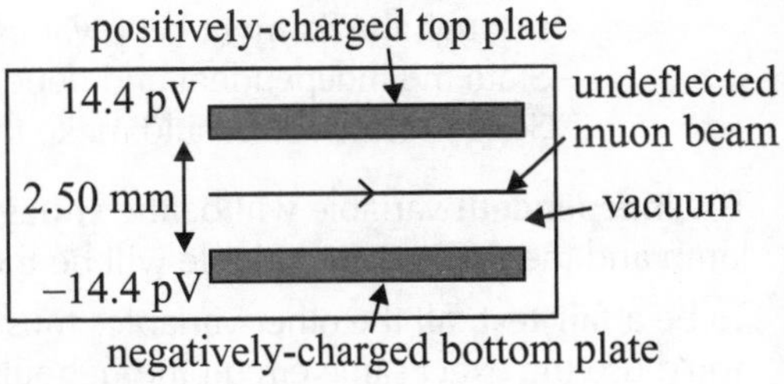

positively-charged top plate

14.4 pV

2.50 mm

−14.4 pV

undeflected muon beam

vacuum

negatively-charged bottom plate

4.2   An electron microscope could theoretically be modified to use muons instead of electrons. Explain why the anode voltage of a muon microscope could be reduced compared to an otherwise similar electron microscope with the same image resolution. Relativistic effects can be ignored.

(3 marks)

In a second experiment, muons are accelerated through a potential difference of 15.0 MV in a vacuum, as shown in **Figure 3**. They accelerate from rest to relativistic speeds.

Figure 3

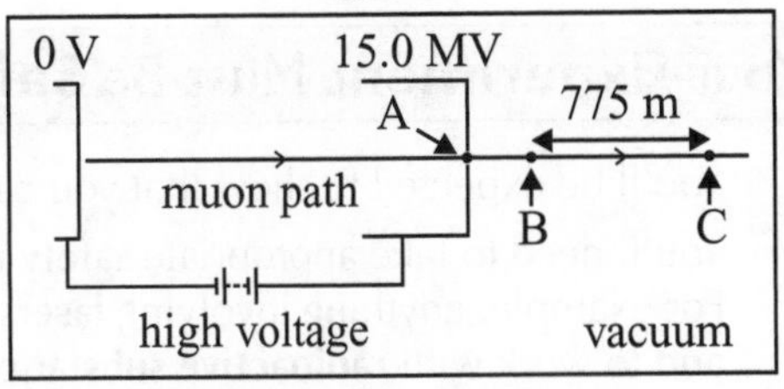

0 V   15.0 MV

A   775 m

muon path

B   C

high voltage   vacuum

4.3   Calculate the total energy of an accelerated muon at point A. (muon rest energy = 105.659 MeV)

(3 marks)

4.4   The muons move at a constant speed of $1.44 \times 10^8 \ \text{ms}^{-1}$ between points B and C. A mean of 768 muons per minute are detected at point B. Muons decaying at rest have a half-life of 1.56 μs. Estimate the mean muon count rate that would be measured at point C. ($c = 3.00 \times 10^8 \ \text{ms}^{-1}$)

(3 marks)

Experiment Design

Science is all about getting good evidence to test your theories... so you need to be able to spot a badly designed experiment or study a mile off, and be able to interpret the results of an experiment or study properly. Here's a quick reference section to show you how to go about designing experiments and doing data-style questions.

Planning **Experiments** to Solve **Problems**

Scientists solve problems by **asking** questions, **suggesting** answers and then **testing** them to see if they're correct. Planning an experiment is an important part of this process to help get accurate and precise results (see p.263).

1) Make a **prediction** — a **specific testable statement** about what will happen in the experiment, based on observation, experience or a **hypothesis** (a **suggested explanation** for a fact or observation).

2) Think about the aims of the experiment and identify the **independent**, **dependent** and other **variables**.

3) Make a **risk assessment** and plan any safety precautions.

4) Select **appropriate equipment** that will give you accurate and precise results.

5) Decide what **data** to collect and how you'll do it.

6) Write out a **clear** and **detailed method** — it should be clear enough that **anyone** could follow it and exactly repeat your experiment.

7) Carry out **tests** — to provide **evidence** that will support the prediction or refute it.

Make Sure Your Experiment is a **Fair Test**

It's important to **control** the **variables** (any quantity that can change) in an experiment. Keeping all variables **constant** apart from the independent and dependent variables, means that the experiment is a **fair test**. This means you can be more confident that any effects you see are **caused** by changing the independent variable. The variables that are kept constant (or at least monitored) in an experiment are called **control variables**.

Independent variable
The thing that you change in an experiment.

Dependent variable
The thing that you measure in an experiment.

Example: The circuit on the right is used to investigate how the current through the filament lamp varies with the voltage across it. State the independent and dependent variables in this experiment. Suggest how you would make this experiment a fair test.

The **independent** variable will be the **voltage** across the lamp and the **dependent** variable will be the **current**.

To be a **fair test**, all the other variables must be kept the **same**. You'd use the exact same circuit throughout the experiment to make sure the length of the leads, the filament bulb and the resistance of the rest of the circuit all remained the same.

You might also use small voltages (and currents) to stop the circuit wires heating up during the experiment.

Power supply.
V_s
Potentiometer (p.95) to vary the supplied voltage
Ⓐ Ammeter
Filament lamp
Voltmeter

Your **Experiment** Must Be **Safe** and **Ethical**

1) You'll be expected to show that you can identify any **risks** and **hazards** in an experiment.

2) You'll need to take appropriate **safety measures** depending on the experiment. For example, anything involving **lasers** will usually need special laser **goggles** and to work with **radioactive substances** you'll probably need to wear **gloves**.

3) You need to make sure you're working **ethically** too — you've got to look after the **welfare** of any people or animals in an experiment to make sure they don't become **ill**, **stressed** or **harmed** in any way.

4) You also need to make sure you're treating the **environment ethically** too, e.g. making sure to not destroy habitats when doing **outdoor** experiments.

Monty was stressed out by the velocity experiment before it even began.

Experiment Design

Nothing is Certain

1) **Every** numerical measurement you take has an **experimental uncertainty**. The smallest uncertainty you can have in a measurement is ± **half** of one division on the measuring instrument used. E.g. using a thermometer with a scale where each division represents 2 °C, a measurement of 30 °C will at **best** be measured to be 30 ± **1 °C**.

2) The ± sign gives you the **range** in which the **true** temperature (the one you'd really like to know) probably lies — 30 ± 0.5 °C tells you the true temperature is very likely to lie in the range of 29.5 to 30.5 °C.

3) To measure a **length** with a ruler, you actually take a measurement at **each end** of the object you're measuring. There's an uncertainty in **each**. E.g. 17.0 cm measured with a mm ruler has an uncertainty of 0.05 + 0.05 = **0.1 cm**.

4) There are **two types** of **error** that cause experimental uncertainty:

Random errors

1) Random errors cause readings to be **spread** about the true value due to the results varying in an **unpredictable** way. They affect **precision** (p.263).

2) They can just be down to **noise**, or measuring a **random process** such as nuclear radiation emission. No matter how hard you try, you **can't** correct them.

3) You get random error in **any** measurement. If you measured the length of a wire 20 times, the chances are you'd get a **slightly different** value each time, e.g. due to your head being in a slightly different position when reading the scale.

4) It could be that you just can't keep controlled variables **exactly** the same throughout the experiment.

Systematic errors

1) Systematic errors cause each reading to be different to the true value by the **same amount** i.e. they **shift** all of your results. They affect the **accuracy** of your results (p.263).

2) Systematic errors are caused by the **environment**, the **apparatus** you're using, or your experimental method, e.g. using an inaccurate clock.

3) The problem is often that you **don't know** they're there. You've got to spot them first to have any chance of correcting for them.

4) If you **suspect** a systematic error, you should **repeat** the experiment with a different **technique** or **apparatus** and compare the results.

There are Loads of Ways You Can Reduce Uncertainties

1) One of the easiest things you can do is **repeat** each measurement **several times**. The **more repeats** you do, and the more **similar** the results of each repeat are, the more precise the data.

2) By taking the **mean** of repeated measurements, you will reduce the **random error** in the result. You calculate a mean by adding up all of the measurements and dividing by the total number of measurements. The **more** measurements you average over, the **less random error** you're likely to have.

3) The **smaller the uncertainty** in a result or measurement, the **smaller the range** of possible values that result could have and the more **precise** your data can be. E.g. two students each measure a length of wire three times. Student A measures the wire to be 30 cm ± 1 cm each time. Student B measures the wire to be 29 cm ± 0.5 cm each time. The **range** that student A's values could take is **larger** than student B's, so student B's data is more **precise**.

4) You should check your data for any **anomalous** results — any results that are **so different** from the **rest of the data** they cannot be explained as variations caused by random uncertainties. For example, a measurement is ten times smaller than all of your other data values. You should not include anomalous results when you take averages.

5) You can also cut down the **uncertainty** in your measurements by using the most **appropriate** equipment. E.g. a micrometer scale has **smaller intervals** than a millimetre ruler — so by measuring a wire's diameter with a micrometer instead of the ruler, you instantly cut down the **random error** in your experiment.

6) **Computers** and **data loggers** can often be used to measure smaller intervals than you can measure by hand and reduce random errors, e.g. timing an object's fall using a light gate rather than a stop watch. You also get rid of any **human error** that might creep in while taking the measurements.

7) There's a limit to how much you can reduce the random uncertainties in your measurements, as all measuring equipment has a **resolution** — the smallest change in what's being measured that can be detected by the equipment.

8) You can **calibrate** your apparatus by measuring a **known value**. If there's a **difference** between the **measured** and **known** value, you can use this to **correct** the inaccuracy of the apparatus, and so reduce your **systematic error**. For example, to calibrate a set of **scales** you could weigh a 10.0 g mass and check that it reads 10.0 g. If these scales measure to the nearest 0.1 g, then you can **only** calibrate to within 0.05 g. Any measurements taken will have an **uncertainty** of ± 0.05 g.

9) **Calibration** can also reduce **zero errors** (caused by the apparatus **failing to read zero** when it should do, e.g. when no current is flowing through an ammeter) which can cause systematic errors.

I'm certain that I need a break...

There's a lot to take in here. Make sure you remember the different kinds of errors and how you can avoid them...

Uncertainty and Errors

Significant figures, uncertainties and error bars are all ways of saying how almost-sure you are about stuff.

Uncertainties Come in Absolute Amounts, Fractions and Percentages

Absolute uncertainty is the uncertainty of a measurement given as certain fixed quantity.

Fractional uncertainty is the uncertainty given as a **fraction** of the measurement taken.

Percentage uncertainty is the uncertainty given as a **percentage** of the measurement.

An uncertainty should also include a **level of confidence** or **probability**, to indicate how **likely** the true value is to lie in the interval. E.g. '5.0 ± 0.4 Ω at a level of confidence of 80%' means you're **80% sure** that the true value is **within** 0.4 Ω of 5.0 Ω. (Don't worry, you **don't need** to calculate the level of confidence.)

> **Example:** The resistance of a filament lamp is given as 5.0 ± 0.4 Ω. Give the absolute, fractional and percentage uncertainties for this measurement.
>
> 1) The **absolute uncertainty** is given in the question — it's **0.4 Ω**.
>
> 2) To calculate **fractional uncertainty**, divide the uncertainty by the measurement and simplify.
>   The fractional uncertainty is $\frac{0.4}{5.0} = \frac{4}{50} = \frac{2}{25}$
>
> 3) To calculate **percentage uncertainty**, divide the uncertainty by the measurement and **multiply** by 100.
>   The percentage uncertainty is $\frac{2}{25} \times 100 = $ **8%**

You can **decrease** the **percentage uncertainty** in your data by taking measurements of **large** quantities. Say you take measurements with a mm ruler, they have an uncertainty of ± 1 mm (see previous page). The **percentage error** in measuring a length of **10 mm** will be **± 10%**, but measuring a length of **20 cm** will give a percentage error of only **± 0.5%**.

The uncertainty on a **mean** of repeated results is equal to **half the range** of the results.
E.g. say the repeated measurement of a current gives the results 0.5 A, 0.3 A, 0.3 A, 0.3 A and 0.4 A.
The range of these results is 0.5 – 0.3 = 0.2 A, so the uncertainty on the mean current would be **± 0.1 A**.

Sometimes You Need to Combine Uncertainties

When you do calculations involving values that have an uncertainty, you have to **combine** the uncertainties to get the **overall** uncertainty for your result.

Adding or Subtracting Data — ADD the Absolute Uncertainties

> **Example:** A wire is stretched from 4.3 ± 0.1 cm to 5.5 ± 0.1 cm. Calculate the extension of the wire.
>
> 1) First subtract the lengths without the uncertainty values: 5.5 – 4.3 = 1.2 cm
>
> 2) Then find the total uncertainty by adding the individual absolute uncertainties: 0.1 + 0.1 = 0.2 cm
>   So, the wire has been stretched **1.2 ± 0.2 cm**.

Multiplying or Dividing Data — ADD the Percentage Uncertainties

> **Example:** A force of 15 ± 3% N is applied to a stationary object which has a mass of 6.0 ± 0.3 kg. Calculate the acceleration of the object and state the percentage uncertainty in this value.
>
> 1) First calculate the acceleration without uncertainty:
> $a = F \div m = 15 \div 6.0 = 2.5$ ms^{-2}
>
> 2) Next, calculate the percentage uncertainty in the mass:
>   % uncertainty in $m = \frac{0.3}{6} \times 100 = 5\%$
>
> 3) Add the percentage uncertainties in the force and mass values to find the total uncertainty in the acceleration:
>   Total uncertainty = 3% + 5% = 8%
>   So, the acceleration = **2.5 ± 8% ms^{-2}**

Raising to a Power — MULTIPLY the Percentage Uncertainty by the Power

> **Example:** The radius of a circle is $r = 40 \pm 2.5\%$ cm. What will the percentage uncertainty be in the area of this circle, i.e. πr^2?

The radius will be raised to the power of **2** to calculate the area.

So, the percentage uncertainty will be 2.5% × 2 = **5%**

Uncertainty and Errors

Error Bars Show the Uncertainty of Individual Points

1) Most of the time, you work out the **uncertainty** in your **final** result using the uncertainty in **each measurement** you make.

2) When you're plotting a **graph**, you show the uncertainty in **each measurement** by using **error bars** to show the **range** the point is likely to lie in.

3) In exams, you might have to **analyse data** from graphs **with** and **without** error bars — so make sure you really understand what error bars are showing.

4) The **error** of **each measurement** when measuring the extension of a material is shown by the **error bars** in the graph to the right.

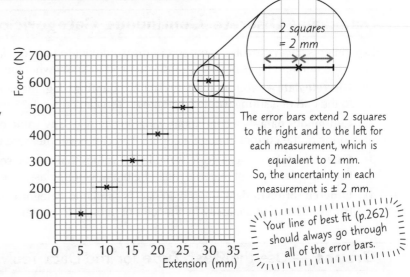

The error bars extend 2 squares to the right and to the left for each measurement, which is equivalent to 2 mm. So, the uncertainty in each measurement is ± 2 mm.

Your line of best fit (p.262) should always go through all of the error bars.

You Can Calculate the Uncertainty of Final Results from a Line of Best Fit

Normally when you draw a graph you'll want to find the **gradient** or **intercept**. For example, you can calculate k, the **spring constant** of the object being stretched, from the **gradient** of the graph on the right — here it's about $20\,000\ Nm^{-1}$. You can find the **uncertainty** in that value by using **worst lines**:

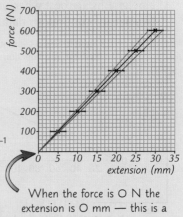

1) Draw lines of best fit which have the **maximum** and **minimum** possible slopes for the data and which should go through all of the **error bars** (see the pink and blue lines on the right). These are the **worst lines** for your data.

2) Calculate the **worst gradient** — the gradient of the slope that is **furthest** from the gradient of the line of best fit. The blue line's gradient is about $21\,000\ Nm^{-1}$ and the pink line's gradient is about $19\,000\ Nm^{-1}$, so you can use either here.

3) The **uncertainty** in the gradient is given by the difference between the **best gradient** (of the line of best fit) and the **worst gradient** — here it's $1000\ Nm^{-1}$. So this is the uncertainty in the value of the spring constant. For this object, the spring constant is $20\,000 \pm 1000\ Nm^{-1}$ (or $20\,000\ Nm^{-1} \pm 5\%$).

When the force is O N the extension is O mm — this is a measurement with no uncertainty.

4) Similarly, the uncertainty in the y-intercept is just the **difference** between the **best** and **worst** intercepts (although there's no uncertainty here since the best and worst lines both go through the origin).

Significant Figures Can Show Uncertainty

1) You always have to assume the **largest** amount of uncertainty in data.

2) Whether you're looking at experimental results or just doing a calculation question in an exam, you must round your results to have the **same number** of significant figures as the given data value with the **least** significant figures. Otherwise you'd be saying there is less uncertainty in your result than in the data used to calculate it.

3) If no uncertainty is given for a value, the number of **significant figures** a value has gives you an estimate of the **uncertainty**. For example, 2 N only has **1 significant figure**, so without any other information you know this value must be $2 \pm 0.5\ N$ — if the value was less than 1.5 N it would have been rounded to 1 N (to 1 s.f.), if it was greater than 2.5 N it would have been rounded to 3 N (to 1 s.f.).

I'd give uncertainties 4 ± 2 for fun...

There's lots of maths to get your head around here, but just keep practising calculating uncertainties and you'll learn the rules in no time. Well... t = 0 ± 4 hours, sorry. Have another read and flip the book over, then scribble down the key points you can remember. Keep doing it until you can remember all the uncertainty joy without having to sneak a look.

Presenting and Evaluating Data

Once you've got results, you have to present them in a sensible way using a graph. Then it's time to evaluate them and use them to form a conclusion that is supported by your results.

Data can be **Discrete, Continuous, Categoric** or **Ordered**

Experiments always involve some sort of measurement to provide data.
There are different types of data — and you need to know what they are.

1) **Discrete data** — you get discrete data by **counting**. E.g. the number of weights added to the end of a spring would be discrete. You can't have 1.25 weights.

2) **Continuous data** — a continuous variable can have **any value** on a scale. For example, the extension of a spring or the current through a circuit. You can never measure the exact value of a continuous variable.

3) **Categoric data** — a categoric variable has values that can be **sorted** into **categories**. For example, types of material might be brass, wood, glass, steel.

4) **Ordered (ordinal) data** — ordered data is similar to **categoric**, but the categories can be put **in order**. For example, if you classify frequencies of light as 'low', 'fairly high' and 'very high' you'd have ordered data.

Graphs — Use the **Best Type** for the Data You've Got

You'll usually be expected to make a **graph** of your results. Not only are graphs **pretty**, they make your data **easier to understand** — so long as you choose the right type. No matter what the type though, make sure you always **label your axes** — including **units**. Choose a **sensible scale** for your axes and **plot points accurately** using a sharp pencil.

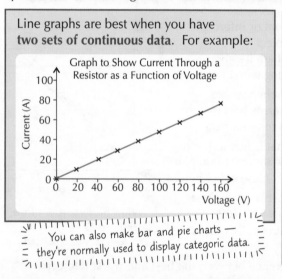

Line graphs are best when you have **two sets of continuous data**. For example:

You can also make bar and pie charts — they're normally used to display categoric data.

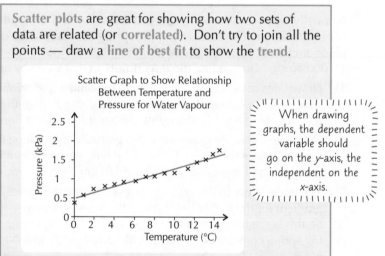

Scatter plots are great for showing how two sets of data are related (or correlated). Don't try to join all the points — draw a line of best fit to show the trend.

When drawing graphs, the dependent variable should go on the y-axis, the independent on the x-axis.

Correlation Shows **Trends** in Data

1) **Correlation** describes the relationship between **two variables** — usually the **independent** and **dependent** ones.

2) Data can show **positive**, **negative** or **no correlation**. An easy way to see correlation is to plot a **scatter graph** of your data. If you can, draw a **line of best fit** to help show the **trend**.

Positive correlation — as one variable increases, the other also increases.

Negative correlation — as one variable increases, the other decreases.

No correlation — there is no relationship between the variables.

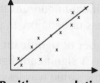
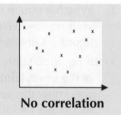

Positive correlation　　**Negative correlation**　　**No correlation**

3) If you've done a **controlled** experiment in a lab and can see **correlation** in your results, you can be fairly certain there's a **causal relationship** between the **independent** and **dependent variables**. This means that a **change** in one **causes** a change in the other.

4) But in experiments or studies **outside** the lab, you can't usually control all the variables. So even if two variables are **correlated**, the change in one may not be causing the change in the other. Both changes might be caused by a **third** variable.

Practical and Investigative Skills

Presenting and Evaluating Data

Evaluating Your Data

Once an experiment's over, you have to **explain** what the data shows.
There are some key words you need to know about (and use) when evaluating data:

Precision is sometimes called reliability.

1) **Precision** — the **smaller** the amount your data spreads from the **mean**, the more precise it is. Precision only depends on the amount of **random error** in your readings.

2) **Repeatable** — **you** can **repeat** an experiment multiple times and get the **same results**.

3) **Reproducible** — if **someone else** can recreate your experiment using different equipment or methods, and gets the **same results** you do, the results are reproducible.

4) **Valid** — the **original question** is **answered** using **precise** data. If you don't keep all variables apart from the one you're testing **constant**, you haven't **only** tested the variable you're investigating and so the results **aren't valid**.

5) **Accurate** — the result is really close to the **true answer**. You can only comment on how accurate a result is if you know the true value of the result.

There's normally loads of stuff to say when you're looking at data. Have a think about...

1) What **patterns** or trends, if any, the results show.

2) Whether the experiment managed to **answer** the question it set out to answer. If it did, is this a **valid** experiment and if not, why not? How **precise** was the data?

3) How close the results are to the **true value**.

4) Did the measuring instruments have enough **resolution**?

5) Any **anomalies** in the results and the possible causes of them.

6) How **large** the **uncertainties** are. If the percentage uncertainty is large, this suggests the data is not precise and a strong conclusion cannot be made.

Nora telling everyone she was 35 was a little inaccurate.

If you're asked to analyse data in the exam, look at how many marks the question is worth — the more **marks** allocated to the question in the exam, the **more detail** you have to go into.

Drawing **Conclusions** From Your **Data**

You need to make sure your conclusion is **specific** to the data you have and is **supported** by the data — don't go making any sweeping generalisations.

Your conclusion is only **valid** if it is supported by **valid data**, known as **evidence**.

Example:

The stress of a material X was measured at strains of 0.002, 0.004, 0.006, 0.008 and 0.010. Each strain reading had an error of 0.001. All other variables were kept constant. A science magazine concluded from a graph of this data that material X's yield point is at a strain of 0.005. Explain whether or not you agree with this conclusion.

Their conclusion **could** be true — but the **data doesn't support this**. You can't tell **exactly** where the yield point is from the data because strain increases of 0.002 at a time were used. The stress at in-between strains wasn't measured — so all you know is that the yield point is somewhere **between** 0.004 and 0.006, as the stress drops between these values.

Also, the graph only gives information about this particular experiment. You can't conclude that the yield point would be in this range for **all experiments** — only this one. And you can't say for sure that doing the experiment at, say, a **different constant temperature** wouldn't give a different yield point.

The error in each reading is 0.001, which gives a **percentage uncertainty** of 50% for the lowest strain reading. This is very large and could mean the results are not valid, so no definite conclusions can be drawn from them.

Stress (Nm⁻²)

0 0.2 0.4 0.6 0.8 1.0

Strain (×10⁻²)

Am I correlated? Well I suppose I'm pretty trendy...

Remember to evaluate the data thoroughly and when you make your conclusions, always back up your points using those evaluations. Use the checklist above to give you an idea of what to say. Suggest ways in which the experiment could be improved — there's some overlap here with how to improve uncertainties, so practising this is extra useful.

Exam Structure and Technique

Good exam technique can make a big difference to your mark, so make sure you read this stuff carefully.

Get Familiar With the **Exam Structure**

For A-level Physics, you'll be sitting **three papers**.
Each paper will be **2 hours** long.

> You'll also do a Practical Endorsement as part of your A-level. It'll involve doing practicals throughout the course, and will be reported separately from your exam results.

Paper 1   **34%** of your A-level
85 marks: **60** for **Section A**
       (**short and long answer** questions)
       25 for **Section B**
       (**multiple choice** questions)
	Covers **sections 1 to 7** of this book.

Paper 2   **34%** of your A-level
85 marks: **60** for **Section A**
       (**short and long answer** questions)
       25 for **Section B**
       (**multiple choice** questions)
	The questions will be on **sections 8 to 12** of this book, but the examiners will assume you know the content of **sections 1 to 7** too.

Paper 3   **32%** of your A-level
80 marks: **45** for **Section A**
       (all **short and long answer** questions).
       35 for **Section B**
       (all **short and long answer** questions).
	Section A is on **practical skills and data analysis** (pages 258-263), but the questions could be based on **any** of the content in sections 1 to 12.
	
	Section B will be on the optional topic you've chosen to study. Options A-D are covered in sections 13 A-D of this book. Option E (electronics) is not covered in this book.

Find out your **exam timetable** and **plan** your revision carefully.
And remember, the Paper 1 material could come up in Paper 2, and
anything from either of the first two papers could crop up in Paper 3.

> If you're taking AS Physics, you'll do different exams altogether, so this information isn't relevant to you.

Make Sure You **Read the Question**

1) It sounds obvious, but it's really important you read each question **carefully**, and give an answer that fits.

2) Look for **command words** in the question — they'll give you an idea of the **kind of answer** you should write. Commonly used command words for written questions are **state**, **describe**, **discuss** and **explain**:

- If a question asks you to **state** something you just need to give a **definition**, **example** or **fact**.
- If you're asked to **describe** what happens in a particular situation, don't waste time explaining why it happens — that's not what the question is after.
- For **discuss** questions, you'll need to include more **detail** — depending on the question you could need to cover what happens, what the effects are, and perhaps include a brief explanation of why it happens.
- If a question asks you to **explain** why something happens, you must give **reasons**, not just a description.

3) Look at **how many marks** a question is worth before you answer it.
It'll tell you roughly **how much information** you need to include.

Watch out for **Practical Questions**

1) Section A of Paper 3 is based on practical skills. You may have to describe an experiment to investigate something, or answer questions on an experiment you've been given.

2) These could be experiments you've met before, or they could be entirely new to you. All the questions will be based on physics that you've covered, but may include bits from different topics put together in ways you haven't seen before. Don't let this put you off, just think carefully about what's going on.

3) Make sure you know the difference between precision, accuracy and validity (page 263). Learn what uncertainty, random errors and systematic errors are (page 259) and make sure you can give some examples of where each might come from.

4) You need to be able to calculate errors and plot and interpret graphs too — anything on pages 260-261 could come up.

Exam Structure and Technique

Be Careful With Calculations

At least **40%** of the marks up for grabs in A-level physics will require maths skills, so make sure you know your stuff.

1) In calculation questions you should always **show your working** — you may get some marks for your **method** even if you get the answer wrong.

2) Don't **round** your answer until the **very end**. A lot of calculations in A-level physics are quite **long**, and if you round too early you could introduce errors to your final answer.

3) Be careful with **units**. Lots of formulas require quantities to be in specific units (e.g. time in seconds), so its best to **convert** any numbers you're given into these before you start. And obviously, if the question **tells** you which units to give your **answer** in, don't throw away marks by giving it in different ones.

4) You should give your final answer to the same number of **significant figures** as the data that you use from the question with the **least number** of significant figures. If you can, write out the **unrounded answer**, then your **rounded** answer with the number of significant figures you've given it to — it shows you know your stuff.

Manage Your Time Sensibly

1) The **number of marks** tells you roughly **how long** to spend on a question. You've got just over a minute per mark, so if you get stuck on a question for too long, it may be best to **move on**.

2) The **multiple choice questions** are only worth **one mark each**, so it's not worth stressing over one for ages if you get stuck — **move on** and come back to it later.

3) You don't have to work through the paper **in order** — you could do all the multiple choice questions first, or leave questions on topics you find harder until the end.

Giles didn't like to brag, but his time-management skills were excellent.

Don't be Put Off if a Question Seems Strange

1) You may get some weird questions that seem to have nothing to do with anything you've learnt. **DON'T PANIC**. Every question will be something you can answer **using physics you know**, it just may be in a new **context**.

2) Check the question for any **keywords** that you recognise. For example, if a question talks about acceleration, think about the rules and equations you know, and whether any of them apply to the situation in the question.

3) Sometimes you might have to **pull together** ideas from different parts of physics, like this:

Example: A windmill is being used to turn a generator. The generator contains of a coil of wire of 32 turns, each with an area of 0.22 m², held in a uniform 1.5 ×10⁻³ T magnetic field. The arms of the windmill are 0.50 m long. A point on the end of one of the arms of the windmill is found to be travelling at 3.4 ms⁻¹. Calculate the maximum e.m.f. induced in the coil.

This question looks ghastly, but there are only two bits of theory you need to use — **electromagnetic induction** and **circular motion** (the windmill).

From page 147, you know that the e.m.f induced in a coil of wire turning in a uniform magnetic field at a given time is given by: $\varepsilon = BAN\,\omega \sin \omega t$.

The question tells you $B = 1.5 \times 10^{-3}$ T, $A = 0.22$ m², and $N = 32$ turns. You want the **maximum e.m.f.**, which will happen when $\sin \omega t = 1$, so the only variable you don't know is ω, the **angular velocity**.

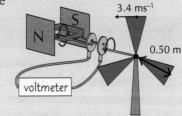

$$\varepsilon = BAN\,\omega \sin \omega t = 1.5 \times 10^{-3} \times 0.22 \times 32 \times \omega \times 1$$

You've been given the **velocity** of a point at the end of the windmill's arms (3.4 ms⁻¹), and the **length** of the arm (0.50 m), so you can find out the **angular velocity** of the windmill (and hence the coil) using the equation from page 98: $\omega = \frac{v}{r}$.

$$\omega = \frac{3.4}{0.50} = 6.8 \text{ rad s}^{-1} \qquad \text{so: } \varepsilon = 1.5 \times 10^{-3} \times 0.22 \times 32 \times 6.8 \times 1 = 0.071808 = \textbf{0.072 V (to 2 s.f.)}$$

Just follow the scouts' motto — if in doubt, tie a knot...

Making sure you're prepared for what the exams will be like. Reading questions carefully and managing your time all sounds like pretty basic advice, but you'd be surprised how many people don't follow it. Make sure you do...

Working with Exponentials and Logarithms

As well as being given some tricky calculations, you could be asked to work with exponentials and logarithms and work out values from log graphs. And it's easy when you know how...

Many Relationships in Physics are **Exponential**

A fair few of the relationships you need to know about in A-level Physics are **exponential** — where the **rate of change** of a quantity is **proportional** to the **amount** of the quantity left. Here are a couple that crop up in the A-level course (if they don't ring a bell, go have a quick read about them)...

Charge on a capacitor — the decay of charge on a discharging capacitor is proportional to the amount of charge left on the capacitor:

$$Q = Q_0 e^{\frac{-t}{RC}}$$ (see p.136)

There are also exponential relationships for I and V and for charging capacitors.

Radioactive decay — the rate of decay of a radioactive sample is proportional to the **number of undecayed nuclei** in the sample:

$$N = N_0 e^{-\lambda t}$$ (see p.163)

The activity of a radioactive sample behaves in the same way.

You can **Model Exponential Relationships** using a **Spreadsheet**

You've seen that for exponential relationships, the **rate of change** of a quantity is proportional to the amount of that quantity left. Rates of change like this can be modelled using an **iterative spreadsheet** that works out the amount of the quantity left over regular time intervals (or intervals of another variable). Models like this make it easier to plot graphs of exponential relationships.

For example, radioactive decay can be described using the formula $\frac{\Delta N}{\Delta t} = -\lambda N$ (see page 162).

If you know the **decay constant**, λ, and the **number of undecayed nuclei** in the initial sample, N_0, you can model ΔN over small intervals of Δt:

1) Set up a spreadsheet with column headings for **total time** (t), ΔN and N, and a data input cell for each of Δt and λ.

   A data input cell is separate from the table and is used to refer to a fixed value that's used throughout your calculations, e.g. decay constant.

λ in s^{-1}	1×10^{-4}
Δt in s	1000

t / s	ΔN	N
$t_0 = 0$		N_0
$t_1 = t_0 + \Delta t$	$(\Delta N)_1 = -\lambda \times N_0 \times \Delta t$	$N_1 = N_0 + (\Delta N)_1$
$t_2 = t_1 + \Delta t$	$(\Delta N)_2 = -\lambda \times N_1 \times \Delta t$	$N_2 = N_1 + (\Delta N)_2$
$t_3 = ...$	$(\Delta N)_3 = ...$	$N_3 = ...$

2) Decide on a Δt that you want to use — this is the **time interval** between the values of N to be calculated.

3) Enter formulas to calculate the number of undecayed nuclei left in the sample after each time interval, as shown. You'll need to use $\Delta N = -\lambda \times N \times \Delta t$ (rearranged from the equation above).

   If you write the formulas properly, the spreadsheet can automatically fill in as many rows as you want, but make sure that the references to the data input cells stay fixed as you do.

4) Plot a graph of the number of undecayed nuclei against time. It should look like this: ⟹ (You may have to fiddle with your value for Δt to get a graph with a nice shape.) This is an **exponential graph** — it's a graph of the equation $N = N_0 e^{-\lambda t}$ above.

You can **Plot** Exponential Relations Using the **Natural Log, ln**

1) Say you've got two variables, x and y, which are related by $y = ke^{-ax}$ (where k and a are constants).

2) The **natural logarithm** of x, **ln** x, is the power to which e (the base) must be raised to to give x.

   A logarithm can be to any base you want. Another common one is 'base 10' which is usually written as '$\log_{10}$' or just '$\log$'.

3) So, by definition, $e^{\ln x} = x$ and $\ln(e^x) = x$. So far so good... now you need some **log rules**:

   These log rules work for all logs (including the natural logarithm). You won't be given them in the exam — so make sure you learn them.

$$\ln(AB) = \ln A + \ln B \qquad \ln\left(\frac{A}{B}\right) = \ln A - \ln B \qquad \ln x^n = n \ln x$$

4) So, for $y = ke^{-ax}$, if you take the natural log of both sides of the equation you get:

   $$\ln y = \ln(ke^{-ax}) = \ln k + \ln(e^{-ax}) \implies \boxed{\ln y = \ln k - ax}$$

5) This is of the form of an equation of a straight line ($y = mx + c$), so all you need to do is plot ($\ln y$) against x, and Eric's your aunty: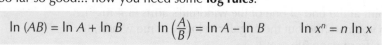

   gradient = $-a$

You get a **straight-line** graph with (**ln** k) as the **vertical intercept**, and $-a$ as the **gradient**.

Working with Exponentials and Logarithms

You Might be Asked to find the **Gradient** of a Log Graph

This log business isn't too bad when you get your head around which bit of the log graph means what.

Example: The graph shows the radioactive decay of isotope X.

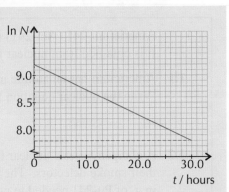

a) Find the initial number of undecayed nuclei, N_0, in the sample.

You know that the number of undecayed nuclei in a sample, N, is related to the initial number of undecayed nuclei, N_0, by the equation $N = N_0 e^{-\lambda t}$.

So: $\ln N = \ln N_0 - \lambda t$

The y-intercept of the graph is $\ln N_0 = 9.2$

$N_0 = e^{9.2} = 9897.129... = 9900$ nuclei (to 2 s.f.)

b) Find the decay constant λ of isotope X.

$-\lambda$ is the gradient of the graph, so:

$$\lambda = \frac{\Delta \ln N}{\Delta t} = \frac{9.2 - 7.8}{30.0 \times 60 \times 60} = 1.296... \times 10^{-5} = 1.3 \times 10^{-5}\,\text{s}^{-1}\,(\text{to 2 s.f.})$$

You can Plot **Any Power Law** as a **Log-Log Graph**

You can use logs to plot a straight-line graph of **any power law** — it doesn't have to be an exponential.

Say the relationship between two variables x and y is:

$$y = kx^n$$

Take the **log** (base 10) of both sides to get:

$$\log y = \log k + n \log x$$

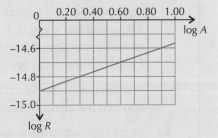

When it came to logs, Geoff always took time to smell the flowers...

So **log k** will be the **y-intercept** and **n** will be the **gradient** of the graph.

Example: A physicist carries out an experiment to determine the nuclear radius R (in m) of various elements, which have nucleon number A. She plots a line of best fit for her results on a graph of $\log R$ against $\log A$. Part of the graph is shown. Using the equation $R = R_0 A^{1/3}$, find the value of the constant R_0 from the graph.

First take logs of both sides:
$\log R = \log (R_0 A^{1/3}) = \log R_0 + \log A^{1/3}$
$\qquad\qquad = \log R_0 + \frac{1}{3} \log A$

Look back at pages 156-157 for more on nuclear radius.

Comparing this to the equation of a straight line (in the form $y = mx + c$), you can see that the gradient of the graph is $\frac{1}{3}$ and the vertical intercept is $\log R_0$.

So, reading from the graph, the vertical intercept is about -14.9.

$\log R_0 = -14.9$, so $R_0 = 10^{-14.9} = 1.258... \times 10^{-15} = 1.3$ fm (to 2 s.f.)

If $a = \log_{10} b$, then $b = 10^a$.

Lumberjacks are great musicians — they have a natural logarhythm...

Well, that's it folks. Crack open the chocolate bar of victory and know you've earned it. Only the tiny detail of the actual exam to go... ahem. Make sure you know which bit means what on a log graph and you'll pick up some nice easy marks. Other than that, stay calm, be as clear as you can and good luck — I've got my fingers, toes and eyes crossed for you.

Synoptic Practice

It's nearly time to say goodbye to gravitational fields, adios to atomic structures, and ciao to circular motion, but not quite yet... Last, but most definitely not least, it's A level synoptic time. The exams are sneaky and can mix together different sections, but don't worry — I've got you covered with a huge bunch of synoptic questions for you to get stuck into. What's that you say? You're right, I am the best...

---

1   Americium-241 (Am-241) is a radioactive isotope commonly used in smoke detectors.
It is obtained from nuclear fission reactors from the decay of plutonium-241 (Pu-241).

1.1   Americium has an atomic number of 95, and plutonium has an atomic number of 94.
Write the nuclear equation for the decay of plutonium-241 into americium-241.

(2 marks)

1.2   A company uses a nuclear fission reactor to produce the americium-241 needed to manufacture their smoke detectors. The reactor produces 0.638 µg of Am-241 per second. Calculate the mass, in g, of Pu-241 needed to produce Am-241 at this rate. The half-life of Pu-241 is 4.42×10^8 s. ($N_A = 6.02 \times 10^{23}$)

(4 marks)

1.3   A stationary americium-241 nucleus in a smoke detector decays into a neptunium-237 (Np-237) nucleus by emitting an alpha particle. 1.70% of the energy emitted by this decay is transferred to the kinetic energy of the alpha particle. Calculate the speed of the emitted alpha particle.

Binding energy per nucleon of Am-241 = 7.54 MeV, binding energy per nucleon of Np-237 = 7.58 MeV, binding energy per nucleon of He-4 = 7.07 MeV.

($e = 1.60 \times 10^{-19}$ C, mass of alpha particle = 6.64×10^{-27} kg)

(3 marks)

1.4   A smoke detector uses an americium-241 alpha source with an activity of 38 kBq.
The detector becomes blocked so that air is trapped inside the detector. The mass of the air trapped in the detector is 3.4×10^{-3} kg and the specific heat capacity of air is 720 Jkg^{-1}K^{-1}.
Calculate the temperature increase of the air inside the detector after 7.0 days.
Assume that all the energy from the radioactive decay in the smoke detector heats the trapped air and no heat is lost to the surroundings. You can also assume that the activity of the source remains constant, and that the decay products of americium-241 do not decay further within the 7.0 days.

(3 marks)

2   A ball game uses a tennis ball attached to the top of a vertical pole with a piece of string as shown in **Figure 1**. The string has a length l. When the ball is hit, it moves around the pole in a horizontal circle with radius r. l and r are the distances to the centre of mass of the ball.

For this question you may assume that air resistance is negligible, and that the angle, θ, is small. For small angles, $\sin\theta \approx \tan\theta$.

Figure 1

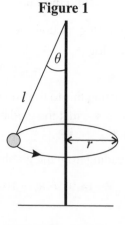

2.1   Show that, when the angle θ is small, the resultant force acting on the ball is equal to $F = \dfrac{mgr}{l}$ where g is the gravitational field strength and m is the mass of the ball.

(3 marks)

2.2   Derive an expression for the time taken for the ball to complete one full circle around the pole, T, in terms of g and l.

(3 marks)

Synoptic Practice

2.3 In one particular game, the length of the string is set to 1.45 m and the ball moves in a circle with a radius of 0.205 m. Whilst the ball is in flight, the string suddenly snaps and the ball moves along the path shown in **Figure 2**.

Figure 2

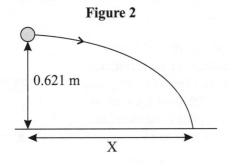

Calculate the distance labelled X. ($g = 9.81 \text{ ms}^{-2}$)

(3 marks)

3 When uranium-235 (U-235) undergoes nuclear fission it can split into a variety of daughter nuclei. The graph in **Figure 3** is obtained by analysing the composition of pure U-235 which has fully fissioned into its daughter nuclei. The percentage of each daughter nuclei present in the sample is measured and plotted against the mass numbers of the daughter nuclei.

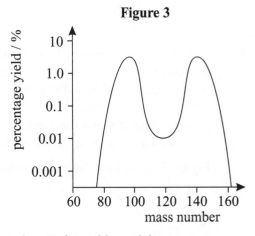

Figure 3

3.1 Explain why the graph in **Figure 3** is symmetrical.

(3 marks)

3.2 Sketch a graph of neutron number, N, against atomic number, Z, for stable nuclei. Use your graph to explain why the daughter nuclei produced by the fission of the U-235 sample are likely to be unstable.

(3 marks)

The fission products of uranium-235 are analysed using a velocity selector, as shown in **Figure 4**. A velocity selector is a device in which an ion is passed through two parallel charged plates within a perpendicular magnetic field. The electric field strength between the plates is E, and the magnetic field strength between the plates is B. The fission products are first vaporised and then heated up until all of the atoms have been ionised. The ions are then passed through the velocity selector, and only ions travelling in a straight line will pass through the slit at the end.

Figure 4

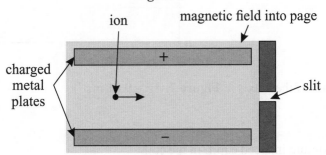

Synoptic Practice

For question parts 3.3 and 3.4, you may ignore any gravitational effects.

3.3 Explain why positive ions will only pass through the slit if they are moving at a velocity of $v = \dfrac{E}{B}$.

(3 marks)

3.4 When the ions pass through the slit at the same velocity, v, they travel between two further metal plates as shown in **Figure 5**. There is no magnetic field between these plates. Detectors are used to locate where the ions hit the plates and therefore the masses of the ions can be measured.

Show that $x \propto m^{1/2}$ where x is the horizontal displacement of an ion as it hits the plate and m is the mass of the ion. Assume all of the ions that pass through the slit have the same charge.

(5 marks)

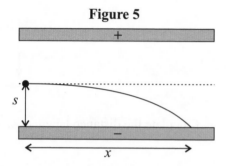

Figure 5

4 A student is investigating the motion of a magnet on a spring. He uses a magnet with a mass of 20.0 g attached to a spring made from a non-magnetic material, as shown in **Figure 6**. When the magnet is attached to the spring, the spring extends by 7.848 mm. The magnet is suspended above a coil. The coil has exactly 300 turns and is connected to a complete circuit. The student pulls the magnet downwards and releases it so that it oscillates vertically above the coil. Air resistance and any magnetic effects from induced e.m.f. can be considered to be negligible.

Figure 7 shows how the magnetic flux through the coil changes with time.

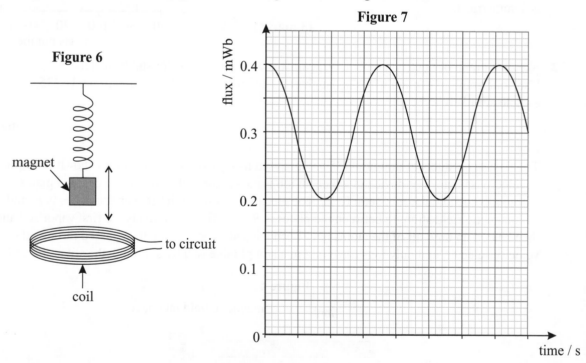

Figure 6

Figure 7

4.1 Determine the scale of the x-axis in **Figure 7**. ($g = 9.81 \text{ ms}^{-2}$)

(3 marks)

4.2 Calculate the maximum induced e.m.f. in the coil.

(2 marks)

Synoptic Practice

4.3 Sketch a graph showing how the induced e.m.f. varies with time. Include a correct scale on each axis. Label the line A.

(3 marks)

4.4 On the same axes as your graph in 4.3, sketch a line to show how the rms induced e.m.f. varies with time. Label this line B.

(2 marks)

4.5 The number of turns on the coil is increased so that any magnetic effects from induced e.m.f. can no longer be treated as negligible. Describe and explain what effect this has on the motion of the magnet as it oscillates.

(3 marks)

5 A graph of how the gravitational field strength below the surface of the Earth varies with the distance from the centre of the Earth is shown in **Figure 8**. It can be assumed that the density of the Earth is constant.

Figure 8

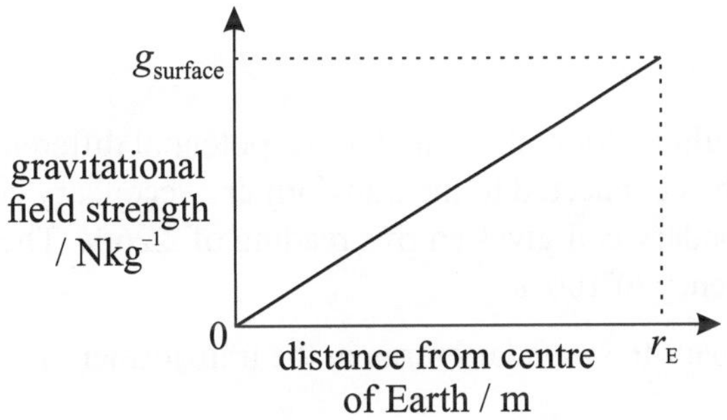

For question 5 you may ignore the effect of air resistance.

5.1 Suggest why the gravitational field strength at the centre of the Earth is 0 Nkg^{-1}.

(1 mark)

5.2 Hypothetically, if a vertical tunnel was to be constructed through the centre of the Earth from the North Pole to the South Pole, calculate the weight of a 1.50 kg object if it was 4.75×10^6 m from the centre of the Earth. ($g_{surface} = 9.81 \text{ ms}^{-2}$, $r_E = 6.37 \times 10^6$ m)

(2 marks)

5.3 Explain why the object would oscillate vertically through the tunnel with simple harmonic motion if it was released from rest in the tunnel at a distance from the Earth's centre.

(1 mark)

5.4 Calculate the time it would take for the object in 5.2 to perform one complete oscillation if released from rest at 4.75×10^6 m from the centre of the Earth.

(2 marks)

5.5 If an object of mass m was placed in the tunnel at the very centre of the Earth, calculate the velocity that the object would need in order to escape Earth's gravitational field from this point. ($G = 6.67 \times 10^{-11} \text{ Nm}^2\text{kg}^{-2}$, $M_E = 5.97 \times 10^{24}$ kg)

(3 marks)

Synoptic Practice

6 **Figure 9** shows a moving coil alternator. A mass is connected to the end slip ring by a piece of string wound around the slip ring. As the mass falls, it rotates the coil. The coil is rotated in a uniform magnetic field of field strength 0.0200 T. The alternator is connected to a transformer.

Figure 9

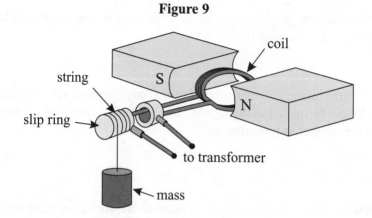

6.1 The mass is assumed to fall at a constant velocity of 0.240 ms⁻¹ and the radius of the slip ring is 1.60 cm. The alternator coil has an area of 15.0 cm² and consists of 415 turns. Calculate the peak e.m.f. induced in the coil.

(2 marks)

The e.m.f. induced in the alternator coil is equal to the potential difference across the transformer's primary coil. A light bulb is connected to the transformer's secondary coil and a voltmeter connected across the secondary coil gives an rms reading of 2.26 V. The whole system can be assumed to have an efficiency of 100%.

6.2 Calculate the ratio of primary to secondary turns in the transformer.

(2 marks)

6.3 The resistance of the light bulb is 1.02 Ω. All other electrical components in the circuit have negligible resistance. Calculate the mass of the falling mass that is operating the alternator. ($g = 9.81$ ms⁻²)

(2 marks)

6.4 When the alternator is disconnected from the transformer, the mass no longer moves at a constant velocity but accelerates uniformly towards the ground. Sketch a graph of how the e.m.f. induced in the alternator's coil varies with time when the transformer is not connected. You do not need to include any calculations.

(2 marks)

7 A plasma ball consists of an inner solid metal sphere and an outer spherical casing made from glass. Gases are contained in the gap between the inner sphere and the outer casing, as shown in **Figure 10**. When the plasma ball is switched on, the inner metal sphere is charged with a high alternating potential difference. Some of the atoms in the gas are ionised synd produce free electrons. The free electrons collide with further atoms in the plasma, which leads to the emission of photons. This causes parts of the gas inside the plasma ball to glow.

Figure 10

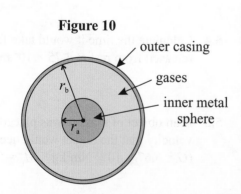

Synoptic Practice

The radius of the inner sphere, r_a, is equal to 3.50 cm and the radius of the outer sphere, r_b, is equal to 12.0 cm. **Table 1** shows information about the composition of the gases within the plasma ball. Both neon and argon exist as single atoms.

Table 1

Element	Percentage abundance	Molecular mass
Neon	99%	20.1797 u
Argon	1%	39.9481 u

When the ball is switched off, the pressure of the gas is 1.01×10^5 Pa and the temperature is 298 K. The gas inside the plasma ball is assumed to be an ideal gas.

7.1 Calculate the mass of argon inside the plasma ball. ($u = 1.661 \times 10^{-27}$ kg, $k = 1.38 \times 10^{-23}$ JK^{-1})

(3 marks)

7.2 When the plasma ball is switched on, the temperature of the gas inside the ball begins to rise. The pressure increases to 1.03×10^5 Pa. Calculate the root mean square speed of the neon gas particles inside the plasma ball at this pressure.

(2 marks)

7.3 Explain why gas in a plasma ball containing both neon and argon glows a different colour to gas in a plasma ball containing just neon.

(3 marks)

An engineer is investigating how the absolute electric potential varies with the distance from the surface of a plasma ball's inner metal sphere. She removes the inner sphere from a plasma ball with unknown dimensions and places it on an insulating stand. She then charges the sphere with a constant potential difference and uses an electric

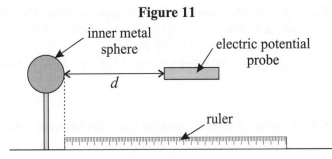

Figure 11

potential probe to measure how the absolute electric potential, V, varies with distance, d, as shown in **Figure 11**. The probe measures the absolute electric potential with a percentage uncertainty of $\pm 5.0\%$. The distance is measured with a ruler with an uncertainty of ± 0.001 m. The engineer uses the following formula to analyse the data:

$$V = \frac{1}{4\pi\varepsilon_0}\frac{Q}{d + A}$$

Where V is the absolute electric potential at a distance d from the surface of the sphere, Q is the charge on the sphere and A is a constant. After collecting results for a range of distances, the engineer plots a graph of d on the y-axis against $\frac{1}{V}$ on the x-axis.

7.4 State what physical quantity is represented by A in the formula above.

(1 mark)

7.5 Explain how the engineer could use her graph in order to calculate the values of Q and A. In your answer you should include an explanation of how the engineer could plot error bars on her graph and use them to calculate the absolute uncertainties in the calculated values of Q and A. You can assume that the engineer knows the value of ε_0 with negligible uncertainty.

(6 marks)

Synoptic Practice

8   Two oppositely charged metal plates are wrapped around each other to form two cylinders, as shown in **Figure 12**.

Figure 12

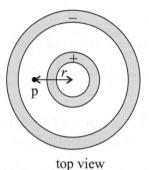

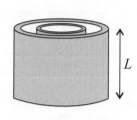

top view   side view

8.1   In the top view in **Figure 12**, draw the electric field lines in the space between the two cylinders. Describe how your diagram shows that the electric field is not uniform between the cylinders.

(2 marks)

The electric field strength at any point, p, between the plates is given by:

$$E = \frac{Q_{cylinder}}{2\pi\varepsilon_0 rL}$$

Where $Q_{cylinder}$ is the charge of the inner cylinder, r is the distance of the point from the centre of the cylinders and L is the length of the cylinders as shown in **Figure 12**.

8.2   An electron is injected into the space between the cylinders so that it moves in a circle with a radius r. The charge of the inner cylinder is 5.66 nC and the length of the cylinder is 25.3 cm. Calculate the speed of the electron.
($\varepsilon_0 = 8.85 \times 10^{-12}$ Fm^{-1}, $m_e = 9.11 \times 10^{-31}$ kg, $e = 1.60 \times 10^{-19}$ C)

(2 marks)

8.3   A proton is injected into the space between the cylinders. Explain whether it is possible for the proton to move in a circle between the two cylinders.

(2 marks)

8.4   The gap between the cylinders is filled with a dielectric material with relative permittivity of 2.25. The cylinders now act like a capacitor with a capacitance:

$$C = \frac{2\pi\varepsilon_0\varepsilon_r}{\ln\left(\frac{b}{a}\right)}$$

where ε_r is the relative permittivity of the dielectric material, a is the radius of the inner cylinder and b is the radius of the outer cylinder, as shown in **Figure 13**. The outer cylinder has double the radius of the inner cylinder.

Figure 13

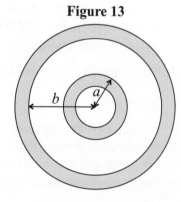

The capacitor is charged so that there is a potential difference of V_0 between the outer cylinder and the inner cylinder. The capacitor is then connected to a circuit with an electrical resistance of 1.85 kΩ, and discharged through the circuit. Calculate the time taken for the potential difference to fall to half of its original value.

(2 marks)

Synoptic Practice

9   **Figure 14** shows a vertical rigid square loop of conducting wire with sides of length 0.250 m. A small block of wood with a mass of 13.5 g is attached to the bottom of the loop. The loop is pivoted at its centre so the block can swing back and forth as shown. A large slab magnet is placed above the wire loop with its north pole facing downwards, so that the top length of the wire loop is in a uniform magnetic field of 5.50 mT. The bottom length of the wire loop is not in the magnetic field.

The wire loop is connected to an external circuit. The switch in the circuit is initially in position 2, and the capacitor charges until it reaches a maximum charge of 3.60 C. The switch is then moved to position 1 and the capacitor is discharged through the wire loop. The time constant of the wire loop and circuit is 0.1875 s.

You may assume that the masses of the wire loop and insulator are negligible, and that the resistance of the wire loop is negligible.

Figure 14

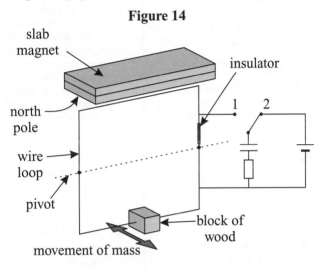

9.1 Calculate the force that acts on the top length of the wire loop, due to the magnetic field, immediately after the switch is moved to position 1.

(2 marks)

9.2 Immediately after the switch is moved to position 1, the block of wood moves a displacement of 5.0 mm. Calculate the time taken after the switch is moved to position 1 for the block to move to a displacement of 1.0 mm from its lowest point. It can be assumed that the displacement of the block is directly proportional to the magnetic force exerted on the wire.

(2 marks)

9.3 The circuit in **Figure 14** is removed and replaced with a signal generator which supplies an alternating current to the wire loop. When the signal generator is switched on, the block oscillates back and forth with simple harmonic motion. Describe and explain what happens to the oscillations of the block as the frequency is gradually increased from 0.01 Hz to 2 Hz. Include calculations to support your answer. ($g = 9.81$ ms^{-2})

Figure 15

(2 marks)

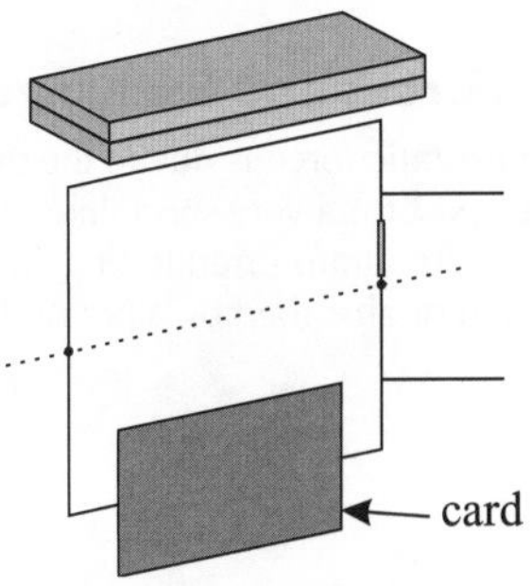

9.4 The block of wood is replaced with a large piece of card with half the mass of the block, as shown in **Figure 15**. Describe and explain how the motion of the card differs to that of the wooden block as the frequency of the signal generator is gradually increased from 0.01 Hz to 2 Hz.

(2 marks)

Answers

Section 1 — Particles

Page 3 — Atomic Structure

1 Inside every atom there is a nucleus which contains protons and neutrons *[1 mark]*. Orbiting this core are the electrons *[1 mark]*.

2 Proton number is 8, so there are 8 protons and electrons (it's neutral) *[1 mark]*. The nucleon number is 16. This is the total number of protons and neutrons. Subtract the 8 protons and that leaves 8 neutrons *[1 mark]*.

3 a) Atoms with the same number of protons but different numbers of neutrons are called isotopes *[1 mark]*.

   b) Any two from: e.g. They have the same chemical properties. / Their nuclei have different stabilities. / They have different physical properties. *[2 marks available — 1 mark for each correct answer.]*

4 A $_2^4$He nucleus has 2 protons and 2 neutrons (but no electrons) *[1 mark]*.
Charge = $2 \times 1.60 \times 10^{-19} = 3.20 \times 10^{-19}$ C *[1 mark]*
Mass = $4 \times 1.67 \times 10^{-27} = 6.68 \times 10^{-27}$ kg *[1 mark]*

Specific charge = $\dfrac{\text{charge}}{\text{mass}} = \dfrac{3.20 \times 10^{-19}}{6.68 \times 10^{-27}} = 4.790... \times 10^7$

= **4.79×10^7 C kg^{-1} (to 3 s.f.)** *[1 mark]*

The actual mass of a helium nucleus is slightly less than this due to energy being released when the nucleus was made. However, you don't need to worry about this at this level.

Page 5 — Stable and Unstable Nuclei

1 a) The strong nuclear force must be repulsive at very small nucleon separations to prevent the nucleus being crushed to a point *[1 mark]*.

   b) The protons repel each other with an electrostatic force and attract each other with the nuclear strong force. The strong force is not large enough to overcome this repulsion *[1 mark]*. When two neutrons are added to the nucleus, they attract each other and the protons via the strong force. The strong force is now able to balance out the force of repulsion between the protons *[1 mark]*.

2 a) $_{88}^{226}$Ra → $_{86}^{222}$Rn + $_2^4\alpha$ *[3 marks available — 1 mark for the alpha particle, 1 mark for the proton number of radon and 1 mark for the nucleon number of radon.]*

   b) $_{19}^{40}$K → $_{20}^{40}$Ca + $_{-1}^{0}\beta$ + $\bar{\nu}_e$ *[4 marks available — 1 mark for the beta particle, 1 mark each for the proton number and nucleon number of calcium, 1 mark for the antineutrino.]*

Page 7 — Particles and Antiparticles

1 $e^+ + e^- \rightarrow \gamma + \gamma$ *[1 mark]* This is called annihilation *[1 mark]*

2 Energy and mass are equivalent *[1 mark]*. When two particles collide, there is a lot of energy at the point of impact. This energy is converted to mass *[1 mark]*.

3 The creation of a particle of matter also requires the creation of its antiparticle. In this case no antineutron has been produced *[1 mark]*.

4 Total energy = $2 \times 9.84 \times 10^{-14} = 1.968 \times 10^{-13}$ J *[1 mark]*

$E = hf$, so $f = \dfrac{E}{h} = \dfrac{1.968 \times 10^{-13}}{6.63 \times 10^{-34}} = 2.968... \times 10^{20}$

= **2.97×10^{20} Hz (to 3 s.f.)** *[1 mark]*

Page 9 — Forces and Exchange Particles

1 The electrostatic force is due to the exchange of virtual photons that only exist for a very short time *[1 mark]*. The force is due to the momentum transferred to or gained from the photons as they are emitted or absorbed by a proton *[1 mark]*.

2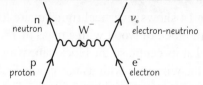

[1 mark for showing a W$^-$ boson being exchanged from the electron to the proton, 1 mark for showing a neutron is produced.]
This is a weak interaction *[1 mark]*.
Don't forget to put the arrows on your diagram.
Remember that the weak interaction uses W bosons, and is the only force that can change protons into neutrons or neutrons into protons.

Page 12 — Classification of Particles

1 Proton, electron and electron-antineutrino *[1 mark]*. The electron and the electron-antineutrino are leptons *[1 mark]*. Leptons are not affected by the strong interaction, so the decay can't be due to the strong interaction *[1 mark]*.
Remember that it's really just the same as beta decay.
Some books might leave out the antineutrino, so don't be misled.

2 Mesons are hadrons but the muon is a lepton *[1 mark]*. The muon is a fundamental particle but mesons are not. Mesons are built up from simpler particles *[1 mark]*. Mesons interact via the strong interaction but the muon does not *[1 mark]*.
You need to classify the muon correctly first and then say why it's different from a meson because of what it's like and what it does.

3 The correct answer is **B** *[1 mark]*.
Protons and neutrons are both baryons, which are a type of hadron. Electrons are leptons.

Page 15 — Quarks

1 a) $\pi^- = d\bar{u}$ *[1 mark]*

   b) Charge of down quark = $-1/3$ unit.
   Charge of anti-up quark = $-2/3$ unit.
   Total charge = -1 unit *[1 mark]*

2 The weak interaction converts a down quark into an up quark plus an electron and an electron-antineutrino *[1 mark]*. The neutron (udd) becomes a proton (uud) *[1 mark]*.
The lepton number L_e is conserved in this reaction.

3 The Baryon number changes from 2 to 1, so baryon number is not conserved *[1 mark]*. The strangeness changes from 0 to 1, so strangeness is not conserved *[1 mark]*.

Section 2 — Electromagnetic Radiation and Quantum Phenomena

Page 17 — The Photoelectric Effect

1 The plate becomes positively charged *[1 mark]*.
Negative electrons in the metal absorb energy from the UV light and leave the surface *[1 mark]*.
There's one mark for saying what happens, and a second mark for saying why.

2 An electron needs to gain a certain amount of energy (the work function) before it can leave the surface of the metal *[1 mark]*. If the energy carried by each photon is less than this work function, no electrons will be emitted *[1 mark]*.

Page 19 — Energy Levels and Photon Emission

1 a) i) E (eV) = V = 12.1 eV *[1 mark]*
      ii) E (J) = E (eV) $\times (1.60 \times 10^{-19})$ = $12.1 \times (1.60 \times 10^{-19})$
      = **1.94×10^{-18} J (to 3 s.f.)** *[1 mark]*

   b) i) The movement of an electron from a lower energy level to a higher energy level by absorbing energy *[1 mark]*.
      ii) $-13.6 + 12.1 = -1.5$ eV. This corresponds to n = 3 *[1 mark]*.

iii) n = 3 → n = 2: –1.5 – (–3.4) = **1.9 eV**   *[1 mark]*
n = 2 → n = 1: –3.4 – (–13.6) = 10.2 eV = **10 eV (to 2 s.f.)**
[1 mark]
n = 3 → n = 1: –1.5 – (–13.6) = 12.1 = **12 eV (to 2 s.f.)**
[1 mark]

Page 21 — Wave-Particle Duality

1 a) Electromagnetic radiation can show characteristics of both a particle and a wave. *[1 mark]*

b) $\lambda = \frac{h}{mv}$ so $mv = \frac{h}{\lambda} = \frac{6.63 \times 10^{-34}}{590 \times 10^{-9}}$ *[1 mark]*
$\qquad\qquad = \mathbf{1.1 \times 10^{-27}\ kg\,m\,s^{-1}}$ **(to 2 s.f.)** *[1 mark]*

2 a) $\lambda = \frac{h}{mv} = \frac{6.63 \times 10^{-34}}{9.11 \times 10^{-31} \times 3.50 \times 10^{6}}$ *[1 mark]*
$\qquad = 2.079... \times 10^{-10} = \mathbf{2.08 \times 10^{-10}\ m}$ **(to 3 s.f.)** *[1 mark]*

b) Either $v = \frac{h}{m\lambda} = \frac{6.63 \times 10^{-34}}{1.67 \times 10^{-27} \times 2.079... \times 10^{-10}}$ *[1 mark]*
$\qquad\qquad = 1909.28... = \mathbf{1910\ ms^{-1}}$ **(to 3 s.f.)** *[1 mark]*
Or momentum of protons = momentum of electrons
so $m_p \times v_p = m_e \times v_e$
$v_p = v_e \times \frac{m_e}{m_p} = 3.50 \times 10^{6} \times \frac{9.11 \times 10^{-31}}{1.67 \times 10^{-27}}$ *[1 mark]*
$\qquad = 1909.28... = \mathbf{1910\ ms^{-1}}$ **(to 3 s.f.)** *[1 mark]*

c) The proton has a larger mass, so it will have a smaller speed, since the two have the same kinetic energy *[1 mark]*.
Kinetic energy is proportional to the square of the speed, while momentum is proportional to the speed, so they will have different momenta *[1 mark]*. Wavelength depends on the momentum, so the wavelengths will be different *[1 mark]*.
This is a really hard question. If you didn't get it right, make sure you understand the answer fully. Do the algebra if it helps.

Extra Exam Practice for Sections 1 and 2

Pages 22-23

2.1 A line spectrum shows that energy can only be absorbed and emitted from an atom in discrete amounts *[1 mark]*. Energy is absorbed and emitted by electrons moving between energy levels. The amount of energy absorbed or emitted is equal to the difference between energy levels, which means electrons in atoms can only exist in discrete energy levels *[1 mark]*.

2.2 Stopping potential is related to the kinetic energy of photoelectrons by $eV_s = E_{k(max)}$
So $hf = \phi + E_{k(max)}$ becomes $hf = \phi + eV_s$
Rearrange $eV_s = hf - \phi$ to look like $y = mx + c$
On Figure 1, $y = V$ and $x = f$
$V_s = \frac{h}{e}f - \frac{\phi}{e}$
So the y-intercept, $c = -\frac{\phi}{e}$ *[1 mark]*
Extend the line back to the y-axis to find the intercept:
E.g.

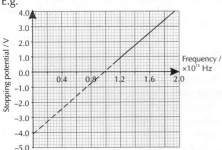

$c = -4.1$ V (accept between –4.0 and –4.2 V) *[1 mark]*
$\phi = -c \times e = 4.1 \times 1.60 \times 10^{-19} = 6.56 \times 10^{-19}$
$\qquad = \mathbf{6.6 \times 10^{-19}\ J}$ **(to 2 s.f.)** *[1 mark]*

2.3 The de Broglie wavelength is $\lambda = \frac{h}{mv}$, so for a photoelectron to have a minimum de Broglie wavelength, it must have a maximum velocity, e.g. $\lambda_{min} = \frac{h}{mv_{max}}$
so $v_{max} = \frac{h}{m\lambda_{min}} = \frac{6.63 \times 10^{-34}}{9.11 \times 10^{-31} \times 415 \times 10^{-12}}$
$\qquad\qquad = 1.753... \times 10^{6}$ *[1 mark]*
Photoelectrons with a velocity of v_{max} have an energy:
$E_k = \frac{1}{2}mv_{max}^2 = 0.5 \times 9.11 \times 10^{-31} \times (1.753... \times 10^{6})^2$
$\qquad = 1.400... \times 10^{-18}$ J *[1 mark]*
The electrons emitted from the aluminium have an initial maximum kinetic energy:
$E_{k(max)} = hf - \phi$
$\qquad\quad = (6.63 \times 10^{-34} \times 2.10 \times 10^{15}) - (6.56 \times 10^{-19})$
$\qquad\quad = 7.363 \times 10^{-19}$ J *[1 mark]*
The difference in energy is the kinetic energy provided by the accelerating voltage:
$1.400... \times 10^{-18} - 7.363 \times 10^{-19} = 6.645... \times 10^{-19}$ J *[1 mark]*
Convert this energy into electron volts, as 1 V provides 1 eV of energy to an electron:
$6.645... \times 10^{-19} \div 1.60 \times 10^{-19} = 4.153...$ eV
So the accelerating potential difference = **4.15 V (to 3 s.f.)**
[1 mark]

3.1 E.g. $\bar{\nu}_e + p \rightarrow e^+ + n$ *[1 mark]*
The antineutrino must be an electron antineutrino to conserve electron lepton number *[1 mark]*. The missing particle must have a baryon number of 1 to conserve baryon number, charge is already conserved so the missing particle is neutral. A neutral particle with a baryon number of 1 is a neutron *[1 mark]*.

3.2 In annihilation, two gamma rays are produced. The total minimum energy of both the gamma rays is equal to the total rest energy of the electron and positron.
$2E_0 = 2E_{min}$ so $E_0 = E_{min} = hf_{min}$, where E_0 is the rest energy of a positron/electron.
$E_0 = 0.511 \times 10^{6} \times 1.60 \times 10^{-19}$
$\quad = 8.176 \times 10^{-14}$ J *[1 mark]*
$E_0 = hf_{min}$ so $f_{min} = E_0 / h$
$\qquad\qquad = 8.176 \times 10^{-14} \div 6.63 \times 10^{-34}$
$\qquad\qquad = 1.233... \times 10^{20}$
$\qquad\qquad = \mathbf{1.23 \times 10^{20}\ Hz}$ **(to 3 s.f.)** *[1 mark]*

3.3 E.g. $c = f\lambda$ so a wave with a long wavelength has a low frequency. In order for a photoelectron to be emitted by the photoelectric effect, f has to be greater than ϕ / h *[1 mark]*. If f is too small, the photomultiplier won't emit photoelectrons when illuminated and therefore won't be able to detect any photons *[1 mark]*.

Section 3 — Waves

Page 25— Progressive Waves

1 a) Use $c = \lambda f$ and $f = 1 / T$, so $c = \lambda / T$, giving $\lambda = cT$
$\lambda = 3.0$ ms^{-1} × 6.0 s *[1 mark]* = **18 m** *[1 mark]*
The vertical movement of the buoy is irrelevant to this part of the question.

b) The trough-to-peak distance is twice the amplitude, so the amplitude is **0.6 m** *[1 mark]*

2 $c = \lambda f$, so $f = c/\lambda = (3.00 \times 10^{8}) \div (7.1 \times 10^{-7})$
$\quad = 4.225... \times 10^{14} = \mathbf{4.2 \times 10^{14}\ Hz}$ **(to 2 s.f.)** *[1 mark]*

3 **B** *[1 mark]*

Page 27 — Longitudinal and Transverse Waves

1 a) The reflected light has been partially polarised *[1 mark]*.
Only transverse waves can be polarised *[1 mark]*.

b) Polaroid material only transmits vibrations in one direction *[1 mark]*. Reflected light mostly vibrates in one direction, so Polaroid sunglasses filter out that direction, reducing glare *[1 mark]*.

2 Sound is a longitudinal wave *[1 mark]*. The vibrations are in the same direction as the energy transfer, so it cannot be polarised *[1 mark]*.

Answers

Page 29 — Superposition and Coherence

1 a) The frequencies and wavelengths of the two sources are equal *[1 mark]* and the phase difference is constant *[1 mark]*.

b) Interference will only be noticeable if the amplitudes of the two waves are approximately equal *[1 mark]*.

2 **B** *[1 mark]*

Remember, displacement and velocity are vector quantities — when two points on a wave are exactly out of phase, the phase difference is 180° and the velocity and displacement of the points are equal in size, but opposite in direction.

Page 31 — Stationary Waves

1 a) The length of the string for a stationary wave at the fundamental frequency is half the wavelength of the wave *[1 mark]*, so $\lambda = 2 \times 1.2 = $ **2.4 m** *[1 mark]*.

b) $f_{new} = \frac{1}{2l}\sqrt{\frac{2T}{\mu}} = \sqrt{2} \times \left(\frac{1}{2l}\sqrt{\frac{T}{\mu}}\right) = \sqrt{2} \times f_{original}$ *[1 mark]*

$f_{new} = \sqrt{2} \times 10$ *[1 mark]* = 14.142...
= **14 Hz (to 2 s.f.)** *[1 mark]*

c) When the string forms a standing wave, its amplitude varies from a maximum at the antinodes to zero at the nodes *[1 mark]*. In a progressive wave all the points vibrate at the same amplitude *[1 mark]*.

Page 33 — Diffraction

1 For noticeable diffraction, the size of the aperture must be roughly equal to the wavelength of the wave passing through it *[1 mark]*. The size of the doorway is roughly equal to the wavelength of sound, so sound waves diffract when they pass through the gap. This allows the person to hear the fire alarm *[1 mark]*. Light has a wavelength much smaller than the size of the doorway, and so diffraction is unnoticeable. This is why the person cannot see the alarm *[1 mark]*.

2 a) E.g. Laser light is monochromatic/only contains one wavelength/frequency of light *[1 mark]*. This provides a clearer pattern than non-monochromatic light sources as different wavelengths diffract by different amounts *[1 mark]*.

b) The central maximum will be wider and less intense *[1 mark]*. Using a narrower slit means more diffraction *[1 mark]* and so there will be fewer photons per unit area, so the intensity will be lower *[1 mark]*.

Page 35 — Two-Source Interference

1 a) Distance between sources (slit width) *[1 mark]*, spacing between two consecutive maxima or minima (fringe spacing) *[1 mark]* and the distance from the sources to the screen *[1 mark]*.

b) Any two from: Don't look into the laser beam / don't point the beam at a person / don't point the laser beam at a reflective surface / display a laser warning sign / wear laser safety goggles / turn the laser off when not in use *[1 mark for two correct suggestions]*
Laser light can permanently damage your eyes/retinas *[1 mark]*.

2 a) $\lambda = c / f = 330 / 1320 = $ **0.25 m** *[1 mark]*

b) Separation $= w = \lambda D / s = (0.25 \times 7.3) / 1.5 = 1.21666...$
= **1.2 m (to 2 s.f.)** *[1 mark]*

Page 37 — Diffraction Gratings

1 a) Use $d \sin \theta = n\lambda$.
For the first order, $n = 1$, so, $\sin \theta = \lambda / d$ *[1 mark]*
No need to actually work out d. The number of lines per metre is $1 / d$. So you can simply multiply the wavelength by that.
$\sin \theta = 6.0 \times 10^{-7} \times 4.0 \times 10^{5} = 0.24$
$\theta = \sin^{-1}(0.24) = 13.886... = $ **14° (to 2 s.f.)** *[1 mark]*
For the second order, $n = 2$ and $\sin \theta = 2\lambda / d$.
You already have a value for λ / d. Just double it to get $\sin \theta$ for the second order.
$\sin \theta = 0.48$, $\theta = \sin^{-1}(0.48) = 28.685... = $ **29° (to 2 s.f.)** *[1 mark]*

b) No. Putting $n = 5$ into the equation gives a value of $\sin \theta$ of 1.2, which is impossible *[1 mark]*.

2 $d \sin \theta = n\lambda$, so for the 1st order maximum, $d \sin \theta = \lambda$
$\sin 14.2° = \lambda \times 3.7 \times 10^{5}$ *[1 mark]*
$\lambda = 6.629... \times 10^{-7} = $ **6.6 × 10⁻⁷ m (or 660 nm) (to 2 s.f.)** *[1 mark]*

Page 39 — Refractive Index

1 a) $n_{diamond} = c / c_{diamond} = (3.00 \times 10^{8}) / (1.24 \times 10^{8}) = 2.419...$
= **2.42 (to 3 s.f.)** *[1 mark]*

b) $n_{air} \sin \theta_1 = n_{diamond} \sin \theta_2$, $n_{air} = 1$
So, $\sin \theta_1 = n_{diamond} \sin \theta_2$ *[1 mark]*
$\sin \theta_2 = \sin 50° / 2.419... = 0.316...$
$\theta_2 = \sin^{-1}(0.316...) = 18.459... = $ **18° (to 2 s.f.)** *[1 mark]*
You can assume the refractive index of air is 1, and don't forget to write the degree sign in your answer.

2 a) When the light is pointing steeply upwards some of it is refracted and some reflected — the beam emerging from the surface is the refracted part *[1 mark]*.
However, when the beam hits the surface at more than the critical angle (to the normal to the boundary) refraction does not occur. All the beam is totally internally reflected to light the tank, hence its brightness *[1 mark]*.

b) The critical angle is $90° - 41.25° = 48.75°$ *[1 mark]*.
$\sin \theta_c = n_{air} / n_{water} = 1 / n_{water}$,
so $n_{water} = 1 / \sin \theta_c = 1 / \sin 48.75°$
= 1.330... = **1.330 (to 4 s.f.)** *[1 mark]*
The question talks about the angle between the light beam and the floor of the aquarium. This angle is 90° minus the incident angle — measured from a normal to the surface of the water.

3 a) The cladding has a lower refractive index than the fibre, to allow total internal reflection *[1 mark]*. It also protects the cable from scratches and damage which may let light escape *[1 mark]*.

b) How to mark your answer (pick the level description that best matches your answer):
5-6 marks:
The answer fully describes several potential causes of signal degradation and correctly explains how to alter the design or operation to reduce the effects.
3-4 marks:
One potential cause of signal degradation has been fully described with a full explanation of how to reduce the effect. Another potential cause is mentioned with incomplete information or suggestions for design/operation alterations.
1-2 marks:
Potential reason(s) for signal degradation suggested but with incomplete description of the effects or of suggestions of how to reduce the effects with design changes.
0 marks:
No relevant information is given.
Here are some points your answer may include:
Absorption of light by the material the fibre is made from causes a loss of signal amplitude.
Dispersion within the fibre causes pulse broadening.
Modal dispersion is caused by light rays taking different paths of different lengths down the fibre.
Material dispersion is caused by different wavelengths of light refracting by different amounts in the fibre.
Designing the fibre so that it only allows light to take one path through it (known as a single-mode fibre) reduces pulse broadening due to modal dispersion.
Sending signals using monochromatic light reduces material dispersion because monochromatic light only has one wavelength/frequency.
Using an optical fibre repeater to boost/regenerate signals can help to reduce signal degradation over long transmission distances.

Answers

Extra Exam Practice for Section 3

Pages 40-41

2.1 The rays of light meet at the boundary.
E.g.

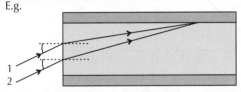

Since they started parallel, ray 1 must bend towards the normal more than ray 2.

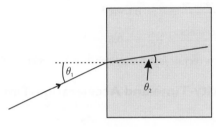

θ_2 for ray 1 must be smaller than θ_2 for ray 2 *[1 mark]*.
Snell's law is $n_1\sin\theta_1 = n_2\sin\theta_2$
n_1 = refractive index for air = 1, n_2 is the refractive index
of glass = n_g
$\sin\theta_2 = \dfrac{\sin\theta_1}{n_g}$
$\sin\theta_1$ is the same for both rays of light, so the only variable
affecting $\sin\theta_2$ is the refractive index. As the refractive index
increases, $\sin\theta_2$ decreases. θ_2 is between 0 and 90 ° so as $\sin\theta_2$
decreases, θ_2 decreases *[1 mark]*.
The blue light has a larger n_g and therefore will have a smaller θ_2,
meaning light ray 1 is the blue light *[1 mark]*.
2.2 The angle that the refracted ray makes with the glass-cladding
boundary is equal to the angle of refraction:

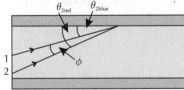

The angle between the two rays of light (ϕ) :

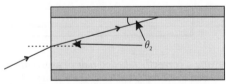

$\phi = \theta_{2red} - \theta_{2blue}$ *[1 mark]*
$n_1\sin\theta_1 = n_2\sin\theta_2$, so $\theta_2 = \sin^{-1}\left(\dfrac{\sin\theta_1}{n_g}\right)$
$\theta_{2red} = \sin^{-1}\left(\dfrac{\sin 15.0}{1.513}\right) = 9.849...$ °
$\theta_{2blue} = \sin^{-1}\left(\dfrac{\sin 15.0}{1.532}\right) = 9.726...$ ° *[1 mark]*
$\phi = 9.849... - 9.726...$
$= 0.1233...$
$= \textbf{0.123 °}$ **(to 3 s.f.)** *[1 mark]*

2.3 Find the distance travelled by the ray of light:

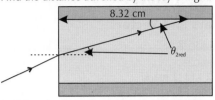

Path length of ray = 8.32×10^{-2} / cos(9.849...)
$= 0.0844...$ m *[1 mark]*
Put this value in your calculator memory for now because you'll need it
again later.
The speed of red light in glass:
$n_g = c / c_g$, so $c_g = c / n_g = 3.00 \times 10^8$ / 1.513
$= 1.982... \times 10^8$ ms^{-1} *[1 mark]*
The wavelength of red light in glass:
$c_g = f\lambda$ so $\lambda = c_g / f = 1.982... \times 10^8$ / 4.57×10^{14}
$= 4.338... \times 10^{-7}$ m *[1 mark]*
Number of cycles = path length / λ
$= 0.0844...$ / $4.338... \times 10^{-7}$
$= 194\ 628.45...$
$= \textbf{195 000 cycles (to 3 s.f.)}$ *[1 mark]*
2.4 For each ray you need to calculate the value of θ_1 when θ_c is
equal to the critical angle, as shown in the diagram below:

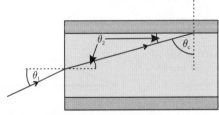

At the critical angle, $\theta_2 = 90 - \theta_c$
$\sin\theta_1 = n_g\sin\theta_2 = n_g\sin(90 - \theta_c)$
so $\theta_1 = \sin^{-1}(n_g\sin(90 - \theta_c))$ *[1 mark]*
$\sin\theta_c = n_2 / n_1$. Here the light is moving from the glass to the
cladding, so $n_1 = n_g$ and $n_2 = n_c$
so $\theta_c = \sin^{-1}(n_c / n_g)$
so $\theta_1 = \sin^{-1}(n_g\sin(90 - \sin^{-1}(n_c / n_g)))$
For red: $\theta_1 = \sin^{-1}(1.513 \times \sin(90 - \sin^{-1}(1.224 / 1.513)))$
$= 62.795...$ ° *[1 mark]*
For blue: $\theta_1 = \sin^{-1}(1.532 \times \sin(90 - \sin^{-1}(1.231 / 1.532)))$
$= 65.777...$ ° *[1 mark]*
The red light will be the first ray to refract into the cladding as it
reaches the critical angle at a smaller angle of θ_1 than the blue
light *[1 mark]*.
2.5 The blue and red lights have different frequencies/wavelengths
so they are not coherent *[1 mark]*. This means that they won't
produce two source interference *[1 mark]*.
2.6 The highest order fringe seen for each colour:
$n\lambda = d\sin\theta$ is a maximum when $\sin\theta = 1$
$n\lambda = d$, and $c = f\lambda$, so $n = df / c$
Red: $n = \dfrac{2.50\times10^{-6} \times 4.57\times10^{14}}{3.00\times10^8} = 3.808...$
So the highest order fringe that could be seen is the 3rd fringe.
Blue: $n = \dfrac{2.50\times10^{-6} \times 6.59\times10^{14}}{3.00\times10^8} = 5.491...$
So the highest order fringe that could be seen is the 5th fringe.
[1 mark]
2.7 The central maximum would be a purple/mixture of red and
blue light *[1 mark]*. The first fringe on both sides of the central
maximum would be blue. This is because $n\lambda = d\sin\theta$ and so
because the wavelength for blue light is smaller, the angle of the
first order diffraction will be smaller *[1 mark]*.

Answers

Section 4 — Mechanics

Page 43 — Scalars and Vectors

1 Start by drawing a diagram:

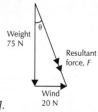
Weight 75 N
θ
Resultant force, F
Wind 20 N

$F^2 = 20^2 + 75^2 = 6025$,
so **F = 78 N (to 2 s.f.)** *[1 mark]*
$\tan \theta = \frac{20}{75} = 0.266...$
So **θ = 15° (to 2 s.f.) to the vertical** *[1 mark]*.
Make sure you know which angle you're finding — and label it on your diagram. You could also answer this question by drawing a scale diagram.

2 Again, start by drawing a diagram:

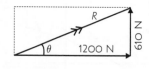
horizontal component, v_H
15°
vertical component, v_v
velocity 20.0 ms⁻¹

Horizontal component
$v_H = 20\cos 15°$
= **19 ms⁻¹ (to 2 s.f.)** *[1 mark]*
Vertical component
$v_V = 20\sin 15° = $ **5.2 ms⁻¹ (to 2 s.f.) downwards** *[1 mark]*
<u>Always</u> draw a diagram.

Page 45 — Forces

1 Weight = vertical component of tension × 2
$8 × 9.81 = 2T\sin 50°$ *[1 mark]*
$78.48 = 0.766... × 2T$
$102.45... = 2T$
T = 51 N (to 2 s.f.) *[1 mark]*

2 By Pythagoras:
$R = \sqrt{1200^2 + 610^2} = 1346.1...$
= **1300 N (to 2 s.f.)** *[1 mark]*

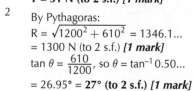
R
θ
1200 N
610 N

$\tan \theta = \frac{610}{1200}$, so $\theta = \tan^{-1} 0.50...$
= 26.95° = **27° (to 2 s.f.)** *[1 mark]*

Page 47 — Moments

1 Moment = force × distance
$60 = 0.40F$ *[1 mark]*, so **F = 150 N** *[1 mark]*

2 Clockwise moment = anticlockwise moment
$W × 2.0 = T × 0.3$
[1 mark for either line of working]
$60 × 9.81 × 2.0 = T × 0.3$
$T = 3924 = $ **4000 N (to 1 s.f.)** *[1 mark]*

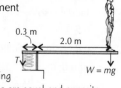
0.3 m
2.0 m
T
W = mg

The moments caused by the tension in the spring and the force exerted by the diver on the spring are equal and opposite.

Page 49 — Mass, Weight and Centre of Mass

1 a) Experiment:
Hang the object freely from a point. Hang a plumb bob from the same point, and use it to draw a vertical line down the object *[1 mark]*. Repeat for a different point and find the point of intersection *[1 mark]*. The centre of mass is halfway through the thickness of the object (by symmetry) at the point of intersection *[1 mark]*.
Identifying and reducing error: e.g.
Source: the object and/or plumb line might move slightly while you're drawing the vertical line *[1 mark]*.
Reduced by: hang the object from a third point to confirm the position of the point of intersection *[1 mark]*.

b) You can find the centre of mass of any regular shape using symmetry. The centre of mass will be at the centre where the lines of symmetry cross, halfway through its thickness *[1 mark]*.

Page 51 — Displacement-Time Graphs

1 Split graph into four sections:
A: Acceleration *[1 mark]*
B: Constant velocity *[1 mark]*
C: Stationary *[1 mark]*
D: Constant velocity in opposite direction to A and B *[1 mark]*

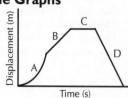
Displacement (m)
A
B
C
D
Time (s)

2 a)

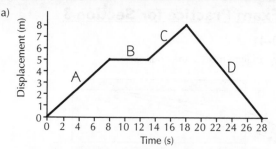
Displacement (m)
8
7
6
5
4
3
2
1
0
0 2 4 6 8 10 12 14 16 18 20 22 24 26 28
Time (s)
A B C D

[4 marks available — 1 mark for each section correctly drawn.]

b) At A: $v = \frac{\text{displacement}}{\text{time}} = \frac{5}{8} = 0.625 = $ **0.6 ms⁻¹ (to 1 s.f.)**
At B: **v = 0**
At C: $v = \frac{\text{displacement}}{\text{time}} = \frac{3}{5} = $ **0.6 ms⁻¹**
At D: $v = \frac{\text{displacement}}{\text{time}} = \frac{-8}{10} = $ **−0.8 ms⁻¹**
[2 marks for all correct or just 1 mark for 2 or 3 correct.]

Page 53 — Velocity-Time and Acceleration-Time Graphs

1 a)

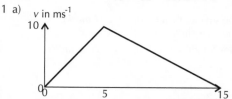
v in ms⁻¹
10
0
5
15
t in s

[1 mark for drawing a correctly labelled pair of axes, with a straight line between v = 0 ms⁻¹, t = 0 s and v = 10 ms⁻¹, t = 5 s. 1 mark for correctly drawing a straight line between v = 10 ms⁻¹, t = 5 s and v = 0 ms⁻¹, t = 15 s.]

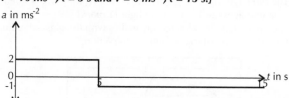
a in ms⁻²
2
0
−1
5
15
t in s

[1 mark for drawing a correctly labelled pair of axes, with a straight line between a = 2 ms⁻², t = 0 s and a = 2 ms⁻², t = 5 s. 1 mark for correctly drawing a straight line from a = 2 ms⁻², t = 5 s and a = −1 ms⁻², t = 5 s, and a straight line between a = −1 ms⁻², t = 5 s and a = −1 ms⁻², t = 15 s.]

b) Distance travelled is equal to the area under v-t graph between t = 0 and t = 5 *[1 mark]* = 0.5 × 5 × 10 = **25 m** *[1 mark]*

Page 55 — Motion With Uniform Acceleration

1 a) $a = -9.81$ ms⁻², $t = 5$ s, $u = 0$ ms⁻¹, $v = ?$
Use: $v = u + at$, $v = 0 + 5 × -9.81$ *[1 mark]*
$v = $ **−49 ms⁻¹ (to 2 s.f.)** *[1 mark]*
NB: It's negative because she's falling downwards and we took upwards as the positive direction.

b) Use: $s = \left(\frac{u+v}{2}\right)t$ or $s = ut + \frac{1}{2}at^2$
$s = \frac{-49}{2} × 5 = -120$ m (to 2 s.f.)
or $s = 0 + \frac{1}{2} × -9.81 × 5^2 = -120$ m (to 2 s.f.)
So she fell **120 m (to 2 s.f.)** *[1 mark for working, 1 mark for answer]*

2 a) $v = 0$ ms⁻¹, $t = 3.2$ s, $s = 40$ m, $u = ?$ Use: $s = \left(\frac{u+v}{2}\right)t$
$40 = 3.2u ÷ 2$ *[1 mark]*, so $u = \frac{80}{3.2} = $ **25 ms⁻¹** *[1 mark]*

b) E.g. use: $v^2 = u^2 + 2as$
$0 = 25^2 + 80a$ *[1 mark]*
$-80a = 625$, so $a = $ **−7.8 ms⁻² (to 2 s.f.)** *[1 mark]*

Answers

3 a) Take upstream as negative:
$v = 5$ ms^{-1}, $a = 6$ ms^{-1}, $s = 1.2$ m, $u = ?$ Use: $v^2 = u^2 + 2as$
$5^2 = u^2 + 2 \times 6 \times 1.2$ **[1 mark]**
$u^2 = 25 - 14.4 = 10.6$
$u = -3.255... = $ **–3 ms^{-1} (to 1 s.f.) [1 mark]**
Take the negative root as we've defined downstream to be positive and initially the boat was travelling upstream.

b) From furthest point: $u = 0$ ms^{-1}, $a = 6$ ms^{-2}, $v = 5$ ms^{-1}, $s = ?$
Use: $v^2 = u^2 + 2as$
$5^2 = 0 + 2 \times 6 \times s$ **[1 mark]**
$s = 25 \div 12 = 2.083... = $ **2 m (to 1 s.f.) [1 mark]**

Page 57 — Acceleration Due to Gravity

1 a) The air resistance on a falling small steel ball will be less than that on a beach ball. The air resistance on the ball used in this experiment needs to be negligible in order to be able to calculate the value of g **[1 mark]**.

b) E.g. the ball's fall might be affected by wind **[1 mark]**. To remove this error, conduct the experiment indoors and close all windows **[1 mark]**. / Not aligning the ball and ruler at eye level can lead to a measuring error **[1 mark]**. This can be reduced by making sure your eye is perpendicular to the measuring scale being used when taking measurements **[1 mark]**.

c) E.g. there may be a delay on the stopwatch/light gates **[1 mark]**. To remove this, ensure they are properly calibrated before conducting the experiment **[1 mark]**. / The ruler may not be aligned properly so would give slightly incorrect vertical height measurements **[1 mark]**. To remove this, use a clamp to ensure the rule is straight and unmoving **[1 mark]**.

d) Use: $s = ut + \frac{1}{2}at^2$ **[1 mark]**
$u = 0$, so $s = \frac{1}{2}at^2$ or $\frac{1}{2}a = \frac{s}{t^2}$ **[1 mark]**
So the gradient of a graph of s against t^2, $\frac{\Delta s}{\Delta t^2}$, is equal to half the acceleration, i.e. $\frac{1}{2}g$ **[1 mark]**.

Page 59 — Projectile Motion

1 a) You only need to worry about the vertical motion of the stone.
$u = 0$ ms^{-1}, $s = -560$ m, $a = -g = -9.81$ ms^{-2}, $t = ?$
You need to find t, so use: $s = ut + \frac{1}{2}at^2$
$-560 = 0 + \frac{1}{2} \times -9.81 \times t^2$ **[1 mark]**
$t = \sqrt{\frac{2 \times (-560)}{-9.81}} = 10.68... = $ **11 s (to 2 s.f.) [1 mark]**

b) You know that in the horizontal direction:
$u = v = 20$ ms^{-1}, $t = 10.68...$ s, $a = 0$, $s = ?$
So use velocity $= \frac{\text{distance}}{\text{time}}$, $v = \frac{s}{t}$
$s = v \times t = 20 \times 10.68...$ **[1 mark]** $= $ **210 m (to 2 s.f.) [1 mark]**

2 You know that for the arrow's vertical motion (taking upwards as the positive direction):
$a = -9.81$ ms^{-2}, $u = 30$ ms^{-1} and the arrow will be at its highest point just before it starts falling back towards the ground, so $v = 0$ ms^{-1}.
$s = $ the vertical distance travelled from the arrow's firing point.
So use $v^2 = u^2 + 2as$
$0 = 30^2 + 2 \times -9.81 \times s$ **[1 mark]**
$900 = 2 \times 9.81s$
$s = \frac{900}{2 \times 9.81} = 45.87... = 45.9$ m **[1 mark]**
So the maximum distance reached from the ground
$= 45.87... + 1 = $ **47 m (to the nearest metre) [1 mark]**

Page 61 — Newton's Laws of Motion

1 a) Force perpendicular to river flow $= 500 - 100 = 400$ N **[1 mark]**
Force parallel to river flow $= 300$ N
Resultant force $= \sqrt{400^2 + 300^2} = $ **500 N [1 mark]**

b) $a = F/m$ (from $F = ma$)
$= 500/250$ **[1 mark]** $= $ **2 ms^{-2} [1 mark]**

2 B **[1 mark]**
The overall acceleration is a, so ma must be equal to the resultant force, which is the force John is pushing with minus the resistance caused by friction. So $F_{\text{John}} - F = ma$, and $F_{\text{John}} = ma + F$.

3 The only force acting on each of them is their weight $= mg$ **[1 mark]**. Since $F = ma$, this gives $ma = mg$, or $a = g$ **[1 mark]**. Their acceleration doesn't depend on their mass — it's the same for both of them — so they reach the water at the same time **[1 mark]**.

Page 63 — Drag, Lift and Terminal Speed

1 a) The velocity increases at a steady rate, which means the acceleration is constant **[1 mark]**.
Constant acceleration means there must be no atmospheric resistance (atmospheric resistance would increase with velocity, leading to a decrease in acceleration). So there must be no atmosphere **[1 mark]**.

b)
velocity
time

[2 marks — 1 mark for drawing a graph that still starts from the origin, 1 mark for showing the graph curving to show the velocity increasing at a decreasing rate until the velocity is constant.]
Your graph must be a smooth curve which levels out. It must NOT go down at the end.

c) The graph becomes less steep because the acceleration is decreasing **[1 mark]** and because air resistance increases with speed **[1 mark]**. The graph levels out because air resistance has become equal to weight **[1 mark]**.
If the question says 'explain', you won't get marks for just describing what the graph shows — you have to say <u>why</u> it is that shape.

Page 65 — Momentum and Impulse

1 a) total momentum before collision = total momentum after **[1 mark]**
$(0.60 \times 5.0) + 0 = (0.60 \times -2.4) + 2v$
$3 + 1.44 = 2v$ **[1 mark]** $v = 2.22... = $ **2.2 ms^{-1} (to 2 s.f.) [1 mark]**

b) Kinetic energy before collision
$= \frac{1}{2} \times 0.6 \times 5^2 + \frac{1}{2} \times 2 \times 0^2 = $ **7.5 J [1 mark]**
Kinetic energy after the collision
$= \frac{1}{2} \times 0.6 \times 2.4^2 + \frac{1}{2} \times 2 \times 2.22^2 = 1.728 + 4.9284$
$= $ **6.7 J (to 2 s.f.) [1 mark]**
The kinetic energy of the two balls is greater before the collision than after (i.e. it's not conserved), so the collision must be inelastic **[1 mark]**.

2 momentum before = momentum after **[1 mark]**
$(0.7 \times 0.3) + 0 = 1.1v \Rightarrow 0.21 = 1.1v$ **[1 mark]** $\Rightarrow$
$v = $ **0.2 ms^{-1} (to 1 s.f.) [1 mark]**

Page 67 — Work and Power

1 a) Force in direction of travel
$= 100 \cos 40° = 76.6...$ N **[1 mark]**
$W = Fs = 76.6... \times 1500 = $
110 000 J (to 2 s.f.) [1 mark]

b) Use $P = Fv$
$= 100 \cos 40° \times 0.8$ **[1 mark]** $= $ **61 W (to 2 s.f.) [1 mark]**

2 a) Use $W = Fs$
$= 20 \times 9.81 \times 3.0$ **[1 mark]** $= $ **590 J (to 2 s.f.) [1 mark]**
Remember that 20 kg is not the force — it's the mass. So you need to multiply it by 9.81 Nkg^{-1} to get the weight.

b) Use $P = Fv$
$= (20 \times 9.81) \times 0.25$ **[1 mark]** $= $ **49 W (to 2 s.f.) [1 mark]**

Answers

Page 69 — Conservation of Energy and Efficiency

1 a) Use $E_k = \frac{1}{2}mv^2$ and $\Delta E_p = mg\Delta h$ **[1 mark]**
   $\frac{1}{2}mv^2 = mg\Delta h$
   $\frac{1}{2}v^2 = g\Delta h$
   $v^2 = 2g\Delta h = 2 \times 9.81 \times 2.0 = 39.24$ **[1 mark]**
   $v = \textbf{6.3 ms}^{-1}$ **(to 2 s.f.) [1 mark]**
   'No friction' allows you to say that the change in kinetic energy is the same as the change in potential energy.

   b) 2 m — no friction means the kinetic energy will all change back into potential energy, so he will rise back up to the same height as he started **[1 mark]**.

   c) Put in some more energy by actively 'skating' **[1 mark]**.

2 a) If there's no air resistance, $E_k = E_p = mg\Delta h$ **[1 mark]**
   $E_k = 0.02 \times 9.81 \times 8.0 = \textbf{1.6 J}$ **(to 2 s.f.) [1 mark]**

   b) If the ball rebounds to 6.5 m, it has gravitational potential energy:
   $E_p = mg\Delta h = 0.02 \times 9.81 \times 6.5 = 1.28$ J **[1 mark]**
   So $1.57 - 1.28 = \textbf{0.29 J}$ is converted to other forms **[1 mark]**

Section 5 — Materials

Page 71 — Properties of Materials

1 a) Hooke's law says that force is proportional to extension. The force is 1.5 times as great, so the extension will be 1.5 times the original value.
   Extension $= 1.5 \times 4.0$ mm $= \textbf{6.0 mm}$ **[1 mark]**

   b) $F = k\Delta L$ so $k = F \div \Delta L$ **[1 mark]**
   $k = 10.0 \div (4.0 \times 10^{-3}) = \textbf{2500 Nm}^{-1}$ **[1 mark]**
   You could also use the values for F and ΔL from part a) to work out k.

   c) Any from e.g. The string now stretches much further for small increases in force **[1 mark]**. / When the string is loosened it is longer than at the start **[1 mark]**.

2 The rubber band does not obey Hooke's law **[1 mark]** because when the force is doubled from 2.5 N to 5.0 N, the extension increases by a factor of 2.3 **[1 mark]**.
   You could also work out k for both 2.5 N and 5.0 N, and show that it varies — i.e. the extension is not proportional to the force.

Page 73 — Stress and Strain

1 a) Area $= \pi r^2$ or $\pi\left(\dfrac{d}{2}\right)^2$
   So area $= \pi \times \dfrac{(1.0 \times 10^{-3})^2}{4} = 7.853... \times 10^7$ **[1 mark]**
   Stress $=$ force/area $= 300 \div (7.853... \times 10^{-7})$
   $= \textbf{3.8} \times \textbf{10}^8$ **Nm**$^{-2}$ **(or Pa) (to 2 s.f.) [1 mark]**

   b) Strain $=$ extension $\div$ length
   $= (4.0 \times 10^{-3}) \div 2.00 = \textbf{2.0} \times \textbf{10}^{-3}$ **(to 2 s.f.) [1 mark]**

2 a) $F = k\Delta L$ and so rearranging $k = F \div \Delta L$ **[1 mark]**
   $k = 50.0 \div (3.0 \times 10^{-3}) = \textbf{1.7} \times \textbf{10}^4$ **Nm**$^{-1}$ **(to 2 s.f.) [1 mark]**

   b) Elastic strain energy $= \frac{1}{2}F\Delta L$
   $= \frac{1}{2} \times 50.0 \times 3.0 \times 10^{-3}$
   $= \textbf{7.5} \times \textbf{10}^{-2}$ **J [1 mark]**
   You could also use $E = \frac{1}{2}k\Delta L^2$ and substitute in your value of k.

3 The force needed to compress the spring is:
   $F = k\Delta L = 40.8 \times 0.05 = 2.04$ N **[1 mark]**
   The elastic strain energy in the spring is then:
   $E = \frac{1}{2}F\Delta L = \frac{1}{2} \times 2.04 \times 0.05 = 0.051$ J **[1 mark]**
   Assume all this energy is converted to kinetic energy in the ball.
   $E = E_{kinetic} = 0.051$ J **[1 mark]**.
   You could also begin by using Hooke's law to replace F in the formula for elastic strain energy, to give $E = \frac{1}{2}k\Delta L^2$, and then substituting into this.

Page 75 — The Young Modulus

1 Cross-sectional area $= \pi r^2$ or $\pi\left(\dfrac{d}{2}\right)^2$
   So area $= \pi \times \dfrac{(0.60 \times 10^{-3})^2}{4} = 2.827... \times 10^{-7}$ m^2 **[1 mark]**
   Stress $=$ force/area $= 80.0 \div (2.827... \times 10^{-7})$
   $= 2.829... \times 10^8$ Nm^{-2} **[1 mark]**
   Strain $=$ extension/length $= (3.6 \times 10^{-3}) \div 2.50$
   $= 1.44 \times 10^{-3}$ **[1 mark]**
   Young modulus $=$ stress/strain
   $= (2.829... \times 10^8) \div (1.44 \times 10^{-3})$
   $= \textbf{2.0} \times \textbf{10}^{11}$ **Nm**$^{-2}$ **(to 2 s.f.) [1 mark]**

2 $E = \dfrac{FL}{\Delta L A}$. Force, original length and extension are
   the same for both wires, so $E \propto \dfrac{1}{A}$.
   The wire B has half the cross-sectional area of the wire A. So the Young modulus of wire B (E_B) must be twice that of the wire A **[1 mark]**.
   $E_B = 2 \times 7.0 \times 10^{10}$ Nm^{-2} $= 1.4 \times 10^{11}$ Nm^{-2}
   $= \textbf{1.4} \times \textbf{10}^{11}$ **Nm**$^{-2}$ **(to 2 s.f.) [1 mark]**

3 a) Young modulus, $E =$ stress/strain and so strain $=$ stress/E
   Strain on wire $= (2.6 \times 10^8) \div (1.3 \times 10^{11})$ **[1 mark]**
   $= \textbf{2.0} \times \textbf{10}^{-3}$ **(to 2 s.f.) [1 mark]**

   b) Stress $=$ force/area and so area $=$ force/stress
   Area $= 100 \div (2.6 \times 10^8)$ **[1 mark]**
   $= 3.846... \times 10^{-7} = \textbf{3.8} \times \textbf{10}^{-7}$ **m**^{2} **(to 2 s.f.) [1 mark]**

   c) Strain energy per unit volume
   $= \frac{1}{2} \times$ stress $\times$ strain $= \frac{1}{2} \times (2.6 \times 10^8) \times (2.0 \times 10^{-3})$ **[1 mark]**
   $= \textbf{2.6} \times \textbf{10}^5$ **Jm**$^{-3}$ **[1 mark]**
   Give the mark if answer is consistent with the value calculated for strain in part a).

Page 77 — Stress-Strain and Force-Extension Graphs

1 a) Liable to break suddenly without deforming plastically **[1 mark]**.

   b) E.g.

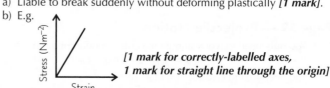

   [1 mark for correctly-labelled axes, 1 mark for straight line through the origin]

2 a) Yield stress $= \textbf{900 MNm}^{-2}$ **[1 mark]**

   b) Energy per unit volume
   $=$ area under the graph **[1 mark]**
   $= (800 \times 0.2) \div 2 = \textbf{80 MJ m}^{-3}$ **(or 8×10^7 J m^{-3}) [1 mark]**

   c) Work done to deform the thread per unit volume is the area between the loading curve and the unloading curve **[1 mark]**.
   So work done $=$ area under loading curve $-$ area under unloading curve **[1 mark]**.

Extra Exam Practice for Sections 4 and 5

Pages 78-81

2.1 Some of the elastic strain energy (E) stored in the spring is converted to the kinetic energy of the pellet. Find the elastic strain energy when the spring is fully compressed:
   $\Delta L = 4.0$ cm $= 0.040$ m, $m = 1.2$ g $= 1.2 \times 10^{-3}$ kg
   Substituting $F = k\Delta L$ into $E = \frac{1}{2}F\Delta L$:
   $E = \frac{1}{2}k\Delta L^2 = \frac{1}{2} \times 275 \times 0.040^2 = 0.22$ J **[1 mark]**
   92% of the elastic strain energy is transferred to kinetic energy, so
   $E_k = 0.92 \times 0.22 = 0.2024$ J **[1 mark]**
   Rearrange $E_k = \frac{1}{2}mv^2$ to make v the subject:
   $v = \sqrt{\dfrac{2E_k}{m}} = \sqrt{\dfrac{2 \times 0.2024}{1.2 \times 10^{-3}}} = 18.366...$ ms^{-1}
   $= \textbf{18 ms}^{-1}$ **(to 2 s.f.) [1 mark]**

Answers

2.2 $F = \dfrac{\Delta(mv)}{\Delta t}$

The gun and pellet are still to begin with ($v = 0$), so the total momentum (mv) before the pellet was fired = 0.
Momentum is always conserved, so the total momentum after the pellet was fired = 0. This means that the change in momentum of the pellet, $\Delta(mv_{\text{pellet}})$, must equal the change in momentum of the gun as it recoils.
$\Delta(mv_{\text{pellet}})$ = pellet's final momentum − pellet's initial momentum
$= ((1.2 \times 10^{-3}) \times 18.366...) - 0$
$= 0.02203...$ kg ms^{-1} $= \Delta(mv_{\text{gun}})$ **[1 mark]**

Resultant force acting on the gun, $F = 4.1$ N
$\Delta t = \dfrac{\Delta(mv)}{F} = \dfrac{0.02203...}{4.1} = 5.3756... \times 10^{-3}$ s
$\qquad\qquad = \mathbf{5.4 \times 10^{-3}\ s}$ **(to 2 s.f.) [1 mark]**

You'd still get the marks if you used 18 ms^{-1} for the initial speed of the pellet.

2.3 It's assumed that gravity is the only force acting on the pellet, so the pellet will move with a constant downwards acceleration, g.
Use the equations for uniform acceleration to find t:
Resolve vertically, taking upwards as positive:
$s = -3.7$ m, $u = (18.366...\sin20)$ ms^{-1}, $a = -9.81$ ms^{-2}, $t = ?$

$s = ut + \dfrac{1}{2}at^2$

$-3.7 = (18.366...\sin20)t + \left(\dfrac{1}{2} \times -9.81 \times t^2\right)$

$4.905t^2 - 6.2817...t - 3.7 = 0$ **[1 mark]**
Use the quadratic formula to solve for t:
$a = 4.905, b = -6.2817..., c = -3.7$
$t = \dfrac{-b \pm \sqrt{b^2 - 4ac}}{2a}$

$= \dfrac{6.2817... \pm \sqrt{(-6.2817...)^2 - (4 \times 4.905 \times -3.7)}}{2 \times 4.905}$ **[1 mark]**

$= \dfrac{6.2817... \pm \sqrt{39.4605... + 72.594}}{9.81}$

$= \dfrac{6.2817... \pm 10.58558}{9.81}$

$t = 1.7194...$ s or $-0.4387...$ s
$t > 0$, so $t = \mathbf{1.7\ s}$ **(to 2 s.f.) [1 mark]**

You'd still get the marks if you used 18 ms^{-1} for the initial speed of the pellet.

2.4 No forces act horizontally, so the pellet maintains a constant horizontal velocity of $(18.366...\cos20)$ ms$^{-1} = 17.2589...$ ms^{-1} throughout its flight.
Resolve vertically, taking upwards as positive to calculate the vertical component of the velocity as the pellet hits the lawn:
$u = (18.366...\sin20)$ ms^{-1}, $v = ?$, $a = -9.81$ ms^{-2}, $t = 1.7194...$ s
$v = u + at = 18.366...\sin20 + (-9.81 \times 1.7194...)$
$\qquad = -10.58558$ ms^{-1} **[1 mark]**
So as the pellet hits the lawn:

Horizontal velocity (v_{h})
$= 17.2589...$ ms^{-1}

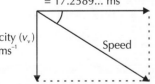

Vertical velocity (v_{v})
$= 10.58558$ ms^{-1}

Speed

Calculate the speed of the pellet using Pythagoras' theorem:
speed $= \sqrt{v_h^2 + v_v^2} = \sqrt{17.2589...^2 + 10.58558^2}$
$\qquad = 20.2466...$ ms$^{-1} = \mathbf{20\ ms^{-1}}$ **(to 2 s.f.) [1 mark]**
Calculate θ using trigonometry:
$\tan\theta = \dfrac{\text{opposite}}{\text{adjacent}}$

$\theta = \tan^{-1}\left(\dfrac{10.58558}{17.2589...}\right) = 31.522...° = \mathbf{32°}$ **(to 2 s.f.) [1 mark]**

You'd still get the marks if you used 18 ms^{-1} for the initial speed of the pellet and 1.7 s for the time taken for the pellet to reach the ground.

2.5 The two forces acting on the pellet during its flight are its weight and the wind.
Weight $= mg = (1.2 \times 10^{-3}) \times 9.81 = 11.772 \times 10^{-3}$ N **[1 mark]**
Find the magnitude of the resultant force using a scale drawing.
E.g. let 1 cm = 2×10^{-3} N, and convert forces to lengths:
length of weight vector $= (11.772 \times 10^{-3}) \div (2 \times 10^{-3}) = 5.886$ cm
length of wind vector $= (5.2 \times 10^{-3}) \div (2 \times 10^{-3}) = 2.6$ cm
[1 mark]

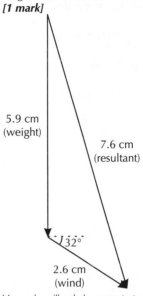

5.9 cm
(weight)

7.6 cm
(resultant)

32°

2.6 cm
(wind)

Your ruler will only be accurate to the nearest mm, so the lengths of the vectors are rounded slightly.
resultant force $= 7.6 \times (2 \times 10^{-3}) = 0.0152$ N
$\qquad\qquad = \mathbf{0.015\ N}$ **(to 2 s.f.) [1 mark]**

3.1 Power = work done ÷ change in time
Work done = force × distance
To find the force applied by the motor, use:
Resultant force = force applied by the motor − weight acting down the ramp − frictional force
Resultant force: $F = ma = 2.4 \times 14.6 = 35.04$ N
Weight acting down the ramp: $mg\sin\theta = 2.4 \times 9.81 \times \sin28$
$\qquad\qquad\qquad\qquad\qquad\qquad = 11.053...$ N

Frictional force: $\mu R = \mu \times mg\cos\theta$
$\qquad\qquad\qquad = 0.81 \times 2.4 \times 9.81 \times \cos28$
$\qquad\qquad\qquad = 16.838...$ N **[1 mark]**
So now find the force applied by the motor:
$35.04 = F_{\text{motor}} - 11.053... - 16.838...$
$F_{\text{motor}} = 62.931...$ N **[1 mark]**
Work done by the motor on the box $= Fs = 62.931... \times 1.4$
$\qquad\qquad\qquad\qquad\qquad\qquad = 88.104...$ J **[1 mark]**
Output power of the motor $= \Delta W \div \Delta t = 88.104... \div 2.2$
$\qquad\qquad\qquad\qquad\qquad\qquad = 40.047...$ W
$\qquad\qquad\qquad\qquad\qquad\qquad = \mathbf{40\ W}$ **(to 2 s.f.) [1 mark]**

Answers

3.2 For the first d m, the box moves up the ramp with a constant acceleration of 14.6 ms^{-2}.

After this, the motor is switched off, so the resultant force acting on the box = weight acting down the ramp + friction
$$= 11.053... + 16.838... = 27.891... \text{ N } \textbf{\textit{[1 mark]}}$$
Acceleration of the box down the ramp after it has travelled d m:
$F = ma$, so $a = F \div m = 27.891... \div 2.4 = 11.621...$ ms^{-2} **[1 mark]**
Use equations for uniform acceleration to calculate the value of d:
For the first d m:
Let the direction of motion of the box be positive.
$s = d$ m, $u = 0$ ms^{-1}, $v = ?$, $a = 14.6$ ms^{-2}
$v^2 = u^2 + 2as = 0^2 + (2 \times 14.6 \times d) = 29.2d$
$v = \sqrt{29.2d}$ ms^{-1} **[1 mark]**
From the point when the motor is switched off until the box reaches the top of the ramp:
$s = (1.4 - d)$ m, $u = \sqrt{29.2d}$ ms^{-1}, $v = 0$ ms^{-1},
$a = -11.621...$ ms^{-2}
$v^2 = u^2 + 2as$
$0^2 = \left(\sqrt{29.2d}\right)^2 + (2a \times (1.4 - d))$
$0 = 29.2d + 2.8a - 2ad$
$29.2d - 2ad = -2.8a$
$(29.2 - 2a)d = -2.8a$
$d = \dfrac{-2.8a}{29.2 - 2a}$
$ = \dfrac{(-2.8) \times (-11.621...)}{29.2 - (2 \times (-11.621...))}$
$ = 0.62048... = \textbf{0.62 m (to 2 s.f.)} \textbf{\textit{[1 mark]}}$

3.3 $F = ma$, so F and m will need to be expressed in terms of W_1, W_2 and g.

Because the box and the mass are attached, they behave as a single moving system. This means the mass of the whole system should be considered when using $F = ma$.

The resultant force acting on the whole system is the force(s) acting in the direction of motion minus the force(s) acting in the opposite direction of motion. The only forces acting on the system are the weights of the box and mass, so:
resultant force $= W_2 - W_1$ **[1 mark]**
$W = mg$, so $m = W \div g$
The mass of the whole system, $m = \dfrac{W_1 + W_2}{g}$ **[1 mark]**
$a = F \div m = (W_2 - W_1) \div \dfrac{W_1 + W_2}{g} = \dfrac{(W_2 - W_1)g}{W_1 + W_2}$ **[1 mark]**

3.4 $P = Fv$, $v = \dfrac{\Delta s}{\Delta t}$

efficiency $= \dfrac{\text{useful output power}}{\text{input power}} \times 100$

useful output power $= \dfrac{\text{efficiency} \times \text{input power}}{100}$
$\phantom{\text{useful output power}} = \dfrac{78 \times 5.4}{100}$
$\phantom{\text{useful output power}} = 4.212$ W **[1 mark]**

Magnitude of the force applied by the motor:
$W_2 - W_1 = 26.5 - m_{box}g = 26.5 - (2.4 \times 9.81) = 2.956$ N **[1 mark]**

$v = \dfrac{P}{F} = \dfrac{4.212}{2.956} = 1.4248...$ ms^{-1} **[1 mark]**

distance travelled $= 82$ cm $= 0.82$ m
$\Delta t = \dfrac{\Delta s}{v} = \dfrac{0.82}{1.4248...} = 0.5754...$ s $= \textbf{0.58 s (to 2 s.f.)}$ **[1 mark]**

4.1 $W = mg$ and $\rho = \dfrac{m}{V}$

Circumference $= 2\pi r = 9.2$ cm $= 0.092$ m
$r = \dfrac{0.092}{2\pi} = 0.01464...$ m
$V_{sphere} = \dfrac{4}{3}\pi r^3 = \dfrac{4}{3}\pi \times 0.01464...^3 = 1.3149... \times 10^{-5}$ m^3 **[1 mark]**
$m_{sphere} = \rho V = \left(0.55 \times 10^3\right) \times \left(1.3149... \times 10^{-5}\right)$
$\phantom{m_{sphere}} = 7.2322... \times 10^{-3}$ kg **[1 mark]**
$W = mg = \left(7.2322... \times 10^{-3}\right) \times 9.81$
$ = 0.07094...$ N $= \textbf{0.071 N (to 2 s.f.)}$ **[1 mark]**

4.2 The mobile is in equilibrium. The principle of moments states that the sum of the clockwise moments will be balanced by the sum of the anticlockwise moments about the pivot.
The pivot is the point where the string is attached to the mobile.
Take moments about the point of suspension:

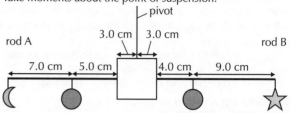

To calculate the moment of each component, use $M = Fd$, where $F =$ weight of a component and $d =$ distance between the pivot and the component.
Anticlockwise moments:
$M_{moon} = 0.025 \times 0.15 = 0.00375$ Nm
$M_{sphere} = 0.071 \times 0.08 = 0.00568$ Nm
The centre of mass of an object is the point at which its whole weight can be considered to act at. For uniform regular solids, the centre of mass is at the centre of the object, so the centre of mass of the cylindrical rod will occur half way along its length.
$M_{rod\,A} = 0.120 \times 0.09 = 0.0108$ Nm **[1 mark]**
The centre of the cube lies directly below the pivot, so it does not exert a moment.
Clockwise moments:
$M_{sphere} = 0.071 \times 0.07 = 0.00497$ Nm
$M_{star} = 0.16\,W_{star}$
$M_{rod\,B} = 0.150 \times 0.095 = 0.01425$ Nm **[1 mark]**
Equating clockwise and anticlockwise moments:
$0.00497 + 0.16\,W_{star} + 0.01425 = 0.00375 + 0.00568 + 0.0108$
$0.16\,W_{star} + 0.01922 = 0.02023$
$0.16\,W_{star} = 0.00101$
$W_{star} = 0.00101 \div 0.16 = 0.0063125$ N
$\phantom{W_{star}} = \textbf{0.0063 N (to 2 s.f.)}$ **[1 mark]**

You still get full marks if you used the unrounded value of the weight of a sphere in your calculation.

4.3 The question is asking for the tensile strain $\left(\dfrac{\Delta L}{L}\right)$ as a percentage.

Young modulus $= \dfrac{\text{tensile stress}}{\text{tensile strain}} = 2.2 \times 10^9$ Pa
stress $= \dfrac{F}{A}$
$F =$ weight of mobile
$ = (4 \times 0.071) + (2 \times 0.025) + (2 \times 0.0063125) + (2 \times 0.120) + (2 \times 0.150) + 1.165$
$ = 2.051625$ N **[1 mark]**
radius of string is 1.0 mm $= 1 \times 10^{-3}$ m
$A = \pi r^2 = \pi \times (1 \times 10^{-3})^2 = 3.1415... \times 10^{-6}$ m^2
stress $= \dfrac{F}{A} = \dfrac{2.051625}{3.1415... \times 10^{-6}} = 6.5305... \times 10^5$ Pa **[1 mark]**

tensile strain $= \dfrac{\text{tensile stress}}{\text{Young modulus}} = \dfrac{6.5305... \times 10^5}{2.2 \times 10^9}$
$\phantom{\text{tensile strain}} = 2.9684... \times 10^{-4}$

As a percentage:
$(2.9684... \times 10^{-4}) \times 100 = 0.029684...\%$
$\phantom{(2.9684... \times 10^{-4}) \times 100} = \textbf{0.030\% (to 2 s.f.)}$ **[1 mark]**

Answers

5.1 When a mass is added to the test wire, it will cause any kinks in the wire to straighten. This gives a larger extension (ΔL) for that mass than is true. Thermal expansion of the test wire during the experiment will also cause a larger value of ΔL to be recorded for a certain mass than is true. Young modulus $= \frac{FL}{\Delta LA}$, so both of these would cause the calculated value of the Young modulus to be lower than the true value *[1 mark]*. To reduce the effect of kinks in the wire, 0.50 kg masses are added to both wires at the start of the experiment to straighten them both out *[1 mark]*. To reduce the effect of thermal expansion, the extension of the test wire is measured relative to an identical control wire. The test wire and control wire will both expand by the same amount, so the thermal expansion will not be included in the measurements of ΔL *[1 mark]*.

5.2 E.g. stress = force ÷ area. The force is the weight (*mg*) of the masses acting on the test wire minus the initial 0.50 kg mass. A mass balance could have been used to measure each mass before it is added to the test wire, so that the total weight can be calculated *[1 mark]*. A (second) micrometer could have been used to measure the diameter of the wire at several points along its length. The average diameter can then be used to calculate the cross-sectional area using $A = \pi r^2$ where *r* is half of the wire's diameter *[1 mark]*. Strain = extension ÷ original length. The extension of the test wire is calculated from $d - d_0$. The original length of the test wire could have been measured using a ruler after the initial 0.50 kg mass had been added *[1 mark]*.
The initial 0.50 kg mass should not be included in the calculation, as it is used to straighten out the test wire. This is also why the extension is measured relative to d_0 (when the 0.50 kg mass is attached to the test wire).

5.3 The elastic limit is the point at which the wire starts to behave plastically *[1 mark]*. The student could e.g. estimate the position of the elastic limit by removing the masses from the test wire after each mass is added. She would then need to adjust the micrometer so that the spirit level is horizontal, before comparing the micrometer reading to d_0. If the two values differ, the wire has been plastically deformed *[1 mark]*. The minimum mass required for plastic deformation to be recorded will approximate the position of the elastic limit, which can be marked on the graph *[1 mark]*.

5.4 Young modulus = tensile stress ÷ tensile strain
= gradient of a stress-strain graph

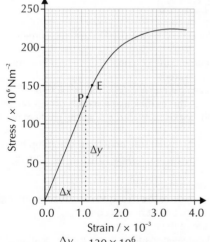

gradient $= \frac{\Delta y}{\Delta x} = \frac{130 \times 10^6}{1.1 \times 10^{-3}} = 1.1818... \times 10^{11}$ Nm^{-2}

$= \mathbf{1.2 \times 10^{11}}$ **Nm^{-2} (to 2 s.f.) *[1 mark]***

5.5 Strain = 0.11% = 0.11 ÷ 100 = 1.1×10^{-3}
This occurs at a lower tensile stress than point E, so the wire behaves elastically as it undergoes a strain of 0.11%. This means that all of the work done on the wire by the masses is stored as elastic strain energy in the wire.
Area under graph gives the elastic strain energy per unit volume.
Area up to a strain of $1.1 \times 10^{-3} = 0.5 \times (130 \times 10^6) \times (1.1 \times 10^{-3})$
$= 71\,500$ Jm^{-3} *[1 mark]*
Calculate the volume of the wire:
initial length of wire = 750 mm = 0.75 m
radius of wire = 0.40 ÷ 2 = 0.20 mm = 2.0×10^{-4} m
cross-sectional area $= \pi r^2 = \pi \times (2.0 \times 10^{-4})^2$
$= 1.2566... \times 10^{-7}$ m^2
volume = length × cross-sectional area
$= 0.75 \times (1.2566... \times 10^{-7})$
$= 9.42477... \times 10^{-8}$ m^3 *[1 mark]*
total elastic strain energy stored in the wire:
$71\,500 \times (9.42477... \times 10^{-8}) = 0.006738...$ J
$= \mathbf{0.0067}$ **J (to 2 s.f.) *[1 mark]***

Section 6 — Electricity

Page 83 — Current, Potential Difference and Resistance

1 Time in seconds = 10.0 × 60 = 600 s. Use the formula $I = \Delta Q / \Delta t$ which gives you $I = 4500 / 600 = \mathbf{7.5}$ **A *[1 mark]***
Write down the formula first. Don't forget the unit in your answer.

2 Rearrange the formula $V = W / Q$ to give $Q = W / V$
so you get $Q = 120 / 12$ *[1 mark]* = **10 C *[1 mark]***

3 a) $R = V/I = 2/12 = 0.166... = \mathbf{0.17}$ **Ω (to 2 s.f.) *[1 mark]***
b) $I = V/R = 35/0.166... = \mathbf{210}$ **A *[1 mark]***
c)

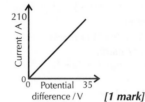

[1 mark]

Page 85 — I/V Characteristics

1 a) The graph is curved, starting steep and then levelling off as voltage/current increases *[1 mark]*.
b) As the current increases, the temperature of the filament increases *[1 mark]*. As the temperature increases, the resistance increases, so the graph gets shallower *[1 mark]*.

2 As the temperature of the thermistor increases, more charge carriers are released *[1 mark]*. More charge carriers available allows more current to flow in the circuit *[1 mark]*. So the current in the circuit can be used to monitor the temperature *[1 mark]*.

Page 87 — Resistivity and Superconductivity

1 a) Area $= \pi (d/2)^2$ and $d = 1.0 \times 10^{-3}$ m
so Area $= \pi \times (0.5 \times 10^{-3})^2$
$= 7.853... \times 10^{-7}$ m^2 *[1 mark]*
$R = \frac{\rho l}{A} = \frac{2.8 \times 10^{-8} \times 4.00}{7.853... \times 10^{-7}} = \mathbf{0.14}$ **Ω (to 2 s.f.)**
[1 mark for correct working, 1 mark for answer and unit.]
b) Resistance will now be zero *[1 mark]*.
Because aluminium is a superconductor below its transition temperature of 1.2 K *[1 mark]*.

2 a) Resistivity varies with temperature *[1 mark]* so she must find the resistivity at 20°C in order to compare it to the resistivities in the table *[1 mark]*.
b) The diameter / cross-sectional area of the wire *[1 mark]* using a micrometer / micrometer caliper / caliper *[1 mark]*.
c) E.g. the wire is cylindrical / has a circular cross section *[1 mark]*.

Answers

Page 89 — Electrical Energy and Power

1 a) $P = VI$, so heater current $= P/V = 920/230 = $ **4.0 A (to 2 s.f.)** *[1 mark]*

b) $V = IR$, so motor current $= V/R = 230/190$
$$= 1.210... = \textbf{1.2 A (to 2 s.f.)} \textit{ [1 mark]}$$

c) Motor power $= V \times I = 230 \times 1.210... = 278.4...$
$$= 280 \text{ W (to 2 s.f.)} \textit{ [1 mark]}$$
Total power $=$ motor power $+$ heater power
$$= 278.4... + 920 = 1198 \text{ W}$$
$$= 1200 \text{ W (to 2 s.f.)} = \textbf{1.2 kW (to 2 s.f.)} \textit{ [1 mark]}$$

2 a) $E = VIt = 12 \times 48 \times 2.0$ *[1 mark]* $= $ **1200 J (to 2 s.f.)** *[1 mark]*

b) Energy wasted $= I^2Rt = 48^2 \times 0.01 \times 2.0$ *[1 mark]*
$$= \textbf{46 J (to 2 s.f.)} \textit{ [1 mark]}$$

Page 91 — E.m.f. and Internal Resistance

1 a) $\varepsilon = I(R + r)$ so $I = \varepsilon/(R + r) = 24/(4.0 + 0.80)$ *[1 mark]*
$$= \textbf{5.0 A (to 2 s.f.)} \textit{ [1 mark]}$$

b) $v = Ir = 5.0 \times 0.80 = $ **4.0 V (to 2 s.f.)** *[1 mark]*
You could have used $\varepsilon = V + v$ and calculated V using $V = IR_{drill}$

2 C *[1 mark]*
$\varepsilon = I(R + r)$, but since there are two cells in series replace r with $2r$, and ε with 2ε, then rearrange to find I.

Page 93 — Conservation of Energy and Charge

1 a) Resistance of parallel resistors:
$$1/R_{parallel} = 1/6.0 + 1/3.0 = 1/2 \Rightarrow R_{parallel} = 2.0 \, \Omega \textit{ [1 mark]}$$
Total resistance:
$$R_{total} = 4.0 + R_{parallel} = 4.0 + 2.0 = \textbf{6.0 } \Omega \textit{ [1 mark]}$$

b) $V = I_3 R_{total} \Rightarrow I_3 = V / R_{total} = 12 / 6.0 = $ **2.0 A** *[1 mark]*

c) $V = IR = 2.0 \times 4.0 = $ **8.0 V** *[1 mark]*

d) E.m.f. $=$ sum of p.d.s in circuit, so $12 = 8.0 + V_{parallel}$
$$V_{parallel} = 12 - 8.0 = \textbf{4.0 V} \textit{ [1 mark]}$$

e) $I = V/R$, so $I_1 = 4.0 / 3.0 = $ **1.3 A (to 2 s.f.)** *[1 mark]*
$I_2 = 4.0 / 6.0 = $ **0.67 A (to 2 s.f.)** *[1 mark]*
You can check your answers by making sure that $I_3 = I_2 + I_1$.

Page 95 — The Potential Divider

1 Parallel circuit, so p.d. across both sets of resistors is 12 V.

a) There are two equal resistors in the top branch of the circuit. The p.d. between points A and B is equal to the potential difference across one of these resistors:
$$V_{AB} = \frac{1}{2} \times 12 = \textbf{6.0 V} \textit{ [1 mark]}$$

b) There are three equal resistors in the bottom branch of the circuit. The p.d. between points A and C is equal to the potential difference across two of them:
$$V_{AC} = \frac{2}{3} \times 12 = \textbf{8.0 V} \textit{ [1 mark]}$$

c) $V_{BC} = V_{AC} - V_{AB} = 8 - 6 = $ **2.0 V** *[1 mark]*

2 a) $V_{AB} = 50/80 \times 12 = $ **7.5 V** *[1 mark]*
(ignore the 10 Ω — no current flows that way)

b) Total resistance of the parallel circuit:
$$1/R_T = 1/50 + 1/(10 + 40) = 1/25 \Rightarrow R_T = 25 \, \Omega \textit{ [1 mark]}$$
p.d. over the whole parallel arrangement $= 25/55 \times 12 = 5.45...$ V *[1 mark]*
p.d. across AB $= 40/50 \times 5.45...$
$$= 4.36... \text{ V} = \textbf{4.4 V (to 2 s.f.)} \textit{ [1 mark]}$$
current through 40.0 Ω resistor $= V/R$
$$= 4.36.../40.0 = \textbf{0.11 A (to 2 s.f.)} \textit{ [1 mark]}$$

Extra Exam Practice for Section 6

Pages 96-97

2.1 E.g. the terminal potential difference supplied by the battery is equal to the e.m.f generated by the battery minus the lost volts ($V = \varepsilon - v$). The lost volts are equal to the current through the battery multiplied by the internal resistance ($V = \varepsilon - Ir$) *[1 mark]*. Because the current supplied is very large, the internal resistance must be very small to avoid a large value for the lost volts/to provide a large enough terminal potential difference for the starter motor to start the engine *[1 mark]*.

2.2 **5-6 marks:**
The answer describes the full experimental procedure including correct suggestions of how to ensure the results are valid and accurate, and includes explanations of why the validity/accuracy is improved. The answer may include a diagram, but this is not essential. The answer has a clear and logical structure. The information given is relevant and detailed.
3-4 marks:
The answer describes most of the experimental procedure with some briefly explained suggestions of how to improve the accuracy or validity of the results. The answer may include a diagram, but this is not essential. The answer has some structure. Most of the information given is relevant and there is some detail involved.
1-2 marks:
A few simple steps for the experiment are described. The answer may not include ways to ensure the results are accurate or valid, or may give one or two simple suggestions without detail or explanation. The answer has no clear structure. The information given is basic and lacking in detail. It may not all be relevant.
0 marks:
No relevant information is given.
Here are some points your answer may include:
The student should connect the battery to a variable resistor, with a voltmeter connected in parallel with the battery and an ammeter in series with the battery.
E.g.

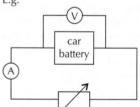

The variable resistor should be adjusted to vary the current through the circuit.
For each value of current, the potential difference across the battery should be measured.
A graph of p.d. (V) against current (I) should be plotted.
$\varepsilon = V - Ir$ so rearrange this to look like $y = mx + c$. V is on the y-axis and I is on the x-axis so $V = -rI + \varepsilon$, so the gradient of the graph is equal to $-r$.
To achieve valid results, make sure only the relationship between current and p.d. is being tested / make sure that the current and the p.d. are the only variables that change / make sure all other variables are controlled.
In order for the resistance of the circuit to remain constant, the temperature of the circuit must remain constant.
Keep the temperature of the room constant.
Turn off the circuit between readings to reduce the heating of the circuit.
Use low currents to minimise heating.
Valid results must be precise. To ensure the results are precise, use a voltmeter and ammeter with small intervals on their scales. This reduces the uncertainty in readings, making them more precise.
Take multiple readings of the p.d. and calculate the mean to reduce the effect of random errors to improve the precision.
To achieve accurate results, calibrate equipment to avoid systematic errors.

Answers

2.3 When the temperature decreases, the resistance of the thermistor increases. This means that the thermistor's share of the total potential difference increases, so the potential difference across the heating wires increases *[1 mark]*. As $V = IR$, an increase in potential difference will increase the current though the wires, which will cause the wires to heat up and heat up the glass *[1 mark]*.

2.4 $\rho = \frac{RA}{l}$, so $R = \frac{\rho l}{A}$. And $A = \pi r^2$ where $r = d \div 2$.

$R = \frac{\rho l}{\pi(d \div 2)^2} = \frac{3.86 \times 10^{-8} \times 1.25}{\pi(0.102 \times 10^{-3} \div 2)^2}$

$= 5.904... = $ **5.90 Ω (to 3 s.f.) *[1 mark]***

2.5 $R = V / I$ so $I = V / R$. To calculate the current through each wire, first calculate the potential difference across each wire. The potential difference across each wire is equal to the potential difference across the thermistor, because they are in parallel.

The potential difference across the thermistor is $V = \frac{R_2}{R_1 + R_2} \times V_s$

where R_2 is the combined resistance of the thermistor and the wires. $R_{\text{thermistor}}$ is 38.0 Ω at 1.0 °C.

$\frac{1}{R_2} = \frac{1}{R_{\text{thermistor}}} + \frac{5}{R_{\text{wire}}} = \frac{1}{38.0} + \frac{5}{5.904...} = 0.873...$

$R_2 = 1 \div 0.873... = 1.145... \ \Omega$ *[1 mark]*

$V = \frac{R_2}{R_1 + R_2} \times V_s = \frac{1.145...}{2.50 + 1.145...} \times 12 = 3.770...$ V *[1 mark]*

$I = \frac{V}{R_{\text{wire}}} = \frac{3.770...}{5.904...} = 0.638... = $ **0.64 A (to 2 s.f.) *[1 mark]***

You could have used the rounded value of $R_{\text{wire}} = 5.90 \ \Omega$ in your calculations here as it was given to you in question 2.4.

2.6 The wires are in series with each other, so the total resistance of the wires is $5 \times R_{\text{wire}}$.

The wires are in parallel with the thermistor, so the total resistance of the wires and thermistor, R_2 is given by:

$\frac{1}{R_2} = \frac{1}{R_{\text{thermistor}}} + \frac{1}{5 \times R_{\text{wire}}} = \frac{1}{38.0} + \frac{1}{5 \times 5.904...} = 0.0601...$

$R_2 = 1 \div 0.0601... = 16.615... \ \Omega$ *[1 mark]*

$V = \frac{R_2}{R_1 + R_2} \times V_s = \frac{16.615...}{2.50 + 16.615...} \times 12 = 10.430...$ V

$I = \frac{V}{R}$ where R is the total resistance of the 5 wires:

$I = \frac{V}{5 \times R_{\text{wire}}} = \frac{10.430...}{5 \times 5.904...} = 0.353... = $ **0.35 A (to 2 s.f.) *[1 mark]***

You could have used the rounded value of $R_{\text{wire}} = 5.90 \ \Omega$ in your calculations here as it was given to you in question 2.4.

2.7 The amount of heating depends on the energy transferred in a certain time/the power.

Figure 2: $P = VI = 3.8 \times 0.64 = 2.4$ W (to 2 s.f.)

The values for V and I here were calculated in the answer to 2.5.

Figure 4: in series, the potential difference is shared between the wires, so each wire will get $\frac{1}{5}$ of the potential difference.

$P = VI = (10 \div 5) \times 0.35 = 0.70$ W (to 2 s.f.) *[1 mark]*

The values for V and I here were calculated in the answer to 2.6.

The power dissipated by the wires in Figure 2 is larger than the power dissipated by the wires in Figure 4, so Figure 2 will heat the rear window faster *[1 mark]*.

You should normally use unrounded values in your calculations. However the rounded values can be used here as the question only asks you to find which setup dissipates the most power, rather than asking for a specific value. If instead you have correctly used your unrounded values in your calculations, then you still get a mark for your calculations and a mark for a correct conclusion.

Section 7 — Further Mechanics

Page 99 — Circular Motion

1 a) $\omega = \frac{\theta}{t}$ *[1 mark]* $= \frac{2\pi}{3.2 \times 10^7} = 1.963... \times 10^{-7}$

$= $ **2.0 $\times$ 10^{-7} rad s^{-1} (to 2 s.f.) *[1 mark]***

b) $v = r\omega = 1.5 \times 10^{11} \times 1.963... \times 10^{-7}$

$= 29\,452.4... \ \text{ms}^{-1} = $ **29 000 ms^{-1} (to 2 s.f.) *[1 mark]***

c) $F = m\omega^2 r = 5.98 \times 10^{24} \times (1.963... \times 10^{-7})^2 \times 1.5 \times 10^{11}$ *[1 mark]*

$= 3.4582... \times 10^{22}$ N $= $ **3.5 $\times$ 10^{22} N (to 2 s.f.) *[1 mark]***

d) The gravitational force between the Sun and the Earth *[1 mark]*.

2 a) Gravity pulling down on the water at the top of the swing gives a centripetal acceleration of 9.81 ms^{-2} *[1 mark]*. If the circular motion of the water has a centripetal acceleration of less than 9.81 ms^{-2}, gravity will pull it in too tight a circle. The water will fall out of the bucket.

Since $a = \omega^2 r$, $\omega = \sqrt{\frac{a}{r}} = \sqrt{\frac{9.81}{1.00}}$,

so $\omega = 3.13...$ rad s^{-1} = **3.13 rad s^{-1} (to 3 s.f.) *[1 mark]***

$\omega = 2\pi f$, so $f = \frac{\omega}{2\pi} = \frac{3.13...}{2\pi} = $ **0.498 rev s^{-1} (to 3 s.f.) *[1 mark]***

b) Centripetal force $= m\omega^2 r$

$= 10.0 \times (5.00)^2 \times 1.00 = 250$ N *[1 mark]*

This force is provided by both the tension in the rope, T, and gravity acting on the water and the bucket (their weight).

$T + (10.0 \times 9.81) = 250$ *[1 mark]*

So $T = 250 - (10.0 \times 9.81) = 151.9$ N

$= $ **152 N (to 3 s.f.) *[1 mark]***

Remember, $W = mg$.

Page 101 — Simple Harmonic Motion

1 a) Simple harmonic motion is an oscillation in which the acceleration of an object is directly proportional to its displacement from the midpoint *[1 mark]*, and is directed towards the midpoint *[1 mark]*.

(*The SHM equation would get you the marks if you defined all the variables*).

b) Acceleration during free fall is constant, not proportional to displacement, which is a requirement of SHM *[1 mark]*.

2 E.g. The total energy of the mass-spring system is constant *[1 mark]*. At the midpoint, the mass's E_p is zero and its E_k is maximum *[1 mark]*. At the maximum displacement (the amplitude) on both sides of the midpoint, the mass's E_k is zero and its E_p is at its maximum *[1 mark]*. As the mass moves away from the midpoint, E_k is transferred into E_p in the spring. As it moves towards the midpoint, E_p in the spring is transferred into E_k *[1 mark]*.

3 a) Maximum speed $= \omega A = (2\pi f)A = 2\pi \times 1.5 \times 0.05$ *[1 mark]*

$= 0.471...$ ms$^{-1} = $ **0.5 ms^{-1} (to 1 s.f.) *[1 mark]***

b) $x = A\cos(\omega t) = A\cos(2\pi f t)$

$= 0.05 \times \cos(2\pi \times 1.5 \times 0.1) = 0.05 \times \cos(0.94...)$ *[1 mark]*

$= 0.0294...$ m $= $ **0.03 m (to 1 s.f.) *[1 mark]***

Remember to make sure your calculator is in radian mode.

c) $x = A\cos(\omega t) = A\cos(2\pi f t)$

$0.01 = 0.05 \times \cos(2\pi \times 1.5t)$

So $0.20 = \cos(3\pi t)$

$\cos^{-1}(0.20) = 3\pi t$ *[1 mark]*

$t = 0.145... = $ **0.1 s (to 1 s.f.) *[1 mark]***

4 $\omega_C = 2\omega_D$ and maximum acceleration $= \omega^2 A$.

$a_{\text{max}(C)} = \omega_C^2 A = (2\omega_D)^2 A = 4\omega_D^2 A$

$a_{\text{max}(D)} = \omega_D^2 A$

So $a_{\text{max}(C)} = 4a_{\text{max}(D)}$

D *[1 mark]*

Page 103 — Simple Harmonic Oscillators

1 a) Extension of spring, $x = 0.20 - 0.10 = 0.10$ m *[1 mark]*

Force $= -$weight $= -9.81$ Nm$^{-1} \times 0.10$ m $= -0.981$ N

$F = -kx$ so $k = -F \div x = -(-9.81 \times 0.10) \div (0.20 - 0.10)$

$= 9.81 = $ **9.8 Nm^{-1} (to 2 s.f.) *[1 mark]***

b) $T = 2\pi\sqrt{\frac{m}{k}} = 2\pi\sqrt{\frac{0.10}{9.81}} = 0.634...$ s

$= $ **0.63 s (to 2 s.f.) *[1 mark]***

c) $m \propto T^2$ so if T is doubled, T^2 is quadrupled and m is quadrupled *[1 mark]*.

So mass needed $= 4 \times 0.10 = $ **0.40 kg *[1 mark]***

2 E.g. $5T_{\text{short pendulum}} = 3T_{\text{long pendulum}}$ *[1 mark]* and $T = 2\pi\sqrt{\frac{l}{g}}$

Let length of long pendulum $= l$

So $5\left(2\pi\sqrt{\frac{0.20}{g}}\right) = 3\left(2\pi\sqrt{\frac{l}{g}}\right)$ *[1 mark]*

Dividing by 2π and squaring gives: $25 \times \frac{0.2}{g} = 9 \times \frac{l}{g}$

Which simplifies to $5 = 9l$

So length of long pendulum $= 5/9 = 0.555...$

$= $ **0.56 m (to 2 s.f.) *[1 mark]***

Answers

Page 105 — Free and Forced Vibrations

1) a) When a system is forced to vibrate at a frequency that's close to, or the same as its resonant frequency *[1 mark]* and oscillates with a much larger than usual amplitude *[1 mark]*.

b)

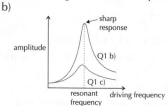

[1 mark] for a peak at the resonant frequency,
[1 mark] for a sharp peak.

c) See graph. *[1 mark]* for a smaller peak around the resonant frequency.

2 a) A system is critically damped if it returns to rest in the shortest time possible when it's displaced from equilibrium and released *[1 mark]*.

b) E.g. suspension in a car *[1 mark]*.

Extra Exam Practice for Section 7

Pages 106-107

2.1 The pilot follows the same circular path as the plane, and will be moving at the same linear speed as the plane, so you can consider the forces acting on the pilot. If the seat is providing a force of 0.00 N, then the only force acting on the pilot is the pilot's weight (mg). This must be providing all of the centripetal force that keeps the pilot moving in a circle.

Centripetal force, $F = \frac{mv^2}{r}$, so $mg = \frac{mv^2}{r}$ *[1 mark]*

$g = \frac{v^2}{r}$, so $v = \sqrt{gr}$

Radius of circle, $r = 185 \div 2 = 92.5$ m

$v = \sqrt{9.81 \times 92.5} = 30.1234...$ ms^{-1} = **30.1 ms^{-1} (to 3 s.f.)** *[1 mark]*

2.2 The pilot is moving at a constant linear speed, so the centripetal force required to keep the pilot moving in a circle is constant (since $F = \frac{mv^2}{r}$). At point A, the centripetal force is equal in magnitude to the pilot's weight, so the same must be true at point D *[1 mark]*. At point D, the centripetal force acts horizontally (towards the centre of the circle). The pilot's weight acts vertically downwards, so cannot contribute to the centripetal force — this must be solely provided by the reaction force on the pilot from the seat *[1 mark]*. The pilot is accelerating horizontally towards the centre of the circle, so there must be no acceleration/resultant force in the vertical direction. This means that the seat must also apply a force on the pilot vertically upwards to balance the weight of the pilot *[1 mark]*. So the seat exerts an overall force on the pilot with vertical and horizontal components of the same magnitude (equal to the pilot's weight), therefore the direction of the overall force is 45° anticlockwise above the horizontal *[1 mark]*.

You could draw a diagram of the forces acting on the pilot to help explain your answer as long as you still write a full explanation, e.g.

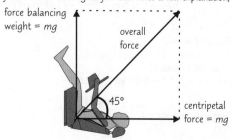

2.3 At the midpoint of the vertical oscillation, the plane will be travelling at its maximum vertical velocity, so $v_{vertical} = \omega A$. $v_{horizontal} = 75$ ms^{-1}, so:

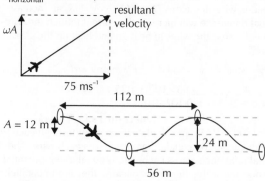

It's always a good idea to draw a diagram at the start of a question like this and label it with the values you know/can figure out (e.g. in this case, the amplitude of simple harmonic motion, and the horizontal distance travelled during one complete oscillation). This helps you to visualise the problem and points you in the right direction as to what to do next.

$\omega = 2\pi f$ and $f = \frac{1}{T}$

Period, T, is the time taken to complete one full oscillation, so

$T = \frac{\text{distance}}{\text{speed}} = \frac{\text{horizontal distance travelled in one oscillation}}{\text{horizontal velocity}}$

$= \frac{112}{75} = 1.49333...$ s *[1 mark]*

So $\omega = \frac{2\pi}{T} = \frac{2\pi}{1.49333...} = 4.2074...$ rad s^{-1} *[1 mark]*

$v_{vertical} = \omega A = 4.2074... \times 12 = 50.4898...$ms^{-1} *[1 mark]*

The magnitude of the resultant velocity can be found using Pythagoras' theorem:

resultant velocity $= \sqrt{v_{horizontal}^2 + v_{vertical}^2}$

$= \sqrt{75^2 + 50.4898...^2}$

$= 90.411...$ ms^{-1} = **90 ms^{-1} (to 2 s.f.)** *[1 mark]*

2.4

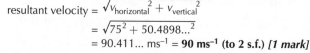

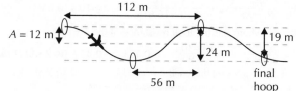

Horizontal distance = 56 m, so to calculate the average horizontal velocity, the time taken to travel between the final two hoops is needed. Vertical velocity still follows the same simple harmonic motion as in 2.3.

$x = A\cos(\omega t)$: $A = 12$ m, $\omega = 4.2074...$ rad s^{-1}

Let $t = 0$ at the last high hoop. At $t = 0$, $x = A = 12$ m.
At time t, the plane reaches the final low hoop, with a displacement of $12 - 19 = -7$ m.

Rearrange $x = A\cos(\omega t)$ to make t the subject:

$t = \frac{1}{\omega}\cos^{-1}\left(\frac{x}{A}\right) = \frac{1}{4.2074...}\cos^{-1}\left(\frac{-7}{12}\right) = 0.5213...$s *[1 mark]*

Average horizontal velocity $= \frac{\text{horizontal distance}}{\text{time}} = \frac{56}{0.5213...}$

$= 107.411...$ ms^{-1}

$= $ **110 ms^{-1} (to 2 s.f.)** *[1 mark]*

3.1 $F = -kx$ and $T = 2\pi\sqrt{\frac{m}{k}}$

$T = \frac{1}{f} = \frac{1}{25} = 0.04$ s *[1 mark]*

$m = 42$ g $= 0.042$ kg

$T = 2\pi\sqrt{\frac{m}{k}}$, so $k = \frac{4\pi^2 m}{T^2} = \frac{4\pi^2 \times 0.042}{0.04^2} = 1036.308...$ Nm^{-1} *[1 mark]*

Restoring force, $F = -kx$

$x = 2.4$ mm $= 2.4 \times 10^{-3}$ m

$F = -1036.308... \times 2.4 \times 10^{-3}$

$= -2.4871...$ N

Magnitude of restoring force is therefore **2.5 N (to 2 s.f.)** *[1 mark]*.

The minus sign can be ignored, as the question just asked for the magnitude of the force.

Answers

3.2 How to grade your answer:

5-6 marks:
A detailed explanation is given on the effects of resonance and damping on the output of loudspeakers, as well as the advantage of using different-sized cones. The answer successfully links these points to improvements in sound quality in a clear and logical way.

3-4 marks:
An explanation is given on the effects of resonance and damping on the output of loudspeakers, and an attempt has been made to explain the advantage of using different-sized cones. The answer tries to link these points to improvements in sound quality, but it lacks some clarity. There is some structure to the answer, and the information is mostly relevant to the question.

1-2 marks:
A brief explanation is given on the effects of resonance and damping on the output of loudspeakers, but no attempt has been made to correctly explain the advantage of using different-sized cones. The answer doesn't link points to improvements in sound quality, lacks detail, and the information given may not be relevant to the question.

0 marks:
No relevant information is given.

Here are some points your answer may include:
An ideal loudspeaker unit will produce a sound with an amplitude that only depends on the amplitude of the electrical (a.c.) signal driving it.
The amplitude of the sound produced should not be dependent on the frequency of sound being produced (otherwise different pitches would have different volumes).
However due to the effects of resonance, a cone forced to vibrate at its resonant frequency will oscillate with a much larger amplitude than at other frequencies.
This means that the loudspeaker cone will produce a louder sound at its resonant frequency compared to at other frequencies, so the relative amplitudes of the sounds produced won't match the input signal.
Damping a loudspeaker cone reduces the effects of resonance — this means the amplitude of the sound produced will be more similar as its frequency varies.
Critically damping the system will make the response as similar as possible at different frequencies whilst still allowing it to oscillate, so this improves the sound quality of a loudspeaker cone.
The graph shows that the amplitude of the sound produced is very small for frequencies that are far away from the resonant frequency.
This can be improved by using different-sized cones with different resonant frequencies, as frequencies that are far from the resonant frequency of one cone will be closer to the resonant frequency of the second cone.
Filtering sounds by frequency and using different cones to produce them means sound can be produced at comparable amplitudes over a much wider range of frequencies.

Section 8 — Thermal Physics

Page 109 — Thermal Energy Transfer

1 Electrical energy supplied: $Q = 90 \times 3 \times 60$
$$= 16\ 200 \text{ J } \textit{[1 mark]}$$
The temperature rise is $12.7 - 4.5 = 8.2$ °C

$c = \dfrac{Q}{m\Delta\theta}$ so $c = \dfrac{16\ 200}{2.0 \times 8.2}$ *[1 mark]*

$= 987.8... = \textbf{990 Jkg}^{-1}\textbf{°C}^{-1}$ **(to 2 s.f.)**

[1 mark for correct number, 1 mark for correct unit.]
You need the right unit for the fourth mark — Jkg^{-1}K^{-1} would be right too.

2 a) Energy required to heat water to boiling point = $Q = mc\Delta\theta$,
$Q = 0.500 \times 4180 \times (100 - 20) = 1.672 \times 10^5$ J *[1 mark]*
Energy required to boil dry = $Q = ml = 0.500 \times 2.26 \times 10^6$
$$= 1.13 \times 10^6 \text{ J } \textit{[1 mark]}$$

So time to boil dry:
$\dfrac{\text{energy required to heat to 100°C and boil dry}}{\text{energy supplied per second}}$ *[1 mark]*

$= \dfrac{(1.672 \times 10^5) + (1.13 \times 10^6)}{3.00 \times 10^3}$ *[1 mark]*

$= 432.4 = \textbf{432 s}$ **(to 3 s.f.)** *[1 mark]*

b) B *[1 mark]*

Page 111 — Gas Laws

1 $107.89 + 273.15 = \textbf{381.04 K}$ *[1 mark]*

2 $V_1 = 2.42$ m^3, $V_2 = 6.43$ m^3, $T_2 = 293$ K.

Charles's Law: $\dfrac{V}{T}$ = constant so $\dfrac{V_2}{T_2} = \dfrac{6.43}{293} = 0.02194...$ *[1 mark]*

$T_1 = \dfrac{V_1}{\text{constant}} = \dfrac{2.42}{0.02194...} = 110.273...$

$= \textbf{110 K}$ **(to 3 s.f.)** *[1 mark]*

3 a) E.g. Connect a tube containing only oil and air to a Bourdon gauge and a bike pump *[1 mark]*. Measure the dimensions of the tube and the depth of the oil, then increase the pressure in the tube using the bike pump *[1 mark]*. Note down the pressure from the Bourdon gauge and measure the depth of the oil again *[1 mark]*. Repeat for different pressures then use your measurements to calculate the volume of the air in the tube. The results should show that as pressure increases, air volume decreases by the same proportion, and vice versa — i.e. pV = constant *[1 mark]*.

b) $V_1 = 0.460$ m^3, $p_1 = 1.03 \times 10^5$ Pa, $p_2 = 3.41 \times 10^5$ Pa.
$p_1 \times V_1$ = constant
$(1.03 \times 10^5) \times 0.460 = 47\ 380$ *[1 mark]*
$V_2 = $ constant $\div p_2 = 47\ 380 \div (3.41 \times 10^5)$
$$= 0.13894... = \textbf{0.139 m}^3 \text{ (to 3 s.f.) } \textit{[1 mark]}$$

Page 113 — Ideal Gas Equation

1 a) i) Number of moles $= \dfrac{\text{mass of gas}}{\text{molar mass}} = \dfrac{0.014}{0.028} = \textbf{0.50}$ *[1 mark]*
ii) Number of molecules = number of moles × Avogadro's constant
$= 0.50 \times 6.02 \times 10^{23} = \textbf{3.0} \times \textbf{10}^{23}$ **(to 2 s.f.)** *[1 mark]*

b) $pV = nRT$, so $p = \dfrac{nRT}{V}$. $T = 27.2 + 273.15 = 300.35$ K *[1 mark]*
$p = \dfrac{0.50 \times 8.31 \times 300.35}{0.0130} = 95\ 996.4...$
$= \textbf{96 000 Pa}$ **(to 2 s.f.)** *[1 mark]*

c) The pressure would also halve *[1 mark]* because it is proportional to the number of molecules — $pV = NkT$ *[1 mark]*.

2 At ground level, $\dfrac{pV}{T} = \dfrac{1.00 \times 10^5 \times 10.0}{293} = 3412.9...$ *[1 mark]*

pV/T is constant, so higher up $pV/T = 3412.9...$ JK^{-1} *[1 mark]*

Higher up, $p = \dfrac{3412.9... \times T}{V} = \dfrac{3412.9... \times 261}{25.0}$

$= 35\ 631.3... = \textbf{35 600 Pa}$ **(to 3 s.f.)** *[1 mark]*

3 Work done $= p\Delta V = p(V_2 - V_1)$
so $V_1 = V_2 - \dfrac{\text{work done}}{p}$

$= 10.3 - \dfrac{470 \times 10^3}{1.12 \times 10^5} = 6.1035...$ *[1 mark]*
$= \textbf{6.10 m}^3$ **(to 3 s.f.)** *[1 mark]*

Answers

Page 115 — The Pressure of an Ideal Gas

1 a) $pV = \frac{1}{3}Nm(c_{rms})^2$ Rearrange the equation: $(c_{rms})^2 = \frac{3pV}{Nm}$

$(c_{rms})^2 = \frac{3 \times (1.03 \times 10^5) \times (7.00 \times 10^{-5})}{(2.17 \times 10^{22}) \times (6.65 \times 10^{-27})}$ *[1 mark]*

$= 149\,890.8... = \mathbf{150\,000\ m^2s^{-2}}$ **(to 3 s.f.)** *[1 mark]*

b) r.m.s. speed $= \sqrt{(c_{rms})^2} = \sqrt{149\,890.8...} = 387.15....$

$= \mathbf{387\ ms^{-1}}$ **(to 3 s.f.)** *[1 mark]*

c) pV is proportional to T, so doubling T will double pV *[1 mark]*.

r.m.s. speed $= \sqrt{(c_{rms})^2} = \sqrt{\frac{3pV}{Nm}}$, so doubling pV will increase

the r.m.s. speed by a factor of $\sqrt{2}$.

r.m.s. speed $= 387.15... \times \sqrt{2}$

$= 547.5... = \mathbf{548\ ms^{-1}}$ **(to 3 s.f.)** *[1 mark]*

Page 117 — Kinetic Energy and the Development of Theories

1 $\frac{1}{2}m(c_{rms})^2 = \frac{3kT}{2}$

Rearranging gives: $(c_{rms})^2 = \frac{3kT}{m}$ *[1 mark]*

m = mass of 1 mole $\div N_A$

$= 2.80 \times 10^{-2} \div 6.02 \times 10^{23}$

$= 4.651... \times 10^{-26}$ kg *[1 mark]*

$(c_{rms})^2 = \frac{3 \times (1.38 \times 10^{-23}) \times 308}{4.651... \times 10^{-26}} = 274\,150.8$ *[1 mark]*

Typical speed = r.m.s. speed $= \sqrt{274\,150.8}$

$= 523.59... = \mathbf{524\ ms^{-1}}$ **(to 3 s.f.)** *[1 mark]*

2 a) Time = distance $\div$ speed = 8.19 m $\div$ 395

$= 0.02073...$

$= \mathbf{0.0207\ s}$ **(to 3 s.f.)** *[1 mark]*

b) Although the particles move at 395 ms^{-1} on average, they frequently collide with fast-moving molecules *[1 mark]*. So the particles move randomly in a zigzag motion — this is Brownian motion *[1 mark]*. So their motion in any one direction is limited and they only move slowly from one end of the room to another *[1 mark]*.

Extra Exam Practice for Section 8

Pages 118-119

2.1 The temperature difference between the surroundings and the ice is 20.0 °C in both experiments, so the rate at which heat is transferred from the surroundings to the ice is the same in both experiments.
The duration of both experiments is 500.0 s, so the total amount of heat energy transferred from the surroundings is the same. This means the extra energy transferred from the heater to the ice in experiment 2 corresponds to the extra mass of ice melted *[1 mark]*.
Energy = power × time
Difference in the energy supplied to ice:
$(50.0 \times 500.0) - (36.0 \times 500.0) = 25\,000 - 18\,000 = 7000$ J
Difference in mass of ice melted = 97.3 − 76.3
$= 21$ g $= 0.021$ kg *[1 mark]*
Substituting into $Q = ml$:
$l = Q \div m = 7000 \div 0.021$
$= 3.333... \times 10^5$ J kg^{-1} $= \mathbf{3.33 \times 10^5\ Jkg^{-1}}$ **(to 3 s.f.)** *[1 mark]*

2.2 The maximum additional pressure in the heater will occur if the 0.21 mg of water is completely vaporised and heated to 150.0 °C (the operating temperature of the heater) without any of it escaping.
$pV = nRT$
$V = 0.10$ cm^3 = 1.0×10^{-7} m^3
moles = mass of a substance (in grams) ÷ relative molecular mass.
mass = 0.21 mg = 2.1×10^{-4} g
Moles of water = $(2.1 \times 10^{-4}) \div 18 = 1.166... \times 10^{-5}$ moles *[1 mark]*.
$T = 150 + 273 = 423$ K
Additional pressure is equivalent to the pressure of $1.166... \times 10^{-5}$ moles of water vapour in a volume of 1.0×10^{-7} m^3 at 423 K:
$p = \frac{nRT}{V} = \frac{(1.166... \times 10^{-5}) \times 8.31 \times 423}{1.0 \times 10^{-7}}$
$= 4.100985 \times 10^5$ Pa $= \mathbf{4.1 \times 10^5\ Pa}$ **(to 2 s.f.)** *[1 mark]*

2.3 $pV = \frac{1}{3}Nm(c_{rms})^2$
$p = 4.100985 \times 10^5$ Pa, $V = 1.0 \times 10^{-7}$ m^3
N is the number of water molecules, and m is the mass of an individual water molecule, so Nm is the total mass of water.
$Nm = 2.1 \times 10^{-4}$ g *[1 mark]*.
Rearranging the equation gives:
$c_{rms} = \sqrt{\frac{3pV}{Nm}} = \sqrt{\frac{3 \times (4.100985 \times 10^5) \times (1.0 \times 10^{-7})}{2.1 \times 10^{-4}}}$
$= 24.2044... $ ms^{-1} $= \mathbf{24\ ms^{-1}}$ **(to 2 s.f.)** *[1 mark]*

2.4 $pV = \frac{1}{3}Nm(c_{rms})^2$ assumes that the water vapour in the heater behaves like an ideal gas with a potential energy of zero. Internal energy = potential energy + kinetic energy, so the internal energy is assumed to be made up only of its kinetic energy *[1 mark]*. In reality, the water vapour will have the same internal energy, but some of this will be the potential energy of the particles, so the kinetic energy of the particles is actually lower *[1 mark]*. Less kinetic energy means the particles will move slower ($E_k = \frac{1}{2}mv^2$), so the root mean square speed of the particles will also be slower *[1 mark]*.

2.5 The operating temperature of the heater is 60 °C higher in experiment 2, so the water vapour can reach a higher maximum temperature than in experiment 1. At a higher temperature, gas molecules have a larger root mean square speed (c_{rms}) *[1 mark]*. A gas containing faster moving particles will exert a greater total force on the walls of the heater. This is because the particles experience a greater change in momentum, so will collide with more force *[1 mark]*, and because collisions are more frequent *[1 mark]*. $p = F \div A$, so the maximum internal pressure in the heater will be greater in experiment 2 than in experiment 1, making it more likely to explode *[1 mark]*.

3.1 Energy is conserved, so all of the heat energy transferred from the steam condensing and cooling to 80.0 °C will be transferred to the milk to heat it from 7.5 °C to 80.0 °C.
Mass of milk = 225 g = 0.225 kg. Mass of steam needed = m_s.
Energy transferred from the steam as it condenses = ml
$= 2.26 \times 10^6 m_s$
Energy transferred from the water as it cools from 100.0 °C to 80.0 °C = $mc\Delta\theta = m_s \times (4.20 \times 10^3) \times (100.0 - 80.0)$
$= 8.4 \times 10^4 m_s$ *[1 mark]*
Energy transferred to the milk = $mc\Delta\theta$
$= 0.225 \times (3.93 \times 10^3) \times (80.0 - 7.5)$
$= 64\,108.125$ J *[1 mark]*
So $(2.26 \times 10^6 m_s) + (8.4 \times 10^4 m_s) = 64\,108.125$
$2.344 \times 10^6 m_s = 64\,108.125$
$m_s = 64\,108.125 \div (2.344 \times 10^6)$
$= 0.02734...$ kg
$= \mathbf{0.027\ kg}$ **(to 2 s.f.)** *[1 mark]*

Answers

3.2 The cocoa particles are suspended in a fluid, so will move with a zigzag, random motion known as Brownian motion as a result of collisions with fast, randomly-moving particles in the fluid *[1 mark]*. As the coffee cools, the kinetic energy of the fluid particles decreases, so less energy is transferred to the cocoa particles during collisions with the fluid particles *[1 mark]*. So the average kinetic energy of the cocoa particles will decrease as the coffee cools *[1 mark]*.

Section 9 — Gravitational and Electric Fields

Page 121 — Gravitational Fields

1 a) $g = \frac{GM}{r^2}$ so $M = \frac{gr^2}{G}$

$M = \frac{9.81 \times (6400 \times 1000)^2}{6.67 \times 10^{-11}}$ *[1 mark]*

$= 6.024... \times 10^{24} = \mathbf{6.0 \times 10^{24}\ kg}$ **(to 2 s.f.)** *[1 mark]*

b) $F = \frac{Gm_1m_2}{r^2} = \frac{6.67 \times 10^{-11} \times 1.99 \times 10^{30} \times 6.024... \times 10^{24}}{(1.5 \times 10^{11})^2}$

[1 mark]

$F = 3.55... \times 10^{22} = \mathbf{3.6 \times 10^{22}\ N}$ **(to 2 s.f.)** *[1 mark]*

2 $g = \frac{GM}{r^2} = \frac{6.67 \times 10^{-11} \times 7.35 \times 10^{22}}{(1740 \times 1000)^2}$

$= 1.619... = \mathbf{1.62\ Nkg^{-1}}$ **(to 2 s.f.)** *[1 mark]*

$F = mg = 25 \times 1.619... = 40.48... = \mathbf{40\ N}$ **(to 2 s.f.)** *[1 mark]*

3 E.g. r is the distance between A and B. r_1 is three quarters of r. r_2 is one quarter of r. $r_1 = 3r_2$

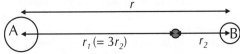

You can write an equation for g due to each planet:

$g = \frac{GM_A}{r_1^2}$ and $g = \frac{GM_B}{r_2^2}$

The force on the object is 0, so $g = 0$.

This means you can equate the two equations for g:

$\frac{GM_A}{r_1^2} = \frac{GM_B}{r_2^2}$

Then replace r_1 with $3r_2$ and simplify:

$\frac{GM_A}{(3r_2)^2} = \frac{GM_B}{r_2^2}$

$\frac{M_A}{9r_2^2} = \frac{M_B}{r_2^2}$

$M_B = \frac{1}{9}M_A$

Answer = **A** *[1 mark]*

Page 123 — Gravitational Potential

1 a) $\Delta V = (-1.52 \times 10^4) - (-1.50 \times 10^4) = 0.02 \times 10^4$

$g = \frac{-\Delta V}{\Delta r} = \frac{-0.02 \times 10^4}{1540}$ *[1 mark]*

$= -0.1298... = \mathbf{-0.130\ ms^{-2}}$ **(to 3 s.f.)** *[1 mark]*

Note: g is negative because it points 'down' towards the asteroid.

b) At the surface:

$V = \frac{-GM}{r}$ so $r = \frac{-GM}{V}$

$r = \frac{-6.67 \times 10^{-11} \times 2.67 \times 10^{19}}{-1.52 \times 10^4}$

$= 117163.8... = \mathbf{117\ 000\ m}$ **(to 3 s.f.)** *[1 mark]*

c) $v = \sqrt{\frac{2GM}{r}} = \sqrt{\frac{2 \times 6.67 \times 10^{-11} \times 2.67 \times 10^{19}}{117\,163.8...}}$

$v = 174.3...... = \mathbf{174\ ms^{-1}}$ **(to 3 s.f.)** *[1 mark]*

d) V at 2020 m above the surface $= \frac{-GM}{r}$

$= \frac{-6.67 \times 10^{-11} \times 2.67 \times 10^{19}}{(117\,163.8... + 2020)}$

$= -1.49423... \times 10^4$ *[1 mark]*

$\Delta W = m\Delta V$

so $\Delta W = 300 \times (-1.49423... \times 10^4 - (-1.52 \times 10^4))$ *[1 mark]*

$= 7.728... \times 10^4 = \mathbf{7.73 \times 10^4\ J}$ **(to 3 s.f.)** *[1 mark]*

Page 125 — Orbits and Gravity

1 $v \propto \frac{1}{\sqrt{r}}$ so if r is doubled, v increases by a factor of $\frac{1}{\sqrt{2}}$

$\frac{1}{\sqrt{2}} = 0.707... = 0.71$ (to 2 s.f.)

So the answer is C *[1 mark]*

2 $v \propto \frac{1}{\sqrt{r}}$ and $T^2 \propto r^3$ *[1 mark]*

So $r \propto \frac{1}{v^2}$ meaning $T \propto \sqrt{\left(\frac{1}{v^2}\right)^3}$ *[1 mark]*

If v becomes $\frac{v}{2}$, then $T \propto \sqrt{\left(\frac{2^2}{v^2}\right)^3}$ *[1 mark]*

So T increases by a factor of $\sqrt{4^3} = 8$

The new orbital period is $8 \times 3 = \mathbf{24\ hours}$ *[1 mark]*

Page 127 — Electric Fields

1 a) Charge on alpha particle, $Q_1 = +2e = 2 \times 1.60 \times 10^{-19}$

$= \mathbf{3.20 \times 10^{-19}\ C}$

Charge on gold nucleus, $Q_2 = +79e = 79 \times 1.60 \times 10^{-19}\ C$

$= 1.264 \times 10^{-17}\ C$ *[1 mark for both]*

$F = \frac{1}{4\pi\varepsilon_0}\frac{Q_1Q_2}{r^2} = \frac{1}{4\pi\varepsilon_0}\frac{3.20 \times 10^{-19} \times 1.264 \times 10^{-17}}{(5.0 \times 10^{-12})^2}$ *[1 mark]*

$= 1.4548... \times 10^{-3} = \mathbf{1.5 \times 10^{-3}\ N}$ **(to 2 s.f.)** *[1 mark]*

away from the gold nucleus *[1 mark]*

2 a) $E = V/d = 1500/(4.5 \times 10^{-3}) = 3.33... \times 10^5$

$= \mathbf{3.3 \times 10^5\ Vm^{-1}}$ **(to 2 s.f.)** *[1 mark]*

The field is perpendicular to the plates *[1 mark]*.

b) $d = 2 \times (4.5 \times 10^{-3}) = 9.0 \times 10^{-3}\ m$

$E = V/d \Rightarrow V = Ed = 3.33... \times 10^5 \times 9 \times 10^{-3} = \mathbf{3000\ V}$ *[1 mark]*

Page 129 — Electric Potential and Work Done

1 $V = \frac{1}{4\pi\varepsilon_0}\frac{Q}{r} = \frac{1}{4\pi \times 8.85 \times 10^{-12}} \times \frac{-1.6 \times 10^{-19}}{6.0 \times 10^{-10}}$ *[1 mark]*

$V = -2.397... = \mathbf{-2.4\ V}$ **(to 2 s.f.)** *[1 mark]*

2 $\Delta W = Q\Delta V$ and $F = \Delta W \div d$ so $F = \frac{Q\Delta V}{d}$ *[1 mark]*

$E = \frac{F}{Q} = \frac{\Delta V}{d}$ *[1 mark]*

3 a) $\Delta W = Q\Delta V = 1.6 \times 10^{-19} \times 200 = \mathbf{3.2 \times 10^{-17}\ J}$ *[1 mark]*

b) It is moving along an equipotential and so ΔV is 0 *[1 mark]*.

Page 131 — Comparing Electric and Gravitational Fields

1 a) Gravitational:

$F = \frac{Gm_1m_2}{r^2} = \frac{6.67 \times 10^{-11} \times (9.11 \times 10^{-31})^2}{(8.00 \times 10^{-10})^2}$

$= -8.649... \times 10^{-53} = \mathbf{-8.65 \times 10^{-53}\ N}$ **(to 3 s.f.)** *[1 mark]*

Electric:

$F = \frac{1}{4\pi\varepsilon_0}\frac{Q_1Q_2}{r^2} = \frac{1}{4\pi\varepsilon_0}\frac{(1.6 \times 10^{-19})^2}{(8.00 \times 10^{-10})^2}$

$= 3.596... \times 10^{-10} = \mathbf{3.60 \times 10^{-10}\ N}$ **(to 3 s.f.)** *[1 mark]*

The force caused by gravity is a factor of 10^{43} smaller than the electrostatic force *[1 mark]*. The gravitational force is attractive (it's negative) and the electrostatic force is repulsive (it's positive) *[1 mark]*.

b) The electric force on each electron is much larger than the gravitational force, by a factor of over 10^{40} — so the gravitational forces are so small they can be ignored *[1 mark]*.

Answers

Section 10 — Capacitors

Page 133 — Capacitors

1 a) Capacitance is the amount of charge stored per unit potential difference *[1 mark]*.

b) $C = \frac{Q}{V} = \frac{660 \times 10^{-6}}{3}$ *[1 mark]*
$= 220 \times 10^{-6} = \textbf{220 μF}$ *[1 mark]*

2 Before the dielectric is removed:
$V = \frac{Q}{C} = \frac{2.47 \times 10^{-9}}{137 \times 10^{-12}} = 18.0...\,V$ *[1 mark]*
When the dielectric is removed, A, d and ε_0 remain constant:
$C_{original} = \frac{A\varepsilon_0\varepsilon_r}{d} = 137 \times 10^{-12}\,F$

$C_{new} = \frac{A\varepsilon_0}{d} = C_{original} \times \frac{1}{\varepsilon_r}$

$C_{new} = \frac{137 \times 10^{-12}}{3.1} = 4.41...\times 10^{-11}\,F$ *[1 mark]*

$V_{new} = \frac{Q}{C_{new}} = \frac{2.47 \times 10^{-9}}{4.41... \times 10^{-11}} = 55.8...\,V$ *[1 mark]*

So the change in potential difference is 55.8... – 18.0...
$= \textbf{38 V (to 2 s.f.)}$ *[1 mark]*

3 $Q = CV = 8.0 \times 10^{-6} \times 12 = 9.6 \times 10^{-5}\,C$ *[1 mark]*
$E = \frac{1}{2}\,QV = \frac{1}{2} \times 9.6 \times 10^{-5} \times 12$ *[1 mark]*
$= 5.76 \times 10^{-4}\,J = \textbf{5.8} \times \textbf{10}^{-4}\,\textbf{J (to 2 s.f.)}$ *[1 mark]*

Page 135 — Charging and Discharging

1 a) $E = \frac{1}{2}\frac{Q^2}{C} = \frac{1}{2} \times \frac{(1.5 \times 10^{-6})^2}{250 \times 10^{-6}}$
$= \textbf{4.5} \times \textbf{10}^{-9}\,\textbf{J}$ *[1 mark]*

b) $E = \frac{1}{2}QV$ so $V = \frac{2E}{Q}$

$V = \frac{2 \times 4.5 \times 10^{-9}}{1.5 \times 10^{-6}}$ *[1 mark]*

$V = 6.0 \times 10^{-3} = \textbf{6.0 mV}$ *[1 mark]*

c)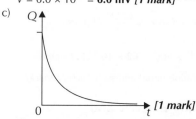

[1 mark]

2 The current decreases exponentially because as charge builds on the plates of the capacitor, it becomes harder and harder to overcome the electrostatic repulsion and deposit electrons onto the plate *[1 mark]*

3 C *[1 mark]*

Page 137 — More Charging and Discharging

1 a) The charge falls to 37% after RC seconds *[1 mark]*,
so $\tau = 1000 \times 2.5 \times 10^{-4} = \textbf{0.25 seconds}$ *[1 mark]*

b) $Q = Q_0 e^{\frac{-t}{RC}}$, so after 0.7 seconds:

$Q = Q_0 e^{\frac{-0.7}{0.25}} = 0.06Q_0$ (to 1 s.f.) *[1 mark]*
6% of the initial charge is left on the capacitor after 0.7 s *[1 mark]*.

c) The total charge stored doubles: V is proportional to Q *[1 mark]*.
The capacitance wouldn't change — this is a fixed property of the capacitor *[1 mark]*.
The time taken to charge wouldn't change, as the charging time depends only on the capacitance of the capacitor and the resistance of the circuit, which don't change *[1 mark]*.

2 $T_{1/2} = 0.69RC$
$= 0.69 \times 1.6 \times 10^3 \times 320 \times 10^{-6}$ *[1 mark]* $= 0.353...\,s$
$= \textbf{0.35 s (to 2 s.f.)}$ *[1 mark]*

Extra Exam Practice for Sections 9 and 10

Pages 138-139

2.1 E.g. $V = \frac{1}{4\pi\varepsilon_0}\frac{Q}{r}$
A proton and an electron have charges of equal magnitude but of different signs and are the same distance from P. This means that at point P the absolute electric potential from the proton is equal to minus the absolute electric potential from the electron *[1 mark]*. The sum of the potentials at P due to the electron and the proton is therefore equal to zero *[1 mark]*.

2.2 An electric field points in the direction that a positive charge would move. Therefore both electric fields point towards the electron, and so the field strength at point P is equal to their magnitudes at point P added together *[1 mark]*.
The distance from the electron/proton to point P:
$r = 1.00 \times 10^{-10} \div 2 = 5.00 \times 10^{-11}\,m$
Magnitude of a proton's electric field strength:
$E = \frac{1}{4\pi\varepsilon_0}\frac{Q}{r^2} = \frac{1}{4\pi\varepsilon_0}\frac{e}{r^2}$
Similarly the magnitude of an electron's electric field strength:
$E = \frac{1}{4\pi\varepsilon_0}\frac{Q}{r^2} = \frac{1}{4\pi\varepsilon_0}\frac{e}{r^2}$
Total electric field strength at point P:
$\frac{1}{4\pi\varepsilon_0}\frac{e}{r^2} + \frac{1}{4\pi\varepsilon_0}\frac{e}{r^2} = \frac{2}{4\pi\varepsilon_0}\frac{e}{r^2}$ *[1 mark]*

$= \frac{2}{4\pi \times 8.85 \times 10^{-12}} \times \frac{1.60 \times 10^{-19}}{(5.00 \times 10^{-11})^2}$
$= 1.150... \times 10^{12}$
$= \textbf{1.15} \times \textbf{10}^{12}\,\textbf{NC}^{-1}\,\textbf{(to 3 s.f.) pointing from the proton to the electron}$ *[1 mark]*

2.3 When the electron has escaped the electric field of the proton, it will be at a potential of 0 V.
Potential of proton's field in electron's current position:
$V = \frac{1}{4\pi\varepsilon_0}\frac{Q}{r} = \frac{1}{4\pi \times 8.85 \times 10^{-12}} \times \frac{1.60 \times 10^{-19}}{1.00 \times 10^{-10}}$
$= 14.386...\,V$ *[1 mark]*
Work done in moving the electron from its current position to escape the proton's electric field:
$\Delta W = Q\Delta V = -1.60 \times 10^{-19} \times (0 - 14.386...)$
$= 2.301... \times 10^{-18}\,J$
The work done is the minimum kinetic energy required for the electron to escape the proton's field.
Kinetic energy $= \textbf{2.30} \times \textbf{10}^{-18}\,\textbf{J (to 3 s.f.)}$ *[1 mark]*

2.4 E.g. The gravitational force between the electron and the proton:
$F = \frac{Gm_e m_p}{r^2} = \frac{6.67 \times 10^{-11} \times 9.11 \times 10^{-31} \times 1.67 \times 10^{-27}}{(1.00 \times 10^{-10})^2}$
$= 1.014... \times 10^{-47}\,N$
The electric force between the electron and the proton:
$F = \frac{1}{4\pi\varepsilon_0}\frac{Q_1 Q_2}{r^2}$
$= \frac{1}{4\pi \times 8.85 \times 10^{-12}} \times \frac{1.60 \times 10^{-19} \times 1.60 \times 10^{-19}}{(1.00 \times 10^{-10})^2}$
$= 2.301... \times 10^{-8}\,N$
The gravitational force between the electron and proton is 10^{39} times smaller than the electrical force, therefore the gravitational force is negligible compared to the electrical force, and so the work done to overcome the gravitational force is negligible.
[1 mark for explanation and 1 mark for supporting calculation]
You could have calculated the work done to move out of the proton's gravitational field to show that this is negligible compared to the work done to move out of its electric field.

3.1 Substitute $V = \frac{1}{4\pi\varepsilon_0}\frac{Q}{r}$ into $C = \frac{Q}{V}$ and rearrange for C:
$C = 4\pi\varepsilon_0 r$ *[1 mark]* $= 4 \times \pi \times 8.85 \times 10^{-12} \times 0.128$
$= 1.423... \times 10^{-11}$
$= \textbf{1.42} \times \textbf{10}^{-11}\,\textbf{F (to 3 s.f.)}$ *[1 mark]*
The potential of the Earth is 0 V, so ΔV across the capacitor is just the potential of the sphere.

Answers

3.2 First calculate the charge on the spheres after 1.15 ms:

$Q = Q_0(1 - e^{-\frac{t}{RC}})$

$= 5.60 \times 10^{-8} \times (1 - e^{-(1.15 \times 10^{-3})/(10.0 \times 10^6 \times 8.43 \times 10^{-11})})$

$= 4.168... \times 10^{-8}$ C *[1 mark]*

So the energy stored after 1.15 ms is:

$E = \frac{1}{2} \times \frac{Q^2}{C} = \frac{1}{2} \times \frac{(4.168... \times 10^{-8})^2}{8.43 \times 10^{-11}}$

$= 1.030... \times 10^{-5} = \mathbf{1.03 \times 10^{-5}}$ **J (to 3 s.f.)** *[1 mark]*

3.3 A dielectric material has polar molecules / molecules where one end has a slight positive charge and the other end has a slight negative charge *[1 mark]*. In the presence of an electric field the molecules line up with the field, the positive end of the molecule faces the negative capacitor plate, and the negative end faces the positive plate *[1 mark]*. The electric field produced by the molecules is in the opposite direction to the electric field, so the electric fields slightly cancel out and reduce the potential difference, because $E = V / d$ *[1 mark]*.

4.1 $g = \frac{GM}{r^2}$, so rearrange this equation to get $G = \frac{gr^2}{M}$.

As G is constant:

$\frac{g_1 r_1^2}{M_1} = \frac{g_2 r_2^2}{M_2}$ *[1 mark]*

(where 1 and 2 denote the planet, and r in this case is the radius of the relevant planet)

so $M_1 = \frac{g_1 r_1^2 M_2}{g_2 r_2^2} = \frac{2g \times (5r)^2 \times M}{g \times r^2}$ *[1 mark]*

$= \frac{50gr^2 M}{gr^2} = \mathbf{50M}$ *[1 mark]*

4.2 $V = -\frac{GM}{r}$ so:

$V_{total} = \left(-\frac{GM_1}{r_1}\right) - \left(-\frac{GM_2}{r_2}\right) = -\frac{GM}{6.65 \times 10^8}$ *[1 mark]*

(where r in this case is the distance from the centre of each planet)

$-\frac{G \times 50M}{(3.10 \times 10^{10})} + \frac{G \times M}{r_2} = -\frac{GM}{6.65 \times 10^8}$

$-\frac{50}{(3.10 \times 10^{10})} + \frac{1}{r_2} = -\frac{1}{6.65 \times 10^8}$

$\frac{1}{r_2} = -\frac{1}{6.65 \times 10^8} + \frac{50}{(3.10 \times 10^{10})}$

$= 1.0914... \times 10^{-10}$

So $r_2 = \frac{1}{1.0914... \times 10^{-10}} = 9.1622... \times 10^9$ m *[1 mark]*

Distance between centres of planets:

$r_1 + r_2 = (3.10 \times 10^{10}) + (9.162... \times 10^9)$

$= 4.0162... \times 10^{10}$

$= \mathbf{4.02 \times 10^{10}}$ **m (to 3 s.f.)** *[1 mark]*

If you got the answer to 4.1 wrong, but carried out the calculations in 4.2 correctly, then you'd still get full marks.

Section 11 — Magnetic Fields

Page 141 — Magnetic Fields

1 a) $F = BIl = 2.00 \times 10^{-5} \times 3.00 \times 0.0400$ *[1 mark]*

$= \mathbf{2.40 \times 10^{-6}}$ **N** *[1 mark]*

b) The force is zero *[1 mark]* because there is no component of the current that is perpendicular to the external magnetic field *[1 mark]*.

2 C *[1 mark]*

Page 143 — Charged Particles in a Magnetic Field

1 $F = BQv$ so $v = \frac{F}{BQ} = \frac{4.91 \times 10^{-15}}{1.10 \times 1.60 \times 10^{-19}}$ *[1 mark]*

$= 27897.7... = \mathbf{27900}$ **ms⁻¹ (to 3 s.f.)** *[1 mark]*

2 Horizontally from south to north *[1 mark]*.

3 a) The particle has a charge and is moving in a magnetic field so $F = BQv$, and the particle is moving in a circle so

$F = \frac{mv^2}{r}$

So $BQv = \frac{mv^2}{r}$ *[1 mark]* which can be rearranged to give

$r = \frac{mv^2}{BQv} = \frac{mv}{BQ}$ *[1 mark]*

b) $r = \frac{mv}{BQ}$ so $v = \frac{rBQ}{m} = \frac{(3.52 \times 10^{-2}) \times 0.00510 \times (1.6 \times 10^{-19})}{9.11 \times 10^{-31}}$

$= 3.1529... \times 10^7$

$= \mathbf{3.15 \times 10^7}$ **ms⁻¹ (to 3 s.f.)** *[1 mark]*

Page 145 — Electromagnetic Induction

1 a) $\phi = BA = (2.00 \times 10^{-3}) \times 0.230 = \mathbf{4.60 \times 10^{-4}}$ **Wb** *[1 mark]*

b) Flux linkage = $BAN = (2.00 \times 10^{-3}) \times 0.230 \times 151 = 0.06946$

$= \mathbf{0.0695}$ **Wb (to 3 s.f.)** *[1 mark]*

c) $\varepsilon = -\frac{\Delta(N\phi)}{\Delta t} = -\frac{\Delta(NBA)}{\Delta t} = -\frac{NA\Delta B}{\Delta t}$ *[1 mark]*

$= -\frac{151 \times 0.230 \times (1.50 \times 10^{-3} - 2.00 \times 10^{-3})}{2.5}$ *[1 mark]*

$= 6.946 \times 10^{-3} = \mathbf{6.95 \times 10^{-3}}$ **V (to 3 s.f.)** *[1 mark]*

2 a) Flux linkage = $BAN = 0.92 \times 0.010 \times 550 = \mathbf{5.06}$ **Wb** *[1 mark]*

b) Flux linkage after movement

$= BAN \cos \theta$

$= 550 \times 0.92 \times 0.010 \times \cos 90° = 0$ Wb *[1 mark]*

$\varepsilon = -\frac{\Delta(N\phi)}{\Delta t} = -\frac{0 - 5.06}{0.5} = 10.12 = \mathbf{10}$ **V (to 2 s.f.)** *[1 mark]*

3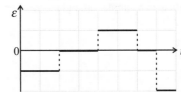

Step graph *[1 mark]* with the first and fifth steps negative and third step positive *[1 mark]* and the last step twice as negative as the others *[1 mark]*.

Page 147 — Induction Laws and Alternators

1 a) The distance travelled by the plane is $v\Delta t$ so area cut, $A = lv\Delta t$ flux linkage = BA so $\Phi = Blv\Delta t$

$\varepsilon = N\frac{\Delta\Phi}{\Delta t} = 1 \times \frac{Blv\Delta t}{\Delta t}$ *[1 mark]* $= Blv$

$= 6.00 \times 10^{-5} \times 33.9 \times 148$ *[1 mark]* $= 0.3010...$

$= \mathbf{0.301}$ **V (to 3 s.f.)** *[1 mark]*

b)

[1 mark]

2 a) $N\Phi = BAN \cos \theta = 0.900 \times 0.0105 \times 521 \times \cos 60.0° = 2.4617...$

$= \mathbf{2.46}$ **Wb (to 3 s.f.)** *[1 mark]*

b) Peak e.m.f. when $\sin \omega t = \pm 1$,

giving $\varepsilon = \pm BAN\omega$ *[1 mark]*

So, peak e.m.f. is:

$\varepsilon = \pm 0.900 \times 0.0105 \times 521 \times 40\pi$ *[1 mark]*

$= \pm 618.698...$

$= \mathbf{\pm 619}$ **V (to 3 s.f.)** *[1 mark]*

Page 149 — Alternating Currents

1 a) Turn on the time base *[1 mark]*.

b) He has used a direct current (d.c.) / non-alternating power supply *[1 mark]*.

2 a) $I_{rms} = \frac{I_0}{\sqrt{2}} = \frac{9.13}{\sqrt{2}} = 6.4558... = \mathbf{6.46}$ **A (to 3 s.f.)** *[1 mark]*

Answers

b) $V_{rms} = \frac{V_0}{\sqrt{2}}$ so $V_0 = V_{rms} \times \sqrt{2} = 119 \times \sqrt{2} = 168.29...$ *[1 mark]*

$V_{peak\ to\ peak} = 2 \times V_0 = 2 \times 168.29... = 336.58...$
$= $ **337 V (to 3 s.f.)** *[1 mark]*

Page 151 — Transformers

1 a) $\frac{N_s}{N_p} = \frac{V_s}{V_p}$ so, $N_s = \frac{V_s \times N_p}{V_p} = \frac{45.0 \times 158}{9.30}$
$= 764.51... = $ **765 turns** *[1 mark]*

b) $\frac{I_s}{I_p} = \frac{V_p}{V_s}$ *[1 mark]* so, $I_s = \frac{V_p \times I_p}{V_s} = \frac{9.30 \times 1.50}{45.0}$
$= $ **0.310 A** *[1 mark]*

c) efficiency $= \frac{I_s V_s}{I_p V_p} = \frac{P_s}{I_p V_p} = \frac{10.8}{1.5 \times 9.3} = 0.7741...$
$= $ **77.4% (to 3 s.f.)** *[1 mark]*

You could also give your answer as a decimal — efficiency = 0.774.

d) Laminating the core with layers of insulation would reduce the effect of eddy currents and improve the efficiency of the transformer *[1 mark]*.

2 power transmitted = power received + power wasted *[1 mark]*
power transmitted $= 943\ 000 + I^2 \times R$
$= 943\ 000 + 15.6^2 \times 132 = 975\ 123.52$
$= $ **975 kW (to 3 s.f.)** *[1 mark]*

Extra Exam Practice for Section 11

Pages 152-153

2.1 Equate the force on a particle in a circular orbit to the force on a charged particle in a magnetic field:

$F = \frac{mv^2}{r} = BQv$ *[1 mark]*

Rearrange for v:

$v = \frac{rBQ}{m}$

The charge of an alpha particle is $2e$ because it is made up of two protons (and two neutrons, but they have no charge).
The mass of an alpha particle is $2m_n + 2m_p$.
As $m_n = m_p$, $m_{alpha} = 4m_p$

$v = \frac{rB \times 2e}{4m_p}$

$= \frac{0.550 \times 0.365 \times 2 \times 1.60 \times 10^{-19}}{4 \times 1.67 \times 10^{-27}}$ *[1 mark]*

$= 9.616... \times 10^6 = $ **9.62 × 10⁶ ms⁻¹ (to 3 s.f.)** *[1 mark]*

2.2 The maximum current in the secondary coil depends on the maximum current in the primary coil. The maximum current in the primary coil is I_0.

$I_{rms} = I_0 \div \sqrt{2}$, so $I_0 = I_{rms} \times \sqrt{2}$
$= 11.8 \times \sqrt{2} = 16.687...$ A *[1 mark]*

efficiency $= \frac{I_s V_s}{I_p V_p}$ so $I_s = \frac{\text{efficiency} \times I_p V_p}{V_s}$

$= \frac{0.850 \times 16.687... \times 238}{1020}$

$= 3.309... = $ **3.31 A (to 3 s.f.)** *[1 mark]*

2.3 Laminating the transformer core reduces the effects of eddy currents in the core *[1 mark]*. Eddy currents cause power losses, so reducing the eddy currents increases the efficiency of the transformer, meaning the current and potential difference in the secondary coil increase *[1 mark]*. If the magnitude of the alternating potential difference increases, the alpha particles will be accelerated more across the gap between the electrodes, and will enter the electrodes with higher speeds *[1 mark]*. Because the speed of the particles increases more, the radius of the circular path they follow increases, so the alpha particles will follow a wider spiral / make fewer loops before they leave the cyclotron *[1 mark]*.

3.1 As the wire is moved downwards through the magnetic field, Lenz's law states that the induced e.m.f. in the wire will act to oppose the motion of the wire *[1 mark]*. This means that as the wire is moved downwards, electrons between A and B will flow from A to B and the electrons between B and C will flow from C to B *[1 mark]*. As electrons flow towards point B from both sides of point B, a negative charge builds up at B *[1 mark]*.
Use Fleming's Left-Hand Rule to work out the direction of movement of the electrons — the force is in the opposite direction to the motion of the wire (Lenz's law), and your second finger shows the direction of motion of a positive charge, so an electron will move in the opposite direction.

3.2 $\varepsilon = N\frac{\Delta\Phi}{\Delta t}$ and $\Phi = BA$ so calculate the area cut by the wire.
The area cut is the area of the square face of the magnet.
$A = (5.5 \times 10^{-2})^2 = 3.025 \times 10^{-3}$ m²
$\Phi = BA = 155 \times 10^{-3} \times 3.025 \times 10^{-3}$
$= 4.68875 \times 10^{-4}$ Wb *[1 mark]*
The time taken for the wire to fall through the magnetic field:
$\Delta v = \frac{\Delta s}{\Delta t}$ so $\Delta t = \frac{\Delta s}{v} = \frac{5.5 \times 10^{-2}}{1.2} = 0.0458...$ s *[1 mark]*
$\varepsilon = N\frac{\Delta\Phi}{\Delta t} = 1 \times \frac{4.68875 \times 10^{-4}}{0.0458...} = 0.01023$
$= $ **0.010 V (to 2 s.f.)** *[1 mark]*

3.3 Between A and B, the direction of the force acting on the wire, due to passing through the magnetic field, is downwards. Between B and C the direction of force acting on the wire, due to passing through the magnetic field, is upwards *[1 mark]*. So overall point A will move downwards faster and point C will move downwards slower, causing the wire to tilt as it falls *[1 mark]*.
Use Fleming's Left-Hand Rule to see the direction of the forces acting on the wire due to the magnetic fields.

Section 12 — Nuclear Physics

Page 155 — Rutherford Scattering and Atomic Structure

1 a) The majority of alpha particles are not scattered because the nucleus is a very small part of the whole atom and so the probability of an alpha particle getting near it is small *[1 mark]*. Most alpha particles pass undeflected through the empty space around the nucleus *[1 mark]*.

b) Alpha particles and atomic nuclei are both positively charged *[1 mark]*. If an alpha particle travels close to a nucleus, there will be a significant electrostatic force of repulsion between them *[1 mark]*. This force deflects the alpha particle from its original path *[1 mark]*.

c) $\frac{Q_{gold} Q_{alpha}}{4\pi\varepsilon_0 r} = E_k$ so $r = \frac{Q_{gold} Q_{alpha}}{4\pi\varepsilon_0 E_k}$

$r = \frac{79 \times (1.60 \times 10^{-19}) \times 2 \times (1.60 \times 10^{-19})}{4\pi \times (8.85 \times 10^{-12}) \times (4.8 \times 10^6 \times 1.60 \times 10^{-19})}$ *[1 mark]*

$r = 4.735... \times 10^{-14}$ m $= $ **4.7 × 10⁻¹⁴ m (to 2 s.f.)** *[1 mark]*

d) 0 J *[1 mark]*
At the distance of closest approach, all of the kinetic energy has been transferred into electric potential energy, so kinetic energy is zero.

Page 157 — Nuclear Radius and Density

1 a) $\theta \approx \sin^{-1}\left(\frac{1.22\lambda}{2r}\right) = \sin^{-1}\left(\frac{1.22 \times (3.0 \times 10^{-15})}{2 \times (2.7 \times 10^{-15})}\right)$ *[1 mark]*

$= 42.67...° = $ **43° (to 2 s.f.)** *[1 mark]*

b)

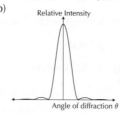

[1 mark for general shape, 1 mark for a central maximum with significantly larger intensity]

Answers

2   For carbon, $A = 12$ so $R = R_0 A^{\frac{1}{3}} = 1.4 \times 10^{-15} \times 12^{\frac{1}{3}}$
$R = 3.205... \times 10^{-15}$ m **[1 mark]**
Volume $= \frac{4}{3}\pi R^3 = \frac{4}{3}\pi(3.205... \times 10^{-15})^3 = 1.379... \times 10^{-43}$m^3
$\rho = \frac{m}{V} = \frac{2.00 \times 10^{-26}}{1.379... \times 10^{-43}} = 1.45... \times 10^{17}$kgm^{-3} **[1 mark]**

For gold, $A = 197$ so $R = R_0 A^{\frac{1}{3}} = 1.4 \times 10^{-15} \times 197^{\frac{1}{3}}$
$R = 8.146... \times 10^{-15}$ m **[1 mark]**
Volume $= \frac{4}{3}\pi R^3 = \frac{4}{3}\pi(8.416... \times 10^{-15})^3 = 2.264... \times 10^{-42}$m^3
$\rho = \frac{m}{V} = \frac{3.27 \times 10^{-25}}{2.264... \times 10^{-42}} = 1.44... \times 10^{17}$kgm^{-3} **[1 mark]**

Page 159 — Radioactive Emissions

1   Place paper then a sheet of aluminium between the source and detector and measure the amount of radiation getting through each time **[1 mark]**. Alpha radiation will be stopped by paper, beta will be stopped by aluminium and gamma radiation isn't stopped by either.

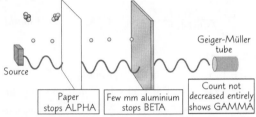

Geiger-Müller tube

Source

| Paper stops ALPHA | Few mm aluminium stops BETA | Count not decreased entirely shows GAMMA |

[1 mark for each material correctly stopping corresponding radiation]

2   E.g. gamma rays are used in the treatment of cancerous tumours **[1 mark]**. The radiation damages cells, including the cancerous ones within the body and can sometimes lead to the patient being cured of cancer **[1 mark]**. However, exposure to gamma radiation can lead to long term side effects like infertility **[1 mark]**.

Page 161 — Investigations of Radioactive Emissions

1 a)   Background radiation = 60 cpm = 1 cps
$20.0 \div 10.0 = 2$
So count rate at 20 cm $= (240 - 1) \div 2^2 = 59.75$ cps **[1 mark]**
Now add back on the contribution of background radiation:
$59.75 + 1 = 60.75$ cps = **61 cps (to 2 s.f.)** **[1 mark]**

   b)   35.0 cm is 3.5 times further away than 10.0 cm, so the count rate will be $(240 - 1) \div 3.5^2 = 19.5102...$
Now add back on the contribution from background radiation:
$19.5102... + 1 = 20.5102... = $ **21 cps (to 2 s.f.)** **[1 mark]**

2   At 40 cm, $x = 0.4$ so $k = Ix^2 = 30 \times 0.4^2 = 4.8$ **[1 mark]**
At A, a distance x times away from the starting position,
$I = 4.8$ cps so $x = \sqrt{\frac{k}{I}} = \sqrt{\frac{4.8}{4.8}} = 1$
So the Geiger counter is 1 m away from the source at A **[1 mark]**.

Page 163— Exponential Law of Decay

1   Any one of: You can't say which atom/nucleus in a sample will decay next. / You can only estimate the fraction of nuclei that will decay or the probability an atom/nucleus will decay in a given time. / You cannot say exactly how many atoms will decay in a given time. **[1 mark]**

2 a)   Activity, A = measured activity – background activity
$= 750 - 50 = 700$ Bq **[1 mark]**
Number of particles = number of moles $\times N_A$
$N = 8.3 \times 10^{-20} \times 6.02 \times 10^{23} = 49\,966$ **[1 mark]**
$A = \lambda N \Rightarrow 700 = 49\,996\,\lambda$ **[1 mark]**
So $\lambda = 700 \div 49\,996 = $ **0.014... s^{-1}** **[1 mark]**
$T_{\frac{1}{2}} = \frac{\ln 2}{\lambda} = \frac{0.693...}{0.014...} = 49.4... = $ **49 s (to 2 s.f.)** **[1 mark]**

   b) $N = N_0 e^{-\lambda t} = 49\,996 \times e^{-0.014... \times 300}$
$= 747.5... = $ **750 (to 2 s.f.)** **[1 mark]**

3   Some parts of radioactive waste have a very long half-life **[1 mark]** and so it must be stored safely and securely to prevent as much damage as possible to people, animals and the environment **[1 mark]**.

Page 165 — Nuclear Decay

1 a) $^{226}_{88}\text{Ra} \rightarrow ^{222}_{86}\text{Rn} + ^{4}_{2}\alpha$ *[1 mark for alpha particle, 1 mark for proton and nucleon number of radon.]*

   b)   Energy

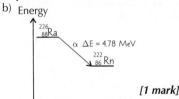

$^{226}_{88}\text{Ra}$

α $\Delta E = 4.78$ MeV

$^{222}_{86}\text{Rn}$

[1 mark]

2     $^{40}_{19}\text{K} \rightarrow ^{40}_{20}\text{Ca} + ^{0}_{-1}\beta + ^{0}_{0}\overline{\nu}_e$ *[1 mark for beta particle, 1 mark each for proton and nucleon number of calcium.]*

Page 167 — Nuclear Fission and Fusion

1 a)   Nuclear fission can be induced by neutrons and produces more neutrons during the process **[1 mark]**. This means that each fission reaction induces more fission reactions, resulting in an ongoing chain of reactions **[1 mark]**. The critical mass is the amount of fuel needed to sustain a chain reaction at a steady rate **[1 mark]**.

   b)   E.g. control rods limit the rate of fission by absorbing neutrons **[1 mark]**. The number of neutrons absorbed by the rods is controlled by varying the amount they are inserted into the reactor **[1 mark]**. A suitable material for the control rods is boron **[1 mark]**.

   c)   In an emergency shut-down, the control rods are released into the reactor **[1 mark]**. The control rods absorb the neutrons, and stop the reaction as quickly as possible **[1 mark]**.

2   E.g. advantages: nuclear power produces less greenhouse gases than burning fossil fuels **[1 mark]** / nuclear power produces huge amounts of energy **[1 mark]**.
Any two disadvantages from e.g.: danger of the reactor getting out of control **[1 mark]** / risks of radiation from radioactive materials used **[1 mark]** / having to store waste products safely **[1 mark]**.

Page 169 — Binding Energy

1 a)   Binding energy $= 931.5 \times m$
$= 931.5 \times 1.864557 = 1736.8...$ MeV **[1 mark]**
$1736.8... \times 1.60 \times 10^{-13} = 2.77893... \times 10^{-10}$ J
$= $ **2.78 $\times 10^{-10}$ J (to 3 s.f.)** **[1 mark]**

   b)   Average binding energy per nucleon $= 1736.8... \div 235$
$= 7.3907...$ MeV
$= $ **7.39 MeV (to 3 s.f.)**
[1 mark]

2 a)   Fusion **[1 mark]**

   b)   There are two deuterium atoms before the reaction, each containing two nucleons, so:
binding energy before reaction $= 2 \times 2 \times 1.11 = 4.44$ MeV **[1 mark]**
There is one helium atom after the reaction, containing three nucleons, and a free neutron with a binding energy of zero, so:
binding energy after reaction $= (3 \times 2.58) + 0 = 7.74$ MeV **[1 mark]**
Energy released = difference in binding energy $= 7.74 - 4.44$
$= $ **3.30 MeV [1 mark]**

Answers

Extra Exam Practice for Section 12

Pages 170-171

2.1 **5-6 marks:**
The answer includes the correct graph with suitable axis labels and the graph shows a clear peak. The answer includes an explanation of how mass defect links to binding energy and how the graph shows the energy absorbed / emitted during fission and fusion. The answer has a clear and logical structure. The information given is relevant and detailed.

3-4 marks:
The answer includes the correct graph with suitable axis labels and with a clear peak. The answer describes mass defect and binding energy with some link to the energy absorbed / emitted during fission and fusion. The answer has some structure. Most of the information given is relevant and there is some detail involved.

1-2 marks:
There is no correct graph, or the graph is of the correct shape, but may have no labels. The answer describes fission and fusion but does not explain mass defect and binding energy and how they relate to energy absorbed / released. The answer has no clear structure. The information given is basic and lacking in detail. It may not all be relevant.

0 marks:
No relevant information is given.

Here are some points your answer may include:
The mass of a nucleus is less than the total mass of the nucleons that make up the nucleus.
The difference in mass is called the mass defect.
The mass defect is caused by mass being converted to energy which is released when nucleons join.
This energy is known as the binding energy.
The change in binding energy per nucleon during a reaction tells you if energy is released or absorbed. An increase in binding energy per nucleon means energy is released.
The graph of binding energy per nucleon against nucleon number looks like:

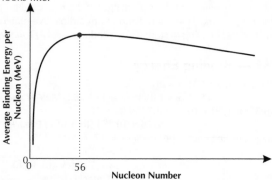

Nuclei combining is known as fusion and nuclei splitting into smaller nuclei is known as fission.
Fusion results in nucleon number increasing.
This leads to an increase in binding energy per nucleon for nucleon numbers below the peak.
This means that fusion releases energy as long as the product has a nucleon number below the peak.
Above the peak, the binding energy per nucleon decreases as nucleon number increases, so energy would be absorbed during fusion.
Fission results in nucleon number decreasing.
This leads to an increase in binding energy per nucleon for nucleon numbers above the peak.
This means that fission releases energy as long as the products have nucleon numbers greater than the peak.
Below the peak, the binding energy per nucleon decreases as nucleon number decreases, so energy would be absorbed during fission.

2.2 Mass before = 235.044 u + 1.00867 u = 236.05267 u
Rest energy = 236.05267 × 931.5 = 219 883.06... MeV
Mass after = 140.914 u + 91.926 u + (3 × 1.00867 u)
= 235.86601 u
Rest energy = 235.86628 × 931.5 = 219 709.18... MeV *[1 mark]*
Total energy before is the total rest energy + KE of the neutron
= 219 883.06... + 11.5 = 219 894.56... MeV *[1 mark]*
Energy difference = 219 894.56... − 219 709.18...
= 185.37... MeV *[1 mark]*
4.20 % of this = 185.37... × 0.042 = 7.785... MeV
This is the total energy of the three released neutrons, the energy of 1 neutron is:
7.785... ÷ 3 = 2.595... MeV = **2.60 MeV (to 3 s.f.)** *[1 mark]*

2.3 The neutrons do not need to be slowed down to thermal neutrons so there is no need for a moderator in the nuclear reactor *[1 mark]*.

3.1 From the graph, θ is the angle of the first minima, so
$\theta = 24.0°$ *[1 mark]*
$\sin\theta \approx \dfrac{1.22\lambda}{2R}$
so $R \approx \dfrac{1.22\lambda}{2\sin\theta}$
$= \dfrac{1.22 \times 4.10 \times 10^{-15}}{2\sin(24.0)} = 6.148... \times 10^{-15}$ m *[1 mark]*
$R = R_0 A^{1/3}$
so $R_0 = R \div A^{1/3}$
$= 6.148... \times 10^{-15} \div 107^{1/3}$ *[1 mark]*
$= 1.295... \times 10^{-15} = \mathbf{1.30 \times 10^{-15}}$ **m (to 3 s.f.)** *[1 mark]*

3.2 E.g. As E_k increases, $E_k = E_{elec} = \dfrac{Q_{alpha}Q_{silver}}{4\pi\varepsilon_0 r}$ increases so r decreases and the alpha particle gets closer to the nucleus. When r gets close to the nuclear radius, the attractive strong nuclear force will overcome the repulsion and the alpha particle will be attracted to the nucleus and absorbed *[1 mark]*. So the proportion of particles deflected will drop very rapidly since the particles are absorbed by the nucleus and don't go any further, this explains why the graph changes at 22.0 MeV *[1 mark]*.

3.3 Assume that at $E_k = 22.0$ MeV, $r \approx$ nuclear radius *[1 mark]*.
$E_k = 22.0$ MeV $= 22.0 \times 10^6 \times 1.60 \times 10^{-19} = 3.52 \times 10^{-12}$ J
$E_k = E_{elec} = \dfrac{Q_{alpha}Q_{silver}}{4\pi\varepsilon_0 r}$,
so $r = \dfrac{Q_{alpha}Q_{silver}}{4\pi\varepsilon_0 E_k}$
$= \dfrac{(2 \times 1.60 \times 10^{-19}) \times (47 \times 1.60 \times 10^{-19})}{4 \times \pi \times 8.85 \times 10^{-12} \times 3.52 \times 10^{-12}}$
$= 6.147... \times 10^{-15}$ m *[1 mark]*
$R = R_0 A^{1/3}$
so $R_0 = R \div A^{1/3}$
$= 6.147... \times 10^{-15} \div 107^{1/3}$
$= 1.294... \times 10^{-15} = \mathbf{1.30 \times 10^{-15}}$ **m (to 3 s.f.)** *[1 mark]*

3.4 R or R_0 can not be directly measured so it's not possible to compare the results in 3.1 and 3.2 to the true value to determine their accuracy *[1 mark]*.

Section 13: Option A — Astrophysics

Page 174 — Optical Telescopes

1 a) $\theta \approx \dfrac{\lambda}{D} = \dfrac{620 \times 10^{-9}}{1.6} = 3.875 \times 10^{-7}$
$= \mathbf{3.9 \times 10^{-7}}$ **rad (to 2 s.f.)** *[1 mark]*

b) A smaller dish means a larger minimum angular resolution. As the resolving power is dependent on the minimum angular resolution (the smaller the minimum angular resolution, the better the resolving power), the resolving power of the telescope decreases. *[1 mark]*

2 a) Separation of lenses needs to be
$f_o + f_e = 5.0 + 0.10 = \mathbf{5.1}$ **m** *[1 mark]*

Answers

b) Angular magnification = angle subtended by image at eye / angle subtended by object at unaided eye *[1 mark]*
$M = f_o/f_e = 5.0 / 0.10 = 50$ *[1 mark]*

Page 177 — Non-Optical Telescopes

1 The collecting power of the telescope is proportional to the area of the objective dish or mirror *[1 mark]*. As both of the dishes have equal areas, their collecting powers are the same *[1 mark]*. Resolving power depends on the wavelength of the radiation and the diameter of the dish *[1 mark]*. Since UV radiation has a much smaller wavelength than radio, UV telescopes have a better resolving power *[1 mark]*.

2 a) The telescope emits infrared radiation, which masks the infrared it is trying to detect *[1 mark]*. The colder the telescope, the less infrared it emits *[1 mark]*.
   b) They are set up at high altitude in dry places *[1 mark]*.

3 a) On high altitude aeroplanes / weather balloons *[1 mark]*, to get above the level of the atmosphere that absorbs the radiation *[1 mark]*.
   b) A UV telescope uses a single parabolic mirror, whereas an X-ray telescope uses a series of nested 'grazing' mirrors *[1 mark]*. This is because UV reflects in the same way as visible light *[1 mark]* but X-rays can only be reflected at very shallow angles / would be absorbed by a parabolic mirror *[1 mark]*.

4 a) power $\propto$ diameter^2 *[1 mark]*.
   b) $\dfrac{\text{power of Arecibo}}{\text{power of Lovell}} = \dfrac{300^2}{76^2}$ *[1 mark]*
   Ratio = 15.6 : 1 = **16 : 1 (to 2 s.f.)** *[1 mark]*

Page 179 — Distances and Magnitude

1 The absolute magnitude is the apparent magnitude *[1 mark]* that the object would have if it were 10 parsecs away from Earth *[1 mark]*.

2 Distance to Sun in parsecs = $1/(2.1 \times 10^5)$
   $= 4.76... \times 10^{-6}$ pc *[1 mark]*
   $-M = 5 \log (d/10)$
   $-27 - M = 5 \log (4.76... \times 10^{-6}/10)$ *[1 mark]*
   $= 5 \log (4.76... \times 10^{-7})$
   $= -31.61... \Rightarrow M = 4.611... = $ **4.6 (to 2 s.f.)** *[1 mark]*

3 a) Sirius *[1 mark]*
   b) For Sirius, $m - M = -1.46 - 1.4 = -2.86$
   For Canopus, $m - M = -0.72 - (-5.5) = 4.78$
   Canopus has the larger difference between apparent and absolute magnitudes, so it is further away *[1 mark]*.
   $m - M = 5 \log (d/10)$
   $4.78 = 5 \log (d/10) \Rightarrow \log (d/10) = 0.956$
   $d/10 = 10^{0.956}$ *[1 mark]*
   So $d = 90.3... = $ **90 pc (to 2 s.f.)** *[1 mark]*

Page 181 — Stars as Black Bodies

1 a) According to Wien's displacement law $\lambda_{max} \times T = 2.9 \times 10^{-3}$, so for this star
   $\lambda_{max} = 2.9 \times 10^{-3} \div 4000 = 7.25 \times 10^{-7}$ m *[1 mark]*
   Curve Y peaks at around 0.7 μm (= 7×10^{-7} m), so could represent the star *[1 mark]*.
   b) Star X is the larger *[1 mark]*.
   From $P = \sigma A T^4$, power output is proportional to temperature (T^4) and to area. Given that the power output of both stars is the same, if one star has a higher temperature than the other, it must have a smaller surface area. The Sun has a higher temperature than star X, so it must have a smaller surface area *[1 mark]*.

2 $\lambda_{max} T = 2.9 \times 10^{-3}$
   So $T = (2.9 \times 10^{-3})/(436 \times 10^{-9}) = 6651.37...$ K *[1 mark]*
   $P = \sigma A T^4$
   So $2.3 \times 10^{27} = 5.67 \times 10^{-8} \times A \times 6651.37...^4$ *[1 mark]*
   which gives $A = 2.07... \times 10^{19}$ m^2
   $= $ **2.1 $\times 10^{19}$ m^2 (to 2 s.f.)** *[1 mark]*

Page 183 — Spectral Classes and the H-R Diagram

1 a) To get strong Balmer lines, the majority of the electrons need to be at the $n = 2$ level *[1 mark]*. At low temperatures, few electrons have enough energy to be at the $n = 2$ level *[1 mark]*. At very high temperatures, most electrons are at $n = 3$ or above, both of which lead to weak Balmer lines *[1 mark]*.
   b) Spectral classes A *[1 mark]* and B *[1 mark]*.
   c) Class F stars are white *[1 mark]*, have a temperature of 6000 – 7500 K *[1 mark]* and show prominent absorption lines from metal ions *[1 mark]*.

2 Molecules are only present in the lowest temperature stars as these are the only stars that are cool enough for molecules to form *[1 mark]*.

3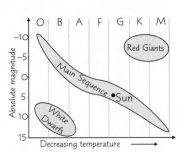

[1 mark for correct axes, 1 mark each for each correctly located and labelled section, 1 mark for correct position of the Sun]

Page 185 — Stellar Evolution

1 Clumps of dust and gas begin to contract under gravity. Eventually, the clumps become dense enough that the cloud of dust and gas breaks into separate regions called protostars *[1 mark]*. As a protostar becomes denser, the temperature increases, until hydrogen nuclei are fused into helium. This releases lots of energy *[1 mark]*. The radiation and gas pressure are now so large that it stops the gravitational collapse, and the protostar becomes a stable main sequence star *[1 mark]*.

2 a) When a star runs out of hydrogen fuel to fuse in the core, the outward radiation pressure stops, so the core of the star begins to contract, causing a rise in temperature *[1 mark]*. The outer layers expand and begin to cool *[1 mark]*.
   b) Red giant *[1 mark]*
   c) a white dwarf *[1 mark]*

Page 187 — Stellar Evolution

1 a) The Schwarzschild radius is the distance *[1 mark]* from the black hole singularity to where the escape velocity is the speed of light (to the event horizon) *[1 mark]*.
   b) $R_s = \dfrac{2GM}{c^2} = \dfrac{2 \times 6.67 \times 10^{-11} \times 6.0 \times 10^{30}}{(3.00 \times 10^8)^2}$ *[1 mark]*
   $= 8.89...$ km = **8.9 km (to 2 s.f.)** *[1 mark]*

2 a) For a star of that mass, the electron degeneracy is not large enough to stop the core contracting *[1 mark]*. The electrons and protons in the core are forced to combine, forming neutrons and neutrinos. The core collapses into a neutron star *[1 mark]*. The outer layers of the star collapse and rebound off the core, leading to massive shockwaves which cause the supernova *[1 mark]*.
   b) E.g. they could destroy the ozone layer and cause mass extinction *[1 mark]* if they were directed towards Earth *[1 mark]*.

Page 189 — The Doppler Effect and Red Shift

1 a) Object A is moving towards us *[1 mark]*.
   b) Object B is part of a binary star system (or is being orbited by a planet) *[1 mark]* with a period of two weeks *[1 mark]*.

2 a) $z = -\dfrac{\Delta\lambda}{\lambda} = -\left(\dfrac{656.28 \times 10^{-9} - 667.83 \times 10^{-9}}{656.28 \times 10^{-9}}\right)$
   $= 0.0175991... = $ **0.017599 (to 5 s.f.)** *[1 mark]*

Answers

b) $v = 0.175991... \times 3.00 \times 10^8 = 5.279... \times 10^6$ ms^{-1}
   = **5.28 × 10^6 ms^{-1} (to 3 s.f.)** *[1 mark]*
   Object C is moving away from Earth as the observed wavelength has been stretched / the velocity is positive *[1 mark]*.

Page 191 — Quasars and Exoplanets

1 a) Their spectra show an enormous red shift *[1 mark]*.
  b) Intensity is proportional to 1/distance^2 *[1 mark]*. So, e.g., if a quasar is 500 000 times further away than, but just as bright as, a star in the Milky Way it must be 500 000^2 times brighter than the star *[1 mark]*.
  c) A supermassive, active black hole *[1 mark]* surrounded by a doughnut-shaped mass of whirling gas *[1 mark]*.
2 a) The transit method detects an exoplanet through a change in the apparent magnitude of a star *[1 mark]*. As an exoplanet's path crosses in front of a star relative to Earth, it blocks some of the light *[1 mark]*. This causes a dip in the star's light curve, which can be used to confirm the existence of an exoplanet and measure its radius *[1 mark]*.

  b)
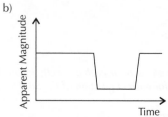
  [1 mark for correct axes, 1 mark for dip in apparent magnitude]

Page 193 — The Big Bang Model of the Universe

1 a) $v = H_0 d$ *[1 mark]* where v is recessional velocity (in kms^{-1}), d is distance (in Mpc) and H_0 is Hubble's constant in (kms^{-1}Mpc^{-1}) *[1 mark]*.
  b) Hubble's law suggests that the Universe originated with the Big Bang *[1 mark]* and has been expanding ever since *[1 mark]*.
  c)i) $H_0 = v \div d = 50$ kms$^{-1} \div 1$ Mpc^{-1}.
      50 kms$^{-1} = 50 \times 10^3$ ms^{-1} and 1 Mpc$^{-1} = 3.08 \times 10^{22}$ m
      So, $H_0 = 50 \times 10^3$ ms$^{-1} \div 3.08 \times 10^{22}$ m
         $= 1.623... \times 10^{-18}$ s$^{-1} =$ **2 × 10^{-18} s^{-1} (to 1 s.f.)**
         [1 mark for the correct value, 1 mark for the correct unit]
   ii) $t = 1/H_0 = 1/1.623... \times 10^{-18} = 6.16 \times 10^{17}$ s *[1 mark]*
      $\approx$ **2 × 10^{10} years (to 1 s.f.)** *[1 mark]*
      The observable Universe has a radius of ~20 billion light years. *[1 mark]*
2 a) $z = v/c$, so $v = 0.37 \times 3.00 \times 10^8 = 1.11 \times 10^8$ ms^{-1} *[1 mark]*
      $d = v/H_0 \approx 1.11 \times 10^8 / 2.4 \times 10^{-18} = 4.625 \times 10^{25}$ m *[1 mark]*
      $= 4.625 \times 10^{25} / 9.46 \times 10^{15}$ ly = **4.9 billion ly (to 2 s.f.)** *[1 mark]*
  b) $z = v/c$ is only valid if $v \ll c$ — it isn't the case here *[1 mark]*
3 **5-6 marks:**
   The answer describes fully how the cosmic microwave background is strong evidence for the HBB.
   The answer has a clear and logical structure.
   3-4 marks:
   Cosmic microwave background radiation is fully described, with some correct attempts made at explaining why it is evidence for the HBB. Most of the information given is relevant.
   1-2 marks:
   Some mention of what the cosmic background radiation is with no explanation as to why it supports the HBB. The information given is basic and lacking in detail. It may not all be relevant.
   0 marks:
   No relevant information is given.

Here are some points your answer may include:
The cosmic background radiation is microwave radiation showing a perfect black body spectrum of a temperature of about 2.73 K. It is very nearly isotropic and homogeneous. This is consistent with the Big Bang model of the universe, which suggests the early universe would have been filled with gamma radiation, that would have been stretched into the microwave region of the electromagnetic spectrum over time due to the expansion of the universe.

Section 13: Option B — Medical Physics

Page 195 — Physics of the Eye

1 a) The distance will be the focal length of the lens *[1 mark]*
      $v = f = 1/$power $= 1/60 =$ **0.017 m (to 2 s.f.)** *[1 mark]*
  b)
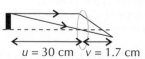
      $u = 30$ cm $v = 1.7$ cm
      [1 mark for correct rays, 1 mark for correctly labelling distances]
  c) $1/u + 1/v = 1/f$, $u = 0.30$ m, $v = 1/60$ m.
      $1/f = 63.33...$ D *[1 mark]*.
      So the extra power needed $= 63.33... - 60$
      $= 3.33...$ D = **3.3 D (to 2 s.f.)** *[1 mark]*.

Page 197 — Defects of Vision

1 Focal length of diverging lens needs to be -4.0 m *[1 mark]*.
   Power $= 1/f =$ **−0.25 D**
   [1 mark for value, 1 mark for negative sign]
2 Lens equation $1/u + 1/v = 1/f$. When $u = 0.25$ m, $v = -2.0$ m
   $1/f = 1/0.25 - 1/2.0$ *[1 mark]* $= 3.5$. Power = **+3.5 D**
   [1 mark for value, 1 mark for sign]
3 a) Cylindrical lenses *[1 mark]*.
  b) The optician gives the angle between the horizontal axes and the vertical lens axis *[1 mark]* and how curved the lens needs to be / the power of the lens needed to correct the astigmatism *[1 mark]*.

Page 199 — Physics of the Ear

1 a) The pinna concentrates the sound energy entering the ear into the auditory canal, increasing its intensity *[1 mark]*.
  b) Sound energy entering the ear causes the tympanic membrane (eardrum) to vibrate *[1 mark]*. The vibrations are transmitted through the middle ear by the malleus, incus and stapes in turn *[1 mark]*. The stapes is connected to the oval window, so causes it to vibrate *[1 mark]*.
  c) The amplitude of a sound is proportional to the square root of its intensity, and the intensity is inversely proportional to the area *[1 mark]*. This means that the amplitude is inversely proportional to the square root of the area *[1 mark]*, so if the area is decreased by a factor of 14, the amplitude is increased by a factor of $\sqrt{14} = 3.7$ (to 2 s.f.) *[1 mark]*.
  d) Pressure waves in the cochlea cause the basilar membrane to vibrate *[1 mark]*, which causes hair cells on the membrane to trigger electrical impulses *[1 mark]*.
  e) Different regions of the basilar membrane have different natural frequencies *[1 mark]*. When the frequency of a sound wave matches the natural frequency of a part of the membrane, that part resonates, causing the hair cells in that area to trigger impulses, so different frequencies trigger different nerve cells *[1 mark]*.

Page 201 — Intensity and Loudness

1 a) 1.0×10^{-12} Wm^{-2} *[1 mark]*
  b) $IL = 10\log\left(\dfrac{I}{I_0}\right) = 10\log\left(\dfrac{0.94}{1.0 \times 10^{-12}}\right) = 119.7...$ dB
     = **120 dB (to 2 s.f.)** *[1 mark]*
  c) The ear is most sensitive at about 3000 Hz, so the siren will sound as loud as possible *[1 mark]*.

Answers

2 The patient has suffered hearing loss at all frequencies, but the loss is worst at high frequencies *[1 mark]*. If the patient's hearing had been damaged by excessive noise, you would expect to see a peak at a particular frequency *[1 mark]*. This isn't present, so the patient's hearing loss is more likely to be age-related *[1 mark]*.

Page 203 — Electrocardiography (ECG)

1 a) Peaks of the waves occur at:
P wave: 3.1 s, QRS wave: 3.3 s, T wave: 3.6 s *[1 mark]*
  b) The P wave *[1 mark]*

2 a) The QRS wave is when the ventricles are contracting, so there may be a problem with the ventricles *[1 mark]*.
  b) Any one from: removed hair and dead skin, apply conductive gel, make sure electrodes are attached securely. *[1 mark]*

Page 205 — Ultrasound Imaging

1 a) $\left(\dfrac{Z_{tissue} - Z_{air}}{Z_{tissue} + Z_{air}}\right)^2 = \left(\dfrac{1630 \times 10^3 - 0.430 \times 10^3}{1630 \times 10^3 + 0.430 \times 10^3}\right)^2$ *[1 mark]*

= 0.9989... = **0.999 (to 3 s.f.)** *[1 mark]*

  b) From part a), 1.00 − 0.998... = 0.1% enters the body when no gel is used *[1 mark]*.
$\left(\dfrac{Z_{tissue} - Z_{gel}}{Z_{tissue} + Z_{gel}}\right)^2 = \left(\dfrac{1630 \times 10^3 - 1500 \times 10^3}{1630 \times 10^3 + 1500 \times 10^3}\right)^2$
= 0.0017... *[1 mark]*,
1 − 0.0017... = 0.9982...
So 99.82...% of the ultrasound is transmitted *[1 mark]*.
99.82...% ÷ 0.1% ≈ 1000, so the ratio is **1000:1** *[1 mark]*.

2 $Z = \rho c$, $c = (1.63 \times 10^6)/(1.09 \times 10^3)$ *[1 mark]*
= 1495 ms^{-1} = **1.50 kms^{-1} (to 3 s.f.)** *[1 mark]*.

3 Advantages: e.g. there are no known hazards / they can obtain real-time images of soft tissue / ultrasound devices are cheap and portable / they are quick and patient can move *[1 mark]*
Disadvantages: e.g. they cannot penetrate bone / ultrasound cannot pass through air spaces / images have a poor resolution / they can't give any information on any solid masses found (i.e. what the solid mass is) *[1 mark]*

Page 207 — Endoscopy

1 a) $\sin \theta_c = n_2/n_1 = 1.30/1.35$ *[1 mark]*
$\theta = 74.35... = $ **74.4° (to 3 s.f.)** *[1 mark]*
  b) When the angle of incidence is greater than or equal to the critical angle, the beam of light will undergo total internal reflection *[1 mark]*. If the angle of incidence falls below the critical angle, then some light will be lost *[1 mark]*.

2 A coherent fibre-optic bundle consists of a large number of very thin fibres *[1 mark]*, arranged in the same way at either end of the bundle *[1 mark]*. Lots of thin fibres are used to increase the resolution of the image *[1 mark]*. The relative positions of the fibres have to remain constant or the image would be jumbled up *[1 mark]*.

Page 209 — X-Ray Production

1

  a) See graph *[1 mark for shape of graph, 1 mark for 30 keV maximum energy and 1 mark for correct labelling of line spectrum]*
  b) Maximum energy = Voltage × e
= 30 × 10³ × 1.60 × 10⁻¹⁹ *[1 mark]* = **4.8 × 10⁻¹⁵ J** *[1 mark]*
  c) See graph *[1 mark for higher intensity and higher maximum energy and 1 mark for a few extra lines in the line spectrum]*

Page 211 — X-Ray Imaging Techniques

1 a) The half-value thickness is the thickness of material required to reduce the intensity of an X-ray beam to half its original value *[1 mark]*.

  b) $\mu = \dfrac{\ln 2}{x_{\frac{1}{2}}} = \dfrac{\ln 2}{3} = 0.231...mm^{-1}$ *[1 mark]*, $\dfrac{I}{I_0} = e^{-\mu x}$

So, $0.01 = e^{-0.231...x}$ for the beam to reach 1% of its initial value. Take the natural log of both sides: $\ln (0.01) = -0.231...x$ *[1 mark]*, $x = 19.9...$ mm = **20 mm (to 1 s.f.)** *[1 mark]*

2 a) A narrow beam of monochromatic X-rays is rotated and fired at a patient *[1 mark]*. Some of the X-rays are absorbed by bones and soft tissue. Thousands of detectors pick up the X-rays which haven't been absorbed *[1 mark]*. A computer calculates the attenuation caused by each part of the body and builds a 2D slice for that section *[1 mark]*.
  b) Either: the patient is subjected to a high dose of ionising radiation or the machines are expensive *[1 mark]*

Page 213 — Magnetic Resonance (MR) Imaging

1 **5-6 marks:**
All steps are covered in detail, with correct usage of terminology. Explanation is clear and concise.
3-4 marks:
The majority of steps are covered with an attempt made to use appropriate terminology. The explanation is legible and logical.
1-2 marks:
Two steps are explained briefly. Explanation is not clear.
0 marks:
No relevant information is given.
Points your answer should include:
The patient lies in the centre of a large superconducting magnet, which produces a magnetic field. The magnetic field aligns hydrogen protons in the patient's body. The protons precess about the magnetic field lines with a precession frequency. The precession frequency of the proton depends on its location within the body. Radio frequency coils are used to transmit radio waves which, if they have the same frequency as the precession frequency of a proton, will cause the aligned protons to absorb energy and change their spin state. When the radio waves stop, the protons emit the stored energy as radio waves with frequency the same as the precession frequency of the proton. These radio waves are recorded by the scanner. A computer analyses the received radio waves to produce a cross-section of the patient's body.

2 E.g. there are no known side effects, so patients have a lower risk when using a MR scanner (unlike with ionising radiation) *[1 mark]*. You can also take a slice at any orientation of the body — saving the patient's and doctor's time *[1 mark]*. A disadvantage is that their imaging of bones is very poor, so alternative methods have to be used which have a higher risk attached to them *[1 mark]*. They're also incredibly expensive, so some hospitals cannot afford them *[1 mark]*.

Page 215 — Medical Uses of Radiation

1 $\dfrac{1}{T_E} = \dfrac{1}{T_B} + \dfrac{1}{T_P} = \dfrac{1}{24} + \dfrac{1}{6} = \dfrac{5}{24}$ *[1 mark]*
So $T_E = 24 \div 5 = 4.8$ hours = **5 hours (to 1 s.f.)** *[1 mark]*

2 E.g. PET scanners give information about the metabolic activity of a patient *[1 mark]* and can be used to monitor brain activity. Some other imaging techniques are unable to penetrate bone, so this is particularly useful *[1 mark]*. One disadvantage is that PET scanners use ionising radiation, which can damage healthy cells inside a patient *[1 mark]*. PET scanners are also very large, which means they cannot easily be transported. Patients have to travel to their nearest hospital with a PET scanner, which can be difficult for some people / The scans can be uncomfortable and claustrophobic *[1 mark]*.

Answers

3   Implants containing beta-emitters could be placed either inside or next to the tumour *[1 mark]*. The ionising radiation would kill off the cancerous cells, but due to the short range of beta radiation, damage to nearby healthy cells would be limited *[1 mark]*.

Section 13: Option C — Engineering Physics

Page 217 — Inertia and Kinetic Energy

1    $I = mr^2 = 0.03 \times 0.8^2 = 0.0192 = \textbf{0.02 kgm}^2$ **(to 1 s.f.)** *[1 mark]*

2   Without the child, the moment of inertia of the roundabout is:
$I = \frac{1}{2}mr^2 = 0.5 \times 130 \times 2.5^2 = 406.25$ *[1 mark]*
Subtract this from the moment of inertia with the child
$531 - 406.25 = 124.75$
As the child is a point mass, $I = mr^2 = 124.75$ *[1 mark]*
So $m = 124.75 \div 2.5^2 = 19.96 = \textbf{20 kg}$ **(to 2 s.f.)** *[1 mark]*

3 a) $I = \frac{2}{3}mr^2 = \frac{2}{3} \times 0.5 \times 0.1^2 = 0.0033...$
    $= \textbf{0.003 kgm}^2$ **(to 1 s.f.)** *[1 mark]*

   b) $E_k = \frac{1}{2}I\omega^2 = \frac{1}{2} \times 0.0033... \times 1.5^2$ *[1 mark]* $= 0.00375$
    $= \textbf{0.004 J}$ **(to 1 s.f.)** *[1 mark]*

   c) $\dfrac{E_{ksolid}}{E_{khollow}} = \dfrac{\frac{1}{2}I_{solid}\omega^2}{\frac{1}{2}I_{hollow}\omega^2} = \dfrac{I_{solid}}{I_{hollow}}$ *[1 mark]* $= \dfrac{\frac{2}{5}mr^2}{\frac{2}{3}mr^2}$
    $= \frac{3}{5}$, so the ratio is **3:5** *[1 mark]*.

Page 219 — Rotational Motion

1    $\omega = \dfrac{\Delta\theta}{\Delta t} = \dfrac{2\pi}{24 \times 60 \times 60} = 0.000072...$
    $= \textbf{7.3} \times \textbf{10}^{-5} \textbf{ rad s}^{-1}$ **(to 2 s.f.)** *[1 mark]*

2   Its initial angular velocity is
    $\omega_1 = \dfrac{30.0 \times 2\pi}{60} = \pi = 3.14... \text{ rad s}^{-1}$ *[1 mark]*
    $\omega_2 = \omega_1 + \alpha t = 3.14... + 1.57 \times 5.00$ *[1 mark]*
    $= 10.99... = \textbf{11.0 rad s}^{-1}$ **(to 3 s.f.)** *[1 mark]*

3

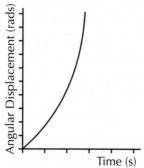

[1 mark for correct axes, 1 mark for correct curved shape]

4 a)   The angular acceleration is constant *[1 mark]* as the graph is a straight line.

   b)   Calculate the gradient of the line
    E.g. $\alpha = \dfrac{\Delta\omega}{\Delta t} = \dfrac{4}{2} = \textbf{2 rad s}^{-2}$ *[1 mark]*

   c)   The displacement is the area under the graph.
    Area of a trapezium $= \dfrac{a + b}{2}h = \dfrac{4 + 10}{2} \times 3$
    So Area = Angular displacement = **21 radians** *[1 mark]*

Page 221 — Torque, Work and Power

1    $T = Fr = 1 \times (0.1 \div 2) = \textbf{0.05 Nm}$ *[1 mark]*

2 a) $Fr = I\alpha$ so $\alpha = \dfrac{Fr}{I} = \dfrac{140 \times 2.5}{500}$ *[1 mark]* $= \textbf{0.7 rad s}^{-2}$ *[1 mark]*

   b) $W = T\theta = Fr\theta = 140 \times 2.5 \times 2\pi$ *[1 mark]*
    $= 2199.1... = \textbf{2200 J}$ **(to 2 s.f.)** *[1 mark]*

3    $T_{friction} = T_{applied} - T_{required} = 0.50 - 0.45 = 0.05$ Nm *[1 mark]*
    Power $= T\omega = 0.05 \times 3.0 = \textbf{0.15 W}$ *[1 mark]*

Page 223 — Flywheels

1 a)   When Taylor's car uses its brakes, a flywheel is engaged. The kinetic energy from the car is transferred to the flywheel, charging it up *[1 mark]*. When the car then next accelerates, the flywheel decelerates and gives kinetic energy back to the car, meaning it needs less energy from the motor to accelerate *[1 mark]*. The flywheel is then disengaged until the car brakes again *[1 mark]*.

   b)   E.g. in a potter's wheel to keep the angular speed smooth, even though the applied torque varies *[1 mark]*.

2   Increasing the mass would increase the maximum amount of energy the flywheel could store, as it would increase the moment of inertia of the flywheel *[1 mark]*. The moment of inertia is proportional to the flywheel's mass, so the maximum energy the flywheel could store would double if its mass was doubled *[1 mark]*. One disadvantage of this is that the flywheel would now be twice as heavy and would need stronger bearings to support it *[1 mark]*. A different improvement which could be made is to use a spoked wheel of the same mass instead of a solid wheel. This also increases the moment of inertia (and thus energy stored) whilst the mass of the flywheel stays the same *[1 mark]*.

Page 225 — Angular Momentum

1   Angular momentum $= I\omega = 0.04 \times 4 = \textbf{0.16 Nms}$ *[1 mark]*

2   A diver tucks into a ball to bring their limbs closer to the axis of rotation, which reduces their moment of inertia *[1 mark]*. As no external forces are being applied, the angular momentum remains constant *[1 mark]*. As the angular momentum remains constant, the diver's angular velocity must increase *[1 mark]*.

3   Angular momentum before = Angular momentum after
    $I_1\omega_1 + I_2\omega_2 = (I_1 + I_2)\omega$ so $\omega = \dfrac{I_1\omega_1 + I_2\omega_2}{(I_1 + I_2)}$ *[1 mark]*
    $\omega = \dfrac{0.10 \times \left(\frac{3000 \times 2\pi}{60}\right) + 0.15 \times \left(\frac{2000 \times 2\pi}{60}\right)}{0.25}$ *[1 mark]*
    $= 251.3... = \textbf{250 rad s}^{-1}$ **(to 2 s.f.)** *[1 mark]*

4 a)   Angular impulse $= \Delta(I\omega) = I\Delta\omega = 0.2 \times (24 - 2.2)$
                 $= 4.36 = \textbf{4.4 Nms}$ **(to 2 s.f.)** *[1 mark]*

   b)   Angular impulse $= T\Delta t = 4.36$
    $T = 4.36 \div 4 = 1.09 = \textbf{1.1 Nm}$ **(to 2 s.f.)** *[1 mark]*

Page 228 — The First Law of Thermodynamics

1 a)   For isothermal processes, pV = constant
    Before compression $pV = 1.2 \times 10^4 \times 0.4 = 4800$ Pa m^3
    So after compression $p = 4800 \div 0.3 = 16\,000$ *[1 mark]*
                        $= \textbf{1.6} \times \textbf{10}^4 \textbf{ Pa}$ **(to 2 s.f.)** *[1 mark]*

   b) $pV = nRT$ so $T = pV \div nR$
    $T = 4800 \div (0.82 \times 8.31)$ *[1 mark]*
    $= 704.4... = \textbf{700 K}$ **(to 2 s.f.)** *[1 mark]*

2    $W = Q - \Delta U = 3000 - 300 = 2700$ J *[1 mark]*
    $W = p\Delta V$ so $\Delta V = 2700 \div (1.1 \times 10^{-4})$
    $= 0.245...$ m^3 *[1 mark]*
    For constant pressure, $\dfrac{V_1}{T_1} = \dfrac{V_2}{T_2}$ so
    $T_2 = \dfrac{V_2 T_1}{V_1} = \dfrac{0.360 \times 300}{0.360 - 0.245...}$ *[1 mark]*
    $T_2 = 942.8... = \textbf{940 K}$ **(to 2 s.f.)** *[1 mark]*

3   The volume is constant, so the work done is zero. This means that $Q = \Delta U$. *[1 mark]* As heat energy is being transferred to the system, this makes Q (and ΔU) positive. ΔU is dependent only on temperature, so the temperature must be increasing. *[1 mark]*
    For isothermal processes, the temperature remains constant. *[1 mark]*
    For adiabatic processes, $Q = 0$ so $W = -\Delta U$. As the gas is being compressed, the work done is negative, meaning that ΔU is positive *[1 mark]*. This means that the temperature must be increasing *[1 mark]*.

Answers

Page 231 — p-V Diagrams

1

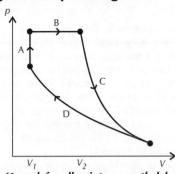

[1 mark for all points correctly labelled, 1 mark for correct straight lines and arrows representing stages A and B, 1 mark for a curve and arrow pointing downwards representing stage C, 1 mark for a shallower curve representing stage D than stage C.]

2 a) Change in volume = 0.8×10^{-4} m^3, $p = 15.0 \times 10^6$ Pa.
$W = p\Delta V = 15.0 \times 10^6 \times 0.8 \times 10^{-4} = $ **1200 J** *[1 mark]*

   b) Horizontally, 10 squares is equal to 2.0×10^{-4} m^3.
   So, one square width equals $(2.0 \times 10^{-4}) \div 10 = 2.0 \times 10^{-5}$ m^3.
   Vertically, 5 squares is equal to 5.0×10^6 Pa.
   So one square height is equal to 1.0×10^6 Pa.
   [1 mark for correct calculation of one square's height or width]
   Work done per square = $2.0 \times 10^{-5} \times 1.0 \times 10^6 = 20$ J *[1 mark]*
   The loop encircles around 66 squares, so net work done per cycle is $66 \times 20 = $ **1320 J** *[1 mark]*.

   c) An adiabatic expansion would have a steeper p-V curve than an isothermal one *[1 mark]*. This would make the p-V diagram loop area smaller. This area represents the work done per cycle, so the net work would decrease if the system adiabatically expanded *[1 mark]*.

Page 233 — Four-Stroke Engines

1 a) During the induction stroke, the piston moves down the cylinder, increasing the volume above it. The air-fuel mixture is sucked in through the inlet valve *[1 mark]*. The pressure stays roughly constant (just below atmospheric pressure) *[1 mark]*. In the compression stroke, the inlet valve is closed and the piston is moved up the cylinder, compressing the air-fuel mixture *[1 mark]*. Just before the end of the stroke, the spark plug creates a spark which ignites the gas inside the cylinder. The temperature and pressure rapidly increase, whilst the volume stays roughly the same *[1 mark]*.

   b)

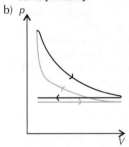

[1 mark for drawing a curved expansion stroke above the compression stroke curve, 1 mark for drawing a horizontal line for the exhaust stroke]

   c)

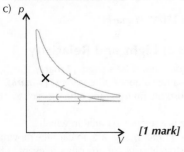

[1 mark]

2 Firstly, on the induction stroke, a four-stroke diesel engine takes in only air instead of an air-fuel mixture like a four-stroke petrol engine *[1 mark]*. There is also no spark plug in a diesel engine, so during the compression stroke, the air inside the cylinder is compressed until it reaches a high enough temperature to ignite diesel *[1 mark]*. Diesel is sprayed in through a fuel injector just before the end of the compression stroke, where it is then ignited *[1 mark]*.

Page 235 — Using Indicator Diagrams

1 a) Indicated power = (area of p-V loop) × (number of cycles per second) × (number of cylinders)
= $120 \times 29 \times 8 = 27\,840 = $ **28 000 W (to 2 s.f.)** *[1 mark]*

   b) Friction power = indicated power – brake power
   Brake power = $T\omega = 130 \times 58\pi = 7540\pi$ W *[1 mark]*
   Friction power = $27\,840 - 7540\pi = 4152.3...$
   $= $ **4200 W (to 2 s.f.)** *[1 mark]*

2 Indicated power is related to the area of the indicator diagram loop. As the loop for engine A has a smaller area than for engine B, engine A has a lower indicated power *[1 mark]*. The frictional power of both engines is the same, so this means that engine A also has a lower output power *[1 mark]*. Output power, $P = T\omega$. Both engines have the same angular velocity, so the torque of engine A must be less than the torque of engine B *[1 mark]*.

Page 237 — Engine Efficiency

1 input power = calorific value × fuel flow rate
= $44.8 \times 10^6 \times 2.8 \times 10^{-3} = 125\,440$ W *[1 mark]*

overall efficiency = $\dfrac{\text{brake power}}{\text{input power}} = \dfrac{44\,700}{125\,440}$ *[1 mark]*
$= 0.356... = $ **36% (to 2 s.f.)** *[1 mark]*

2 a) Theoretical maximum efficiency = $\dfrac{T_H - T_C}{T_H}$
$= \dfrac{1200 - 290}{1200}$ *[1 mark]* $= 0.758... = $ **76% (to 2 s.f.)** *[1 mark]*

   b) $W = Q_H - Q_C = 1000 - 550 = 450$ J *[1 mark]*
   Efficiency = $\dfrac{W}{Q_H} = \dfrac{450}{1000} = 0.45 = $ **45%** *[1 mark]*

   c) E.g. frictional forces inside the engine, energy is needed to move internal parts *[1 mark for one correct reason]*.

Page 239 — Reversed Heat Engines

1 a) $W = Q_H - Q_C$ so $Q_H = W + Q_C$
$= 2.02 \times 10^6 + 5.66 \times 10^6 = $ **7.68×10^6 J** *[1 mark]*

   b) $COP_{ref} = \dfrac{Q_C}{W} = \dfrac{5.66 \times 10^6}{2.02 \times 10^6} = 2.801... = $ **2.80 (to 3 s.f.)** *[1 mark]*

2 a) $T_H = 25 + 273 = 298$ K
$T_C = 3 + 273 = 276$ K
$COP_{hp} = \dfrac{T_H}{T_H - T_C} = \dfrac{298}{22} = 13.5... = $ **14 (to 2 s.f.)** *[1 mark]*

   b) $W = \dfrac{Q_H}{COP} = \dfrac{4.10 \times 10^6}{3.5}$ *[1 mark]*

   $= 1.17... \times 10^6 = $ **1.2 MJ (to 2 s.f.)** *[1 mark]*

Section 13: Option D — Turning Points in Physics

Page 241 — Specific Charge of the Electron

1 a) 1000 eV *[1 mark]*
   b) 1000 eV $\times 1.60 \times 10^{-19}$ J/eV $= $ **1.60×10^{-16} J (to 3 s.f.)** *[1 mark]*
   c) Kinetic energy = $\frac{1}{2}mv^2 = 1.60 \times 10^{-16}$ J *[1 mark]*
   $v^2 = (2 \times 1.60 \times 10^{-16}) \div (9.11 \times 10^{-31}) = 3.512... \times 10^{14}$
   $v = \sqrt{3.512... \times 10^{14}} = 1.874... \times 10^7$ ms^{-1}
   $= $ **1.87×10^7 ms^{-1}** *[1 mark]*
   $\dfrac{1.874... \times 10^7}{3.00 \times 10^8} \times 100\% = 6.247...$
   $= $ **6.25% (to 3 s.f.) of the speed of light** *[1 mark]*

Answers

2   Your answer will depend on which experiment you describe, e.g.:
Electrons are accelerated using an electron gun *[1 mark]*.
A magnetic field *[1 mark]* exerts a centripetal force *[1 mark]* on
the electrons, making them trace a circular path. By measuring
the radius of this path and equating the magnetic and centripetal
forces *[1 mark]* you can calculate e/m_e.
[1 mark for quality of written communication].

Page 243 — Millikan's Oil-Drop Experiment

1 a) The forces acting on the drop are its weight, acting downwards
[1 mark] and the equally sized force due to the electric field,
acting upwards *[1 mark]*.

b) Weight = electric force, so $mg = \frac{QV}{d}$, and $Q = \frac{mgd}{V}$

$Q = \frac{1.63 \times 10^{-14} \times 9.81 \times 3.00 \times 10^{-2}}{4995}$

$= 9.603... \times 10^{-19}$ C *[1 mark]*
Divide by e: $9.603... \times 10^{-19} \div 1.60 \times 10^{-19} = 6.002...$ *[1 mark]*
So $Q = $ **6.00e (to 3 s.f.)** *[1 mark]*

c) The forces on the oil drop as it falls are its weight and the
viscous force from the air *[1 mark]*. As the oil drop accelerates,
the viscous force increases until it equals the oil drop's weight
[1 mark]. At this point, there is no resultant force on the oil
drop, so it stops accelerating, but continues to fall at terminal
velocity *[1 mark]*.

d) At terminal velocity, $F = mg = 6\pi\eta rv$
Rearranging, $v = \frac{mg}{6\pi\eta r}$
Find the radius of the oil drop,
using mass = volume × density: $m = \frac{4}{3}\pi r^3\rho$.

So $r^3 = \frac{3m}{4\pi\rho} = \frac{3 \times 1.63 \times 10^{-14}}{4 \times \pi \times 885}$ *[1 mark]*
$= 4.396... \times 10^{-18}$

$r = \sqrt[3]{4.396... \times 10^{-18}} = 1.638... \times 10^{-6}$ *[1 mark]*

So, $v = \frac{1.63 \times 10^{-14} \times 9.81}{6\pi \times 1.84 \times 10^{-5} \times 1.638... \times 10^{-6}} = 2.814... \times 10^{-4}$

$= $ **2.81×10^{-4} ms^{-1} (to 3 s.f.)** *[1 mark]*

Page 246 — Light — Particles vs Waves

1 a) Light consists of particles *[1 mark]*. The theory was based on
Newton's laws of motion, with the straight-line motion of light as
evidence *[1 mark]*.

b) Newton's corpuscular theory intuitively explained reflection and
refraction and fitted with existing laws of physics *[1 mark]*.
There was no experimental evidence for Huygens' theory
[1 mark], and scientists didn't think it could explain double
refraction *[1 mark]*. Newton became a very successful physicist
with a strong reputation *[1 mark]*.

2   Young's double-slit experiment proved that light could diffract and
interfere like a wave, which particles couldn't do *[1 mark]*. Fizeau
measured the speed of light *[1 mark]*, which allowed Maxwell
to show that light travelled at the same speed as electromagnetic
waves, and so was likely to be an electromagnetic wave *[1 mark]*.
Hertz discovered radio waves and showed that their speed was
the same as electromagnetic waves, proving Maxwell's prediction
of a spectrum of electromagnetic waves including light to be
correct *[1 mark]*.

Page 249 — The Photoelectric Effect and the Photon Model

1 a) Wave theory was unable to explain why, for a given metal,
radiation below a certain frequency doesn't cause any
photoelectrons to be emitted *[1 mark]*, or why the kinetic energy
of photoelectrons doesn't vary with intensity, but has a maximum
value for a given frequency of radiation *[1 mark]*. Wave theory
predicted that photoelectrons would be emitted due to radiation
of any frequency, but that it would take longer for electrons to be
emitted by lower frequency waves *[1 mark]*, and that the higher
the intensity of the radiation, the higher the kinetic energy of the
photoelectrons emitted should be *[1 mark]*.

b) The photon model says each photon has a particular energy given
by its frequency *[1 mark]*. When a photon hits a free electron
in the metal, this energy is transferred to the electron, and if it is
greater than the work function of the metal, the electron can be
emitted *[1 mark]*. As each electron can only absorb one photon
at a time, only photons with energy greater than the work function
can cause photoelectrons to be emitted, hence the threshold
frequency *[1 mark]*. Because electrons only absorb one photon at
a time, the maximum kinetic energy a photoelectron can have is
only dependent on the frequency of the photons, not the intensity
of the radiation, which increases the number of photoelectrons
emitted, but not their energy *[1 mark]*.

2   The ultraviolet catastrophe was the prediction by wave theory that
the peak radiation emitted from a black body would be infinitely
high *[1 mark]* towards the ultraviolet region of the spectrum
[1 mark]. It meant that wave theory must be incorrect as it
couldn't correctly explain the behaviour of light *[1 mark]*.

Page 251 — Wave-Particle Duality

1 a) i)   Velocity is given by $\frac{1}{2}mv^2 = eV$ so $v = \sqrt{\frac{2eV}{m}}$ *[1 mark]*

$v = \sqrt{\frac{2 \times 1.60 \times 10^{-19} \times 515}{9.11 \times 10^{-31}}} = 1.3449... \times 10^7$
$= $ **1.34×10^7 ms^{-1} (to 3 s.f.)** *[1 mark]*

ii)   de Broglie equation $p = \frac{h}{\lambda}$ so wavelength $\lambda = \frac{h}{mv}$ *[1 mark]*

so $\lambda = \frac{6.63 \times 10^{-34}}{9.11 \times 10^{-31} \times 1.3449... \times 10^7} = 5.4109... \times 10^{-11}$
$= $ **5.41×10^{-11} m (to 3 s.f.)** *[1 mark]*

b) This is in the X-ray region of the EM spectrum *[1 mark]*.

2 a) A stream of electrons is accelerated towards the sample using an
electron gun *[1 mark]*. The beam of electrons is focused onto
the sample using magnetic and electric fields *[1 mark]*. The parts
of the beam that pass through the sample are projected onto a
screen to form an image of the sample *[1 mark]*.

b) To resolve detail around the size of an atom, the electron
wavelength needs to be around 0.100 nm *[1 mark]*. The
relationship between anode voltage and electron wavelength is
given by $\lambda = \frac{h}{\sqrt{2meV}}$, which rearranges to give

$V = \frac{h^2}{2me\lambda^2}$ *[1 mark]*.
Substituting $m = 9.11 \times 10^{-31}$ kg, $e = 1.60 \times 10^{-19}$ C,
$\lambda = 0.100 \times 10^{-9}$ m gives:

$v = \frac{(6.63 \times 10^{-34})^2}{2 \times 9.11 \times 10^{-31} \times 1.60 \times 10^{-19} \times (0.100 \times 10^{-9})^2}$
$= 150.78... = $ **151 V (to 3 s.f.)**, showing that the minimum anode

voltage has to be around 150 V *[1 mark]*.

Page 253 — The Speed of Light and Relativity

1 a) The interference pattern would move/be shifted *[1 mark]*.
b) The speed of light has the same value for all observers *[1 mark]*.
It is impossible to detect absolute motion / the ether doesn't exist
[1 mark].

2 a) An inertial reference frame is a reference frame in which
Newton's 1st law is obeyed *[1 mark]*, e.g. a train carriage moving
at constant speed along a straight track (or any other relevant
example) *[1 mark]*.

Answers

b) The speed of light is unaffected by the motion of the observer *[1 mark]* or the motion of the light source *[1 mark]*.

Page 255 — Special Relativity

1 time $t = \dfrac{t_0}{\sqrt{1 - \dfrac{v^2}{c^2}}}$ and $t_0 = 20.0 \times 10^{-9}$ s *[1 mark]*

$t = \dfrac{20.0 \times 10^{-9}}{\sqrt{1 - \dfrac{(0.995c)^2}{c^2}}}$ *[1 mark]*

$= 2.0025... \times 10^{-7}$

$= 2.00 \times 10^{-7}$ s **(to 3 s.f.)** *[1 mark]*

You could also give your answer as **200 ns (to 3 s.f.)**.

2 Your description must include:
A diagram or statement showing relative motion *[1 mark]*.
An event of a specified duration in one reference frame *[1 mark]*.
Measurement of the time interval by a moving observer *[1 mark]*.
Time interval for "external" observer greater than time interval for the "stationary" observer or equivalent *[1 mark]*.

3 a) $E = \dfrac{m_0 c^2}{\sqrt{1 - \dfrac{v^2}{c^2}}}$ and $E = mc^2$ so $m = \dfrac{E}{c^2} = \dfrac{m_0}{\sqrt{1 - \dfrac{v^2}{c^2}}}$ *[1 mark]*

$m = \dfrac{1.67 \times 10^{-27}}{\sqrt{1 - \dfrac{(2.80 \times 10^8)^2}{(3.00 \times 10^8)^2}}} = 4.6516... \times 10^{-27}$

$= \mathbf{4.65 \times 10^{-27}}$ **kg (to 3 s.f.)** *[1 mark]*

b) $E = mc^2 = 4.6516... \times 10^{-27} \times (3.00 \times 10^8)^2 = 4.1865... \times 10^{-10}$
$= \mathbf{4.19 \times 10^{-10}}$ **J (to 3 s.f.)** *[1 mark]*

Extra Exam Practice for Section 13

Pages 256-257

1.1 Type 1a supernovae have high luminosities, so they can be observed from a long way away *[1 mark]*. They also have the same absolute magnitude curve with time/the same peak absolute magnitude, so they can be used (as a standard candle) to measure their distance from Earth with $m - M = 5\log\left(\dfrac{d}{10}\right)$ / using their absolute and apparent magnitudes *[1 mark]*.

1.2 $v = H_0 d$, age of universe $= \dfrac{1}{H_0}$
Use the absolute and apparent magnitude of the supernova to calculate its distance, d, from Earth:

$m - M = 5\log\left(\dfrac{d}{10}\right)$

$\dfrac{15.0 - (-19.0)}{5} = \log\left(\dfrac{d}{10}\right)$

$\log\left(\dfrac{d}{10}\right) = 6.8$

$10^{6.8} = \dfrac{d}{10}$, so $d = 6.30... \times 10^7$ pc
1 pc $= 3.08 \times 10^{16}$ m, so $d = (6.30... \times 10^7) \times (3.08 \times 10^{16})$
$= 1.94... \times 10^{24}$ m *[1 mark]*
Use the red shift of the absorption line to calculate the recessional velocity, v, of the supernova:

$-\dfrac{\Delta\lambda}{\lambda} = \dfrac{v}{c}$

$\Delta\lambda = \lambda_{emitted} - \lambda_{observed} = 636.0 - 645.6 = -9.6$ nm

$v = -\dfrac{\Delta\lambda}{\lambda} \times c = -\dfrac{-9.6\,\text{nm}}{636.0\,\text{nm}} \times (3.00 \times 10^8)$

$= 4.52... \times 10^6$ ms^{-1} *[1 mark]*

$v = H_0 d$, so $\dfrac{1}{H_0} = \dfrac{d}{v} = \dfrac{1.94... \times 10^{24}}{4.52... \times 10^6}$

$= 4.291... \times 10^{17}$ s

$= \mathbf{4.29 \times 10^{17}}$ **s (to 3 s.f.)** *[1 mark]*

1.3 How to grade your answer:
5-6 marks:
A detailed explanation of using both methods to identify a binary star system is given in a clear and logical way. Limitations of both methods are clearly explained.
3-4 marks:
An explanation of using both methods to identify a binary star system is given, but it lacks some clarity. The limitations may be briefly discussed but not fully explained. There is some structure to the answer, and the information is mostly relevant to the question.
1-2 marks:
A brief explanation that details at least telescope use to identify a binary star system is given. The limitations are not made clear. The answer lacks detail, and the information given may not be relevant to the question.
0 marks:
No relevant information is given.
Here are some points your answer may include:
A telescope could be used to directly observe the two stars in a binary system.
For a given telescope with an aperture diameter, D, light of wavelength λ, can be resolved if the angle between the sources is more than the minimum angular resolution, $\theta = \dfrac{\lambda}{D}$.
This method is therefore limited by the angular separation of the two stars, θ, which will be lower the further the system is from Earth, and the closer the stars are together.
Therefore this method is limited by distance from Earth, distance between the stars in the system, and the maximum diameter of a telescope.
Another method that can be used to detect a binary system is to observe how the absorption spectra of the star system changes with time.
If the stars have a component of motion parallel to our line of sight from Earth, the two stars will be moving in different directions relative to Earth.
This means the Doppler effect on the two stars will be different, and the corresponding absorption lines will be separated every half cycle when observed from Earth.
However, this method does not work if the stars are only moving in the plane perpendicular to our line of sight, as the absorption lines from each star will experience the same Doppler effect and line up.

2.1 An X-ray tube potential difference of about 30 kV would produce the best image *[1 mark]*, because the difference between the mass attenuation coefficient of iodine and lung tissue is largest here *[1 mark]*. A larger difference in the mass attenuation coefficient means a larger difference in the amount of X-rays absorbed. This means the image with the best contrast between lung tissue and blood vessels containing iodine contrast will be produced when around 30 kV is used *[1 mark]*.
You can give yourself the mark if you've suggested an X-ray tube potential difference of between 25-35 kV.

2.2 The effective half-life of Xe-133 is much shorter than Tc-99m, even though the physical half-life of Xe-133 is much longer.
$\dfrac{1}{T_E} = \dfrac{1}{T_B} + \dfrac{1}{T_P}$, so the biological half-life of the gas containing Xe-133 is much shorter than for the Tc-99m *[1 mark]*. This could be because the patient breathes out most of the gas containing the Xe-133 almost straight away, whereas the body takes longer to remove the Tc-99m from the blood *[1 mark]*.

304

Answers

2.3 $\frac{I_r}{I_i} = \left(\frac{Z_2 - Z_1}{Z_2 + Z_1}\right)^2$

When the ultrasound reaches a tissue-air boundary, the proportion of the ultrasound energy that is reflected is:

$\frac{I_r}{I_i} = \left(\frac{400 - (1.8 \times 10^5)}{400 + (1.8 \times 10^5)}\right)^2 = 0.99115... = 99.115...\%$

You would end up with the same answer if you calculated the proportion of ultrasound energy reflected as they go from air to lung tissue (instead of from lung tissue to air).

So almost all of the ultrasound energy will be reflected from the first air-tissue boundary it meets *[1 mark]*. The lungs contain a lot of air-tissue boundaries, so it is difficult for the ultrasound to reach all parts of the lungs *[1 mark]*.

3.1 $p_1 V_1^\gamma = p_2 V_2^\gamma$

$\frac{p_1}{p_2} = \frac{V_2^\gamma}{V_1^\gamma} = \left(\frac{V_2}{V_1}\right)^\gamma$

$p_1 = 1.0 \times 10^5$ Pa, $p_2 = 1.8 \times 10^6$ Pa

V_2 is 8 times smaller than V_1, so $V_1 = 8V_2$

$\frac{1.0 \times 10^5}{1.8 \times 10^6} = \left(\frac{V_2}{8V_2}\right)^\gamma$

$\frac{1}{18} = \left(\frac{1}{8}\right)^\gamma$ *[1 mark]*

Take $\log\frac{1}{8}$ of each side to get:

$\gamma = \log\frac{1}{8}\left(\frac{1}{18}\right) = 1.389975 = \mathbf{1.4}$ **(to 2 s.f.)** *[1 mark]*

3.2 $E_k = \frac{1}{2}I\omega^2$, angular momentum $= I\omega$

$\omega = 2400$ rpm $= 2400 \div 60 = 40$ revolutions per second

One complete revolution is 2π rad

$\omega = 40 \times 2\pi = 80\pi$ rad s^{-1} *[1 mark]*

$E_k = \frac{1}{2}I\omega^2 = \frac{1}{2} \times$ angular momentum $\times \omega$

$= \frac{1}{2} \times 13.07 \times 80\pi$

$= 1642.42...$ J $= \mathbf{1600}$ **J (to 2 s.f.)** *[1 mark]*

3.3 mechanical efficiency = brake power ÷ indicated power

brake power $= T\omega = 340 \times 80\pi = 85\ 451.32...$ W *[1 mark]*

friction power = indicated power – brake power

indicated power = friction power + brake power

$= 21\ 400 + 85\ 451.32...$

$= 106\ 851.32...$ W *[1 mark]*

mechanical efficiency $= 85\ 451.32... \div 106\ 851.32...$

$= 0.7997... = \mathbf{0.80}$ **(to 2 s.f.)** *[1 mark]*

3.4 How to grade your answer:

5-6 marks:

A detailed explanation of how each change would affect indicated power and thermal efficiency is given in a clear and logical way.

3-4 marks:

An explanation of how a change would affect indicated power and thermal efficiency is given, but it lacks some clarity. There is some structure to the answer, and the information is mostly relevant to the question.

1-2 marks:

A brief explanation is given that attempts to detail how either indicated power or thermal efficiency varies. The answer lacks detail, and the information given may not be relevant to the question.

0 marks:

No relevant information is given.

Here are some points your answer may include:

If the engine contained 6 cylinders instead of 4 cylinders:

Indicated power = (area of *p-V* loop) × (number of cycles per second) × (number of cylinders)

Area of *p-V* loop and the number of cycles per second remains the same, and the number of cylinders has increased by a factor of 1.5, so the indicated power of the engine will increase by a factor of 1.5.

Input power = calorific value × fuel flow rate

The calorific value of the fuel remains the same, as the type of fuel isn't changing. The fuel flow rate to each cylinder is the same, so the fuel flow rate to the engine will increase by a factor of 1.5. The input power to the engine will also therefore increase by a factor of 1.5.

Thermal efficiency of the engine $= \frac{\text{indicated power of the engine}}{\text{input power of the engine}}$,

so the thermal efficiency of the engine will remain the same.

If the compression ratio was increased to 10:1:

During the compression stroke, the *p-V* curve will start at the same point and will follow the same adiabatic curve as with an 8:1 compression ratio. However, the adiabatic curve will continue to lower volumes than that in an 8:1 cylinder. The pressure will be higher when the fuel is ignited, so the final pressure of the compression stroke will be higher.

The area of the *p-V* loop will therefore be larger, as the area would span a wider range of volumes and pressures.

The number of cycles per second and the number of cylinders remains the same, so this would increase the indicated power of the engine.

The input power remains constant, so the thermal efficiency would increase.

4.1 Specific charge $= Q \div m$

The two forces acting on the muon are the electric force $\left(\frac{QV}{d}\right)$ acting upwards (since it's negatively-charged) and the weight of the muon (*mg*) acting downwards.

The beam is not deflected towards either of the charged plates, so the muon's weight must balance the electric force.

$\frac{QV}{d} = mg$, so $\frac{Q}{m} = \frac{gd}{V}$ *[1 mark]*

$d = 2.50$ mm $= 2.50 \times 10^{-3}$ m

$V = 28.8$ pV $= 2.88 \times 10^{-11}$ V

$\frac{Q}{m} = \frac{9.81 \times (2.50 \times 10^{-3})}{2.88 \times 10^{-11}} = 8.515... \times 10^8$ C kg^{-1}

$= 8.52 \times 10^8$ C kg^{-1} *[1 mark]*

4.2 The resolution of an electron microscope depends on the de Broglie wavelength of the electrons used. This means that to make a muon microscope with this same resolution, the de Broglie wavelength of the muons used should match that of the electrons in an electron microscope *[1 mark]*.

$\lambda = \frac{h}{\sqrt{2mQV}}$

Muons have the same charge but a much smaller specific charge $\left(\frac{Q}{m}\right)$ than electrons, so muons must have a much larger mass than electrons *[1 mark]*.

For the de Broglie wavelength/resolution to remain constant, the anode voltage must be lower in a muon microscope to balance the larger mass of a muon *[1 mark]*.

4.3 The total energy of a muon travelling at relativistic speeds is the sum of its kinetic energy and rest energy.

rest energy = 105.659 MeV $= 1.05659 \times 10^8$ eV

$= (1.05659 \times 10^8) \times (1.60 \times 10^{-19})$ J

$= 1.690... \times 10^{-11}$ J *[1 mark]*

$V = 15.0$ MV $= 1.50 \times 10^7$ V

Work done on a muon by the electric field $= QV$

$= (1.60 \times 10^{-19}) \times (1.50 \times 10^7) = 2.4 \times 10^{-12}$ J *[1 mark]*

The muons do not have any kinetic energy initially, as they are accelerated from rest. This means the work done by the electric field = total kinetic energy of the muon at point A.

Total energy $= (1.690... \times 10^{-11}) + (2.4 \times 10^{-12})$

$= 1.930... \times 10^{-11}$

$= \mathbf{1.93 \times 10^{-11}}$ **J (to 3 s.f.)** *[1 mark]*

Answers

Answers

4.4 In the reference frame of the muon, the muon is stationary, and the external observer is moving at a relative speed of 1.44×10^8 ms^{-1}. The muon experiences the proper time, t_0, and the external observer measures time $t = 775 \div (1.44 \times 10^8)$ $= 5.3819... \times 10^{-6}$ s.

$t = \dfrac{t_0}{\sqrt{1 - \dfrac{v^2}{c^2}}}$ so

$t_0 = t \times \sqrt{1 - \dfrac{v^2}{c^2}} = 5.3819... \times 10^{-6} \times \sqrt{1 - \dfrac{(1.44 \times 10^8)^2}{(3.00 \times 10^8)^2}}$

$= 4.7214... \times 10^{-6}$ s *[1 mark]*

The half life of a muon is 1.56 μs $= 1.56 \times 10^{-6}$ s, so in the reference frame of the muon, the number of half lives it experiences between points B and C is

$\dfrac{4.7214... \times 10^{-6}}{1.56 \times 10^{-6}} = 3.026... \approx 3$ half lives *[1 mark]*.

Since you've been asked to estimate, it's OK to round to 3 half lives here.
After every half life, the number of muons detected should halve, so after 3 half lives, the number of muons should change by a factor of $\dfrac{1}{8}$.

The count rate at point B is 768 muons per minute, so at point C, the count rate $= 768 \times \dfrac{1}{8} = $ **96 muons per minute** *[1 mark]*

Synoptic Practice

Pages 268-275

1.1 $^{241}_{94}\text{Pu} \rightarrow ^{241}_{95}\text{Am} + ^{0}_{-1}\beta + \bar{\nu}_e$
[1 mark for all correct symbols before and after reaction, 1 mark for correct mass numbers and atomic numbers]
You'd still get full marks if you put atomic and mass numbers of zero on the neutrino.

1.2 First calculate the number of Am-241 atoms produced per second:

$N = nN_A = \dfrac{\text{mass (in g)}}{\text{molar mass}} \times N_A = \dfrac{0.638 \times 10^{-6}}{241} \times 6.02 \times 10^{23}$
$= 1.593... \times 10^{15}$ atoms *[1 mark]*

The number of Am-241 atoms produced per second by the Pu-241 is equal to the activity of the Pu-241 source, so $A = 1.593... \times 10^{15}$ Bq.
$A = \lambda N$ so calculate the decay constant, λ, of Pu-241:
$T_{1/2} = \dfrac{\ln 2}{\lambda}$ so $\lambda = \dfrac{\ln 2}{T_{1/2}} = \dfrac{\ln 2}{4.42 \times 10^8}$
$= 1.568... \times 10^{-9}$ s^{-1} *[1 mark]*
$A = \lambda N$ so $N = \dfrac{A}{\lambda} = \dfrac{1.593... \times 10^{15}}{1.568... \times 10^{-9}}$
$= 1.016... \times 10^{24}$ atoms *[1 mark]*
Calculate the mass in grams:
$N = \dfrac{\text{mass (in g)}}{\text{molar mass}} \times N_A$
so mass $= \dfrac{N}{N_A} \times$ molar mass
$= \dfrac{1.016... \times 10^{24}}{6.02 \times 10^{23}} \times 241$
$= 406.834... = $ **407 g (to 3 s.f.)** *[1 mark]*

1.3 The energy released is the difference in the binding energy (BE) per nucleus before and after the reaction. The binding energy per nucleus is the binding energy per nucleon × mass number:
BE per nucleus: Am-241 $= 7.54 \times 241 = 1817.14$ MeV
Np-237 $= 7.58 \times 237 = 1796.46$ MeV
He-4 $= 7.07 \times 4 = 28.28$ MeV *[1 mark]*
Energy released = BE after − BE before
$= (1796.46 + 28.28) - 1817.14$
$= 7.6$ MeV *[1 mark]*
1.70% of this energy is transferred to the KE of the alpha particle.
$E_k = $ energy per decay × percentage energy transferred to alpha
$= 7.6 \times 10^6 \times 0.0170 = 129\,200$ eV
Convert E_k into joules: $129\,200 \times 1.60 \times 10^{-19} = 2.0672 \times 10^{-14}$ J
$E_k = \dfrac{1}{2}mv^2$
so $v = \sqrt{\dfrac{2E_k}{m}} = \sqrt{\dfrac{2 \times 2.0672 \times 10^{-14}}{6.64 \times 10^{-27}}} = 2.495... \times 10^6$
$= $ **2.50×10^6 ms^{-1} (to 3 s.f.)** *[1 mark]*

1.4 The activity is the number of decays per second, so the number of decays in 7.0 days is:
$7.0 \times 24 \times 60 \times 60 \times 38 \times 10^3 = 2.29824 \times 10^{10}$ decays *[1 mark]*
Energy released per decay $= 7.6$ MeV
The energy released per decay was calculated in part 2.3.
Convert this energy to joules:
$7.6 \times 10^6 \times 1.60 \times 10^{-19} = 1.216 \times 10^{-12}$ J
Total energy released = number of decays × energy per decay
$= 2.29824 \times 10^{10} \times 1.216 \times 10^{-12}$
$= 0.0279...$ J *[1 mark]*
$Q = mc\Delta\theta$ so $\Delta\theta = \dfrac{Q}{mc} = \dfrac{0.279...}{3.4 \times 10^{-3} \times 720}$
$= 0.0114... = $ **0.011 K (to 2 s.f.)** *[1 mark]*
You could also have given your answer in °C. $\Delta\theta = $ 0.011 °C (to 2 s.f.).

2.1 Find $\sin\theta$ using the length and radius.

So $\sin\theta = \dfrac{r}{l}$ *[1 mark]*
Find $\tan\theta$ using the forces acting on the ball.

So $\tan\theta = \dfrac{F}{mg}$ *[1 mark]*
The small angle approximation states that $\sin\theta \approx \tan\theta$
so $\dfrac{r}{l} = \dfrac{F}{mg}$ which rearranges to give $F = \dfrac{mgr}{l}$ *[1 mark]*.

2.2 The centripetal force on the ball is $F = m\omega^2 r$ and $\omega = 2\pi f = \dfrac{2\pi}{T}$,
so $F = m \times \left(\dfrac{2\pi}{T}\right)^2 \times r$ *[1 mark]*
The centripetal force is equal to the resultant force:
$F = m \times \left(\dfrac{2\pi}{T}\right)^2 \times r = \dfrac{mgr}{l}$ *[1 mark]*
Rearrange for T:
$\left(\dfrac{2\pi}{T}\right)^2 = \dfrac{g}{l}$ so $T = 2\pi\sqrt{\dfrac{l}{g}}$ *[1 mark]*

2.3 The ball is moving with projectile motion. Its initial horizontal velocity is equal to its speed when it was in circular motion.
$\omega = \dfrac{v}{r}$ and $\omega = \dfrac{2\pi}{T}$, so $v = \dfrac{2\pi r}{T}$
$T = 2\pi\sqrt{\dfrac{l}{g}}$ so $v = r\sqrt{\dfrac{g}{l}} = 0.205 \times \sqrt{\dfrac{9.81}{1.45}}$
$= 0.5332...$ ms^{-1} *[1 mark]*
Use the ball's vertical motion to calculate the time taken for the ball to reach the ground.
$s = ut + \dfrac{1}{2}at^2$ and the initial vertical speed = 0, so $s = \dfrac{1}{2}at^2$,
so $t = \sqrt{\dfrac{2s}{a}} = \sqrt{\dfrac{2 \times 0.621}{9.81}} = 0.3558...$ s *[1 mark]*
The horizontal distance travelled:
$v = \dfrac{\Delta s}{\Delta t}$ so $\Delta s = v\Delta t = 0.5332... \times 0.3558...$
$= 0.1897... = $ **0.190 m (to 3 s.f.)** *[1 mark]*

Answers

3.1 When an atom undergoes fission it produces a pair of daughter nuclei and a few neutrons *[1 mark]*. This means that when uranium-235 undergoes fission, the total mass number of the pair of daughter nuclei will add up to just slightly less than 235. If one of the daughter nuclei has a mass number A, the other will have a mass number of roughly $235 - A$ *[1 mark]*. This means that the percentage yield of the two daughter nuclei with atomic numbers A and $235 - A$ will be the same, meaning the curve will be symmetrical *[1 mark]*.

3.2 E.g.

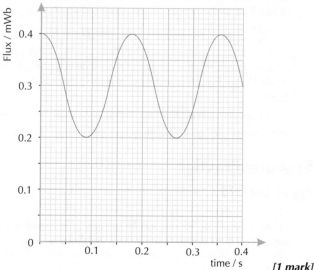

[1 mark for a curve with a slowly increasing gradient]
The stability curve shows that stable heavy nuclides have a larger neutron to proton ratio than stable lighter nuclides *[1 mark]*. Therefore, if a heavy nuclide splits into two, the daughter nuclei will also have a large neutron to proton ratio and will not be stable, as the graph shows that they require a lower neutron to proton ratio in order to be stable *[1 mark]*.

3.3 The force on a charge in a uniform electric field is $F = EQ$ and the force on a moving charge in a magnetic field is $F = BQv$ *[1 mark]*. Fleming's left-hand rule shows that the magnetic force on the ion is acting upwards. The electric force on the ion is acting downwards so the magnetic and electric forces on the ion are acting in opposite directions *[1 mark]*. This means that the ions will travel in a straight line when the magnitude of the force due to the electric field equals the magnitude of the force due to the magnetic field:

$F = EQ = BQv$, so $v = \dfrac{EQ}{BQ} = \dfrac{E}{B}$ *[1 mark]*.

3.4 The ions have a constant horizontal velocity, so $v = \dfrac{x}{t}$ where t is the time taken before the ion hits the charged plate *[1 mark]*. To find t, consider the vertical motion of the ion:
The ions have a constant vertical acceleration due to the electric force on the ion. $F = ma$ and $F = EQ$, so the vertical acceleration of the ion is $a = \dfrac{EQ}{m}$ *[1 mark]*. For the vertical motion, $s = ut + \dfrac{1}{2}at^2$ and the initial vertical speed $= 0$, so $s = \dfrac{1}{2}at^2$.
This rearranges to give $t^2 = \dfrac{2s}{a}$. Substitute $a = \dfrac{EQ}{m}$ into this:
$t^2 = \dfrac{2sm}{EQ}$, so $t = \sqrt{\dfrac{2sm}{EQ}}$ *[1 mark]*
Horizontal velocity, $v = \dfrac{x}{t}$ so $x = vt = v\sqrt{\dfrac{2sm}{EQ}}$ *[1 mark]*.
v, s, E and Q are all constant, therefore $x \propto m^{1/2}$ *[1 mark]*.

4.1 To work out the scale of the x-axis, calculate the period of the oscillations. $T = 2\pi\sqrt{\dfrac{m}{k}}$, so calculate k first:
$F = k\Delta L$ and when the magnet is attached to the spring, the force acting on the spring due to the magnet is equal to $F = mg$,
so $k = \dfrac{F}{\Delta L} = \dfrac{mg}{\Delta L} = \dfrac{20.0 \times 10^{-3} \times 9.81}{7.848 \times 10^{-3}} = 25$ Nm^{-1} *[1 mark]*
$T = 2\pi\sqrt{\dfrac{m}{k}} = 2\pi\sqrt{\dfrac{20.0 \times 10^{-3}}{25}} = 0.1777...$ s *[1 mark]*
One full oscillation in the graph in Figure 7 takes roughly 3.6 large squares on the x-axis. One large square must be equal to $0.1777... \div 3.6 \approx 0.05$ s, so the scale of the x-axis must be 0.05 s per large square:

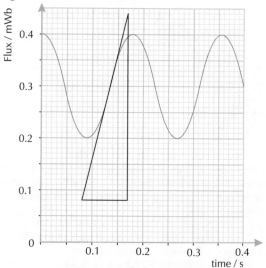

[1 mark]

There are 2.25 oscillations shown on the graph in Figure 7, so to work out the scale you could also have calculated the time taken for the 2.25 oscillations to take place: $0.1777... \times 2.25 = 0.399... \approx 0.4$ s. So the final scale marking is 0.4 s.

4.2 The magnitude of the e.m.f. is $\varepsilon = N\dfrac{\Delta\Phi}{\Delta t}$, and $\dfrac{\Delta\Phi}{\Delta t}$ is the gradient of the graph. So the e.m.f. is a maximum when the graph is steepest. Draw a tangent to one of the steepest parts of the graph and calculate the gradient of the tangent:
E.g.

gradient $= \dfrac{\Delta y}{\Delta x} = \dfrac{(0.44 \times 10^{-3}) - (0.08 \times 10^{-3})}{0.17 - 0.08}$
$= 4 \times 10^{-3}$ Wbs^{-1} *[1 mark]*

$\varepsilon = N\dfrac{\Delta\Phi}{\Delta t} = N \times$ gradient
$= 300 \times 4 \times 10^{-3}$
$= \textbf{1.2 V }$*[1 mark]*

You'd get 1 mark for calculating a gradient between 3.7×10^{-3} Wbs^{-1} and 4.5×10^{-3} Wbs^{-1}, and 1 mark for correctly using your value of the gradient to find ε.

Answers

4.3 E.g.

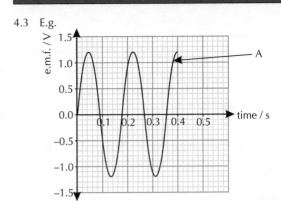

[1 mark for a sine graph (starting at zero and with an initial positive gradient), 1 mark for the maximum and minimum values being equal to ± the value calculated in part 4.2 and 1 mark for a period of 0.1777... s]

The induced e.m.f. can be found using the change in flux in the coil. So when the gradient of the flux graph is negative, the value of the induced e.m.f. is positive, and when the gradient is positive, the value of the induced e.m.f. is negative. This also means that the induced e.m.f. will be equal to zero when the gradient of the flux graph is equal to zero.

4.4 $V_{rms} = \frac{V_0}{\sqrt{2}} = \frac{1.2}{\sqrt{2}} = 0.848...$ V *[1 mark]*

E.g.

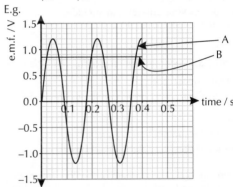

[1 mark for straight horizontal line at the calculated value of V_{rms}]

If you got the answer to 4.2 wrong, you still get full marks here for correctly using your value of V_O that you calculated in part 4.2.

4.5 The moving magnet will induce an e.m.f., which will cause a current to flow in the coil, which will induce a magnetic field around the coil *[1 mark]*. Lenz's law states that the induced e.m.f. will act to oppose the change that caused it, i.e. the motion of the oscillating magnet *[1 mark]*. The amplitude of oscillation of the magnet will therefore decrease as the magnetic force from the coil acts to slow it down *[1 mark]*.

5.1 The gravitational force on an object at the centre of the Earth would be of equal magnitude in all directions. This is because the Earth is assumed to have a constant density, and therefore there would be the same mass in every direction around an object at the centre of the Earth. This means that all the forces would cancel out to give zero *[1 mark]*.

5.2 The graph in Figure 8 shows that the gravitational field strength, g, is directly proportional to the distance from the centre of the Earth, r. This means that $\frac{g}{r} = $ constant, so $\frac{g_1}{r_1} = \frac{g_2}{r_2}$

$g_2 = \frac{g_1 r_2}{r_1} = \frac{9.81 \times 4.75 \times 10^6}{6.37 \times 10^6} = 7.315...$ Nkg^{-1} *[1 mark]*

$W = mg = 1.50 \times 7.315... = 10.972...$
$= \textbf{11.0 N (to 3 s.f.)}$ *[1 mark]*

5.3 The graph shows that the acceleration, g, is directly proportional to the distance from the centre of the Earth, r. The acceleration always acts towards the centre of the Earth. These are the two requirements for simple harmonic motion *[1 mark]*.

Remember, the gravitational field strength is the same as the acceleration due to gravity.

5.4 $\omega = 2\pi f = 2\pi \div T$ so first calculate ω:
$a_{max} = \omega^2 A$ and the maximum acceleration is equal to the acceleration due to gravity calculated in part 5.2 (g_2).

$\omega = \sqrt{\frac{a_{max}}{A}} = \sqrt{\frac{7.315...}{4.75 \times 10^6}} = 1.240... \times 10^{-3}$ rads^{-1} *[1 mark]*
$\omega = 2\pi \div T$ so $T = 2\pi \div \omega = 2\pi \div 1.240... \times 10^{-3}$
$= 5063.083...$
$= \textbf{5060 s (to 3 s.f.)}$ *[1 mark]*

5.5 To escape the Earth's gravitational field, the mass must do work against the gravitational force.
Work done, $\Delta W = m\Delta V$, so first find the change in gravitational potential. The change in gravitational potential as the mass moves from the centre of the Earth to the surface of the Earth is equal to the area under the g-r graph in Figure 8:

$\Delta V = \frac{1}{2} \times 9.81 \times 6.37 \times 10^6 = 3.124... \times 10^7$ Jkg^{-1} *[1 mark]*

When the mass has escaped Earth's gravitational field, it will have a gravitational potential of 0. The gravitational potential at the surface of the Earth is $V = -\frac{GM}{r_E}$, so ΔV from the surface of the Earth to being completely out of Earth's gravitational field is:

$\Delta V = 0 - -\frac{GM}{r_E} = \frac{GM}{r_E} = \frac{6.67 \times 10^{-11} \times 5.97 \times 10^{24}}{6.37 \times 10^6}$
$= 6.251... \times 10^7$ Jkg^{-1} *[1 mark]*

Total $\Delta V = (3.124... \times 10^7) + (6.251... \times 10^7) = 9.375... \times 10^7$ Jkg^{-1}

Equate the work done and the kinetic energy of the mass:
$m\Delta V = \frac{1}{2}mv^2$, so $v = \sqrt{2\Delta V} = \sqrt{2 \times 9.375... \times 10^7}$
$= 13\,693.536...$
$= \textbf{13 700 ms}^{-1}$ **(to 3 s.f.)** *[1 mark]*

6.1 $\varepsilon = BAN\omega \sin \omega t$, so the peak e.m.f. occurs when $\sin \omega t = 1$, so $\varepsilon = BAN\omega$.
ω is the angular frequency of the spinning slip ring:
$\omega = \frac{v}{r}$ where v is the velocity of the falling mass and r is the radius of the slip ring.

$\omega = \frac{v}{r} = \frac{0.240}{1.60 \times 10^{-2}} = 15$ rads^{-1} *[1 mark]*

$\varepsilon = BAN\omega = 0.0200 \times 15.0 \times 10^{-4} \times 415 \times 15$
$= 0.18675 = \textbf{0.187 V (to 3 s.f.)}$ *[1 mark]*

To convert the area from cm^2 to m^2, multiply by $(1 \times 10^{-2})^2 = 1 \times 10^{-4}$.

6.2 $\frac{N_s}{N_p} = \frac{V_s}{V_p}$

To find the ratio of primary to secondary turns, rearrange the equation to $\frac{N_p}{N_s} = \frac{V_p}{V_s}$.

The secondary voltage given is an rms value, so to find the voltage ratio, first calculate the rms value of the primary voltage.

$V_{rms} = \frac{V_0}{\sqrt{2}} = \frac{0.18675}{\sqrt{2}} = 0.132...$ V *[1 mark]*

$\frac{V_p}{V_s} = \frac{0.132...}{2.26} = 0.05843...$
$= \textbf{0.0584 (to 3 s.f.)}$ *[1 mark]*

You could also have calculated the peak secondary voltage (V_O) and divided the peak primary voltage from part 6.1 by V_O to find the ratio.

6.3 The power of the light bulb is:
$P = \frac{V^2}{R} = \frac{2.26^2}{1.02} = 5.007...$ W *[1 mark]*

Power is energy supplied per second, so the generator needs to produce 5.007... J of energy per second. This energy comes from the change in gravitational potential energy of the falling mass, $\Delta E_p = mg\Delta h$. The mass falls 0.240 m in 1 second (because the velocity is 0.240 ms^{-1}).

$\Delta E_p = mg\Delta h$, so $m = \frac{\Delta E_p}{g\Delta h} = \frac{5.007...}{9.81 \times 0.240}$
$= 2.126...$
$= \textbf{2.13 kg (to 3 s.f.)}$ *[1 mark]*

Answers

6.4 E.g.

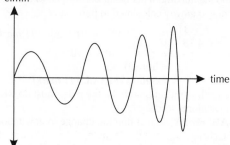

[1 mark for a sinusoidal wave with a continuously increasing amplitude and 1 mark for a decreasing period]

As the mass accelerates, its velocity increases and so the angular velocity of the rotating coil increases. The peak e.m.f. = $BAN\omega$, so as the angular velocity increases, the amplitude of the e.m.f. increases. $\omega = 2\pi f$ so as the angular velocity increases, the frequency of rotation increases. $T = 1 \div f$ so the period of the induced e.m.f. decreases.

7.1 First calculate the volume of gas in the plasma ball. Volume of gas = volume of outer sphere – volume of inner sphere.

$V_{total} = \frac{4}{3}\pi(r_b)^3 - \frac{4}{3}\pi(r_a)^3 = \frac{4}{3}\pi((r_b)^3 - (r_a)^3)$

$\qquad = \frac{4}{3}\pi((12.0 \times 10^{-2})^3 - (3.50 \times 10^{-2})^3)$

$\qquad = 7.058... \times 10^{-3}$ m³ *[1 mark]*

$pV = NkT$ so the total number of gas atoms:

$N = \frac{pV}{kT} = \frac{1.01 \times 10^5 \times 7.058... \times 10^{-3}}{1.38 \times 10^{-23} \times 298}$

$\qquad = 1.733... \times 10^{23}$ *[1 mark]*

1% of these are argon atoms, so the total number of argon atoms:
$1.733... \times 10^{23} \times 0.01 = 1.733... \times 10^{21}$

Total mass = number of argon atoms × mass of 1 argon atom

$\qquad = 1.733... \times 10^{21} \times 39.9481 \times u$

$\qquad = 1.733... \times 10^{21} \times 39.9481 \times 1.661 \times 10^{-27}$

$\qquad = 1.150... 10^{-4} =$ **1.15 × 10⁻⁴ kg (to 3 s.f.) *[1 mark]***

7.2 $pV = NkT$ so $\frac{p}{T} = \frac{Nk}{V}$ = constant, so $\frac{p_1}{T_1} = \frac{p_2}{T_2}$.

$T_2 = \frac{p_2 T_1}{p_1} = \frac{1.03 \times 10^5 \times 298}{1.01 \times 10^5} = 303.900...$ K *[1 mark]*

$\frac{1}{2}m(c_{rms})^2 = \frac{3}{2}kT$

so $c_{rms} = \sqrt{\frac{3kT}{m}} = \sqrt{\frac{3 \times 1.38 \times 10^{-23} \times 303.900...}{20.1797 \times 1.661 \times 10^{-27}}}$

$\qquad = 612.666... =$ **613 ms⁻¹ (to 3 s.f.) *[1 mark]***

7.3 Light is produced by excited electrons in the neon and argon atoms moving from a higher energy level to a lower energy level and emitting photons of a specific frequency *[1 mark]*. The frequency of the emitted photons depends on the difference in the energy levels *[1 mark]*. The energy levels in argon and neon are different, so photons of a different frequency (and hence colour) would be emitted *[1 mark]*.

7.4 A is the radius of the inner sphere *[1 mark]*.

Electric potential is given by $\frac{1}{4\pi\varepsilon_0}\frac{Q}{r}$, and comparing this to the given equation shows that $r = d + A$. r is the total distance from the centre of the sphere to the detector, which equals the distance from the surface of the inner sphere to the detector (d), plus the radius of the inner sphere, so A must equal the radius of the inner sphere.

7.5 ***5-6 marks:***
The formula has been rearranged correctly for d, and this has been used to explain fully how the gradient and the y-intercept can be used to calculate Q and A. A full explanation of how the error bars should be drawn has been given, including how to use them to determine the absolute uncertainties of Q and A. The answer has a clear and logical structure. The information given is relevant and detailed.

3-4 marks:
The formula has been rearranged for d and this has been linked to how Q and A can be calculated. A brief description of how the error bars should be drawn has been included. There is some description of how error bars can be used to calculate the absolute uncertainties. The answer has some structure. Most of the information given is relevant and there is some detail involved.

1-2 marks:
An attempt at rearranging the formula for d has been made. There is some attempt to link the formula to finding Q and A. A description of error bars and uncertainties may not be included, or may be included with little detail. The answer has no clear structure. The information given is basic and lacking in detail. It may not all be relevant.

0 marks:
No relevant information is given.

Here are some points your answer may include:
Rearranging the formula to make d the subject gives:

$d = \frac{Q}{4\pi\varepsilon_0}\frac{1}{V} - A$.

This formula gives a straight line when plotting d on the y-axis against $\frac{1}{V}$ on the x-axis.

Comparing this to $y = mx + c$ shows that the gradient of the line is equal to $\frac{Q}{4\pi\varepsilon_0}$.

The y-intercept of the straight line is equal to $-A$.

The engineer should draw a straight line of best fit through her results.

She should then calculate the gradient of the line (by drawing an appropriate triangle) and find the y-intercept (by extrapolating the line backwards until it crosses the y-axis).

The value of Q = gradient × $4\pi\varepsilon_0$.

The value of A = $-$ y-intercept.

The uncertainty in d is ±0.001 m. Therefore the engineer should draw vertical error bars that extend 0.001 m (on the scale of the y-axis) above and below each plotted data point.

The uncertainty in V is 5%, so the uncertainty in $\frac{1}{V}$ is also 5%.

The engineer should calculate 5% of each $\frac{1}{V}$ value and draw errors bars horizontally by this value to the left and right for each plotted data point.

The engineer should find the uncertainty in Q by drawing lines with maximum and minimum gradients that still pass within the range of the error bars.

The worst gradient is the gradient of the line furthest from the gradient of the line of best fit.

Use the worst gradient to calculate the worst value of Q, i.e. Q_{worst} = worst gradient × $4\pi\varepsilon_0$.

The absolute uncertainty in Q is the difference between the value of Q calculated using the line of best fit, and the value of Q_{worst}.

To find the uncertainty in A, find the y-intercept from the line that is furthest away from the y-intercept of the line of best fit.

The absolute uncertainty of A equals the difference between their y-intercepts.

Answers

8.1 E.g.

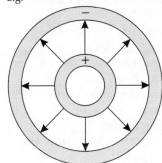

[1 mark for straight lines between the inner and outer cylinders that are perpendicular to the surfaces of the cylinders and pointing from the inner to the outer cylinder]
The strength of a field is indicated by how close together the field lines are, and the distance between the field lines changes depending on the distance from the centre, which shows that the electric field strength is not constant and so the electric field is not uniform *[1 mark]*.

8.2 Equate centripetal force and the force on a charge in an electric field:

$E = \frac{F}{Q}$ so $F = EQ$

$F = \frac{mv^2}{r} = EQ$

$E = \frac{Q_{cylinder}}{2\pi\varepsilon_0 rL}$ and $Q = e$

$\frac{mv^2}{r} = \frac{Q_{cylinder}}{2\pi\varepsilon_0 rL} \times e$ *[1 mark]*

$v = \sqrt{\frac{Q_{cylinder}e}{2\pi\varepsilon_0 Lm_e}}$

$= \sqrt{\frac{5.66\times10^{-9}\times1.60\times10^{-19}}{2\pi\times8.85\times10^{-12}\times25.3\times10^{-2}\times9.11\times10^{-31}}}$

$= 8.405... \times 10^6$

$= \mathbf{8.41 \times 10^6\ ms^{-1}}$ **(to 3 s.f.)** *[1 mark]*

8.3 A proton is positively charged, so the electric force on the proton will be towards the outer, negative cylinder *[1 mark]*. For circular motion to happen, there needs to be a force towards the centre of the circle, so the proton will not move in a circle *[1 mark]*.

8.4 The time taken for the potential difference to halve is $T_{1/2} = 0.69RC$.

$C = \frac{2\pi\varepsilon_0\varepsilon_r}{\ln\left(\frac{b}{a}\right)}$ and the outer radius (b) is double that of the inner radius (a), so $b = 2a$.

$C = \frac{2\pi\varepsilon_0\varepsilon_r}{\ln\left(\frac{2a}{a}\right)} = \frac{2\pi\varepsilon_0\varepsilon_r}{\ln(2)}$

$T_{1/2} = 0.69R \times \frac{2\pi\varepsilon_0\varepsilon_r}{\ln(2)}$ *[1 mark]*

$= 0.69 \times 1.85 \times 10^3 \times \frac{2\pi\times8.85\times10^{-12}\times2.25}{\ln(2)}$

$= 2.304... \times 10^{-7} = \mathbf{2.30 \times 10^{-7}\ s}$ **(to 3 s.f.)** *[1 mark]*

You could have done this question by substituting $V = \frac{V_0}{2}$ into $V = V_0e^{-t/(RC)}$ and rearranging for t to find the time taken for V to halve. If you used this method you'd get an answer of 2.31×10^{-7} s (to 3 s.f.).

9.1 $F = BIl$ so calculate the current through the wire first.
$R = \frac{V}{I}$ and $C = \frac{Q}{V}$, so $I = \frac{Q}{RC}$. RC is equal to the time constant.

$I = \frac{3.60}{0.1875} = 19.2$ A *[1 mark]*
$F = BIl = 5.50 \times 10^{-3} \times 19.2 \times 0.250 = \mathbf{0.0264\ N}$ *[1 mark]*

9.2 The displacement (x) of the wooden block is directly proportional to the force on the wire, and the force is proportional to the current through the circuit $(F = BIl)$. This means that $I \propto x$. When the current is equal to I_0, the displacement is $x = 5.0$ mm. So a displacement of 1.0 mm occurs when the current has fallen to $\frac{1}{5}$ of I_0. $I = I_0 \times \frac{1}{5}$, so $\frac{I}{I_0} = \frac{1}{5}$ *[1 mark]*.

$I = I_0e^{-t/(RC)}$ so $\frac{I}{I_0} = e^{-t/(RC)}$

Take the natural logarithm of both sides of the equation:

$\ln(\frac{I}{I_0}) = \frac{-t}{RC}$, so $t = -RC \times \ln(\frac{I}{I_0})$
$= -0.1875 \times \ln(\frac{1}{5})$
$= 0.3017... = \mathbf{0.30\ s}$ **(to 2 s.f.)** *[1 mark]*

9.3 The wire loop and wooden block act as a simple pendulum. The resonant frequency of the pendulum is:

$f = \frac{1}{T} = 1 \div \left(2\pi\sqrt{\frac{l}{g}}\right)$ where l is the distance from the block to the pivot, which is equal to half the length of the sides of the wire.

$f = 1 \div \left(2\pi\sqrt{\frac{0.250\div2}{9.81}}\right) = 1 \div 0.709...$
$= 1.409...$ Hz *[1 mark]*

The amplitude of oscillation of the block will remain small until the frequency of the signal generator reaches 1.409... Hz. When the frequency supplied by the signal generator reaches 1.409... Hz, the driving frequency will match the resonant frequency of the block and so the amplitude of oscillation will increase greatly. When the frequency increases beyond 1.409... Hz, the amplitude of oscillation will decrease again *[1 mark]*.

9.4 The force of air resistance against the card will be larger so the system will be more damped *[1 mark]*. The amplitude of oscillation will still increase before 1.409... Hz and decrease after 1.409... Hz, however the maximum amplitude will decrease *[1 mark]*.

The resonant frequency of the oscillations is only dependent on l, so the mass of the card doesn't affect the resonant frequency. You could also have said that the maximum amplitude will occur at a slightly lower frequency due to the increase in damping.

Index

A

absolute electric potential 128-130
absolute magnitude 179, 183
absolute zero 110
absorption (of a signal) 39
absorption spectra 182
acceleration 50-60
  centripetal 99
acceleration-time graphs 53
accuracy 263
acoustic impedance 204
adiabatic processes 227, 230, 234
air resistance 62, 63
Airy discs 173, 250
alpha radiation 4, 158, 159, 164
  scattering 154, 155
alternating current (ac) 148, 149
alternators 147
ammeters 82
amplitude 24
angle of incidence 38
angle of refraction 38
angular magnification 172
angular motion 98, 99, 216-225
annihilation 7, 215
antibaryons 10
antimatter 6, 7
antineutrinos 5, 6, 9, 11
antineutrons 6, 10
antinodes 30
antiparticles 6, 7
antiprotons 6, 10
antiquarks 13-15
arc-length 98
A-Scan 205
astigmatism 196
atomic number 2, 164
atomic radius 156
atoms 2
atria 202, 203
atrioventricular node 202
attenuation 202, 204, 210
Avogadro's constant (N_A) 112

B

background radiation 160
Balmer series 182, 190
barium meal 210
baryon number 10, 11, 13, 14
baryons 10, 11
  quark composition 13
basilar membrane 198, 199
beam splitters 252
Bertozzi 255
beta radiation 5, 9, 11, 14,
    158, 159, 164, 215
Big Bang theory 188, 192, 193

binary stars 189
binding energy 168, 169
biological half-life 214
black body radiation 180, 181, 248
black holes 186, 190
blue shift 188, 189
Boltzmann's constant (k) 112
Boyle's law 110, 111, 116
breaking stress 72
bremsstrahlung 208
brightness
  B-Scans 205
  of stars 178
brittle materials 76, 77
Brownian motion 117
B-Scan 205

C

calibration 259
calorific value (fuel) 236
cancer treatments 159, 215
capacitors 132-137
  time constant 136, 137
Cassegrain arrangement 173
categoric data 262
cathode rays 240
centre of mass 48, 49
centripetal acceleration 99
centripetal force 99, 124, 241
ceramics 76
chain reactions (nuclear) 166
characteristic X-rays 208
charge 82
  carriers 84, 85
  conservation 92
  on a capacitor 132-137
  relative 2
  specific 3
charge-coupled devices (CCDs)
    174, 176
Charles's law 110, 111, 116
chromatic aberration 173
circuits 82-95
circular motion 98, 99
cladding (optical fibres) 38
closed systems 108, 226
cochlea 198, 199
coefficient of performance 238, 239
coherence 29
collecting power of a telescope 177
collisions 64, 65
  gas particles 114, 115, 117
colour perception 195
combined heat and power plants 237
computed tomography (CT) scans 210
conclusions 263
cone cells 194, 195
conservation
  in particle interactions 13, 14

of angular momentum 224
of charge 92
of energy 64, 68, 69, 92
of momentum 64
rules (nuclear reactions) 165
continuous data 262
continuous-flow calorimeters 109
control rods 166
converging lenses
    172, 173, 194, 196, 197
coolant 166
cornea 194
corpuscular theory 244
correlation 262
cosmic background radiation 193
cosmological principle 192
cosmological red shift 188
Coulomb's law 126
couples 47, 220
coupling media 205
critical angle 38, 206
critical mass 166
crumple zones 65
current 82, 92
cycle (of a wave) 24
cyclic processes 231-235
cyclotrons 143
cylindrical lenses 196

D

damping 104, 105
dark energy 192
data 262, 263
data-loggers 53
dBA scale 200
de Broglie wavelength
    20, 21, 250, 251
decay constant (radioactivity) 162
decibels 200
density 70
  nuclear 157
dependent variables 258
diffraction 32, 33, 245
  electrons 20, 156, 250, 251
  gratings 36, 37
  patterns 20, 21, 32, 33, 36, 37
  Young's double slit 34, 35, 245
diodes 85
dioptres 194
direct current (dc) 148
discrete data 262
dispersion (of a signal) 39
displacement 42
  displacement-time graphs 50-53
  of a wave 24
diverging lenses 196, 197
Doppler effect 188, 189
Doppler shift method 191
double refraction 244, 245

drag 62
driving force 62
driving frequency 104, 105
dynamos 147

E

ears 198-201
eddy currents 150
efficiency 68
  of engines 236
  of transformers 150
elastic collisions 64
  of gas particles 114, 115
elastic deformation 71, 76, 77
elastic limit 70, 72, 76, 77
elastic potential energy 68, 100
elastic strain energy 68, 71-73, 75
electric fields 126-131
  of capacitors 132-137
electric field strength 126, 127, 130
electric potential (absolute) 128-130
electrocardiography (ECG) 202, 203
electromagnetic forces 8, 9
electromagnetic induction
        144-147, 150
electromagnetic radiation 6, 24, 26
  diffraction 32-37
  nature of light 244-251
  photons 6, 16, 247, 248
  polarisation 26, 27
  refraction 24, 38
  spectrum 6
  wave-particle duality
        20, 21, 250, 251
  wave speed 25
  Young's double slit 34, 35, 245
electromotive force (e.m.f.)
        90-92, 144, 145
electrons 2
  capture 9, 165
  degeneracy pressure 184
  diffraction 20, 156, 250, 251
  electron guns 240
  excitation 18
  fluorescent tubes 18
  in beta-minus decay 5, 11
  microscopes 251
  pair production 7
  photoelectrons 16, 17, 247
  properties 2, 6, 12
  specific charge 240, 241
electronvolts 18, 240
electrostatic force between nucleons
        4, 126
elliptical orbits 125
empirical laws 116
endolymph 198
endoscopy 206, 207

energy
  carried by a photon 6, 16
  conservation 64, 68, 69, 92
  elastic potential 68, 100
  elastic strain 68, 71-73, 75
  energy levels of atoms 18, 19
  internal 108
  kinetic 64, 68, 108, 116, 117
  levels in atomic hydrogen 182
  mass-energy equivalence
        6, 7, 168, 255
  of a photoelectron 17
  potential energy
        68, 73, 100, 122, 128
  rest energies 6, 7
  stored by a flywheel 222
  transfer 24, 66-69, 88-90, 92
engine efficiency 236, 237
engine torque 235
equations of motion 54, 55, 58, 59
  uniform angular acceleration 218
equilibrium 44, 46
equipotentials 123, 129, 130
error bars 261
escape velocity 122
ether 252
Eustachian tube 198
event horizon 186
exchange particles 8
exoplanets 190, 191
exponential relationships 266
eye lens 172, 173
eyes 194-197

F

Faraday's law 146
far point 194
field lines
  electric 126, 130
  gravitational 120, 123, 130
fields
  electrical 126-131
  gravitational 120-125, 129, 130
  magnetic 140-151
filament lamps 84
first law of thermodynamics 226-228
fission 166-169
flat panel detectors (FTP) 211
Fleming's left-hand rule 140
fluorescent tubes 18
fluoroscopy 210
flux 144
flux linkage 144, 146, 147
flywheels 222, 223
focal length 172, 194, 196, 197
force-extension graphs 70, 72, 77
force fields 120, 126

forces
  compressive 70
  due to gravity 44, 56, 120
  electromagnetic 8, 10, 11
  electrostatic 4, 126
  free-body diagrams 44
  friction 62, 63, 68
  fundamental forces 8
  moments 46, 47
  Newton's Laws 60, 61, 65
  on a current-carrying wire 140
  on charged particles in fields 142
  resolving 44, 45, 66
  restoring 100
  strong nuclear 4, 8, 10
  tensile 70
  weak 8, 14
  within nuclei 4
forward bias 85
four-stroke engines 232-234
fovea 194
fractional uncertainties 260
fracture 76, 77
frequency 24, 25
  alternating current 148
  circular motion 98
  Doppler effect 188
  resonant 30, 31, 104
  simple harmonic motion 100, 101
  sound 200, 204
friction 62, 63, 68
frictional torque 221, 222
friction power 235
fringe spacing 35
fundamental forces 8
fundamental particles 12, 13
fusion 167-169, 184

G

galactic nuclei 190
gamma radiation 158-160, 165
  from supernovae 186, 187
  in medicine 214, 215
gas constants 112
gas laws 110-112, 116, 226-228
gauge bosons 8, 9
Geiger counters 158, 160, 161
generators 147
geostationary orbits 125
graphs
  error bars 261
  force-extension 70, 72, 77
  I/V characteristics 84, 85
  line graphs 262
  scatter plots 262
  stress-strain 72, 75-77

Index

gravitational
   fields 48, 120-125, 129, 130
   force 8, 120
   potential 68, 122, 123, 130
gravity, acceleration due to
         56-58, 60

H

hadrons 10, 11
half-life 162, 163, 214
half-value thickness 210
harmonics 30, 31
hearing 198-201
hearing loss 201
hearts 202, 203
heat engines 236-239
heat pumps 238
Hertzsprung-Russell (H-R) diagram
         183, 185
high mass stars 186
Hooke's law 70, 76
Hubble's law 192
hypermetropia (long-sight) 196, 197

I

ideal gas equation 112, 226-228
ideal gases 112-116
imaging techniques
   comparison 213
   CT scans 210, 211
   MRI scans 212, 213
   PET scans 215
   ultrasound 204, 205
impedance 204, 205
impulse 65
incus 199
independent variables 258
indicator diagrams 232-235
induction (electromagnetic) 144-147
induction stroke (engines) 232, 233
inelastic collisions 64
inertial frames 253
inner ear 198, 199
intensity
   of diffracted electrons 156
   of gamma radiation 160
   of light 33
   sound 198-201
   stars 178, 180
   X-ray production 209
interference 28, 29, 34-36
interferometers 252
internal combustion engines 232, 233
internal energy 108, 226, 227
internal resistance 90, 91

inverse square law
   brightness 180, 181, 190
   fields 120, 126, 127
   ionising radiation 160, 161
ionisation 18
ionising radiation 158, 159, 214, 215
isothermal processes 227, 229
isotopes 3, 162
   tracers 214, 215
I/V characteristics 84, 85

K

kaons 11, 14
kelvins 110
keyhole surgery 207
kinetic energy 68
   conservation 64, 68, 69
   gas particles 108, 110, 116, 117
   in SHM 100
   photoelectric effect
         16, 17, 247, 249
kinetic theory 114, 117
Kirchhoff's laws 92, 93

L

lasers 34
length contraction 254
lenses 172, 173, 194, 196, 197
Lenz's law 146
lepton number 12, 14
leptons 12
levers 46
lift 62
light 244, 245
   corpuscular theory 244
   diffraction 32-37, 245
   double refraction 244
   electromagnetic spectrum 6
   interference 28, 29, 34-36
   photon emission 18
   photon model 6, 16, 248, 249
   polarisation 26, 27, 244
   reflection 24, 244
   refraction 24, 38, 244
   signals 38, 39
   spectra 18, 19, 32, 37, 182
   speed (measuring) 245, 252
   wave-particle duality
         20, 21, 250, 251
   wave theory 244, 245
light-dependent resistors (LDRs) 94
light emitting diodes (LEDs) 85
light-years (ly) 179
limit of proportionality 70, 76, 77
linear magnification 196
linear particle accelerators (Linacs) 255
line graphs 262

line of best fit 261, 262
line spectra 18, 19, 182, 188
logarithms 266, 267
longitudinal waves 26
long-sightedness 196, 197
loudness 198, 200, 201
luminosity 178-180, 183

M

magnetic fields 140-151, 241
   field lines 140, 144
   flux 144
   flux density 140, 141, 145
   flux linkage 144-147
magnetic resonance imaging (MRI)
         212, 213
magnification 172, 173, 196
main sequence 183-185
malleus 199
mass 48
   centre of 48, 49
   number 2, 157, 164
mass attenuation coefficient 210
mass defect 168
mass-energy equivalence
         6, 7, 168, 255
material dispersion 39
matter 6, 7
mean square speed 114
mechanical efficiency 236
medical tracers 159, 163, 214, 215
mesons 10, 11, 13, 14
microwaves 30, 34
Millikan's oil drop experiment
         242, 243
modal dispersion 39
moderator (nuclear) 166
molar gas constant (R) 112
molar mass 112
molecular mass 112
moles 112
moments 46, 47
   of inertia 216, 217, 220, 222, 224
momentum 20, 64, 65
   angular momentum 224, 225
   gas particle collisions 114
monochromatic 32
muons 12, 254
myopia (short-sight) 196, 197

N

national grid, the 151
near point 194, 196, 197
neutrinos 5, 6, 12
neutrons 2, 3, 6, 10
   nuclear decay 5, 11, 14
   quark composition 13

Index

neutron stars 186
Newton's law of gravitation 120
Newton's laws 60, 61, 65, 114
nodes 30
non-flow processes 226-230
NTC thermistors 85, 94
nuclear density 157
nuclear model of the atom 2
nuclear power 166-169
nuclear radius 155-157
nuclear reactions 164-169
nuclear separation 4
nuclei 2, 4
nucleon number 2, 3, 157, 164, 168
nucleons 2-4
nuclide notation 2, 164

O

objective lens 172
ohm (definition of) 82
ohmic conductors 83, 84
Ohm's law 83
oil drop experiment 242, 243
optical fibres 38, 39, 206, 207
optic nerve 194
orbits 124, 125
ordered (ordinal) data 262
oscillations 100-105
  simple harmonic motion 100-103
oscilloscopes 145, 148, 205
ossicles 198, 199
outer ear 198, 199

P

pair production 6, 7, 15
parallel circuits 92
parsecs 178
particle exchange 8
particle interaction diagrams 8, 9
path difference 29
peak-to-peak voltages 148
peak wavelength 180
peer review 21
pendulums 103
percentage uncertainties 260
perilymph 198
period 24, 101
  of a simple pendulum 103
  of circular motion 98
  of mass-spring systems 102
permittivity 126, 132
PET scans 215
phase difference 24, 28, 29, 104
phase (of a wave) 24, 28, 29
phons 201
photodiode pixels 211
photoelectric effect
    16, 17, 20, 247-249

photomultiplier tubes 214
photons 6
  annihilation 7
  pair production 7
  photon model of light
    16, 17, 248, 249
photoreceptors 194
piezoelectric effect 204
pinna 198, 199
pions 11, 14
pitch 200
planetary nebulae 184
plastic deformation 71, 76, 77, 105
plum pudding model 154
polarisation 26, 27, 244
potential difference 82
  across a capacitor 132, 134-136
  electric 128
  electromotive force (e.m.f.)
    90-92, 144, 146, 147
  gravitational 123
  terminal 90
potential dividers 94, 95
power
  electrical 88
  lenses 194
  luminosity 178-180, 190
  mechanical 67
  rotating objects 220
  sound 198
precession frequency 212
precision 263
pressure law 110, 116
pressure of an ideal gas 114, 116
principal axis 172, 194
principal focus 172, 194, 197
probability waves 250
progressive waves 24, 25
proton number 2, 155, 164
protons 2, 6, 10
  nuclear decay 5, 11, 14
  quark composition 13
protostars 184
pulsars 186
pulse broadening 39
p-V diagrams 229-234

Q

quantum efficiency 174
quarks 13-15
quasars 190

R

radial velocity method 191
radians 98
radiation treatment 159, 215
radioactive decay 158-169

radioactive isotopes 3
radioactive tracers 159, 163, 214, 215
radioactive waste 163, 167
radio frequency (RF) coils 212
random errors 259
rate of radioactive decay 162, 266
ray diagrams 172, 194
Rayleigh criterion 173, 175, 177
reaction force 58, 61
recessional velocity 188, 192
red giants 183, 184
red shift 188-193
reflection 24, 244
refraction 24, 38, 194, 206, 244
  double refraction 244
  refractive index 38
refractive index 38
refrigerators 238
regenerative braking 223
relative intensity (sound) 200
relative molecular mass 112
relative permittivity 132
relativistic energy 255
relativistic mass 255
repeatability 263
resistance 82-86
  internal resistance 90, 91
  I/V characteristics 84, 85
resistivity 86, 87
resolution 173, 174, 195
resolving power of a telescope
    173, 175, 177
resolving vectors 43-45
resonance 104, 105, 199
resonant frequencies 30, 31, 104, 105
restoring forces 100
resultant forces 45, 60, 62
retina 194-196
reverse bias 85
reversed heat engines 238, 239
right-hand rule 140
risk assessments 258
rods (eyes) 194
root mean square (rms) 115, 148
rotational motion 98, 99, 216-225
Rutherford scattering 154, 155

S

satellites 124, 125
scanning tunnelling microscopes
    (STMs) 251
scatter plots 262
Schwarzchild radius 186
scintillator material 211, 214
search coils 145
seat belts 65
semiconductors 84
series circuits 90, 92
short-sightedness 196, 197

signal degradation 39
simple harmonic motion (SHM)
        100-103
simple pendulums 103
Snell's law 38
sound waves 24, 29, 30
  diffraction 32
  hearing 198-201
spatial resolution 174, 195
special relativity 252-255
specific charge 3
  of an electron 240, 241
specific heat capacity 108, 109
specific latent heat 109
spectra
  absorption 19, 182, 189
  black body 180
  diffraction gratings 37
  emission 18, 19, 182
  X-ray 208
spectral classes 182, 183
spectral lines 182, 188, 189
spectroscopic binary stars 189
speed
  angular 98
  of the Earth 252
  terminal 62, 63
spherical aberration 173
spring constant 70, 102
springs
  Hooke's law 70
  SHM 100, 102
stability of objects 49
standard candles 179
standard notation 164
stapes 199
stars
  black bodies 180, 181
  classification 182, 183
  distance to 178
  evolution 184-187
  luminosity 178-180, 183
  magnitude 178, 179, 183, 185
state changes 108, 109
stationary waves 30, 31
  microwaves 30
Stefan's law 180, 181
stiffness 70, 102
Stokes' law 242
stopping potential 17
strain (tensile) 72, 74, 75
strangeness 13, 14
stress-strain graphs 72, 75-77
stress (tensile) 72, 74, 75
strong nuclear force 4, 8, 10
superconductors 87
supernovae 179, 184, 186, 187
superposition 28, 29
synchronous orbits 125
systematic errors 259

T

telescopes 172-177
television signals 27
temperature scale 110
temperature sensors 94
tensile strain 72, 74, 75
tensile stress 72, 74, 75
terminal potential difference 90
terminal speed 62, 63
teslas 140
theoretical indicator diagrams 234
theories 116
thermal efficiency 236
thermal (heat) energy
        108, 109, 226-228, 236-238
thermionic emission 240
thermistors 85, 94
thermodynamic processes 227, 228
threshold frequency 16, 17, 247, 249
threshold of feeling 200
threshold of hearing 200
time constant, RC 136
time dilation 254
torque 220-222, 225
total internal reflection 38, 206
tracers 159, 214, 215
transducers 204, 205
transformers 150, 151
transit method 191
transmission electron microscopes
        (TEMs) 251
transverse waves 26, 27
two-source interference
        29, 34, 35, 245
tympanic membrane (ear drum)
        198, 199
type la supernovae 179, 187

U

ultimate tensile stress 72
ultrasound 204, 205, 213
ultraviolet catastrophe 248
uncertainties 260, 261
universe, the 192, 193

V

validating theories 21
valid results 263
vector quantities 42-44
velocity 50-55, 64
  angular 98, 99, 218
  simple harmonic motion 100, 101
velocity-time graphs 52
ventricles 202, 203
V/I characteristics 84, 85
virtual images 172, 196, 197
virtual particles 8

viscosity 62
viscous drag 62, 242
volts 82
volumes (of objects) 70

W

watts 88
wave cycle 24
wavelength 24, 25, 175, 176
wave-packets 248
wave-particle duality 20, 21,
        250, 251
waves
  coherence 29
  diffraction 32, 33, 36, 37
  diffraction gratings 36, 37
  dispersion 39
  frequency 24
  interference 28, 29, 36, 37, 252
  polarisation 26, 27
  progressive waves 24, 25
  reflection 24
  refraction 24, 38
  speed 25
  stationary 30, 31
  superposition 28, 29
  theory of light 16, 20, 244-248
  wave equation 25
  Young's double slit 34, 35, 245
W bosons 8, 9
weak interaction 8, 9, 11, 12, 14
webers 140
weight 48
white dwarfs 183, 184
Wien's displacement law 180, 181
work 66, 67, 226-228
  from p-V diagrams 229-231
  heat engines 236-238
  in cyclic processes 231, 235
  in electric fields 128, 130
  in gravitational fields 123, 129, 130
  rotating objects 220
work function 16, 17, 248, 249

X

X-rays 208-211, 213
  crystallography 37
  telescopes 176

Y

yellow spot 194
yield point 76
Young modulus 74-76
Young's double-slit experiment
        34, 35, 245